Everyman, I will go with thee,
and be thy guide

THE EVERYMAN
LIBRARY

*The Everyman Library was founded by J. M. Dent
in 1906. He chose the name Everyman because he wanted
to make available the best books ever written in every
field to the greatest number of people at the cheapest possible
price. He began with Boswell's 'Life of Johnson';
his one-thousandth title was Aristotle's 'Metaphysics',
by which time sales exceeded forty million.*

*Today Everyman paperbacks remain true to
J. M. Dent's aims and high standards, with a wide range
of titles at affordable prices in editions which address
the needs of today's readers. Each new text is reset to give
a clear, elegant page and to incorporate the latest thinking
and scholarship. Each book carries the pilgrim logo,
the character in 'Everyman', a medieval morality play,
a proud link between Everyman
past and present.*

LIBERTINE PLAYS
OF THE RESTORATION

Edited by
GILLIAN MANNING

EVERYMAN
J. M. DENT · LONDON
CHARLES E. TUTTLE
· VERMONT

Selection, introduction and other critical apparatus
© J. M. Dent 2001

This edition first published by
Everyman Paperbacks in 2001

J. M. Dent
Orion Publishing Group
Orion House, 5 Upper St Martin's Lane
London WC2H 9EA
and
Tuttle Publishing
Airport Industrial Park
364 Innovation Drive
North Clarendon
VT 05759-9436
USA

Typeset by Deltatype Ltd, Birkenhead
Printed in Great Britain by
The Guernsey Press Co. Ltd, Guernsey, C.I.

British Library Cataloguing-in-Publication Data
is available upon request.

ISBN 0 460 87745 3

For Elizabeth Howe

CONTENTS

NOTE ON THE AUTHORS AND EDITOR

APHRA BEHN (*c*.1640–1689)
JOHN DRYDEN (1631–1700)
THOMAS OTWAY (1652–1685)
THOMAS SHADWELL (*c*.1640–1692)
THOMAS SOUTHERNE (1660–1746)

Further information concerning these dramatists may be found in the Chronology and in the Introduction.

GILLIAN MANNING has taught for the Open University and in the School of English at the Queen's University of Belfast. Her doctoral thesis was on Rochester's poetry, and her publications include articles on seventeenth-century writing. She is a contributor to *That Second Bottle: Essays on John Wilmot, Earl of Rochester*, ed. Nicholas Fisher (Manchester: University of Manchester Press, 2000). A book on Rochester's poetry is in preparation.

EDITOR'S NOTE

I should like to thank staff at the British Library for helping me to acquire microfilm and printout copies of early editions of the plays. I am most grateful also to staff at the libraries of the University of Exeter, and of the Queen's University of Belfast, for their courtesy and assistance. In addition, I owe innumerable debts to the many friends and colleagues from whom I have sought information, help and advice over the past months. In particular, I would like to thank: Mark Thornton Burnett, David Farley-Hills, Robert D. Hume, Derek Hughes, Peg Katritsky, Edward A. Langhans, Harold Love, Judith Milhous, Jessica Munns, Lynda Pratt, Penny Richards and James A. Winn. I am especially indebted also to David Farley-Hills, Derek Hughes, John Manning and Jessica Munns for their care in reading the Introduction, and for their incisive and valuable comments. My grateful thanks, too, to Malcolm Andrew for his long-standing support and encouragement for the project, and to my editors, Hilary Laurie and Kate Shearman, for their friendly efficiency and unfailing patience. Above all, I would like to offer my heartfelt thanks to Carol and Ken Mulholland, without whose technical expertise, painstaking help and shrewd advice, this edition would never have seen the light of day.

CHRONOLOGY

Dates given for plays are those of first recorded performance.
Dates for other works are those of first publication, unless otherwise stated.
Approximate dates are signified by *
Boldface entries concern dramatists with plays included in this edition.

Date	Historical & Cultural Contexts	British Dramatists' Dates & Key Plays
1631	John Donne d.	**John Dryden b.**
1633	Samuel Pepys b.	
1635		Sir George Etherege b.*
1637	René Descartes, *Discours de la Méthode*	
1639		Sir Charles Sedley b.
1640	1st Civil War began (ended 1646)	**Aphra Behn b.*** **Thomas Shadwell b.***
1641		William Wycherley b.
1642	Theatres closed by Parliament	
1643	Charles Sackville, Earl of Dorset b.	
1647	John Wilmot, Earl of Rochester b. Pierre Gassendi, *De Vita et Moribus Epicuri*	
1648	2nd Civil War	
1649	Charles I executed	
1651	Thomas Hobbes, *Leviathan*	

Date	Historical & Cultural Contexts	British Dramatists' Dates & Key Plays
1652	1st Dutch War began (ended 1654)	**Thomas Otway b.**
1653–5	Madeleine de Scudéry, *Artamenes, or the Grand Cyrus*, trans. in 5 vols.	
1655–62	Thomas Stanley, *History of Philosophy*	
1656	Charleton, Walter, *Epicurus's Morals* John Evelyn, *An Essay on the First Book of T. Lucretius Carus, De Rerum Natura*	Sir William Davenant, *The Siege of Rhodes* (staged at his house)
1658	Oliver Cromwell d.	
1660	Restoration of Charles II Royal Society founded Theatres re-open: creation of King's Company & Duke's Company by royal patent, granted to Thomas Killigrew, & Sir William Davenant, respectively **Dryden, *Astræa Redux*** Pepys begins diary (ends 1669)	**Thomas Southerne b.**
1661	Daniel Defoe b. Robert Boyle, *The Sceptical Chemist* Cowley, *A Proposition for the Advancement of Experimental Philosophy* Joseph Glanvill, *The Vanity of Dogmatizing* Molière, *L'École Des Maris*	Abraham Cowley, *Cutter of Coleman-Street*

Date	Historical & Cultural Contexts	British Dramatists' Dates & Key Plays
1662	Act of Uniformity Licensing Act Samuel Butler, *Hudibras*, 1 Smock Alley Theatre, Dublin, opens Margaret Cavendish, *Plays* Molière, *L'École Des Femmes*	Sir Robert Howard, *The Committee*
1663	Butler, *Hudibras*, 2	**Dryden, *The Wild Gallant*** Sir Samuel Tuke, *The Adventures of Five Hours*
1664		Sir John Vanbrugh b. Etherege, *The Comical Revenge* **Dryden, *The Rival Ladies*** **Dryden & Howard, *The Indian Queen***
1665	2nd Dutch War (ended 1667) Plague: all theatres closed François, duc de La Rochefoucauld, *Maxims*	**Dryden, *The Indian Emperor*** Roger Boyle, Earl of Orrery, *Mustapha*
1666	Great Fire of London Theatres re-opened (29 Nov.) John Bunyan, *Grace Abounding* Margaret Cavendish, *The Blazing World* Molière, *Le Misanthrope*	
1667	Dutch fleet burns English ships in the Medway Charles II's chief minister, Edward Hyde, Earl of Clarendon, impeached: flees into exile	

Date	Historical & Cultural Contexts	British Dramatists' Dates & Key Plays
	Dryden, *Annus Mirabilis* John Milton, *Paradise Lost* Katherine Philips, *Poems* Thomas Sprat, *History of the Royal Society* Abraham Cowley d. Jonathan Swift b. Molière, *Tartuffe* Jean Racine, *Andromaque*	Dryden, *Secret Love* Dryden, *Sir Martin Mar-all*
1668	Dryden made Poet Laureate Cowley, *Works* Dryden, *Essay of Dramatic Poesy* Margaret Cavendish, *Plays, never before Printed* Henry Nevile, *The Isle of Pines*	Davenant d. Dryden, *An Evening's Love* Etherege, *She Would If She Could* Katherine Philips & John Denham, *Horace* (perf. at Court) Sedley, *The Mulberry Garden* Shadwell, *The Sullen Lovers*
1669		Susannah Centlivre b. Dryden, *Tyrannic Love*
1670	Isaac Walton, *Lives of Donne, Wotton, Hooker, Herbert* Molière, *Le Bourgeois Gentilhomme*	William Congreve b. Dryden, *The Conquest of Granada*, 1 & 2 Behn, *The Forced Marriage* Shadwell, *The Humourists*
1671	Dorset Garden Theatre opened Milton, *Paradise Regained*; *Samson Agonistes*	Colley Cibber b. George Villiers, Duke of Buckingham, *The Rehearsal* Dryden, *Marriage A-la-Mode** Shadwell, *Epsom Wells*
1672	3rd Dutch War Joseph Addison b. Richard Steele b. Declaration of Indulgence to Catholics and Dissenters	

Date	Historical & Cultural Contexts	British Dramatists' Dates & Key Plays
1673	The Test Act Richard Allestree, *The Ladies Calling* Molière, *Le Malade Imaginaire* Molière d.	**Behn, The Dutch Lover** Elkanah Settle, *Empress of Morocco*
1674	Milton d. Earl of Clarendon d. Rochester, *A Satyr Against Reason & Mankind* (circulating in MS)*	
1675	Elizabeth Barry begins acting career	John Crowne, *Calisto* **Dryden, Aurengzebe** **Shadwell, The Libertine** Wycherley, *The Country Wife*
1676		**Behn, The Town Fop** Etherege, *The Man of Mode* **Shadwell, The Virtuoso** Wycherley, *The Plain Dealer*
1677	Thomas Rymer, *Tragedies of the Last Age Considered* Racine, *Phèdre*	**Behn, The Rover, 1** Crowne, *The Destruction of Jerusalem*, 1 & 2 **Dryden, All For Love** Thomas Durfey, *A Fond Husband* Nathaniel Lee, *The Rival Queens*
1678	The Popish Plot Bunyan, *Pilgrim's Progress*, 1 Andrew Marvell d. Richard Flecknoe d.*	**Behn, Sir Patient Fancy** **Dryden, The Kind Keeper** Farquhar b.* **Otway, Friendship in Fashion** **Shadwell, Timon of Athens** **Shadwell, A True Widow**

Date	Historical & Cultural Contexts	British Dramatists' Dates & Key Plays
1679	James, Duke of York sent from England Exclusion Bill introduced Hobbes d. Licensing Act expires (allowing a brief period of press freedom) Charles Blount, *Anima Mundi* Titus Oates, *A True Narrative of the Horrid Plot* . . .	Behn, *The Feigned Courtesans* Shadwell, *The Woman-Captain* Orrery d.
1680	Rochester d. Butler d. Comédie Française founded Robert Filmer, *Patriarcha* (composed 1630*) Gilbert Burnet, *Some Passages of the Life & Death of John, Earl of Rochester* Charles Blount (trans.), *The Two First Books of Philostratus*	Dryden, *The Spanish Friar* Lee, *Lucius Junius Brutus* Otway, *The Orphan* Otway, *The Soldier's Fortune* Settle, *The Female Prelate*
1681	Charles II dissolves Oxford Parliament Dryden, *Absalom & Achitophel*, 1	John Banks, *The Unhappy Favourite* Behn, *The Rover*, 2 Behn, *The Roundheads* Behn, *The False Count* Lee, *The Princess of Cleve** Edward Ravenscroft, *The London Cuckolds* Shadwell, *The Lancashire Witches*

Date	Historical & Cultural Contexts	British Dramatists' Dates & Key Plays
1682	Dryden, *MacFlecknoe* (written 1676*); *Religio Laici*; with Tate, *Absalom & Achitophel*, 2 United Company formed (after failure of King's Company) Thomas Creech (trans.), *T. Lucretius Carus ... De Natura Rerum*	Banks, *Virtue Betrayed* Behn, *The City Heiress* Otway, *Venice Preserved* Southerne, *The Loyal Brother*
1683	Rye House Plot John Oldham, *Poems* **Warrant issued for Behn's arrest after she attacks Monmouth in an epilogue**	Otway, *The Atheist** Crowne, *City Politics* Thomas Killigrew d. Nahum Tate, *A Duke & No Duke*
1684	**Behn, *Love-Letters* between a Nobleman & His Sister, 1; *Poems Upon Several Occasions***	Rochester, *Valentinian* Southerne, *The Disappointment*
1685	Charles II d. Accession of James II Theatres closed for 3 months Duke of Monmouth's rebellion fails **Behn, *Love-Letters*, 2** Anne Killigrew, *Poems**	Otway d. John Gay b. Crowne, *Sir Courtly Nice* Dryden, *Albion & Albanius*
1686		**Behn, *The Lucky Chance***
1687	Nell Gwyn d. **Behn, *Love-Letters*, 3** Sir Isaac Newton, *Principia* **Dryden, *The Hind & The Panther***	Buckingham d. **Behn, *The Emperor of the Moon*** Sedley, *Bellamira*

Date	Historical & Cultural Contexts	British Dramatists' Dates & Key Plays
1688	The Revolution: James II goes into exile Bunyan d. Alexander Pope b. George Savile, Earl of Halifax, *Advice to a Daughter; The Character of a Trimmer* (written 1684) **Behn, *Oroonoko***	**Shadwell, *The Squire of Alsatia***
1689	Accession of William & Mary Toleration Act War of the League of Augsburg (ended 1697) Richardson b. **Shadwell made Poet Laureate**	**Dryden, *Don Sebastian*** **Shadwell, *Bury Fair*** **Behn d.** **Behn, *The Widow Ranter***
1690	Battle of the Boyne (James II defeated in Ireland) John Locke, *An Essay Concerning Human Understanding; Two Treatises of Government*	**Dryden, *Amphitryon*** **Shadwell, *The Scourers**** **Southerne, *Sir Anthony Love***
1691	Gerard Langbaine, *An Account of the English Dramatists* Rochester, *Poems on Several Occasions* George Fox d. Racine, *Athalie*	Etherege d.* **Dryden & Henry Purcell, *King Arthur*** Durfey, *Love for Money* **Southerne, *The Wives' Excuse****
1692	Tate made Poet Laureate Congreve, *Incognita*	**Dryden, *Cleomenes, the Spartan Hero*** Settle & Purcell, *The Fairy Queen* **Shadwell, *The Volunteers*** Lee d. **Shadwell d.**

Date	Historical & Cultural Contexts	British Dramatists' Dates & Key Plays
1693	Thomas Skipwith & Christopher Rich take over the United Company Thomas Rymer, *A Short View of Tragedy* Blount, *The Oracles of Reason*	Congreve, *The Old Bachelor*; *The Double Dealer* Durfey, *The Richmond Heiress* **Southerne, *The Maid's Last Prayer*** George Lillo b.
1694	Queen Mary d. Fox, *Journal*	**Southerne, *The Fatal Marriage***
1695	Betterton & other leading actors secede to act in Lincoln's Inn Fields Halifax d. Purcell d.	'Ariadne', *She Ventures & He Wins* Congreve, *Love For Love* **Southerne, *Oroonoko*** Catharine Trotter, *Agnes de Castro*
1696		Anon, *The Female Wits* (mocks Manley, Pix & Trotter) **Behn, *The Younger Brother*** Cibber, *Love's Last Shift* Mary de La Rivière Manley, *The Lost Lover* Manley, *The Royal Mischief* Mary Pix, *The Innocent Mistress* Pix, *The Spanish Wives* John Vanbrugh, *The Relapse*
1697	Treaty of Ryswick **Dryden, *Alexander's Feast***	Congreve, *The Mourning Bride* Vanbrugh, *The Provoked Wife*
1698	Jeremy Collier, *A Short View of the Immorality & Prophaneness of the English Stage*	George Farquhar, *Love and a Bottle*

Date	Historical & Cultural Contexts	British Dramatists' Dates & Key Plays
1699		Farquhar, *The Constant Couple*
1700	**Dryden, Fables**	Congreve, *The Way of the World*
		Dryden, The Secular Masque
		Pix, *The Beau Defeated*
		Southerne, The Fate of Capua
		Trotter, *Love at a Loss*
		Dryden d.
1746		**Southerne d.**

INTRODUCTION

> Why should a foolish marriage vow
> Which long ago was made,
> Oblige us to each other now
> When passion is decayed?
> [John Dryden, *Marriage A-la-Mode* (1671), 1.1.4–7.]

> Since liberty, Nature for all has designed,
> A pox on the fool who to one is confined.
> [Thomas Shadwell, *The Libertine* (1675), 2.1.317–18.]

Libertine Drama: Definitions and Development

Libertine plays are by definition works centring upon rakish characters whose speech and conduct are geared to confront, with varying degrees of forcefulness, conventional codes of morals and manners. Each of the seven plays in this volume includes at least one such key character who decries or interrogates marriage, upholding instead a concept of individual licence flatly opposed to the sexual and social mores generally endorsed by late seventeenth-century English society. In a few cases, too, stage rakes may also maintain heterodox religious and philosophical ideas of a nature equally guaranteed to raise contemporary hackles. In addition, these libertine characters, who are usually, but not invariably, male, witty and charismatic, are shown as (at least) attempting to put their irregular views into practice, and often, also, as indulging in more routine forms of dissipation, such as excessive drinking and swearing. Clearly in a class of his own, however, being by far the most extreme and transgressive of these figures, is the ebullient Don John in *The Libertine*, Thomas Shadwell's reworking of the Don Juan legend. Don John is unique among stage rakes in being accredited conservatively with 'Some thirty murders, rapes innumerable, frequent sacrilege, parricide' (1.1.132–3). He is also unusual in seeking to underpin his libertine lifestyle with declarations of commitment to a rag-bag of sensationalist, sceptical and irreligious ideas, stoutly asserting, '[t]here is no right or wrong, but what conduces to, or hinders pleasure' (1.1. 136–8), and exhorting his friends and followers to join him in further excess: 'Let's on, and live the noble life of sense' (1.1.159).

As the above comments suggest, and as a number of recent studies have argued, Restoration stage libertines do not all conform rigidly to one pattern, despite having some basic features in common.[1] Moreover, though critical discussion of these figures has mainly focused upon their presence in comedies of the period, libertine elements are by no means confined to any particular dramatic genre, nor indeed to the drama *per se*. Libertine characters and ideas self-evidently dominate in *The Libertine*, a work which, if somewhat problematic generically, is at least nominally a tragedy; while they also contribute significantly to a number of other Restoration tragedies, among them, in the present collection, Otway's *The Orphan*. The categorisation of rakish characters has proved a task both tempting and tricky for critics, but has resulted (together with much else of value) in the coining of a number of descriptive terms which may assist the differentiation process, and hence, our understanding of the plays. Of these terms, perhaps the most useful are the following: 'the extravagant rake'; 'the vicious rake'; and 'the judicious rake', (also called 'the philosophical libertine').[2]

Briefly, the first of these categories comprises characters who are predominantly comic, likeable and entertaining, as well as promiscuous, and (often) wild and madcap. In the present volume, Willmore and Woodall, the sexually profligate protagonists of Behn's *The Rover*, and Dryden's *The Kind Keeper*, respectively, may be classed as 'extravagant rakes', and, like many of their kind, both are finally induced to exchange their much-prized freedom for financially advantageous marriages with pleasing partners. Nevertheless, it is debatable how seriously fifth-act agreements of this type should be taken as genuine tokens of moral 'reform'. This is particularly the case with plays of the 1670s such as the two just noted, despite Dryden's somewhat glib assurance that a stage rake's marriage equates with reformation: '[dramatists] make not vicious persons happy, but only as heaven makes sinners so: that is by reclaiming them first from vice. For so 'tis to be suppos'd they are, when they resolve to marry'.[3]

By contrast, the term 'vicious rake' has been used to denote a more disturbing category of hard-core libertine, who either wholly eschews marriage, or shows total contempt and disregard for the married state. Characters of this kind, such as Nemours in Lee's *The Princess of Cleve* (c. 1681), or the eponymous Valentinian in Rochester's tragedy (1684), are often presented as cynical sexual predators who may have wit, but are rarely designed to win audience sympathy or approval. Notable examples in this volume are (inevitably) Don John and his cronies in *The Libertine*, together with a whole clutch of assembled rakes in Southerne's comedy, *The Wives' Excuse*: Friendall, Lovemore, Wilding and (arguably) Mrs Witwoud.

The third category, 'the judicious rake', or 'the philosophical libertine', has been taken to comprise quite a broad band of rakish characters. Though diverse in many respects, they share a courtly smoothness, polish and self-control, together with qualities of wit and intelligence – all of which may combine to lend them a certain glamour and appeal, and to win them (with reservations) general endorsement within the social contexts of their respective plays. Such figures may in fact *be* courtiers, as are Palamede and Rhodophil in Dryden's *Marriage A-la-Mode*; or, at least *would-be* courtiers, like the affected Melantha in the same play; or, from very different motives, Polydore, in *The Orphan*. But, in any case, they are usually depicted as subscribing to a libertine lifestyle akin to the one that prevailed during the 1670s among the so-called 'merry gang' of Charles II's intimate friends and courtiers.[4] The most notable members of this circle, who were themselves all gifted writers, included: Sir George Etherege; Charles Sackville, Lord Buckhurst (later, Earl of Dorset); Sir Charles Sedley; George Villiers, Duke of Buckingham; and John Wilmot, Earl of Rochester. More specifically, Rochester, the most brilliant of the court wits, was the dedicatee of *Marriage A-la-Mode*, and was reputed to have provided the model for Dorimant, the 'philosophical libertine' in Etherege's *The Man of Mode*. Unlike the libertine wits of Charles II's court, however, stage rakes of this species rarely profess overt support for any current heterodox religious or philosophical ideas. As one scholar has recently warned: 'the amount of philosophy behind the aggressive sexual behaviors of the young males depicted on stage can be exaggerated'.[5] Nevertheless, they may at times show traces of the same counter-cultural, intellectual influences more openly avowed by their real-life court contemporaries: notably, sceptical and materialist ideas gleaned from Thomas Hobbes's *Leviathan* (1651), as well as from the newly fashionable, classical philosophies, Epicureanism and Pyrrhonism.[6]

The crucial issue of how far (or whether) we should view rakish plays of the period as endorsing libertinism has been magisterially surveyed with regard to the comedies by R. D. Hume. He finds that 'there is no instance in late seventeenth-century comedy in which "libertinism" is presented both seriously and favorably', and concludes that, 'reputation notwithstanding, "Restoration comedy" gives precious little support to libertinism'. Moreover, as Hume also points out, *any* representation of libertinism on the public stage, irrespective of the viewpoint from which it was presented, would have been anathema to the Restoration moral majority.[7] All of which raises a number of intriguing questions concerning the reception and development of plays of this kind, and the nature of their evident importance for late seventeenth-century drama and culture. However, before considering the works in this volume individually in relation to these issues, it may be useful to outline a general trajectory for libertine drama of the period, noting briefly en route where and how these particular plays fit in.

The earliest work in this collection, *Marriage A-la-Mode*, was first performed *c.* November 1671, and the latest, *The Wives' Excuse*, either in late 1691 or early 1692. Relatively few plays that could be fairly described as 'libertine' were written in the years immediately after 1660, when the Stuart monarchy was restored and the theatres officially re-opened, and *Marriage A-la-Mode* is often taken as a convenient marker for the beginning of the most intensive phase of libertine drama. Similarly, though *The Wives' Excuse* was by no means the last libertine play to appear, and in fact formed part of a brief resurgence of works of this kind, its poor reception may be read at least in part as a sign of the times. Stage libertinism was under threat in the 1690s and in its death throes, as far as the production of new plays was concerned, by the turn of the century. The majority of libertine plays were produced during the reign of Charles II (1660–85) and are therefore termed 'Carolean', with the vogue for this kind of drama peaking in the mid-to-late 1670s. It should be stressed, however, that even during this period, and for all their undoubted influence, such works formed only a relatively small proportion of the totality of new plays, which were very varied in kind. Nevertheless, among the 1670s libertine plays, many of them sex comedies, may be numbered some of the most celebrated theatrical successes of the age. These plays included Wycherley's *The Country Wife* (1675), Shadwell's *The Libertine* (1675), Etherege's *The Man of Mode* (1676), and Behn's *The Rover* (1677), which were all highly successful, as well as one of the decade's most intriguing failures, Dryden's *The Kind Keeper* (1678).

By 1680, the profound political unrest which accompanied the Popish Plot and the Exclusion Crisis resulted in declining support for the two London theatre companies, until in 1682, the financial straits of the King's Company forced it to unite with its stronger rival, the Duke's Company. In this period of political and theatrical crisis that extended from the late 1670s to the early 1680s, there were, nevertheless, some outstanding plays. Many dramatists declared their Royalist or Opposition sympathies, and plays of most kinds became increasingly politicised.[8] Of the works in the present volume, for instance, both *The Orphan* (1680) and *The Rover*, Part 2 (1681) are politically highly charged, despite the fact that neither is directly nor centrally concerned with politics. In these years, too, more tragedies were produced, while dramatic writing in general was marked by a darkening of tone and heightening of satiric input. In keeping with the latter tendency, and despite the presence of some lively farcical episodes, *The Rover*, Part 2, Behn's sequel to her hugely successful comedy of 1677, is a noticeably more serious and obsessive work than its high-spirited predecessor.

After the two companies amalgamated, fewer new plays of any kind were produced, and this pattern continued almost to the end of the decade. Various reasons have been suggested for this, and factors would seem to have included the lack of competition for the newly formed United Company, and the death of Charles II (1685), a keen patron of the drama, together with the gradual dissolution of a strong theatre-culture at court. Also of key importance were the political upheavals surrounding his brother James's accession to the throne and subsequent rapid ejection in favour of William and Mary (1688). Not only did the number of libertine plays decline during this period, however, but, as the decade advanced, such plays tended to be less favourably received than had formerly been the case, with notable casualties evidently including Behn's *The Lucky Chance* (1686) and Sedley's *Bellamira* (1687).[9]

This latter trend was confirmed in the early 1690s, when new plays were once more being produced in greater numbers, and there became apparent a perceptible shift in audience tastes, especially among the 'ladies', towards more moral and 'humane', and occasionally, even 'exemplary', plays.[10] Interestingly, revivals of older libertine plays seem to have been more successful than productions of new ones. Yet even here, there is perhaps some evidence of changing tastes, as instanced by the famous actor-dramatist, Colley Cibber's account of William Mountfort in the role of Willmore, at a court performance of *The Rover* (November 1690):

> The *agreeable* was so natural to him, that even in the dissolute character of the Rover he seem'd to wash off the guilt from vice, and give it charms and merit. For tho' it may be a reproach to the poet, to draw such characters, not only unpunish'd, but rewarded; the actor may still be allow'd his due praise in his excellent performance. And this is a distinction which ... Queen

Mary was pleas'd to make in favour of Monfort, notwithstanding her disapprobation of the play.[11]

During this decade there were repeated calls for the moral reform of the stage, most notoriously in Jeremy Collier's intemperate attack on contemporary dramatists, *A Short View of the Immorality and Profaneness of the English Stage* (1698).[12] Libertine successes still occurred, however, prime examples among the comedies being: Southerne's *Sir Anthony Love* (1690), which figures a lively female rake *en travestie* in the title role; and Congreve's *The Old Bachelor* (March 1693). Both these younger dramatists were strongly promoted by Dryden, and were among those writers keen to 're-visit' libertine concerns and features of the earlier drama, though often to bleaker, sourer effect than their 1670s predecessors. However, Congreve's next work in this vein, *The Double Dealer* (November 1693), failed to win the popular applause gained by his first effort. Similarly, Southerne's *The Wives' Excuse*, his finest libertine play and perhaps his most impressive work, proved a failure relative to the runaway success enjoyed by its immediate predecessor, *Sir Anthony Love*. After the lukewarm reception accorded to another of his libertine comedies, *The Maid's Last Prayer* (February 1693), Southerne turned instead to writing tragedies of pathos. *The Fatal Marriage* (1694) and *Oroonoko* (1695) both won him instant acclaim.

Unsurprisingly, dramatists who employed libertine materials during these years seem to have been increasingly concerned to present them tactically, often intermingling them with 'softer', less potentially offensive elements. In general, too, as, for instance, in *The Wives' Excuse* and *The Maid's Last Prayer*, stage rakes of this period are subjected to critiques of a much harsher kind than those found in plays of the 1670s. Moreover, the rake-hero figure characteristic of earlier libertine plays virtually disappears in 1690s drama, or, rather, his attributes tend to be divided there between two or more characters. Thus, his wit and charisma may devolve on a new type of hero, now presented as a more prudent and moral kind of character: an *honnête homme*, or at least a genuinely 'reformed' libertine. On the other hand, the amoral, appetitive qualities seen in the old-style rake-hero often fall instead to the hero's 'friend' or associate, who may in consequence emerge as something of a villain. Effectively, this method of presentation signals the rejection and defeat of libertinism, and while brilliantly managed, for example, in Congreve's last and greatest play, *The Way of the World* (1700), its deployment there pointed also to the imminent demise of libertine drama. Though old, stock libertine plays, including, eventually, Congreve's own, continued to be regularly performed until the mid-eighteenth century, the production of new plays containing significant libertine elements virtually ceased in 1707 with the death of Farquhar.[13]

The Plays and their Contexts

While libertine drama in general was clearly more popular in the 1670s than it became by the end of the century, it is evident that moral objections were raised by some almost as soon as the first plays of this kind began to appear. Nor did all the complaints come from pious non-theatre-goers, or clerics, of the type later represented by Jeremy Collier. As early as 1668, Thomas Shadwell famously denounced what he viewed as the unacceptable aspects of some (unspecified) contemporary comedies:

> . . . in the *Playes* which have been wrote of late . . . the two chief persons are most commonly a Swearing, Drinking, Whoring, Ruffian for a Lover, and an impudent ill-bred *tomrig* for a Mistress, and these are the fine People of the *Play*; and there is that Latitude in this, that almost any thing is proper for them to say; but their chief Subject is bawdy, and profaneness . . .
>
> [Preface to *The Sullen Lovers*][14]

In fact, only a handful of plays written in the first eight years of the Restoration even approximately fit this description. Several of these are by Dryden, already Poet Laureate (April 1668) and a highly successful dramatist, and Shadwell, who undoubtedly has Dryden in his sights here, is using the Preface to his own first play to snipe at his famous rival's theory and practice of comedy. Nevertheless, though Shadwell's complaints may be somewhat jaundiced and exaggerated, his ethical stance would seem to be sincere, being widely reflected throughout his works, most of which seek to endorse traditional moral, social and religious values. Moreover, despite the obvious bias and short-comings of Shadwell's assessment of contemporary comedies, the features which he identifies so pejoratively, if not much in evidence by 1668, were certainly about to become both widespread and popular. By the mid-1670s, many comic dramatists were busy ringing the changes on the so-called 'gay couple', who typically comprise a witty, outspoken rake-hero, matched with, and against, in bouts of lively repartee, an equally witty, daringly outspoken, but (usually) chaste heroine.[15] The latter, though almost invariably intent on retaining her virginity until marriage, is yet a far cry in style and manner from the models of female behaviour widely upheld in former times. Thus, in early seventeenth-century sermons and conduct books, women were typically exhorted (mainly by men) to be chaste, silent and obedient.[16] While such patriarchal notions had already begun to be questioned in the Renaissance period, and continued to be challenged throughout the late seventeenth century, they were by no means eradicated, and presumably Shadwell was not alone in finding the representation on stage of 'impudent ill-bred *tomrig[s]*' disturbing.[17] The impact of witty, outspoken, female characters would have been further enhanced for audiences by the fact that these roles were now played by women, rather than boys: the post-1660 introduction of profes-sional actresses on the public stage in England having consti-tuted one of the prime innovations of Restoration theatre.[18]

Marriage A-la-Mode offers sparkling female roles of this kind, and takes in much entertainingly risqué dialogue and action. In addition it includes one highly suggestive song ('Whilst Alexis lay pressed', 4.2.47), and another, sung by a young wife, which sets the tone in the first scene by scorning the restrictions of 'a foolish marriage vow' (1.1.4). The Epilogue assures the audience that the dramatist's aim is moral improvement (l.2), and stresses that he drew the line at portraying adultery: 'Though 'twas well offered, there was nothing done' (l.12). Nevertheless, it is clear that Dryden is in part trying to have his cake and eat it, and that a considerable portion of his comedy would have been more than capable of causing affront. *Marriage A-la-Mode* was a huge popular success, but there is also evidence that it aroused considerable opposition and critical debate. In consequence, vehement pamphlets were produced for and against libertinism and marriage, with one anti-libertine theatre-goer particularly incensed to see 'both Boxes and Pitt [i.e. the most expensive seats] so damnably crouded'.[19]

Though the controversy probably did the play more good than harm, the mixed response of the audience set a pattern that was repeated throughout the decade with regard to a number of libertine plays. The reasons for the continued success of such plays during this period, despite ongoing protests, are complex and hard to determine precisely. Obvious and immediate causes must have included the examples of Charles II and his court circle who were notorious for their libertine lifestyles, and who were also powerful and enthusiastic patrons of the London stage. Dryden, for example, in the Dedication of *Marriage A-la-Mode*, attributes any exceptional merit that may be found in his play to 'the favour of being admitted into [Rochester's] conversation' and claims it is to Rochester that 'we [writers] generally owe our protection and patronage' (ll.16–17 & 63–4). Less specific influences on the keen interest in representations of libertinism would seem likely to be located among such widespread Carolean phenomena as the rationalistic, pragmatic and sceptical questioning of old certainties and authorities, whether in social, scientific, religious or political spheres.[20] In an essay of 1673, Dryden argues that, since the king's return from Continental exile, English manners and conversation had begun to acquire something of the stylish ease and elegance displayed at Charles II's Francophile court. He attributes this change to the king's influence and remarks: 'insensibly, our way of living became more free'. Given the high profile of 1670s libertinism, however, some modern critics have understandably been led to perceive more far-reaching significance in Dryden's comment than its immediate context might otherwise admit.[21]

Marriage A-la-Mode (1671)

In *Marriage A-la-Mode*, which Dryden thought 'perhaps . . . the best of [his] comedies' (Dedication [1673], l.96), there are two plots juxtaposed: a comic plot in prose, and a serious plot in verse, the latter sourced mainly from Madame de Scudéry's best-selling, heroic romance, *Artamène: ou le Grand Cyrus* (1649–53).[22] In the comic plot, Dryden presents not one, but two 'gay couples'. However, he varies the pattern he had himself helped to establish by depicting one of these pairs of courtly lovers, Rhodophil and Doralice, as already disaffected and bored with each other after two years of marriage. The other couple, Palamede and Melantha, have not yet met as the play begins, but are subject to a pre-arranged engagement imposed on them by their respective fathers. Rhodophil is already secretly courting Melantha, while his friend, Palamede, newly returned from foreign travel, soon becomes attracted to Doralice and vice versa. The scene is thus rapidly set for potential intrigue and exchange of partners, attended, amid much witty repartee, by cross-dressing, mistaken identity, jealousy and confusion. There is lively and sophisticated debate concerning the key issue of extramarital sex. The problems of parentally enforced marriage, still a highly topical concern in Restoration England, are lightly reviewed, while also on the agenda are 'modern' notions of 'open' marriage. For all their efforts, however, the lovers fail to encompass their libertine desires. Though Rhodophil and Doralice teeter on the brink of adultery, and both men hanker briefly after a 'blessed community' (5.1.396.) in which partner swapping would be *de rigueur*, they finally opt pragmatically, and with due reluctance, for a good-humoured settlement of their differences and the reassuring confines of conventional marriage.

Throughout the comic plot, issues of sexual and emotional autonomy are uppermost, with the desires of the individual set up in opposition to a broader nexus of familial and social demands and expectations. In apparent contrast, the romance plot turns on 'high' politics, and concerns the convoluted process whereby Leonidas, the lost heir and true ruler of the usurped kingdom, is discovered and eventually restored to power. Though the kingdom in question is ostensibly Sicily, the situation would have held obvious, more immediate connotations for 1670s audiences, especially since the popular Royalist theme of legitimate rule restored would have been already familiar from a number of recent works. The comic and serious actions are kept separate until the play's last scene, though, despite the contrast of modes, there is significant parallelism of ideas and circumstance. Issues of legitimacy, unstable identity, shifting attitudes and personal autonomy are central to both plots, with difficult choices being similarly posed between private desires and the duties and responsibilities owed to the family, society and the state. In the last scene, both plot strands are united as the courtiers and would-be libertines, Rhodophil and Palamede, turn from resolving their tangled private lives to intervene crucially in affairs of state. By force of arms they bring about the final dénouement, in which Leonidas is saved from imminent execution and restored both to his crown and to Palmyra, his first love. The restoration of a traditional, patriarchal order is therefore apparently achieved in both the comic and serious plots, with the humorous, negotiated consensus of the former anticipating, in its cautious pragmatism, the conservatism of some of Dryden's arguments in his great Tory satire, *Absalom and Achitophel* (1681).[23]

Whatever one makes of the play's conservative conclusion, which some critics have found less than convincing, Dryden's portrayal of his rakish characters as inherent and active royalists helped confirm a pattern of association which persisted in much libertine drama until the late 1680s. Certainly, the majority of libertine protagonists in plays of the 1670s are more immediately concerned with sex than with 'high' politics. However, it has recently been persuasively argued that such characters may still hold political significance in that they convey 'the *élan* of the court through the charismatic presence of [figures] so often affiliated with it'.[24] Moreover, as *Marriage A-la-Mode* and some other libertine plays would seem to suggest, rakes and tyrants may be viewed as comparable in their desire for autonomy and arbitrary power, whether in the sexual, or in the political sphere.[25]

The Libertine (1675)

Unlike the royalist rakes in *Marriage A-la-Mode*, Shadwell's rakish aristocrat, Don John, acknowledges no extrinsic authority, temporal or divine. As his servant, Jacomo, informs the hapless Leonora, one of Don John's many abused mistresses: 'He owns no deity but his voluptuous appetite, whose satisfaction he will compass by murders, rapes, treasons, or aught else' (1.1.224–6.) Conspicuous excess is Don John's watchword, and though *The Libertine* borrows copiously from other plays based on the Don Juan legend, Shadwell's characters and incidents are presented in a much more extreme and sensational manner than those of his predecessors.[26] Speed and brevity are essential elements here, and, throughout a relatively short play, Shadwell brilliantly orchestrates a series of brief, episodic scenes in which Don John and his fellow libertines, Don Antonio and Don Lopez, plunge recklessly from crime to crime. They blaze a defiant trail of multiple rape, murder, pillage and sacrilege right up to the point of their inevitable, final damnation. Then, in a grand, climactic church-scene, surrounded by the ghosts of their former victims, they disdain all calls to repent, and are swallowed up by hell to the vigorous accompaniment of a chorus of devils.

There has been much critical debate as to what we are to make of all this and arguments have turned largely on the vexed question of the play's genre. *The Libertine* is described as 'A Tragedy' on the title page of the first edition (1676), but while the central protagonist is undeniably dead by the end of the play, as indeed are most of the other characters, the general tone of the piece is hardly tragic. This may be partly attributed to the nature of the basic materials, since all dramatists who have worked with the Don Juan legend have had to deal with the problematic issue of its serio-comic aspects. Shadwell's version exaggerates these aspects, however, and though some have seen *The Libertine* as a horror tragedy, its tone has been aptly described elsewhere as 'furiously unstable' and 'frequently closer to that of black comedy'.[27] The action is too breathless and sensational to admit of any very lasting or serious emotion on the audience's part; and the characters, whether villains or victims, are too sketchily drawn to inspire much by way of sympathy, or psychological interest. In addition, there is a fair admixture of entertaining satiric humour and farce. The former is mainly supplied by the witty cynicism of Don John and his followers; the latter, largely by the cowardly, much put-upon, but indestructible Jacomo, who not only survives the action, but reappears to deliver an amusing and suggestive Epilogue.

Shadwell himself apologises for *The Libertine*'s 'irregularities' (Preface, l.12), and describes it in the Prologue as: 'The most irregular play upon the stage / As wild and as extravagant as th'age' (ll.15–16). He would seem to be referring primarily here to his own disregard for the classical 'rules' of dramatic construction, but may also be glancing at the immoral actions of his vicious rakes. In the Preface, he is careful to express his 'hope that the severest reader will not be offended at the representation of those vices on which they will see a dreadful punishment inflicted' (ll.16–18). Nevertheless, we are often more inclined to be impressed by 'the liberating energy of those who question or defy authority' than by 'conventionally moral endings',[28] and it is doubtful if the huge success enjoyed by early performances of *The Libertine* should be attributed to its impeccable moral stance. Produced by the Duke's Company at their new, splendidly equipped Dorset Garden Theatre, it was evidently also a 'diverting' spectacular, which comprised much song and dance, and many scene changes and special effects. Above all, though no cast list survives, Thomas Betterton, the greatest actor of the age, is recorded as having 'Crown'd the Play' in the title role.[29]

It might seem that, in writing his 'Tragedy', Shadwell's prime concern was merely to provide something for everyone: from horror and spectacle to farce and cynical humour, while also including elements of burlesque and parody en route to a moralising conclusion. Some recent criticism, however, has seen the play predominantly as a harsh satire against libertinism, whether as manifested in real life (notably by Rochester and the other court wits), or as presented on stage.[30] There is considerable evidence to support this approach, in addition to Shadwell's well-known objections to the immorality of some contemporary comedies. Of obvious relevance are Don John's irreligion and his defiantly sensationalist stance, together with his sardonic view of human nature and emphatic rejection of all civil and religious restraints on the free expression of his sexual appetites. These notions would seem to echo, in a deliberately crude and exaggerated manner, some of the Hobbesian and sceptical ideas fashionable in the court wits' circle. There are also some general similarities between Don John's views and those argued in Rochester's most famous poem, *A Satyr Against Reason and Mankind* (1674), a work which played a major role in the ongoing hostilities between contemporary 'atheists' and prominent members of the Anglican clergy.[31] Moreover, given the perceived link between libertinism and the court, the revival of the play at a time of political crisis with the title, *The Libertine Destroy'd* (May 1682), suggests that the Whig Opposition thought it likely to prove effective as a piece of satiric, anti-court propaganda.[32]

Against the view of Shadwell's play as a savage satire against libertinism, one might cite its varied, but largely ebullient tone, and the fact that the play's pace, energy, and sheer spectacle could well tend to divert audience sympathies from Don John's succession of pious and innocent victims. Shadwell was also apparently on good terms with the court wits at this period. In fact, he was soon to receive a favourable mention (in marked contrast to his rival, Dryden) in Rochester's satiric assessment of contemporary writers, *An Allusion to Horace* (winter 1675-6). On balance, therefore, it seems more likely that Shadwell was trying to cater to all tastes by seeking to write an entertaining, mixed-mode play that hooked into the fashionable phenomenon of libertinism, but strove at the same time to portray it as deeply offensive and reprehensible. It may be that these aims were not wholly compatible or, indeed, realisable. Certainly, a terse note in Robert Hooke's diary suggests that any anti-libertine satire present in Shadwell's play may have proved too slippery for at least one contemporary theatre-goer. His entry for 25 June 1675 reads: 'Mr Hoskins and I at Shadwell. Atheistical wicked play'.[33]

The Rover (1677)

Behn was not only the first woman to work as a professional playwright in England, but also the first English, female dramatist to write libertine plays. As we have seen, libertine writers often encountered considerable opposition and hostility even when their plays were successful, and in Behn's case such disapprobation was compounded by the fact of her gender. The basic premise of the period was still that a woman who writes for money is morally suspect, since she is breaking with traditional codes of reticent, decorous female conduct, and is, in effect, selling herself – albeit in the literary market-place. As the misogynist satirist, Robert Gould, crudely puts it: 'For Punk [i.e. whore] and Poesie [sic] agree so pat / You cannot well be this and not be that'.[34] The fact that much of Behn's work, whether dramatic, or non-dramatic, is outspoken, as well as often erotic and sexually explicit, merely exacerbated her difficulties of gaining her due as a writer. Even Dryden exemplifies to some degree the kind of disapproval her work frequently incurred, when he cautions an aspiring young woman poet to avoid 'the licences which Mrs Behn allowed herself, of writing loosely [i.e. indecently], and giving . . . some scandal to the Modesty of her Sex'. However, he has the grace to add: 'I confess, I am the last Man who ought, in justice, to arraign her, who have been too much a Libertine in most of my poems'.[35]

Possibly because of previous charges of plagiarism, the earliest printed copies of The Rover appeared without Behn's name, despite the fact that only a few months earlier the play had scored her first, major stage success.[36] Behn based The Rover on Thomas Killigrew's unperformed play, Thomaso; Or, The Wanderer (written 1654; published 1663/4), and her own play is heavily indebted to its source as regards both basic materials and verbal detail.[37] However, Behn's skilful reshaping and alteration of these, together with her own many additions, make The Rover a wholly independent and much more dramatically effective work. The action takes place in Naples during the 1650s, and concerns the lively amatory adventures of a group of young, exiled, English cavaliers who arrive in the city at carnival time. Willmore, the Rover of the title, is so called because he is at once a wandering rake and the captain of a privateer, out for plunder in both capacities. Behn shared Dryden's monarchist loyalties, and while *The Rover* is only lightly politicised, she depicts Willmore and his friends as fervent royalists whose estates have been confiscated by the Puritan government, and who roam Europe (as did Killigrew himself) in support of the exiled king. In changing the setting of her play from Killigrew's Madrid to Naples, Behn sets up some telling points of comparison with English politics past and present. Naples at this time was a Spanish colony, and Behn depicts a sharp culture-clash between the sophisticated, tolerant, pleasure-loving Italians and their pompous, morally strict, and often hypocritical Spanish rulers. From a royalist viewpoint, the parallel between the situation portrayed in Naples, and that in England in the 1650s under Puritan rule is not far to seek. In addition, the cultural divisions depicted in *The Rover* reflect obliquely on those political and religious rifts in English society which had persisted after the interregnum, and which had not been effectively healed by the Restoration settlement.[38]

Behn's main preoccupation in *The Rover*, however, is with sexual politics, and though her comedy is predominantly humorous and light-hearted, she presents some acute insights into issues relating to the abuse and commodification of women, including attitudes to rape, prostitution and forced marriage. Moreover, Behn's stance as a convinced monarchist does not preclude her from critiquing some aspects of the male libertinism associated with royalist culture, and she subjects her band of English cavaliers to an entertaining and fairly relentless, satiric scrutiny. Despite the fact that Willmore is depicted as attractively witty, and courageous, he is also revealed to be flawed, fallible and, often, ridiculous in his capacity for drunken blunders, and his comic eagerness to engage sexually with almost any and every woman he encounters. Behn subverts and interrogates patriarchy with some panache in *The Rover*, but subscribes here (as she does not in the play's sequel) to the conventional comedy ending of multiple marriages. Thus, Hellena, the spirited other half of Behn's 'gay couple', outwits her dour brother, Pedro, so that together with Florinda, her more decorous sister, she may engage in carnival adventures. She contrives also to displace her rival, the beautiful courtesan, Angellica Bianca, in Willmore's fickle affections, hang on to her virginity, and hold out successfully for marriage – admittedly, as regards the last, with the help of a large fortune.

The character of Angellica appears as a somewhat enigmatic and discordant element within the comedy. Behn's portrayal of the proud and famous courtesan who succumbs to love for the first time, only to be betrayed, is tragicomic in tone, and the intensity of the passionate scenes of struggle between Angellica and Willmore is heightened by the intermittent use of loose blank verse rather than prose. After a melodramatic attempt to shoot the faithless Willmore, Angellica's predicament is left unresolved at the close of the play. In *The Rover*, Part 2, however, Behn chose to reprise and re-think this type of situation in a rather similar love triangle between Willmore (now conveniently widowed), Ariadne, a rich young virgin, and La Nuche, a Spanish courtesan. Consequently, this time round, Willmore eschews a conventional, wealthy match, opting instead for La Nuche as his life's partner, 'without the formal foppery of marriage' (5.4.248–9).

The Kind Keeper (1678)

The Kind Keeper had a short and inglorious stage career, despite its author's subsequent claim 'that this comedy is of the first rank of those which I have written' (Dedication, ll.109–10). Dryden's 'roaring, dirty farce' survived for only three performances in March 1678, and was then 'stopped' by the authorities, though for what reason, and at whose behest, still remains obscure.[39] In the Dedication, Dryden specifically denies that his play contains any personal satire ('It has nothing of particular satire in it', ll.111–12), though it is true that such denials were fairly routine. From the eighteenth century onwards, however, scholars have suggested a range of influential candidates who may have thought they had been attacked in *The Kind Keeper*, or perhaps whom others may have identified (rightly or wrongly) with characters in the play. Whatever the case, it seems clear that the comedy was also found offensive on moral grounds, though this alone, according to one modern critic, would hardly have been enough to get it banned, especially considering the number of equally risqué plays performed with some success in 1677-8.[40] At all events, Dryden himself maintains that the play has a moral end in view, being 'intended for an honest satire against our crying sin of keeping [mistresses]'. Nevertheless, he notes that he felt obliged to revise the work before its first publication (1680), and has therefore 'taken a becoming care that those things which offended on the stage might be either altered, or omitted in the press' (Dedication, ll.84-5, & 97-9). The original manuscript version of the play is lost, though a few intriguing notes on it have survived.[41]

Dryden seems to have had considerable problems with *The Kind Keeper*, not the least being that while writing the play he had to cope with having the king as his adviser and part-collaborator. In a letter of 1677, he refers to the project as 'the Kings comedy', and remarks that 'it will be almost such another piece of businesse as the fond Husband, for such the King will have it, who is parcell poet with me in the plott'. Thomas Durfey had recently had a smash hit with *A Fond Husband* (1677) which, as Dryden's letter implies, was a particular favourite of the king's. Durfey's play is an amoral, farcical, sex comedy of the kind then highly popular. Its main action centres upon cuckolding, and several parallels with *The Kind Keeper* suggest that Dryden, in writing the latter work, was mindful of the king's wishes. Evidently, also, the king had ideas of his own concerning the plot. Dryden mentions in his letter that 'one of the designes' in *The Kind Keeper* derives from 'a story [the king] was pleasd formerly to tell me', adding somewhat glumly, 'and therefore I hope he will keep the jeast in countenance by laughing at it'.[42] Attempts to identify the episode in question have proved inconclusive, though several attractive possibilities have been mooted.[43]

Dryden may have been writing against the grain in *The Kind Keeper*. Despite his later boast in the Dedication, the Prologue implies that he viewed the play as catering to a fickle and undiscerning audience, and consequently as falling below his usual standards. However, it is never less than a lively and amusing sex romp which touches in addition on more significant issues of class and sexual politics. For reasons unknown, Dryden changed companies for this play, offering *The Kind Keeper* to the Duke's Company at the Dorset Garden Theatre, rather than, as usual, to the King's Company. Dorset Garden was situated in the less fashionable 'City' sector of London, and depended more for its clientele on middle-class businessmen and tradespeople than did its rival in Drury Lane. Dryden's choice of setting and characters in *The Kind Keeper* may therefore have had some influence on his decision to change venues. At all events, he is concerned here with depicting a very different social scene from the courtly milieu of his earlier comedies. *The Kind Keeper* is set in the small, claustrophobic world of a distinctly down-market and dubious London boarding-house, presided over by the landlady, Mrs Saintly, a devout Dissenter, and (especially in matters sexual) a confirmed hypocrite. Her ill-assorted lodgers include the eponymous Mr Limberham[44] and his dominating mistress, Tricksy, together with the Brainsicks, an inharmonious married couple. Also in the household is Mrs Saintly's supposed daughter, the sharp-tongued Mrs Pleasance, while its mainstay is 'father' Aldo, described in the cast list as an 'honest, good-natured, free-hearted old gentleman of the town'. Aldo's once rampant libertinism is now perforce largely confined to a paternal role, in particular the overseeing of a group of whores who meet regularly at his rooms for advice and succour.

The highly farcical plot turns on the arrival of a young rake from travels in France. Bent on evading his wealthy father and an arranged marriage, he has changed his name from Aldo to Woodall, and plans to lie low at the boarding-house and continue to enjoy his accustomed libertine lifestyle. With the reluctant aid of his sententious servant, Gervase, Woodall cuts a swath through the female members of the household. He speedily seduces Tricksy, Mrs Brainsick, and the maid, Judith, while endeavouring, at the same time, to outwit Brainsick and Limberham; fob off his predatory landlady; negotiate the satiric sniping of Mrs Pleasance, and avoid recognition by his father.

After a series of narrow escapes, all (or most) is finally revealed. The besotted Limberham offers Tricksy marriage *and* a separate maintenance. The Aldos, father and son, are reconciled, and the latter agrees to marry Mrs Pleasance, now identified as wholly unrelated to Mrs Saintly, and as a suitably wealthy match.

Clearly, Dryden's main concern here is with fast-moving, titillating entertainment, and *The Kind Keeper* is admittedly lightweight relative to some of his other comedies. Nevertheless, in the course of the play, a number of sharp points are notched up regarding issues of gender, class and libertinism. One function of Woodall's cuckolding of the two 'cits' is to assert his class superiority as a 'gentleman', as Limberham points out resentfully in the epilogue (ll.7–16). Such social one-upmanship is somewhat undermined, however, by the fact that Woodall's intrigues often lead him to appear ridiculous (albeit still engaging). Urged on by his resourceful mistresses, he is led, for instance, to masquerade as an Italian perfume seller, or conceal himself in a chest, a still room, or an insalubrious closet, to avoid detection. The effects of this inadvertent self-mockery are enhanced by the officious Gervase, who constantly disputes his master's authority and pours scorn on his rakish habits, advising him that libertinism has now grown outmoded: 'Debauchery is upon its last legs in England. Witty men began the fashion; and, now the fops are got into't, 'tis time to leave it' (2.1.26–8).

Woodall and Mrs Pleasance hardly qualify as a 'gay couple', since they are neither outstandingly witty, nor partners in an intrigue. Moreover, Mrs Pleasance's role is not equally weighted with Woodall's: in fact she does not appear until Act III. However, she bears some resemblance to the witty heroines of 'gay couple' comedies in her capacity for outspoken, malicious comments on Woodall's antics. Like those characters, too, she envies the sexual licence assumed by male rakes, remarking: 'He [Woodall] makes love to one of 'em . . . It may be to both; for methinks I should have done so, if I had been a man; but the damned petticoats have perverted me to honesty' (3.1.10–13). Despite his attraction to Mrs Pleasance, Woodall objects, not merely to 'the noose of matrimony' *per se*, but, more especially, on socio-political grounds, to the prospect of acquiring a lower-middle-class 'fanatic' (i.e. a Dissenter) for a mother-in-law (4.1.321–2). Gervase, too, gives due weight to considerations of class and property, even placing them above those of gender, when he opts for the title of 'Mr Saintly' on marrying his landlady, explaining that 'When a man is married to his betters, 'tis but decency to take her name' (5.1.637–8). Dryden's conclusion in *The Kind Keeper* is characteristically, if rather perfunctorily, conservative: marriage is endorsed, and traditional hierarchies are upheld. Throughout the comedy, however, there is consistent, fairly even-handed mockery both of libertinism, and of conventional morals and mores. Hence, the final reassertion of the latter may seem less than wholly convincing, not least in the 'reformed' rake's ambiguous avowal to his prospective wife: 'All I can say is, I do not now begin to love you' (5.1.602–3).

The Orphan (1680)

Two years later, when Otway's *The Orphan* was first performed (February or March 1680), England was in a state of high political tension. In October 1678, the Popish Plot Crisis had broken, with lurid allegations circulating of a Catholic conspiracy to kill the king and leading Protestants, overturn the government and impose Catholicism on the nation by armed force. Widespread unrest and a species of witch-hunt followed, which was to result in the trial and execution of numerous innocent Catholics. Fears of Popery had meanwhile strengthened popular distrust and dislike of James, Duke of York, the king's brother and heir, whose conversion to Catholicism had long been an open secret. In May 1679, the newly elected and fiercely anti-Catholic parliament, mistrustful also of absolutist sympathies and corruption at court, attempted to have James barred from the succession. The Exclusion Crisis was thus under way, and politics rapidly polarised between the royalist supporters of James and the king on one side, and the 'country' or opposition party on the other, the two hostile factions becoming known by 1681 as 'Tories' and 'Whigs', respectively. The king had already ordered his brother abroad (March 1679), and James remained effectively in voluntary exile during most of the ensuing, heated, political struggle, only returning permanently to England in 1682.

Otway's royalist allegiance is plain, both from *The Orphan*'s Dedication, addressed to the Duchess of York, and from the play's politicised Prologue. The latter celebrates James's former military successes, together with his recent return home (ll.23–36), though in fact the subsequent peaking of the Exclusion Crisis (October 1680) ensured that his stay in England on this occasion was strictly temporary. The play itself, however, is not directly concerned with contemporary politics, but appears (ostensibly, at least) as a tragedy of private life, based on *The History of Brandon*, Part 1 of *The English Adventures* (1676) probably written by Roger Boyle, Earl of Orrery. Unlike its source, which is set in England, the action of *The Orphan* takes place on a remote country estate in Bohemia, and details the unhappy involvement of twin brothers, Castalio and Polydore, with their father's ward, Monimia, the beautiful and virtuous orphan of the title. The bones of the plot are simple, unlikely, but powerfully emotive. Courted by both brothers, Monimia marries Castalio, but the marriage is kept secret for reasons which (again, in contrast to the source) are never wholly satisfactorily explained. Polydore, the more rakish brother, overhears the couple arrange what he takes to be an illicit nocturnal assignation; substitutes himself for his twin and unknowingly commits incest with the unsuspecting Monimia. Consequently, when Castalio arrives soon after for his wedding-night tryst, Monimia's maid refuses him admittance, taking him for Polydore. From this point onward, events spiral ineluctably and disastrously out of control, until, finally, with all secrets revealed, the three main protagonists commit suicide, while death also seems imminent for the aged, grief-stricken Acasto, the father of the family.

The Orphan's 'tremendous power' to move audiences has been widely acknowledged, notably with reference to its early performances when Elizabeth Barry triumphed as Monimia – her first starring role in tragedy. As Downes records, 'she forc't

Tears from the Eyes of her Auditory, especially those who have any Sense of Pity for the Distress't'. In other respects, however, the play has long been seen as problematic, even in those periods when it was highly popular on stage. Collier included *The Orphan* among the many plays he lambasted for being 'smutty' and 'profane', and objected also to the abusive, anti-clerical sentiments expressed by Monimia's soldier brother, Chamont. By the mid-eighteenth century, some critics found the 'Circumstance on which the Catastrophe turns' to be 'gross and shocking', while nineteenth- and early twentieth-century commentators fastened on the plot as faulty and improbable.[45] More positively, recent criticism has focused on previously neglected areas of *The Orphan*, such as its political and psychological aspects, which together have proved crucial in advancing our understanding of the play.[46]

As noted above, *The Orphan* is not overtly political, but there are nevertheless numerous ways in which it reflects obliquely on current political concerns. One such resides in that very quality of indirection which is endemic to politics (especially, perhaps, of this period) and which also characterises Otway's play. Not only are the protagonists themselves largely preoccupied with problems of duality, deceit, secrecy, mistrust and suspicion, but also, throughout the play, matters tend to be implied or hinted at, rather than plainly stated. Often, these are suggested through the use of natural imagery, though in the key instance of Chamont's nightmare vision and its aftermath, an inset, extended, symbolic narrative is employed (2.1.221–58). In much the same allusive mode, Otway's decision to set his play in Bohemia enables him to set up a distanced, pastoral paradigm that both critiques, and eventually partly mirrors, the corrupt fragmented nature of contemporary English politics. Acasto's decision to reside in seclusion on his country estate is presented from the outset as a form of exile – one which he himself undergoes voluntarily, and with pride, but which he imposes autocratically and damagingly on his ambitious sons. Though he has fought valorously for his ruler in recent civil wars, and his loyalty remains absolute, he loathes the corrupt court where true honour and merit now go unrewarded, and which is frequented more by libertines, flatterers and hypocrites, than by honest men. This attitude has been taken to reflect something of Otway's own sympathies and impoverished state, and it clearly has relevance (from a royalist, but anti-court, perspective) to the English political scene of c.1680.

As the tragedy unwinds, and Acasto's family grows increasingly dysfunctional, those marks of libertinism which earlier were mainly seen as defining the immoral, atheistic 'Other' of the court, now become inscribed upon the once innocent, aristocratic household.[47] As regards the twins, this is adumbrated in the first scene, when they recount the hazards of the day's hunt. Their pursuit of the savage, 'foaming boar', a threatening image of lust and death, clearly features as a compensatory activity for that longed-for engagement in public and military life that is denied them by Acasto.[48] Not only Polydore, the more rakish twin, but Castalio also, becomes susceptible to libertine modes of thought and behaviour. This gradual transition is signalled at first when Castalio merely 'affects a libertine carelessness': decrying marriage and scorning woman as he seeks to conceal his serious love for Monimia (1.1.156–65). Polydore, however, is soon planning in earnest to seduce Monimia, and invokes misanthropic, theriophilic ideas of the kind to be found in Rochester's *Satyr Against Reason and Mankind* (1674), a work then widely viewed as a notorious encouragement to irreligion and vice.[49] Eventually, Castalio, too, comes to share similar sentiments, seeing man as a monstrous 'beast of reason', warped by his intellectual capacity, and far removed in his guilty depravity from the happily instinctive and innocent animals (5.1.17–28). By the play's close, all three main protagonists regard themselves as irredeemably polluted, and Acasto's increasing frailty after a sudden seizure figures the destructive moral sickness which has overtaken his household. Evocations of the Fall proliferate in the latter stages of Otway's ominous parable, and the dying Castalio's projections of universal chaos arguably carry more resonance than the play's stoical concluding couplet.

The Rover, Part 2 (1681)

Early in 1681, when England was still in the throes of political
crisis, Behn nailed her Tory colours to the mast by dedicating
Part 2 of The Rover to James, Duke of York. This Dedication is
both more stridently partisan and more personal than that of
The Orphan to Mary, Duchess of York, in the previous year,
and reflects, by comparison with Otway, Behn's greater intimacy and sympathy with the court, as well as a shift in current
politics. Evidently, The Rover was already a favourite with
James, and, in dedicating its sequel to him, Behn is at pains to
draw a parallel between the duke's position and that of her
exiled cavalier-hero. Thus, she compares James's predicament
past and present, as a courageous, wandering exile, fighting
abroad for king and country, with that of the impecunious,
dispossessed Willmore, 'a wanderer, too: distressed, beloved,
though unfortunate, and ever constant to loyalty' (ll.43–4).

Like The Rover, Behn's sequel is based on Killigrew's
Thomaso; Or, The Wanderer, and shares its 1650s setting.
However, in The Rover, Part 2, Behn retains Killigrew's Madrid
as the scene of the play's action, rather than changing it to
Naples, as she had done in Part 1. Willmore and Ned Blunt are
the only characters to appear in both plays and in early
performances of Part 2, William Smith and the great comic
actor, Cave Underhill, resumed the roles of Willmore and Blunt,
respectively, which they had created to such applause in March
1677. The now famous Elizabeth Barry again took the female
lead, having previously played Hellena, the spirited young
heiress who marries Willmore at the end of Part 1. In the sequel,
however, Barry was cast as the beautiful courtesan, La Nuche,
with whom Willmore is in love, and whose extramarital partner
he finally becomes, Hellena having been killed off by Behn prior
to the beginning of Part 2. The casting implications are
significant here, as so often with plays of this period, when a
relatively small theatre-going public would have been familiar
with the personnel of the two main companies, and frequently
also with their personal histories. It seems likely in this case, for
instance, that, in addition to drawing on Thomaso for
the character of Willmore, Behn derived some hints for her

rake-hero from a non-fictional libertine model: her friend and fellow poet, John Wilmot, Earl of Rochester, who had died the previous summer. Rochester had allegedly coached the previously unsuccessful Barry for the role of Hellena (reputedly for a wager), and had also engaged in a passionate affair with her, resulting in the birth of a much-loved daughter (December 1677).[50] In each part of *The Rover*, therefore, Barry played the character, whether virgin or whore, who is finally united with Willmore. Presumably, for those in the know, Behn's pairing off of Willmore and La Nuche at the end of Part 2 must have reflected intriguingly on the former relationship of her two celebrated friends, besides lending further resonance to the play's already urgent interrogation of marriage.

Though *The Rover*, Part 2 was successful on stage, it never won the long-standing popularity achieved by its predecessor. This may have been due in some measure to the difficulties caused by the current political unrest, which Behn complains of so vigorously in the Epilogue. The play itself, however, is intrinsically less high-spirited and immediately appealing than Part 1, though, arguably, in some respects more interesting. Early audiences may therefore have been unprepared for the sequel's generally harsher and often disturbing tone, especially, perhaps, in such bleakly farcical episodes as those concerning the exploitation and abuse of the two wealthy Jewish 'monsters' – the 'woman giant' and her dwarfish sister. Behn's retention of the Spanish setting from her source, possibly partly in compliment to the Duke of York, underlines the difference in mood between her two comedies. Madrid provides a more sombre backdrop than the lively scene of Naples in carnival time that figures in Part 1, and there is greater emphasis in the later work on the hardships and poverty endured by the expatriate, British, Royalist forces in Spain.[51] Even the familiar figure of Willmore, though still characterised by wit, energy and cheerful promiscuity, is somewhat less madcap and 'extravagant' than he appears in *The Rover*. Equally, Ariadne, the wealthy young virgin of Part 2, is less humorously witty and inventive than Hellena, her counterpart in the earlier play; though, like Hellena, she makes use of disguise and cross-dressing in her pursuit of Willmore. Moreover, the bouts of wit between Ariadne and Willmore are relatively lacklustre, and her prime motive in pursuing him appears to be her determination to avoid an arranged marriage with her cousin, Beaumond, who is also smitten with La Nuche, and therefore likely to prove an unsatisfactory, 'keeping husband' (2.2.128).

In addition, *The Rover*, Part 2, is distinguished by an intense, obsessive quality that Part 1 lacks. This derives largely from its close focus on the passionate but embattled relationship between Willmore and La Nuche, which forms the emotional centre of the play. The main bone of contention here is La Nuche's fear both of total commitment, and of the lack of security, emotional and financial, that commitment to the libertine Willmore may entail. For many of the characters, in fact, the bottom line is 'interest' – i.e. an individual's own mercenary advantage – and this key term resounds throughout the play, seemingly supporting La Nuche's sharp rebuke to the disguised Willmore that 'all the universe is swayed by interest' (3.1.240–1). In the corrupt world of the play, virtually everything and everybody is for sale, although delivery is not guaranteed, even when the asking price has been paid: a fact underlined by Willmore's trickery in his assumed role as a mountebank.[52] By and large, in Behn's dark comedy, vice in its grosser forms is punished and (relative) virtue rewarded: vice here being largely defined as hypocrisy, repressive morality and selfish greed; and virtue, as the capacity for generosity, love, loyalty and trust. A graphic instance of the former occurs in the final scene, when the cowardly Fetherfool steals some pearls belonging to the 'woman giant'. As he swallows them for 'safekeeping', he invokes Cleopatra, but the contrast between the Egyptian queen's famous gesture of reckless extravagance, and his own mean-minded, hoarding acquisitiveness is blatant, and his action receives its swift, farcical come-uppance in the form of a 'clyster' (5.4.364).

As in Part 1, morals and mores are politicised, but recent critics have disagreed in their readings of the later play's ideology. The fact that Behn was (in Hill's phrase) a 'radical royalist' has proved the main stumbling-block, since her radical

sexual politics have been seen as problematic in the light of her
fervent Royalism and 'her avowed intention of celebrating
cavaliers'.[53] Thus, from one viewpoint, Part 2 of *The Rover* has
been defined as a 'feminist interrogation' – and near 'excoria-
tion' – of the libertine ethos, despite the traditional association
of libertinism with Royalism (stressed here by the linking of
Willmore with James in the Dedication).[54] Conversely, it has
been persuasively argued that Behn successfully unites her stance
on sexual politics with her Royalism, and presents 'a polemic
intended to disseminate Royalist – and quasi-utopian – values',
more particularly among the 'Almighty rabble' (Prologue,
l.26).[55] Both views are perhaps somewhat overstated. Part 2 of
The Rover certainly critiques some aspects of Willmore's
libertinism, as does Part 1, but while it might be argued that the
critique offered in the later, darker play is more incisive,
Willmore is still presented positively, rather than negatively,
overall. The question of Behn's possible promotion of a Royalist
and 'quasi-utopian' vision is intriguing. An attractive ideal of
'free' yet committed love, between partners equal in sexual
desire, is surely invoked at the play's close, but there is also a
strong element of escapist, wish-fulfilment fantasy in the 'all for
love' pairing of her favoured protagonists: the courtesan and the
rake. As several critics have observed, Willmore and La Nuche
are 'outsiders', whose chosen lifestyle both excludes and frees
them from the security and trammels of conventional society.[56]
Moreover, the play also concludes in a routine, but amicable,
upper-class match between Ariadne and Beaumond, both, by
now, rather more thoughtful and willing to compromise. And
though Behn may not endorse this couple with as much feeling
as she does her maverick wanderers, they may yet perhaps be
seen to adumbrate the species of pragmatic, legally constrained
Royalism more likely to endure.

The Wives' Excuse (1691/2)

By contrast with Behn's expatriate, interregnum fantasy, *The
Wives' Excuse* offers a detailed, realistic evocation of contemporary life in London society. The latter play, though probably

Southerne's most brilliant work, was (as noted above) relatively unsuccessful when first performed, and seems not to have been revived on the professional stage until the recent Royal Shakespeare Company production (1994). There would appear to have been various likely reasons for the play's early failure, in addition to more general factors such as the changing moral and political climate. As several scholars have suggested, contemporary audiences may have been misled in their expectations, and hence disappointed by what they got.[57] Thus, for instance, the popular success of Southerne's previous, more light-hearted comedy, *Sir Anthony Love* (1690), may have led audiences to expect more of the same, though, as Southerne proudly notes, his mentor, Dryden, at once perceived the superior quality of *The Wives' Excuse* (Dedication, ll.43–5). It has been further proposed that the play's subtitle – *Cuckolds Make Themselves* – may have proved misleading: causing audiences to anticipate farcical cuckolding scenes far removed in kind from Southerne's dark study of a tormented, but determinedly virtuous, wife. The play had a star cast which included Barry, Betterton, Kynaston, and Susanna and William Mountfort, but it may be, as Holland has convincingly argued, that the casting itself proved deceptive with regard to audience expectations.[58] Whatever early audiences may have envisaged, however, the reality was, and is, a complex, subtly nuanced 'problem' comedy, that makes strenuous demands on actors and audience alike.

The play concerns the intrigues of a social circle centred upon a wealthy, recently married, but ill-matched couple – a scenario that may suggest some similarity with the comic plot in Dryden's *Marriage A-la-Mode*. But though Southerne, like other dramatists of the 1690s, was keen to 're-visit' concerns of earlier libertine comedy, his writing appears at times to have as much in common with Ibsen or Chekhov, in terms of its general approach and effect, as with Dryden, Behn, Etherege or Wycherley.[59] *The Wives' Excuse* is often witty and thought-provoking, but rarely humorous, and certainly not high-spirited, in the manner of *The Rover*, or the comic scenes in *Marriage A-la-Mode*. In his shrewd complimentary verses, Dryden commends Southerne's comedy for its wit, 'clean' language and moral decorum. However, he also suggests that his friend's 'laboured drama' may appeal more to the judicious reader than to the average theatre-goer, and recommends two 1670s dramatists as future models: Etherege, for his apparently effortless and accessible style of writing, and Wycherley, for his fund of inspired witty humour. The tactful implication here would seem to be that, for all its undoubted merits, Southerne's play is something of a tough nut for audiences to crack.

Modern scholarship would seem to concur with this view in part, and it has been persuasively argued that in effect Southerne 'radically re-invents' the way in which materials familiar from earlier libertine comedy might be dramatised.[60] The opening scene provides a striking instance of such innovation, since unusually for a play of this period it includes none of the central characters, but presents instead a group of footmen unnamed in the cast list. In a parody of upper-class social life, the servants while away the time with gaming and gossip as they wait for their employers to emerge from a fashionable 'music-meeting'. The audience thus receives a somewhat oblique and distanced account of the main protagonists, Mr and Mrs Friendall, and their various friends and acquaintances, as the cynical and self-interested servants comment sardonically on their employers' characters and relationships. Clearly the scene is a challenging one both for actors and audience, with the former being called on, as often throughout the play, for finely judged ensemble work requiring subtle orchestration. The audience, for their part, have to cope with the puzzle of working out who's who among the servants and their (as yet unseen) masters and mistresses, while also digesting the hints thrown out concerning a complex web of intrigues, actual and potential, involving the main characters. The scene is sharply satiric with the servants aping their employers even as they mock them, and the point is underlined by a brief, inset exchange between two saucy young pages who mimic, for their own amusement, a typical social encounter between their respective, affected ladies.

The Wives' Excuse has been termed an 'angry, ugly, and effective' satire,[61] and the sophisticated society under scrutiny is portrayed in general as hypocritical and corrupt. 'Vicious rakes'

predominate among the characters, and though the play scath-
ingly critiques such figures, Southerne makes it clear that the
society in which they move is for the most part quite prepared to
condone, if not openly to endorse, their activities, provided these
are kept relatively discreet. The play's moral minority is largely
female, comprising two attractive women of conscience – Mrs
Friendall and Mrs Sightly; and the plain-speaking, and, consequently, much mocked, Mrs Teazall, who represents an older,
more conservative and easily outraged, generation. The sole
male bastion of morality is Wellvile, Mrs Sightly's longtime
admirer. Presumably, Wellvile is also to some extent the
author's spokesman, since in an entertaining passage of meta-
drama he reveals to his friends, Wilding and Friendall, that he is
in the throes of composing a play called *The Wives' Excuse; or,
Cuckolds Make Themselves*. His project concerns an unhappy
young wife 'married to an impertinent, nonsensical, silly,
intriguing, cowardly, good-for-nothing coxcomb'. Amusingly,
however, Friendall, the egotistical 'blockhead' in question, fails
to recognise himself as the model for Wellvile's unflattering
portrait, just as he fails to perceive that the predicament outlined
is plainly his wife's (3.2.275–95). Wellvile's artistic 'problem' –
whether or not to have his heroine pay back her husband in his
own coin – is thus highlighted as the key issue in Southerne's
comedy. Southerne's self-referential layering points up, in
addition, the crucial importance of observation and appearances
for the society he portrays. As recent critics have noted, many
scenes in *The Wives' Excuse* take place either in fashionable
'open' spaces, such as public concert rooms, The Mall, or St
James's Park; or else amid social occasions at the Friendalls',
who are satirically dubbed 'a public private family' (1.1.54–5).[62]
Even the most intimate exchanges, therefore, are often conducted under constant threat of disclosure to the public gaze –
the most striking example occurring in the final scene, when
Friendall and Mrs Witwoud are discovered *in flagrante* at the
Friendalls' masquerade.

Southerne uses Wellvile's play-writing problem to foreground
Mrs Friendall's anguished state of indecision. Scornful and
resentful of her husband's folly and disregard, she is the victim

of an arranged match, and is effectively trapped in a humiliating marriage, since divorce in this period was not a viable option. She is, however, unwilling to revenge herself by the obvious means, despite the persistent attentions of the rakish Lovemore, and the knowledge that 'the town' would be unlikely to condemn her. Thus, even Mrs Teazall advises: 'use [Mr Friendall] as you please, nobody will think you wrong him' (3.2.41–2); while Springame, Mrs Friendall's rakish, younger brother, comments: 'She has satisfied her relations enough in marrying this coxcomb; now let her satisfy herself, if she pleases, with anybody she likes better' (1.2.47–50). The degree of acumen and subtle self-knowledge revealed in Mrs Friendall's speeches underlines her moral and intellectual complexity, as well as indicating how far Southerne's comedy diverges in its approach and techniques from libertine plays of the 1670s. As Cordner notes, Southerne's writing here is 'inventive and distinctive', and Mrs Friendall's prime motive for remaining 'honest' – the need to retain her own self-respect – would seem to owe little to conventional religious morality, or external pressures.[63]

The Wives' Excuse offers a rich diversity of strong, female characters, and the most compelling of these – Mrs Friendall apart – is her libertine antitype, Mrs Witwoud. In the play's first production, Susanna Mountfort took this role, having previously proved hugely popular as the witty, cross-dressing heroine in *Sir Anthony Love*. Though both these roles are rakish ones, that of Mrs Witwoud represents a far darker, more complex, and (for the period) somewhat unusual species of female libertine. Unlike many such characters, she is neither a courtesan nor a kept mistress, nor yet a *demi-mondaine*, but an unmarried society woman of respectable family, though the latter are (admittedly) close to disowning her. Seen by one scholar as, 'an evil, isolated, aging bawd', whose 'problem is her despair at her own unattractiveness', it seems possible that this is indeed the general impression Southerne wished to convey of her character.[64] However, as the recent RSC production has shown, Mrs Witwoud may be convincingly portrayed as a considerably more lively, powerful, and, in some respects, attractive, figure than the above description would suggest. While her scheming is certainly both malicious and potentially dangerous, it is arguable that such machinations arise from a more complex source than that of 'despair at her own unattractiveness'. She is, in any case, apparently involved in a liaison with a mysterious married man, her 'plague and pleasure' (2.1.68), and is clearly still capable of attracting the youthful rake, Springame. In all, Witwoud would seem more likely to be motivated by her often palpable frustration and resentment at her inability to live openly as a rakish wit – in other words, to enjoy the same degree of licence as that deemed (more or less) socially acceptable for male libertines. Inevitably, the deadly double standard then pertaining in sexual matters weighed even more harshly against female rakes. Thus, in the final scene, the publicly disgraced and confounded Mrs Witwoud is extruded from the social circle, while Friendall, her foolish, unintended partner in crime, is merely temporarily discomforted. Essentially, he is free to resume his accustomed role in society – even to the extent of incorporating his now estranged wife into his social round.

The activities of the more dangerous among the male rakes also pass relatively unregarded, with Wilding receiving no more than a tongue-lashing from Mrs Teazall for his brutal seduction of her young niece, Fanny. Lovemore, too, despite his apparent rejection by Mrs Friendall, has clearly not abandoned all hopes of achieving success with her (5.3.381–3), and perhaps with some reason. Though Mrs Friendall has consistently held out against his siege, this was clearly no easy victory, and, for all her shrewd insight, the audience alone are privy to the full extent of Lovemore's baseness (5.3.111–17). Some critics, also, have seen the play's ending as inconclusive regarding Mrs Friendall's predicament, and this would clearly be an interpretative option for an actor. In fact, it would seem likely to have been employed by Barry herself, as Dryden's commendatory verses suggest (ll.22–5). *The Wives' Excuse*, then, offers an ironic and pessimistic perspective on contemporary London society, and one which, perhaps understandably, failed to appeal to early audiences invited to view themselves in Southerne's dark mirror.

[1] See especially Robert D. Hume, 'The Myth of the Rake in "Restoration Comedy"', in *The Rakish Stage, Studies in English Drama, 1660–1800* (Carbondale & Edwardsville, 1983), pp.138–75; Robert Jordan, 'The Extravagant Rake in Restoration Comedy', in *Restoration Literature: Critical Approaches*, ed. Harold Love (London, 1973), pp.69–90; Richard Braverman, 'The Rake's Progress Revisited: Politics and Comedy in the Restoration', in *Cultural Readings of Restoration and Eighteenth-Century English Theater*, ed. J. Douglas Canfield & Deborah Payne (Athens, USA & London, 1995), pp.141–68.

[2] For the first and third terms, see Jordan, pp.69–73, 84; for the others, see Hume, p.159. My account of the rakish types is heavily indebted to both these essays.

[3] Preface to *An Evening's Love* (1671), in *Essays of John Dryden*, ed. W. P. Ker, 2 vols (Oxford, 1900), I, 143–4.

[4] *The Poems & Letters of Andrew Marvell*, ed. H. M. Margoliouth, 3rd edition, 2 vols (Oxford, 1971), II, p.355.

[5] Jessica Munns, 'Change, skepticism, and uncertainty', chapter 9 in *The Cambridge Companion to Restoration Theatre*, ed. Deborah Payne Fisk (Cambridge, 2000), p.142.

[6] For a detailed account of libertine philosophy in relation to Restoration comedy, see especially chapter 2 in Dale Underwood, *Etherege and the Seventeenth-Century Comedy of Manners*, (New Haven, 1957).

[7] 'Myth of the Rake', pp.175, 172.

[8] For a stimulating survey of the interrelations between politics and plays at this time, see Susan J. Owen, *Restoration Theatre and Crisis* (Oxford, 1996).

[9] Both dramatists in their respective prefaces to these plays complain of an adverse response from 'the ladies' to the works in question.

[10] See David Roberts, *The Ladies: Female Patronage of Restoration Drama 1660–1700* (Oxford, 1989).

[11] Cibber, Colley. *An Apology for the Life of Mr Colley Cibber, Comedian*, ed. B. S. Fone (1968), p.75.

[12] Collier's attack drew spirited ripostes from two of his chief targets, Congreve and Vanbrugh.

[13] For further discussion of the change of taste issue, see Arthur H. Scouten & Robert D. Hume, '"Restoration Comedy" and its Audiences, 1660–1776', *The Rakish Stage*, pp.46–81.

[14] *The Works of Thomas Shadwell*, ed. Montague Summers, 5 vols (1927), I, 11.

[15] See John Harrington Smith's pioneering study, *The Gay Couple in Restoration Comedy* (Cambridge, Mass., 1948).

[16] See, e.g., Suzanne W. Hull, *Chaste, Silent and Obedient: English Books for Women, 1475–1640* (San Marino, Calif., 1982).

[17] Sir Robert Filmer presents a classic argument for patriarchy in his political treatise, *Patriarcha* (composed *c.* 1630; pub. posth. 1680). By the time of its first publication, it proved something of a rearguard action. See *Patriarcha & Other Writings*, ed. Johann P. Sommerville (Cambridge, 1991).

[18] See Elizabeth Howe, *The First English Actresses: Women and Drama 1660–1700* (Cambridge, 1992).

[19] Anon., *Marriage Asserted . . .* (1674), cited in *A Register of English Theatrical Documents 1660–1737*, ed. Judith Milhous, & Robert D. Hume (1991), I, 159.

[20] For comment on these contexts, see Derek Hughes, *English Drama 1660–1700* (Oxford, 1996), chapter 1; Munns, 'Change, skepticism, and uncertainty'. For broader coverage of the intellectual context, see Don Cameron Allen, *Doubt's Boundless Sea: Skepticism and Faith in the Renaissance* (Baltimore, 1964); Richard H. Popkin, *The History of Scepticism from Erasmus to Descartes* (New York, 1964); Michael Hunter & David Wootton (eds), *Atheism from the Reformation to the Enlightenment* (Oxford, 1992).

[21] Dryden, 'Defence of the Epilogue', in Ker, I, 176. For comment on Dryden's remarks here, see, e.g., Maximilian E. Novak, 'Margery Pinchwife's "London Disease": Restoration Comedy and the Libertine Offensive of the 1670's', *Studies in the Literary Imagination*, vol.10 (1977), 4–5; Braverman, 151–2.

[22] An equally popular English version soon appeared: *Artamenes, or the Grand Cyrus*, trans. F.G., 5 vols (1653–5).

[23] See especially, ll.796–810.

[24] Braverman, 143.

[25] For the linking of libertinism with tyranny and absolutism, see Michael Neill on Shadwell's *Libertine*: 'Heroic Heads and Humble Tails: Sex, Politics, and The Restoration Comic Rake', *The Eighteenth Century*, vol. 24, no. 2 (1983), 118–20.

[26] For Shadwell's sources, see *The Works of Thomas Shadwell*, ed. Montague Summers, 5 vols (1927), III, 9–10.

[27] Neill, 128. Neill also notes Shadwell's use of burlesque and parody, 129–30.

[28] Munns, p.150.

[29] Gerard Langbaine, *An Account of the English Dramatick Poets* (1691; rptd New York, 1973), p.448; John Downes, *Roscius Anglicanus* (1708), ed. Judith Milhous & Robert D. Hume (1987), p.78.

[30] See, e.g., Owen, pp.176–7, 181; Laura Brown, *English Dramatic*

Form, 1660–1760: An Essay in Generic History (New Haven, 1981), p.106; Brean Hammond & Paulina Kewes, 'A Satyre against Reason and Mankind from Page to Stage', in *That Second Bottle: Essays on John Wilmot, Earl of Rochester*, ed. Nicholas Fisher (Manchester & New York, 2000), pp. 133–52.

[31] For comment on these similarities, see Ramon Selden, 'Rochester and Shadwell', in *Spirit of Wit: Reconsiderations of Rochester*, ed. Jeremy Treglown (Oxford, 1982), pp.177–90; Hammond & Kewes, pp.143–7. For the 'atheists' v. clergy debate, see Gillian Manning, 'Rochester's *Satyr Against Mankind* and Contemporary Religious Debate', in *The Seventeenth Century*, 8, 1 (1993), 99–121.

[32] For the play as Whig propaganda during the Tory reaction of 1682, see Owen, p.177. *The Libertine Destroy'd* seems also to have been used as an alternative title in the 1670s.

[33] *The Diary of Robert Hooke, 1672–80*, ed. Henry W. Robinson & Walter Adams (1935).

[34] *A Satyrical Epistle to the Female Author of a Poem called Sylvia's Revenge Etc.* (1691), p.19. For comment on attitudes to women writers, see Catherine Gallagher, 'Who Was That Masked Woman? The Prostitute and the Playwright in the Comedies of Aphra Behn', in *Rereading Aphra Behn: History, Theory and Criticism*, ed. Heidi Hutner (Charlottesville & London, 1993), 65–85. For a critique of Gallagher's views, see Derek Hughes, 'The Masked Woman Revealed: or, the Prostitute and the Playwright in Aphra Behn Criticism', *Women's Writing*, 7, 2 (2000), 149–64.

[35] *The Letters of John Dryden*, ed. Charles E. Ward (Durham, NC, 1942), p.127.

[36] Behn's name does not appear on the title page until the 3rd issue of the 1st edition.

[37] In the Postscript, which appears only in Q1, Behn is disingenuous about the extent of her borrowings.

[38] Despite protests from Presbyterians and other religious sects, Parliament had passed a series of stringent statutes (1660–65), the so-called Clarendon Code (after Charles II's chief minister, Edward Hyde, Earl of Clarendon). These effectively excluded nonconformists from any share in central or local government.

[39] Robert D. Hume, *The Development of English Drama in the Late Seventeenth Century* (Oxford, 1976), p.329; Dedication, l.75.

[40] See *The Works of John Dryden*, ed. E. Hooker et al., 20 vols (Berkeley, 1992), XIV, 374–5; Susan Staves, 'Why Was Dryden's *Mr Limberham* Banned? A Problem in Restoration Theatre History',

Restoration and Eighteenth-Century Theatre Research, 13 (1974), 1–11.

[41] See *Works*, XIV, 365–6.

[42] *Letters*, pp.11–12.

[43] See *Works*, XIV, 370.

[44] It seems that the play's title was originally to have been *Limberham*, 'and it is often so called' (See *Works*, XIV, 365, n.).

[45] Hume, *The Development of English Drama*, p.350; Downes, p.79; Collier, *A Short View*, pp.146, 100–101. Views of 18th- & 19th-century critics are cited in *The Orphan*, ed. A. Mackenzie Taylor (1977), pp. xvii–xviii.

[46] See especially the following (to which my comments on *The Orphan* are heavily indebted): Derek Hughes, *English Drama 1660–1700* (Oxford, 1996), pp.283–6; Jessica Munns, *Restoration Politics and Drama: The Plays of Thomas Otway, 1675–83* (Newark & London, 1995), pp.129–66; Owen, pp.214–19.

[47] For intimations of earlier corruption, see Taylor, p.xxviii.

[48] For the boar as a traditional emblem of lust and death, cf. Shakespeare, *Venus and Adonis*, especially ll.1105–16; Spenser, *The Faerie Queene*, Book 3, Canto vi, 48.

[49] E.g. I, 1. 393–9. Taylor (p. xxv) cites an eighteenth-century contemporary of Barton Booth's who comments on the appropriateness of the 'gay libertine air' assumed by that actor in the role of Polydore.

[50] See 'Memoirs of Mrs Barry', in *The History of the English Stage from the Restauration to the Present Time . . .* compiled by Edmund Curll & William Oldys from the notes of T. Betterton (1741), pp.13–23.

[51] James, Duke of York, commanded an international brigade under the Spanish flag (against France) from 1657. The regiments involved were notoriously underfunded, and hence, ill-equipped and ill-disciplined.

[52] The word 'interest' occurs 12 times in the play. Willmore's mountebank disguise echoes a similar escapade on Rochester's part. For the latter's 'quack' pamphlet, see *The Works of John Wilmot, Earl of Rochester,* ed. Harold Love (Oxford, 1999), pp.112–17, 437–40.

[53] Hill's phrase is cited in Robert Markley, '"Be impudent, be saucy, forward, bold, touzing, and leud": The Politics of Masculine Sexuality and Feminine Desire in Behn's Tory Comedies', in *Cultural Readings of Restoration and Eighteenth-Century English Theater*, p.114. Susan J. Owen, 'Sexual Politics and Party Politics in Behn's Drama, 1678–83', in *Aphra Behn Studies*, ed. Janet Todd (Cambridge, 1996), p.20.

[54] Susan J. Owen, '"Suspect my loyalty when I lose my virtue": Sexual Politics and Party in Aphra Behn's Plays of the Exclusion Crisis,

1678–83', *Restoration: Studies in English Literary Culture, 1660–1700*, vol. 18, no. 1 (Spring, 1994), 40.

[55] Markley, p.118.

[56] Ibid., p.124; Peter Holland, *The Ornament of Action: Text and Performance in Restoration Comedy* (Cambridge, 1979), p.68.

[57] See, e.g., Michael Cordner, Introduction to *Four Restoration Marriage Plays* (World's Classics Series, Oxford, 1995), p.xli.

[58] Holland, pp.145–6.

[59] Brean S. Hammond's description of the play as 'Restoration Chekhov' is cited by Cordner in his edition, p.xlii.

[60] Cordner, p.xli.

[61] Hume, *The Development of English Drama*, p.387.

[62] See, e.g., Cordner, p.xli; Holland, pp.167–8.

[63] Cordner, p.xliii.

[64] Holland, p.146.

NOTE ON THE TEXTS

All seven plays have been freshly edited from the earliest printed editions, which are as follows: *Marriage A-la-Mode* (1673); *The Libertine* (1676); *The Rover* (1677); *The Kind Keeper* (1680); *The Orphan* (1680); *The Rover*, Part 2 (1681); *The Wives' Excuse* (1692). Other early editions have been consulted. In the case of each play, I have used the first printed edition as my copy text, and have recorded in the notes substantive departures from this text, except in a few instances where obvious errors (as in the cast list of *The Libertine*) have been silently corrected. Editorial changes and amplifications regarding, e.g., the stage directions or cast lists, are indicated by angled brackets. Spelling and punctuation have been modernised throughout.

I am heavily indebted to the labours of all previous editors, but especially to the following works: volumes XI (1978) and XIV (1992) of the California edition of Dryden's *Works*, edited by John Loftis, David Stuart Rodes et al.; and by Vincent A. Dearing and Alan Roper, respectively; *The Complete Works of Thomas Shadwell*, ed. Montague Summers, 5 vols (1927); *The Works of Aphra Behn*, ed. Montague Summers, 6 vols (1915); *The Works of Aphra Behn*, ed. Janet Todd, 7 vols (Columbus, Ohio, 1992–6); *The Works of Thomas Otway*, ed. J. C. Ghosh, 2 vols (Oxford, 1932, reprtd 1968); *The Works of Thomas Southerne*, ed. Robert Jordan & Harold Love, 2 vols (Oxford, 1988); *Four Restoration Marriage Plays*, ed. Michael Cordner with Ronald Clayton (World's Classics Series, Oxford, 1995). I have also consulted the following editions: *Marriage A-la-Mode*, ed. David Crane (New Mermaids Series, 1991); *The Libertine*, ed. Helen Pellegrin (New York & London, 1987); *The Rover*, ed. Frederick M. Link (Lincoln, Neb., 1967); *'The Rover' and Other Plays*, ed. Jane Spencer (World's Classics Series, Oxford, 1995); *The Rover*, ed. Anne Russell (Broadview Series, Ontario,

1994); *The Orphan*, ed. Aline Mackenzie Taylor (1977); *The Wives' Excuse*, ed. Ralph R. Thornton (Wynnewood, Pa., 1973).

MARRIAGE A-LA-MODE

A COMEDY

BY

JOHN DRYDEN

Quicquid sum ego, quamvis
Infra Lucilli censum ingeniumque, tamen me
Cum magnis vixisse, invita fatebitur usque
Invidia, et fragili quaerens illidere dentem
Offendet solido.*

[Horace, *Satires*, II.1.74–9]

<DEDICATION>
To the Right Honourable, the Earl of Rochester *

My Lord,

I humbly dedicate to your Lordship that poem of which you were pleased to appear an early patron before it was acted on the stage. I may yet go farther, with your permission, and say that it received amendment from your noble hands ere it was fit to be presented. You may please 5 likewise to remember with how much favour to the author, and indulgence to the play, you commended it to the view of His Majesty, then at Windsor,* and by his approbation of it in writing, made way for its kind reception on the theatre. In this dedication, therefore, I may seem to imitate a custom of 10 the ancients, who offered to their gods the firstlings of the flock, which I think they called *ver sacrum*,* because they helped 'em to increase. I am sure if there be anything in this play, wherein I have raised myself beyond the ordinary lowness of my comedies, I ought wholly to acknowledge it 15 to the favour of being admitted into your Lordship's conversation.* And not only I, who pretend not to this way,* but the best comic writers of our age will join with me to acknowledge that they have copied the gallantries of courts, the delicacy of expression and the decencies of 20 behaviour from your Lordship, with more success than if they had taken their models from the court of France. But this, my Lord, will be no wonder to the world, which knows the excellency of your natural parts, and those you have acquired in a noble education. That which with more 25 reason I admire is that being so absolute a courtier, you have not forgot either the ties of friendship or the practice of generosity. In my little experience of a court (which I confess I desire not to improve) I have found in it much of interest* and more of detraction. Few men there have that 30 assurance of* a friend as not to be made ridiculous by him when they are absent. There are a middling sort of courtiers who become happy by their want* of wit, but they supply

that want by an excess of malice to those who have it. And
there is no such persecution as that of fools: they can never   35
be considerable enough to be talked of themselves, so that
they are safe only in their obscurity, and grow mischievous
to witty men by the great diligence of their envy, and by
being always present to represent and aggravate their faults.
In the meantime they are forced, when they endeavour to be   40
pleasant, to live on the offals of their wit* whom they decry,
and either to quote it (which they do unwillingly) or to pass
it upon others for their own. These are the men who make it
their business to chase wit from the knowledge of princes,
lest it should disgrace their ignorance. And this kind of   45
malice your Lordship has not so much avoided, as sur-
mounted. But if by the excellent temper of a royal master
always more ready to hear good than ill, if by his inclination
to love you, if by your own merit and address, if by the
charms of your conversation, the grace of your behaviour,   50
your knowledge of greatness and habitude* in courts, you
have been able to preserve yourself with honour in the midst
of so dangerous a course; yet at least the remembrance of
those hazards has inspired you with pity for other men, who
being of an inferior wit and quality to you, are yet   55
persecuted for being that in little which your Lordship is in
great. For the quarrel of those people extends itself to
anything of sense and, if I may be so vain to own it amongst
the rest of the poets, has sometimes reached to the very
borders of it, even to me. So that if our general good fortune   60
had not raised up your Lordship to defend us, I know not
whether anything had been more ridiculous in court than
writers. 'Tis to your Lordship's favour we generally owe our
protection and patronage, and to the nobleness of your
nature, which will not suffer the least shadow of your wit to   65
be contemned* in other men. You have been often pleased
not only to excuse my imperfections but to vindicate what
was tolerable in my writings from their censures. And what
I never can forget, you have not only been careful of my
reputation, but of my fortune. You have been solicitous to   70
supply my neglect of myself, and to overcome the fatal

modesty of poets which submits them to perpetual wants
rather than to become importunate with those people who
have the liberality of kings in their disposing; and who,
dishonouring the bounty of their master, suffer such to be in   75
necessity who endeavour at least to please him, and for
whose entertainment he has generously provided, if the
fruits of his royal favour were not often stopped in other
hands. But your Lordship has given me occasion not to
complain of courts whilst you are there. I have found the   80
effects of your mediation in all my concernments; and they
were so much the more noble in you because they were
wholly voluntary. I became your Lordship's (if I may
venture on the similitude) as the world was made, without
knowing him who made it; and brought only a passive   85
obedience to be your creature. This nobleness of yours I
think myself the rather obliged to own, because otherwise it
must have been lost to all remembrance: for you are endued
with that excellent quality of a frank nature, to forget the
good which you have done.   90

But, my Lord, I ought to have considered that you are as
great a judge as you are a patron; and that in praising you
ill, I shall incur a higher note of ingratitude than that I
thought to have avoided. I stand in need of all your
accustomed goodness for the dedication of this play, which   95
though, perhaps, it be the best of my comedies, is yet so
faulty that I should have feared you for my critic, if I had
not with some policy* given you the trouble of being my
protector. Wit seems to have lodged itself more nobly in this
age than in any of the former; and people of my mean   100
condition are only writers because some of the nobility, and
your Lordship in the first place, are above the narrow
praises which poesy could give you. But let those who love
to see themselves exceeded encourage your Lordship in so
dangerous a quality. For my own part, I must confess that I   105
have so much of self-interest as to be content with reading
some papers* of your verses, without desiring you should
proceed to a scene or play,* with the common prudence of
those who are worsted in a duel, and declare they are

satisfied when they are first wounded. Your Lordship has 110
but another step to make, and from the patron of wit you
may become its tyrant, and oppress our little reputations
with more ease than you now protect them.* But these, my
Lord, are designs which I am sure you harbour not – any
more than the French king is contriving the conquest of the 115
Swissers.* 'Tis a barren triumph which is not worth your
pains, and would only rank him amongst your slaves who is
already,

    My Lord,

      Your Lordship's

        Most obedient and most faithful servant,

                        John Dryden

Prologue

Lord, how reformed and quiet we are grown,
Since all our braves* and all our wits are gone.*
Fop-corner* now is free from civil war:
White-wig* and vizard-mask* no longer jar.*
France* and the fleet have swept the town so clear,   5
That we can act in peace and you can hear.*
'Twas a sad sight before they marched from home
To see our warriors, in red waistcoats, come,
With hair tucked up, into our tiring-room.*
But 'twas more sad to hear their last adieu: 10
The women sobbed, and swore they would be true.
And so they were, as long as e'er they could:
But powerful guinea cannot be withstood,
And they were made of playhouse flesh and blood.
Fate did their friends* for double use ordain: 15
In wars abroad they grinning honour* gain,
And mistresses, for all that stay, maintain.
Now they are gone, 'tis dead vacation here,
For neither friends nor enemies appear.
Poor pensive punk* now peeps ere plays begin,   20
Sees the bare bench, and dares not venture in:
But manages her last half-crown* with care,
And trudges to the Mall,* on foot, for air.
Our city friends* so far will hardly come,
They can take up with pleasures nearer home;   25
And see gay shows and gaudy scenes elsewhere:*
For we presume they seldom come to hear.
But they have now ta'en up a glorious trade,
And cutting Moorcraft struts in masquerade.*
There's all our hope, for we shall show today   30
A masquing ball, to recommend our play:
Nay, to endear 'em more, and let 'em see
We scorn to come behind in courtesy,
We'll follow the new mode which they begin,
And treat 'em with a room, and couch within:*   35

For that's one way, how e'er the play fall short,
T' oblige the town, the city, and the court.

DRAMATIS PERSONAE

The play was first performed *c*. November 1671 by the King's Company at the Theatre Royal, Bridges Street, Drury Lane, with the cast listed below.

POLYDAMAS usurper of Sicily	Mr Wintershall
LEONIDAS the rightful prince, unknown	Mr Kynaston
ARGALEON favourite to Polydamas	Mr Lydall
HERMOGENES foster-father to Leonidas	Mr Cartwright
EUBULUS his friend and companion	Mr Watson
RHODOPHIL captain of the guards	Mr Mohun
PALAMEDE a courtier	Mr Hart
<STRATON servant to Palamede's father>	
PALMYRA daughter to the usurper	Mrs Cox
AMALTHEA sister to Argaleon	Mrs James
DORALICE wife to Rhodophil	Mrs Marshall
MELANTHA an affected lady	Mrs Boutell
PHILOTIS woman to Melantha	Mrs Reeves
BELIZA woman to Doralice	Mrs Slade
ARTEMIS a court lady	Mrs Uphill

<MESSENGER, COURTIERS, GUARDS, ATTENDANTS, SERVANTS, CITIZENS>

Scene: Sicily

Act 1, Scene 1

Walks near the court

(*Enter* DORALICE *and* BELIZA)

DORALICE Beliza, bring the lute into this arbour, the walks
are empty: I would try the song the Princess Amalthea
bade me learn.

(*They go in, and sing*)

1

Why should a foolish marriage vow
Which long ago was made,   5
Oblige us to each other now
When passion is decayed?
We loved, and we loved, as long as we could,
Till our love was loved out in us both.
But our marriage is dead, when the pleasure is fled: 10
'Twas pleasure first made it an oath.

2

If I have pleasures for a friend,
And farther love in store,
What wrong has he whose joys did end,
And who could give no more?   15
'Tis a madness that he should be jealous of me,
Or that I should bar him of another:
For all we can gain is to give ourselves pain,
When neither can hinder the other.

(*Enter* PALAMEDE, *in riding habit, and hears the song.*
Re-enter DORALICE *and* BELIZA)

BELIZA Madam, a stranger.   20
DORALICE I did not think to have had witnesses of my bad
singing.
PALAMEDE If I have erred, madam, I hope you'll pardon

the curiosity of a stranger; for I may well call myself so, after five years' absence from the court. But you have 25 freed me from one error.

DORALICE What's that, I beseech you?

PALAMEDE I thought good voices and ill faces had been inseparable; and that to be fair and sing well had been only the privilege of angels. 30

DORALICE And how many more of these fine things can you say to me?

PALAMEDE Very few, madam, for if I should continue to see you some hours longer, you look so killingly, that I should be mute with wonder. 35

DORALICE This will not give you the reputation of a wit with me. You travelling monsieurs live upon the stock you have got abroad, for the first day or two: to repeat with a good memory, and apply with a good grace, is all your wit. And commonly your gullets are sewed up like 40 cormorants.* When you have regorged what you have taken in, you are the leanest things in nature.

PALAMEDE Then, madam, I think you had best make that use of me. Let me wait on you for two or three days together, and you shall hear all I have learnt of extraordi- 45 nary in other countries. And one thing which I never saw till I came home, that is, a lady of a better voice, better face, and better wit, than any I have seen abroad. And after this, if I should not declare myself most passionately in love with you, I should have less wit than yet you think 50 I have.

DORALICE A very plain and pithy declaration. I see, sir, you have been travelling in Spain or Italy, or some of the hot countries, where men come to the point immediately. But are you sure these are not words of course?* For I 55 would not give my poor heart an occasion of complaint against me, that I engaged it too rashly, and then could not bring it off.

PALAMEDE Your heart may trust itself with me safely; I shall use it very civilly while it stays, and never turn it 60 away, without fair warning to provide for itself.

DORALICE First, then, I do receive your passion with as
little consideration on my part, as ever you gave it me on
yours. And now see what a miserable wretch you have
made yourself.   65

PALAMEDE Who, I miserable? Thank you for that. Give me
love enough, and life enough, and I defy Fortune.

DORALICE Know then, thou man of vain imagination,
know, to thy utter confusion, that I am virtuous.

PALAMEDE Such another word, and I give up the ghost.   70

DORALICE Then, to strike you quite dead, know that I am
married too.

PALAMEDE Art thou married? O thou damnable virtuous
woman!

DORALICE Yes, married to a gentleman; young, handsome,   75
rich, valiant, and with all the good qualities that will
make you despair, and hang yourself.

PALAMEDE Well, in spite of all that, I'll love you. Fortune
has cut us out for one another, for I am to be married
within these three days. Married past redemption, to a   80
young, fair, rich and virtuous lady. And it shall go hard,
but I will love my wife as little as I perceive you do your
husband.

DORALICE Remember, I invade no propriety.* My servant* you are only till you are married.   85

PALAMEDE In the meantime, you are to forget you have a
husband.

DORALICE And you, that you are to have a wife.

BELIZA (aside to her lady) Oh madam, my lord's just at the
end of the walks, and if you make not haste will discover   90
you.

DORALICE Some other time, new servant, we'll talk further
of the premises.* In the meanwhile, break not my first
commandment, that is, not to follow me.

PALAMEDE But where, then, shall I find you again?   95

DORALICE At court. Yours for two days, sir.

PALAMEDE And nights, I beseech you, madam.

[*Exit* DORALICE *and* BELIZA]

PALAMEDE Well, I'll say that for thee, thou art a very

dextrous executioner; thou hast done my business at one
stroke. Yet I must marry another – and yet I must love 100
this; and if it lead me into some little inconveniencies, as
jealousies, and duels, and death, and so forth; yet while
sweet love is in the case, Fortune do thy worst, and
avaunt mortality.*

(*Enter* RHODOPHIL, *who seems speaking to one within*)

RHODOPHIL Leave 'em with my lieutenant, while I fetch 105
new orders from the king. (*sees* PALAMEDE) How?
Palamede!

PALAMEDE Rhodophil!

RHODOPHIL Who thought to have seen you in Sicily?

PALAMEDE Who thought to have found the court so far 110
from Syracuse?

RHODOPHIL The king best knows the reason of the
progress. But answer me, I beseech you, what brought
you home from travel?

PALAMEDE The commands of an old rich father.   115

RHODOPHIL And the hopes of burying him?

PALAMEDE Both together, as you see, have prevailed on my
good nature. In few words: my old man has already
married me; for he has agreed with another old man, as
rich and as covetous as himself. The articles are drawn, 120
and I have given my consent, for fear of being disinherited; and yet know not what kind of woman I am to
marry.

RHODOPHIL Sure your father intends you some very ugly
wife; and has a mind to keep you in ignorance, till you 125
have shot the gulf.*

PALAMEDE I know not that; but obey I will, and must.

RHODOPHIL Then, I cannot choose but grieve for all the
good girls* and courtesans of France and Italy. They have
lost the most kind-hearted, doting, prodigal, humble 130
servant, in Europe.

PALAMEDE All I could do in these three years I stayed
behind you, was to comfort the poor creatures for the

loss of you. But what's the reason that in all this time, a
friend could never hear from you?   135

RHODOPHIL Alas, dear Palamede, I have had no joy to
write, nor indeed to do anything in the world to please
me. The greatest misfortune imaginable is fallen upon me.

PALAMEDE Prithee, what's the matter?

RHODOPHIL In one word, I am married, wretchedly   140
married, and have been above these two years. Yes, faith,
the devil has had power over me, in spite of my vows and
resolutions to the contrary.

PALAMEDE I find you have sold yourself for filthy lucre.
She's old, or ill-conditioned.*   145

RHODOPHIL No, none of these. I'm sure she's young; and,
for her humour, she laughs, sings, and dances eternally;
and, which is more, we never quarrel about it, for I do the
same.

PALAMEDE You're very unfortunate indeed. Then the case   150
is plain: she is not handsome.

RHODOPHIL A great beauty too, as people say.

PALAMEDE As people say? Why, you should know that
best yourself.

RHODOPHIL Ask those who have smelt to a strong   155
perfume two years together, what's the scent.

PALAMEDE But here are good qualities enough for one
woman.

RHODOPHIL Aye, too many, Palamede, if I could put 'em
into three or four women, I should be content.   160

PALAMEDE Oh, now I have found it: you dislike her for no
other reason but because she's your wife.

RHODOPHIL And is not that enough? All that I know of
her perfections now is only by memory. I remember,
indeed, that about two years ago I loved her passionately;   165
but those golden days are gone, Palamede. Yet I loved her
a whole half year, double the natural term of any
mistress, and think in my conscience I could have held out
another quarter; but then the world began to laugh at me,
and a certain shame of being out of fashion seized me. At   170
last, we arrived at that point, that there was nothing left

in us to make us new to one another. Yet still I set a good
face upon the matter, and am infinite fond of her before
company. But when we are alone, we walk like lions in a
room, she one way, and I another; and we lie with our 175
backs to each other so far distant, as if the fashion of
great beds* was only invented to keep husband and wife
sufficiently asunder.

PALAMEDE The truth is, your disease is very desperate; but,
though you cannot be cured, you may be patched up a 180
little. You must get you a mistress, Rhodophil. That,
indeed, is living upon cordials;* but, as fast as one fails,
you must supply it with another. You're like a gamester
who has lost his estate; yet, in doing that, you have
learned the advantages of play, and can arrive to live 185
upon 't.

RHODOPHIL Truth is, I have been thinking on't, and have
just resolved to take your counsel; and, faith, considering
the damned disadvantages of a married man, I have
provided well enough, for a poor humble sinner, that is 190
not ambitious of great matters.

PALAMEDE What is she, for a woman?

RHODOPHIL One of the stars of Syracuse, I assure you:
young enough, fair enough, and, but for one quality, just
such a woman as I would wish. 195

PALAMEDE O friend, this is not an age to be critical in
beauty. When we had good store of handsome women
and but few chapmen,* you might have been more
curious in your choice. But now the price is enhanced
upon us, and all mankind set up for mistresses, so that 200
poor little creatures, without beauty, birth, or breeding,
but only impudence, go off at unreasonable rates. And a
man in these hard times snaps at 'em, as he does at broad-
gold,* never examines the weight, but takes light or heavy
as he can get it. 205

RHODOPHIL But my mistress has one fault that's almost
unpardonable; for, being a town-lady, without any
relation to the court, yet she thinks herself undone, if she
be not seen there three or four times a day with the

Princess Amalthea. And for the king, she haunts and 210
watches him so narrowly in a morning, that she prevents*
even the chemists* who beset his chamber, to turn their
mercury into his gold.

PALAMEDE Yet, hitherto, methinks, you are no very
unhappy man.   215

RHODOPHIL With all this, she's the greatest gossip in
nature; for, besides the court, she's the most eternal
visitor of the town: and yet manages her time so well, that
she seems ubiquitary.* For my part, I can compare her to
nothing but the sun; for, like him, she takes no rest, nor 220
ever sets in one place, but to rise in another.

PALAMEDE I confess she had need be handsome with these
qualities.

RHODOPHIL No lady can be so curious of a new fashion,
as she is of a new French word; she's the very mint of the 225
nation; and as fast as any bullion comes out of France,
coins it immediately into our language.

PALAMEDE And her name is –

RHODOPHIL No naming; that's not like a cavalier. Find
her, if you can, by my description; and I am not so ill a 230
painter, that I need write the name beneath the picture.

PALAMEDE Well then, how far have you proceeded in your
love?

RHODOPHIL 'Tis yet in the bud, and what fruit it may bear
I cannot tell; for this insufferable humour of haunting the 235
court is so predominant, that she has hitherto broken all
her assignations with me, for fear of missing her visits
there.

PALAMEDE That's the hardest part of your adventure. But,
for ought I see, Fortune has used us both alike: I have a 240
strange kind of mistress too in court, besides her I am to
marry.

RHODOPHIL You have made haste to be in love then; for,
if I am not mistaken, you are but this day arrived.

PALAMEDE That's all one, I have seen the lady already 245
who has charmed me, seen her in these walks, courted

her, and received, for the first time, an answer that does
not put me into despair.

(*To them,* ARGALEON, AMALTHEA, ARTEMIS)

I'll tell you at more leisure my adventures. The walks fill
apace, I see. Stay, is not that the young Lord Argaleon, 250
the king's favourite?

RHODOPHIL Yes, and as proud as ever, as ambitious, and
as revengeful.

PALAMEDE How keeps he the king's favour with these
qualities?   255

RHODOPHIL Argaleon's father helped him to the crown.
Besides, he gilds over all his vices to the king, and,
standing in the dark to him,* sees all his inclinations,
interests and humours, which he so times and soothes,
that, in effect, he reigns.   260

PALAMEDE His sister Amalthea, who, I guess, stands by
him, seems not to be of his temper.

RHODOPHIL Oh, she's all goodness and generosity.

ARGALEON Rhodophil, the king expects you earnestly.

RHODOPHIL 'Tis done, my lord, what he commanded. I 265
only waited his return from hunting. Shall I attend your
lordship to him?

ARGALEON No; I go first another way.

[*Exit hastily*]

PALAMEDE He seems in haste, and discomposed.

AMALTHEA (*to* RHODOPHIL, *after a short whisper*) Your 270
friend? Then he must needs be of much merit.

RHODOPHIL When he has kissed the king's hand, I know
he'll beg the honour to kiss yours. Come, Palamede.

[*Exeunt* RHODOPHIL *and* PALAMEDE, *bowing to*
AMALTHEA]

ARTEMIS Madam, you tell me most surprising news.

AMALTHEA The fear of it, you see,   275
Has discomposed my brother; but to me
All that can bring my country good, is welcome.

ARTEMIS It seems incredible, that this old king,

Whom all the world thought childless,
Should come to search the farthest parts of Sicily,   280
In hope to find an heir.
AMALTHEA To lessen your astonishment, I will
Unfold some private passages of state,
Of which you yet are ignorant. Know, first,
That this Polydamas, who reigns, unjustly   285
Gained the crown.
ARTEMIS Somewhat of this I have confus'dly heard.
AMALTHEA I'll tell you all in brief. Theagenes,
Our last great king,
Had by his queen one only son, an infant   290
Of three years old, called after him, Theagenes.
The general, this Polydamas, then married:
The public feasts for which were scarcely past,
When a rebellion in the heart of Sicily
Called out the king to arms.
ARTEMIS   Polydamas   295
Had then a just excuse to stay behind.
AMALTHEA His temper was too warlike to accept it:
He left his bride, and the new joys of marriage,
And followed to the field. In short, they fought,
The rebels were o'ercome; but in the fight   300
The too bold king received a mortal wound.
When he perceived his end approaching near,
He called the general, to whose care he left
His widow queen, and orphan son; then died.
ARTEMIS Then false Polydamas betrayed his trust?   305
AMALTHEA He did; and with my father's help, for which
Heaven pardon him, so gained the soldiers' hearts,
That in few days he was saluted king:
And when his crimes had impudence enough
To bear the eye of day,   310
He marched his army back to Syracuse.
But see how heaven can punish wicked men
In granting their desires: the news was brought him
That day he was to enter it, that Eubulus,
Whom his dead master had left governor,   315

Was fled, and with him bore away the queen,
And royal orphan; but, what more amazed him,
His wife, now big with child, and much detesting
Her husband's practices, had willingly
Accompanied their flight.   320

ARTEMIS How I admire her virtue!

AMALTHEA   What became
Of her, and them, since that, was never known;
Only, some few days since, a famous robber
Was taken with some jewels of vast price,
Which, when they were delivered to the king,   325
He knew had been his wife's; with these, a letter,
Much torn and sullied, but which yet he knew
To be her writing.

ARTEMIS   Sure from hence he learned
He had a son.

AMALTHEA It was not left so plain:
The paper only said she died in childbed: 330
But when it should have mentioned son, or daughter,
Just there it was torn off.

ARTEMIS   Madam, the king.

(*To them*, POLYDAMAS, ARGALEON, GUARD, *and*
ATTENDANTS)

ARGALEON The robber, though thrice racked, confessed
    no more
But that he took those jewels near this place.

POLYDAMAS But yet the circumstances strongly argue,   335
That those for whom I search are not far off.

ARGALEON I cannot easily believe it.

ARTEMIS (*aside*)   No,
You would not have it so.

POLYDAMAS Those I employed have, in the
    neighbouring hamlet,
Amongst the fishers' cabins, made discovery
Of some young persons, whose uncommon beauty,   340
And graceful carriage, make it seem suspicious
They are not what they seem. I therefore sent

The captain of my guards this morning early,
With orders to secure and bring 'em to me.   345

    (*Enter* RHODOPHIL *and* PALAMEDE)

Oh here he is. Have you performed my will?
RHODOPHIL Sir, those whom you commanded me to
    bring,
Are waiting in the walks.
POLYDAMAS   Conduct 'em hither.
RHODOPHIL First, give me leave
To beg your notice of this gentleman.   350
POLYDAMAS He seems to merit it. His name and
    quality?
RHODOPHIL Palamede, son to Lord Cleodemus of
    Palermo,
And new returned from travel.

(PALAMEDE *approaches, and kneels to kiss the king's*
hand)

POLYDAMAS   You're welcome.
I knew your father well, he was both brave
And honest. We two once were fellow-soldiers   355
In the last civil wars.
PALAMEDE I bring the same unquestioned honesty
And zeal to serve your majesty; the courage
You were pleased to praise in him,
Your royal prudence, and your people's love,   360
Will never give me leave to try like him
In civil wars; I hope it may in foreign.
POLYDAMAS Attend the court, and it shall be my care
To find out some employment worthy you.
Go, Rhodophil, and bring in those without.   365
             [*Exit* RHODOPHIL *and* PALAMEDE]

(RHODOPHIL *returns again immediately, and with him*
enter HERMOGENES, LEONIDAS, *and* PALMYRA)

Behold two miracles! (*looking earnestly on* LEONIDAS
and PALMYRA)

Of different sexes, but of equal form:
So matchless both, that my divided soul
Can scarcely ask the gods a son, or daughter,
For fear of losing one. If from your hands,   370
You powers, I shall this day receive a daughter,
Argaleon, she is yours; but if a son,
Then Amalthea's love shall make him happy.

ARGALEON Grant, heaven, this admirable nymph may
    prove
That issue which he seeks.   375

AMALTHEA Venus Urania,* if thou art a goddess,
Grant that sweet youth may prove the prince of Sicily.

POLYDAMAS (*to* HERMOGENES)
Tell me, old man, and tell me true, from whence
Had you that youth and maid?

HERMOGENES   From whence you had
Your sceptre, sir: I had 'em from the gods.   380

POLYDAMAS The gods then have not such another gift.
Say who their parents were.

HERMOGENES   My wife, and I.

ARGALEON It is not likely,
A virgin of so excellent a beauty
Should come from such a stock.   385

AMALTHEA Much less, that such a youth, so sweet, so
    graceful,
Should be produced from peasants.

HERMOGENES Why, nature is the same in villages,
And much more fit to form a noble issue
Where it is least corrupted.   390

POLYDAMAS He talks too like a man that knew the
    world
To have been long a peasant. But the rack
Will teach him other language. Hence with him.

(*As the* GUARD *are carrying him away, his peruke**
    falls off*)

Sure I have seen that face before. Hermogenes!
'Tis he, 'tis he who fled away with Eubulus,   395

And with my dear Eudoxia.

HERMOGENES Yes, sir, I am Hermogenes.
  And if to have been loyal be a crime,
  I stand prepared to suffer.

POLYDAMAS If thou wouldst live, speak quickly.   400
  What is become of my Eudoxia?
  Where is the queen and young Theagenes?
  Where Eubulus? And which of these is mine?

(*Pointing to* LEONIDAS *and* PALMYRA)

HERMOGENES Eudoxia is dead, so is the queen,
  The infant king her son, and Eubulus.   405

POLYDAMAS Traitor, 'tis false: produce 'em, or –

HERMOGENES   Once more
  I tell you, they are dead; but leave* to threaten,
  For you shall know no further.

POLYDAMAS Then prove indulgent to my hopes, and be
  My friend for ever. Tell me, good Hermogenes,   410
  Whose son is that brave youth?

HERMOGENES   Sir, he is yours.

POLYDAMAS Fool that I am, thou seest that so I wish
    it,
  And so thou flatter'st me.

HERMOGENES   By all that's holy.

POLYDAMAS Again. Thou canst not swear too deeply.
  Yet hold, I will believe thee: – yet I doubt.   415

HERMOGENES You need not, sir.

ARGALEON Believe him not; he sees you credulous,
  And would impose his own base issue on you,
  And fix it to your crown.

AMALTHEA Behold his goodly shape and feature, sir,   420
  Methinks he much resembles you.

ARGALEON I say, if you have any issue here,
  It must be that fair creature;
  By all my hopes I think so.

AMALTHEA Yes, brother, I believe you by your hopes. 425
  (*aside*) For they are all for her.

POLYDAMAS   Call the youth nearer.

HERMOGENES Leonidas, the king would speak with you.

POLYDAMAS Come near, and be not dazzled with the splendour
And greatness of a court.

LEONIDAS I need not this encouragement.   430
I can fear nothing but the gods.
And for this glory, after I have seen
The canopy of state spread wide above
In the abyss of heaven, the court of stars,
The blushing morning, and the rising sun,   435
What greater can I see?

POLYDAMAS (*embracing him*) This speaks thee born a prince, thou art thyself
That rising sun, and shalt not see on earth
A brighter than thyself. – All of you witness,
That for my son I here receive this youth,   440
This brave, this – but I must not praise him further,
Because he now is mine.

LEONIDAS (*kneeling*) I wonnot,* sir, believe
That I am made your sport,
For I find nothing in myself but what   445
Is much above a scorn. I dare give credit
To whatsoe'er a king like you can tell me.
Either I am, or will deserve to be your son.

ARGALEON I yet maintain it is impossible
This young man should be yours; for, if he were,   450
Why should Hermogenes so long conceal him,
When he might gain so much by his discovery?

HERMOGENES I stayed a while to make him worthy, sir, of you.
But in that time I found
Somewhat within him which so moved my love,   455
I never could resolve to part with him.

LEONIDAS (*to* ARGALEON) You ask too many questions, and are
Too saucy for a subject.

ARGALEON You rather over-act your part and are
Too soon a prince.

LEONIDAS   Too soon you'll find me one.   460
POLYDAMAS Enough, Argaleon;
  I have declared him mine. And you, Leonidas,
  Live well with him I love.
ARGALEON Sir, if he be your son, I may have leave
  To think your queen had twins. Look on this virgin: 465
  Hermogenes would enviously deprive you
  Of half your treasure.
HERMOGENES   Sir, she is my daughter.
  I could perhaps, thus aided by this lord,
  Prefer her to be yours; but truth forbid
  I should procure her greatness by a lie.   470
POLYDAMAS Come hither, beauteous maid; are you not
    sorry
  Your father will not let you pass for mine?
PALMYRA I am content to be what heaven has made me.
POLYDAMAS Could you not wish yourself a princess,
    then?
PALMYRA Not to be sister to Leonidas.   475
POLYDAMAS Why, my sweet maid?
PALMYRA   Indeed I cannot tell;
  But I could be content to be his handmaid.
ARGALEON (aside) I wish I had not seen her.
PALMYRA (to LEONIDAS) I must weep for your good
    fortune;
  Pray pardon me, indeed I cannot help it.   480
  Leonidas, (alas, I had forgot,
  Now I must call you prince) but must I leave you?
LEONIDAS (aside) I dare not speak to her; for if I
    should,
  I must weep too.
POLYDAMAS No, you shall live at court, sweet
    innocence,   485
  And see him there. Hermogenes,
  Though you intended not to make me happy,
  Yet you shall be rewarded for th' event.
  Come, my Leonidas, let's thank the gods;
  Thou for a father, I for such a son.   490

[*Exeunt all but* LEONIDAS *and* PALMYRA]

LEONIDAS My dear Palmyra, many eyes observe me,
And I have thoughts so tender, that I cannot
In public speak 'em to you. Some hours hence
I shall shake off these crowds of fawning courtiers,
And then –   495

[*Exit* LEONIDAS]

PALMYRA Fly swift, you hours, you measure time for me
    in vain,
Till you bring back Leonidas again.
Be shorter now; and to redeem that wrong,
When he and I are met, be twice as long.

[*Exit*]

Act 2, Scene 1

(MELANTHA *and* PHILOTIS)

PHILOTIS Count Rhodophil's a fine gentleman indeed,
madam; and I think deserves your affection.

MELANTHA Let me die but he's a fine man; he sings and
dances *en français*, and writes the *billets doux** to a
miracle.   5

PHILOTIS And those are no small talents to a lady that
understands and values the French air,* as your ladyship
does.

MELANTHA How charming is the French air! And what an
*étourdie bête** is one of our untravelled islanders! When 10
he would make his court to me, let me die, but he is just
Aesop's ass,* that would imitate the courtly French in his
addresses; but, instead of those, comes pawing upon me,
and doing all things so *maladroitly.**

PHILOTIS 'Tis great pity Rhodophil's a married man, that 15
you may not have an honourable intrigue* with him.

MELANTHA Intrigue, Philotis! That's an old phrase. I have
laid that word by: *amour* sounds better. But thou art heir
to all my cast words, as thou art to my old wardrobe. Oh,

Count Rhodophil! Ah *mon cher*! I could live and die with   20
him.

(*Enter* PALAMEDE *and a* SERVANT)

SERVANT   Sir, this is my lady.

PALAMEDE   Then this is she that is to be divine, and
nymph, and goddess, and with whom I am to be
desperately in love. (*bows to her, delivering a letter*) This   25
letter, madam, which I present you from your father, has
given me both the happy opportunity, and the boldness,
to kiss the fairest hands in Sicily.

MELANTHA   Came you lately from Palermo, sir?

PALAMEDE   But yesterday, madam.   30

MELANTHA   (*reading the letter*) 'Daughter, receive the
bearer of this letter, as a gentleman whom I have chosen
to make you happy.' (O Venus, a new servant sent me!
And let me die, but he has the air of a gallant *homme*.)
'His father is the rich Lord Cleodemus, our neighbour. I   35
suppose you'll find nothing disagreeable in his person or
his converse, both which he has improved by travel. The
treaty is already concluded, and I shall be in town within
these three days; so that you have nothing to do but to
obey your careful father.'   40
(*to* PALAMEDE) Sir, my father, for whom I have a blind
obedience, has commanded me to receive your passionate
addresses; but you must also give me leave to avow that I
cannot merit 'em, from so accomplished a cavalier.

PALAMEDE   I want many things, madam, to render me   45
accomplished; and the first and greatest of 'em, is your
favour.

MELANTHA   Let me die, Philotis, but this is extremely
French; but yet Count Rhodophil – a gentleman, sir, that
understands the *grand monde** so well, who has haunted   50
the best *conversations*, and who (in short) has *voyaged*,
may pretend to the good *grâces* of any lady.

PALAMEDE   (*aside*) Hey day! *Grand monde! Conversation!
Voyaged!* And good *grâces*! I find my mistress is one of
those that run mad in new French words.   55

MELANTHA I suppose, sir, you have made the *tour* of
France; and having seen all that's fine there, will make a
considerable reformation in the rudeness* of our court:
for, let me die, but an unfashioned, untravelled, mere
Sicilian, is a *bête*; and has nothing in the world of an   60
honnête homme.*

PALAMEDE I must confess, madam, that –

MELANTHA And what new *menuets** have you brought
over with you? Their *menuets* are to a miracle! And our
Sicilian jigs are so dull and *fade** to 'em!   65

PALAMEDE For *menuets*, madam –

MELANTHA And what new plays are there in vogue? And
who danced best in the last *grand ballet*? Come, sweet
servant, you shall tell me all.

PALAMEDE (*aside*) Tell her all? Why, she asks all, and will   70
hear nothing – To answer in order, madam, to your
demands –

MELANTHA I am thinking what a happy couple we shall be!
For you shall keep up your correspondence abroad, and
everything that's new writ in France and *fine*, I mean all   75
that's delicate, and *bien tourné*,* we will have first.

PALAMEDE But, madam, our fortune –

MELANTHA I understand you, sir; you'll leave that to me:
for the *ménage** of a family, I know it better than any
lady in Sicily.   80

PALAMEDE Alas, madam, we –

MELANTHA Then, we will never make visits together, nor
see a play, but always apart. You shall be every day at the
king's *levée*;* and I at the queen's; and we will never
meet, but in the drawing-room.   85

PHILOTIS Madam, the new prince is just passed by the end
of the walk.

MELANTHA The new prince, sayst thou? Adieu, dear
servant; I have not made my court to him these two long
hours. O, 'tis the sweetest prince! So *obligeant, charmant,*   90
ravissant,* that – Well, I'll make haste to kiss his hands;
and then make half a score visits more, and be with you
again in a twinkling.

[*Exit, running, with* PHILOTIS]

PALAMEDE (*solus*)* Now heaven, of thy mercy, bless me
from this tongue! It may keep the field against a whole   95
army of lawyers, and that in their own language, French
gibberish. 'Tis true, in the day-time, 'tis tolerable, when a
man has field-room to run from it; but, to be shut up in a
bed with her, like two cocks in a pit; humanity cannot
support it. I must kiss all night, in my own defence, and   100
hold her down, like a boy at cuffs,* nay, and give her the
rising blow* every time she begins to speak.

(*Enter* RHODOPHIL)

But here comes Rhodophil. 'Tis pretty odd that my
mistress should so much resemble his: the same news-
monger, the same passionate lover of a court, the same –   105
But *basta*,* since I must marry her, I'll say nothing,
because he shall not laugh at my misfortune.

RHODOPHIL Well, Palamede, how go the affairs of love?
You've seen your mistress?

PALAMEDE I have so.   110

RHODOPHIL And how, and how? Has the old Cupid, your
father, chosen well for you? Is he a good woodman?*

PALAMEDE She's much handsomer than I could have
imagined. In short, I love her, and will marry her.

RHODOPHIL Then you are quite off from your other   115
mistress?

PALAMEDE You are mistaken, I intend to love 'em both, as
a reasonable man ought to do. For since all women have
their faults and imperfections, 'tis fit that one of 'em
should help out t' other.   120

RHODOPHIL This were a blessed doctrine, indeed, if our
wives would hear it; but they're their own enemies: if they
would suffer us but now and then to make excursions, the
benefit of our variety would be theirs. Instead of one
continued, lazy, tired love, they would, in their turns,   125
have twenty vigorous, fresh, and active loves.

PALAMEDE And I would ask any of 'em, whether a poor
narrow brook, half dry the best part of the year, and

running ever one way, be to be compared to a lusty
stream that has ebbs and flows? 130

RHODOPHIL Aye, or is half so profitable for navigation?

(*Enter* DORALICE, *walking by, and reading*)

PALAMEDE 'Ods* my life, Rhodophil, will you keep my
counsel?

RHODOPHIL Yes: where's the secret?

PALAMEDE (*showing* DORALICE) There 'tis. I may tell you, 135
as my friend, *sub sigillo** etc., this is that very numerical*
lady, with whom I am in love.

RHODOPHIL (*aside*) By all that's virtuous, my wife!

PALAMEDE You look strangely. How do you like her? Is
she not very handsome? 140

RHODOPHIL (*aside*) Sure, he abuses me. (*to him*) Why the
devil do you ask my judgment?

PALAMEDE You are so dogged* now, you think no man's
mistress handsome but your own. Come, you shall hear
her talk too; she has wit, I assure you. 145

RHODOPHIL (*going back*) This is too much, Palamede.

PALAMEDE (*pulling him forward*) Prithee, do not hang
back so. Of an old tried lover, thou art the most bashful
fellow!

DORALICE (*looking up*) Were you so near, and would not 150
speak, dear husband?

PALAMEDE (*aside*) Husband, quoth a!* I have cut out a
fine piece of work for myself.

RHODOPHIL Pray, spouse, how long have you been
acquainted with this gentleman? 155

DORALICE Who, I acquainted with this stranger? To my
best knowledge, I never saw him before.

(*Enter* MELANTHA, *at the other end*)

PALAMEDE (*aside*) Thanks, Fortune, thou hast helped me.

RHODOPHIL Palamede, this must not pass so. I must know
your mistress a little better. 160

PALAMEDE It shall be your own fault else. Come, I'll
introduce you.

RHODOPHIL Introduce me! Where?

PALAMEDE There. To my mistress.

(*Pointing to* MELANTHA, *who swiftly passes over the stage*)

RHODOPHIL Who? Melantha! O heavens, I did not see 165
her.

PALAMEDE But I did: I am an eagle where I love. I have
seen her this half hour.

DORALICE (*aside*) I find he has wit, he has got off so
readily; but it would anger me, if he should love 170
Melantha.

RHODOPHIL (*aside*) Now I could e'en wish it were my wife
he loved: I find he's to be married to my mistress.

PALAMEDE Shall I run after, and fetch her back again, to
present you to her?   175

RHODOPHIL No, you need not. I have the honour to have
some small acquaintance with her.

PALAMEDE (*aside*) O Jupiter! What a blockhead was I not
to find it out! My wife that must be, is his mistress. I did a
little suspect it before. Well, I must marry her, because 180
she's handsome, and because I hate to be disinherited for
a younger brother, which I am sure I shall be if I disobey;
and yet I must keep in with Rhodophil, because I love his
wife. (*to* RHODOPHIL) I must desire you to make my
excuse to your lady, if I have been so unfortunate to cause 185
any mistake; and, withall, to beg the honour of being
known to her.

RHODOPHIL Oh, that's but reason. Hark you, spouse, pray
look upon this gentleman as my friend; whom, to my
knowledge, you have never seen before this hour.   190

DORALICE I'm so obedient a wife, sir, that my husband's
commands shall ever be a law to me.

(*Enter* MELANTHA *again, hastily, and runs to embrace* DORALICE)

MELANTHA O, my dear, I was just going to pay my
*devoirs** to you; I had not time this morning, for making

my court to the king, and our new prince. Well, never 195
nation was so happy and all that, in a young prince; and
he's the kindest person in the world to me, let me die, if he
is not.

DORALICE He has been bred up far from court, and
therefore – 200

MELANTHA That imports not. Though he has not seen the
grand monde, and all that, let me die but he has the air of
the court, most absolutely.

PALAMEDE But yet, madam, he –

MELANTHA O servant, you can testify that I am in his good 205
graces. Well, I cannot stay long with you, because I have
promised him this afternoon to – But hark you, my dear,
I'll tell you a secret. (*whispers to* DORALICE)

RHODOPHIL (*aside*) The devil's in me, that I must love this
woman. 210

PALAMEDE (*aside*) The devil's in me, that I must marry this
woman.

MELANTHA (*raising her voice*) So the prince and I – But
you must make a secret of this, my dear, for I would not
for the world your husband should hear it, or my tyrant 215
there, that must be.

PALAMEDE (*aside*) Well, fair impertinent, your whisper is
not lost, we hear you.

DORALICE I understand then, that –

MELANTHA I'll tell you, my dear, the prince took me by the 220
hand, and pressed it *à la dérobée*,* because the king was
near, made the *doux yeux** to me, and *en suite*,* said a
thousand *galanteries*,* or let me die, my dear.

DORALICE Then I am sure you –

MELANTHA You are mistaken, my dear. 225

DORALICE What, before I speak?

MELANTHA But I know your meaning; you think, my dear,
that I assumed something of *fierté** into my countenance,
to *rebute** him; but quite contrary, I regarded him, I
know not how to express it in our dull Sicilian language, 230
d'un air enjoué,* and said nothing but *à d'autre, à*

d'autre, * and that it was all *grimace,* * and would not pass
upon* me.

(*Enter* ARTEMIS; MELANTHA *sees her, and runs away
from* DORALICE)

(*to* ARTEMIS) My dear, I must beg your pardon, I was
just making a loose* from Doralice, to pay my respects to 235
you. Let me die, if I ever pass time so agreeably as in your
company, and if I would leave it for any lady's in Sicily.

ARTEMIS The Princess Amalthea is coming this way.

(*Enter* AMALTHEA: MELANTHA *runs to her*)

MELANTHA O dear madam! I have been at your lodgings,
in my new *galèche,** so often, to tell you of a new *amour,* 240
betwixt two persons whom you would little suspect for it,
that, let me die, if one of my coach-horses be not dead,
and another quite tired and sunk under the *fatigue.*

AMALTHEA O, Melantha, I can tell you news, the prince is
coming this way.   245

MELANTHA The prince, O sweet prince! He and I are to –
and I forgot it. – Your pardon, sweet madam, for my
abruptness. Adieu, my dears. Servant, Rhodophil. –
Servant, servant, servant all.

[*Exit running*]

AMALTHEA Rhodophil, a word with you. (*whispers*)   250

DORALICE (*to* PALAMEDE) Why do you not follow your
mistress, sir?

PALAMEDE Follow her? Why, at this rate she'll be at the
Indies within this half hour.

DORALICE However, if you can't follow her all day, you'll 255
meet her at night, I hope?

PALAMEDE But can you, in charity, suffer me to be so
mortified, without affording me some relief? If it be but to
punish that sign of a husband there; that lazy matrimony,
that dull insipid taste, who leaves such delicious fare at 260
home, to dine abroad, on worse meat, and to pay dear
for't into the bargain.

DORALICE All this is in vain. Assure yourself, I will never admit of any visit from you in private.

PALAMEDE That is to tell me, in other words, my condition 265 is desperate.

DORALICE I think you in so ill a condition, that I am resolved to pray for you, this very evening, in the close walk, behind the terrace; for that's a private place, and there I am sure nobody will disturb my devotions. And so, 270 good night, sir.

[Exit]

PALAMEDE This is the newest way of making an appointment, I ever heard of. Let women alone to contrive the means; I find we are but dunces to 'em. Well, I will not be so profane a wretch as to interrupt her devotions; but to 275 make 'em more effectual, I'll down upon my knees, and endeavour to join my own with 'em.

[Exit]

AMALTHEA (to RHODOPHIL) I know already they do not love each other; and that my brother acts but a forced obedience to the king's commands; so that, if a quarrel 280 should arise betwixt the prince and him, I were most miserable on both sides.

RHODOPHIL There shall be nothing wanting in me, madam, to prevent so sad a consequence.

(Enter the king, LEONIDAS; the king whispers <to>
AMALTHEA)

(to himself) I begin to hate this Palamede because he is to 285 marry my mistress; yet break with him I dare not, for fear of being quite excluded from her company. 'Tis a hard case when a man must go by his rival to his mistress: but 'tis at worst but using him like a pair of heavy boots in a dirty journey; after I have fouled him all day, I'll throw 290 him off at night.

[Exit]

AMALTHEA (to the KING) This honour is too great for me to hope.

POLYDAMAS You shall this hour have the assurance of
  it.
  Leonidas, come hither; you have heard,
  I doubt not, that the father of this princess   295
  Was my most faithful friend, while I was yet
  A private man; and when I did assume
  This crown, he served me in that high attempt.
  You see, then, to what gratitude obliges me;
  Make your addresses to her.   300
LEONIDAS Sir, I am yet too young to be a courtier.
  I should too much betray my ignorance,
  And want of breeding, to so fair a lady.
AMALTHEA Your language speaks you not bred up in
  deserts,
  But in the softness of some Asian court,   305
  Where luxury and ease invent kind words,
  To cozen* tender virgins of their hearts.
POLYDAMAS You need not doubt
  But in what words soe'er a prince can offer
  His crown and person, they will be received.   310
  You know my pleasure, and you know your duty.
LEONIDAS Yes, sir, I shall obey, in what I can.
POLYDAMAS In what you can, Leonidas? Consider,
  He's both your king, and father, who commands you.
  Besides, what is there hard in my injunction?   315
LEONIDAS 'Tis hard to have my inclination forced.
  I would not marry, sir, and, when I do,
  I hope you'll give me freedom in my choice.
POLYDAMAS View well this lady,
  Whose mind as much transcends her beauteous face,   320
  As that excels all others.
AMALTHEA My beauty, as it ne'er could merit love,
  So neither can it beg: and, sir, you may
  Believe that, what the king has offered you,
  I should refuse, did I not value more   325
  Your person than your crown.
LEONIDAS   Think it not pride,
  Or my new fortunes swell me to contemn you.

Think less, that I want eyes to see your beauty;
And least of all think duty wanting in me
T' obey a father's will, but –   330
POLYDAMAS   But what, Leonidas?
For I must know your reason; and be sure
It be convincing too.
LEONIDAS   Sir, ask the stars,
Which have imposed love on us, like a fate,
Why minds are bent to one, and fly another?
Ask why all beauties cannot move all hearts?   335
For though there may
Be made a rule for colour, or for feature;
There can be none for liking.
POLYDAMAS Leonidas, you owe me more
Than to oppose your liking to my pleasure.   340
LEONIDAS I owe you all things, sir; but something too
I owe myself.
POLYDAMAS You shall dispute no more; I am a king,
And I will be obeyed.
LEONIDAS You are a king, sir; but you are no god;   345
Or if you were, you could not force my will.
POLYDAMAS (aside) But you are just, you gods, O you
    are just,
In punishing the crimes of my rebellion
With a rebellious son!
Yet I can punish him, as you do me.   350
(to him) Leonidas, there is no jesting with
My will. I ne'er had done so much to gain
A crown, but to be absolute in all things.
AMALTHEA O, sir, be not so much a king, as to
Forget you are a father. Soft indulgence   355
Becomes that name. Though nature gives you power
To bind his duty, 'tis with silken bonds:
Command him, then, as you command yourself:
He is as much a part of you, as are
Your appetite, and will, and those you force not,   360
But gently bend, and make 'em pliant to your reason.
POLYDAMAS It may be I have used too rough a way:

Forgive me, my Leonidas; I know
I lie as open to the gusts of passion,
As the bare shore to every beating surge: 365
I will not force thee now, but I entreat thee,
Absolve a father's vow to this fair virgin:
A vow, which hopes of having such a son
First caused.

LEONIDAS Show not my disobedience by your pray'rs,   370
For I must still deny you, though I now
Appear more guilty to myself, than you.
I have some reasons, which I cannot utter,
That force my disobedience; yet I mourn
To death, that the first thing you e'er enjoined me,   375
Should be that only one command in nature
Which I could not obey.

POLYDAMAS I did descend too much below myself
When I intreated him. Hence, to thy desert,
Thou'rt not my son, or art not fit to be.   380

AMALTHEA (*kneeling*) Great sir, I humbly beg you, make
    not me
The cause of your displeasure. I absolve
Your vow: far, far from me be such designs,
So wretched a desire of being great,
By making him unhappy. You may see   385
Something so noble in the prince his* nature,
As grieves him more not to obey, than you
That you are not obeyed.

POLYDAMAS   Then, for your sake,
I'll give him one day longer, to consider,
Not to deny; for my resolves are firm   390
As fate, that cannot change.

                    [*Exeunt* KING *and* AMALTHEA]

LEONIDAS   And so are mine.
This beauteous princess, charming as she is,
Could never make me happy. I must first
Be false to my Palmyra, and then wretched.
But, then, a father's anger!   395
Suppose he should recede from his own vow,

He never would permit me to keep mine.

(*Enter* PALMYRA; ARGALEON *following her, a little after*)

See, she appears!
I'll think no more of anything, but her.
Yet I have one hour good* ere I am wretched.   400
But, oh! Argaleon follows her! So night
Treads on the footsteps of a winter's sun,
And stalks all black behind him.
PALMYRA   O Leonidas,
(For I must call you still by that dear name)
Free me from this bad man.   405
LEONIDAS I hope he dares not be injurious to you.
ARGALEON I rather was injurious to myself,
Than her.
LEONIDAS That must be judged when I hear what you
said.
ARGALEON I think you need not give yourself that
trouble: 410
It concerned us alone.
LEONIDAS You answer saucily, and indirectly:
What interest can you pretend in her?
ARGALEON It may be, sir, I made her some expressions
Which I would not repeat, because they were   415
Below my rank, to one of hers.
LEONIDAS What did he say, Palmyra?
PALMYRA I'll tell you all. First, he began to look,
And then he sighed, and then he looked again;
At last, he said my eyes wounded his heart: 420
And, after that, he talked of flames, and fires;
And such strange words, that I believed he conjured.
LEONIDAS O my heart! Leave me, Argaleon.
ARGALEON Come, sweet Palmyra,
I will instruct you better in my meaning: 425
You see he would be private.
LEONIDAS   Go yourself,
And leave her here.
ARGALEON   Alas, she's ignorant,

And is not fit to entertain a prince.

LEONIDAS First learn what's fit for you; that's to obey.

ARGALEON I know my duty is to wait on you.   430
A great king's son, like you, ought to forget
Such mean converse.

LEONIDAS   What? A disputing subject?
Hence, or my sword shall do me justice on thee.

ARGALEON (going) Yet I may find a time –

LEONIDAS   (going after him) What's that you mutter,
To find a time?   435

ARGALEON   To wait on you again –
(softly) In the meanwhile I'll watch you.
                    [Exit, and watches during the scene]

LEONIDAS How precious are the hours of love in courts!
In cottages, where love has all the day,
Full, and at ease, he throws it half away.
Time gives himself, and is not valued, there;   440
But sells at mighty rates each minute, here.
There, he is lazy, unemployed, and slow;
Here, he's more swift; and yet has more to do.
So many of his hours in public move,
That few are left for privacy, and love.   445

PALMYRA The sun, methinks, shines faint and dimly,
    here;
Light is not half so long, nor half so clear.
But, oh! When every day was yours and mine,
How early up! What haste he made to shine!

LEONIDAS Such golden days no prince must hope to see; 450
Whose ev'ry subject is more blessed than he.

PALMYRA Do you remember, when their tasks were
    done,
How all the youth did to our cottage run?
While winter winds were whistling loud without,
Our cheerful hearth was circled round about.   455
With strokes in ashes* maids their lovers drew;
And still you fell to me, and I to you.

LEONIDAS When love did of my heart possession take,
I was so young, my soul was scarce awake:

I cannot tell when first I thought you fair; 460
But sucked in love, insensibly as air.

PALMYRA I know too well when first my love began,
When, at our wake,* you for the chaplet* ran:
Then I was made the lady of the May,
And, with the garland, at the goal did stay: 465
Still, as you ran, I kept you full in view;
I hoped, and wished, and ran, methought, for you.
As you came near, I hastily did rise,
And stretched my arm outright, that held the prize.
The custom was to kiss whom I should crown: 470
You kneeled; and, in my lap, your head laid down.
I blushed, and blushed, and did the kiss delay:
At last, my subjects forced me to obey;
But, when I gave the crown, and then the kiss,
I scarce had breath to say, 'Take that – and this.' 475

LEONIDAS I felt, the while, a pleasing kind of smart;
The kiss went, tingling, to my very heart.
When it was gone, the sense of it did stay;
The sweetness clinged upon my lips all day
Like drops of honey, loath to fall away. 480

PALMYRA Life, like a prodigal, gave all his store
To my first youth, and now can give no more.
You are a prince; and, in that high degree,
No longer must converse with humble me.

LEONIDAS 'Twas to my loss the gods that title gave; 485
A tyrant's son is doubly born a slave:
He gives a crown; but, to prevent my life
From being happy, loads it with a wife.

PALMYRA Speak quickly; what have you resolved to do?

LEONIDAS To keep my faith inviolate to you. 490
He threatens me with exile, and with shame,
To lose my birthright, and a prince his name;
But there's a blessing which he did not mean,
To send me back to love and you again.

PALMYRA Why was not I a princess for your sake? 495
But heav'n no more such miracles can make:
And, since that cannot, this must never be;

You shall not lose a crown for love of me.
Live happy, and a nobler choice pursue;
I shall complain of fate; but not of you.   500
LEONIDAS Can you so easily without me live?
Or could you take the counsel which you give?
Were you a princess would you not be true?
PALMYRA I would; but cannot merit it from you.
LEONIDAS Did you not merit, as you do, my heart;   505
Love gives esteem; and then it gives desert.
But if I basely could forget my vow,
Poor helpless Innocence, what would you do?
PALMYRA In woods and plains, where first my love
     began,
There would I live, retired from faithless man: 510
I'd sit all day within some lonely shade,
Or that close arbor which your hands have made:
I'd search the groves and ev'ry tree to find
Where you had carved our names upon the rind.
Your hook, your scrip,* all that was yours, I'd keep,   515
And lay 'em by me when I went to sleep.
Thus would I live: and maidens, when I die,
Upon my hearse white true-love-knots should tie:
And thus my tomb should be inscribed above,
Here the forsaken virgin rests from love.   520
LEONIDAS Think not that time or fate shall e'er divide
Those hearts, which love and mutual vows have tied.
But we must part; farewell, my love.
PALMYRA   Till when?
LEONIDAS Till the next age of hours we meet again.
Meantime – we may,   525
When near each other we in public stand,
Contrive to catch a look, or steal a hand:
Fancy will every touch, and glance improve;
And draw the most spirituous parts of love.
Our souls sit close, and silently within;   530
And their own web from their own entrails spin.
And when eyes meet far off, our sense is such,
That, spider-like, we feel the tender'st touch.   [*Exeunt*]

Act 3, Scene 1

(*Enter* RHODOPHIL, *meeting* DORALICE *and* ARTEMIS.
RHODOPHIL *and* DORALICE *embrace*)

RHODOPHIL My own dear heart!

DORALICE My own true love! (*she starts back*) I had forgot
myself to be so kind. Indeed, I am very angry with you,
dear. You are come home an hour after you appointed: if
you had stayed a minute longer, I was just considering   5
whether I should stab, hang, or drown myself. (*embracing
him*)

RHODOPHIL Nothing but the king's business could have
hindered me; and I was so vexed, that I was just laying
down my commission, rather than have failed my dear.
(*kissing her hand*)

ARTEMIS Why, this is love as it should be, betwixt man and   10
wife: such another couple would bring marriage into
fashion again. But is it always thus betwixt you?

RHODOPHIL Always thus! This is nothing. I tell you there
is not such a pair of turtles* in all Sicily; there is such an
eternal cooing and kissing betwixt us, that indeed it is   15
scandalous before civil company.

DORALICE Well, if I had imagined I should have been this
fond fool, I would never have married the man I loved. I
married to be happy, and have made myself miserable by
over-loving. Nay, and now, my case is desperate; for I   20
have been married above these two years, and find myself
every day worse and worse in love. Nothing but madness
can be the end on't.

ARTEMIS Dote on to the extremity, and you are happy.

DORALICE He deserves so infinitely much, that the truth is   25
there can be no doting in the matter. But to love well, I
confess, is a work that pays itself: 'tis telling* gold, and
after, taking it for one's pains.

RHODOPHIL By that I should be a very covetous person;
for I am ever pulling out my money, and putting it into   30
my pocket again.

DORALICE O, dear Rhodophil!

RHODOPHIL O, sweet Doralice! (*embracing each other*)

ARTEMIS (*aside*) Nay, I am resolved, I'll never interrupt lovers. I'll leave 'em as happy as I found 'em. (*steals away*) 35

RHODOPHIL (*looking up*) What, is she gone?

DORALICE Yes, and without taking leave.

RHODOPHIL Then there's enough for this time. (*parting from her*)

DORALICE Yes sure, the scene's done, I take it.

(*They walk contrary ways on the stage: he, with his hands in his pocket, whistling; she, singing a dull melancholy tune*)

RHODOPHIL Pox o' your dull tune, a man can't think for 40 you.

DORALICE Pox o' your damned whistling; you can neither be company to me yourself, nor leave me to the freedom of my own fancy.

RHODOPHIL Well, thou art the most provoking wife! 45

DORALICE Well, thou art the dullest husband, thou art never to be provoked.

RHODOPHIL I was never thought dull, till I married thee; and now thou hast made an old knife of me; thou hast whetted me so long till I have no edge left. 50

DORALICE I see you are in the husbands' fashion; you reserve all your good humours for your mistresses, and keep your ill for your wives.

RHODOPHIL Prithee leave me to my own cogitations; I am thinking over all my sins, to find for which of them it was 55 I married thee.

DORALICE Whatever your sin was, mine's the punishment.

RHODOPHIL My comfort is, thou art not immortal; and when that blessed, that divine day comes, of thy departure, I'm resolved I'll make one holy-day more in the 60 almanac, for thy sake.

DORALICE Aye, you had need make a holy-day for me, for I am sure you have made me a martyr.

RHODOPHIL Then, setting my victorious foot upon thy

head in the first hour of thy silence, (that is, the first hour   65
thou art dead, for I despair of it before) I will swear by
thy ghost, an oath as terrible to me as Styx* is to the
gods, never more to be in danger of the banes* of
matrimony.

DORALICE And I am resolved to marry the very same day   70
thou diest, if it be but to show how little I'm concerned
for thee.

RHODOPHIL Prithee, Doralice, why do we quarrel thus a-
days? Ha? This is but a kind of heathenish life, and does
not answer the ends of marriage. If I have erred,   75
propound what reasonable atonement may be made,
before we sleep, and I shall not be refractory: but withall
consider, I have been married these three years, and be
not too tyrannical.

DORALICE What should you talk of a peace abed, when   80
you can give no security for performance of articles?*

RHODOPHIL Then, since we must live together, and both
of us stand upon our terms, as to matter of dying first, let
us make ourselves as merry as we can with our misfortunes. Why there's the devil on't! If thou couldst make my   85
enjoying thee but a little less easy, or a little more
unlawful, thou shouldst see what a termagant lover I
would prove. I have taken such pains to enjoy thee,
Doralice, that I have fancied thee all the fine women in the
town, to help me out. But now there's none left for me to   90
think on, my imagination is quite jaded. Thou art a wife,
and thou wilt be a wife, and I can make thee another no
longer.

[*Exit* RHODOPHIL]

DORALICE Well, since thou art a husband, and wilt be a
husband, I'll try if I can find out another! 'Tis a pretty   95
time we women have on't, to be made widows, while we
are married. Our husbands think it reasonable to complain that we are the same, and the same to them, when
we have more reason to complain, that they are not the
same to us. Because they cannot feed on one dish,   100
therefore we must be starved. 'Tis enough that they have

a sufficient ordinary* provided, and a table ready spread
for 'em. If they cannot fall to and eat heartily, the fault is
theirs; and 'tis pity, methinks, that the good creature
should be lost, when many a poor sinner would be glad 105
on't.

(*Enter* MELANTHA, *and* ARTEMIS *to her*)

MELANTHA Dear, my dear, pity me; I am so *chagrin**
today, and have had the most signal affront at court! I
went this afternoon to do my *devoir* to Princess
Amalthea, found her, conversed with her, and helped to 110
make her court some half an hour; after which, she went
to take the air, chose out two ladies to go with her, that
came in after me, and left me most barbarously behind
her.

ARTEMIS You are the less to be pitied, Melantha, because 115
you subject yourself to these affronts, by coming perpetually to court, where you have no business nor
employment.

MELANTHA I declare, I had rather of the two, be *raillied*,
nay, *mal traitée** at court, than be deified in the town; for 120
assuredly, nothing can be so *ridicule* as a mere town lady.

DORALICE Especially at court. How I have seen 'em crowd
and sweat in the drawing-room, on a holiday-night!* For
that's their time to swarm, and invade the presence. O,
how they catch at a bow, or any little salute from a 125
courtier, to make show of their acquaintance! And rather
than be thought to be quite unknown, they curtsy to one
another. But they take true pains to come near the circle,*
and press and peep upon the princess, to write letters into
the country how she was dressed, while the ladies that 130
stand about make their court to her with abusing them.

ARTEMIS These are sad truths, Melantha; and therefore I
would e'en advise you to quit the court, and live either
wholly in the town, or, if you like not that, in the country.

DORALICE In the country! Nay, that's to fall beneath the 135
town, for they live there upon our offals here. Their
entertainment of wit is only the remembrance of what

they had when they were last in town. They live this year
upon the last year's knowledge, as their cattle do all night,
by chewing the cud of what they eat in the afternoon.   140

MELANTHA   And they tell, for news, such unlikely stories. A
letter from one of us is such a present to 'em, that the
poor souls wait for the carrier's day* with such devotion
that they cannot sleep the night before.

ARTEMIS   No more than I can, the night before I am to go a   145
journey.

DORALICE   Or I, before I am to try on a new gown.

MELANTHA   A song that's stale here, will be new there a
twelvemonth hence; and if a man of the town by chance
come amongst 'em, he's reverenced for teaching 'em the   150
tune.

DORALICE   A friend of mine, who makes songs sometimes,
came lately out of the west, and vowed he was so put out
of countenance with a song of his. For at the first country
gentleman's he visited, he saw three tailors cross-legged   155
upon the table in the hall, who were tearing out as loud as
ever they could sing:
– 'After the pangs of a desperate lover, etc.'*
and all that day he heard nothing else but the daughters of
the house and the maids humming it over in every corner,   160
and the father whistling it.

ARTEMIS   Indeed I have observed of myself, that when I am
out of town but a fortnight, I am so humble, that I would
receive a letter from my tailor or mercer* for a favour.

MELANTHA   When I have been at grass in the summer and   165
am new come up again, methinks I'm to be turned into
ridicule by all that see me; but when I have been once or
twice at court, I begin to value myself again, and to
despise my country acquaintance.

ARTEMIS   There are places where all people may be adored,   170
and we ought to know ourselves so well as to choose 'em.

DORALICE   That's very true. Your little courtier's wife, who
speaks to the king but once a month, need but go to a
town lady, and there she may vapour,* and cry, 'the king
and I', at every word. Your town lady, who is laughed at   175

in the circle, takes her coach into the city, and there she's
called your honour, and has a banquet from the merchant's wife, whom she laughs at for her kindness. And,
as for my finical cit,* she removes but to her country
house, and there insults over the country gentlewoman 180
that never comes up; who treats her with frumity* and
custard, and opens her dear bottle of *mirabilis* * beside,
for a gill-glass* of it at parting.

ARTEMIS At last, I see, we shall leave Melantha where we
found her; for, by your description of the town and 185
country, they are become more dreadful to her, than the
court, where she was affronted. But you forget we are to
wait on the Princess Amalthea. Come, Doralice.

DORALICE Farewell, Melantha.

MELANTHA Adieu, my dear.   190

ARTEMIS You are out of charity with her, and therefore I
shall not give your service.

MELANTHA Do not omit it, I beseech you; for I have such a
tender * for the court, that I love it ev'n from the drawing-
room to the lobby, and can never be *rebutée* * by any 195
usage. But, hark you, my dears, one thing I had forgot of
great concernment.

DORALICE Quickly then, we are in haste.

MELANTHA Do not call it my service, that's too vulgar; but
do my *baise mains* * to the Princess Amalthea; that is 200
spirituelle!*

DORALICE To do you service then, we will *prendre* the
carrosse * to court, and do your *baise mains* to the
Princess Amalthea, in your phrase, *spirituellé*.

[*Exeunt* ARTEMIS *and* DORALICE]

(*Enter* PHILOTIS, *with a paper in her hand*)

MELANTHA O, are you there, minion? And, well, are not 205
you a most precious damsel, to retard all my visits for
want of language, when you know you are paid so well
for furnishing me with new words for my daily conversation? Let me die, if I have not run the *risque* already, to
speak like one of the vulgar; and if I have one phrase left 210

in all my store that is not threadbare and *usé*,* and fit for
nothing but to be thrown to peasants.

PHILOTIS Indeed, madam, I have been very diligent in my
vocation; but you have so drained all the French plays
and romances, that they are not able to supply you with   215
words for your daily expences.

MELANTHA Drained? What a word's there! *Epuisé*, you sot
you! Come, produce your morning's work.

PHILOTIS 'Tis here, madam. (*shows the paper*)

MELANTHA O, my Venus! Fourteen or fifteen words to   220
serve me a whole day! Let me die, at this rate I cannot last
till night. Come, read your works: twenty to one half of
'em will not pass muster neither.

PHILOTIS (*reads*) *Sottises.**

MELANTHA *Sottises*: *bon*. That's an excellent word to begin   225
withall: as for example, he, or she said a thousand *sottises*
to me. Proceed.

PHILOTIS *Figure*: as what a *figure* of a man is there! *Naïve*,
and *naïveté*.

MELANTHA *Naïve*! As how?   230

PHILOTIS Speaking of a thing that was naturally said. It
was so *naïve*. Or such an innocent piece of simplicity:
'twas such a *naïveté*.

MELANTHA Truce with your interpretations. Make haste.

PHILOTIS *Foible, chagrin, grimace, embarrasse, double-*   235
*entendre, équivoque,** *éclaircissement,** *suite, bévue,**
*façon,** *penchant, coup d'étourdi,** and *ridicule*.

MELANTHA Hold, hold. How did they begin?

PHILOTIS They began at *sottises*, and ended *en ridicule*.

MELANTHA Now give me your paper in my hand, and hold   240
you my glass, while I practise my postures for the day.
(MELANTHA *laughs in the glass*) How does that laugh
become my face?

PHILOTIS Sovereignly well, madam.

MELANTHA Sovereignly! Let me die, that's not amiss. That   245
word shall not be yours. I'll invent it, and bring it up
myself. My new *point gorget** shall be yours upon't. Not
a word of the word, I charge you.

PHILOTIS I am dumb, madam.

MELANTHA (*looking in the glass again*) That glance, how 250
suits it with my face?

PHILOTIS 'Tis so *languissant.**

MELANTHA *Languissant*! That word shall be mine too, and
my last Indian gown* thine for't. (*looks again*) That sigh?

PHILOTIS 'Twill make many a man sigh, madam. 'Tis a 255
mere* incendiary.

MELANTHA Take my gimp* petticoat for that truth. If thou
hast more of these phrases, let me die but I could give
away all my wardrobe, and go naked for 'em.

PHILOTIS Go naked? Then you would be a Venus, madam. 260
O Jupiter! What had I forgot? This paper was given me
by Rhodophil's page.

MELANTHA (*reading the letter*) – 'Beg the favour from you
– gratify my passion – so far – assignation – in the grotto
– behind the terrace – clock this evening' – Well, for the 265
billets doux there's no man in Sicily must dispute with
Rhodophil. They are so French, so *gallant*, and so *tendre*,
that I cannot resist the temptation of the assignation.
Now go you away, Philotis; it imports me to practise
what I shall say to my servant when I meet him.   270

[*Exit* PHILOTIS]

Rhodophil, you'll wonder at my assurance to meet you
here. Let me die, I am so out of breath with coming, that I
can render you no reason of it. Then he will make this
repartee:* madam, I have no reason to accuse you for that
which is so great a favour to me. Then I reply, but why 275
have you drawn me to this solitary place? Let me die, but
I am apprehensive of some violence from you. Then, says
he: solitude, madam, is most fit for lovers; but by this fair
hand – Nay, now I vow you're rude, sir. O fie, fie, fie; I
hope you'll be honourable? – You'd laugh at me if I 280
should, madam – What do you mean to throw me down
thus? Ah me! Ah, ah, ah.

(*Enter* POLYDAMAS, LEONIDAS, *and* GUARDS)

O Venus! The king and court. Let me die but I fear they
have found my *foible*, and will turn me into *ridicule*.

[*Exit running*]

LEONIDAS Sir, I beseech you.
POLYDAMAS   Do not urge my patience.   285
LEONIDAS I'll not deny
But what your spies informed you of is true.
I love the fair Palmyra; but I loved her
Before I knew your title to my blood.

(*Enter* PALMYRA, *guarded*)

See, here she comes; and looks, amidst her guards,   290
Like a weak dove under the falcon's gripe.*
O heav'n, I cannot bear it.
POLYDAMAS   Maid, come hither.
Have you presumed so far, as to receive
My son's affection?
PALMYRA Alas, what shall I answer? To confess it   295
Will raise a blush upon a virgin's face;
Yet I was ever taught 'twas base to lie.
POLYDAMAS You've been too bold, and you must love
    no more.
PALMYRA Indeed I must; I cannot help my love;
I was so tender when I took the bent,   300
That now I grow that way.
POLYDAMAS He is a prince, and you are meanly born.
LEONIDAS Love either finds equality, or makes it
Like death, he knows no difference in degrees,
But planes, and levels all.   305
PALMYRA Alas, I had not rendered up my heart,
Had he not loved me first; but he preferred me
Above the maidens of my age and rank;
Still shunned their company, and still sought mine;
I was not won by gifts, yet still he gave;   310
And all his gifts, though small, yet spoke his love.
He picked the earliest strawberries in woods,
The clustered filberts,* and the purple grapes:
He taught a prating stare* to speak my name;

And when he found a nest of nightingales,   315
Or callow linnets, he would show 'em me,
And let me take 'em out.
POLYDAMAS This is a little mistress, meanly born,
Fit only for a prince his vacant hours,
And then, to laugh at her simplicity,   320
Not fix a passion there. Now hear my sentence.
LEONIDAS Remember, ere you give it, 'tis pronounced
Against us both.
POLYDAMAS   First, in her hand
There shall be placed a player's painted sceptre,   325
And, on her head, a gilded pageant crown;
Thus shall she go,
With all the boys attending on her triumph.
That done, be put alone into a boat,
With bread and water only for three days;   330
So on the sea she shall be set adrift,
And who relieves her, dies.
PALMYRA I only beg that you would execute
The last part first: let me be put to sea.
The bread and water, for my three days' life,   335
I give you back. I would not live so long;
But let me 'scape the shame.
LEONIDAS   Look to me, Piety;
And you, O gods, look to my piety:
Keep me from saying that which misbecomes a son;
But let me die before I see this done.   340
POLYDAMAS If you for ever will abjure her sight,
I can be yet a father; she shall live.
LEONIDAS Hear, O you pow'rs, is this to be a father?
I see 'tis all my happiness and quiet
You aim at, sir; and take 'em: 345
I will not save ev'n my Palmyra's life
At that ignoble price; but I'll die with her.
PALMYRA So had I done by you,
Had fate made me a princess. Death, methinks,
Is not a terror now: 350
He is not fierce, or grim, but fawns, and soothes me,

And slides along, like Cleopatra's aspic,*
Off'ring his service to my troubled breast.

LEONIDAS Begin what you have purposed when you
    please,
Lead her to scorn, your triumph shall be doubled.   355
As holy priests
In pity go with dying malefactors,
So will I share her shame.

POLYDAMAS You shall not have your will so much; first
    part 'em,
Then execute your office.   360

LEONIDAS (draws his sword)   No; I'll die
In her defence.

PALMYRA   Ah, hold, and pull not on
A curse, to make me worthy of my death:
Do not by lawless force oppose your father,
Whom you have too much disobeyed for me.

LEONIDAS Here, take it, sir, and with it, pierce my
    heart: 365

(Presenting his sword to his father upon his knees)

You have done more, in taking my Palmyra.
You are my father, therefore I submit.

POLYDAMAS Keep him from anything he may design
Against his life, whilst the first fury lasts;
And now perform what I commanded you.   370

LEONIDAS In vain; if sword and poison be denied me,
I'll hold my breath and die.

PALMYRA Farewell, my last Leonidas; yet live,
I charge you live, till you believe me dead.
I cannot die in peace, if you die first.   375
If life's a blessing, you shall have it last.

POLYDAMAS Go on with her, and lead him after me.

(Enter ARGALEON hastily, with HERMOGENES)

ARGALEON I bring you, sir, such news as must amaze
    you,
And such as will prevent you from an action

Which would have rendered all your life unhappy.   380

(HERMOGENES *kneels*)

POLYDAMAS Hermogenes, you bend your knees in vain,
My doom's* already past.
HERMOGENES I kneel not for Palmyra, for I know
She will not need my pray'rs; but for myself.
With a feigned tale I have abused your ears,   385
And therefore merit death; but since, unforced,
I first accuse myself, I hope your mercy.
POLYDAMAS Haste to explain your meaning.
HERMOGENES Then, in few words, Palmyra is your
daughter.
POLYDAMAS How can I give belief to this impostor?   390
He who has once abused me, often may.
I'll hear no more.
ARGALEON   For your own sake, you must.
HERMOGENES A parent's love (for I confess my crime)
Moved me to say, Leonidas was yours;
But when I heard Palmyra was to die,   395
The fear of guiltless blood so stung my conscience,
That I resolved, ev'n with my shame, to save
Your daughter's life.
POLYDAMAS But how can I be certain, but that interest,
Which moved you first to say your son was mine,   400
Does not now move you too, to save your daughter?
HERMOGENES You had but then my word; I bring you
now
Authentic testimonies. Sir, in short, (*delivers on his
knees a jewel, and a letter*)
If this will not convince you, let me suffer.
POLYDAMAS (*looking first on the jewel*) I know this   405
jewel well; 'twas once my mother's,
Which, marrying, I presented to my wife.
And this, O this, is my Eudocia's* hand.
(*reads*) 'This was the pledge of love given to Eudocia,
Who, dying, to her young Palmyra leaves it.
And this when you, my dearest lord, receive,   410

Own her, and think on me, dying Eudocia.'
Take it; 'tis well there is no more to read,
My eyes grow full, and swim in their own light.

(*He embraces* PALMYRA)

PALMYRA I fear, sir, this is your intended pageant.
You sport yourself at poor Palmyra's cost;   415
But if you think to make me proud,
Indeed I cannot be so: I was born
With humble thoughts, and lowly, like my birth.
A real fortune could not make me haughty,
Much less a feigned.   420
POLYDAMAS   This was her mother's temper.
I have too much deserved thou shouldst suspect
That I am not thy father; but my love
Shall henceforth show I am. Behold my eyes,
And see a father there begin to flow:
This is not feigned, Palmyra.   425
PALMYRA I doubt no longer, sir; you are a king,
And cannot lie. Falsehood's a vice too base
To find a room in any royal breast;
I know, in spite of my unworthiness,
I am your child; for when you would have killed me,   430
Methought I loved you then.
ARGALEON Sir, we forget the prince Leonidas,
His greatness should not stand neglected thus.
POLYDAMAS Guards, you may now retire. Give him his
    sword,
And leave him free.   435
LEONIDAS Then the first use I make of liberty
Shall be, with your permission, mighty sir,
To pay that reverence to which Nature binds me.

(*Kneels to* HERMOGENES)

ARGALEON Sure you forget your birth, thus to misplace
This act of your obedience; you should kneel   440
To nothing but to heaven, and to a king.
LEONIDAS I never shall forget what nature owes,

Nor be ashamed to pay it. Though my father
Be not a king, I know him brave and honest,
And well deserving of a worthier son.   445
POLYDAMAS He bears it gallantly.
LEONIDAS (to HERMOGENES) Why would you not
     instruct me, sir, before
   Where I should place my duty?
   From which, if ignorance have made me swerve,
   I beg your pardon for an erring son.   450
PALMYRA I almost grieve I am a princess, since
   It makes him lose a crown.
LEONIDAS And next, to you, my king, thus low I kneel,
   T' implore your mercy; if in that small time
   I had the honour to be thought your son,   455
   I paid not strict obedience to your will
   I thought, indeed, I should not be compelled,
   But thought it as your son; so what I took
   In duty from you, I restored in courage;
   Because your son should not be forced.   460
POLYDAMAS You have my pardon for it.
LEONIDAS To you, fair princess, I congratulate
   Your birth; of which I ever thought you worthy:
   And give me leave to add, that I am proud
   The gods have picked me out to be the man   465
   By whose dejected fate yours is to rise;
   Because no man could more desire your fortune,
   Or franklier part with his to make you great.
PALMYRA I know the king, though you are not his son,
   Will still regard you as my foster-brother,   470
   And so conduct you downward from a throne,
   By slow degrees, so unperceived and soft,
   That it may seem no fall; or, if it be,
   May Fortune lay a bed of down beneath you.
POLYDAMAS He shall be ranked with my nobility,   475
   And kept from scorn by a large pension given him.
LEONIDAS (bowing) You are all great and royal in your
     gifts;
   But at the donor's feet I lay 'em down:

Should I take riches from you, it would seem
As I did want a soul to bear that poverty   480
To which the gods designed my humble birth:
And should I take your honours without merit,
It would appear I wanted manly courage
To hope 'em, in your service, from my sword.

POLYDAMAS Still brave, and like yourself.   485
The court shall shine this night in its full splendour,
And celebrate this new discovery.
Argaleon, lead my daughter: as we go,
I shall have time to give her my commands,
In which you are concerned.   490

[*Exeunt all but* LEONIDAS]

LEONIDAS Methinks I do not want*
That huge long train of fawning followers,
That swept a furlong after me.
'Tis true, I am alone;
So was the godhead ere he made the world,   495
And better served himself, than served by nature.
And yet I have a soul
Above this humble fate. I could command,
Love to do good; give largely to true merit;
All that a king should do. But though these are not   500
My province, I have scene enough within
To exercise my virtue.
All that a heart, so fixed as mine, can move,
Is, that my niggard fortune starves my love.

[*Exit*]

Act 3, Scene 2

(PALAMEDE *and* DORALICE *meet: she, with a book in
her hand, seems to start at sight of him*)

DORALICE 'Tis a strange thing that no warning will serve
your turn; and that no retirement will secure me from

your impertinent addresses! Did not I tell you that I was
to be private here at my devotions?

PALAMEDE Yes; and you see I have observed my cue   5
exactly: I am come to relieve you from them. Come, shut
up, shut up your book; the man's come who is to supply
all your necessities.

DORALICE Then, it seems, you are so impudent to think it
was an assignation? This, I warrant, was your lewd   10
interpretation of my innocent meaning.

PALAMEDE Venus forbid that I should harbour so unreasonable a thought of a fair young lady, that you should
lead me hither into temptation. I confess I might think
indeed it was a kind of honourable challenge, to meet   15
privately without seconds, and decide the difference
betwixt the two sexes; but heaven forgive me if I thought
amiss.

DORALICE You thought too, I'll lay my life on't, that you
might as well make love to me, as my husband does to   20
your mistress.

PALAMEDE I was so unreasonable to think so too.

DORALICE And then you wickedly inferred, that there was
some justice in the revenge of it, or at least but little
injury; for a man to endeavour to enjoy that, which he   25
accounts a blessing, and which is not valued as it ought
by the dull possessor. Confess your wickedness, did you
not think so?

PALAMEDE I confess I was thinking so, as fast as I could;
but you think so much before me, that you will let me   30
think nothing.

DORALICE 'Tis the very thing that I designed. I have
forestalled all your arguments, and left you without a
word more, to plead for mercy. If you have anything
farther to offer, ere sentence pass – poor animal, I   35
brought you hither only for my diversion.

PALAMEDE That you may have, if you'll make use of me
the right way; but I tell thee, woman, I am now past
talking.

DORALICE But it may be, I came hither to hear what fine 40
things you could say for yourself.

PALAMEDE You would be very angry, to my knowledge, if
I should lose so much time to say many of 'em – by this
hand you would –

DORALICE Fie, Palamede, I am a woman of honour. 45

PALAMEDE I see you are; you have kept touch with your
assignation. And before we part, you shall find that I am a
man of honour – yet I have one scruple of conscience –

DORALICE I warrant you will not want some naughty
argument or other to satisfy yourself – I hope you are 50
afraid of betraying your friend?

PALAMEDE Of betraying my friend! I am more afraid of
being betrayed by you to my friend. You women now are
got into the way of telling first yourselves. A man who has
any care of his reputation will be loath to trust it with 55
you.

DORALICE Oh, you charge your faults upon our sex. You
men are like cocks, you never make love, but you clap
your wings, and crow when you have done.

PALAMEDE Nay, rather you women are like hens. You 60
never lay, but you cackle an hour after, to discover your
nest. But I'll venture it for once.

DORALICE To convince you that you are in the wrong, I'll
retire into the dark grotto, to my devotion, and make so
little noise, that it shall be impossible for you to find me. 65

PALAMEDE But if I find you –

DORALICE Aye, if you find me – but I'll put you to search
in more corners than you imagine.

(She runs in, and he after her)

(Enter RHODOPHIL *and* MELANTHA*)*

MELANTHA Let me die, but this solitude, and that grotto
are scandalous. I'll go no further; besides, you have a 70
sweet lady of your own.

RHODOPHIL But a sweet mistress now and then, makes my
sweet lady so much more sweet.

MELANTHA I hope you will not force me?

RHODOPHIL But I will, if you desire it.   75
PALAMEDE (*within*) Where the devil are you, madam?
S'death, I begin to be weary of this hide and seek. If you
stay a little longer, till the fit's* over, I'll hide in my turn,
and put you to the finding me.

(*He enters, and sees* RHODOPHIL *and* MELANTHA)

How! Rhodophil and my mistress!   80
MELANTHA (*aside*) My servant to apprehend me! This is
*surprenant au dernier.**
RHODOPHIL (*aside*) I must on; there's nothing but impu-
dence can help me out.
PALAMEDE Rhodophil, how came you hither in so good   85
company?
RHODOPHIL As you see, Palamede; an effect of pure
friendship. I was not able to live without you.
PALAMEDE But what makes my mistress with you?
RHODOPHIL Why, I heard you were here alone, and could   90
not in civility but bring her to you.
MELANTHA You'll pardon the effects of a passion which I
may now avow for you, if it transported me beyond the
rules of *bienséance.**
PALAMEDE But who told you I was here? They that told   95
you that, may tell you more, for ought I know.
RHODOPHIL Oh, for that matter, we had intelligence.
PALAMEDE But let me tell you, we came hither so very
privately that you could not trace us.
RHODOPHIL Us? What us? You are alone.   100
PALAMEDE <*aside*> Us! The devil's in me for mistaking.
<*to him*> Me, I meant. Or us; that is, you are me, or I
you, as we are friends: that's us.
DORALICE (*within*) Palamede, Palamede.
RHODOPHIL I should know that voice. Who's within there 105
that calls you?
PALAMEDE Faith, I can't imagine; I believe the place is
haunted.
DORALICE (*within*) Palamede, Palamede. All-cocks
hidden.*   110

PALAMEDE <aside> Lord, lord, what shall I do? <to him>
Well, dear friend, to let you see I scorn to be jealous, and
that I dare trust my mistress with you, take her back. For
I would not willingly have her frighted, and I am resolved
to see who's there. I'll not be daunted with a bugbear,*   115
that's certain. Prithee, dispute it not, it shall be so. Nay,
do not put me to swear, but go quickly. There's an effect
of pure friendship for you now.

(*Enter* DORALICE, *and looks amazed, seeing them*)

RHODOPHIL Doralice! I am thunderstruck to see you
here.   120

PALAMEDE So am I! Quite thunderstruck. Was it you that
called me within? (*aside*) I must be impudent.

RHODOPHIL How came you hither, spouse?

PALAMEDE Aye, how came you hither? And, which is
more, how could you be here without my knowledge?   125

DORALICE (*to her husband*) O, gentleman, have I caught
you i'faith? Have I broke forth in ambush upon you? I
thought my suspicions would prove true.

RHODOPHIL Suspicions! This is very fine, spouse! Prithee
what suspicions?   130

DORALICE Oh, you feign ignorance! Why, of you and
Melantha. Here have I stayed these two hours, waiting
with all the rage of a passionate, loving wife, but infinitely
jealous, to take you two in the manner;* for hither I was
certain you would come.   135

RHODOPHIL But you are mistaken, spouse, in the occasion; for we came hither on purpose to find Palamede on
intelligence he was gone before.

PALAMEDE I'll be hanged then if the same party who gave
you intelligence I was here, did not tell your wife you   140
would come hither. Now I smell the malice on't on both
sides.

DORALICE Was it so, think you? Nay, then, I'll confess my
part of the malice too. As soon as ever I spied my husband
and Melantha come together, I had a strange temptation   145
to make him jealous in revenge; and that made me call

Palamede, Palamede, as though there had been an intrigue
between us.

MELANTHA Nay, I avow, there was an appearance of an
intrigue between us too.   150

PALAMEDE To see how things will come about!

RHODOPHIL And was it only thus, my dear Doralice?
(*embraces*)

DORALICE And did I wrong none,* Rhodophil, with a false
suspicion? (*embracing him*)

PALAMEDE (*aside*) Now am I confident we had all four the 155
same design. 'Tis a pretty odd kind of game this, where
each of us plays for double stakes. This is just thrust and
parry with the same motion: I am to get his wife, and yet
to guard my own mistress. But I am vilely suspicious that
while I conquer in the right wing, I shall be routed in the 160
left. For both our women will certainly betray their party,
because they are each of them for gaining of two, as well
as we. And I much fear:
If their necessities and ours were known,
They have more need of two, than we of one.   165
                    [*Exeunt, embracing one another*]

Act 4, Scene 1

(*Enter* LEONIDAS, *musing,* AMALTHEA *following him*)

AMALTHEA Yonder he is, and I must speak, or die;
And yet 'tis death to speak. Yet he must know
I have a passion for him, and may know it
With a less blush; because to offer it
To his low fortunes, shows I loved, before,   5
His person, not his greatness.

LEONIDAS First scorned, and now commanded from the
     court!
The king is good; but he is wrought to this
By proud Argaleon's malice.
What more disgrace can love and fortune join   10
T' inflict upon one man? I cannot now

Behold my dear Palmyra: she, perhaps, too
Is grown ashamed of a mean ill-placed love.
AMALTHEA (*aside*) Assist me, Venus, for I tremble when
I am to speak, but I must force myself.   15
(*to him*) Sir, I would crave but one short minute with
    you,
And some few words.
LEONIDAS (*aside*)   The proud Argaleon's sister!
AMALTHEA (*aside*) Alas, it will not out; shame stops my
    mouth.
(*to him*) Pardon my error, sir, I was mistaken,
And took you for another.   20
LEONIDAS (*aside*) In spite of all his guards, I'll see
    Palmyra;
Though meanly born, I have a kingly soul yet.
AMALTHEA (*aside*) I stand upon a precipice, where fain
I would retire, but love still thrusts me on.
Now I grow bolder, and will speak to him.   25
(*to him)* Sir, 'tis indeed to you that I would speak, and
    if –
LEONIDAS O, you are sent to scorn my fortunes.
Your sex and beauty are your privilege.
But should your brother –
AMALTHEA (*aside*) Now he looks angry, and I dare not
    speak.   30
(*to him*) I had some business with you, sir,
But 'tis not worth your knowledge.
LEONIDAS Then 'twill be charity to let me mourn
My griefs alone, for I am much disordered.
AMALTHEA 'Twill be more charity to mourn 'em with
    you: 35
Heaven knows I pity you.
LEONIDAS   Your pity, madam,
Is generous, but 'tis unavailable.*
AMALTHEA You know not till 'tis tried.
Your sorrows are no secret; you have lost
A crown, and mistress.
LEONIDAS   Are not these enough?   40

Hang two such weights on any other soul,
And see if it can bear 'em.

AMALTHEA More; you are banished, by my brother's
    means,
And ne'er must hope again to see your princess;
Except as pris'ners view fair walks and streets,   45
And careless passengers going by their grates,*
To make 'em feel the want of liberty.
But, worse than all,
The king this morning has enjoined his daughter
T' accept my brother's love.

LEONIDAS   Is this your pity?   50
You aggravate my griefs, and print 'em deeper
In new and heavier stamps.

AMALTHEA 'Tis as physicians show the desperate ill
T' endear their art, by mitigating pains
They cannot wholly cure. When you despair   55
Of all you wish, some part of it, because
Unhoped for, may be grateful;* and some other –

LEONIDAS What other?

AMALTHEA Some other may –
    (aside) My shame again has seized me, and I can go   60
No farther –

LEONIDAS These often failings, sighs, and interruptions,
Make me imagine you have grief like mine.
Have you ne'er loved?

AMALTHEA   I? Never. (aside) 'Tis in vain;
I must despair in silence.   65

LEONIDAS You come as I suspected then, to mock,
At least observe my griefs. Take it not ill
That I must leave you. (is going)

AMALTHEA You must not go with these unjust opinions.
Command my life, and fortunes; you are wise,   70
Think, and think well, what I can do to serve you.

LEONIDAS I have but one thing in my thoughts and
    wishes.
If by your means I can obtain the sight
Of my adored Palmyra; or, what's harder,

One minute's time, to tell her I die hers.   75

(*She starts back*)

I see I am not to expect it from you;
Nor could, indeed, with reason.
AMALTHEA Name any other thing. Is Amalthea
So despicable, she can serve your wishes
In this alone?   80
LEONIDAS If I should ask of heav'n,
I have no other suit.
AMALTHEA To show you, then, I can deny you nothing,
Though 'tis more hard to me than any other,
Yet I will do't for you.
LEONIDAS Name quickly, name the means, speak, my
   good angel.   85
AMALTHEA Be not so much o'erjoyed; for, if you are,
I'll rather die than do't. This night the court
Will be in masquerade.
You shall attend on me; in that disguise
You may both see and speak to her,   90
If you dare venture it.
LEONIDAS Yes, were a god her guardian,
And bore in each hand thunder, I would venture.
AMALTHEA Farewell then; two hours hence I will expect
   you:
My heart's so full, that I can stay no longer.   95
LEONIDAS Already it grows dusky; I'll prepare
With haste for my disguise. But who are these?

(*Enter* HERMOGENES *and* EUBULUS)

HERMOGENES 'Tis he; we need not fear to speak to him.
EUBULUS Leonidas.
LEONIDAS   Sure I have known that voice.
HERMOGENES You have some reason, sir; 'tis Eubulus,   100
Who bred you with the princess; and, departing,
Bequeathed you to my care.
LEONIDAS (*kneeling*) My foster-father! Let my knees
   express

My joys for your return!
EUBULUS Rise, sir, you must not kneel.
LEONIDAS   E'er since you left me,   105
  I have been wand'ring in a maze of fate,
  Led by false fires* of a fantastic glory,
  And the vain lustre of imagined crowns,
  But, ah! Why would you leave me? Or how could you
  Absent yourself so long?   110
EUBULUS I'll give you a most just account of both.
  And something more I have to tell you, which
  I know must cause your wonder; but this place,
  Though almost hid in darkness, is not safe.
  (torches appear) Already I discern some coming
    towards us   115
  With lights, who may discover me. Hermogenes,
  Your lodgings are hard by, and much more private.
HERMOGENES There you may freely speak.
LEONIDAS   Let us make haste;
  For some affairs, and of no small importance,
  Call me another way.   120
                        [Exeunt]

(Enter PALAMEDE and RHODOPHIL, with vizor masks*
in their hands, and torches before 'em)

PALAMEDE We shall have noble sport tonight, Rhodophil;
  this masquerading is a most glorious invention.
RHODOPHIL I believe it was invented first by some jealous
  lover, to discover the haunts of his jilting mistress; or,
  perhaps, by some distressed servant, to gain an opportu- 125
  nity with a jealous man's wife.
PALAMEDE No, it must be the invention of a woman, it has
  so much of subtlety and love in it.
RHODOPHIL I am sure 'tis extremely pleasant; for to go
  unknown, is the next degree to going invisible.   130
PALAMEDE What with our antique habits,* and feigned
  voices, do you know me, and I know you? Methinks we
  move and talk just like so many overgrown puppets.

RHODOPHIL Masquerade is only vizor-mask improved, a heightening of the same fashion.   135

PALAMEDE No; masquerade is vizor-mask in debauch;* and I like it the better for't. For with a vizor-mask we fool ourselves into courtship, for the sake of an eye that glanced; or a hand that stole itself out of the glove sometimes, to give us a sample of the skin. But in 140 masquerade there is nothing to be known, she's all *terra incognita*, and the bold discoverer leaps ashore, and takes his lot among the wild Indians and savages, without the vile consideration of safety to his person, or of beauty or wholesomeness in his mistress.   145

(*Enter* BELIZA)

RHODOPHIL Beliza, what make you here?

BELIZA Sir, my lady sent me after you, to let you know, she finds herself a little indisposed, so that she cannot be at court, but is retired to rest in her own apartment, where she shall want the happiness of your dear embraces 150 tonight.

RHODOPHIL A very fine phrase, Beliza, to let me know my wife desires to lie alone.

PALAMEDE I doubt,* Rhodophil, you take the pains some- times to instruct your wife's woman in these elegancies. 155

RHODOPHIL Tell my dear lady, that since I must be so unhappy as not to wait on her tonight, I will lament bitterly for her absence. 'Tis true, I shall be at court, but I will take no divertisement there; and when I return to my solitary bed, if I am so forgetful of my passion as to 160 sleep, I will dream of her; and betwixt sleep and waking, put out my foot towards her side, for midnight consola- tion; and not finding her, I will sigh, and imagine myself a most desolate widower.

BELIZA I shall do your commands, sir.   165

[*Exit*]

RHODOPHIL (*aside*) She's sick as aptly for my purpose as if she had contrived it so. Well, if ever woman was a helpmate for man, my spouse is so; for within this hour I

received a note from Melantha, that she would meet me
this evening in masquerade in boy's habit, to rejoice with 170
me before she entered into fetters. For I find she loves me
better than Palamede only because he's to be her
husband. There's something of antipathy in the word
'marriage' to the nature of love; marriage is the mere ladle
of affection, that cools it when 'tis never so fiercely 175
boiling over.

PALAMEDE Dear Rhodophil, I must needs beg your pardon. There is an occasion fallen out which I had forgot: I
cannot be at court tonight.

RHODOPHIL Dear Palamede, I am sorry we shall not have 180
one course together at the herd;* but I find your game lies
single. Good fortune to you with your mistress.

[Exit]

PALAMEDE He has wished me good fortune with his wife.
There's no sin in this then, there's fair leave given. Well, I
must go visit the sick; I cannot resist the temptations of 185
my charity. O what a difference will she find betwixt a
dull resty* husband, and a quick vigorous lover! He sets
out like a carrier's horse, plodding on, because he knows
he must, with the bells of matrimony chiming so melancholy about his neck, in pain till he's at his journey's end, 190
and despairing to get thither, he is fain to fortify
imagination with the thoughts of another woman. I take
heat after heat, like a well-breathed courser,* and –
(*clashing of swords within*) But hark, what noise is that?
Swords! Nay, then, have with you. 195

[Exit PALAMEDE]

(*Re-enter* PALAMEDE, *with* RHODOPHIL: *and* DORALICE
in man's habit)

RHODOPHIL Friend, your relief was very timely, otherwise
I had been oppressed.

PALAMEDE What was the quarrel?

RHODOPHIL What I did was in rescue of this youth.

PALAMEDE What cause could he give 'em? 200

DORALICE The cause was nothing but only the common cause of fighting in masquerades: they were drunk, and I was sober.

RHODOPHIL Have they not hurt you?

DORALICE No; but I am exceeding ill, with the fright on't. 205

PALAMEDE Let's lead him to some place where he may refresh himself.

RHODOPHIL Do you conduct him then.

PALAMEDE (aside) How cross this happens to my design of going to Doralice! For I am confident she was sick on 210 purpose that I should visit her. Hark you, Rhodophil, could not you take care of the stripling? I am partly engaged tonight.

RHODOPHIL You know I have business: but come, youth, if it must be so.   215

DORALICE (to RHODOPHIL) No, good sir, do not give yourself that trouble. I shall be safer, and better pleased with your friend here.

RHODOPHIL Farewell then; once more I wish you a good adventure.   220

PALAMEDE Damn this kindness! Now must I be troubled with this young rogue, and miss my opportunity with Doralice.

[Exit RHODOPHIL alone; PALAMEDE with DORALICE]

Act 4, Scene 2

(Enter POLYDAMAS)

POLYDAMAS Argaleon counselled well to banish him,
He has, I know not what
Of greatness in his looks, and of high fate,
That almost awes me; but I fear my daughter,
Who hourly moves* me for him, and I marked   5
She sighed when I but named Argaleon to her.
But see, the maskers. Hence my cares, this night,
At least take truce, and find me on my pillow.

(*Enter the* PRINCESS *in masquerade, with ladies: at the
other end,* ARGALEON *and gentlemen in masquerade:
then* LEONIDAS *leading* AMALTHEA. *The* KING *sits. A
dance. After the dance*)

AMALTHEA (*to Leonidas*) That's the princess;
  I saw the habit ere she put it on.   10
LEONIDAS I know her by a thousand other signs,
  She cannot hide so much divinity.
  Disguised and silent, yet some graceful motion
  Breaks from her, and shines round her like a glory.

(*Goes to* PALMYRA)

AMALTHEA Thus she reveals herself, and knows it not.   15
  Like love's dark lantern* I direct his steps,
  And yet he sees not that which gives him light.
PALMYRA (*to* LEONIDAS) I know you; but, alas,
    Leonidas,
  Why should you tempt this danger on yourself?
LEONIDAS Madam, you know me not, if you believe   20
  I would not hazard greater for your sake:
  But you, I fear, are changed.
PALMYRA No, I am still the same;
  But there are many things became Palmyra
  Which ill become the princess.
LEONIDAS   I ask nothing   25
  Which honour will not give you leave to grant:
  One hour's short audience, at my father's house,
  You cannot sure refuse me.
PALMYRA Perhaps I should, did I consult strict virtue;
  But something must be given to love and you.   30
  When would you I should come?
LEONIDAS This evening, with the speediest opportunity.
  I have a secret to discover to you,
  Which will surprise, and please you.
PALMYRA   'Tis enough.
  Go now; for we may be observed and known.   35
  I trust your honour; give me not occasion

To blame myself, or you.

LEONIDAS (*kisses her hand*) You never shall repent your
    good opinion.

                                     [*Exit*]

ARGALEON I cannot be deceived; that is the princess:
    One of her maids betrayed the habit to me;   40
    But who was he with whom she held discourse?
    'Tis one she favours, for he kissed her hand.
    Our shapes are like, our habits near the same:
    She may mistake, and speak to me for him.
    I am resolved, I'll satisfy my doubts,   45
    Though to be more tormented.

                                       [*Exit*]

Song

I

Whilst Alexis lay pressed
In her arms he loved best,
With his hands round her neck,
And his head on her breast,   50
He found the fierce pleasure too hasty to stay,
And his soul in the tempest just flying away.

2

When Cœlia saw this,
With a sigh, and a kiss,
She cried, Oh my dear, I am robbed of my bliss;   55
'Tis unkind to your love, and unfaithfully done,
To leave me behind you, and die* all alone.

3

The youth, though in haste,
And breathing his last,
In pity died slowly, while she died more fast;   60
Till at length she cried, Now, my dear, now let us go,

Now die, my Alexis, and I will die too.

4

Thus entranced they did lie,
Till Alexis did try
To recover new breath, that again he might die: 65
Then often they died; but the more they did so,
The nymph died more quick, and the shepherd more
  slow.

(*Another dance. After it,* ARGALEON *re-enters, and stands
    by the* PRINCESS)

PALMYRA (*to* ARGALEON) Leonidas, what means this
  quick return?
ARGALEON (*aside*) O heaven! 'Tis what I feared.
PALMYRA Is aught of moment happened since you went?   70
ARGALEON No, madam, but I understood not fully
  Your last commands.
PALMYRA   And yet you answered to 'em.
  Retire; you are too indiscreet a lover.
  I'll meet you where I promised.
                                                [*Exit*]

ARGALEON O my cursed fortune! What have I
  discovered?   75
But I will be revenged.

              (*Whispers to the* KING)

POLYDAMAS But are you certain you are not deceived?
ARGALEON Upon my life.
POLYDAMAS   Her honour is concerned.
  Somewhat I'll do; but I am yet distracted,
  And know not where to fix. I wished a child,   80
  And heaven, in anger, granted my request.
  So blind we are, our wishes are so vain,
  That what we most desire, proves most our pain.
                                      [*Exeunt omnes*]

Act 4, Scene 3

An eating-house. Bottles of wine on the table.
PALAMEDE, *and* DORALICE *in man's habit*

DORALICE (*aside*) Now cannot I find in my heart to discover myself, though I long he should know me.

PALAMEDE I tell thee, boy, now I have seen thee safe, I must be gone. I have no leisure to throw away on thy raw* conversation. I am a person that understands better   5
things, I.

DORALICE Were I a woman, oh how you'd admire me! Cry up every word I said, and screw your face into a submissive smile, as I have seen a dull gallant act wit, and counterfeit pleasantness, when he whispers to a great   10
person in a play-house; smile, and look briskly when the other answers, as if something of extraordinary had passed betwixt 'em, when, heaven knows, there was nothing else but, 'What a clock does your lordship think it is?' and my lord's repartee is, ''Tis almost park-time';*   15
or, at most, 'Shall we out of the pit, and go behind the scenes for an act or two?' And yet such fine things as these would be wit in a mistress's mouth.

PALAMEDE Aye, boy; there's Dame Nature in the case: he who cannot find wit in a mistress, deserves to find nothing   20
else, boy. But these are riddles to thee, child, and I have not leisure to instruct thee. I have affairs to dispatch, great affairs; I am a man of business.

DORALICE Come, you shall not go: you have no affairs but what you may dispatch here, to my knowledge.   25

PALAMEDE I find now, thou art a boy of more understanding than I thought thee; a very lewd, wicked boy.* O' my conscience thou wouldst debauch me, and hast some evil designs upon my person.

DORALICE You are mistaken, sir. I would only have you   30
show me a more lawful reason why you would leave me, than I can why you should not. And I'll not stay you; for I am not so young, but I understand the necessities of flesh

and blood, and the pressing occasions of mankind, as well
as you.   35

PALAMEDE A very forward and understanding boy! Thou
art in great danger of a page's wit, to be brisk at fourteen,
and dull at twenty. But I'll give thee no further account; I
must and will go.

DORALICE My life on't, your mistress is not at home.   40

PALAMEDE (aside) This imp will make me very angry. I tell
thee, young sir, she is at home; and at home for me; and,
which is more, she is abed for me, and sick for me.

DORALICE For you only?

PALAMEDE Aye, for me only.   45

DORALICE But how do you know she's sick abed?

PALAMEDE She sent her husband word so.

DORALICE And are you such a novice in love, to believe a
wife's message to her husband?

PALAMEDE Why, what the devil should be her meaning   50
else?

DORALICE It may be, to go in masquerade as well as you;
to observe your haunts, and keep you company without
your knowledge.

PALAMEDE Nay, I'll trust her for that. She loves me too   55
well to disguise herself from me.

DORALICE If I were she, I would disguise on purpose to try
your wit; and come to my servant like a riddle, read me,
and take me.*

PALAMEDE I could know her in any shape. My good genius   60
would prompt me to find out a handsome woman.
There's something in her that would attract me to her
without my knowledge.

DORALICE Then you make a loadstone of your mistress?

PALAMEDE Yes, and I carry steel* about me, which has   65
been so often touched, that it never fails to point to the
north pole.

DORALICE Yet still my mind gives me, that you have met
her disguised tonight, and have not known her.

PALAMEDE (aside) This is the most pragmatical,* conceited   70
little fellow, he will needs understand my business better

than myself. <*to the 'boy'*> I tell thee, once more, thou dost not know my mistress.

DORALICE And I tell you, once more, that I know her better than you do.   75

PALAMEDE (*aside*) The boy's resolved to have the last word. I find I must go without reply.

[*Exit*]

DORALICE Ah mischief, I have lost him with my fooling. Palamede, Palamede.

(*He returns. She plucks off her peruque, and puts it on again when he knows her*)

PALAMEDE O heavens! Is it you, madam?   80

DORALICE Now, where was your good genius, that would prompt you to find me out?

PALAMEDE Why, you see I was not deceived; you, yourself, were my good genius.

DORALICE But where was the steel, that knew the load-   85
stone? Ha?

PALAMEDE The truth is, madam, the steel has lost its virtue; and therefore, if you please, we'll new touch it.

(*Enter* RHODOPHIL; *and* MELANTHA *in boy's habit.*
RHODOPHIL *sees* PALAMEDE *kissing* DORALICE*'s hand*)

RHODOPHIL Palamede again! Am I fall'n into your quarters? What? Engaging with a boy? Is all honourable?   90

PALAMEDE O, very honourable on my side. I was just chastising this young villain; he was running away, without paying his share of the reckoning.

RHODOPHIL Then I find I was deceived in him.

PALAMEDE Yes, you are deceived in him. 'Tis the archest*   95
rogue, if you did but know him.

MELANTHA Good Rhodophil, let us get off *à la dérobée*, for fear I should be discovered.

RHODOPHIL <*to* MELANTHA> There's no retiring now; I warrant you for discovery.* Now have I the oddest   100
thought, to entertain you before your servant's face, and

he never the wiser. 'Twill be the prettiest juggling trick to cheat him when he looks upon us.

MELANTHA This is the strangest *caprice* in you.

PALAMEDE (*to* DORALICE) This Rhodophil's the unluck- 105 iest fellow to me! This is now the second time he has barred the dice when we were just ready to have nicked* him; but if ever I get the box again –

DORALICE Do you think he will not know me? Am I like myself?   110

PALAMEDE No more than a picture in the hangings.*

DORALICE Nay, then he can never discover me, now the wrong side of the arras is turned towards him.

PALAMEDE At least, 'twill be some pleasure to me, to enjoy what freedom I can while he looks on. I will storm the 115 outworks of matrimony even before his face.

RHODOPHIL What wine have you there, Palamede?

PALAMEDE Old Chios,* or the rogue's damned that drew it.

RHODOPHIL Come: to the most constant of mistresses. 120 That, I believe is yours, Palamede.

DORALICE Pray spare your seconds. For my part I am but a weak brother.*

PALAMEDE Now: to the truest of turtles. That is your wife, Rhodophil, that lies sick at home in the bed of honour. 125

RHODOPHIL Now let's have one common health, and so have done.

DORALICE Then, for once, I'll begin it. Here's to him that has the fairest lady of Sicily in masquerade tonight.

PALAMEDE This is such an obliging health, I'll kiss thee, 130 dear rogue, for thy invention.

(*Kisses her*)

RHODOPHIL He who has this lady is a happy man, without dispute. (*aside*) I'm most concerned in this, I am sure.

PALAMEDE Was it not well found out,* Rhodophil?   135

MELANTHA Aye, this was *bien trouvé* indeed.

DORALICE (*to* MELANTHA) I suppose I shall do you a
  kindness to enquire if you have not been in France, sir?

MELANTHA To do you service, sir.

  DORALICE (*saluting* her) O, *monsieur, votre valet bien* 140
  *humble.**

MELANTHA (*returning the salute*) *Votre esclave, monsieur,*
  *de tout mon coeur.**

DORALICE I suppose, sweet sir, you are the hope and joy of
  some thriving citizen, who has pinched himself at home to 145
  breed you abroad, where you have learnt your exercises,
  as it appears, most awkwardly, and are returned with the
  addition of a new-laced bosom* and a clap* to your good
  old father, who looks at you with his mouth,* while you
  spout French with your man *monsieur.**   150

PALAMEDE Let me kiss thee again for that, dear rogue.

MELANTHA And you, I imagine, are my young master
  whom your mother durst not trust upon salt water,* but
  left you to be your own tutor at fourteen, to be very brisk
  and *entreprenant*,* to endeavour to be debauched ere you 155
  have learnt the knack on't, to value yourself upon a clap
  before you can get it, and to make it the height of your
  ambition to get a player for your mistress.

RHODOPHIL (*embracing* MELANTHA) O dear young bully,
  thou hast tickled him with a repartee i'faith.   160

MELANTHA You are one of those that applaud our country
  plays, where drums, and trumpets, and blood, and
  wounds, are wit.

RHODOPHIL Again, my boy? Let me kiss thee most
  abundantly.   165

DORALICE You are an admirer of the dull French poetry,
  which is so thin that it is the very leaf-gold of wit, the very
  wafers and whipped cream of sense, for which a man
  opens his mouth and gapes, to swallow nothing; and to be
  an admirer of such profound dullness, one must be 170
  endowed with a great perfection of impudence and
  ignorance.

PALAMEDE Let me embrace thee most vehemently.

MELANTHA (*advancing*) I'll sacrifice my life for French
poetry.   175

DORALICE I'll die upon the spot for our country wit.

RHODOPHIL (*to* MELANTHA) Hold, hold, young Mars.*
Palamede, draw back your hero.

PALAMEDE 'Tis time: I shall be drawn in for a second else
at the wrong weapon.   180

MELANTHA O that I were a man for thy sake!

DORALICE You'll be a man as soon as I shall.

(*Enter a* MESSENGER *to* RHODOPHIL)

MESSENGER Sir, the king has instant business with you.
I saw the guard drawn up by your lieutenant
Before the palace gate, ready to march.   185

RHODOPHIL 'Tis somewhat sudden. Say that I am
coming.

[*Exit* MESSENGER]

Now, Palamede, what think you of this sport?
This is some sudden tumult: will you along?

PALAMEDE Yes, yes, I will go; but the devil take me if ever
I was less in humour. Why the pox could they not have   190
stayed their tumult till tomorrow? Then I had done my
business, and been ready for 'em. Truth is, I had a little
transitory crime to have committed first, and I am the
worst man in the world at repenting, till a sin be
thoroughly done. But what shall we do with the two   195
boys?

RHODOPHIL Let them take a lodging in the house till the
business be over.

DORALICE What, lie with a boy? For my part, I own it, I
cannot endure to lie with a boy.   200

PALAMEDE The more's my sorrow, I cannot accommodate
you with a better bedfellow.

MELANTHA Let me die, if I enter into a pair of sheets with
him that hates the French.

DORALICE Pish, take no care for us, but leave us in the   205
streets. I warrant you, as late as it is, I'll find my lodging
as well as any drunken bully of 'em all.

RHODOPHIL (*aside*) I'll fight in mere revenge, and wreak
  my passion
  On all that spoil this hopeful assignation.
PALAMEDE I'm sure we fight in a good quarrel: 210
  Rogues may pretend religion, and the laws;
  But a kind mistress is the Good Old Cause.*

                                    [*Exeunt*]

Act 4, Scene 4

(*Enter* PALMYRA, EUBULUS, HERMOGENES)

PALMYRA You tell me wonders; that Leonidas
  Is Prince Theagenes, the late king's son.
EUBULUS It seemed as strange to him, as now to you,
  Before I had convinced him. But, besides
  His great resemblance to the king his father,   5
  The queen his mother lives, secured by me
  In a religious house; to whom each year
  I brought the news of his increasing virtues.
  My last long absence from you both was caused
  By wounds which, in my journey, I received,   10
  When set upon by thieves; I lost those jewels
  And letters, which your dying mother left.
HERMOGENES The same he means, which, since, brought
  to the King,
  Made him first know he had a child alive
  'Twas then my care of Prince Leonidas   15
  Caused me to say he was th' usurper's son;
  Till, after forced by your apparent danger,
  I made the true discovery of your birth,
  And once more hid my prince's.

                    (*Enter* LEONIDAS)

LEONIDAS Hermogenes and Eubulus, retire;   20
  Those of our party, whom I left without,
  Expect your aid and counsel.

                            [*Exeunt ambo*]*

PALMYRA   I should, Leonidas, congratulate
  This happy change of your exalted fate;
  But, as my joy, so you my wonder move;   25
  Your looks have more of business, than of love:
  And your last words some great design did show.
LEONIDAS   I frame not any to be hid from you.
  You, in my love, all my designs may see;
  But what have love and you designed for me?   30
  Fortune, once more, has set the balance right:
  First, equalled us, in lowness; then, in height.
  Both of us have so long like gamesters thrown,
  Till fate comes round, and gives to each his own.
  As fate is equal, so may love appear: 35
  Tell me, at least, what I must hope, or fear.
PALMYRA   After so many proofs, how can you call
  My love in doubt? Fear nothing, and hope all.
  Think what a prince, with honour, may receive,
  Or I may give, without a parent's leave.   40
LEONIDAS   You give, and then restrain the grace you
    show;
  As ostentatious priests, when souls they woo,
  Promise their heaven to all, but grant to few:
  But do for me, what I have dared for you.
  I did no argument from duty bring: 45
  Duty's a name; and love's a real thing.
PALMYRA   Man's love may, like wild torrents, overflow;
  Woman's as deep, but in its banks must go.
  My love is mine, and that I can impart;
  But cannot give my person with my heart.   50
LEONIDAS   Your love is then no gift:
  For when the person it does not convey,
  'Tis to give gold, and not to give the key.
PALMYRA   Then ask my father.
LEONIDAS   – He detains my throne:
  Who holds back mine, will hardly give his own.   55
PALMYRA   What then remains?
LEONIDAS   – That I must have recourse
  To arms; and take my love and crown, by force.

Hermogenes is forming the design;
And with him all the brave and loyal join.

PALMYRA And is it thus you court Palmyra's bed?   60
Can she the murd'rer of her parent wed?
Desist from force: so much you well may give
To love and me, to let my father live.

LEONIDAS Each act of mine my love to you has shown;
But you, who tax my want of it, have none.   65
You bid me part with you, and let him live;
But they should nothing ask, who nothing give.

PALMYRA I give what virtue and what duty can,
In vowing ne'er to wed another man.

LEONIDAS You will be forc'd to be Argaleon's wife.   70

PALMYRA I'll keep my promise, though I lose my life.

LEONIDAS Then you lose love, for which we both
   contend;
For life is but the means, but love's the end.

PALMYRA Our souls shall love hereafter.

LEONIDAS   I much fear,
That soul which could deny the body here,   75
To taste of love, would be a niggard there.

PALMYRA Then 'tis past hope: our cruel fate, I see,
Will make a sad divorce 'twixt you and me.
For, if you force employ, by heav'n I swear,
And all blessed beings, –

LEONIDAS   Your rash oath forbear.   80

PALMYRA I never –

LEONIDAS   Hold once more. But yet, as he
Who scapes a dang'rous leap, looks back to see;
So I desire, now I am past my fear,
To know what was that oath you meant to swear.

PALMYRA I meant that if you hazarded your life,   85
Or sought my father's, ne'er to be your wife.

LEONIDAS See now, Palmyra, how unkind you prove!
Could you, with so much ease, forswear my love?

PALMYRA You force me with your ruinous design.

LEONIDAS Your father's life is more your care, than
   mine.   90

PALMYRA You wrong me, 'tis not; though it ought to
   be;
  You are my care, heav'n knows, as well as he.
LEONIDAS If now the execution I delay,
  My honour, and my subjects, I betray.
  All is prepared for the just enterprise;   95
  And the whole city will tomorrow rise.
  The leaders of the party are within,
  And Eubulus has sworn that he will bring,
  To head their arms, the person of their king.
PALMYRA In telling this, you make me guilty too;   100
  I therefore must discover* what I know.
  What honour bids you do, nature bids me prevent;
  But kill me first, and then pursue your black intent.
LEONIDAS Palmyra, no; you shall not need to die;
  Yet I'll not trust so strict a piety.   105
  <calls> Within there.

(Enter EUBULUS)

             Eubulus, a guard prepare.
  Here, I commit this pris'ner to your care.

(Kisses PALMYRA's hand; then gives it to EUBULUS)

PALMYRA Leonidas, I never thought these bands*
  Could e'er be giv'n me by a lover's hands.
LEONIDAS (kneeling) Palmyra, thus your judge himself
  arraigns;   110
  He who imposed these bonds still wears your chains:
  When you to love or duty false must be,
  Or* to your father guilty, or to me,
  These chains alone remain to set you free.

(Noise of swords clashing)

POLYDAMAS (within) Secure these, first; then search the
  inner room.   115
LEONIDAS From whence do these tumultuous clamours
  come?

(Enter HERMOGENES, hastily)

HERMOGENES We are betrayed; and there remains alone
This comfort, that your person is not known.

(*Enter the* KING, ARGALEON, RHODOPHIL, PALAMEDE,
GUARDS; *some like* CITIZENS *as prisoners*)

POLYDAMAS What mean these midnight consultations
here,
Where I, like an unsummoned guest, appear?   120
LEONIDAS Sir –
ARGALEON   There needs no excuse; 'tis understood;
You were all watching for your prince's good.
POLYDAMAS My reverend city friends, you are well met!
On what great work were your grave wisdoms set?
Which of my actions were you scanning here?   125
What French invasion have you found to fear?*
LEONIDAS They are my friends; and come, sir, with
intent
To take their leaves before my banishment.
POLYDAMAS (*seeing* PALMYRA)
Your exile in both sexes friends can find:
I see the ladies, like the men, are kind.   130
PALMYRA (*kneeling*) Alas, I came but –
POLYDAMAS   – Add not to your crime
A lie: I'll hear you speak some other time.
How? Eubulus! Nor time, nor thy disguise,
Can keep thee undiscovered from my eyes.
A guard there, seize 'em all.   135
RHODOPHIL Yield, sir, what use of valour can be
shown?
POLYDAMAS One, and unarmed, against a multitude!
LEONIDAS Oh for a sword!

(*He reaches at one of the guard's halberds, and is seized
behind*)

                              I w'not* lose my breath
In fruitless pray'rs; but beg a speedy death.
PALMYRA O spare Leonidas, and punish me.   140

POLYDAMAS Mean* girl, thou want'st an advocate for
    thee.
  Now the mysterious knot will be untied,
  Whether the young king lives, or where he died.
  Tomorrow's dawn shall the dark riddle clear,
  Crown all my joys, and dissipate my fear.   145

                              [*Exeunt omnes*]

Act 5, Scene 1

(<*Enter*> PALAMEDE, STRATON; PALAMEDE *with a letter
                  in his hand*)

PALAMEDE This evening, sayst thou? Will they both be
    here?
STRATON Yes, sir; both my old master, and your mistress's
    father. The old gentlemen ride hard this journey. They say
    it shall be the last time they will see the town; and   5
    both of 'em are so pleased with this marriage which they
    have concluded for you, that I am afraid they will live
    some years longer to trouble you, with the joy of it.
PALAMEDE But this is such an unreasonable thing, to
    impose upon me to be married tomorrow; 'tis hurrying a   10
    man to execution, without giving him time to say his
    prayers.
STRATON Yet, if I might advise you, sir, you should not
    delay it: for your younger brother comes up with 'em, and
    is got already into their favours. He has gained much   15
    upon my old master by finding fault with innkeepers'
    bills, and by starving us, and our horses, to show his
    frugality; and he is very well with your mistress's father,
    by giving him receipts* for the spleen, gout, and scurvy,
    and other infirmities of old age.   20
PALAMEDE I'll rout him, and his country education. Pox on
    him, I remember him before I travelled; he had nothing in
    him but mere jockey;* used to talk loud, and make
    matches,* and was all for the crack of the field.* Sense

and wit were as much banished from his discourse, as 25
they are when the court goes out of town to a horse-race.
Go now and provide your master's lodgings.

STRATON I go, sir.

[*Exit*]

PALAMEDE It vexes me to the heart, to leave all my designs
with Doralice unfinished; to have flown her so often to a 30
mark,* and still to be bobbed at retrieve.* If I had but
once enjoyed her, though I could not have satisfied my
stomach with the feast, at least I should have relished my
mouth a little; but now –

(*Enter* PHILOTIS)

PHILOTIS Oh, sir, you are happily met; I was coming to 35
find you.

PALAMEDE From your lady, I hope.

PHILOTIS Partly from her, but more especially from
myself. She has just now received a letter from her father,
with an absolute command to dispose herself to marry 40
you tomorrow.

PALAMEDE And she takes it to the death?

PHILOTIS Quite contrary: the letter could never have come
in a more lucky minute, for it found her in an ill humour
with a rival of yours that shall be nameless, about the 45
pronunciation of a French word.

PALAMEDE Count Rhodophil; never disguise it, I know the
amour. But I hope you took the occasion to strike in for
me?

PHILOTIS It was my good fortune to do you some small 50
service in it. For your sake I discommended him all over:
clothes, person, humour,* behaviour, everything; and to
sum up all, told her it was impossible to find a married
man that was otherwise. For they were all so mortified at
home with their wives' ill humours, that they could never 55
recover themselves to be company abroad.

PALAMEDE Most divinely urged!

PHILOTIS Then I took occasion to commend your good

qualities: as, the sweetness of your humour, the comeli-
ness of your person, your good mien,* your valour; but,   60
above all, your liberality.

PALAMEDE I vow to gad I had like to have forgot that good
quality in myself, if thou hadst not remembered me on't:
here are five pieces* for thee.

PHILOTIS Lord, you have the softest hand, sir! It would do   65
a woman good to touch it. Count Rhodophil's is not half
so soft; for I remember I felt it once, when he gave me ten
pieces for my New Year's gift.

PALAMEDE O, I understand you, madam; you shall find my
hand as soft again as Count Rhodophil's. There are   70
twenty pieces for you; the former was but a retaining fee.
Now I hope you'll plead for me.

PHILOTIS Your own merits speak enough. Be sure only to
ply her with French words, and I'll warrant you'll do your
business. Here are a list of her phrases for this day. Use   75
'em to her upon all occasions, and foil her at her own
weapon; for she's like one of the old Amazons,* she'll
never marry, except it be the man who has first conquered
her.

PALAMEDE I'll be sure to follow your advice: but you'll   80
forget to further my design.

PHILOTIS What, do you think I'll be ungrateful? But,
however, if you distrust my memory, put some token on
my finger to remember it by. That diamond there would
do admirably.   85

PALAMEDE There 'tis, and I ask your pardon heartily for
calling your memory into question. I assure you I'll trust
it another time without putting you to the trouble of
another token.

(*Enter* PALMYRA *and* ARTEMIS)

ARTEMIS Madam, this way the prisoners are to pass.   90
Here you may see Leonidas.

PALMYRA Then here I'll stay, and follow him to death.

(*Enter* MELANTHA *hastily*)

MELANTHA O, here's her Highness! Now is my time to introduce myself, and to make my court to her, in my new French phrases. Stay, let me read my catalogue: 'suite, 95 figure, chagrin, naïveté;' and 'let me die' for the parenthesis of all.*

PALAMEDE (aside) Do, persecute her; and I'll persecute thee as fast in thy own dialect.

MELANTHA Madam, the princess! Let me die, but this is a 100 most horrid spectacle, to see a person who makes so grand a figure in the court, without the suite of a princess, and entertaining your chagrin all alone. <aside> Naïveté should have been there, but the disobedient word would not come in. 105

PALMYRA What is she, Artemis?

ARTEMIS An impertinent lady, madam; very ambitious of being known to your Highness.

PALAMEDE (to MELANTHA) Let me die, madam, if I have not waited you here these two long hours without so 110 much as the suite of a single servant to attend me; entertaining myself with my own chagrin, till I had the honour to see your ladyship, who are a person that makes so considerable a figure in the court.

MELANTHA Truce with your douceurs,* good servant; you 115 see I am addressing to the princess. Pray do not embarrass me – embarrass me! What a delicious French word do you make me lose upon you too! (to the PRINCESS) Your Highness, madam, will please to pardon the bévue which I made, in not sooner finding you out to be a princess: but 120 let me die if this éclaircissement which is made this day of your quality does not ravish me; and give me leave to tell you –

PALAMEDE But first give me leave to tell you, madam, that I have so great a tendre for your person, and such a 125 penchant to do you service, that –

MELANTHA What, must I still be troubled with your sottises? (There's another word lost, that I meant for the princess, with a mischief to you.) But your Highness, madam – 130

PALAMEDE But your ladyship, madam –

(*Enter* LEONIDAS *guarded, and led over the stage*)

MELANTHA Out upon him, how he looks, madam! Now
he's found no prince, he is the strangest *figure* of a man;
how could I make that *coup d'étourdi* to think him one?

PALMYRA Away, impertinent – My dear Leonidas!   135

LEONIDAS My dear Palmyra!

PALMYRA Death shall never part us;
My destiny is yours.

[*He is led off; she follows*]

MELANTHA Impertinent! Oh I am the most unfortunate
person this day breathing: that the princess should thus   140
rompre en visière,* without occasion. Let me die but I'll
follow her to death, till I make my peace.

PALAMEDE (*holding her*) And let me die, but I'll follow you
to the infernals till you pity me.

MELANTHA (*turning towards him angrily*) Aye, 'tis long   145
of* you that this *malheur* is fall'n upon me. Your
impertinence has put me out of the good graces of the
princess, and all that, which has ruined me and all that,
and therefore let me die but I'll be revenged, and all that.

PALAMEDE *Façon, façon*,* you must and shall love me,   150
and all that. For my old man is coming up, and all that;
and I am *désespéré au dernier*,* and will not be disinherited, and all that.

MELANTHA How durst you interrupt me so *mal à propos*,*
when you knew I was addressing to the princess?   155

PALAMEDE But why would you address yourself so much *à
contretemps** then?

MELANTHA Ah, *mal peste*!*

PALAMEDE Ah, *j'enrage*!*

PHILOTIS *Radoucissez-vous, de grâce, madame; vous êtes* 160
bien en colère pour peu de chose. Vous n'entendez pas la
raillerie gallante.*

MELANTHA (*cries*) *A d'autres, à d'autres.* He mocks himself
of me,* he abuses me. Ah me, unfortunate!

PHILOTIS You mistake him, madam, he does but accom-   165

modate his phrase to your refined language. *Ah, qu'il est
un cavalier accompli!** (*<aside> to him*) Pursue your
point, sir –

PALAMEDE (*singing*)
Ah, qu'il fait beau dans ces bocages;
*Ah, que le ciel donne un beau jour!**   170
There I was with you, with a *menuet.**

MELANTHA (*laughs*) Let me die now, but this singing is
fine, and extremely French in him. (*crying*) But then, that
he should use my own words, as it were in contempt of
me, I cannot bear it.   175

   PALAMEDE (*singing*)
Ces beaux séjours, ces doux ramages –

MELANTHA (*singing after him*)
Ces beaux séjours, ces doux ramages,
*Ces beaux séjours, nous invitent a l'amour!**
(*laughing*) Let me die but he sings *en cavalier,** and so
humours* the cadence.   180

PALAMEDE (*singing again*)
Vois, ma Climène,
Vois sous ce chêne,
*S'entrebaiser ces oiseaux amoureux!**
Let me die now, but that was fine. Ah, now, for three or
four brisk Frenchmen to be put into masquing habits, and 185
to sing it on a theatre, how witty it would be! And then to
dance helter-skelter to a *chanson à boire:** 'toute la terre,
toute la terre est à moi!'* What's matter though it were
made and sung two or three years ago in *cabarets,** how
it would attract the admiration, especially of every one 190
that's an *éveillé!**

MELANTHA Well, I begin to have a *tendre* for you; but yet,
upon condition, that – when we are married, you –
(PALAMEDE *sings, while she speaks*)

PHILOTIS You must drown her voice. If she makes her
French conditions, you are a slave for ever.   195

MELANTHA   First, will you engage that –

PALAMEDE (*louder*) Fa, la, la, la, etc.

MELANTHA Will you hear the conditions?

PALAMEDE No, I will hear no conditions! I am resolved to
win you *en français*: to be very airy, with abundance of 200
noise, and no sense. Fa, la, la, la, etc.

MELANTHA Hold, hold: I am vanquished with your *gaieté
d'esprit.** I am yours, and will be yours, *sans nulle
reserve, ni condition.** And let me die, if I do not think
myself the happiest nymph in Sicily. My dear French dear, 205
stay but a *minute*, till I *raccommode** myself with the
princess; and then I am yours, *jusqu' à la mort.** <to
PHILOTIS> *Allons donc –* *

> [*Exeunt* MELANTHA, PHILOTIS]

PALAMEDE (*solus,** fanning himself with his hat*) I never
thought before that wooing was so laborious an exercise; 210
if she were worth a million, I have deserved her. And
now, methinks too, with taking all this pains for her, I
begin to like her. 'Tis so; I have known many who never
cared for hare nor partridge, but those they caught
themselves would eat heartily. The pains, and the story a 215
man tells of the taking of 'em, makes the meat go down
more pleasantly. Besides, last night I had a sweet dream of
her, and, gad, she I have once dreamed of, I am stark mad
till I enjoy her, let her be never so ugly.

> (*Enter* DORALICE)

DORALICE Who's that you are so mad to enjoy, Palamede? 220

PALAMEDE You may easily imagine that, sweet Doralice.

DORALICE More easily than you think I can. I met just
now with a certain man, who came to you with letters
from a certain old gentleman, yclept* your father;
whereby I am given to understand that tomorrow you are 225
to take an oath in the church to be grave henceforward, to
go ill-dressed and slovenly, to get heirs for your estate,
and to dandle 'em for your diversion; and, in short, that
love and courtship are to be no more.

PALAMEDE Now have I so much shame to be thus 230
apprehended in the manner, that I can neither speak nor
look upon you; I have abundance of grace in me, that I
find. But if you have any spark of true friendship in you,

retire a little with me to the next room that has a couch or
bed in't, and bestow your charity upon a poor dying man. 235
A little comfort from a mistress, before a man is going to
give himself in marriage, is as good as a lusty dose of
strong water* to a dying malefactor; it takes away the
sense of hell and hanging from him.

DORALICE No, good Palamede, I must not be so injurious 240
to your bride. 'Tis ill drawing from the bank today, when
all your ready money is payable tomorrow.

PALAMEDE A wife is only to have the ripe fruit, that falls of
itself; but a wise man will always preserve a shaking for a
mistress. 245

DORALICE But a wife for the first quarter is a mistress.

PALAMEDE But when the second comes –

DORALICE When it does come, you are so given to variety,
that you would make a wife of me in another quarter.

PALAMEDE No, never, except I were married to you. 250
Married people can never oblige one another, for all they
do is duty, and consequently there can be no thanks. But
love is more frank and generous than he is honest; he's a
liberal giver, but a cursed pay-master.

DORALICE I declare I will have no gallant; but, if I would, 255
he should never be a married man. A married man is but a
mistress's half-servant, as a clergyman is but the king's
half-subject. For a man to come to me that smells o' th'
wife! 'S life,* I would as soon wear her old gown after
her, as her husband. 260

PALAMEDE Yet 'tis a kind of fashion to wear a princess's
cast shoes; you see the country ladies buy 'em to be fine in
them.

DORALICE Yes, a princess's shoes may be worn after her,
because they keep their fashion, by being so very little 265
used; but generally a married man is the creature of the
world the most out of fashion. His behaviour is dumpish,
his discourse his wife and family, his habit so much
neglected, it looks as if that were married too. His hat is
married, his peruke is married, his breeches are married, 270

and if we could look within his breeches, we should find
him married there too.

PALAMEDE Am I then to be discarded forever? Pray, do but
mark how terrible that word sounds: forever! It has a very
damned sound, Doralice.   275

DORALICE Aye, forever! It sounds as hellishly to me, as it
can do to you, but there's no help for't.

PALAMEDE Yet if we had but once enjoyed one another;
but then once only, is worse than not at all: it leaves a
man with such a lingering after it.   280

DORALICE For ought I know 'tis better that we have not.
We might upon trial have liked each other less, as many a
man and woman that have loved as desperately as we,
and yet when they came to possession, have sighed and
cried to themselves, 'Is this all?'   285

PALAMEDE That is only if the servant were not found a
man of this world; but if upon trial we had not liked each
other, we had certainly left loving; and faith, that's the
greater happiness of the two.

DORALICE 'Tis better as 'tis; we have drawn off* already   290
as much of our love as would run clear. After possessing,
the rest is but jealousies, and disquiets, and quarrelling,
and piecing.*

PALAMEDE Nay, after one great quarrel, there's never any
sound piecing; the love is apt to break in the same place   295
again.

DORALICE I declare I would never renew a love; that's like
him who trims an old coach for ten years together. He
might buy a new one better cheap.*

PALAMEDE Well, madam, I am convinced, that 'tis best for 300
us not to have enjoyed; but gad, the strongest reason is,
because I can't help it.

DORALICE The only way to keep us new to one another, is
never to enjoy, as they keep grapes by hanging 'em upon a
line; they must touch nothing if you would preserve 'em   305
fresh.

PALAMEDE But then they wither, and grow dry in the very
keeping. However, I shall have a warmth for you, and an

eagerness, every time I see you; and if I chance to outlive
Melantha –   310

DORALICE And if I chance to outlive Rhodophil –

PALAMEDE Well, I'll cherish my body as much as I can
upon that hope. 'Tis true, I would not directly murder the
wife of my bosom; but to kill her civilly, by the way of
kindness, I'll put as fair as another man. I'll begin   315
tomorrow night, and be very wrathful with her, that's
resolved on.

DORALICE Well, Palamede, here's my hand. I'll venture to
be your second wife, for all your threatenings.

PALAMEDE In the meantime I'll watch you hourly, as I   320
would the ripeness of a melon, and I hope you'll give me
leave now and then to look on you, and to see if you are
not ready to be cut yet.

DORALICE No, no, that must not be, Palamede, for fear the
gardener should come and catch you taking up the glass.* 325

(*Enter* RHODOPHIL)

RHODOPHIL (*aside*) Billing* so sweetly! Now I am confirmed in my suspicions. I must put an end to this, ere it
go further. (*to* DORALICE) Cry you mercy, spouse; I fear I
have interrupted your recreations.

DORALICE What recreations?   330

RHODOPHIL Nay, no excuses, good spouse. I saw fair
hand conveyed to lip, and pressed, as though you had
been squeezing soft wax together for an indenture.*
Palamede, you and I must clear this reckoning; why
would you have seduced my wife?   335

PALAMEDE Why would you have debauched my mistress?

RHODOPHIL What do you think of that civil couple, that
played at a game called hide-and-seek, last evening, in the
grotto?

PALAMEDE What do you think of that innocent pair who 340
made it their pretence to seek for others, but came,
indeed, to hide themselves there?

RHODOPHIL All things considered, I begin vehemently to
suspect that the young gentleman I found in your

company last night, was a certain youth of my acquaint-   345
ance.

PALAMEDE And I have an odd imagination that you could
never have suspected my small gallant, if your little
villainous Frenchman had not been a false brother.

RHODOPHIL Farther arguments are needless. Draw off. I   350
shall speak to you now by the way of bilbo.*

(*Claps his hand to his sword*)

PALAMEDE And I shall answer you by the way of
Dangerfield.*

(*Claps his hand on his*)

DORALICE Hold, hold; are not you two a couple of mad
fighting fools, to cut one another's throats for nothing?   355

PALAMEDE How for nothing? He courts the woman I must
marry.

RHODOPHIL And he courts you whom I have married.

DORALICE But you can neither of you be jealous of what
you love not.   360

RHODOPHIL Faith, I am jealous, and that makes me partly
suspect that I love you better than I thought.

DORALICE Pish! A mere jealousy of honour.

RHODOPHIL Gad, I am afraid there's something else in't.
For Palamede has wit, and if he loves you, there's   365
something more in ye than I have found: some rich mine,
for ought I know, that I have not yet discovered.

PALAMEDE 'S life, what's this? Here's an argument for me
to love Melantha; for he has loved her, and he has wit
too, and, for ought I know, there may be a mine: but, if   370
there be, I am resolved I'll dig for't.

DORALICE (*to* RHODOPHIL) Then I have found my
account in raising your jealousy. O! 'tis the most delicate
sharp sauce to a cloyed stomach; it will give you a new
edge, Rhodophil.   375

RHODOPHIL And a new point too, Doralice, if I could be
sure thou art honest.

DORALICE If you are wise, believe me for your own sake.

Love and religion have but one thing to trust to; that's a
good sound faith. Consider, if I have played false, you can 380
never find it out by any experiment you can make upon
me.

RHODOPHIL No? Why, suppose I had a delicate screwed
gun.* If I left her clean, and found her foul, I should
discover to my cost, she had been shot in.   385

DORALICE But if you left her clean, and found her only
rusty, you would discover, to your shame, she was only so
for want of shooting.

PALAMEDE Rhodophil, you know me too well to imagine I
speak for fear; and therefore in consideration of our past 390
friendship, I will tell you, and bind it by all things holy,
that Doralice is innocent.

RHODOPHIL Friend, I will believe you, and vow the same
for your Melantha; but the devil on't is, how we shall
keep 'em so?   395

PALAMEDE What dost think of a blessed community
betwixt us four, for the solace of the women, and relief of
the men? Methinks it would be a pleasant kind of life:
wife and husband for the standing dish,* and mistress and
gallant for the desert.   400

RHODOPHIL But suppose the wife and the mistress should
both long for the standing dish, how should they be
satisfied together?

PALAMEDE In such a case they must draw lots: and yet that
would not do neither; for they would both be wishing for 405
the longest cut.*

RHODOPHIL Then I think, Palamede, we had as good
make a firm league, not to invade each other's propriety.

PALAMEDE Content, say I. From henceforth let all acts of
hostility cease betwixt us; and that in the usual form of 410
treaties, as well by sea as by land, and in all fresh waters.

DORALICE I will add but one proviso: that whoever breaks
the league, either by war abroad, or by neglect at home,
both the women shall revenge themselves, by the help of
the other party.   415

RHODOPHIL That's but reasonable. Come away, Doralice,
  I have a great temptation to be sealing articles in private.
PALAMEDE Hast thou so? (*claps him on the shoulder*)
  'Fall on, Macduff,
  And cursed be he that first cries, "Hold, enough."'*   420

(*Enter* POLYDAMAS, PALMYRA, ARTEMIS, ARGALEON:
  after them EUBULUS, *and* HERMOGENES, *guarded*)

PALMYRA Sir, on my knees I beg you.
POLYDAMAS Away, I'll hear no more.
PALMYRA For my dead mother's sake. You say you
  loved her,
  And tell me I resemble her. Thus she
  Had begged.
POLYDAMAS   – And thus had I denied her.   425
PALMYRA You must be merciful.
ARGALEON   – You must be constant.
POLYDAMAS Go, bear 'em to the torture. You have
  boasted
  You have a king to head you: I would know
  To whom I must resign.
EUBULUS   This is our recompense
  For serving thy dead queen.
HERMOGENES   And education   430
Of thy daughter.
ARGALEON You are too modest, in not naming all
  His obligations to you: why did you
  Omit his son, the prince Leonidas?
POLYDAMAS That imposture   435
  I had forgot; their tortures shall be doubled.
HERMOGENES You please me, I shall die the sooner.
EUBULUS No; could I live an age, and still be racked,
  I still would keep the secret.

  (*As they are going off, enter* LEONIDAS, *guarded*)

LEONIDAS Oh whither do you hurry innocence?   440
  If you have any justice, spare their lives;
  Or if I cannot make you just, at least

I'll teach you to more purpose to be cruel.

PALMYRA Alas, what does he seek?

LEONIDAS Make me the object of your hate and
    vengeance!   445
    Are these decrepid bodies worn to ruin,
    Just ready of themselves, to fall asunder,
    And to let drop the soul,
    Are these fit subjects for a rack and tortures?
    Where would you fasten any hold upon 'em?   450
    Place pains on me: united fix 'em here,
    I have both youth, and strength, and soul to bear 'em:
    And if they merit death, then I much more;
    Since 'tis for me they suffer.

HERMOGENES   Heav'n forbid
    We should redeem our pains, or worthless lives,   455
    By our exposing yours.

EUBULUS Away with us. Farewell, sir.
    I only suffer in my fears for you.

ARGALEON (aside) So much concerned for him? Then
    my
    Suspicion's true. (whispers the KING)   460

PALMYRA Hear yet my last request for poor Leonidas,
    Or take my life with his.

ARGALEON (to the KING) Rest satisfied: Leonidas is he.

POLYDAMAS I am amazed: what must be done?

ARGALEON Command his execution instantly;   465
    Give him not leisure to discover it;
    He may corrupt the soldiers.

POLYDAMAS Hence with that traitor; bear him to his
    death:
    Haste there, and see my will performed.

LEONIDAS Nay, then I'll die like him the gods have
    made me.   470
    Hold, gentlemen; I am –

        (ARGALEON stops his mouth)

ARGALEON Thou art a traitor; 'tis not fit to hear thee.

LEONIDAS (getting loose a little) I say I am the –

ARGALEON (*again stopping his mouth*) So; gag him, and
   lead him off.

(LEONIDAS, HERMOGENES, EUBULUS, *led off.*
    POLYDAMAS *and* ARGALEON *follow*)

PALMYRA Duty and love by turns possess my soul,   475
   And struggle for a fatal victory.
   I will discover he's the king. Ah, no.
   That will perhaps save him,
   But then I am guilty of a father's ruin.
   What shall I do, or not do? Either way   480
   I must destroy a parent, or a lover.
   Break heart; for that's the least of ills to me,
   And death the only cure. (*swoons*)
ARTEMIS Help, help the princess.
RHODOPHIL   Bear her gently hence,
   Where she may have more succour.   485

(*She is borne off;* ARTEMIS *follows her. Shouts within,
     and clashing of swords*)

PALAMEDE What noise is that?

(*Enter* AMALTHEA *running*)

AMALTHEA Oh, gentlemen, if you have loyalty
   Or courage, show it now. Leonidas
   Broke on the sudden from his guards, and snatching
   A sword from one, his back against the scaffold,   490
   Bravely defends himself; and owns aloud
   He is our long-lost king, found for this moment;
   But, if your valours help not, lost for ever.
   Two of his guards, moved by the sense of virtue,
   Are turned for him, and there they stand at bay   495
   Against an host of foes.
RHODOPHIL   Madam, no more;
   We lose time. My command, or my example,
   May move the soldiers to the better cause.
   (*to* PALAMEDE) You'll second me?
PALAMEDE Or die with you. No subject e'er can meet   500

A nobler fate, than at his sovereign's feet.

[*Exeunt*]

(*Clashing of swords within, and shouts. Enter*
PALAMEDE, EUBULUS, HERMOGENES, *and their party,*
victorious; POLYDAMAS *and* ARGALEON, *disarmed*)

LEONIDAS That I survive the dangers of this day,
  Next to the gods, brave friends, be yours the honour.
  And let heav'n witness for me, that my joy
  Is not more great for this my right restored,   505
  Than 'tis, that I have power to recompense
  Your loyalty and valour. Let mean princes
  Of abject souls, fear to reward great actions.
  I mean to show
  That whatsoe'er subjects like you dare merit,   510
  A king like me dares give —
RHODOPHIL You make us blush, we have deserved so
    little.
PALAMEDE And yet instruct us how to merit more.
LEONIDAS And as I would be just in my rewards,
  So should I in my punishments. These two,   515
  This the usurper of my crown, the other
  Of my Palmyra's love, deserve that death
  Which both designed for me.
PALAMEDE   And we expect it.
ARGALEON I have too long been happy to live wretched.
POLYDAMAS And I too long have governed, to desire   520
  A life without an empire.
LEONIDAS You are Palmyra's father; and as such,
  Though not a king, shall have obedience paid
  From him who is one. Father, in that name,
  All injury's forgot, and duty owned. (*embraces him*)   525
POLYDAMAS O, had I known you could have been this
    king,
  Thus god-like, great and good, I should have wished
  T' have been dethroned before. 'Tis now I live,
  And more than reign; now all my joys flow pure,
  Unmixed with cares, and undisturbed by conscience.   530

(*Enter* PALMYRA, AMALTHEA, ARTEMIS, DORALICE, *and*
MELANTHA)

LEONIDAS See, my Palmyra comes! The frighted blood
  Scarce yet recalled to her pale cheeks,
  Like the first streaks of light broke loose from
    darkness,
  And dawning into blushes. (*to* POLYDAMAS) Sir, you
    said,
  Your joys were full. Oh, would you make mine so!   535
  I am but half-restored without this blessing.
POLYDAMAS (*gives her hand to* LEONIDAS)
  The gods, and my Palmyra, make you happy,
  As you make me.
PALMYRA   Now all my prayers are heard:
  I may be dutiful, and yet may love.
  Virtue, and patience, have at length unravelled   540
  The knots which fortune tied.
MELANTHA Let me die, but I'll congratulate his majesty.
  How admirably well his royalty becomes him! Becomes!
  That is *lui sied*, but our damned language expresses 545
  nothing.
PALAMEDE How? Does it become him already? 'Twas but
  just now you said he was such a *figure* of a man.
MELANTHA True, my dear, when he was a private man he
  was a *figure*; but since he is a king, methinks he has
  assumed another *figure*. He looks so *grand*, and so 550
  auguste.

(*Going to the* KING)

PALAMEDE Stay, stay; I'll present you when it is more
  convenient. <*aside*> I find I must get her a place at court;
  and when she is once there, she can be no longer
  ridiculous; for she is young enough, and pretty enough, 555
  and fool enough, and French enough, to bring up a
  fashion there to be affected.
LEONIDAS (*to* RHODOPHIL) Did she then lead you to
  this brave attempt?
  (*to* AMALTHEA) To you, fair Amalthea, what I am,

And what all these, from me, we jointly owe: 560
First, therefore, to your great desert, we give
Your brother's life; but keep him under guard,
Till our new power be settled. What more grace
He may receive, shall from his future carriage*
Be given, as he deserves.   565

ARGALEON I neither now desire, nor will deserve it;
My loss is such as cannot be repaired,
And to the wretched, life can be no mercy.

LEONIDAS Then be a prisoner always: thy ill fate,
And pride will have it so: but since, in this, I cannot,   570
Instruct me, generous Amalthea, how
A king may serve you.

AMALTHEA   I have all I hope,
And all I now must wish; I see you happy.
Those hours I have to live, which heav'n in pity
Will make but few, I vow to spend with vestals:*   575
The greatest part, in pray'rs for you; the rest
In mourning my unworthiness.
Press me not farther to explain myself;
'Twill not become me, and may cause <you>* trouble.

LEONIDAS (aside) Too well I understand her secret grief,   580
But dare not seem to know it. – (to PALMYRA) Come
    my fairest,
Beyond my crown I have one joy in store:
To give that crown to her whom I adore.

                                           [Exeunt omnes]

Epilogue

<Spoken by RHODOPHIL>

Thus have my spouse and I informed the nation,
And led you all the way to reformation:
Not with dull morals, gravely writ, like those,
Which men of easy phlegm* with care compose;
Your poets* of stiff* words, and limber* sense,   5
Born on the confines of indifference;
But by examples drawn, I dare to say,
From most of you, who hear and see the play.
There are more Rhodophils in this theatre,
More Palamedes, and some few wives, I fear.   10
But yet too far our poet would not run,
Though 'twas well offered, there was nothing done.
He would not quite the women's frailty bare,
But stripped 'em to the waist, and left 'em there.
And the men's faults are less severely shown,   15
For he considers that himself is one.
Some stabbing wits, to bloody satire bent,
Would treat both sexes with less compliment:
Would lay the scene at home, of husbands tell
For wenches taking up their wives i' th' Mall,   20
And a brisk bout which each of them did want,
Made by mistake of mistress and gallant.
Our modest author thought it was enough
To cut you off a sample of the stuff:
He spared my shame, which you, I'm sure, would not,   25
For you were all for driving on the plot:
You sighed when I came in to break the sport,
And set your teeth when each design fell short.
To wives and servants all good wishes lend,
But the poor cuckold seldom finds a friend.   30
Since therefore court and town will take no pity,
I humbly cast myself upon the city.*

THE LIBERTINE

A Tragedy

By

THOMAS SHADWELL

To the Most Illustrious Prince, William, Duke,
Marquis and Earl of Newcastle,* etc.

May it please Your Grace,

The favours have been so many and so great which Your
Grace's unwearied bounty has conferred upon me, that I
cannot omit this opportunity of telling the world how much
I have been obliged, and by whom. My gratitude will not
suffer me to smother the favours in silence; nor the pride   5
they have raised me to, let me conceal the name of so
excellent a patron. The honour of being favoured by the
great Newcastle is equal with any real merit; I am sure,
infinitely above mine. Yet the encouragement I receive from
Your Grace is the certain way to make the world believe I   10
have some desert, or to create in me the most favourable
thoughts of myself. My name may thus, when otherwise it
would perish, live in after ages under the protection of Your
Grace's, which is famous abroad and will be eternized in
this nation: for your wit beyond all poets; judgement and   15
prudence above all statesmen; courage and conduct above
all generals; constancy and loyalty beyond all subjects;
virtue and temperance above all philosophers; for skill in
weapons and horsemanship, and all other arts befitting your
quality, excelling all noblemen; and, lastly, for those   20
eminent services in defence of your king and country, with
an interest and power much exceeding all, and with loyalty
equalling any nobleman. And, indeed, the first was so great
that it might justly have made the greatest prince afraid of
it, had it not been so strongly secured by the latter.   25

All these heroic qualities I admired and worshipped at a
distance, before I had the honour to wait upon Your Grace
at your house. For so vast was your bounty to me as to find
me out in my obscurity, and oblige me several years before
you saw me at Welbeck;* where (when I arrived) I found a   30
respect so extremely above the meanness of my condition,
that I still received it with blushes; having had nothing to

recommend me but the birth and education, without the fortune of a gentleman, besides some writings of mine which Your Grace was pleased to like. Then was soon 35 added to my former worship and admiration, infinite love and infinite gratitude; and a pride of being favoured by one in whom I observed a majesty equal with greatest princes, yet affability exceeding ordinary gentlemen. A greatness that none e'er approached without awe, or parted from without 40 satisfaction.

Then, by the great honour I had to be daily admitted into Your Grace's public and private conversation, I observed that admirable experience and judgement surmounting all the old; and that vigorousness of wit, and smartness of 45 expression, exceeding all the young, I ever knew: and not only in sharp and apt replies, the most excellent way of pursuing a discourse; but (which is much more difficult) by giving easy and unforced occasions; the most admirable way of beginning one; and all this adapted to men of all 50 circumstances and conditions; Your Grace being able to discourse with every man in his own way, which, as it shows you to be a most accurate observer of all men's tempers, so it shows your excellency in all their arts. But when I had the favour daily to be admitted to Your Grace's 55 more retired conversation, when I alone enjoyed the honour, I must declare I never spent my hours with that pleasure or improvement. Nor shall I ever enough acknowledge that, and the rest of the honours done me by Your Grace, as much above my condition as my merit. 60

And now, my Lord, after all this, imagine not I intend this small present of a play (though favoured here by those I might wish it should be) as any return; for all the services of my life cannot make a sufficient one. I only lay hold on this occasion to publish to the world your great favours, and the 65 grateful acknowledgements of,

My most noble Lord,
Your Grace's most obliged, humble and obedient servant,

Thomas Shadwell

PREFACE

The story from which I took the hint of this play is famous all over Spain, Italy and France. It was first put into a Spanish play,* as I have been told, the Spaniards having a tradition (which they believe) of such a vicious Spaniard as is represented in this play. From them, the Italian comedians* took it, and from them the French took it, and four several* French plays* were made upon the story.

The character of the Libertine and, consequently, those of his friends, are borrowed;* but all the plot, till the latter end of the fourth act, is new. And all the rest is very much varied from anything which has been done upon the subject.

I hope the readers will excuse the irregularities of the play, when they consider that the extravagance of the subject forced me to it. And I had rather try new ways to please, than to write on in the same road, as too many do. I hope that the severest reader will not be offended at the representation of those vices on which they will see a dreadful punishment inflicted. And I have been told by a worthy gentleman that, many years ago, when first a play was made upon the story in Italy, he has seen it acted there by the name of *Atheisto Fulminato* in churches on Sundays, as a part of devotion. And some not of the least judgement and piety here have thought it rather an useful moral, than an encouragement to vice.

I have no reason to complain of the success of this play, since it pleased those whom, of all the world, I would please most. Nor was the town unkind to it; for which reason I must applaud my good fortune, to have pleased with so little pains: there being no act which cost me above five days' writing; and the last two (the playhouse having great occasion for a play) were both written in four days, as several can testify. And this I dare declare, notwithstanding the foul, coarse and ill-mannered censure passed upon them who write plays in three, four, or five weeks' time, by a rough, hobbling rhymer in his postscript to another man's play, which he spoiled and called *Love and Revenge*:* I having before publicly owned the writing two plays in so short a time. He ought not to have measured any man's abilities who writes for the stage with his own; for some may write that in three weeks which he cannot in three years. But he is angry that any man should write sense so easily, when he finds it so laborious a thing to write even fustian* that he is believed to have been three years drudging upon *The Conquest of China*.* But he ought not to be called a poet who cannot write ten times a better in three weeks.

I cannot here pass by his saucy epistle to this *Conquest*, which (instead of expressions of just respect, due to the birth and merit of his patron) is stuffed with railing against others. And first he begins with the 'Vanity of [his] Tribe'.* What 'tribe' that really is, is not hard to guess; but all the poets will bear me witness it is not theirs, who are sufficiently satisfied that he is no more a poet, than 'Servant to His Majesty',* as he presumes to write himself; which I wonder he will do, since protections are taken off.* I know not what place he is sworn into 'in extraordinary', but I am sure there is no such thing as 'Poet in Extraordinary'.*

But I wonder, after all his railing, he will call these poets his brethren. If they were, methinks he might have more natural affection than to abuse his brethren; but he might have spared that title, for we can find no manner of relation betwixt him and them. For they are all gentlemen that will not own him, or keep him company; and that, perhaps, is the cause which makes him so angry with them to tax them, in his ill-mannered epistle, with impudence, which he (having a particular affection for his own vice) calls by the name of frailty.* Impudence, indeed, is a very pretty frailty.

But, whatever the poets are guilty of, I wish he had as much of poetry in him as he has of that frailty, for the good of the Duke's Theatre. They might then have hopes of gaining as much by his good sense, as they have lost by his fustian.

Thus much I thought fit to say in vindication of the poets,

though I think he has not authority enough with men of sense to fix any calumny upon the tribe, as he calls it. For which reason I shall never trouble myself to take notice of him hereafter, since all men of wit will think that he can do the poets no greater injury than pretending to be one. Nor had I said so much in answer to his coarse railing, but to reprehend his arrogance and lead him to a little better knowledge of himself; nor does his base language in his postscript deserve a better return.

Prologue

Our author sent me hither for a scout,
To spy what bloody critics were come out:
Those picaroons* in wit wh' infest this road,
And snap both friend and foe that come abroad.
This savage party crueller appears   5
Than, in the Channel, Ostend privateers.*
You in this road, or sink or* plunder all;
Remorseless as a storm, on us you fall.
But as a merchant, when by storms distressed,
Flings out his bulky goods to save the rest,   10
Hoping a calm may come, he keeps the best.
In this black tempest which o'er us impends,
Near rocks and quicksands, and no ports of friends,
Our poet gives this over to your rage,
The most irregular play upon the stage,   15
As wild and as extravagant as th' age.
Now, angry men, to all your spleens give vent;
When all your fury has on this been spent,
Elsewhere you with much worse shall be content.
The poet has no hopes you'll be appeased,   20
Who come on purpose but to be displeased.
Such corrupt judges should excepted be,
Who can condemn before they hear or see.
Ne'er were such bloody critics yet in fashion:
You damn by absolute predestination.   25
But why so many to run one man down?
It were a mighty triumph when y' have done.
Our scarcity of plays you should not blame,
When by foul poaching you destroy the game.
Let him but have fair play, and he may then   30
Write himself into favour once again.
If after this your anger you'll reveal,
To Caesar* he must make his just appeal:
There, mercy and judgement equally do meet,
To pardon faults, and to encourage wit.   35

DRAMATIS PERSONAE

The play was first performed June 1675 at the Dorset Garden Theatre by the Duke's Company. No cast is recorded.

DON JOHN the Libertine; a rash, fearless man, guilty of all vice
DON ANTONIO }
DON LOPEZ   } his two friends
DON OCTAVIO <in love with> Maria
DON FRANCISCO father to Clara and Flavia
JACOMO Don John's man

LEONORA Don John's mistress; abused by him, yet follows him for love
CLARA }
FLAVIA } daughters to Don Francisco
MARIA <in love with Don Octavio> abused by Don John, and follow<s> him for revenge
<FLORA her maid>

SIX WOMEN all wives to Don John
BROTHER TO MARIA
HERMIT
TWO GENTLEMEN intended for husbands to Clara and Flavia

<COUNTRY FELLOWS, DEVILS, NUNS, SHIP'S CAPTAIN, SHIP'S MASTER, SAILORS> GHOSTS, SHEPHERDS and SHEPHERDESSES, OLD WOMAN, OFFICERS and SOLDIERS, SINGERS, SERVANTS, ATTENDANTS

Act I, Scene I

<A street in Seville>

(*Enter* DON JOHN, DON LOPEZ, DON ANTONIO,
JACOMO, *Don John's valet*)

DON JOHN Thus far without a bound we have enjoyed
  Our prosperous pleasures, which dull fools call sins:
  Laughed at old feeble judges and weak laws,
  And at the fond, fantastic thing called conscience,
  Which serves for nothing but to make men cowards: 5
  An idle fear of future misery;
  And yet is worse than all that we can fear.
DON LOPEZ Conscience, made up of dark and horrid
    thoughts,
  Raised from the fumes of a distempered spleen.
DON ANTONIO A senseless fear, would make us
    contradict   10
  The only certain guide, infallible Nature;
  And at the call of melancholy fools,
  (Who style all actions which they like not, sins)
  To silence all our natural appetites.
DON JOHN Yet those conscientious fools, that would
    persuade us   15
  To I know not what, which they call piety,
  Have in reserve private delicious sins,
  Great as the happy libertine enjoys,
  With which, in corners, wantonly they roll.
DON LOPEZ Don John, thou art our oracle; thou hast   20
  Dispelled the fumes which once clouded our brains.
DON ANTONIO By thee, we have got loose from
    education,
  And the dull slavery of pupillage,
  Recovered all the liberty of nature;
  Our own strong reason now can go alone,   25
  Without the feeble props of splenetic fools,
  Who contradict our common mother, Nature.

DON JOHN Nature gave us our senses, which we please;
Nor does our reason war against our sense.
By nature's order, sense should guide our reason,   30
Since to the mind all objects sense conveys.
But fools for shadows lose substantial pleasures,
For idle tales abandon true delight,
And solid joys of day, for empty dreams at night.
Away, thou foolish thing, thou colic of the mind,   35
Thou worm by ill-digesting stomachs bred:
In spite of thee, we'll surfeit in delights,
And never think aught can be ill that's pleasant.
JACOMO A most excellent sermon, and no doubt, gentle-
men, you have edified much by it.   40
DON JOHN Away, thou formal, phlegmatic coxcomb!
Thou
Hast neither courage nor yet wit enough
To sin thus. Thou art my dull conscientious pimp.
And when I am wanton with my whore within,
Thou, with thy beads and prayer book, keep'st the
door.   45
JACOMO Sir, I find your worship is no more afraid to be
damned, than other fashionable gentlemen of the age: but,
methinks, halters and axes should terrify you. With
reverence to your worships, I've seen civiller men hanged;
and men of as pretty parts too. There's scarce a city in   50
Spain but is too hot for you: you have committed such
outrages wheresoe'er you come.
DON LOPEZ Come, for diversion, pray let's hear your fool
preach a little.
JACOMO For my part, I cannot but be troubled that I shall   55
lose my honour by you, sir; for people will be apt to say,
like master, like man.
DON JOHN Your honour, rascal? A sow-gelder may better
pretend to it.
JACOMO But I have another scruple, sir.   60
DON JOHN What's that?
JACOMO I fear I shall be hanged in your company.

DON JOHN That's an honour you will ne'er have courage
to deserve.

JACOMO It is an honour I am not ambitious of.   65

DON LOPEZ Why does the fool talk of hanging? We scorn
all laws.

JACOMO It seems so, or you would not have cut your elder
brother's throat, Don Lopez.

DON LOPEZ Why, you coxcomb, he kept a good estate   70
from me and I could not whore and revel sufficiently
without it.

DON ANTONIO Look you, Jacomo, had he not reason?

JACOMO Yes, Antonio, so had you, to get both your sisters
with child; 'twas very civil, I take it.   75

DON ANTONIO Yes, you fool, they were lusty, young,
handsome wenches, and pleased my appetite. Besides, I
saved the honour of the family by it: for if I had not,
somebody else would.

JACOMO O horrid villainy!   80
But you are both saints to my hopeful master;
I'll turn him loose to Beelzebub himself,
He shall outdo him at his own weapons.

DON JOHN I, you rascal?

JACOMO Oh no, sir, you are as innocent. To cause your   85
good old father to be killed was nothing.

DON JOHN It was something, and a good thing too, sirrah!
His whole design was to debar me of my pleasures: he
kept his purse from me, and could not be content with
that, but still would preach his senseless morals to me, his   90
old dull foolish stuff against my pleasure. I caused him to
be sent I know not whither. But he believed he was to go
to heaven; I care not where he is, since I am rid of him.

JACOMO Cutting his throat was a very good return for his
begetting of you.   95

DON JOHN That was before he was aware on't; 'twas for
his own sake, he ne'er thought of me in the business.

JACOMO Heaven bless us!

DON JOHN You dog, I shall beat out your brains, if you
dare be so impudent as to pray in my company.   100

JACOMO Good sir, I have done, I have done.

DON LOPEZ Prithee, let the insipid fool go on.

DON ANTONIO Let's hear the coxcomb number up your
crimes,
The patterns we intend to imitate.

JACOMO Sir, let me lay your horrid crimes before you: 105
The unhappy minute may perhaps arrive,
When the sense of 'em may make you penitent.

DON ANTONIO 'Twere better thou wert hanged.

DON LOPEZ Repent? Cowards and fools do that.

DON JOHN Your valiant well-bred gentlemen never
repent: 110
But what should I repent of?

JACOMO After the murder of your father;
The brave Don Pedro, governor of Seville,
For whom the town are still in grief,
Was, in his own house, barb'rously killed by you.   115

DON JOHN Barbarously? You lie, you rascal, 'twas finely
done. I run him through the lungs as handsomely, and
killed him as decently and as like a gentleman, as could
be. The jealous coxcomb deserved death; he kept his sister
from me. Her eyes would have killed me if I had not   120
enjoyed her, which I could not do without killing him.
Besides, I was alone, and killed him hand to fist.

JACOMO I never knew you go to church but to take
sanctuary for a murder, or to rob churches of their plate.

DON JOHN Heaven needs not be served in plate, but I had 125
use on't.

JACOMO How often have you scaled the walls of monas-
teries? Two nuns, I know, you ravished, and a third you
dangerously wounded for her violent resistance.

DON JOHN The perverse jades were uncivil, and deserved 130
such usage.

JACOMO Some thirty murders, rapes innumerable, frequent
sacrilege, parricide: in short, not one in all the catalogue
of sins have 'scaped you.

DON JOHN My business is my pleasure; that end I will   135
always compass, without scrupling the means. There is no

right or wrong, but what conduces to, or hinders, pleasure. But, you tedious insipid rascal, if I hear more of your morality, I will carbonado* you.

DON ANTONIO We live the life of sense, which no fantastic 140 thing, called reason, shall control.

DON LOPEZ My reason tells me, I must please my sense.

DON JOHN My appetites are all I'm sure I have from heaven, since they are natural, and them I always will obey.   145

JACOMO I doubt it not, sir, therefore I desire to shake hands and part.

DON JOHN D' ye hear, dog, talk once more of parting, and I will saw your windpipe! I could find in my heart to cut your rascal's nose off, and save the pox a labour.* I'll 150 do't, sirrah, have at you!

JACOMO Good sir, be not so transported. I will live, sir, and will serve you in anything. I'll fetch a wench or anything in the world, sir. (aside) Oh, how I tremble at this tyrant's rage.   155

DON ANTONIO Come, 'tis night, we lose time to our adventures.

DON LOPEZ I have bespoke music for our serenading.

DON JOHN Let's on, and live the noble life of sense.
To all the powers of love and mighty lust,   160
In spite of formal fops I will be just.
What ways soe'er conduce to my delight,
My sense instructs me, I must think 'em right.
On, on, my soul, and make no stop in pleasure,
They're dull insipid fools that live by measure!   165
                              [*Exeunt all but* JACOMO]

JACOMO What will become of me? If I should leave him, he's so revengeful, he would travel o'er all Spain to find me out and cut my throat. I cannot live long with him neither: I shall be hanged, or knocked o'th'head, or share some dreadful fate or other with him. 'Tis just between 170 him and me, as between the devil and the witch: who repents her bargain, and would be free from future ills, but for the fear of present durst not venture.

(*Enter* LEONORA)

Here comes Leonora, one of those multitudes of ladies, he
has sworn, lied to, and betrayed.   175

LEONORA Jacomo, where is Don John? I could not live to
endure a longer absence from him. I have sighed and wept
myself away. I move, but have no life left in me. His
coldness and his absence have given me fearful and killing
apprehensions. Where is my dear?   180

JACOMO Your dear, madam? He's yours no more.

LEONORA Heaven! What do I hear? Speak, is he dead?

JACOMO To you he is.

LEONORA Ah me, has he forgot his vows and oaths?
Has he no conscience, faith, or honour left?   185

JACOMO Left, madam? He ne'er had any.

LEONORA It is impossible; you speak this out of malice,
sure.

JACOMO There's no man knows him better than I do.
I have a greater respect for you than for any he has   190
betrayed, and will undeceive you. He is the most perfidious wretch alive.

LEONORA Has he forgot the sacred contract, which was
made privately betwixt us, and confirmed before the altar,
during the time of holy Mass?   195

JACOMO All times and places are alike to him.

LEONORA Oh, how assiduous was he in his passion!
How many thousand vows and sighs he breathed!
What tears he wept, seeming to suffer all
The cruel pangs which lovers e'er endured!   200
How eloquent were all his words and actions!

JACOMO His person and his parts are excellent,
But his base vices are beyond all measure.
Why would you believe him?

LEONORA My own love bribed me to believe him.   205
I saw the man I loved more than the world,
Oft on his knees, with his eyes up to heaven,
Kissing my hand with such an amorous heat,
And with such ardour, breathing fervent vows
Of loyal love, and venting sad complaints   210

Of extreme sufferings. I, poor easy soul,
Flattering myself to think he meant as I did,
Lost all my sex's faculty, dissembling.
And in a month must I be thus betrayed?

JACOMO Poor lady! I cannot but have bowels* for you; 215
your sad narration makes me weep in sadness. But you
are better used than others. I ne'er knew him constant a
fortnight, before.

LEONORA Then, then he promised he would marry me.

JACOMO If he were to live here one month longer, he 220
would marry half the town: ugly and handsome, old and
young. Nothing that's female comes amiss to him.

LEONORA Does he not fear a thunderbolt from heaven?

JACOMO No, nor a devil from hell. He owns no deity but
his voluptuous appetite, whose satisfaction he will com- 225
pass by murders, rapes, treasons, or aught else. But pray,
let me ask you one civil question: did you not give him
earnest of your body, madam?

LEONORA Mock not my misery.
Oh, that confounds me! Ah! I thought him true,   230
And loved him so, I could deny him nothing.

JACOMO Why, there 'tis; I fear you have, or else he would
have married you. He has married six within this month,
and promised fifteen more, all of whom he has enjoyed
and left; and is this night gone on to some new adventure, 235
some rape or murder, some such petty thing.

LEONORA Oh, monster of impiety!
O false Don John! Wonder of cruelty!

(She swounds) *

JACOMO What a pox, does she swound at the news? Alas,
poor soul, she has moved me now to pity, as she did to 240
love. Hah, the place is private! If I should make use of a
natural receipt to refresh her, and bring her to life again,
'twould be a great pleasure to me, and no trouble to her.
Hum! 'tis very private, and I dare sin in private. A deuce
take her, she revives, and prevents me.   245

LEONORA Where is the cruel tyrant? Inhuman monster!

But I will strive to fortify myself.
But oh, my misfortune! Oh, my misery!
Under what strange enchantments am I bound?
Could he be yet a thousand times more impious, 250
I could not choose but love his person still.

JACOMO Be not so passionate. If you could be discreet and love yourself, I'd put you in a way to ease your grief now, and all your cares hereafter.

LEONORA If you can now ease an afflicted woman 255
Who else must shortly rid herself of life,
Employ your charity; 'twas never placed yet
On a wretch needed it more than I.

JACOMO If loyalty in a lover be a jewel, say no more! I can tell you where you may have it. 260

LEONORA Speak not of truth in man, it is impossible.

JACOMO Pardon me, I speak on my own knowledge.

LEONORA Is your master true, then? And have you happily deceived me? Speak.

JACOMO As true as all the power of hell can make him. 265

LEONORA If he be false, let all the world be so.

JACOMO There's another-guess man* than he, madam.

LEONORA Another! Who can that be?
(aside) No, no, there's no truth found in the sex.

JACOMO He is a civil, virtuous and discreet, sober person. 270

LEONORA Can there be such a man? What does he mean?

JACOMO There is, madam, a man of goodly presence, too –
something inclining to be fat; of a round plump face, with
quick and sparkling eyes, and mouth of cheerful overture.
His nose, which is the only fault, is somewhat short, but 275
that's no matter; his hair and eye-brows black, and so
forth.

LEONORA How? <aside> He may perhaps be bribed by
some other man, and what he said of his master may be
false. 280

JACOMO (aside) How she surveys me! Fa-la-la – (sings, and
struts about)

LEONORA Who is this you speak of?

JACOMO A man who, envy must confess, has excellent parts; but those are gifts, gifts – mere gifts; thanks be to heaven for them.   285

LEONORA But shall I never know his name?

JACOMO He's one whom many ladies have honoured with their affection, but no more of that. They have met disdain, and so forth. But he'll be content to marry. Fa-la-la-la – (sings)   290

LEONORA Again I ask you who he is?

JACOMO (aside) Lord, how inapprehensive* she is? Can you not guess?

LEONORA No.

JACOMO Your humble servant, madam.   295

LEONORA Yours, sir.

JACOMO It is myself in person; and upon my honour, I will be true and constant to you.

LEONORA Insolent varlet! Am I fallen so low to be thy scorn?   300

JACOMO Scorn? As I am a Christian soul, I am in earnest.

LEONORA Audacious villain! Impudence itself!

JACOMO Ah, madam, your servant, your true lover, must endure a thousand such bobs* from his mistress. I can bear, madam, I can.   305

LEONORA Because thy master has betrayed me, am I become so infamous?

JACOMO 'Tis something hard, madam, to preserve a good reputation in his company; I can scarce do't myself.

LEONORA Am I so miserable to descend to his man?   310

JACOMO Descend, say you? Ha, ha, ha!

LEONORA Now I perceive all's false which you have said of him. Farewell, you base ingrateful fellow.

JACOMO Hold, madam, come in the morning and I will place you in the next room, where you shall overhear our 315 discourse. You'll soon discover the mistake, and find who 'tis that loves you. Retire, madam, I hear somebody coming.

[Exeunt JACOMO, LEONORA]

Act 1, Scene 2

(*Enter* DON JOHN *in the street*)

DON JOHN Let me see, here lives a lady. I have seen Don
Octavio haunting about this house, and making private
signs to her. I never saw her face, but am resolved to
enjoy her because he likes her; besides, she's another
woman.   5

(*Enter* DON ANTONIO)

Antonio, welcome to our place of rendezvous. Well, what
game? What adventure?

(*Enter* DON LOPEZ)

Come, dear Lopez.

DON ANTONIO I have had a rare adventure.

DON LOPEZ What, dear Antonio?   10

DON ANTONIO I saw at a villa not far off, a grave, mighty-
bearded fool, drinking lemonado with his mistress. I
misliked his face, plucked him by the whiskers, pulled all
one side of his beard off, fought with him, run him
through the thigh, carried away his mistress, served her in   15
her kind, and then let her go.

DON JOHN Gallantly performed, like a brave soldier in an
enemy's country. When they will not pay contribution,
you fight for forage.

DON LOPEZ Pox on't, I have been damnably unfortunate. I   20
have neither beat man nor lain with woman tonight, but
fallen in love most furiously. I dogged my new mistress to
her lodging; she's Don Bernardo's sister, and shall be my
punk.*

DON JOHN I could meet with no willing dame, but was fain   25
to commit a rape to pass away the time.

DON ANTONIO Oh, a rape is the joy of my heart! I love a
rape, upon my *clavis*,* exceedingly.

DON JOHN But mine, my lads, was such a rape, it ought to
be registered, a noble and heroic rape.   30

DON LOPEZ Ah, dear Don John!

DON ANTONIO How was it?
DON JOHN 'Twas in a church, boys.
DON ANTONIO Ah, gallant leader!
DON LOPEZ Renowned Don John!   35
DON ANTONIO Come, let's retire, you have done enough
  for once.
DON JOHN Not yet, Antonio, I have an intrigue here.

(*Enter* FIDDLERS)

Here are my fiddlers. Rank yourselves under this window,
and sing the song I prepared.   40

Song

Thou joy of all hearts, and delight of all eyes,
Nature's chief treasure, and beauty's chief prize,
Look down, you'll discover,
Here's a faithful young vigorous lover:
With a heart full as true,   45
As e'er languished for you;
Here's a faithful, young, vigorous lover.

The heart that was once a monarch in's breast,
Is now your poor captive, and can have no rest;
'Twill never give over,   50
But about your sweet bosom will hover.
Dear Miss, let it in,
By heaven, 'tis no sin;
Here's a faithful, young, vigorous, vigorous lover.

DON JOHN Now fiddlers, be gone.   55

(*Window opens,* MARIA *looks out, and flings a paper
down*)

MARIA Retire, my dear Octavio; read that note. Adieu.
                                            [*Exit* MARIA]

DON JOHN Good, she takes me for Octavio. I warrant you,
boys, I shall succeed in this adventure. Now my false light
assist me.

(Reads by a dark lantern)*

(*reads*) 'Go from this window. Within eight minutes you   60
shall be admitted to the garden door. You know the sign.'
Hah, the sign! Gad, she lies! I know not the sign.

DON ANTONIO   What will you do? You know not the sign.
Let's away, and be contented this night.

DON JOHN   My friends, if you love me, retire. I'll venture,   65
though thunderbolts should fall upon my head.

DON LOPEZ   Are you mad? As soon as she discovers the
deceit, she'll raise the house upon you, and you'll be
murdered.

DON JOHN   She'll not raise the house for her own sake, but   70
rather grant me all I ask to keep her counsel.

DON ANTONIO   'Tis very dangerous; be careful of yourself.

DON JOHN   The more danger, the more delight. I hate the
common road of pleasure. What! Can I fear at such a time
as this? The cowardly deer are valiant in their rutting   75
time. I say, be gone.

DON ANTONIO   We'll not dispute your commands. Good
luck to you.

[*Exeunt* DON ANTONIO, DON LOPEZ]

DON JOHN   How shall I know this devilish sign?

(*Enter* DON OCTAVIO *with* FIDDLERS, *and stands under*
MARIA's *window*)

Ha! Whom have we here? Some serenading coxcomb.   80
Now shall we have some damned song or other, a
Chloris, or a Phyllis at least.

Song

Chloris, when you disperse* your influence,
Your dazzling beams are quick and clear,
You so surprise and wound the sense,   85
So bright a miracle y'appear,
Admiring mortals you astonish so,
No other deity they know,

But think that all divinity's below.

One charming look from your illustrious face,   90
Were able to subdue mankind,
So sweet, so powerful a grace
Makes all men lovers but the blind.
Nor can they freedom by resistance gain,
For each embraces the soft chain,   95
And never struggles with the pleasant pain.

DON OCTAVIO <to the FIDDLERS> Be gone! Be gone! The
window opens.
DON JOHN 'Sdeath! This is Octavio. I must dispatch him,
or he'll spoil all, but I would fain hear the sign first.   100

<MARIA and her maid, FLORA, at the window>

MARIA What strange mistake is this? Sure, he did not
receive my note, and then I am ruined!
DON OCTAVIO She expects the sign. Where's my whistle?
Oh, here.

(Whistles)

DON JOHN I have found it, that must be the sign!   105
MARIA <whispers to DON OCTAVIO> I dare not speak
aloud; go to the garden door.

(DON JOHN runs upon DON OCTAVIO, and snatches the
whistle out of his hand)

DON OCTAVIO 'Sdeath, what ruffian's this?
DON JOHN One that will be sure to cut your throat.
DON OCTAVIO Make not a promise to yourself of what   110
you can't perform.

(Fight)

DON JOHN I warrant you. Have at you!
MARIA O heaven! Octavio's fighting! Oh, my heart!
DON OCTAVIO (falls) Oh! I am slain –
DON JOHN I knew I should be as good as my word. I think 115
you have it, sir – Hah, he's dying! Now for the lady – I'll

draw him further off, that his groans may not disturb our pleasure. Stay – by your leave, sir, I'll change hat and cloak with you, it may help me in my design.

DON OCTAVIO O barbarous villain!   120

(*Dies*)

MARIA They have done fighting and I hear no noise. Oh, unfortunate woman! My dear Octavio's killed!

FLORA Perhaps, madam, he has killed the other. I'll down to the garden door. If he be well, he'll come hither, as well to satisfy his appointment as to take refuge. Your   125 brother's safe,* he may come in securely –

[*Exit to the door*]

MARIA Haste, haste! Fly, fly! Oh, Octavio! I'll follow her.

(*She follows*)

DON JOHN Now for the garden door. This whistle will do me excellent service. Now, good luck!

(*Goes to the door and whistles*)

FLORA Octavio?   130
DON JOHN The same.
FLORA Heaven be praised, my lady thought you had been killed.
DON JOHN I am unhurt; let's quickly to her.
FLORA Oh, she'll be overjoyed to see you alive!   135
DON JOHN <*aside*> I'll make her more overjoyed before I have done with her. This is a rare adventure!

(*Enter* MARIA, *at the door*)

FLORA Here's your jewel, madam, speak softly.
MARIA <*embraces* DON JOHN> O my dear Octavio, have I got you within these arms?   140
DON JOHN Aye, my dear, unpierced by anything, but by your eyes.
MARIA Those will do you no hurt. But are you sure you are not wounded?

DON JOHN I am. Let me embrace my pretty dear! <aside> 145
 And yet she may be a blackamoor for ought I know!
MARIA We'll retire to my chamber. Flora, go out and
 prepare us a collation.
DON JOHN O admirable adventure! Come, my delight.

                                              [Exeunt]

     (Enter DON LOPEZ, DON ANTONIO, JACOMO)

JACOMO Where's my pious master?   150
DON ANTONIO We left him hereabouts. I wonder what he
 has done in his adventure. I believe he has had some
 bustle.
DON LOPEZ I thought I heard fighting hereabout.
JACOMO Gad forgive me! Fighting? Where, where?   155
DON ANTONIO O thou incorrigible coward!
DON LOPEZ See, here's some of his handiwork: here's a
 man killed.
JACOMO (aside) Another murder! Heaven, what will
 become of me? I shall be hanged, yet dare not run away 160
 from him.

     (Enter an OFFICER with a GUARD, going the round)

OFFICER Stand! Who are there?
DON LOPEZ We do stand, rascal, we never use to run.
JACOMO (aside) Now shall I be taken and hanged for my
 master's murder.   165

                    (Offers to run)

DON ANTONIO Stand, you dog! Offer once more to run,
 and I'll put bilbo* in your guts.
JACOMO Gad forgive me! What will become of me?
OFFICER What's here? A man murdered? Yield: you are
 my prisoners.   170
  JACOMO With all my heart! But as I hope to be saved,
 we did not kill him, sir.
OFFICER These must be the murderers, disarm 'em.
DON ANTONIO How now, rascal! Disarm us?

DON LOPEZ We are not used to part with our swords. 175

JACOMO I care not a farthing for my sword, 'tis at your service.

DON ANTONIO <aside to JACOMO> Do you hear, rascal? Keep it and fight, or I'll swear the murder against you.

DON LOPEZ (aside to JACOMO) Offer to flinch, and I'll run 180 you through.

OFFICER Take their swords, or knock 'em down.

(*They fight.* JACOMO *offers to run; some of the* GUARDS *stop him*)

JACOMO A pox on't, I had as good fight and die, as be taken and be hanged.

(GUARDS *are beaten off*)

DON LOPEZ Are you gone, you dogs? I have pinked* some 185 of you.

JACOMO Ah, rogues! Villains! I have met with you.

DON ANTONIO O brave Jacomo! You fought like an imprisoned rat! The rogue had concealed courage and did not know it. 190

JACOMO O cowards! Rascals! A man can get no honour by fighting with such poltroons! But for all that, I will prudently withdraw; this place will suddenly be too hot for us.

DON LOPEZ Once in your life you are in the right, Jacomo. 195

JACOMO O good sir, there is as much to be ascribed to conduct, as to courage, I assure you.

[*Exeunt*]

(*Enter* DON JOHN *and* MARIA *in her chamber*)

MARIA Speak softly, my dear; should my brother hear us, we are ruined.

DON JOHN (*aside*) Though I can scarce contain my joy, I 200 will. Oh, she's a rare creature in the dark, pray heaven she be so in the light.

(*Enter* FLORA *with a candle; as soon as they discover*

DON JOHN, *they shriek out*)

MARIA   Oh, heaven! I am ruined and betrayed.

FLORA   He has Octavio's clothes on.

MARIA   Oh, he has murdered him. My brother shall revenge   205
it.

DON JOHN   I will cut his throat if he offers it.

MARIA & FLORA   *<calling out>* Thieves! Murder! Murder!
Thieves!

DON JOHN   I will stop your shrill windpipes.   · 210

(*Enter Maria's* BROTHER, *with his sword drawn*)

BROTHER   'Sdeath! A man in my sister's chamber! Have at
you, villain!

DON JOHN   Come on, villain.

(DON JOHN *kills the* BROTHER)

MARIA   O villain, thou hast killed my brother, and dishonoured me!   215

(*Enter* FIVE *or* SIX SERVANTS, *with drawn swords*)

Oh, your master's murdered!

DON JOHN   So many of you? 'Tis no matter: your heroes in
plays beat five times as many. Have at you, rogues.

(MARIA *runs away shrieking, and* DON JOHN *beats the*
SERVANTS *off and stops* FLORA)

Now give me the key of the garden, or I'll murder
thee.   220

FLORA   Murder! Murder! *<gives him the key>* There, take
it –

(*She runs away*)

DON JOHN   So, thus far it is well; this was a brave
adventure.
'Mongst all the joys which in the world are sought,   225
None are so great as those by dangers bought.

[*Exit*]

Act 2, Scene 1

JACOMO *solus**

JACOMO What will this lewd master of mine do? This town of Seville will not much care for his company after his last night's achievements. He must either fly or hang for't. Ha! Methinks my blood grows chill at the naming of that dreadful word, 'hang'. What will become of me? I 5 dare not leave him, and yet I fear that I shall perish with him. He's certainly the first that ever set up a religion to the devil.

(*Enter* LEONORA)

LEONORA I come to claim your promise; is Don John within? 10

JACOMO No, madam, but I expect him every minute. You see, madam, what honour I have for you, for I venture my ears to do this.

LEONORA You oblige me extremely. So great is the present pain of doubt that we desire to lose it, though in exchange 15 of certainty that must afflict us more.

JACOMO I hear him coming, withdraw quickly.

(*She withdraws*)

(*Enter* DON JOHN)

DON JOHN How now, sir, what wise thoughts have you in your noddle?

JACOMO Why, sir, I was considering how well I could 20 endure to be hanged.

DON JOHN And why so, buffle?*

JACOMO Why, you will force me to wait upon you in all your fortunes, and you are making what haste you can to the gallows. 25

DON JOHN Again, your reproofs. You insipid rascal! I shall cut your ears off, dog –

JACOMO Good sir, I have done; yet I cannot but admire,* since you are resolved to go to the devil, that you cannot

be content with the common way of travelling, but must 30
ride post to him.

DON JOHN Leave off your idle tales, found out by priests
to keep the rabble in awe.*

JACOMO Oh horrid wickedness! If I may be bold to ask,
what noble exploits did your chivalry perform last night? 35

DON JOHN Why, sir, I committed a rape upon my father's
monument.

JACOMO Oh horror!

DON JOHN Do you start, you villain? Hah!

JACOMO I, sir? Who I, sir? Not I, sir. 40

DON JOHN D'ye hear, rascal, let me not see a frown upon
your face: if I do, I will cut your throat, you rogue.

JACOMO No, sir; no, sir; I warrant you; I am in a very
good humour, I assure you – (aside) Heaven deliver me!

DON JOHN Now listen and learn. I killed a lady's lover, 45
and supplied his place; by stratagem enjoyed her. In came
her foolish brother and surprised me, but perished by my
hand; and I doubt not but I mauled three or four of his
servants.

(JACOMO starts)

JACOMO (aside) Oh, horrid fact! 50

DON JOHN Again, villain? Are you frowning?

JACOMO No, no, sir; don't think ill of me, sir. (aside)
Heaven fend me from this wicked wretch! What will
become of us, sir? We shall be apprehended.

DON JOHN Can you fear your rascally carcass, when I 55
venture mine? I observe always those that have the
most despicable persons, are most careful to preserve
them.

JACOMO Sir, I beg your pardon; but I have an odd
humour makes me something unfit for your worship's 60
service.

DON JOHN What's that, sirrah?

JACOMO 'Tis a very odd one, I am almost ashamed to tell it
to you.

DON JOHN Out with it, fool! 65

JACOMO Why, sir, I cannot tell what is the reason, but I have a most unconquerable antipathy to hemp. I could never endure a bell-rope. Hanging is a kind of death I cannot abide; I am not able to endure it.

DON JOHN I have taken care to avoid that. My friends are 70 gone to hire a vessel, and we'll to sea together to seek a refuge and a new scene of pleasure.

JACOMO All three, sir?

DON JOHN Yes, sir.

JACOMO Three as civil, discreet, sober persons, as a man 75 would wish to drink with.

(*Enter* LEONORA)

LEONORA I can hold no longer!

DON JOHN 'Sdeath, you dog, how came she here?

JACOMO I don't know, sir, she stole in –

<*Exit* JACOMO>

LEONORA (*aside*) What witchcraft do I suffer under, that 80 when I abhor his vices, I still love his person? – Ah, Don John, have I deserved that you should fly me? Are all your oaths and vows forgotten by you?

DON JOHN No, no. In these cases I always remember my oaths, and never forget to break them. 85

LEONORA Oh impiety! Did I, for this, yield up my honour to you? After you had sighed and languished many months, and showed all signs of a sincere affection, I trusted in your truth and constancy without the bond of marriage; yielded up a virgin's treasure, all my innocence; 90 believed your solemn contract, when you invoked all the powers above to testify your vows.

DON JOHN They think much of us; why don't they witness 'em for you? Pish, 'tis nothing but a way of speaking, which young amorous fellows have gotten. 95

LEONORA Did you not love me then? What injury had I e'er done you, that you should feign affection to betray me?

DON JOHN Yes, faith, I did love you, and showed you as

frequent and as hearty signs of it as I could. And, egad, 100
y'are an ungrateful woman if you say the contrary.

LEONORA Oh, heaven! Did you, and do not now? What
crime have I committed that could make you break your
vows and oaths, and banish all your passion? Ah, with
what tenderness have I received your feigned affection, 105
and ne'er thought I lived but in your presence. My love
was too fervent to be counterfeit.

DON JOHN That I know not: for since your sex are such
dissemblers, they can hold out against, and seem to hate
the men they love. Why may they not seem to love the 110
men they hate?

LEONORA O cruel man! Could I dissemble? Had I a
thousand lives, I ventured all each time I saw your face.
Nay, were I now discovered, I should instantly be
sacrificed to my raging brother's fury; and can I dissemble? 115

DON JOHN I do not know whether you do or no; you see I
don't: I am something free with you.

LEONORA And do you not love me, then?

DON JOHN Faith, madam, I loved you as long as I could for
the heart and blood of me, and there's an end of it, what a 120
devil would you have more?

LEONORA O cruel man! How miserable have you made
me!

DON JOHN Miserable! Use variety as I do, and you'll not
be miserable. Ah, there's nothing so sweet to frail human 125
flesh as variety.

LEONORA Inhuman creature! What have I been guilty of
that thou shouldst thus remove thy affections from me?

DON JOHN Guilty, no: but I have had enough of you, and I
have done what I can for you, and there's no more to be 130
said.

LEONORA Tigers would have more pity than thou hast.

DON JOHN Unreasonable woman! Would you have a man
love after enjoyment? I think the devil's in you.

LEONORA Do you upbraid me with the rash effects of love, 135
which you caused in me? And do you hate me for what
you ought to love me for? Were you not for many months

with vows and oaths betraying me to that weakness?
Ungrateful monster!

DON JOHN Why the devil did you not yield before? You 140
women always rook* in love; you'll never play upon the
square with us.

LEONORA False man! I yielded but too soon. Unfortunate
woman!

DON JOHN Your dissembling arts and jilting tricks, taught 145
you by your mothers, and the phlegmatic coldness of your
constitutions, make you so long in yielding; that we love
out almost all our love before you begin, and yet you
would have our love last as long as yours. I got the start
of you a long way, and have reason to reach the goal 150
before you.

LEONORA Did you not swear you would forever love me?

DON JOHN Why there 'tis; why did you put me to the
trouble to swear it? If you women would be honest, and
follow the dictates of sense and nature, we should agree 155
about the business presently, and never be forsworn for
the matter.

LEONORA Are oaths so slighted by you? Perfidious man!

DON JOHN Oaths! Snares to catch conceited women with. I
would have sworn all the oaths under the sun – why, 160
I would have committed treason for you; and yet I knew I
should be weary of you.

LEONORA I thought such love as mine might have deserved
your constancy, false and ungrateful man!

DON JOHN Thus your own vanity, not we, betray you. 165
Each woman thinks, though men are false to others, that
she is so fine a person, none can be so to her. You should
not take our words of course in earnest.

LEONORA Thus devils do in hell, who cruelly upbraid those
whom they have tempted thither.   170

DON JOHN In short, my constitution will not let me love
you longer: and whatever some hypocrites pretend,
all mankind obey their constitutions, and cannot do
otherwise.

LEONORA Heaven, sure, will punish this vile treachery.   175
DON JOHN Do you, then, leave it to heaven, and trouble
   yourself no farther about it.
LEONORA Ye sacred powers, who take care of injured
   innocence, assist me.

(*Enter* JACOMO)

JACOMO Sir, sir! Stand upon your guard.   180
DON JOHN How now! What's the matter?
JACOMO Here's a whole battalion of courageous women
   come to charge you.

(*Enter* SIX WOMEN)

DON JOHN Keep 'em out, you villain.
JACOMO I cannot, they overrun me.   185
DON JOHN What an inundation of strumpets is here?
LEONORA Oh, heaven! I can stay no longer to be a witness
   of his falsehood.

[*Exit* LEONORA]

1ST WOMAN My dear, I desire a word in private with
   you.   190
DON JOHN Faith, my dear, I am something busy, but I love
   thee dearly. (*aside*) A pox on thee!
2ND WOMAN Don John, a word. 'Tis time, now, we should
   declare our marriage: 'tis now above three weeks.
DON JOHN Aye, we will do it suddenly.*   195
3RD WOMAN Prithee, honey, what business can these idle
   women have? Send them packing, that we may confer
   about our affairs.
4TH WOMAN Lord! How I am amazed at the confidence of
   some women! Who are these that will not let one   200
   converse with one's own husband? By your leave,
   ladies.
JACOMO (*aside*) Now it works! Tease him, ladies, worry
   him soundly!
5TH WOMAN Nay, by your leave, good madam; if you go   205
   to that.

(*Pulls* DON JOHN *from the other*)

6TH WOMAN   Ladies, by all your leaves. Sure, none of you will have the confidence to pretend an interest in this gentleman –

DON JOHN   (*aside*) I shall be torn in pieces. Jacomo, stand 210 by me.

1ST WOMAN   Lord, madam, what's your meaning? None ought to claim a right to another woman's husband, let me tell you that.

2ND WOMAN   You are in the right, madam. (*to* DON JOHN) 215 Therefore, prithee, dear, let's withdraw, and leave them; I do not like their company.

DON JOHN   Aye, presently, my dear. (*aside*) What an excellent thing is a woman before enjoyment, and how insipid after it!   220

4TH WOMAN   Come, prithee, put these women out of doubt, and let them know our marriage.

DON JOHN   Tomorrow we'll declare and celebrate our nuptials.

6TH WOMAN   Ladies, the short and the long on't is, you 225 are very uncivil to press upon this gentleman. (*to* DON JOHN) Come, love, e'en tell 'em the truth of the story.

4TH WOMAN   Uncivil, madam? Pardon me; one cannot be so in speaking to one's own.   230

3RD WOMAN   That's true; she little thinks who that is.

6TH WOMAN   To their own! Ha, ha, ha! That's true – Come, honey, keep 'em no longer in ignorance.

4TH WOMAN   Come, ladies, I will undeceive you all. Think no further of this gentleman, I say, think no further 235 of him.

1ST WOMAN   What can this mean?

DON JOHN   Hold, for heaven's sake; you know not what you do.

4TH WOMAN   Yes, yes, I do; it shall all out. I'll send 'em 240 away with fleas in their ears. Poor silly creatures!

DON JOHN   (*aside*) Now will civil wars arise.

4TH WOMAN Trouble yourselves no longer about Don John, he is mine – he is mine, ladies –

ALL Yours!   245

DON JOHN Pox on't, I must set a good face on the business. I see murder will out.

6TH WOMAN Yours! That's pleasant; he's mine!

5TH WOMAN I have been too long patient; he is my husband.   250

1ST WOMAN Yours? How can that be? I am sure I am his wife.

3RD WOMAN Are you not ashamed, ladies, to claim my husband?

2ND WOMAN Are you all mad? I am sure I am married to   255 him.

ALL You!

DON JOHN Look you, ladies, a man's but a man: here's my body, tak't among you as far as 'twill go. The devil can't please you all.   260

JACOMO Pray, ladies, will you dispatch? For there are a matter of fifteen more that are ready to put in their claims and must be heard in their order.

DON JOHN How now, rogue? This is your fault, sirrah.

JACOMO My fault, sir? No, the ladies shall see I am no   265 traitor. Look you, ladies –

DON JOHN Peace, villain, or I will cut your throat. Well, ladies, know then, I am married to one in this company; and tomorrow morning, if you will repair to this place, I will declare my marriage, which now, for some secret   270 reasons, I am obliged to conceal. (*aside*) Now will each strumpet think 'tis her I mean.

1ST WOMAN That's well enough.

4TH WOMAN I knew he would own me at last.

3RD WOMAN Now they will soon see their errors.   275

5TH WOMAN (*to* DON JOHN) Now we'll conceal it no longer, dearest.

DON JOHN No, no, I warrant you.

6TH WOMAN Lord, how blank these ladies will look.

2ND WOMAN Poor ladies.   280

JACOMO Ladies, pray let me ask a question: which of you is really married to him?

OMNES* I, I, I –

DON JOHN 'Sdeath, you son of a baboon. Come, pox on't, why should I dally any longer! Why should I conceal my good actions! In one word, I am married to every one of you, and have above fourscore more. Nor will I ever give over, till I have as many wives and concubines as the Grand Seignior.* 285

JACOMO A very modest, civil person, truly. 290

4TH WOMAN O horrid villain!

6TH WOMAN Perfidious monster!

(*Enter* DON LOPEZ *and* DON ANTONIO)

DON ANTONIO How now, Don John. Hah! You are a ravenous bird of prey, indeed! Do you fly at no less than a whole covey of whores at once? You scorn a single strumpet for your quarry. 295

<DON LOPEZ> What, in tears too! Fie, Don John! Thou art the most ungentlemanly knight alive. Use your ladies civilly, for shame!

DON JOHN Aye, before the victory, I grant you; but after it, they should wear chains, and follow the conqueror's chariot. 300

DON LOPEZ Alas, poor harlots!

DON JOHN Peace, peace, good words. These are certain animals called wives, and all of 'em are my wives. Do you call a man of honour's wives, harlots? Out, on't! 305

1ST WOMAN Perfidious monster!

DON ANTONIO Excellent!

DON JOHN Come on; you are come very opportunely to help to celebrate my several and respective weddings. Come, my dears; faith, we will have a ballad at our weddings. Where are my fiddlers? 310

6TH WOMAN O savage beast!

4TH WOMAN Inhuman villain! Revenge shall follow.

DON JOHN Pox on revenge. Call in my minstrels. 315

(*Enter* FIDDLERS)

Come, sing my epithalamium.

Song

Since liberty, Nature for all has designed,
A pox on the fool who to one is confined.
All creatures besides,
When they please change their brides;   320
All females they get when they can.
Whilst they nothing but Nature obey,
How happy, how happy are they!
But the silly fond animal, man,
Makes laws 'gainst himself, which his appetites sway;   325
Poor fools, how unhappy are they!
(*Chorus*) Since liberty, Nature for all has designed,
A pox on the fool who to one is confined.

At the first going down, a woman is good,
But whene'er she comes up, I'll ne'er chew the cud,   330
But out she shall go,
And I'll serve them all so.
When with one my stomach is cloyed,
Another shall soon be enjoyed.
Then how happy, how happy are we!   335
Let the coxcomb, when weary, drudge on,
And foolishly stay when he would fain be gone.
Poor fool, how unhappy is he!
(*Chorus*) At the first going down, etc.

Let the rabble obey, I'll live like a man   340
Who, by Nature, is free to enjoy all he can:
Wise Nature does teach
More truth than fools preach;
They bind us, but she gives us ease.
I'll revel and love where I please;   345
She, she's my infallible guide.
But were the blessed freedom denied
Of variety in the things we love best,
Dull man were the slavishest beast.
(*Chorus*) Let the rabble obey, etc.   350

DON JOHN Come, how do you like this? Let's be merry,
my brides.

4TH WOMAN O monstrous traitor! Do you mock our
misery?

DON JOHN Good spouse, be not passionate – faith, we'll   355
have a dance. Strike up!

(*Dance*)

DON LOPEZ Be comforted, good ladies; you have companions in your misfortunes.

DON ANTONIO He has been married in all the cities of
Spain; what a breed of Don Johns shall we have?   360

DON JOHN Come, sweethearts; you must be civil to these
gentlemen; they are my friends, and men of honour.

6TH WOMAN Men of honour! They are devils if they be
your friends.

DON JOHN I hate unreasonable, unconscionable fellows   365
who when they are weary of their wives, will still keep
'em from other men. Gentlemen, ye shall command mine.

4TH WOMAN Thinkest thou I will outlive this affront?

DON JOHN I'll trust you for that: there's ne'er a Lucrece*
nowadays, the sex has learnt more wit since. Let me see,   370
Antonio, thou shalt have for thy present use, let me see –
my sixth wife. Faith, she's a pretty, buxom wench, and
deserves hearty usage from thee.

6TH WOMAN Traitor! I'll be revenged on all thy
treachery.   375

DON ANTONIO A mettled girl, I like her well: she'll endure
a rape gallantly. I love resistance, it endears the pleasure.

DON JOHN And, Lopez, thou shalt have, let me see, aye,
my fourth spouse, she's a brave virago; and gad, if I had
not been something familiar with her already, I would   380
venture my life for her.

4TH WOMAN Vile wretch! Think'st thou I will outlive this
affront? Impious villain! Though thou hast no sense of
virtue or honour left, thou shalt find I have.

DON JOHN Virtue and honour! There's nothing good or ill,   385
but as it seems to each man's natural appetite, if they will

consent freely. You must ravish, friends! That's all I
know: you must ravish!

1ST WOMAN Unheard-of villainy! Fly from this hellish
place.   390

DON ANTONIO Ladies, you shall fly, but we must ravish
first.

DON LOPEZ Yes, I assure you, we must ravish –

4TH WOMAN No, monster – I'll prevent you!

(*Stabs herself*)

DON ANTONIO 'Sdeath, she's as good as her word. The 395
first time I e'er knew a woman so.

DON LOPEZ Pox on't, she has prevented me; she's dead.

DON JOHN Say you so? Well, go thy ways. Thou wert a girl
of pretty parts, that's the truth on't; but I ne'er thought
this had been in thee.   400

2ND WOMAN These, sure, are devils in the shape of
men.

DON JOHN Now, see my providence: if I had been married
to none but her, I had been a widower!

1ST WOMAN Oh, horror! Horror! Fly! Fly!   405

6TH WOMAN No, I'll be revenged first on this barbarous
wretch.

DON JOHN Why, look you, here's a wench of mettle for
you! Go ravish quickly!

6TH WOMAN Let's fly, and call for help; some in the street 410
may hear us.

(*They all run off, crying, 'Help! Murder, murder!'*)

DON ANTONIO Let 'em go, they are confined, they can't get
out.

DON JOHN It shall ne'er be said that a woman went out of
this house *re infecta*;* but after that 'twill be time for us 415
to fly.

DON LOPEZ We have hired a vessel; the master is a brave
rogue of my acquaintance. He has been a bandit.

DON ANTONIO A brave, honest, wicked fellow as heart can
wish: I have ravished, robbed and murdered with him.   420

DON JOHN That's well. Hey, where are my rogues? Hey!

(*Enter* SERVANT<S> *and* JACOMO)

Here, sirrah, do you send my goods on board.

DON ANTONIO My man will direct you.

[*Exit* SERVANT]

DON JOHN Come, sirrah, do you remove this body to another room.   425

JACOMO O horrid fact! What, another murder! What shall I do?

DON JOHN Leave your complaints, you dog; I'll send you after her.

JACOMO Oh! I shall be hanged, I shall be hanged.   430

DON JOHN Take her up, rascal; or I'll cut your throat.

JACOMO I will, sir. (*aside*) Oh, mercy upon me! I shall be hanged!

DON JOHN <*to the* SERVANT> Now, sirrah, do you run into the streets and force in the next woman you meet, or 435
I'll cut your windpipe; and let nobody out.

<*Exit* SERVANT>

JACOMO (*aside*) What hellish fact will he now commit?

DON JOHN Take her up, you hen-hearted, compassionate rascal.

JACOMO (*aside*) Heaven! What will become of me? Oh! 440
Oh!

(*Carries her off*)

DON JOHN Now, gentlemen, you shall see I'll be civil to you: you shall not ravish alone. Indeed, I am loath to meddle with mine old acquaintance, but if my man can meet with a woman I have not lain withal, I'll keep you 445
company; let her be old or young, ugly or handsome, no matter.

DON LOPEZ Faith, I will ever say, you are a well-bred man.

DON ANTONIO A very civil person, a man of honour.

(*Enter* SERVANT, *forcing in an ugly* OLD WOMAN, *who cries out*)

DON JOHN This unlucky rogue has made but a scurvy 450
choice, but I'll keep my word. Come, bawd, you must be
ravished, bawd.

OLD WOMAN Oh, murder! Murder! Help! Help! I was
never ravished in my life.

DON JOHN That I dare swear; but to show I am a very 455
vigorous man, I'll begin with you. But you, rascal, jackal:
I'll make you cater better next time!

SERVANT Indeed, sir, this was the first I met.

DON JOHN Come on, beldam, thy face shall not protect
thee.   460

OLD WOMAN Oh, my honour! My honour! Help, help, my
honour!

DON JOHN Come, to our business.

(*Enter* JACOMO)

JACOMO O sir, sir! Shift for yourself; we shall all be
hanged. The house is beset. Oh, what shall we do?   465

DON JOHN Away, coward! Were the king of Spain's army
beleaguering us, it should not divert me from this exploit.

DON ANTONIO Nor me.

DON LOPEZ Nor me: let's on.

DON JOHN Keep the doors fast, sirrah. Come on.   470

JACOMO Oh what will become of me! Oh, heaven! Mercy
on me! Oh! Oh!

[*Exeunt*]

(*In man's habit, enter* MARIA, *and her maid*, FLORA)

MARIA Thus I have abandoned all my fortune,
And laid by my sex, Revenge, for thee.
Assist me now, you instruments of blood,   475
For my dear brother's, and for my much more dear
Octavio's, sake. Where are my bravoes?

FLORA They have beset the villain's house,
And he shall ne'er come out alive.

MARIA O let 'em show no more remorse,   480
Than hungry lions o'er their prey will.
How miserable am I made by that

Inhuman monster! No savage beast,
Wild deserts e'er brought forth, provoked
By all its hunger, and its natural rage,   485
Could yet have been so cruel.
Oh, my Octavio! Whither art thou fled
From the most loving and most wretched
Creature of her sex? What ages of delight
Each hour with thee brought forth!   490
How much, when I had thee, was all the world
Unenvied by me! Nay, I pitied all my sex
That could have nothing worth their care,
Since all the treasure of mankind was mine.
Methought I could look down on queens when he   495
Was with me: but now, compared to me,
How happy is the wretched, whose sinews
Crack upon the merciless engine
Of his torture! I live with greater torments then* he
    dies.
FLORA Leave your complaints. Tears are no sacrifice for
    blood.   500
MARIA Now my just grief to just revenge give place.
I am ashamed of these soft tears, till I've
Revenged thy horrid murder. Oh, that I could
Make the villain linger out an age in
Torments! But I will revel in his blood! Oh,   505
I could suck the last drop that warms the
Monster's heart, that might inspire me with
Such cruelty as vile man, with all his horrid
Arts of power, is yet a stranger to;
Then I might root out all his cursed race.   510
FLORA I'll follow all your fortunes, my dear lady;
Had I ten thousand lives, in this cause I'd
Venture one by one to my last stake.
MARIA Thou art my dear and faithful creature;
Let not thy fortunes thus be wracked with mine.   515
Be gone, and leave thy most unhappy mistress;
One that has miseries enow* to sink the sex.
FLORA I will not leave you, till death takes me from

you.

MARIA Oh, that I had been some poor, lost, mountain
    girl,
  Nursed up by goats, or suckled by wild beasts,   520
  Exposed to all the rage of heats and killing colds.
  I ne'er could have been abandoned to such fury.
  More savage cruelty reigns in cities,
  Than ever yet in deserts among the
  Most venomous serpents and remorseless   525
  Ravenous beasts, could once be found.
  So much has barb'rous art debauched
  Man's innocent nature.
FLORA Lay by your tears, till your revenge be finished;
  Then, then you may have leisure to complain.   530
MARIA I will; 'tis blood I now must spill, or
  Lose my own in th'attempt. But if I can
  Have the fortune, with my own hand, to reach
  The dog's vile heart, then I shall die
  Contented; and in the other world I'll   535
  Torture him so, devils shall learn of me to
  Use the damned.
FLORA Let's to our sacred instruments of revenge.
MARIA Come on. So just a cause would turn the
  Vilest ruffian to a saint.   540

                      [Exeunt]

(BRAVOES *watch at* DON JOHN's *house*)

(MARIA *and* FLORA *re-enter*)

MARIA Come, friends, let once a woman preach courage
  To you, inspired by my just rage this arm
  Shall teach you wonders. I'll show you now
  What love with just revenge can do.
1ST BRAVO We are so practised in the trade of death,   545
  We need no teaching.
MARIA There's gold, good store. If you dispatch the dog,
  I'll give you yet much more; if not,
  If all the wealth I have can buy your lives,
  I'll have 'em instead of his.   550

1ST BRAVO For half the sum, I'd kill a bishop at th' altar.

[*They retire*]

(*Enter* DON JOHN, DON ANTONIO, DON LOPEZ,
JACOMO)

DON JOHN Now we have finished our design; let's make a
sally, and raise the siege.

DON ANTONIO Jacomo, do you lead the van.

DON LOPEZ Lead on, Jacomo, or we are sure to lose you; 555
you are not good at bringing up the rear.

JACOMO Nay, good gentlemen, I know myself better than
to take place of men of quality, especially upon this
occasion.

DON JOHN Sirrah, go on. I'll prick him forward. Remem- 560
ber, if you do not fight, I am behind you.

JACOMO Oh, heaven! Oh, Jacomo, what will become of
thy dear person? Is this your courage, to put me forward
to what you dare not meet yourselves?

DON JOHN No words, rogue! On, on, I say. 565

JACOMO Oh, I shall be murdered! Murdered! Oh! Oh!

DON JOHN On, on, you dog.

JACOMO Inhuman master! It must be so! Heaven have
mercy on my better part.

(*Enter* MARIA)

MARIA Fall on, fall on! That's the villain! Have at you, 570
dog!

DON JOHN Courage, Jacomo.

JACOMO Oh! Oh!

(*They fight, and are driven off, but* MARIA *and* FLORA
remain)

MARIA Oh cowardly villains! The traitor will escape their
hands. Oh, dogs! More feeble than the feeblest of our sex. 575
Let's after him, and try our strength.

(*Enter* DON JOHN)

He is returned – fall on!

DON JOHN Ha! Must I encounter boys?

<Fights>

FLORA Oh, I am slain –

(<DON JOHN> kills FLORA)

MARIA At thy heart, base villain!   580

(DON JOHN disarms MARIA)

DON JOHN There, take your sword. I'll not nip roguery in
the bud; thou may'st live to be as wicked as myself.

MARIA Poor Flora! But, dog, I'll be revenged on thee yet ere
I die.

[Exit]

(Enter DON LOPEZ, DON ANTONIO, JACOMO)

JACOMO What? No thanks! No reward!   585

DON JOHN What's the matter, sirrah?

JACOMO What, no acknowledgement? You are but an
ungrateful man, let me tell you that, to treat a man of my
prowess thus.

DON JOHN What has your valour done?   590

JACOMO Nothing, nothing; saved your life only, that's all.
But men of valour are nothing nowadays. 'Tis an
ungrateful age. I fought like a hero –

DON ANTONIO Called a stag at bay!

DON LOPEZ You can fight, when there's no way of escape 595
without it.

JACOMO (sees FLORA's body) Oh, what's here? Another
murder! Fly, fly; we shall be hanged.

DON JOHN Come on! Let's now to sea to try our fortunes.

JACOMO Aye, make haste. I've laid horses and will shift by 600
land. Farewell, sir; a good voyage –

DON JOHN I will murder you, if you refuse to go to sea.

JACOMO O, good sir, consider; do but consider. I am so
sea-sick always; that wicked element does not agree with
me.   605

DON JOHN Dare you dispute? Go on, I say.

JACOMO O, good sir, think, think a little: the merciless
waves will never consider a man of parts. Besides, sir, I
can swim no more than I can fly.

DON JOHN I'll leave you dead upon the place, if you refuse. 610

JACOMO O sir, on my knees, I beg you'll let me stay. I am
the last of all my family; my race will fail, if I should fail.

DON JOHN Damn your race!

DON ANTONIO Do we not venture with you?

JACOMO You have nothing but your lives to venture, but I 615
have a whole family to save: I think upon posterity.
Besides, gentlemen, I can look for no safety in such
wicked company.

DON JOHN I'll kill the villain. His fear will else betray us.

JACOMO Oh, hold, hold! For heaven's sake hold –   620

(Ghost of DON JOHN's *father rises)*

GHOST Hold! Hold!

JACOMO Aye, hold, hold! Oh, heaven! Your father's ghost
– a ghost! A ghost! Oh! Oh!

(Falls down and roars)

DON JOHN 'Sdeath! What's here? My father alive!

GHOST No, no; inhuman murderer, I am dead.   625

DON JOHN That's well; I was afraid the old gentleman had
come for his estate again. If you would have that, 'tis too
late; 'tis spent.

gGHOST Monster! Behold these wounds.

DON JOHN I do. They were well-meant, and well per- 630
formed, I see.

DON ANTONIO This is strange! How I am amazed!

DON LOPEZ Unheard-of wonder! –

GHOST Repent, repent of all thy villainies!
My clamorous blood to heaven for vengeance cries.   635
Heaven will pour out his judgements on you all;
Hell gapes for you, for you each fiend does call,
And hourly waits your unrepenting fall.
You with eternal horrors they'll torment,
Except of all your crimes you suddenly repent.   640

(Ghost sinks)

JACOMO Oh! Oh! Heaven deliver me from these monsters.

DON JOHN Farewell, thou art a foolish ghost. Repent, quoth he! What could this mean? Our senses are all in a mist, sure.

DON ANTONIO They are not: 'twas a ghost.   645

DON LOPEZ I ne'er believ'd those foolish tales before.

DON JOHN Come, 'tis no matter; let it be what it will, it must be natural.

DON ANTONIO And nature is unalterable in us too.

DON JOHN 'Tis true, the nature of a ghost cannot change 650 ours.

DON LOPEZ It was a silly ghost, and I'll no sooner take his word than a whore's.

DON JOHN Thou art in the right. Come, fool. Fool, rise; the ghost is gone.   655

JACOMO Oh! I die, I die; pray let me die in quiet.

DON ANTONIO Oh, if he be dying, take him up; we'll give him burial in the sea. Come on.

JACOMO Hold, hold, gentlemen; bury me not till I am dead, I beseech you.   660

DON JOHN If you be not, sirrah, I'll run you through.

JACOMO Hold, hold, sir; I'll go, I'll go.

DON LOPEZ
DON ANTONIO } Let's on.

DON JOHN Should all the bugbears cowards feign appear, I would urge on without one thought of fear.   665

DON ANTONIO And I.

DON LOPEZ And I.

[Exeunt omnes]

Act 3, Scene 1

Aboard a ship

(*Enter* DON JOHN, DON LOPEZ, DON ANTONIO, JACOMO, CAPTAIN *of the Ship*, MASTER *and* SAILORS)

MASTER Mercy upon us! What sudden, dreadful storm is this? We are all lost; we shall split upon the rocks. Luff,* luff –

JACOMO Oh! Oh! Mercy! Oh, I was afraid of this! See what your wickedness has brought me to? Mercy! Mercy! 5

DON JOHN Take away thy cowardly face – it offends me, rascal.

CAPTAIN Such dreadful claps of thunder I never yet remembered.

DON JOHN Let the clouds roar on, and vomit all their 10
sulphur out, they ne'er shall fright me.

DON ANTONIO These are the squibs and crackers of the sky.

DON LOPEZ Fire on, fire on; we are unmoved.

CAPTAIN The heavens are all on fire; these unheard-of 15
prodigies amaze me.

DON JOHN Can you, that have stood so many cannons, be frighted at the farting and belching of a cloud?

MASTER Bless me, captain! Six of our foremast men are even now struck dead with lightning. 20

SAILOR Oh! That clap has rent our masts in sunder.

JACOMO Oh, we are lost! You can swim, sir; pray save me, sir, for my own and family's sake.

DON JOHN Toss these cowardly rogues overboard. Captain, courage! Let the heavens do their worst, 'tis but 25
drowning at last.

JACOMO But – in the name of heaven, but drowning, quoth he! Your drowning will prepare you for burning, though. Oh! Oh! Oh! –

SAILOR Captain, captain, the ship's on fire in the 30
forecastle –

CAPTAIN All hands to work upon the forecastle. Heaven, how it blazes already!

[*Exit* CAPTAIN]

JACOMO Oh! Oh! We burn, we drown, we sink! Oh, we
perish, we are lost, we are lost! Oh! Oh! Oh! –   35
MASTER O horrid apparitions! Devils stand and guard the
fire, and will not suffer us to quench it. We are lost!

(*Enter* CAPTAIN)

CAPTAIN In all the dangers I have been, such horrors I
never knew; I am quite unmanned.
DON LOPEZ A man and fear! 'Tis but dying at last.   40
DON JOHN I never yet could know what that foolish thing
fear is.
CAPTAIN Help, help, the fire increases. What horrid sights
are these? Where'er I turn me, fearful spirits appear.
[*Exeunt* CAPTAIN *and* SAILORS]

DON JOHN Let's into the boat, and with our swords keep   45
out all others.
DON ANTONIO While they are busy 'bout the fire we may
'scape.
DON LOPEZ If we get from hence, we certainly shall perish
on the rocks –   50
DON JOHN I warrant you.
JACOMO O good gentlemen, let us shift for ourselves and
let the rest burn, or drown, and be damned and they will.
DON JOHN No, you have been often leaving me: now shall
be the time we'll part. Farewell.   55
JACOMO Oh! I'll stand by you while I live. Oh the devil,
the devil! What horrors do I feel? Oh I am killed, I am
dead!

(*A thunderclap strikes* DON JOHN *and* JACOMO *down*)

DON JOHN 'Sdeath, why this to me? You paltry, foolish
bugbear, thunder, am I the mark of your senseless rage?   60
DON LOPEZ Nothing but accident. Let's leap into the boat.
DON ANTONIO The sailors all make towards us; they'll in
and sink it.

DON JOHN Sirrah, if you come on, you run upon my
  sword.   65
JACOMO O cruel tyrant! I burn, I drown, I sink! Oh, I die, I
  am lost!
CAPTAIN All shift aboard! We perish, we are lost.
MASTER All lost, all lost!

  (*A great shriek, they all leap overboard*)

Act 3, Scene 2

The shore, near a HERMIT's *cave*

(*Enter an old* HERMIT)

HERMIT This forty years I've lived in this neighbouring
  cave; and from these dreadful cliffs, which are always
  beaten by the foaming surges of the sea, beheld the ocean
  in its wildest rage, yet ne'er saw a storm so dreadful. Such
  horrid flashes of lightning, and such claps of thunder,   5
  never were in my remembrance. Yon ship is all on fire,
  and the poor miserable wretches must all perish. The
  dreadful object melts my heart and brings a flood of tears
  into my eyes. It is prodigious: for on the sudden, all the
  heavens are clear again, and the enraged sea is become   10
  more patient.

(*Enter* DON FRANCISCO)

DON FRANCISCO Oh, father, have you not been frighted at
  this prodigious storm, and at yon dreadful spectacle?
HERMIT No man that has an apprehension, but would have
  been moved with horror.   15
DON FRANCISCO 'Twas the most violent tempest I ever
  saw. Hold, yonder are some coming in a small vessel, and
  must necessarily split upon the rock. I'll go and help to
  succour 'em.
HERMIT Here are some this way, just come in a small boat.   20
  Go you to those, and these I will assist –
DON FRANCISCO I'll haste to their relief.

[*Exit* DON FRANCISCO]

HERMIT Hah! These are come safe to land – three men,
goodly men they seem to be; I am bound in charity to
serve them. They come towards me.   25

(*Enter* DON JOHN, DON ANTONIO *and* DON LOPEZ)

DON JOHN Much ado we are safe, but my man's lost. Pox
on him, I shall miss the fool; it was a necessary
blockhead.

DON ANTONIO But you have lost your goods, which were
more necessary.   30

DON LOPEZ Our jewels and money we have all about us.

DON JOHN It makes me laugh to think how the fools we
left behind were puzzled which death to choose, burning
or drowning.

DON ANTONIO But how shall we dispose of ourselves, we   35
are plaguy wet and cold? Hah! What old fool is that?

DON LOPEZ It is an hermit, a fellow of mighty beard and
sanctity.

DON JOHN I know not what sanctity he may have, but he
has beard enough to make an owl's nest, or stuff a saddle   40
with.

HERMIT Gentlemen, I see you are shipwrecked, and in
distress; and my function obliges me in charity to succour
you in what I may.

DON ANTONIO Alas, what canst thou help us to? Dost   45
thou know of ever a house near hand, where we may be
furnished with some necessaries?

HERMIT On the other side of this vast rock, there is a fertile
and pleasant valley, where one Don Francisco, a rich and
hospitable man, has a sweet dwelling; he will entertain   50
you nobly. He's gone to assist some shipwrecked persons,
and will be here presently. In the meantime, what my
poor cave can afford, you shall be most welcome to.

DON LOPEZ What can that afford? You oblige yourself to
fasting and abstinence.   55

HERMIT I have studied physic for the relief of needy people,

and I have some cordials which will refresh you. I'll bring
one to you.

[*Exit* HERMIT]

DON JOHN A good, civil, old hypocrite. But this is a
pleasant kind of religion, that obliges 'em to nastiness and   60
want of meat. I'll none on't.

DON ANTONIO No, nor of any other, to my knowledge.

(*Enter* HERMIT, *with a cordial*)

HERMIT Gentlemen, pray taste of this vial, it will comfort
your cold stomachs.

DON JOHN Hah, 'tis excellent, faith! Let it go round.   65

HERMIT Heaven bless it to you.

DON LOPEZ How it warms.

DON ANTONIO Thank thee, thou art a very honest old
fellow i'faith.

DON JOHN I see thou art very civil; but you must supply us   70
with one necessary more; a very necessary thing, and very
refreshing.

HERMIT What's that, sir?

DON JOHN It is a whore, a fine young buxom whore.

DON ANTONIO }
DON LOPEZ   } A whore, old man, a whore!   75

HERMIT Bless me, are you men or devils?

DON JOHN Men, men! And men of lust and vigour!
Prithee, old sot, leave thy prating, and help me to a
strumpet – a fine salacious strumpet! I know you zealots
have enough of 'em. Women love your godly whore-   80
masters.

HERMIT O monsters of impiety! Are you so lately scaped
the wrath of heaven, thus to provoke it?

DON ANTONIO How! By following the dictates of nature,
who can do otherwise?   85

DON LOPEZ All our actions are necessitated: none
command their own wills.

HERMIT Oh horrid blasphemy! Would you lay your dreadful and unheard-of vices upon heaven? No, ill men: that
has given you free will to good.   90

DON JOHN I find thou retir'st here, and never read'st or
think'st.
Can that blind faculty, the will, be free,
When it depends upon the understanding
Which argues first, before the will can choose?   95
And the last dictate of the judgement sways
The will; as in a balance, the last weight
Put in the scale, lifts up the other end,
And with the same necessity.

HERMIT But foolish men and sinners act against   100
Their understandings, which inform 'em better.

DON ANTONIO None willingly do anything against the
last
Dictates of their judgements; whatsoe'er men do,
Their present opinions lead 'em to.

DON LOPEZ As fools that are afraid of sin, are by the
thought   105
Of present pleasure, or some other reason,
Necessarily biased to pursue
The opinion they are of at that moment.

HERMIT The understanding yet is free, and might persuade
'em better.   110

DON JOHN The understanding never can be free;
For what we understand, spite of ourselves we do.
All objects are ready formed and placed
To our hands, and these, the senses to the mind
convey,
And as those represent them, this must judge.   115
How can the will be free, when the understanding,
On which the will depends, cannot be so?

HERMIT Lay by your devilish philosophy, and change the
dangerous and destructive course of your lewd lives.

DON ANTONIO Change our natures? Go bid a blackamoor 120
be white! We follow our constitutions, which we did not
give ourselves.

DON LOPEZ What we are, we are by Nature; our reason
tells us we must follow that.

DON JOHN Our constitutions tell us one thing, and yours 125

another; and which must we obey? If we be bad, 'tis
Nature's fault that made us so.

HERMIT Farewell. I dare no longer hear your impious
discourse. Such hardened wretches I ne'er heard of yet.

[*Exit* HERMIT]

DON ANTONIO Farewell, old fool.   130

DON JOHN Thus sots condemn what they can never
answer.

(*Enter* DON FRANCISCO)

(*aside*) This, I believe, is Francisco whom he spoke of; if
he has but a handsome wife, or daughters, we are happy.

DON LOPEZ Sir, we are shipwrecked men, and if you can 135
direct us to a place where we may be furnished with some
necessaries, you will oblige us.

DON FRANCISCO Gentlemen, I have a house hard by, you
shall be welcome to it. I even now endeavoured to
succour a youth and beauteous woman who, with two 140
sailors, in a boat, were driven towards these rocks, but
were forced back again, and I fear are lost by this time. I
desire nothing more than to assist men in extremes, and
am o'erjoyed at the opportunity of serving you.

DON JOHN We thank you.   145

DON FRANCISCO You shall command my house as long as
you please. I see you are cavaliers, and hope you will bear
with some inconvenience. I have two young and, though I
say it, handsome daughters who are tomorrow morning
to be married. The solemnity will bring much company 150
together, which, I fear, may incommode my house and
you.

DON ANTONIO You pose* us with this kindness.

DON JOHN Whatever pleases you, cannot be inconvenient
to us.   155

DON LOPEZ On the contrary, we shall be glad to assist you
at the ceremony, and help to make up the joyful chorus.

DON FRANCISCO You shall command my house and me;
I'll show you the way to it.

DON JOHN Your humble servant. We'll follow you.   160

[*Exit* DON FRANCISCO]

This is an admirable adventure:
He has daughters, boys, and to be married too.
If they have been so foolish to preserve those
Toys they call maidenheads, their senseless
Husbands shall not be troubled with them: 165
I'll ease them of those. Pox, what should those dull,
Drudging animals called husbands do with such
treasures?
No, they are for honest whore-masters, boys.

DON ANTONIO Well said, Don; we will not be wanting in 170
our endeavours to succeed you.

DON LOPEZ To you alone we must give place. *Allons!*

[*Exeunt*]

(*Enter* HERMIT, MARIA *in man's habit, and* LEONORA)

HERMIT Heaven be praised, you are safely now on land.

MARIA We thank you, reverend Father, for your assistance.

LEONORA We shall never forget the obligation.   175

HERMIT I am happy to be so good an instrument.

LEONORA We followed a vessel, which we saw fired with
lightning, and we fear that none of 'em escaped.

MARIA I hope the villain I pursue has scaped. I would not
be revenged by heaven, but my own hand; or, if not by 180
that, by the hangman's.

LEONORA Did any come to land? For I most nearly am
concerned for one, the grief for whom, if he be lost, will
soon, I fear, destroy me.

HERMIT Here were three of that company come safe to 185
land; but such impious wretches as did not deserve to
escape, and such as no virtuous person can be concerned
for, sure. I was stiff with fear and horror when I heard
'em talk.

MARIA Three, say you?   190

LEONORA (*aside*) By this sad description, it must be Don
John, and his two wicked associates. I am ashamed to
confess the tenderness I have for him. Why should I love
that wretch? Oh, my too violent passion hurries me I

know not whither! Into what fearful dangerous labyrinths 195
of misery will it conduct me?

MARIA   Were they gentlemen?

HERMIT   By their outsides they seemed so, but their insides
declared them devils.

MARIA (*aside*)   Heaven! It must be the villain and his
    barbarous   200
Companions! They are reserved for my revenge:
Assist me, heaven, in that just cause.
Oh, villain, villain! Inhuman villain!
Each minute is, methinks, a tedious age,
Till I have dipped my hands in thy heart's blood.   205

HERMIT   You seem o'erjoyed at the news of their safe
arrival. Can any have a kindness for such dissolute
abandoned atheists?

MARIA   No, 'tis revenge that I pursue against the basest of
all villains.   210

HERMIT   Have a care; revenge is heaven's, and must not be
usurped by mortals.

MARIA   Mine is revenge for rapes and cruel murders; and
those, heaven leaves to earth to punish.

HERMIT   They are horrid crimes, but magistrates must 215
punish them.

LEONORA (*aside*)   What do I hear? Were he the basest of all
men, my love is so headstrong and so wild within me, I
must endeavour to preserve him, or destroy myself. To
what deplorable condition am I fallen? What chains are 220
these that hold me? Oh, that I could break them! And yet
I would not if I could. Oh, my heart!

HERMIT   They are gone to one Don Francisco's house; that
road will bring you to it. 'Tis on the other side of this
rock, in a pleasant valley. I have not stirred these forty 225
years from these small bounds, or I would give him notice
what devils he harbours in his house. You will do well to
do it.

JACOMO (*within*)   Help, help, murder! I am drowned, I am
dead! Help, help!   230

HERMIT   Hah! What voice is that? I must assist him –

MARIA Father, farewell. Come, madam, will you go to this
house? – Now, monster, for my revenge.

LEONORA I will, but for different ends we go:
'Tis love conducts me, but revenge brings you.   235

[*Exeunt* MARIA, LEONORA]

JACOMO Oh help, help! I sink, I sink!

HERMIT Poor man, sure he is almost drowned.

JACOMO No, not yet, I have only drunk something too
much of a scurvy unpleasant liquor.

HERMIT Reach me your hand.   240

(*Pulls him out*)

JACOMO Aye, and my heart too! Oh! Oh!
Sir, a thousand thanks to you. I vow to gad, y'are a very
civil person, and, as I am an honest man, have done me
the greatest kindness in the world, next to the piece of the
mast which I floated upon, which I must ever love and   245
honour. I am sorry it swam away: I would have preserved
it, and hung it up in the seat of our ancient family.

HERMIT Thank heaven for your deliverance, and leave such
vain thoughts.

JACOMO I do with all my heart; but I am not settled   250
enough to say my prayers yet. Pray, Father, do you for
me; 'tis nothing with you, you are used to it, it is your
trade.

HERMIT Away, vain man; you speak as if you had drunk
too deeply of another liquor than sea-water.   255

JACOMO No, I have not, but I would fain. Where may a
man light of a good glass of wine? I would gladly have an
antidote to my poison. Methinks – pah! – these fishes
have but a scurvy time; I am sure they have very ill
drinking.   260

HERMIT Farewell, and learn more devotion and thankful-
ness to heaven.

[*Exit* HERMIT]

JACOMO Ha! 'Tis uncivilly done to leave a man in a
strange country. But these hermits have no breeding. Poor

Jacomo, dear Jacomo, how I love thy person; how glad 265
am I to see thee safe! For I swear, I think thou art as
honest a fellow as e'er I met with. Well, farewell, thou
wicked element; if ever I trust thee again – Well,
haddocks, I defy you, you shall have none of me, no, not
a collop.* No, no; I will be eaten by worms, as all my 270
ancestors have been. If heaven will but preserve me from
the monsters of the land, my master and his two
companions who, I hope, are drowned, I'll preserve
myself from those of the sea. Let me see, here is a path.
This must lead to some house. I'll go, for I am plaguy sick 275
with this salt water. Pah!

                        [*Exit* JACOMO]

(*Enter* CLARA *and* FLAVIA, *with* <their> *two* MAIDS)

CLARA Oh, Flavia, this will be our last happy night,
tomorrow is our execution day; we must marry.

FLAVIA Aye, Clara, we are condemned without reprieve.
'Tis better to live as we have done, kept from all men, 280
than for each to be confined to one whom yet we never
saw and a thousand to one, shall never like.

CLARA Out on't, a Spanish wife has a worse life than a
cooped chicken.

FLAVIA A singing bird in a cage is a princely creature, 285
compared to that poor animal, called a wife, here.

CLARA Birds are made tame by being caged, but wives are
made wild by confinement, and that, I fear, my husband
will find to his cost.

FLAVIA None live pleasantly here but those who should be 290
miserable, strumpets. They can choose their mates, but
we must be like slaves confined to the galleys; we have not
liberty to sell ourselves, or venture one throw for our
freedom.

CLARA O that we were in England! There, they say, a lady 295
may choose a footman and run away with him, if she
likes him, and no dishonour to the family.

FLAVIA That's because the families are so very honourable,
that nothing can touch them. There, wives run and

ramble* whither and with whom they please, and defy all 300
censure.

CLARA Aye, and a jealous husband is a more monstrous
creature there, than a wittol* here, and would be more
pointed at. They say if a man be jealous there, the women
will all join and pull him to pieces.   305

FLAVIA O happy country! We ne'er touch money. There,
the wives can spend their husbands' estates for 'em. O
blessed country!

CLARA Aye, there, they say, the husbands are the prettiest,
civil, easy, good-natured, indifferent persons in the whole 310
world. They ne'er mind what their wives do, not they.

FLAVIA Nay, they say they love those men best that are
kindest to their wives. Good men! Poor hearts. And here,
if an honest gentleman offer a wife a civility by the by,
our bloody butcherly husbands are cutting of throats 315
presently.

CLARA O that we had those frank, civil Englishmen,
instead of our grave, dull, surly, Spanish blockheads;
whose greatest honour lies in preserving their beards and
foreheads inviolable.   320

FLAVIA In England, if a husband and wife like not one
another, they draw two several ways and make no bones
on't. While the husband treats his mistress openly in his
glass-coach, the wife, for decency's sake, puts on her
vizor,* and whips away in a hackney with a gallant, and 325
no harm done.

CLARA Though, of late, 'tis as unfashionable for a husband
to love his wife there, as 'tis here; yet 'tis fashionable for
her to love somebody else, and that's something.

FLAVIA Nay, they say gentlemen will keep company with a 330
cuckold there, as soon as another man, and ne'er wonder
at him.

CLARA O happy country! There a woman may choose for
herself, and none will into the trap of matrimony, unless
she likes the bait; but here we are tumbled headlong and 335
blindfold into it.

FLAVIA We are used as they use hawks: never unhooded,*
or whistled off, till they are just upon the quarry.

CLARA And 'tis for others, not ourselves, we fly, too.

FLAVIA No more, this does but put us in mind of our 340
misery.

CLARA It does so. But prithee, let's be merry one night,
tomorrow is our last. Farewell all happiness.

FLAVIA O that this happy day would last our lives-time!
But prithee, my dear, let's have thy song, and divert 345
ourselves as well as we can in the meantime.

CLARA 'Tis a little too wanton.

FLAVIA Prithee, let's be a little wanton this evening,
tomorrow we must take our leaves on't.

CLARA Come on then, our maids shall join in the chorus. 350
Here they are.

Song

Woman, who is by nature wild,
Dull, bearded men encloses;
Of nature's freedom we're beguiled
By laws which man imposes: 355
Who still himself continues free,
Yet we poor slaves must fettered be.

Chorus: A shame on the curse
Of 'for better, for worse';
'Tis a vile imposition on nature: 360
For women should change,
And have freedom to range,
Like to every other wild creature.

So gay a thing was ne'er designed.
To be restrained from roving;   365
Heaven meant so changeable a mind
Should have its change in loving.
By cunning we could make men smart,
But they by strength o'ercome our art.

Chorus: A shame on the curse   370
Of 'for . . .' etc.

How happy is the village maid,
Whom only Love can fetter;
By foolish Honour ne'er betrayed,
She serves a power much greater: 375
That lawful prince the wisest rules,
Th' usurper, Honour, rules but fools.

Chorus: A shame on the curse
Of 'for . . .' etc.

Let us resume our ancient right,   380
Make man at distance wonder:
Though he victorious be in fight,
In love we'll keep him under.
War and ambition hence be hurled,
Let love and beauty rule the world.   385

Chorus: A shame on the curse
Of 'for . . .' etc.

FLAVIA Oh, dear Clara, that this were true! But now let's
home, our father will miss us.
CLARA No, he's walked abroad with the three shipwrecked 390
gentlemen.
FLAVIA They're proper handsome gentlemen; but the chief,
whom they call Don John, exceeds the rest.
CLARA I never saw a finer person; pray heaven either of our
husbands prove as good.   395
FLAVIA Do not name 'em. Let the maids go home, and if
my father be there, let him know we are here.
                                        [<*Exeunt*> MAIDS]

CLARA In the meantime, if he be thereabouts, do you go
down that walk, and I'll go this way, and perhaps one of
us shall light upon him.   400
FLAVIA Agreed.
                                        [<*Exeunt*> *ambo*]*

(*Enter* DON JOHN, DON LOPEZ, DON ANTONIO)

DON JOHN Where have you left the old man, Don
Francisco?

DON LOPEZ He's very busy at home, seeing all things
prepared for his daughters' weddings tomorrow.   405

DON JOHN His daughters are gone this way. If you have
any friendship for me, go and watch the old man; and if
he offers to come towards us, divert him, that I may have
freedom to attack his daughters.

DON ANTONIO You may be sure of us, that have served   410
you with our lives; besides, the justice of this cause will
make us serve you. Adieu.

[*Exeunt* DON LOPEZ, DON ANTONIO]

DON JOHN Now for my virgins. Assist me, love. Fools, you
shall have no maidenheads tomorrow-night. Husbands
have maidenheads! No, no – poor sneaking fools!   415

(*Enter* JACOMO)

JACOMO I have lost my way; I think I shall never find this
house. But I shall never think myself out of my way,
unless I meet my impious master. Heaven grant he be
drowned.

DON JOHN How now, rascal, are you alive?   420

JACOMO *<aside>* Oh, heaven! He's here. Why was this
lewd creature saved? I am in a worse condition than ever.
Now I have scaped drowning, he brings hanging fresh
into my memory.

DON JOHN What, mute, sirrah?   425

JACOMO Sir, I am no more your servant; you parted with
me. I thank you, sir; I am beholding to you. Farewell,
good sir, I am my own man now –

DON JOHN No; though you are a rogue, you are a
necessary rogue, and I'll not part with you.   430

JACOMO I must be gone, I dare not venture further with
you.

DON JOHN Sirrah, do you know me, and dare you say this
to me? *<draws>* Have at your guts! I will rip you from the
navel to the chin.   435

JACOMO O good sir, hold, hold. *<aside>* He has got me in
his clutches, I shall never get loose – Oh! Oh! –

DON JOHN Come, dog, follow me close, stinking rascal.

JACOMO I am too well pickled in salt water to stink, I
thank you; I shall keep a great while. But you were a very 440
generous man to leave a gentleman, your friend, in
danger, as you did me. I have reason to follow you; but if
I serve you not in your kind, then am I a soused sturgeon.

DON JOHN Follow me, sirrah; I see a lady.

JACOMO Are you so fierce already?   445

(*Enter* CLARA, *singing, 'A shame on the curse', etc.*)

CLARA <*aside*> Hah! This is the stranger. What makes him
here?

DON JOHN <*aside*> A delicate creature! Hah! This is the
lady. <*to* CLARA> How happy am I to meet you here.

CLARA What mean you, sir?   450

DON JOHN I was undone enough before, with seeing your
picture in the gallery; but I see you have more excellencies
than beauty: your voice needed not have conspired with
that to ruin me.

CLARA Have you seen my picture?   455

DON JOHN And loved it beyond all things I ever saw, but
the original. I am lost beyond redemption, unless you can
pity me.

JACOMO (*aside*) He has been lost a hundred times, but he
always finds himself again – and me too, a pox on him. 460

DON JOHN When love had taken too fast hold on me ever
to let me go, I too late found you were tomorrow to be
married.

CLARA Yes, I am condemned to one I never saw, and you
are come to rally* me and my misfortunes.   465

JACOMO Ah, madam, say not so, my master is always in
earnest.

DON JOHN So much I am in earnest now, that if you have
no way to break this marriage off and pity me, I soon
shall repent I ever came to land. I shall suffer a worse 470
wrack upon the shore. Here, I shall linger out my life in
the worst of pains, despairing love; there, I should have
perished quickly.

JACOMO Ah, poor man! He's in a desperate condition, I
pity him with all my heart –   475

DON JOHN Peace, rascal. Madam, this is the only opportunity I am like to have; give me leave to improve it.

CLARA Sure, sir, you cannot be in earnest.

DON JOHN If all the oaths under the sun can convince you,
madam, I swear –   480

JACOMO O sir, sir, have a care of swearing, for fear you
should once in your life be forsworn.

DON JOHN Peace, dog, or I shall slit your windpipe.

JACOMO Nay, I know if he be forsworn, 'tis the first time,
that's certain.   485

CLARA But, sir, if you be in earnest, and I had an
inclination, 'tis impossible to bring it about. My father
has disposed of me.

DON JOHN Dispose of yourself, I'll do well enough with
him; and my fortune and quality are too great for him, for 490
whom you are intended, to dispute with me.

CLARA If this be true, would you win a woman at first
sight?

DON JOHN Madam, this is likely to be the first and last;
tomorrow is the fatal day that will undo me.   495

JACOMO Courage, Don, matters go well.

CLARA (aside) Nay, I had rather have a peasant of my own
choosing, than an emperor of another's. He is a handsome gentleman, and seems to be of quality. Oh, that he
could rid me of my intended slavery. – Sir, talk not of 500
impossible things: for could I wish this, my father's
honour will not suffer him to dispense with his promise.

DON JOHN I'll carry you beyond his power, and your
intended husband's too.

CLARA It cannot be; but I must leave you, I dare not be seen 505
with you.

DON JOHN Remember the short time you have to think on
this. Will you let me perish without relief? If you will have
pity on a wretched man, I have a priest in my company;
I'll marry you, and we'll find means to fly early in the 510
morning, before the house are stirring.

CLARA I confess I am to be condemned to a slavery, that
nothing can be worse; yet this were a rash attempt.

DON JOHN If you will not consent to my just desires, I am
resolved to kill myself and fall a sacrifice to your disdain. 515
Speak, speak my doom!

(*Holds his sword to his breast*)

CLARA Hold, hold –

JACOMO *<aside>* Aye, hold, hold! Poor foolish woman, she
should not need to bid him hold.

CLARA I'll find a means this night to speak with you alone; 520
but I fear this is but for your diversion.

JACOMO *<aside>* Yes, 'tis for diversion indeed; the common diversion of all the world.

DON JOHN By all that's great and good, my intentions are
honourable.   525

CLARA Farewell, sir, I dare not stay longer.

DON JOHN Will you keep your word, madam?

JACOMO You'll keep yours, no doubt –

CLARA I will; anything, rather than marry one I cannot
love, as I can no man of another's choosing.   530

DON JOHN Remember, madam, I perish if you do not. I
have only one thing to say: keep this secret from your
sister, till we have effected it. I'll give you sufficient reason
for what I say.

[*Exit* CLARA]

Victoria, victoria! I have her fast, she's my own.   535

JACOMO You are a hopeful man, you may come to good in
time.

(*Enter* FLAVIA)

DON JOHN Here is the other sister; have at her.

JACOMO Why, sir, sir; have you no conscience?
Will not one at once serve your turn?   540

DON JOHN Stand by, fool. – Let me see, you are the
lady.

FLAVIA What say you, sir?

DON JOHN You have recently taken up a stray heart of

mine; I hope you do not intend to detain it, without giving 545
me your own in exchange.

FLAVIA I a heart of yours? Since when, good sir? You were
but this day shipwrecked on this coast, and never saw my
face before.

DON JOHN I saw your picture, and I saw your motion, 550
both so charming, I could not resist them; but now I have
a nearer view, I see plainly I am lost.

FLAVIA (aside) A goodly handsome man! But what can this
mean?

DON JOHN Such killing beauties I ne'er saw before; my 555
heart is irrevocably gone.

FLAVIA Whither is it gone, sir? I assure you I have no such
thing about me, that I know of.

DON JOHN Ah, madam, if you would give me leave to
search you, I should find it in some little corner about you 560
that shall be nameless.

FLAVIA It cannot be about me; I have none but my own,
and that I must part with tomorrow to I know not whom.

DON JOHN If the most violent love that e'er man knew can
e'er deserve that treasure, it is mine; if you give that away, 565
you lose the truest lover that e'er languished yet.

JACOMO What can be the end of this? Sure, blood must
follow this dishonour of the family and I, unfortunate,
shall have my throat cut for company.

FLAVIA Do you know where you are? 570

DON JOHN Yes, madam, in Spain, where opportunities are
very scarce, and those that are wise make use of 'em as
soon as they have 'em!

FLAVIA You have a mind to divert yourself; but I must
leave you, I am disposed to be more serious. 575

DON JOHN Madam, I swear by all –

JACOMO Hold, hold; will you be forsworn again?

DON JOHN Peace, villain, I shall cut that tongue out.

FLAVIA Farewell, I cannot stay.

[*Exit* FLAVIA]

DON JOHN I'll not leave her. I'll thaw her, if she were ice, 580
before I have done with her.

JACOMO There is no end of this lewdness. Well, I must be killed or hanged once for all, and there's an end on't.

[*Exeunt*]

(*Enter* MARIA *and* LEONORA)

LEONORA I am faint with what I suffered at sea, and with my wandering since. Let us repose a little, we shall not 585 find this house tonight.

MARIA I shall not rest till I have found Don Francisco's house; but I'll sit down a while.

LEONORA (*aside*) I hope he will not find it till I have found means to give Don John warning of his cruel intentions. I 590 would save his life, who, I fear, would not do that for me. But in the miserable case that I am in, if he denies his love, death would be the welcom'st thing on earth to me.

MARIA (*aside*) Oh, my Octavio! How does the loss of thee perplex me with despair; the honour of mankind is gone 595 with thee. Why do I whine? Grief shall no longer usurp the place of my revenge. How could I gnaw the monster's heart! Villain, I'll be with you! When I have reveng'd dear Octavio's loss, I then shall die contented.

(*Enter* DON LOPEZ *and* DON ANTONIO)

DON LOPEZ The old man's safe; I long to know Don John's 600 success.

DON ANTONIO He's engaged upon a noble cause. If he succeeds, 'twill be a victory worth the owning.

DON LOPEZ Hah, whom have we here? A young man well habited, with a lady too. They seem to be strangers.   605

DON ANTONIO A mischief comes into my head, that's worth the doing.

DON LOPEZ What's that, dear Antonio?

DON ANTONIO We are in a strange country, and may want money; I would rob that young fellow. We have not 610 robbed a good while, methinks 'tis a new wickedness to me.

DON LOPEZ Thou art in the right. I hate to commit the

same dull sin over and over again, as if I were married to
it. Variety makes all things pleasant.   615

DON ANTONIO But there's one thing we'll ne'er omit.
When we have robbed the man, we'll ravish the woman.

DON LOPEZ Agreed; let's to't, man. Come on, young
gentleman, we must see what riches you have about you.

MARIA O villains! Thieves! Thieves! These are the inhu-   620
man companions of that bloody monster.

LEONORA Have pity on poor miserable strangers.

DON ANTONIO Peace; we'll use you kindly, very kindly.

DON LOPEZ Do you carry that young gentleman, bind him
to a tree, and bring the money, while I wait upon the lady. 625

DON ANTONIO Will you play me no foul play in the
meantime then? For we must cast lots about the business
you wot of.

DON LOPEZ No, upon my honour.

MARIA Honour, you villain?   630

DON ANTONIO Come, young gentleman, I'll tame you.

MARIA Help! Help! –

[*Exit* DON ANTONIO *haling* MARIA]

<Re-enter DON ANTONIO>

LEONORA Have you no humanity in you? Take our money,
but leave us liberty; be not so barbarously cruel.

DON ANTONIO Come, I have made haste with him; now let 635
us draw cuts who enjoys the lady first.

LEONORA O heaven assist me! What do I hear? Help! Help!

(*Enter* FOUR *or* FIVE COUNTRY FELLOWS, *coming from
work*)

1ST COUNTRY FELLOW What, two men a-robbing of a
lady! Be gone, and let her alone; or we have sower*
cudgels shall wasler* your bones, I tell you that.   640

DON ANTONIO How now, rogues?

(*Fight off the stage*)

LEONORA Thanks to heaven. I fly! I fly! Where shall I hide
myself?

[Exit]

(*Enter* DON JOHN *and* JACOMO)

DON JOHN I shall conquer 'em both. Now, sirrah, what
   think you?   645

JACOMO Why I think you manage your business as
   discreetly, and take as much pains to have your throat
   cut, as any man in Spain.

DON JOHN Your fear o'errules your sense; mine is a life
   monarchs might envy.   650

JACOMO 'Tis like to be a very short one at this rate.

DON JOHN Away, fool; 'tis dark, I must be gone; I shall
   scarce find the way home.

(*Enter* LEONORA)

LEONORA Heaven, guard me from these wicked wretches.
   Help! Help! They are here.   655

DON JOHN How now, madam? What, afraid of a man!

LEONORA Don John, no, not of you; you are the man i'the
   world I would have met.

DON JOHN Leonora, you are the woman i'the world I
   would have avoided. (*aside*) 'Sdeath! She will spoil my   660
   new designs, but I have a trick for her. – What miracle
   brought you hither?

LEONORA Love, that works the greatest miracles, made me
   follow you; and the same storm drove me on this shore on
   which you were thrown, and thus far I have wandered till   665
   I have found you.

DON JOHN (*aside*) This is the most unreasonable, unsatia-
   ble, loving lady that ever was abused by man. She has a
   kind of spaniel love, the worse you use her, the more
   loving she is. Pox on her, I must be rid of her.   670

LEONORA I am very faint and weary, yet I was resolved not
   to rest till I had found you.

DON JOHN Your unwearied love has o'ercome and convinced me there is not such a woman breathing.

LEONORA This is a sovereign medicine for all my sorrows. 675

I now, methinks, am happier than ever; but I am faint and
ill.

DON JOHN Here, madam, I have an excellent cordial; 'twill
refresh you; and I'll conduct you where you shall never be
unhappy more.   680

LEONORA From that dear hand, 'tis welcome – (drinks) –
To your health!

DON JOHN And to your own destruction; you have drunk
your last.

LEONORA What means my love?   685

DON JOHN Y'have drunk the subtlest poison that art e'er
yet invented.

JACOMO Oh, murder! Murder! What have you done?

DON JOHN Peace, villain, leave your unseasonable pity.
<to LEONORA> You cannot live two minutes.   690

LEONORA O ungrateful tyrant! Thou hast murdered the
only creature living that could love thee. Heaven will
revenge it, though to me 'tis kindness. Here all my
sorrows shall forever cease.

DON JOHN Why would you persecute me with your love?   695

LEONORA I could not help it. I came to preserve you, and
am destroyed for't.

JACOMO Oh horrid fact!

DON JOHN To preserve me! I wear my safety by my   700
side!

LEONORA Oh, I faint! Guard yourself. There's a young
Gentleman pursues your life. Have a care –
I came to tell you this, and thus I am rewarded.
Heaven pardon you. Farewell. I can no more.

(Dies)

JACOMO This object, sure, will strike your heart! Tigers   705
would melt at this. Oh, the earth will open and swallow
you up; and me for company. There's no end of your
murders.

DON JOHN This is the first time I ever knew compassion.
Poor fool, I pity her, but 'tis too late.   710
Farewell all senseless thoughts of a remorse,

I would remove whate'er would stop my course.

[*Exeunt*]

Act 4, Scene 1

<DON FRANCISCO'S *house*>

(*Enter* DON JOHN, DON LOPEZ, DON ANTONIO,
JACOMO)

DON JOHN This night's success exceeded all my hopes. I
had admittance to their several chambers, and I have been
contracted to both the sisters, and this day resolve to
marry 'em, and at several times enjoy them; and, in my
opinion, I shall have a brace of as pretty wives as any man   5
in Spain.

DON ANTONIO Brave Don John! You are master of your
art; not a woman in Spain can stand before you.

DON LOPEZ We can but envy you, and, at a distance,
imitate. But both their maids shall to pot, I assure you.   10

JACOMO How far will the devil hurry you?

DON JOHN 'Tis not the devil, 'tis the flesh, fool.

JACOMO Here will be fine cutting of throats. Poor Jacomo,
must thou be cut off in the flower of thy age?

(*Enter* DON FRANCISCO)

DON FRANCISCO Gentlemen, your servant. I hope you   15
rested well this night.

DON LOPEZ We thank you, sir; never better.

DON ANTONIO We never shall requite this obligation.

JACOMO I warrant you my master will; he's a very grateful
civil person indeed.   20

DON JOHN The favour is too great to be suddenly requited;
but I shall study to deserve it.

JACOMO Good man, you will deserve it.

(*Enter* TWO BRIDEGROOMS)

DON FRANCISCO Gentlemen, you are come; you are early.

1ST BRIDEGROOM This joyful occasion made us think 25
it late.

2ND BRIDEGROOM The expectation of so great a blessing
as we this day hope to enjoy, would let us have but little
rest last night.

1ST BRIDEGROOM And the fruition will afford us 30
less tonight.

DON JOHN <aside> Poor fools, you shall be bobbed!* How
it tickles my spleen to think on't.

DON FRANCISCO These are to be my sons-in-law.

DON JOHN <aside> And my cuckolds beforehand. 35

DON FRANCISCO Pray know 'em, gentlemen; they are men
of honour.

DON JOHN I shall be glad to serve them. (aside) But first I'll
serve their ladies.

DON FRANCISCO Come, gentlemen, I'll now conduct you 40
to my daughters; and beg your pardon for a moment. I'll
wait on you again.

[*Exit* DON FRANCISCO *and* BRIDEGROOMS]

DON ANTONIO These fools will spoil your design.

DON JOHN No, poor sots; I have persuaded the ladies to
feign sickness, and put off their marriage till tomorrow 45
morning, to gain time. In the meanwhile I have 'em safe,
boys.

DON LOPEZ But will not the sisters betray you to one
another?

DON JOHN No, I have wheedled each into a jealousy of the 50
other; and each believes that if the other knows it, she, in
honour, will reveal it to the father.

JACOMO Sir, if you be so very weary of your life, why
don't you make use of a convenient beam? 'Tis the easier
way; so you may die without the filthy pother you keep 55
about it.

DON JOHN Away, coward; 'tis a sign I am not weary of my
life, that I make so much use on't.

JACOMO Oh, Jacomo, thou art lost! 'Tis pity a fellow of
thy neat, spruce parts should be destroyed. 60

(*Enter* DON FRANCISCO)

DON FRANCISCO Come, gentlemen, will you not refresh yourselves with some cool wines this morning?

DON LOPEZ We thank you, sir, we have already.

(*Enter a* SERVANT)

SERVANT Sir, here's a young gentleman, a stranger, desires to speak with you.   65

DON FRANCISCO Admit him.

(*Enter* MARIA, *in man's habit*)

Your humble servant.

MARIA Sir, when I've told you what I come for, I doubt not but I shall deserve your thanks. I come to do you service.

DON FRANCISCO You have 'em, sir, already.   70

MARIA You have lodged within your house some ship-wrecked men, who are greater villains than the earth e'er bore. I come to give you warning of 'em, and to beg your power to revenge such horrid actions, as heart could never yet conceive, or tongue could utter. Ha, they are   75
these! Revenge, revenge cruel, unnatural rapes and murders! They are devils in the shapes of men.

DON FRANCISCO What say you, sir?

JACOMO Now the snare is fallen upon me; methinks I feel cold steel already in my body. Too well I know that face.   80

DON JOHN <*aside*> I know that face. Now, impudence, assist me. – What mad young man is that?

DON FRANCISCO These, by their habits and their miens, are gentlemen, and seem to be men of honour.

MARIA By these two, last night, I was robbed and bound to   85
a tree, and there have been all night, and but this morning was relieved by peasants. I had a lady with me whom they said they would ravish, and this morning I saw her dead. They must have murdered her.

DON FRANCISCO Heaven! What do I hear?   90

JACOMO Oh, I am noosed already! I feel the knot, methinks, under my left ear.

DON ANTONIO The youth raves; we never saw his face, we

never stirred from the bounds of this house since we came
hither.   95

DON LOPEZ 'Sdeath, let me kill the villain. Shall he thus
affront men of our quality and honour?

DON FRANCISCO Hold, consider I am a magistrate.

DON JOHN The youth was robbed, and with the fright has
lost his wits. Poor fool! Let him be bound in's bed.   100

DON FRANCISCO Do not persist in this, but have a care:
These injuries to men of honour shall not go unpunished.

MARIA Whither shall injured innocence fly for succour, if
you so soon can be corrupted? Monster, I'll revenge   105
myself; have at thy heart!

<draws>

DON FRANCISCO: What means the youth? Put up your
sword.

DON ANTONIO We told you, sir, he was mad.

MARIA Oh impudent villains! I ask your pardon, sir: my   110
griefs and injuries transport me so, I scarce can utter
them. That villain is Don John, who basely murdered the
governor of Seville in his house, and then dishonoured his
fair sister.

DON JOHN Death and hell! This injury is beyond all   115
sufferance.

<DON FRANCISCO> Hold, sir, think in whose house you
are.

JACOMO O lord, what will this come to? Ah, Jacomo, thy
line of life is short!   120

MARIA This is the villain, who killed the lover of Antonio's
sister; deflowered her and murdered her brother in his
own house.

DON JOHN I'll have no longer patience.

DON ANTONIO Such a villain should have his throat cut,   125
though in a church.

DON LOPEZ No man of honour will protect those who
offer such injuries.

DON JOHN *<draws>* Have at you, villain!

DON FRANCISCO Nay then — within there, ho! I will 130
protect him, or perish with him.

(*Enter* TWO BRIDEGROOMS)

1ST BRIDEGROOM What's the matter?

DON JOHN (*to* DON ANTONIO *<and>* DON LOPEZ) This
rashness will spoil my design upon the daughters. If I had
perfected that, I would have owned* all this for half a 135
ducatoon.* *<to* DON FRANCISCO>* I ask your pardon for
my ill manners; I was provoked too far. Indeed, the
accusations are so extravagant and odd I rather should
have laughed at 'em. Let the young fool have a vein
opened, he's stark staring mad.   140

DON ANTONIO A foolish impostor. We ne'er saw Seville
till last night.

MARIA Oh, impudence!

JACOMO No, not we; we were never there till yesterday.
Pray, sir, lay that young fellow by the heels for lying on us 145
men of honour.

DON FRANCISCO What is the matter, friend, you tremble
so?

DON LOPEZ 'Sdeath, the dog's fear will betray us.

JACOMO I, tremble, sir? No, no, sir. I, tremble? — Though it 150
would make anyone tremble to hear one lie as that young
gentleman does. Have you no conscience in you?

MARIA Heaven can witness for me, I speak not false.
Octavio, my dear Octavio, being dearest to me of all the
world, I would in Seville have revenged his murder; but 155
the villain there escaped me. I followed him to sea, and in
the same storm in which their ship perished, I was thrown
on shore. Oh, my Octavio! If this foul unnatural murder
be not revenged, there is no justice left among mankind.
His ghost, and all the rest whom he has barbarously 160
murdered, will interrupt your quiet; they'll haunt you in
your sleep. Revenge, revenge!

2ND BRIDEGROOM This is wonderful.

DON FRANCISCO There must be something in this; his
passion cannot be counterfeited, nor your man's fear.   165
JACOMO My fear? I scorn your words. I fear nothing under
the sun. I, fear? Ha, ha, ha –
DON JOHN Will you believe this one false villain against
three who are gentlemen, and men of honour?
JACOMO Nay, against four who are gentlemen, and men of   170
honour.
MARIA O villain, that I had my sword imbrued in thy
heart's blood. Oh, my dear Octavio! Do justice, sir, or
heaven will punish you.

(*Enter* CLARA)

DON FRANCISCO Gentlemen, he is too earnest in his grief   175
and anger, to be what you would have him, an impostor.
My house has been your sanctuary, and I am obliged in
honour not to act as a magistrate, but your host. No
violence shall here be offered to you; but you must
instantly leave this house and, if you would have safety,   180
find it somewhere else. Be gone.
DON JOHN This is very well.
MARIA Oh! Will you let 'em go unpunished?
Whither shall I fly for vengeance?
DON FRANCISCO Pray leave this place immediately.   185
JACOMO Ah, good sir, let's be gone. Sir, your most humble
servant.
CLARA Oh, sir, consider what you do. Do not banish Don
John from hence.
1ST BRIDEGROOM Ha! What means she?   190
DON FRANCISCO What say you?
CLARA Oh, sir, he is my husband; we were last night
contracted.
DON FRANCISCO Oh, heaven! What do I hear?
1ST BRIDEGROOM I am dishonoured, abused. Villain,   195
thou diest.
DON JOHN Villain, you lie; I will cut your throat first.
DON FRANCISCO Hey, where are my people here!

(*Enter* SERVANTS *and* FLAVIA)

FLAVIA Oh, sir, hold; if you banish Don John I am lost
forever.   200
DON FRANCISCO Oh, devil! What do I hear?
FLAVIA He is my husband, sir; we were last night
contracted.
CLARA Your husband? Heaven! What's this?
2ND BRIDEGROOM Hell and damnation!   205
DON FRANCISCO Oh! I have lost my senses.
MARIA Oh, monster! Now am I to be believed?
JACOMO Oh, spare my life! I am innocent, as I hope to live
and breathe.
DON JOHN Dog, you shall fight for your life, if you have it. 210
DON FRANCISCO First, I'll revenge myself on these.
DON JOHN Hold, hold; they are both my wives, and I will
have them.

(<DON FRANCISCO> *runs at his* DAUGHTERS; *they run
out*)

DON FRANCISCO Oh, devil! Fall on!
MARIA Fall on, I will assist you.   215

(*They fight.* MARIA *and* DON FRANCISCO *are killed; the*
TWO BRIDEGROOMS *are hurt;* JACOMO *runs away*)

DON JOHN Now we've done their business.
Ah, cowardly rogue! Are you not a son of a whore?
JACOMO Aye, sir, what you please. A man had better be a
living son of a whore, than a dead hero, by your favour.
DON JOHN I could find it in my heart to kill the rascal; his   220
fear, some time or other, will undo us.
JACOMO Hold, sir; I went, sir, to provide for your escape.
Let's take horses out of the stable, and fly. Abundance of
company are coming, expecting the wedding, and we are
incomparably lost if we take not this time. I think my fear 225
will now preserve you.
DON ANTONIO I think he counsels well. Let's fly to a new
place of pleasure.
DON JOHN But I shall leave my business undone with the
two women.   230

DON LOPEZ 'Tis now scarce feasible. Let's fly; you'll light
on others as handsome where we come next.

DON JOHN Well, dispose of me as you please; and yet it
troubles me.

JACOMO Haste, haste, or we shall be apprehended.   235

[*Exeunt*]

(*Enter* CLARA *and* FLAVIA)

FLAVIA Oh, that I ever lived to see this day!
This fatal day! 'Twas our vile disobedience
Caused our poor father's death, which heaven
Will revenge on us. So lewd a villain
As Don John was never heard of yet.   240

CLARA That we should be so credulous! Oh dreadful
Accident! Dear father, what expiation can
We make? Our crime's too foul for
Tears to wash away, and all our lives will
Be too short to spend in penitence for this,   245
Our levity and disobedience. He was the
Best of fathers, and of men.

FLAVIA What will become of us, poor miserable maids,
Lost in our fortunes and our reputations?
Our intended husbands, if they recover of their   250
Wounds, will murder us; and 'tis but justice.
Our lives too, now, cannot be worth the keeping.
Those devils in the shape of men are fled.

CLARA Let us not waste our time in fruitless grief;
Let us employ some to pursue the murderers.   255
And for ourselves, let's to the next monastery,
And there spend all our weary life in penitence.

FLAVIA Let's fly to our last sanctuary in this world,
And try, by a religious life, to expiate this crime:
There is no safety, or no hope but there.   260
Let's go, and bid a long farewell to all the
World: a thing too vain, and little worth our care.

CLARA Agreed. Farewell to all the vanity on earth,
Where wretched mortals, tossed 'twixt hope and fear,
Must of all fixed and solid joy despair.   265

[*Exeunt*]

Act 4, Scene 2

The scene is a delightful grove

(*Enter* TWO SHEPHERDS *and* TWO NYMPHS)

1ST SHEPHERD Come nymphs and shepherds, haste away
  To th' happy sports within these shady groves;
  In pleasant lives time slides away apace,
  But with the wretched seems to creep too slow.
1ST NYMPH Our happy leisure, we employ in joys   5
  As innocent as they are pleasant. We,
  Strangers to strife, and to tumultuous noise,
  To baneful envy, and to wretched cares,
  In rural pleasures spend our happy days,
  And our soft nights in calm and quiet sleeps.   10
2ND SHEPHERD No rude ambition interrupts our rest,
  Nor base and guilty thoughts how to be great.
2ND NYMPH In humble cottages we have such contents,
  As uncorrupted Nature does afford,
  Which the great, that surfeit under gilded roofs,   15
  And wanton in down beds, can never know.
1ST SHEPHERD Nature is here not yet debauched by art,
  'Tis as it was in Saturn's happy days.*
  Minds are not here by luxury invaded:
  A homely plenty, with sharp appetite,   20
  Does lightsome health, and vigorous strength impart.
1ST NYMPH A chaste, cold spring does here refresh our
    thirst,
  Which by no feverish surfeit is increased;
  Our food is such as Nature meant for men,
  Ere, with the vicious, eating was an art.   25
2ND NYMPH In noisy cities riot is pursued
  And lewd luxurious living softens men,
  Effeminates fools in body and in mind,
  Weakens their appetites, and decays their nerves.
2ND SHEPHERD With filthy steams from their excess of
    meat,   30
  And cloudy vapours raised from dangerous wine;
  Their heads are never clear or free to think,

They waste their lives in a continual mist.

1ST SHEPHERD Some subtle and ill men choose
    temperance,
    Not as a virtue, but a bawd to vice,   35
    And vigilantly wait to ruin those,
    Whom luxury and ease have lulled asleep.

2ND SHEPHERD Yes, in the clamorous courts of tedious
    law,
    Where what is meant for a relief's a grievance;
    Or in kings' palaces, where cunning strives   40
    Not to advance kings' interests, but its own.

1ST NYMPH There, they in a continual hurry live,
    And seldom can, for all their subtle arts,
    Lay their foundations sure; but some
    Are undermined, others blown down by storms.   45

2ND NYMPH Their subtlety is but a common road
    Of flattering great men, and oppressing little,
    Smiling on all they meet, and loving none.

1ST SHEPHERD In populous cities, life is all a storm;
    But we enjoy a sweet perpetual calm.   50
    Here, our own flocks we keep, and here
    I and my Phyllis can embrace unenvied.

2ND SHEPHERD And I and Celia, without jealousy.
    But hark, the pipes begin; now for our sports.

             (*A symphony of rustic music*)

Nymphs and shepherds come away,   55
In these groves let's sport and play:
Where each day is a holy-day,
Sacred to ease and happy love;
To dancing, music, poetry.
Your flocks may now securely rove,   60
Whilst you express your jollity.

    (*Enter* SHEPHERDS *and* SHEPHERDESSES, *singing in*
                      chorus)

We come, we come, no joy like this.
Now let us sing, rejoice, and kiss.

The great can never know such bliss
1 As this.   65
2 As this.
3 As this.
ALL As this.
The great can never know such bliss.

1 All th' inhabitants o' th' wood,   70
   Now celebrate the spring,
   That gives fresh vigour to the blood
   Of every living thing.
   (*Chorus*) The birds have been singing and billing
      before us,
   And all the sweet choristers join in the chorus.   75

2 The nightingales with jugging throats,
   Warble out their pretty notes,
   So sweet, so sweet, so sweet:
   And thus our loves and pleasures greet.
   (*Chorus*) Then let our pipes sound, let us dance, let us
      sing,   80
   Till the murmuring groves with loud echoes shall ring.

(Dance begins)

3 How happy are we,
   From all jealousy free;
   No dangers or cares can annoy us.
   We toy and we kiss,   85
   And love's our chief bliss,
   A pleasure that never can cloy us.
   (*Chorus*) Our days we continue in unenvied delights,
   And in love and soft rest our happy long nights.

4 Each nymph does impart   90
   Her love without art,
   To her swain who thinks that his chief treasure.
   No envy is feared,
   No sighs are e'er heard,
   But those which are caused by our pleasure.   95
   (*Chorus*) When we feel the blessed raptures of innocent

love,
No joys exceed ours but the pleasures above.

(*General chorus*) In these delightful fragrant groves,
Let's celebrate our happy loves.
Let's pipe, and dance, and laugh, and sing;   100
Thus every happy living thing,
Revels in the cheerful spring.

(*Dance continues*)

(*Enter* DON JOHN, DON LOPEZ, DON ANTONIO,
JACOMO)

DON JOHN So, thus far we are safe, we have almost killed
    our horses with riding cross out of all roads.
JACOMO Nay, you had as little mercy on them as if they 105
    had been men or women. But yet we are not safe, let us fly
    farther.
DON JOHN The house I lighted at was mine during my life,
    which I sold to that fellow. He, since he holds by that
    tenure, will carefully conceal us.   110
JACOMO 'Tis a tenure I will not give him two months'
    purchase for.
DON JOHN Besides, our swords are used to conquest.
DON ANTONIO At worst, there is a church hard by; we'll
    put it to its proper use, take refuge in't.   115
DON LOPEZ Look, here are shepherds, and young pretty
    wenches; shall we be idle, Don?
DON ANTONIO By no means; 'tis a long time, methinks,
    since we were vicious.
DON JOHN We'll serve 'em as the Romans did the   120
    Sabines,* we'll rob 'em of their women. Only we'll return
    the punks again, when we have used 'em.
JACOMO For heaven's sake, hold.
DON JOHN Sirrah, no more. Do as we do: ravish, rascal, or
    by my sword, I'll cut thee into so many pieces, it shall   125
    pose an arithmetician to sum up the fractions of thy body.
JACOMO I, ravish! Oh, good sir! My courage lies not that
    way. Alas, I am almost famished, I have not eat today.

DON JOHN Sirrah, by heaven, do as I bid thee, or thou
shalt never eat again. Shall I keep a rascal for a cypher? 130
JACOMO Oh, what will become of me? I must do it.
DON JOHN Come on, rogue, fall on.
DON ANTONIO Which are you for?
DON JOHN 'Tis all one, I am not in love but in lust, and to
such a one a bellyful's a bellyful, and there's an end on't. 135
1ST SHEPHERDESS What means this violence?
2ND SHEPHERDESS Oh, heaven protect us!
JACOMO Well, I must have one too. If I be hanged, I had as
good be hanged for something.

(*Everyone runs off with a woman*)

DON LOPEZ Rogues, come not on; we'll be in your guts. 140
ALL SHEPHERDESSES Help, help!

(*They cry out*)

1ST SHEPHERD What devils are these?

[*Exeunt*]

(THREE *or* FOUR SHEPHERDS *return with* JACOMO)

1ST SHEPHERD Here's one rogue. Have we caught you,
sir? We'll cool your courage.
JACOMO Am I taken prisoner? I shall be kept as an 145
honourable hostage, at least –
2ND SHEPHERD Where are the villains, these ravishers?
JACOMO Why you need not keep such a stir, gentlemen,
you will have all your women again, and no harm done.
Let me go, I'll fetch 'em to you.   150
1ST SHEPHERD No, you libidinous swine; we'll revenge the
rapes on you.
JACOMO Good, kind, civil people pass this by. 'Tis true my
master's a very Tarquin;* but I ne'er attempted to ravish
before.   155
2ND SHEPHERD I'll secure you from ever doing of it again.
Where's your knife?
JACOMO Heaven! What do you mean? Oh spare me! I am
unprepared; let me be confessed.

1ST SHEPHERD We'll not kill you, we'll but geld 160
you. Are you so hot, sir?

JACOMO Oh, bloody villains! Have a care, 'tis not a season
for that, the sign's in Scorpio.*

2ND SHEPHERD Down with him –

JACOMO Oh help, help! Murder, murder! Have a care 165
what you do, I am the last of all my race – Will you
destroy a whole stock, and take away my representers of
my family?

1ST SHEPHERD There shall be no more of the breed of
you. 170

JACOMO I am of an ancient family. Will you cut off all
hopes of a son and heir? Help! help! Master! Don John!
Oh! Oh! Oh!

(*Enter* DON JOHN, DON LOPEZ, DON ANTONIO)

DON JOHN How now, rogues? Do you abuse my man?

<*The* SHEPHERDS *flee*>

JACOMO Oh, sir, this is the first good thing you ever did. If 175
you had not come just in the nick, I had lost my
manhood.

DON ANTONIO 'Tis no matter for the use you make on't.

DON LOPEZ But come, let's now to supper.

JACOMO Come on, I am almost starved. 180

[*Exeunt*]

(SHEPHERDS *return*)

1ST SHEPHERD Let's not complain, but dog the rogues;
and when we have housed 'em, we will to the next
magistrate, and beg his power to apprehend 'em.

[*Exeunt*]

Act 4, Scene 3

The scene changes to a church, with a statue of DON
PEDRO *on horseback in it*

(*Enter* DON JOHN, DON ANTONIO, DON LOPEZ,
JACOMO)

DON JOHN Let's in, and see this church.

JACOMO Is this a time to see churches? But let me see
whose statue's this? Oh, heaven! This is Don Pedro's,
whom you murdered at Seville.

DON JOHN Say you so? Read the inscription.   5

JACOMO 'Here lies Don Pedro, governor of Seville, barbarously murdered by that impious villain, Don John, 'gainst
whom his innocent blood cries still for vengeance.'

DON JOHN Let it cry on. Art thou there i'faith? Yes, I killed
thee, and would do't again upon the same occasion.   10
Jacomo, invite him to supper.

JACOMO What, a statue? Invite a statue to supper? Ha, ha
– can marble eat?

DON JOHN I say, rascal, tell him I would have him sup
with me.   15

JACOMO Ha, ha, ha! Who the devil put this whimsy into
your head? Ha, ha, ha! Invite a statue to supper?

DON JOHN I shall spoil your mirth, sirrah; I will have it
done.

JACOMO Why, 'tis impossible. Would you have me such a   20
coxcomb, invite marble to eat? Ha, ha, ha.

(*He goes several times towards the* STATUE, *and returns,
laughing*)

Good Mr Statue, if it shall please your worship, my
master desires you to make collation with him presently –

(*The* STATUE *nods his head,* JACOMO *falls down and
roars*)

Oh, I am dead! Oh, oh, oh!

DON JOHN The statue nods its head; 'tis odd.   25

DON ANTONIO 'Tis wonderful.

DON LOPEZ I am amazed.

JACOMO Oh, I cannot stir! Help, help!

DON JOHN Well, governor, come, take part of a collation
with me; 'tis by this time ready. Make haste, 'tis I invite   30
you.

(STATUE *nods again*)

Say you so? Come on, let's set all things in order quickly.

JACOMO Oh fly, fly.

DON ANTONIO This is prodigious.

[*Exeunt* DON JOHN, DON LOPEZ, DON ANTONIO,
JACOMO]

Act 4, Scene 4

The scene is a dining-room, a table spread, SERVANTS
setting meat and wine

(*Enter* DON JOHN, DON ANTONIO, DON LOPEZ,
JACOMO)

DON JOHN Come, our meat is ready, let's sit. Pox on this
foolish statue, it puzzles me to know the reason on't.
Sirrah, I'll give you leave to sit.

DON ANTONIO Let's eat, ne'er think on't.

JACOMO Aye, come, let's eat; I am too hungry now to   5
think on the fright.

(JACOMO *eats greedily*)

DON JOHN This is excellent meat. How the rogue eats.
You'll choke yourself.

JACOMO I warrant you, look to yourself.

DON ANTONIO Why, Jacomo, is the devil in you?   10

JACOMO No, no; if he be, 'tis a hungry devil.

DON LOPEZ Will you not drink?

JACOMO I'll lay a good foundation first.

DON JOHN The rascal eats like a cannibal.

JACOMO Aye, 'tis no matter for that.   15

DON JOHN Some wine, sirrah.

JACOMO There, sir, take it; I am in haste.

DON ANTONIO 'Sdeath, the fool will be strangled.

JACOMO The fool knows what he does.

DON JOHN Here's to Don Pedro's ghost, he should have   20
been welcome!

JACOMO Oh, name him not.

DON LOPEZ The rascal is afraid of you after death.

JACOMO (*almost choked*) Oh! Oh! Some wine, give me
some wine.   25

DON ANTONIO Take it.

JACOMO So, now 'tis down.

DON ANTONIO Are you not satisfied yet?

JACOMO Peace, peace; I have but just begun.

(*One knocks hard at the door*)

Who's there? Come in, I am very busy.   30

DON JOHN Rise, and do your duty.

JACOMO But one morsel more, I come.

(*Knocks again*)

What a pox, are you mad?

(*Opens the door*)

(*Enter* GHOST)

Oh! The devil, the devil!

DON JOHN Hah! It is the ghost, let's rise and receive him. 35

DON ANTONIO I am amazed.

DON LOPEZ Not frighted are you?

DON ANTONIO I scorn the thoughts of fear.

(*They salute the* GHOST)

DON JOHN Come, governor, you are welcome, sit there. If
we had thought you would have come, we would have   40
stayed for you. But come on, sirrah, give me some wine.

(*The* GHOST *sits*)

JACOMO Oh! I am dead! What shall I do? I dare not come near you.

DON JOHN Come, rascal, or I'll cut your throat.

JACOMO I come, I come. Oh! Oh!   45

       (*Fills wine, his hand trembles*)

DON JOHN Why do you tremble, rascal? Hold it steadily.

JACOMO Oh! I cannot.

(JACOMO *snatches meat from the table, and runs aside*)

DON JOHN Here, governor, your health. Friends, put it about. Here's excellent meat; taste of this ragout.* If you had a body of flesh, I would have given you *cher entire*,*   50
but the women care not for marble. Come, I'll help you. Come, eat and let old quarrels be forgotten.

GHOST I come not here to take repast with you.
Heaven has permitted me to animate
This marble body, and I come to warn   55
You of that vengeance is in store for you,
If you amend not your pernicious lives.

JACOMO Oh, heaven!

DON ANTONIO What, are you come to preach to us?

DON LOPEZ Keep your harangues for fools that will believe   60
'em.

DON JOHN We are too much confirmed. Pox o' this dry discourse, give me some wine. Come, here's to your mistress! You had one when you were living. Not forgetting your sweet sister. Sirrah, more wine.   65

JACOMO Aye, sir. Good sir, do not provoke the ghost; his marble fists may fly about your ears, and knock your brains out.

DON JOHN Peace, fool.

GHOST Tremble, you impious wretches, and repent;   70
Behold the powers of hell wait for you.

       (DEVILS *rise*)

JACOMO Oh! I will steal from hence. Oh, the devil!

DON JOHN Sirrah, stir not; by heaven I'll use thee worse

than devils can do. Come near, coward.

JACOMO Oh, I dare not stir; what will become of me?   75

DON JOHN Come, sirrah, eat.

JACOMO Oh, sir, my appetite is satisfied.

DON JOHN Drink, dog, the ghost's health. Rogue, do't, or
I'll run my sword down your throat.

JACOMO Oh! Oh! Here, Mr Statue, your health.   80

DON JOHN Now, rascal, sing to entertain him.

JACOMO Sing, quoth he! Oh! I have lost my voice. I cannot
be merry in such company. Sing!

DON ANTONIO Who are these with ugly shapes?

DON LOPEZ Their manner of appearing is something   85
strange.

GHOST They're devils that wait for such hard impious men.
They're heaven's instruments of eternal vengeance.

DON JOHN Are they some of your retinue? Devils, say you?
I am sorry I have no burnt brandy to treat 'em with, that's   90
drink fit for devils. Hah! They vanish!

(*They sink*)

GHOST Cannot the fear of hell's eternal tortures,
Change the horrid course of your abandoned lives?
Think on those fires, those everlasting fires,
That shall without consuming, burn you ever.   95

DON JOHN Dreams, dreams, too slight to lose my
pleasure for.
In spite of all you say I will go on,
Till I have surfeited on all delights.
Youth is a fruit that can but once be gathered,
And I'll enjoy it to the full.   100

DON ANTONIO Let's push it on. Nature chalks out the way
that we should follow.

DON LOPEZ 'Tis her fault, if we do what we should not.
Let's on, here's a brimmer to our leader's health.

JACOMO What hellish fiends are these?   105

DON JOHN Let me tell you, 'tis something ill bred to rail at
your host, that treats you civilly. You have not yet forgot
your quarrel to me.

GHOST 'Tis for your good. By me heaven warns you of its
wrath, and gives you a longer time for your repentance. I   110
invite you this night to a repast of mine.

DON JOHN Where?

GHOST At my tomb.

DON ANTONIO What time?

GHOST At dead of night.   115

DON JOHN We'll come.

GHOST Fail not.

DON LOPEZ I warrant you.

GHOST Farewell, and think upon your lost condition.

DON JOHN Farewell, governor; I'll see what treat you'll   120
give us.

DON ANTONIO ⎫
DON LOPEZ   ⎬ And I.

JACOMO That will not I. Pox on him, I have had enough of
his company, I shall not recover it this week. If I eat with
such an host, I'll be hanged.   125

DON JOHN If you do not, by heaven you shall be hanged.

JACOMO Whither will your lewdness carry me? I do not
care for having a ghost for my landlord. Will not these
miracles do good upon you?

DON JOHN There's nothing happens but by natural
causes,   130
Which in unusual things fools cannot find,
And then they style 'em miracles. But no accident
Can alter me from what I am by nature.
Were there –
Legions of ghosts and devils in my way,   135
One moment in my course of pleasure I'd not stay.

[*Exeunt omnes*]

Act 5, Scene 1

(*Enter* JACOMO, *with back, breast and headpiece*)

JACOMO Well, this damned master of mine will not part
with me; and we must fight five or six times a day, one

day with another, that's certain. Therefore, thou art wise,
honest Jacomo, to arm thyself, I take it. Sa, sa, sa –
Methinks I am very valiant on the sudden. Sa, sa, sa.   5
Hah! There I have you. Paph – Have at you! Hah – there,
I have you through. That was a fine thrust in tierce.* Hah
– Death! What noise is that?

(*Enter* DON JOHN)

DON JOHN How now, sirrah, what are you doing?
JACOMO Nothing, but practising to run people through the   10
bodies, that's all; for I know somebody's throat must be
cut, before midnight.
DON JOHN In armour, too! Why, that cannot help you,
you are such a cowardly fool. Fear will betray you faster
within, than that can defend you without.   15
JACOMO I fear nobody breathing, I! Nothing can terrify me
but the devilish ghost. Ha! Who's that coming? Oh,
heaven!

(*Leaps back*)

DON JOHN Is this your courage? You are preparing for
flight before an enemy appears.   20
JACOMO No, no, sir, not I. I only leapt back to put myself
upon my guard. Fa, la, la –

(*Enter* DON LOPEZ *and* DON ANTONIO)

DON JOHN Whom have we here?
JACOMO Oh, where, where, where? Who are they?
DON JOHN Oh, my friends! Where have you been?   25
DON ANTONIO We went to view the stately nunnery hard
by, and have been chatting with the poor sanctified fools
till it's dark. We have been chaffering* for nuns'-flesh.
DON LOPEZ There, I made such a discovery; if you do not
assist me, I am ruined forever. Don Bernardo's sister,   30
whom I fell in love with in Seville, is this day placed there
for probation; and if you cannot advise me to some way
or other of getting her out, for some present occasion I
have for her, I am a lost man, that's certain.

DON ANTONIO The business is difficult, and we resolve to 35
manage it in council.

JACOMO (*aside*) Now will they bring me into some wicked
occasion or other of showing my prowess. A pox on 'em.

DON JOHN Have you so long followed my fortunes to
boggle at difficulty upon so honourable an occasion? 40
Besides, here is no difficulty.

DON LOPEZ No? The walls are so high, and the nunnery so
strongly fortified, 'twill be impossible to do it by force; we
must find some stratagem.

DON JOHN The stratagem is soon found out. 45

DON ANTONIO As how, Don John?

DON JOHN Why, I will set fire on the nunnery; fire the hive,
and the drones must out, or be burnt within. Then may
you, with ease, under pretence of succour, take whom you
will. 50

DON LOPEZ 'Tis a gallant design.

DON ANTONIO I long to be about it. Well, Don, thou art
the bravest fellow breathing.

JACOMO Gentlemen, pray what became of that brave
fellow that fired the temple at Ephesus?* Was he not 55
hanged, gentlemen, hum?

DON ANTONIO We are his rivals, fool; and who would not
suffer for so brave an action?

DON JOHN He's a scoundrel and a poltroon that would
not have his death for his fame. 60

DON LOPEZ That he is, a damned son of a whore, and not
fit to drink with.

JACOMO 'Tis a rare thing to be a martyr for the devil. But
what good will infamy do you when you are dead; when
honour is nothing but a vapour to you, while you are 65
living? For my part I'd not be hanged to be Alexander the
Great.

DON ANTONIO What a phlegmatic, dull rascal is that, who
has no ambition in him.

JACOMO Ambition! What, to be hanged? Besides, what's 70
the intrinsic value of honour when a man is under
ground? Let 'em but call me honest Jacomo, as I am,

while I live, and let 'em call me, when I am dead, Don
John if they will.

DON JOHN Villain, dare you profane my name?   75

JACOMO Hold, sir, think what you do. You cannot hurt
me, my arms are pistol-proof.

(*Enter a* SERVANT)

SERVANT I come to give you notice of an approaching
danger. You must fly. An officer with some shepherds
have found you were at our house, and are come to   80
apprehend you, for some outrage you have committed. I
came to give you notice, knowing our family has a great
respect for you.

DON JOHN Yes, I know your family has a great respect for
me; for I have lain with everyone in it, but thee and thy   85
master.

JACOMO Why look you now, I thought what 'twould come
to. Fly, sir, fly; the darkness of the night will help us.
Come, I'll lead the way.

DON JOHN Stay, sirrah, you shall have one occasion more   90
of showing your valour.

DON ANTONIO Did ever any knight errant fly, that was so
well appointed?

DON LOPEZ No, you shall stay and get honour, Jacomo.

JACOMO Pox of honour, I am content with the stock I have 95
already.

DON JOHN You are easily satisfied. But now let's fire the
nunnery.

DON ANTONIO Come on.

DON LOPEZ I long to be at it.   100

JACOMO Oh, Jacomo, thy life is not worth a piece of eight!
'Tis in vain to dissuade 'em, sir. I will never trouble you
with another request, if you'll be graciously pleased to
leave me out of this adventure.

DON JOHN Well, you have your desire.   105

JACOMO A thousand thanks; and when I see you again, I
will be humbly content with a halter.

DON JOHN But, do you hear, fool: stand sentinel here; and
if anything happens extraordinary, give us notice of it.

JACOMO Oh, good sir, what do you mean? That's as bad 110
as going with you.

DON JOHN Let me find you here when I come again, or you
are a dead man.

[*Exeunt* DON JOHN, DON LOPEZ, DON ANTONIO]

JACOMO I am sure I am a dead man, if you find me here.
But would my armour were off now, that I might run the 115
lighter. Night assist me. Heaven! What noise is that? To
be left alone in the dark, and fear ghosts and devils, is
very horrible. But oh! Who are these?

(*Enter* OFFICER, GUARDS, *and* SHEPHERDS)

1ST SHEPHERD We are thus far right; the ravishers went
this way.   120

2ND SHEPHERD For heaven's sake take 'em, dead or alive;
such desperate villains ne'er were seen.

JACOMO So: if I be catched, I shall be hanged; if not, I shall
be killed. 'Tis very fine. These are the shepherds. I'll hide
myself.   125

(*He stands up close against the wall*)

1ST SHEPHERD If we catch the rogues, we will broil
'em alive; no death can be painful enough for such
wretches.

JACOMO O bloody-minded men –

2ND SHEPHERD O impious, vile wretches! That we had 130
you in our clutches! Open your dark lantern, and let's
search for 'em.

JACOMO What will become of me? My armour will not do
now.

1ST SHEPHERD Thus far we hunted them upon a good 135
scent; but now we are at a fault.

JACOMO Let me see; I have one trick left. I have a disguise
will fright the devil.

2ND SHEPHERD They must be hereabouts.

JACOMO I'll in amongst them, and certainly this will fright 140
'em.

1ST SHEPHERD Oh, heaven! What horrid object's this?

JACOMO The devil.

2ND SHEPHERD Oh fly, fly! The devil, the devil! Fly!

[*Exeunt* SHEPHERDS, *frighted*]

JACOMO Farewell, good gentlemen. This is the first time 145
my face e'er did me good. But I'll not stay, I take it. Yet
whither shall I fly? Oh, what noise is that? I am in the
dark, in a strange place too. What will follow? There lie,
O my arms! Hah! Who's there? Let me go this way – Oh,
the ghost! Oh, the ghost! Gad forgive me, 'twas nothing 150
but my fear.

(*A noise within, 'Fire, fire, the nunnery's on fire'*)

Oh, vile wretches! They have done the deed. There is no
flying: now the place will be full of people, and wicked
lights that will discover me, if I fly.

WITHIN Fire, fire, fire! The nunnery's on fire. Help, help! 155

(SEVERAL PEOPLE *cross the stage, crying 'Fire'*)

JACOMO What shall I do? There's no way but one. I'll go
with the crowd. Fire! Fire – Murder! Help! Help! Fire!
Fire!

(MORE PEOPLE *cross the stage, he runs with them*)

(*Enter* DON JOHN, DON ANTONIO, DON LOPEZ, FOUR
NUNS)

DON JOHN Fear not, ladies, we'll protect you.

1ST NUN Our sex and habits will protect us.   160

DON JOHN Not enough, we will protect you better.

1ST NUN Pray leave us, we must not consort with men.

DON ANTONIO What, would you run into the fire to avoid
mankind? You are zealous ladies, indeed.

DON JOHN Come, ladies, walk with us; we'll put you in a 165
place of safety.

1ST NUN We'll go no further, we are safe enough. Be gone,

and help to quench the fire.

DON JOHN We have another fire to quench; come along
with us.   170

DON LOPEZ Aye, come, you must go.

DON ANTONIO Come along, we know what's good for
you; you must go with us.

1ST NUN Heaven! What violence is this? What impious
men are these? Help! Help!   175

(*All cry 'Help'*)

(*Enter* FLAVIA *and* CLARA <*as*> *probationers*)*

FLAVIA Here are the bloody villains, the causes of our
misery.

CLARA Inhuman butchers! Now we'll have your lives.

DON JOHN Hah! Here are a brace of my wives. If you have
a mind to this fool, take her betwixt you; for my part, I'll   180
have my own. Come, wives, along with me; we must
consummate, my spouses, we must consummate.

CLARA What monsters are these?

ALL NUNS Help! Help!

DON ANTONIO 'Sdeath! These foolish women are their   185
own enemies.

DON LOPEZ Here are so many people, if they cry out more,
they'll interrupt us in our brave design.

DON JOHN I warrant you. When they cry out, let us out-
noise 'em. Come, women, you must go along with us.   190

1ST NUN Heaven! What shall we do? Help! Help!

DON JOHN Help! Help! Fire! Fire! Fire!

DON LOPEZ
                          } Help! Help!
DON ANTONIO

(*They hale the* WOMEN *by the hands, who still cry out,
and they with them*)

(*Enter* SEVERAL PEOPLE, *crying out 'Fire',* JACOMO *in
the rear*)

JACOMO Fire! Fire! Fire! Help! Help! (*aside*) 'Sdeath, here's
my master!   195

DON JOHN Sirrah, come along with me, I have use of you.

JACOMO I am caught.

DON JOHN Here, sirrah, take one of my wives, and force her after me. Do you refuse, villain?

(*Enter* SHEPHERDS, *with* OFFICER *and* GUARDS)

NUNS Help, help! Good people, help! Rescue us from 200 these villains.

1ST SHEPHERD Who are you, committing violence on women?

2ND SHEPHERD Heavens! They are the villains we seek for. 205

JACOMO Where is my armour now? Oh, my armour.

OFFICER Fall on.

(*They fight.* WOMEN *fly;* JACOMO *falls down as killed;* TWO SHEPHERDS *and the* OFFICER *are killed*)

DON JOHN Say you so, rogues?

DON LOPEZ So, the field's our own.

DON JOHN But a pox on't, we have bought a victory too 210 dear, we have lost the women.

DON ANTONIO We'll find 'em again. But poor Jacomo's kill'd.

JACOMO (*aside*) That's a lie.

DON LOPEZ Faith, let's carry off our dead. 215

DON JOHN Agreed; we'll bury him in the church. While the ghost treats us, we'll treat the worms with the body of a rascal.

JACOMO (*aside*) Not yet awhile.

DON ANTONIO Let's take away the fool. 220

JACOMO No, the fool can take up himself. 'Sdeath, you resolve not to let me alone dead or alive!
Here are more murders. Oh!

DON LOPEZ Oh, counterfeiting rascal! Are you alive?

(*The clock strikes twelve*)

DON ANTONIO The clock strikes twelve. 225

DON JOHN 'Slife, our time's come, we must to the tomb; I

would not break my word with the ghost for a thousand
doubloons.

JACOMO Nor I keep it for ten times the money.

DON JOHN But you shall keep your word, sir.   230

JACOMO Sir, I am resolved to fast tonight, 'tis a vigil.
Besides, I care not for eating in such base company.

WITHIN Follow, follow, follow.

DON LOPEZ D'ye hear that noise? The remaining rogues
have raised the mobile* and are coming upon us.   235

JACOMO Oh! Let's fly – fly! What will become of me?

DON ANTONIO Let's to the church, and give the rogues the
go-by.

DON JOHN Come on; since 'tis my time and I have
promised the governor, I'll go. You had best stay, sirrah, 240
and be taken.

JACOMO No. Now must I to the church whether I will or
no. Away, away, fly!

(*Enter* TWO SHEPHERDS, *with a great* RABBLE)

<SHEPHERDS> Here they went. Follow, follow!

[*Exeunt omnes*]

Act 5, Scene 2

The scene: the church; the statue of DON PEDRO *on
horseback. On each side of the church:* DON JOHN'S
<FATHER'S> GHOST; <GHOSTS *of* >MARIA, DON
FRANCISCO, LEONORA, FLORA, MARIA'S BROTHER *and*
OTHERS, *with torches in their hands*

(*Enter* DON JOHN, DON ANTONIO, DON LOPEZ, JACOMO)

JACOMO Good sir, let's go no farther. Look what horrid
attendants are here. This wicked ghost has no good
meaning in him.

DON JOHN He resolves to treat us in state. I think he has
robbed all the graves hereabouts of their dead, to wait   5
upon us.

DON ANTONIO I see no entertainment prepared.

DON LOPEZ He has had the manners to light off his horse
and entertain us.

DON JOHN He would not sure be so ill bred, to make us   10
wait on him on foot.

JACOMO Pox on his breeding, I shall die with fear. I had as
good have been taken and hanged. What horror seizes
me!

DON JOHN Well, governor, you see we are as good as our   15
words.

DON ANTONIO Where's your collation?

DON LOPEZ Bid some of your attendants give us some
wine.

(GHOST *descends*)

STATUE Have you not thought yet on your lost
condition?   20
Here are the ghosts of some whom you have
murdered,
That cry for vengeance on you.

FATHER'S GHOST Repent, repent of all your horrid
crimes.
Monster, repent, or hell will swallow you.

DON JOHN That's my old man's voice. D'ye hear, old   25
gentleman, you talk idly.

JACOMO I do repent. Oh, spare me! I do repent of all my
sins, but especially of following this wicked wretch.

(*Kneels*)

DON ANTONIO (*kicks him*) Away, fool!

DON FRANCISCO'S GHOST My blood cries out upon thee,   30
barbarous wretch.

DON JOHN That's my host Francisco; 'faith thou wert a
good honest blockhead, that's the truth on't.

FLORA'S GHOST Thou shalt not escape vengeance for all
thy crimes.   35

DON JOHN What fool's that? I am not acquainted with her.

LEONORA'S GHOST In time lay hold on mercy, and repent.

DON JOHN That was Leonora, a good-natured, silly wench; something too loving, that was all her fault.

MARIA Villain, this is the last moment of thy life, 40
And thou in flames eternally shall howl.

DON JOHN Thou liest. This is the young hot-headed fool we killed at Francisco's. Pox on him, he disappointed me in my design upon the daughters. Would thou wert alive again, that I might kill thee once more. 45

DON LOPEZ No more of this old foolish stuff; give us some wine to begin with.

DON ANTONIO Aye, give us some wine, governor.

DON JOHN What, do you think to treat us thus? I offered you a better entertainment. Prithee, trouble us no more, 50 but bid some of your attendants give us some wine. I'll drink to you and all the good company.

STATUE Give 'em the liquor they have most delighted in.

(TWO *of the* GHOSTS *go out, and bring four glasses full of blood, then give 'em to* DON JOHN, DON ANTONIO, DON LOPEZ)

DON LOPEZ This is something.

DON JOHN This is civil. 55

DON LOPEZ I hope a good dessert will follow.

(GHOST *offers a glass to* JACOMO, *who runs round* DON JOHN, DON ANTONIO, DON LOPEZ, *roaring*)

JACOMO Are you stark distracted? Will you drink of that liquor? Oh! Oh! What d'you mean? Good, sweet ghost, forbear your civility. Oh, I am not dry I thank you –

DON JOHN Give it me. Here, take it, sirrah. 60

JACOMO By no means, sir. I never drink between meals. Oh, sir –

DON JOHN Take it, rascal.

JACOMO Oh, heavens!

DON JOHN Now, governor, your health; 'tis the reddest 65 drink I ever saw.

DON LOPEZ Hah! Pah! 'Tis blood.

DON ANTONIO Pah! It is.

JACOMO Oh! I'll have none of it.

   (*They throw the glasses down*)

DON JOHN 'Sdeath, do you mean to affront us?   70

STATUE 'Tis fit for such blood-thirsty wretches.

DON JOHN Do you upbraid me with my killing of you? I
 did it, and would do it again. I'd fight with all your family
 one by one; and cut off root and branch to enjoy your
 sister. But will you treat us yet no otherwise? 75

STATUE Yes, I will, ye impious wretches.

   (*A flourish*)

DON LOPEZ What's here? Music to treat us with?

DON ANTONIO There is some pleasure in this.

SONG OF DEVILS

1ST DEVIL Prepare, prepare, new guests draw near,
 And on the brink of hell appear.   80

2ND DEVIL Kindle fresh flames of sulphur there;
 Assemble all ye fiends:
 Wait for the dreadful end
 Of impious men, who far excel
 All th'inhabitants of hell.   85

CHORUS OF DEVILS Let 'em come, let 'em come;
 To an eternal, dreadful doom,
 Let 'em come, let 'em come.

3RD DEVIL In mischiefs they have all the damned
 outdone;
 Here they shall weep, and shall unpitied groan, 90
 Here they shall howl, and make eternal moan.

1ST DEVIL By blood and lust they have deserved so
 well,
 That they shall feel the hottest flames of hell.

2ND DEVIL In vain they shall here their past mischiefs
 bewail,
 In exquisite torments that never shall fail. 95

3RD DEVIL Eternal darkness they shall find,
 And them eternal chains shall bind

To infinite pain of sense and mind.

CHORUS OF ALL Let 'em come, let 'em come;
To an eternal dreadful doom,   100
Let 'em come, let 'em come.

STATUE Will you not relent, and feel remorse?
DON JOHN Couldst thou bestow another heart on me, I
might; but with this heart I have, I cannot.
DON LOPEZ These things are prodigious.   105
DON ANTONIO I have a kind of grudging to relent, but
something holds me back.
DON LOPEZ If we could, 'tis now too late; I will not.
DON ANTONIO We defy thee.
STATUE Perish, ye impious wretches, go and find   110
The punishments laid up in store for you.

(*It thunders;* DON LOPEZ *and* DON ANTONIO *are
swallowed up*)

Behold their dreadful fates, and know that thy last
moment's come.
DON JOHN Think not to fright me, foolish ghost; I'll break
your marble body in pieces, and pull down your horse.
JACOMO If fear has left me my strength, I'll steal away.   115
[*Exit*]

DON JOHN These things I see with wonder, but no fear.
Were all the elements to be confounded,
And shuffled all into their former chaos;
Were seas of sulphur flaming round about me,
And all mankind roaring within those fires,   120
I could not fear or feel the least remorse.
To the last instant I would dare thy power.
Here I stand firm, and all thy threats contemn;
Thy murderer stands here, now do thy worst.

(*It thunders and lightens,* DEVILS *descend and sink with*
DON JOHN, *who is covered with a cloud of fire as he
sinks*)

STATUE Thus perish all   125

Those men who, by their words and actions, dare
Against the will and power of heaven, declare.

(*Scene shuts*)

Epilogue

(*Spoken by* JAÇOMO)

Through all the perils of the play I've run,
But know not how your fury I may shun.
I'm in new dangers now to be undone:
I had but one fierce master there,
But I have many cruel tyrants here   5
Who do most bloodily my life pursue;
Who takes my livelihood, may take that too.
'Gainst little players you great factions raise,
Make solemn leagues and cov'nants* against plays.
We, who by no allies assisted are,   10
Against the great confederates must make war.
You need not strive our province to o'errun,
By our own stratagems we are undone.
We've laid out all our pains, nay, wealth for you,
And yet, hard-hearted men, all will not do.   15
'Tis not your judgements sway, for you can be
Pleased with damned plays as heart can wish to see.
'Ounds, we do what we can, what would you more?
Why do you come, and rant, and damn, and roar?
'Sdeath, what a devil would you have us do?   20
Each take a prison, and there humbly sue,
Angling for single money with a shoe?*
What, will you be Don Johns? Have you no remorse?
Farewell, then, bloody men, and take your course.
Yet stay –   25
If you be civil, we will treat of peace,
And th'articles o'th'treaty shall be these:
'First: to the men of wit we all submit;
The rest shall swagger too within the pit,
And may roar out their little or no wit.   30
But do not swear so loud to fright the city,
Who neither care for wicked men, nor witty;
They start at ills they do not like to do,

But shall in shops be wickeder than you.
Next: you'll no more be troubled with machines.   35
Item: you shall appear behind our scenes,
And there make love with the sweet chink of guineas,
The unresisted eloquence of ninnies.
Some of our women shall be kind to you,
And promise free ingress and egress too.   40
But if the faces which we have won't do,
We will find out some of sixteen for you.
We will be civil when nought else will win ye;
We will new bait our trap, and that will bring ye.'
Come, faith, let all old breaches now be healed,   45
And the said articles shall be signed and sealed.

THE ROVER
or
THE BANISHED CAVALIERS

A COMEDY

BY

APHRA BEHN

Prologue

Wits, like physicians, never can agree
When of a different society.*
And Rabel's drops* were never more cried down
By all the learned doctors of the town,
Than a new play whose author is unknown.   5
Nor can those doctors with more malice sue
(And powerful purses) the dissenting few,
Than those with an insulting pride do rail
At all who are not of their own cabal.*
    If a young poet hit your humour right,   10
You judge him then out of revenge and spite.
So amongst men there are ridiculous elves,*
Who monkeys hate for being too like themselves.
So that the reason of the grand debate,
Why wit so oft is damned when good plays take,   15
Is that you censure as you love, or hate.
    Thus like a learned conclave poets sit,
Catholic* judges both of sense and wit,
And damn or save as they themselves think fit.
Yet those who to others' faults are so severe,   20
Are not so perfect but themselves may err.
Some write correct indeed, but then the whole
(Bating* their own dull stuff i' th' play) is stole.
As bees do suck from flowers their honeydew,
So they rob others, striving to please you.   25
    Some write their characters genteel and fine,
But then they do so toil for every line,
That what to you does easy seem and plain,
Is the hard issue of their labouring brain.
And some th'effects of all their pains we see,   30
Is but to mimic good extempore.
Others by long converse about the town,
Have wit enough to write a lewd lampoon,
But their chief skill lies in a bawdy song.
In short, the only wit that's now in fashion,   35

Is but the gleanings of good conversation.
As for the author of this coming play,
I asked him* what he thought fit I should say,
In thanks for your good company today:
He called me fool, and said it was well known,   40
You came not here for our sakes, but your own.
New plays are stuffed with wits, and with debauches,
That crowd and sweat like cits* in May-Day coaches.*

                    Written by a person of quality.

DRAMATIS PERSONAE

The play's first recorded performance was in March 1677 at the Dorset Garden Theatre by the Duke's Company with the cast listed below.

DON ANTONIO the viceroy's son*	Mr Jevon
DON PEDRO a noble Spaniard, his friend	Mr Medbourne
BELVILE an English colonel in love with Florinda	Mr Betterton
WILLMORE the Rover	Mr Smith
FREDERICK an English gentleman, and friend to Belvile and Blunt	Mr Crosby
BLUNT an English country gentleman	Mr Underhill
STEPHANO servant to Don Pedro	Mr Richards
PHILIPPO Lucetta's gallant	Mr Percival
SANCHO pimp to Lucetta	Mr John Lee
BISKEY SEBASTIAN } two bravoes* to Angellica	
OFFICERS and SOLDIERS,	
<DIEGO> page to Don Antonio	
FLORINDA sister to Don Pedro	Mrs Betterton
HELLENA a gay young woman designed for a nun, and sister to Florinda	Mrs Barry*
VALERIA a kinswoman to Florinda	Mrs Hughes
ANGELLICA BIANCA a famous courtesan	Mrs Quin
MORETTA her woman	Mrs Leigh
CALLIS governess to Florinda and Hellena	Mrs Norris
LUCETTA a jilting wench	Mrs Gillow

SERVANTS, OTHER MASQUERADERS (Men and Women)

Scene: Naples, in carnival time

Act 1, Scene 1

A chamber

(Enter FLORINDA and HELLENA)

FLORINDA What an impertinent thing is a young girl bred in
a nunnery! How full of questions! Prithee no more,
Hellena, I have told thee more than thou understand'st
already.

HELLENA The more's my grief. I would fain know as much   5
as you, which makes me so inquisitive; nor is't enough I
know you're a lover, unless you tell me too, who 'tis you
sigh for.

FLORINDA When you're a lover, I'll think you fit for a
secret of that nature.   10

HELLENA 'Tis true, I never was a lover yet – but I begin to
have a shrewd guess what 'tis to be so, and fancy it very
pretty to sigh and sing, and blush and wish, and dream
and wish, and long and wish to see the man; and when I
do, look pale and tremble; just as you did when my   15
brother brought home the fine English colonel to see you
– what do you call him, Don Belvile?

FLORINDA Fie, Hellena.

HELLENA That blush betrays you – I am sure 'tis so – or is
it Don Antonio, the viceroy's son? Or perhaps the rich old   20
Don Vincentio, whom my father designs you for a
husband? Why do you blush again?

FLORINDA With indignation, and how near soever my
father thinks I am to marrying that hated object, I shall let
him see I understand better what's due to my beauty,   25
birth and fortune, and more to my soul, than to obey
those unjust commands.

HELLENA Now hang me, if I don't love thee for that dear
disobedience. I love mischief strangely, as most of our sex
do who are come to love nothing else – but tell me, dear   30
Florinda, don't you love that fine *Anglese*?* – For I vow,

next to loving him myself, 'twill please me most that you do, for he is so gay and so handsome.

FLORINDA Hellena, a maid designed for a nun ought not to be so curious in a discourse of love.   35

HELLENA And dost thou think that ever I'll be a nun? Or at least till I'm so old, I'm fit for nothing else – faith no, sister; and that which makes me long to know whether you love Belvile, is because I hope he has some mad companion or other that will spoil my devotion. Nay,   40 I'm resolved to provide myself this carnival, if there be e'er a handsome proper* fellow of my humour above ground, though I ask first.

FLORINDA Prithee be not so wild.

HELLENA Now you have provided yourself of a man you   45 take no care for poor me – prithee tell me, what dost thou see about me that is unfit for love? Have I not a world of youth? A humour gay? A beauty passable? A vigour desirable? Well-shaped? Clean-limbed? Sweet-breathed? And sense enough to know how all these ought to be   50 employed to the best advantage? Yes, I do, and will. Therefore lay aside your hopes of my fortune by my being a devote,* and tell me how you came acquainted with this Belvile – for I perceive you knew him before he came to Naples.   55

FLORINDA Yes, I knew him at the siege of Pamplona.* He was then a colonel of French horse,* who, when the town was ransacked, nobly treated my brother and myself, preserving us from all insolences; and I must own (besides great obligations) I have I know not what that pleads   60 kindly for him about my heart, and will suffer no other to enter. – But see, my brother.

(*Enter* DON PEDRO, STEPHANO *with a masquing habit,** *and* CALLIS)

PEDRO Good morrow, sister – pray, when saw you your lover Don Vincentio?

FLORINDA I know not, sir – Callis, when was he here? For   65 I consider it so little, I know not when it was.

PEDRO I have a command from my father here to tell you you ought not to despise him, a man of so vast a fortune, and such a passion for you – Stephano, my things.

(Puts on his masquing habit)

FLORINDA A passion for me? 'Tis more than e'er I saw, or   70
he had a desire should be known. I hate Vincentio, sir, and I would not have a man so dear to me as my brother follow the ill custom of our country, and make a slave of his sister – and, sir, my father's will I'm sure you may divert.   75

PEDRO I know not how dear I am to you, but I wish only to be ranked in your esteem equal with the English colonel Belvile – why do you frown and blush? Is there any guilt belongs to the name of that cavalier?

FLORINDA I'll not deny I value Belvile. When I was   80
exposed to such dangers as the licensed lust of common soldiers threatened, when rage and conquest flew through the city; then Belvile, this criminal for my sake, threw himself into all dangers to save my honour, and will not you allow him my esteem?   85

PEDRO Yes, pay him what you will in honour – but you must consider Don Vincentio's fortune, and the jointure* he'll make you.

FLORINDA Let him consider my youth, beauty and fortune, which ought not to be thrown away on his age and   90
jointure.

PEDRO 'Tis true he's not so young and fine a gentleman as that Belvile – but what jewels will that cavalier present you with? Those of his eyes and heart?

HELLENA And are not those better than any Don Vincentio   95
has brought from the Indies?

PEDRO Why, how now! Has your nunnery breeding taught you to understand the value of hearts and eyes?

HELLENA Better than to believe Vincentio's deserve value from any woman – he may perhaps increase her bags* but   100
not her family.

PEDRO This is fine! Go – up to your devotion. You are not
designed for the conversation of lovers.

HELLENA (*aside*) Nor saints yet awhile, I hope. – Is't not
enough you make a nun of me, but you must cast my 105
sister away too, exposing her to a worse confinement than
a religious life?

PEDRO The girl's mad! It is a confinement to be carried
into the country, to an ancient villa belonging to the
family of the Vincentios these five hundred years, and 110
have no other prospect than that pleasing one of seeing all
her own that meets her eyes – a fine air, large fields, and
gardens, where she may walk and gather flowers!

HELLENA When, by moonlight? For I am sure she dares not
encounter with the heat of the sun. That were a task only 115
for Don Vincentio and his Indian breeding,* who loves it
in the dog days.* And if these be her daily divertisements,
what are those of the night? To lie in a wide moth-eaten
bedchamber, with furniture in the fashion in the reign of
King Sancho the First;* – the bed, that which his 120
forefathers lived and died in.

PEDRO Very well.

HELLENA This apartment (new furbished and fitted out for
the young wife), he (out of freedom) makes his dressing-
room, and being a frugal and jealous coxcomb, instead of 125
a valet to uncase* his feeble carcass, he desires you to do
that office – signs of favour I'll assure you, and such as
you must not hope for unless your woman be out of the
way.

PEDRO Have you done yet?   130

HELLENA That honour being past, the giant stretches itself,
yawns and sighs a belch or two loud as a musket, throws
himself into bed, and expects you in his foul sheets, and
ere you can get yourself undressed, calls you with a snore
or two – and are not these fine blessings to a young lady? 135

PEDRO Have you done yet?

HELLENA And this man you must kiss, nay you must kiss
none but him, too – and nuzzle through his beard to find

his lips. And this you must submit to for threescore years, and all for a jointure.   140

PEDRO For all your character of Don Vincentio, she is as like to marry him as she was before.

HELLENA Marry Don Vincentio! Hang me! Such a wedlock would be worse than adultery with another man. I had rather see her in the Hôtel de Dieu,* to waste her youth 145 there in vows, and be a handmaid to lazars and cripples, than to lose it in such a marriage.

PEDRO You have considered, sister, that Belvile has no fortune to bring you to, banished his country, despised at home, and pitied abroad.   150

HELLENA What then? The viceroy's son is better than that old Sir Fifty. Don Vincentio! Don Indian! He thinks he's trading to Gambo* still, and would barter himself (that bell and bauble*) for your youth and fortune.

PEDRO Callis, take her hence, and lock her up all this 155 carnival, and at Lent she shall begin her everlasting penance in a monastery.

HELLENA I care not, I had rather be a nun than be obliged to marry as you would have me, if I were designed for't.

PEDRO Do not fear the blessing of that choice – you shall 160 be a nun.

HELLENA Shall I so? You may chance to be mistaken in my way of devotion – a nun! Yes, I am like to make a fine nun! I have an excellent humour for a grate.* (aside) No, I'll have a saint of my own to pray to shortly, if I like any 165 that dares venture on me.

PEDRO Callis, make it your business to watch this wild cat. As for you, Florinda, I've only tried you all this while and urged my father's will; but mine is that you would love Antonio. He is brave and young, and all that can 170 complete the happiness of a gallant maid. This absence of my father will give us opportunity to free you from Vincentio by marrying here, which you must do tomorrow.

FLORINDA Tomorrow!   175

PEDRO Tomorrow, or 'twill be too late. 'Tis not my

friendship to Antonio which makes me urge this, but love to thee, and hatred to Vincentio – therefore resolve upon tomorrow.

FLORINDA Sir, I shall strive to do as shall become your   180 sister.

PEDRO I'll both believe and trust you. Adieu.

                    [*Exeunt* PEDRO *and* STEPHANO]

HELLENA As becomes his sister! That is to be as resolved your way, as he is his.

                (HELLENA *goes to* CALLIS)

FLORINDA I ne'er till now perceived my ruin near: 185
I've no defence against Antonio's love,
For he has all the advantages of nature,
The moving arguments of youth and fortune.

HELLENA But hark you, Callis, you will not be so cruel to lock me up indeed, will you?   190

CALLIS I must obey the commands I have – besides, do you consider what a life you are going to lead?

HELLENA Yes, Callis, that of a nun: and till then I'll be indebted a world of prayers to you if you let me now see, what I never did, the divertisements of a carnival.   195

CALLIS What, go in masquerade? 'Twill be a fine farewell to the world I take it – pray what would you do there?

HELLENA That which all the world does, as I am told – be as mad as the rest, and take all innocent freedoms. Sister, you'll go too, will you not? Come, prithee be not sad. 200 We'll outwit twenty brothers, if you'll be ruled by me. Come, put off this dull humour with your clothes, and assume one as gay, and as fantastic as the dress my cousin Valeria and I have provided, and let's ramble.*

FLORINDA Callis, will you give us leave to go?   205

CALLIS (*aside*) I have a youthful itch of going myself. – Madam, if I thought your brother might not know it, and I might wait on you, for by my troth I'll not trust young girls alone.

FLORINDA Thou see'st my brother's gone already, and   210 thou shalt attend and watch us.

(*Enter* STEPHANO)

STEPHANO Madam, the habits are come, and your cousin
Valeria is dressed and stays for you.

FLORINDA 'Tis well. I'll write a note, and if I chance to see
Belvile and want* an opportunity to speak to him, that 215
shall let him know what I've resolved in favour of him.

HELLENA Come, let's in and dress us.

[*Exeunt*]

Act 1, Scene 2

A long street

(*Enter* BELVILE, *melancholy;* BLUNT *and* FREDERICK)

FREDERICK Why* what the devil ails the colonel? In a time
when all the world is gay, to look like mere Lent thus?
Hadst thou been long enough in Naples to have been in
love, I should have sworn some such judgement had
befallen thee.   5

BELVILE No, I have made no new amours since I came to
Naples.

FREDERICK You have left none behind you in Paris?

BELVILE Neither.

FREDERICK I cannot divine the cause then, unless the old   10
cause, the want of money.

BLUNT And another old cause, the want of a wench –
would not that revive you?

BELVILE You are mistaken, Ned.

BLUNT Nay, 'sheartlikins,* then thou'rt past cure.   15

FREDERICK I have found it out: thou hast renewed thy
acquaintance with the lady that cost thee so many sighs at
the siege of Pamplona – pox on't, what d'ye call her – her
brother's a noble Spaniard – nephew to the dead general –
Florinda – aye, Florinda – and will nothing serve thy turn 20
but that damned virtuous woman? Whom on my conscience thou lovest in spite too, because thou seest little or
no possibility of gaining her?

BELVILE Thou art mistaken. I have interest enough in that lovely virgin's heart to make me proud and vain, were it 25 not abated by the severity of a brother, who, perceiving my happiness –

FREDERICK Has civilly forbid thee the house?

BELVILE 'Tis so, to make way for a powerful rival, the viceroy's son, who has the advantage of me in being a 30 man of fortune, a Spaniard, and her brother's friend; which gives him liberty to make his court, while I have recourse only to letters, and distant looks from her window, which are as soft and kind as those which heaven sends down on penitents. 35

BLUNT Heyday! 'Sheartlikins, simile! By this light, the man is quite spoiled. Fred, what the devil are we made of, that we cannot be thus concerned for a wench? 'Sheartlikins, our cupids are like the cooks of the camp, they can roast or boil a woman, but they have none of the fine tricks to 40 set 'em off, no hogoes* to make the sauce pleasant and the stomach sharp.

FREDERICK I dare swear that I have had a hundred as young, kind and handsome as this Florinda; and dogs eat me, if they were not as troublesome to me i' the morning, 45 as they were welcome o'er night.

BLUNT And yet I warrant he would not touch another woman if he might have her for nothing.

BELVILE That's thy joy, a cheap whore.

BLUNT Why 'sheartlikins, I love a frank soul – when did 50 you ever hear of an honest woman that took a man's money? I warrant 'em good ones – but gentlemen, you may be free, you have been kept so poor with parliaments and protectors* that the little stock you have is not worth preserving – but I thank my stars, I had more grace than 55 to forfeit my estate by cavaliering.*

BELVILE Methinks only following the court* should be sufficient to entitle 'em to that.

BLUNT 'Sheartlikins, they know I follow it to do it no good, unless they pick a hole in my coat for lending you money 60 now and then, which is a greater crime to my conscience, gentlemen, than to the Commonwealth.

(*Enter* WILLMORE)

WILLMORE Ha! Dear Belvile! Noble colonel!

BELVILE Willmore! Welcome ashore, my dear rover! What happy wind blew us this good fortune?   65

WILLMORE Let me salute* my dear Fred, and then command me. How is't, honest lad?

FREDERICK Faith, sir, the old compliment, infinitely the better to see my dear mad Willmore again. Prithee, why cam'st thou ashore? And where's the prince?*   70

WILLMORE He's well, and reigns still lord of the watery element. I must aboard again within a day or two, and my business ashore was only to enjoy myself a little this carnival.

BELVILE Pray know our new friend, sir; he's but bashful, a   75
raw traveller, but honest, stout, and one of us. (*Embraces* BLUNT)

WILLMORE That you esteem him gives him an interest here.

BLUNT Your servant, sir.

WILLMORE But well – faith, I'm glad to meet you again in   80
a warm climate, where the kind sun has its god-like power still over the wine and women. Love and mirth are my business in Naples, and if I mistake not the place, here's an excellent market for chapmen* of my humour.

BELVILE See, here be those kind merchants of love you   85
look for.

(*Enter several men in masquing habits, some playing on
music, others dancing after; women dressed like
courtesans, with papers pinned on their breasts, and
baskets of flowers in their hands*)

BLUNT 'Sheartlikins, what have we here?

FREDERICK Now the game begins.

WILLMORE Fine pretty creatures! May a stranger have

leave to look and love? What's here – (*reads the papers*) 90
'Roses for every month'?

BLUNT 'Roses for every month'? What means that?

BELVILE They are, or would have you think they're
courtesans, who here in Naples are to be hired by the
month. 95

WILLMORE Kind and obliging to inform us – pray, where
do these roses grow? I would fain plant some of 'em in a
bed of mine.

WOMAN Beware such roses, sir.

WILLMORE A pox of fear! I'll be baked with thee between a 100
pair of sheets, and that's thy proper still;* so I might but
strew such roses over me and under me. Fair one, would
you give me leave to gather at your bush this idle month, I
would go near to make somebody smell of it all the year
after. 105

BELVILE And thou hast need of such a remedy, for
thou stink'st of tar and ropes' ends like a dock or a
pest-house.*

[*The woman puts herself into the hands of a man and
exeunt*]

WILLMORE Nay, nay, you shall not leave me so.

BELVILE By all means use no violence here. 110

WILLMORE Death! Just as I was going to be damnably in
love, to have her led off! I could pluck that rose out of his
hand, and even kiss the bed the bush grew in.

FREDERICK No friend to love like a long voyage at sea.

BLUNT Except a nunnery, Fred. 115

WILLMORE Death! But will they not be kind? Quickly be
kind? Thou know'st I'm no tame fighter, but a rampant
lion of the forest.

(*Advances from the farther end of the scenes two men
dressed all over with horns* of several sorts, making
grimaces at one another, with papers pinned on their
backs*)

BELVILE Oh the satirical rogues, how they're dressed! 'Tis
a satire against the whole sex. 120

WILLMORE Is this a fruit that grows in the warm country?

BELVILE Yes, 'tis pretty to see these Italians start, swell and stab at the word cuckold, and yet stumble at horns on every threshold.

WILLMORE See what's on their back – (*reads*) 'Flowers of 125 every night.' Ah, rogue! And more sweet than roses of every month! This is a gardener of Adam's own breeding.

(*They dance*)

BELVILE What think you of those grave people? Is a wake in Essex half so mad or extravagant?

WILLMORE I like their sober, grave way; 'tis a kind of legal 130 authorised fornication, where the men are not chid for't, nor the women despised, as amongst our dull English; even the monsieurs* want that part of good manners.

BELVILE But here in Italy, a monsieur is the humblest, best-bred gentleman. Duels are so baffled by bravoes that an 135 age shows not one but between a Frenchman and a hangman, who is as much too hard for him on the piazza* as they are for a Dutchman on the New Bridge* – but see, another crew.

(*Enter* FLORINDA, HELLENA *and* VALERIA, *dressed like gypsies;* CALLIS *and* STEPHANO, LUCETTA, PHILIPPO *and* SANCHO *in masquerade*)

HELLENA Sister, there's your Englishman, and with him a 140 handsome proper fellow – I'll to him, and instead of telling him his fortune, try my own.

WILLMORE Gypsies, on my life. Sure these will prattle if a man cross their hands.* (*goes to* HELLENA) Dear, pretty (and I hope) young devil, will you tell an amorous 145 stranger what luck he's like to have?

HELLENA Have a care how you venture with me, sir, lest I pick your pocket, which will more vex your English humour than an Italian fortune will please you.

WILLMORE How the devil cam'st thou to know my country 150 and humour?

HELLENA The first I guess by a certain forward impudence,

which does not displease me at this time; and the loss of
your money will vex you, because I hope you have but
very little to lose.   155

WILLMORE Egad, child, thou'rt i'th'right; it is so little I
dare not offer it thee for a kindness – but cannot you
divine what other things of more value I have about me,
that I would more willingly part with?

HELLENA Indeed, no, that's the business of a witch, and I   160
am but a gypsy yet. Yet without looking in your hand, I
have a parlous* guess, 'tis some foolish heart you mean,
an inconstant English heart, as little worth stealing as
your purse.

WILLMORE Nay, then thou dost deal with the devil, that's   165
certain – thou hast guessed as right as if thou hadst been
one of that number it has languished for. I find you'll be
better acquainted with it, nor can you take it in a better
time; for I am come from sea, child, and Venus not being
propitious to me in her own element,* I have a world of   170
love in store – would you would be good-natured, and
take some on't off my hands.

HELLENA Why – I could be inclined that way – but for a
foolish vow I am going to make – to die a maid.

WILLMORE Then thou art damned without redemption,   175
and as I am a good Christian, I ought in charity to divert
so wicked a design – therefore prithee, dear creature, let
me know quickly when and where I shall begin to set a
helping hand to so good a work.

HELLENA If you should prevail with my tender heart (as I   180
begin to fear you will, for you have horrible loving eyes),
there will be difficulty in't that you'll hardly undergo for
my sake.

WILLMORE Faith, child, I have been bred in dangers, and
wear a sword that has been employed in a worse cause   185
than for a handsome kind woman. Name the danger – let
it be anything but a long siege – and I'll undertake it.

HELLENA Can you storm?

WILLMORE Oh, most furiously.

HELLENA What think you of a nunnery wall? For he that 190
wins me must gain that first.

WILLMORE A nun! Oh, how I love thee for't! There's no
sinner like a young saint – nay, now there's no denying
me, the old law* had no curse (to a woman) like dying a
maid; witness Jephthah's daughter.*   195

HELLENA A very good text this, if well handled, and I
perceive, Father Captain, you would impose no severe
penance on her who were inclined to console herself
before she took orders.*

WILLMORE If she be young and handsome.   200

HELLENA Aye, there's it – but if she be not –

WILLMORE By this hand, child, I have an implicit faith, and
dare venture on thee with all faults – besides 'tis more
meritorious to leave the world when thou hast tasted and
proved the pleasure on't. Then 'twill be a virtue in thee, 205
which now will be pure ignorance.

HELLENA I perceive, good Father Captain, you design only
to make me fit for heaven – but if, on the contrary, you
should quite divert me from it and bring me back to the
world again, I should have a new man to seek I find. And 210
what a grief that will be – for when I begin, I fancy I shall
love like anything; I never tried yet.

WILLMORE Egad, and that's kind. Prithee, dear creature,
give me credit for a heart, for faith I'm a very honest
fellow. Oh, I long to come first to the banquet of love! 215
And such a swingeing* appetite I bring – oh, I'm
impatient. Thy lodging, sweetheart, thy lodging, or I'm a
dead man!

HELLENA Why must we be either guilty of fornication or
murder if we converse with you men – and is there no 220
difference between leave to love me, and leave to lie with
me?

WILLMORE Faith, child, they were made to go together.

LUCETTA Are you sure this is the man? (*pointing to
BLUNT*)

SANCHO When did I mistake your game?   225

LUCETTA This is a stranger, I know by his gazing; if he be

brisk he'll venture to follow me, and then, if I understand
my trade, he's mine. He's English too, and they say that's
a sort of good-natured, loving people, and have generally
so kind an opinion of themselves, that a woman with any 230
wit may flatter 'em into any sort of fool she pleases.

(She often passes by BLUNT, *and gazes on him; he struts
and cocks, and walks and gazes on her)*

BLUNT 'Tis so – she is taken – I have beauties which my
false glass at home did not discover.

FLORINDA This woman watches me so, I shall get no
opportunity to discover myself to him, and so miss the 235
intent of my coming – but as I was saying, sir – *(looking
in his hand)* by this line you should be a lover.

BELVILE I thought how right you guessed, all men are in
love, or pretend to be so – come, let me go, I'm weary of
this fooling. 240

(Walks away)

FLORINDA I will not, till you have confessed whether the
passion that you have vowed for Florinda be true or false.

*(She holds him, he strives to get from her. Turns quick
towards her)*

BELVILE Florinda!

FLORINDA Softly.

BELVILE Thou hast named one will fix me here for ever. 245

FLORINDA She'll be disappointed then, who expects you
this night at the garden gate, and if you fail not as – let me
see the other hand – you will go near to do – she vows to
die or make you happy.

(Looks on CALLIS *who observes 'em)*

BELVILE What canst thou mean? 250

FLORINDA That which I say. Farewell. *(offers to go)*

BELVILE Oh, charming sibyl,* stay, complete that joy
which as it is will turn into distraction! Where must I be?

At the garden gate? I know it – at night you say? I'll
sooner forfeit heaven than disobey.   255

(*Enter* DON PEDRO *and other masquers, and pass over
the stage*)

CALLIS Madam, your brother's here.
FLORINDA Take this to instruct you farther.

(*Gives him a letter, and goes off*)

FREDERICK Have a care, sir, what you promise. This may
be a trap laid by her brother to ruin you.
BELVILE Do not disturb my happiness with doubts.   260

(*Opens the letter*)

WILLMORE My dear pretty creature, a thousand blessings
on thee! Still in this habit you say? And after dinner at
this place?
HELLENA Yes, if you will swear to keep your heart and not
bestow it between this and that.   265
WILLMORE By all the little gods of love, I swear I'll leave it
with you, and if you run away with it, those deities of
justice will revenge me.
[*Exeunt all the women <except* LUCETTA>]

FREDERICK Do you know the hand?
BELVILE 'Tis Florinda's.   270
All blessings fall upon the virtuous maid.
FREDERICK Nay, no idolatry; a sober sacrifice I'll allow
you.
BELVILE Oh friends, the welcom'st news! The softest letter!
Nay, you shall all see it! And could you now be serious, I   275
might be made the happiest man the sun shines on!
WILLMORE The reason of this mighty joy?
BELVILE See how kindly she invites me to deliver her from
the threatened violence of her brother – will you not assist
me?   280
WILLMORE I know not what thou mean'st, but I'll make
one at any mischief where a woman's concerned – but
she'll be grateful to us for the favour, will she not?

BELVILE How mean you?

WILLMORE How should I mean? Thou know'st there's but 285
one way for a woman to oblige me.

BELVILE Do not profane – the maid is nicely* virtuous.

WILLMORE Who, pox, then she's fit for nothing but a
husband. Let her e'en go, colonel.

FREDERICK Peace, she's the colonel's mistress, sir. 290

WILLMORE Let her be the devil; if she be thy mistress, I'll
serve her – name the way.

BELVILE Read here this postscript. (*gives him a letter*)

WILLMORE (*reads*) 'At ten at night – at the garden gate – of
which, if I cannot get the key, I will contrive a way over 295
the wall – come attended with a friend or two.' Kind
heart, if we three cannot weave a string to let her down a
garden wall, 'twere pity but the hangman wove one for us
all.

FREDERICK Let her alone for that; your woman's wit, your 300
fair kind woman will out-trick a broker or a Jew, and
contrive like a Jesuit in chains!* But see, Ned, Blunt is
stolen out after the lure of a damsel.

[*Exeunt* BLUNT *and* LUCETTA]

BELVILE So, he'll scarce find his way home again unless we
get him cried by the bellman* in the market-place, and 305
'twould sound prettily – a lost English boy of thirty.

FREDERICK I hope 'tis some common crafty sinner, one
that will fit him.* It may be she'll sell him for Peru:* the
rogue's sturdy and would work well in a mine. At least I
hope she'll dress him for our mirth, cheat him of all, then 310
have him well-favouredly banged,* and turned out naked
at midnight.

WILLMORE Prithee, what humour is he of, that you wish
him so well?

BELVILE Why, of an English elder brother's humour: 315
educated in a nursery, with a maid to tend him till fifteen,
and lies with his grandmother till he's of age. One that
knows no pleasure beyond riding to the next fair, or
going up to London with his right worshipful father in
parliament-time; wearing gay clothes, or making honour- 320

able love to his lady mother's laundry maid; gets drunk at
a hunting match, and ten to one then gives some proof of
his prowess. A pox upon him, he's our banker, and has all
our cash about him, and if he fail, we are all broke.

FREDERICK Oh, let him alone for that matter, he's of a 325
damned stingy quality that will secure our stock. I know
not in what danger it were indeed if the jilt should pretend
she's in love with him, for 'tis a kind believing coxcomb.
Otherwise, if he part with more than a piece of eight* –
geld him – for which offer he may chance to be beaten if 330
she be a whore of the first rank.

BELVILE Nay, the rogue will not be easily beaten, he's stout
enough. Perhaps if they talk beyond his capacity, he may
chance to exercise his courage upon some of them, else
I'm sure they'll find it as difficult to beat as to please him. 335

WILLMORE 'Tis a lucky devil to light upon so kind a
wench!

FREDERICK Thou hadst a great deal of talk with thy little
gypsy, couldst thou do no good upon her? For mine was
hard-hearted.   340

WILLMORE Hang her, she was some damned honest*
person of quality I'm sure, she was so very free and witty.
If her face be but answerable to her wit and humour, I
would be bound to constancy this month to gain her – in
the meantime, have you made no kind acquaintance since 345
you came to town? You do not use to be honest so long,
gentlemen.

FREDERICK Faith, love has kept us honest: we have been
all fired with a beauty newly come to town, the famous
Paduana* Angellica Bianca.   350

WILLMORE What, the mistress of the dead Spanish
general?

BELVILE Yes, she's now the only adored beauty of all the
youth in Naples, who put on all their charms to appear
lovely in her sight, their coaches, liveries, and themselves, 355
all gay as on a monarch's birthday,* to attract the eyes of
this fair charmer, while she has the pleasure to behold all
languish for her that see her.

FREDERICK 'Tis pretty to see with how much love the men
   regard her, and how much envy the women.   360
WILLMORE What gallant has she?
BELVILE None, she's exposed to sale, and four days in the
   week she's yours – for so much a month.
WILLMORE The very thought of it quenches all manner of
   fire in me – yet prithee, let's see her.   365
BELVILE Let's first to dinner, and after that we'll pass the
   day as you please – but at night ye must all be at my
   devotion.
WILLMORE I will not fail you.

                                                    [*Exeunt*]

Act 2, Scene 1

The long street

(*Enter* BELVILE *and* FREDERICK *in masquing habits, and*
   WILLMORE *in his own clothes, with a vizard* in his
   hand*)

WILLMORE But why thus disguised and muzzled?
BELVILE Because whatever extravagances we commit in
   these faces, our own may not be obliged to answer 'em.
WILLMORE I should have changed my eternal buff* too;
   but no matter, my little gypsy would not have found me   5
   out then, unless I should hear her prattle. A pox on't, I
   cannot get her out of my head: pray heaven, if I ever do
   see her again, she prove damnably ugly, that I may fortify
   myself against her tongue.
BELVILE Have a care of love, for o' my conscience she was   10
   not of a quality to give thee any hopes.
WILLMORE Pox on 'em, why do they draw a man in then?
   She has played with my heart so, that 'twill never lie still
   till I have met with some kind wench that will play the
   game out with me. Oh, for my arms full of soft, white,   15
   kind – woman! Such as I fancy Angellica.
BELVILE This is her house, if you were but in stock to get

admittance. They have not yet dined yet; I perceive the picture is not out.

(*Enter* BLUNT)

WILLMORE I long to see the shadow of the fair substance; a 20
man may gaze on that for nothing.

BLUNT Colonel, thy hand – and thine, Fred. I have been an ass, a deluded fool, a very coxcomb from my birth till this hour, and heartily repent my little faith.

BELVILE What the devil's the matter with thee, Ned? 25

<BLUNT> Oh, such a mistress, Fred, such a girl!

WILLMORE Ha! Where?

FREDERICK Aye, where?

<BLUNT> So fond, so amorous, so toying and so fine! And all for sheer love, ye rogue! Oh, how she looked and 30 kissed! And soothed my heart from my bosom – I cannot think I was awake, and yet methinks I see and feel her charms still – Fred, try if she have not left the taste of her balmy breath upon my lips. (*kisses him*)

BELVILE Ha! Ha! Ha! 35

WILLMORE Death, man, where is she?

<BLUNT> What a dog was I to stay in dull England so long. How have I laughed at the colonel when he sighed for love! But now the little archer* has revenged him! And by this one dart I can guess at all his joys, which then I took 40 for fancies, mere dreams and fables. Well, I'm resolved to sell all in Essex, and plant here forever.

BELVILE What a blessing 'tis thou hast a mistress thou dar'st boast of, for I know thy humour is rather to have a proclaimed clap* than a secret amour. 45

WILLMORE Dost know her name?

BLUNT Her name? No, 'sheartlikins, what care I for names? She's fair, young, brisk and kind – even to ravishment! And what a pox care I for knowing her by any other title? 50

WILLMORE Didst give her anything?

BLUNT Give her! Ha, ha, ha! Why, she's a person of quality – that's a good one, give her! 'Sheartlikins, dost think

such creatures are to be bought? Or are we provided for
such a purchase? Give her, quoth ye? Why, she presented   55
me with this bracelet for the toy of a diamond I used to
wear. No, gentlemen, Ned Blunt is not everybody – she
expects me again tonight.

WILLMORE Egad, that's well; we'll all go.

BLUNT Not a soul. No, gentlemen, you are wits; I am a dull   60
country rogue, I.

FREDERICK Well, sir, for all your person of quality, I shall
be very glad to understand your purse be secure; 'tis our
whole estate at present, which we are loath to hazard in
one bottom.* Come, sir, unlade.   65

BLUNT Take the necessary trifle useless now to me, that am
beloved by such a gentlewoman – 'sheartlikins, money!
Here, take mine, too.

FREDERICK No, keep that to be cozened,* that we may
laugh.   70

WILLMORE Cozened – death! would I could meet with one
that would cozen me of all the love I could spare tonight.

FREDERICK Pox, 'tis some common whore, upon my life.

BLUNT A whore? Yes, with such clothes, such jewels, such
a house, such furniture, and so attended! A whore!   75

BELVILE Why yes, sir, they are whores, though they'll
neither entertain you with drinking, swearing, or bawdry;
are whores in all those gay clothes and right jewels; are
whores with those great houses richly furnished with
velvet beds, store of plate, handsome attendance and fine   80
coaches; are whores, and arrant* ones.

WILLMORE Pox on't, where do these fine whores live?

BELVILE Where no rogues in office ycleped* constables
dare give 'em laws, nor the wine-inspired bullies of the
town break their windows; yet they are whores, though   85
this Essex calf* believe 'em persons of quality.

BLUNT 'Sheartlikins, y'are all fools. There are things about
this Essex calf that shall take with the ladies, beyond all
your wit and parts – this shape and size, gentlemen, are
not to be despised – my waist too, tolerably long, with   90
other inviting signs that shall be nameless.

WILLMORE Egad, I believe he may have met with some
person of quality that may be kind to him.

BELVILE Dost thou perceive any such tempting things
about him that should make a fine woman, and of 95
quality, pick him out from all mankind to throw away her
youth and beauty upon, nay, and her dear heart too? No,
no, Angellica has raised the price too high.

WILLMORE May she languish for mankind till she die, and
be damned for that one sin alone.   100

(*Enter two* BRAVOES *and hang up a great picture of
Angellica's against the balcony, and two little ones at
each side of the door*)

BELVILE See there, the fair sign to the inn where a man
may lodge that's fool enough to give her price.

(WILLMORE *gazes on the picture*)

BLUNT 'Sheartlikins, gentlemen, what's this?

BELVILE A famous courtesan, that's to be sold.

BLUNT How? To be sold? Nay then, I have nothing to say 105
to her – sold! What impudence is practised in this
country! With what order and decency whoring's estab-
lished here by virtue of the Inquisition. Come, let's be
gone, I'm sure we're no chapmen for this commodity.

FREDERICK Thou art none, I'm sure, unless thou couldst 110
have her in thy bed at the price of a coach in the street.

WILLMORE How wondrous fair she is – 'a thousand
crowns a month' – by heaven, as many kingdoms were
too little. A plague of this poverty – of which I ne'er
complain but when it hinders my approach to beauty, 115
which virtue ne'er could purchase.

(*Turns away from the picture*)

BLUNT What's this? (*reads*) 'A thousand crowns a month'!
'Sheartlikins, here's a sum! Sure 'tis a mistake. – Hark
you friend, does she take or give so much by the month?

FREDERICK A thousand crowns! Why, 'tis a portion for the 120
Infanta.*

BLUNT Hark ye friends, won't she trust?

BRAVO This is a trade, sir, that cannot live by credit.

(*Enter* DON PEDRO *in masquerade, followed by*
STEPHANO)

BELVILE See, here's more company, let's walk off a while.
[*Exeunt <the* ENGLISH>]

(PEDRO *reads*)

(*Enter* ANGELLICA *and* MORETTA *in the balcony, and
draw a silk curtain*)

PEDRO Fetch me a thousand crowns, I never wished to buy 125
this beauty at an easier rate.
[*Passes off <the stage>*]

ANGELLICA Prithee, what said those fellows to thee?

BRAVO Madam, the first were admirers of your beauty
only, but no purchasers: they were merry with your price
and picture, laughed at the sum, and so passed off.   130

ANGELLICA No matter, I'm not displeased with their
rallying; their wonder feeds my vanity, and he that wishes
but to buy gives me more pride than he that gives my
price can make my pleasure.

BRAVO Madam, the last I knew through all his disguises to 135
be Don Pedro, nephew to the general, and who was with
him at Pamplona.

ANGELLICA Don Pedro! My old gallant's nephew. When
his uncle died he left him a vast sum of money; it is he
who was so in love with me at Padua, and who used to 140
make the general so jealous.

MORETTA Is this he that used to prance before our
window, and took such care to show himself an amorous
ass? If I am not mistaken, he is the likeliest man to give
your price.   145

ANGELLICA The man is brave and generous, but of an
humour so uneasy and inconstant that the victory over his
heart is as soon lost as won, a slave that can add little to
the triumph of the conqueror. But inconstancy's the sin of

all mankind, therefore I'm resolved that nothing but 150
gold shall charm my heart.

MORETTA I'm glad on't; 'tis only interest that women of
our profession ought to consider, though I wonder what
has kept you from that general disease of our sex so long
– I mean that of being in love.   155

ANGELLICA A kind but sullen star, under which I had the
happiness to be born. Yet I have had no time for love; the
bravest and noblest of mankind have purchased my
favours at so dear a rate, as if no coin but gold were
current with our trade – but here's Don Pedro again, fetch 160
me my lute – for 'tis for him or Don Antonio, the
viceroy's son, that I have spread my nets.

(*Enter at one door* DON PEDRO, STEPHANO, DON
ANTONIO *and* DIEGO *at the other door, with people
following him in masquerade, anticly* attired, some with
music; they both go up to the picture*)

ANTONIO A thousand crowns! Had not the painter flattered her, I should not think it dear.

PEDRO Flattered her! By heaven, he cannot; I have seen the 165
original, nor is there one charm here more than adorns
her face and eyes; all this soft and sweet, with a certain
languishing air that no artist can represent.

ANTONIO What I heard of her beauty before had fired my
soul, but this confirmation of it has blown it to a flame. 170

PEDRO Ha!

PAGE Sir, I have known you throw away a thousand
crowns on a worse face, and though y'are near your
marriage, you may venture a little love here, Florinda will
not miss it.   175

PEDRO (*aside*) Ha! Florinda! Sure 'tis Antonio.

ANTONIO Florinda! Name not those distant joys, there's
not one thought of her will check my passion here.

PEDRO Florinda scorned! And all my hopes defeated of the
possession of Angellica. Her injuries, by heaven, he shall 180
not boast of!

(*A noise of a lute above.* ANTONIO *gazes up. Song to a
lute above*)

Song

When Damon first began to love
He languished in a soft desire,
And knew not how the gods to move,
To lessen or increase his fire.   185
For Celia in her charming eyes
Wore all love's sweets, and all his cruelties.

2

But as beneath a shade he lay,
Weaving of flowers for Celia's hair,
She chanced to lead her flock that way,   190
And saw the am'rous shepherd there.
She gazed around upon the place,
And saw the grove (resembling night)
To all the joys of love invite,
Whilst guilty smiles and blushes dressed her face.   195
At last the bashful youth all transport grew,
And with kind force he taught the virgin how
To yield what all his sighs could never do.

(ANGELLICA *throws open the curtains and bows to*
ANTONIO, *who pulls off his vizard and bows and blows
up kisses.* PEDRO *unseen looks in his face.* <*The curtains
close*>)

ANTONIO By heaven, she's charming fair!
PEDRO 'Tis he, the false Antonio!   200
ANTONIO (*to the* BRAVO) Friend, where must I pay my
offering of love? My thousand crowns, I mean.
PEDRO That offering I have designed to make.
And yours will come too late.
ANTONIO Prithee begone, I shall grow angry else.   205
And then thou art not safe.
PEDRO My anger may be fatal, sir, as yours;
And he that enters here may prove this truth.

ANTONIO I know not who thou art, but I am sure thou'rt
worth my killing for aiming at Angellica.   210

(*They draw and fight. Enter* WILLMORE *and* BLUNT)

BLUNT 'Sheartlikins, here's fine doings.
WILLMORE Tilting for the wench I'm sure – nay, gad, if
that would win her, I have as good a sword as the best
of ye.

(<WILLMORE *and* BLUNT> *draw and part* <PEDRO *and*
ANTONIO>)

Put up, put up, and take another time and place, for this 215
is designed for lovers only.

(*They all put up*)

PEDRO We are prevented; dare you meet me tomorrow on
the Molo?*
For I've a title to a better quarrel,
That of Florinda, in whose credulous heart   220
Thou'st made an interest and destroyed my hopes.
ANTONIO Dare!
I'll meet thee there as early as the day.
PEDRO We will come thus disguised, that whosoever
chance to get the better, he may escape unknown.   225
ANTONIO It shall be so.

[*Exeunt* PEDRO *and* STEPHANO]

Who should this rival be, unless the English colonel, of
whom I've often heard Don Pedro speak?
It must be he, and time he were removed,
Who lays a claim to all my happiness.   230

(WILLMORE, *having gazed all this while on the picture,
pulls down a little one*)

WILLMORE This posture's loose and negligent,
The sight on't would beget a warm desire
In souls whom impotence and age had chilled.
This must along with me.

BRAVO What means this rudeness, sir? Restore the 235
picture.

ANTONIO Ha! Rudeness committed to the fair Angellica!
Restore the picture, sir –

WILLMORE Indeed I will not, sir.

ANTONIO By heaven, but you shall. 240

WILLMORE Nay, do not show your sword; if you do, by
this dear beauty – I will show mine too.

ANTONIO What right can you pretend to't?

WILLMORE That of possession which I will maintain – you
perhaps have a thousand crowns to give for the original. 245

ANTONIO No matter, sir, you shall restore the picture.

(ANGELLICA *and* MORETTA *above*)

ANGELLICA Oh, Moretta! What's the matter?

WILLMORE Death! You lie – I will do neither.

(*They fight; the* SPANIARDS *join with* ANTONIO; BLUNT
laying on like mad)

ANGELLICA Hold, I command you, if for me you fight.

(*They leave off and bow*)

WILLMORE How heavenly fair she is! Ah, plague of her 250
price.

ANGELLICA You sir, in buff, you that appear a soldier, that
first began this insolence –

WILLMORE 'Tis true, I did so, if you call it insolence for a
man to preserve himself. I saw your charming picture and 255
was wounded: quite through my soul each pointed beauty
ran, and wanting a thousand crowns to procure my
remedy, I laid this little picture to my bosom – which if
you cannot allow me, I'll resign.

ANGELLICA No, you may keep the trifle. 260

ANTONIO You shall first ask me leave, and this.

(*Fight again as before*)

(*Enter* BELVILE *and* FREDERICK *who join with the
English*)

ANGELLICA Hold! Will you ruin me? Biskey – Sebastian –
part 'em.
[*The* SPANIARDS *are beaten off.* <Exeunt all the MEN>]

MORETTA Oh madam, we're undone. A pox upon that
rude fellow, he's set on to ruin us; we shall never see good 265
days till all these fighting poor rogues are sent to the
galleys.

(*Enter* BELVILE, BLUNT, FREDERICK *and* WILLMORE
with his shirt bloody)

BLUNT 'Sheartlikins, beat me at this sport and I'll ne'er
wear sword more.

BELVILE (*to* WILLMORE) The devil's in thee for a mad 270
fellow, thou art always one at an unlucky adventure –
come, let's be gone whilst we're safe, and remember these
are Spaniards; a sort of people that know how to revenge
an affront.

FREDERICK You bleed! I hope you are not wounded.   275

WILLMORE Not much – a plague on your dons, if they fight
no better they'll ne'er recover Flanders.* What the devil
was't to them that I took down the picture?

BLUNT Took it! 'Sheartlikins, we'll have the great one too;
'tis ours by conquest. Prithee help me up, and I'll pull it 280
down –

ANGELLICA Stay, sir, and ere you affront me farther, let me
know how you durst commit this outrage – to you I
speak, sir, for you appear a gentleman.

WILLMORE To me, madam? – Gentlemen, your servant. 285

(BELVILE *stays him*)

BELVILE Is the devil in thee? Dost know the danger of
entering the house of an incensed courtesan?

WILLMORE I thank you for your care – but there are other
matters in hand, there are, though we have no great
temptation. Death! Let me go!   290

FREDERICK Yes, to your lodging if you will, but not in
here. Damn these gay harlots – by this hand, I'll have as

sound and handsome a whore for a patacoon.* Death, man, she'll murder thee.

WILLMORE Oh, fear me not. Shall I not venture where a 295 beauty calls? A lovely charming beauty! For fear of danger! When, by heaven, there's none so great as to long for her whilst I want money to purchase her.

PEDRO Therefore 'tis loss of time unless you had the thousand crowns to pay.   300

WILLMORE It may be she may give a favour; at least I shall have the pleasure of saluting her when I enter, and when I depart.

BELVILE Pox, she'll as soon lie with thee as kiss thee, and sooner stab than do either – you shall not go.   305

ANGELLICA Fear not, sir, all I have to wound with is my eyes.

BLUNT Let him go, 'sheartlikins, I believe the gentlewoman means well.

BELVILE Well, take thy fortune, we'll expect you in the 310 next street. Farewell, fool – farewell.

WILLMORE 'Bye, colonel – (goes in)

FREDERICK The rogue's stark mad for a wench.

[Exeunt]

Act 2, Scene 2

A fine chamber

(Enter WILLMORE, ANGELLICA and MORETTA)

ANGELLICA Insolent sir, how durst you pull down my picture?

WILLMORE Rather, how durst you set it up, to tempt poor amorous mortals with so much excellence? Which I find you have but too well consulted by the unmerciful price 5 you set upon't. Is all this heaven of beauty shown to move despair in those that cannot buy? And can you think th'effects of that despair should be less extravagant than I have shown?

ANGELLICA I sent for you to ask my pardon, sir, not to   10
aggravate your crime – I thought I should have seen you
at my feet imploring it.

WILLMORE You are deceived; I came to rail at you, and rail
such truths too, as shall let you see the vanity of that pride
which taught you how to set such price on sin.   15
For such it is, whilst that which is love's due
Is meanly bartered for.

ANGELLICA Ha! Ha! Ha! Alas, good captain, what pity 'tis
your edifying doctrine will do no good upon me –
Moretta! Fetch the gentleman a glass and let him survey   20
himself to see what charms he has – (*aside in a soft tone*)
and guess my business.

MORETTA He knows himself of old; I believe those
breeches and he have been acquainted ever since he was
beaten at Worcester.*   25

ANGELLICA Nay, do not abuse the poor creature –

MORETTA Good weather-beaten corporal, will you march
off? We have no need of your doctrine, though you have
of our charity, but at present we have no scraps, we can
afford no kindness for God's sake. In fine, sirrah, the   30
price is too high i'th'mouth* for you, therefore troop, I
say.

WILLMORE Here, good forewoman of the shop, serve me,
and I'll be gone.

MORETTA Keep it to pay your laundress, your linen stinks   35
of the gunroom; for here's no selling by retail.

WILLMORE Thou hast sold plenty of thy stale ware at a
cheap rate.

MORETTA Aye, the more silly kind heart I, but this is an
age wherein beauty is at higher rates. In fine, you know   40
the price of this.

WILLMORE I grant you 'tis here set down a thousand
crowns a month – pray how much may come to my share
for a pistole?* Bawd, take your black lead* and sum it
up, that I may have a pistole's worth of this vain gay   45
thing, and I'll trouble you no more.

MORETTA Pox on him, he'll fret me to death. – Abominable
   fellow, I tell thee, we only sell by the whole piece.
WILLMORE 'Tis very hard, the whole cargo or nothing.
   Faith, madam, my stock will not reach it; I cannot be   50
   your chapman. Yet I have countrymen in town, merchants of love like me: I'll see if they'll put in for a share.
   We cannot lose much by it, and what we have no use for
   we'll sell upon the Friday's mart at 'Who gives more?' I
   am studying, madam, how to purchase you, though at   55
   present I am unprovided of money.
ANGELLICA (aside) Sure, this from any other man would
   anger me – nor shall he know the conquest he has made. –
   Poor angry man, how I despise this railing.
WILLMORE Yes, I am poor – but I'm a gentleman,   60
   And one that scorns this baseness which you practise;
   Poor as I am, I would not sell myself,
   No, not to gain your charming high-prized person.
   Though I admire you strangely for your beauty,
   Yet I contemn* your mind.   65
   – And yet I would at any rate enjoy you,
   At your own rate – but cannot – see here
   The only sum I can command on earth;
   I know not where to eat when this is gone.
   Yet such a slave I am to love and beauty   70
   This last reserve I'll sacrifice to enjoy you.
   – Nay, do not frown, I know you're to be bought,
   And would be bought by me, by me,
   For a mean trifling sum if I could pay it down;
   Which happy knowledge I will still repeat,   75
   And lay it to my heart, it has a virtue in't,
   And soon will cure those wounds your eyes have
      made.
   – And yet – there's something so divinely powerful
   there –
   Nay, I will gaze – to let you see my strength.

   (Holds her, looks on her, and pauses and sighs)

By heaven, bright creature, I would not for the world   80

Thy fame were half so fair as is thy face.

(*Turns her away from him*)

ANGELLICA (*aside*) His words go through me to the very
    soul.
  – If you have nothing else to say to me –
WILLMORE Yes, you shall hear how infamous you are –
    For which I do not hate thee –   85
    But that secures my heart, and all the flames it feels
    Are but so many lusts –
    I know it by their sudden bold intrusion.
    The fire's impatient and betrays, 'tis false –
    For had it been the purer flame of love,   90
    I should have pined and languished at your feet,
    Ere found the impudence to have discovered it.
    I now dare stand your scorn and your denial.
MORETTA Sure, she's bewitched that she can stand thus
    tamely and hear his saucy railing. – Sirrah, will you be 95
    gone?
ANGELLICA (to MORETTA) How dare you take this liberty!
    Withdraw. – Pray tell me, sir, are not you guilty of the
    same mercenary crime? When a lady is proposed to you
    for a wife, you never ask how fair, discreet, or virtuous 100
    she is; but what's her fortune – which if but small, you cry
    'She will not do my business', and basely leave her,
    though she languish for you. Say, is not this as poor?
WILLMORE It is a barbarous custom, which I will scorn to
    defend in our sex, and do despise in yours.   105
ANGELLICA Thou'rt a brave fellow! Put up thy gold, and
    know,
    That were thy fortune large as is thy soul,
    Thou shouldst not buy my love,
    Couldst thou forget those mean effects of vanity
    Which set me out to sale,   110
    And, as a lover, prize my yielding joys?
    Canst thou believe they'll be entirely thine,
    Without considering they were mercenary?

WILLMORE I cannot tell, I must bethink me first. (*aside*) –
Ha, death, I'm going to believe her.   115

ANGELLICA Prithee confirm that faith – or if thou canst
not – Flatter me a little, 'twill please me from thy
mouth.

WILLMORE (*aside*) Curse on thy charming tongue! Dost
thou return
My feigned contempt with so much subtlety?   120
Thou'st found the easiest way into my heart,
Though I yet know that all thou say'st is false.

(*Turning from her in rage*)

ANGELLICA By all that's good, 'tis real;
I never loved before, though oft a mistress.
Shall my first vows be slighted?   125

WILLMORE (*aside*) What can she mean?

ANGELLICA (*in an angry tone*) I find you cannot credit
me.

WILLMORE I know you take me for an arrant ass,
An ass that may be soothed into belief,   130
And then be used at pleasure.
– But, madam, I have been so often cheated
By perjured, soft, deluding hypocrites,
That I've no faith left for the cozening sex;
Especially for women of your trade.   135

ANGELLICA The low esteem you have of me, perhaps
May bring my heart again:
For I have pride, that yet surmounts my love.

(*She turns with pride; he holds her*)

WILLMORE Throw off this pride, this enemy to bliss,
And show the power of love: 'tis with those arms   140
I can be only vanquished, made a slave.

ANGELLICA Is all my mighty expectation vanished?
No, I will not hear thee talk – thou hast a charm
In every word that draws my heart away.
And all the thousand trophies I designed   145
Thou hast undone – why art thou soft?

Thy looks are bravely rough, and meant for war.
Couldst thou not storm on still?
I then perhaps had been as free as thou.
WILLMORE (aside) Death, how she throws her fire about
   my soul!   150
– Take heed, fair creature, how you raise my hopes,
Which once assumed pretend* to all dominion.
There's not a joy thou hast in store,
I shall not then command.
For which I'll pay thee back my soul, my life!   155
Come, let's begin th'account this happy minute!
ANGELLICA And will you pay me then the price I ask?
WILLMORE Oh, why dost thou draw me from an awful
   worship
By showing thou art no divinity?
Conceal the fiend, and show me all the angel!   160
Keep me but ignorant, and I'll be devout
And pay my vows for ever at this shrine.

(*Kneels and kisses her hand*)

ANGELLICA The pay I mean is but thy love for mine. Can
   you give that?
WILLMORE Entirely – come, let's withdraw! Where I'll 165
renew my vows, and breathe 'em with such ardour thou
shalt not doubt my zeal.
ANGELLICA Thou hast a power too strong to be resisted.
       [*Exeunt* WILLMORE *and* ANGELLICA]

MORETTA Now, my curse go with you – is all our project
fallen to this? To love the only enemy to our trade? Nay, 170
to love such a shameroon,* a very beggar, nay a pirate
beggar, whose business is to rifle and be gone; a no-
purchase, no-pay tatterdemalion,* and English picaroon.* A rogue that fights for daily drink, and takes a
pride in being loyally lousy! Oh, I could curse now, if I 175
durst. This is the fate of most whores.
Trophies, which from believing fops we win,
Are spoils to those who cozen us again.

Act 3, Scene 1

A street

(*Enter* FLORINDA, VALERIA, HELLENA, *in antic different dresses from what they were in before;* CALLIS *attending*)

FLORINDA I wonder what should make my brother in so ill a humour? I hope he has not found out our ramble this morning.

HELLENA No, if he had, we should have heard on't at both ears, and have been mewed up* this afternoon; which I   5
would not for the world should have happened – hey ho, I'm as sad as lover's lute.

VALERIA Well, methinks we have learnt this trade of gypsies as readily as if we had been bred upon the road to Loretto;* and yet I did so fumble when I told the stranger   10
his fortune that I was afraid I should have told my own and yours by mistake – but, methinks Hellena has been very serious ever since.

FLORINDA I would give my garters she were in love, to be revenged upon her for abusing me – how is't, Hellena?   15

HELLENA Ah – would I had never seen my mad monsieur – and yet for all your laughing, I am not in love – and yet this small acquaintance, o' my conscience, will never out of my head.

VALERIA Ha, ha, ha, – I laugh to think how thou art fitted   20
with a lover, a fellow that I warrant loves every new face he sees.

HELLENA Hum – he has not kept his word with me here – and may be taken up – that thought is not very pleasant to me – what the deuce should this be now, that I feel?   25

VALERIA What is't like?

HELLENA Nay, the Lord knows – but if I should be hanged I cannot choose but be angry and afraid, when I think that mad fellow should be in love with anybody but me. What to think of myself, I know not – would I could meet   30
with some true damned gypsy, that I might know my fortune.

VALERIA Know it! Why there's nothing so easy; thou wilt

love this wandering inconstant till thou find thyself
hanged about his neck, and then be as mad to get free   35
again.

FLORINDA Yes, Valeria, we shall see her astride his
baggage horse, and follow him to the campaign.

HELLENA So, so, now you are provided for, there's no care
taken of poor me. But since you have set my heart a-   40
wishing, I am resolved to know for what; I will not die of
the pip,* so I will not.

FLORINDA Art thou mad to talk so? Who will like thee
well enough to have thee, that hears what a mad wench
thou art?   45

HELLENA Like me! I don't intend every he that likes me
shall have me, but he that I like. I should have stayed in
the nunnery still, if I had liked my Lady Abbess as well as
she liked me – no, I came thence not (as my wise brother
imagines) to take an eternal farewell of the world, but to   50
love and to be beloved, and I will be beloved, or I'll get
one of your men, so I will.

VALERIA Am I put into the number of lovers?

HELLENA You? Why, coz, I know thou'rt too good-natured
to leave us in any design: thou wouldst venture a cast   55
though thou comest off a loser, especially with such a
gamester. I observe your man, and your willing ear incline
that way; and if you are not a lover, 'tis an art soon learnt
– that I find. (sighs)

FLORINDA I wonder you learnt to love so easily, I had a   60
thousand charms to meet my eyes and ears e'er I could
yield, and 'twas the knowledge of Belvile's merit, not the
surprising person, took my soul. Thou art too rash, to
give a heart at first sight.

HELLENA Hang your considering lover! I never thought   65
beyond the fancy that 'twas a very pretty, idle, silly kind
of pleasure to pass one's time with, to write little soft
nonsensical billets,* and with great difficulty and danger
receive answers in which I shall have my beauty praised,
my wit admired (though little or none), and have the   70
vanity and power to know I am desirable; then I have the

more inclination that way because I am to be a nun, and so shall not be suspected to have any such earthly thoughts about me – but when I walk thus – and sigh thus – they'll think my mind's upon my monastery, and cry 75 'How happy 'tis she's so resolved'. – But not a* word of man.

FLORINDA What mad creature's this?

HELLENA I'll warrant if my brother hears either of you sigh, he cries (gravely) – 'I fear you have the indiscretion 80 to be in love, but take heed the honour of our house, and your own unspotted fame', and so he conjures on till he has laid the soft-winged god in your hearts, or broke the bird's nest – but see, here comes your lover, but where's my inconstant? Let's step aside, and we may learn 85 something.

(*Go aside*)

(*Enter* BELVILE, FREDERICK *and* BLUNT)

BELVILE What means this? The picture's taken in.

BLUNT It may be the wench is good-natured, and will be kind gratis. Your friend's a proper, handsome fellow.

BELVILE I rather think she has cut his throat and is fled: I 90 am mad he should throw himself into dangers – pox on't, I shall want him, too, at night – let's knock and ask for him.

HELLENA My heart goes a-pit-a-pat, for fear 'tis my man they talk of. 95

(*Knock;* MORETTA *above*)

MORETTA What would you have?

BELVILE Tell the stranger that entered here about two hours ago, that his friends stay here for him.

MORETTA A curse upon him for Moretta, would he were at the devil – but he's coming to you. 100

(*Enter* WILLMORE)

HELLENA Aye, aye, 'tis he! Oh, how this vexes me.

BELVILE And how and how, dear lad, has fortune smiled?

Are we to break her windows?* Or raise up altars to her, hah?

WILLMORE Does not my fortune sit triumphant on my 105 brow? Dost not see the little wanton god there all gay and smiling? Have I not an air about my face and eyes that distinguish me from the crowd of common lovers? By heaven, Cupid's quiver has not half so many darts as her eyes! Oh, such a *bona roba*!* To sleep in her arms is lying 110 in *fresco*,* all perfumed air about me.

HELLENA (*aside*) Here's fine encouragement for me to fool on.

WILLMORE Harkee, where didst thou purchase that rich Canary we drank today? Tell me, that I may adore the 115 spigot* and sacrifice to the butt! The juice was divine, into which I must dip my rosary, and then bless all things that I would have bold or fortunate.

BELVILE Well, sir, let's go take a bottle, and hear the story of your success. 120

FREDERICK Would not French wine do better?

WILLMORE Damn the hungry balderdash;* cheerful sack* has a generous virtue in't, inspiring a successful confidence, gives eloquence to the tongue, and vigour to the soul! And has in a few hours completed all my hopes and 125 wishes! There's nothing left to raise a new desire in me – come, let's be gay and wanton – and, gentlemen, study, study what you want, for here are friends, that will supply gentlemen. (*jingles gold*) Hark what a charming sound they make! 'Tis he and she gold whilst here, and shall 130 beget new pleasures every moment.

BLUNT But harkee, sir, you are not married are you?

WILLMORE All the honey of matrimony, but none of the sting, friend!

BLUNT 'Sheartlikins, thou'rt a fortunate rogue! 135

WILLMORE I am so, sir, let these – inform you! – Ha, how sweetly they chime! – Pox of poverty, it makes a man a slave, makes wit and honour sneak. My soul grew lean and rusty for want of credit.

BLUNT 'Sheartlikins, this I like well; it looks like my lucky 140 bargain! Oh how I long for the approach of my squire, that is to conduct me to her house again. Why, here's two provided for!

FREDERICK By this light y'are happy men.

BLUNT Fortune is pleased to smile on us, gentlemen – to 145 smile on us.

(*Enter* SANCHO *and pulls down* BLUNT *by the sleeve*)

SANCHO Sir, my lady expects you –

(*They go aside*)

– She has removed all that might oppose your will and pleasure, and is impatient till you come.

BLUNT Sir, I'll attend you – oh, the happiest rogue! I'll take 150 no leave, lest they either dog me, or stay me.

[*Exit with* SANCHO]

BELVILE But then the little gypsy is forgot?

WILLMORE A mischief on thee for putting her into my thoughts! I had quite forgot her else, and this night's debauch had drunk her quite down.   155

HELLENA Had it so, good captain? (*claps him on the back*)

WILLMORE (*aside*) Hah! I hope she did not hear me.

HELLENA What, afraid of such a champion?

WILLMORE Oh! You're a fine lady of your word, are you not? To make a man languish whole day –   160

HELLENA In tedious search of me.

WILLMORE Egad, child, thou'rt in the right. Hadst thou seen what a melancholy dog I have been ever since I was a lover, how I have walked the streets like a Capuchin* with my hands in my sleeves – faith, sweetheart, thou 165 wouldst pity me.

HELLENA <*aside*> Now if I should be hanged, I can't be angry with him, he dissembles so heartily. – Alas, good captain, what pains you have taken – now were I ungrateful not to reward so true a servant.   170

WILLMORE Poor soul! That's kindly said, I see thou bearest a conscience. Come then, for a beginning show me thy dear face.

HELLENA I'm afraid, my small acquaintance, you have
been staying that swingeing stomach you boasted of this 175
morning; I then remember my little collation* would have
gone down with you without the sauce of a handsome
face – is your stomach so queasy now?

WILLMORE Faith, long fasting, child, spoils a man's appetite – yet if you durst treat, I could so lay about me still – 180

HELLENA And would you fall to, before a priest says grace?

WILLMORE Oh fie, fie! What an old, out-of-fashioned thing
hast thou named! Thou couldst not dash me more out of
countenance shouldst thou show me an ugly face.

(*Whilst he is seemingly courting* HELLENA, *enter*
ANGELLICA, MORETTA, BISKEY *and* SEBASTIAN *all in
masquerade.* ANGELLICA *sees* WILLMORE *and stares*)

ANGELLICA Heavens, 'tis he! And passionately fond to see 185
another woman.

MORETTA What could you less expect from such a
swaggerer?

ANGELLICA Expect? As much as I paid him, a heart
    entire,
Which I had pride enough to think whene'er I gave,   190
It would have raised the man above the vulgar,
Made him all soul, and that all soft and constant.

HELLENA You see, captain, how willing I am to be friends
with you till time and ill luck make us lovers, and ask you
the question first, rather than put your modesty to the 195
blush by asking me. For (alas!) I know you captains are
such strict men, and such severe observers of your vows
to chastity, that 'twill be hard to prevail with your tender
conscience to marry a young willing maid.

WILLMORE Do not abuse me, for fear I should take thee at 200
thy word and marry thee indeed, which I'm sure will be
revenge sufficient.

HELLENA O' my conscience, that will be our destiny,
because we are both of one humour. I am as inconstant as
you, for I have considered, captain, that a handsome 205
woman has a great deal to do whilst her face is good, for

then is our harvest-time to gather friends; and should I in these days of my youth, catch a fit of foolish constancy, I were undone; 'tis loitering by daylight in our great journey. Therefore, I declare I'll allow but one year for 210 love, one year for indifference, and one year for hate, and then – go hang yourself – for I profess myself the gay, the kind, and the inconstant – the devil's in't if this won't please you.

WILLMORE Oh, most damnably – I have a heart with a 215 hole quite through it too, no prison mine to keep a mistress in.

ANGELLICA (aside) Perjured man! How I believe thee now.

HELLENA Well, I see our business as well as humours are alike; yours to cozen as many maids as will trust you, and 220 I as many men as have faith – see if I have not as desperate a lying look as you can have for the heart of you.

(Pulls off her vizard: he starts)

– How do you like it, captain?

WILLMORE Like it! By heaven, I never saw so much 225 beauty! Oh the charms of those sprightly black eyes! That strangely fair face, full of smiles and dimples! Those soft round melting cherry lips! And small even white teeth! Not to be expressed, but silently adored! <she replaces her mask> – Oh, one look more! And strike me dumb, or I 230 shall repeat nothing else till I'm mad.

(He seems to court her to pull off her vizard: she refuses)

ANGELLICA I can endure no more – nor is it fit to interrupt him, for if I do, my jealousy has so destroyed my reason, I shall undo him – therefore I'll retire. (to one of her BRAVOES) And you, Sebastian, follow that woman, and 235 learn who 'tis; (to the other BRAVO) while you tell the fugitive, I would speak to him instantly.

[Exit]

(This while FLORINDA is talking to BELVILE, who stands sullenly; FREDERICK courting VALERIA)

VALERIA Prithee, dear stranger, be not so sullen, for
though you have lost your love, you see my friend frankly
offers you hers to play with in the meantime.   240

BELVILE Faith, madam, I am sorry I can't play at her game.

FREDERICK Pray leave your intercession, and mind your
own affair. They'll better agree apart; he's a modest
sigher in company, but alone no woman 'scapes him.

FLORINDA Sure, he does but rally – yet if it should be true 245
– I'll tempt him farther. Believe me, noble stranger, I'm no
common mistress – and for a little proof on't – wear this
jewel – nay, take it, sir, 'tis right,* and bills of exchange*
may sometimes miscarry.

BELVILE Madam, why am I chose out of all mankind to be 250
the object of your bounty?

VALERIA That's another civil question asked.

FREDERICK Pox of 's modesty, it spoils his own markets
and hinders mine.

FLORINDA Sir, from my window I have often seen you, and 255
women of my quality have so few opportunities for love,
that we ought to lose none.

FREDERICK Aye, this is something! Here's a woman! (to
VALERIA) When shall I be blest with so much kindness
from your fair mouth?   260
(aside to BELVILE) Take the jewel, fool.

BELVILE You tempt me strangely, madam, every way.

FLORINDA (aside) So, if I find him false, my whole repose is
gone.

BELVILE And but for a vow I've made to a very lady, this 265
goodness had subdued me.

FREDERICK Pox on't, be kind, in pity to me be kind, for I
am to thrive here but as you treat her friend.

HELLENA Tell me what you did in yonder house, and I'll
unmask.   270

WILLMORE Yonder house? – Oh – I went to – a – to – why,
there's a friend of mine lives there.

HELLENA What a she, or a he friend?

WILLMORE A man upon honour! A man – A she friend? –
No, no, madam, you have done my business, I thank you. 275

HELLENA And was't your man friend that had more darts in his eyes than Cupid carries in's whole budget* of arrows?

WILLMORE So –

HELLENA 'Ah, such a *bona roba*! To be in her arms is lying 280 in *fresco*, all perfumed air about me' – was this your man friend too?

WILLMORE So –

HELLENA That gave you the he and the she gold, that begets young pleasures? 285

WILLMORE Well, well, madam, then you see there are ladies in the world that will not be cruel – there are, madam, there are –

HELLENA And there be men too, as fine, wild inconstant fellows as yourself, there be, captain, there be, if you go 290 to that now – therefore I'm resolved –

WILLMORE Oh!

HELLENA To see your face no more –

WILLMORE Oh!

HELLENA Till tomorrow. 295

WILLMORE Egad, you frighted me.

HELLENA Nor then neither, unless you'll swear never to see that lady more.

WILLMORE See her! – Why, never to think of womankind again. 300

HELLENA Kneel – and swear.

(*<He> kneels, she gives him her hand*)

WILLMORE I do, never to think – to see – to love – nor lie – with any but thyself.

HELLENA Kiss the book.

WILLMORE Oh, most religious. (*kisses her hand*) 305

HELLENA Now, what a wicked creature am I, to damn a proper fellow.

CALLIS (*to* FLORINDA) Madam, I'll stay no longer, 'tis e'en dark.

FLORINDA However, sir, I'll leave this with you – that 310

when I'm gone, you may repent the opportunity you have
lost by your modesty.

(*Gives him the jewel which is her picture, and exit. He
gazes after her*)

WILLMORE 'Twill be an age till tomorrow, and till then I
will most impatiently expect you. Adieu, my dear pretty
angel.   315

[*Exeunt all the women*]

BELVILE Ha! Florinda's picture – 'twas she herself – what a
dull dog was I! I would have given the world for one
minute's discourse with her.

FREDERICK This comes of your modesty! Ah, pox o'your
vow, 'twas ten to one, but we had lost the jewel by 't. 320

BELVILE Willmore! The blessed'st opportunity lost!
Florinda, friends, Florinda!

WILLMORE Ah, rogue! Such black eyes! Such a face! Such a
mouth! Such teeth – and so much wit!

BELVILE All, all, and a thousand charms besides.   325

WILLMORE Why, dost thou know her?

BELVILE Know her! Aye, aye, and a pox take me with all
my heart for being modest.

WILLMORE But harkee, friend of mine, are you my rival?
And have I been only beating the bush all this while?   330

BELVILE I understand thee not – I'm mad – see here –
(*shows the picture*)

WILLMORE Ha! Whose picture's this? 'Tis a fine wench!

FREDERICK The colonel's mistress, sir.

WILLMORE Oh, oh here – I thought 't had been another
prize – come, come, a bottle will set thee right again. 335
(*gives the picture back*)

BELVILE I am content to try, and by that time 'twill be late
enough for our design.

WILLMORE Agreed.
Love does all day the soul's great empire keep,
But wine at night lulls the soft god asleep.   340

[*Exeunt*]

Act 3, Scene 2

Lucetta's house

(*Enter* BLUNT *and* LUCETTA *with a light*)

LUCETTA Now we are safe and free; no fears of the coming
home of my jealous old husband, which made me a little
thoughtful when you came in first – but now love is all the
business of my soul.

BLUNT I am transported! (*aside*) Pox on't, that I had but   5
some fine things to say to her, such as lovers use – I was a
fool not to learn of Fred a little by heart before I came –
something I must say – 'Sheartlikins sweet soul! I am not
used to compliment, but I'm an honest gentleman, and
thy humble servant.   10

LUCETTA I have nothing to pay for so great a favour, but
such a love as cannot but be great, since at first sight of
that sweet face and shape, it made me your absolute
captive.

BLUNT (*aside*) Kind heart! How prettily she talks! Egad, I'll   15
show her husband a Spanish trick; send him out of the
world and marry her. She's damnably in love with me,
and will ne'er mind settlements,* and so there's that
saved.

LUCETTA Well, sir, I'll go and undress me, and be with you   20
instantly.

BLUNT Make haste then, for 'sheartlikins, dear soul, thou
canst not guess at the pain of a longing lover, when his
joys are drawn within the compass of a few minutes.

LUCETTA You speak my sense, and I'll make haste to prove   25
it.

[*Exit*]

BLUNT 'Tis a rare girl! And this one night's enjoyment with
her will be worth all the days I ever passed in Essex.
Would she would go with me into England, though to say
truth there's plenty of whores already. But a pox on 'em,   30
they are such mercenary prodigal whores, that they want

such a one as this, that's free and generous, to give 'em
good examples. Why, what a house she has, how rich and
fine!

(*Enter* SANCHO)

SANCHO Sir, my lady has sent me to conduct you to her   35
chamber.

BLUNT Sir, I shall be proud to follow – here's one of her
servants too! 'Sheartlikins, by this garb and gravity he
might be a Justice of Peace in Essex, and is but a pimp
here.   40

[*Exeunt*]

Act 3, Scene 3

*The scene changes to a chamber with an alcove bed in't,
a table, etc.,* LUCETTA *in bed*

(*Enter* SANCHO *and* BLUNT, *who takes the candle of*
SANCHO *at the door*)

SANCHO Sir, my commission reaches no farther.

BLUNT I'll excuse your compliment – what, in bed, my
sweet mistress?

LUCETTA You see, I still outdo you in kindness.

BLUNT And thou shalt see what haste I'll make to quit   5
scores – oh, the luckiest rogue!

(*He undresses himself*)

LUCETTA Should you be false or cruel now!

BLUNT False! 'Sheartlikins, what dost thou take me for? A
Jew? An insensible heathen? A pox of thy old jealous
husband: an* he were dead, egad, sweet soul, it should be 10
none of my fault if I did not marry thee.

LUCETTA It never should be mine.

BLUNT Good soul! I'm the fortunest dog!

LUCETTA Are you not undressed yet?

BLUNT As much as my impatience will permit.   15

   (*Goes towards the bed in his shirt, drawers, etc.*)

LUCETTA Hold, sir, put out the light, it may betray us else.
BLUNT Anything; I need no other light but that of thine
eyes! 'Sheartlikins, there, I think I had it.

  (*Puts out the candle, the bed descends,* he gropes about
to find it*)

  – Why – why – where am I got? What, not yet? – Where
are you sweetest? Ah, the rogue's silent now – a pretty   20
love-trick this – How she'll laugh at me anon! You need
not, my dear rogue, you need not! I'm on fire already –
come, come, now call me in pity. Sure, I'm enchanted! I
have been round the chamber, and can find neither
woman, nor bed. I locked the door, I'm sure she cannot   25
go that way – or if she could, the bed could not. Enough,
enough, my pretty wanton, do not carry the jest too far –
(*lights on a trap, and is let down*) Ha, betrayed! Dogs!
Rogues! Pimps! – Help! Help!

  (*Enter* LUCETTA, PHILIPPO, *and* SANCHO *with a light*)

PHILIPPO Ha, ha, ha, he's dispatched finely.   30
LUCETTA Now, sir, had I been coy, we had missed of this
booty.
PHILIPPO Nay, when I saw 'twas a substantial fool, I was
mollified; but when you dote upon a serenading coxcomb,
upon a face, fine clothes, and a lute, it makes me rage.   35
LUCETTA You know I was never guilty of that folly, my
dear Philippo, but with yourself – but come, let's see what
we have got by this.
PHILIPPO A rich coat! Sword and hat – these breeches, too,
are well lined! See here, a gold watch! A purse – Ha, gold! 40
At least two hundred pistoles! A bunch of diamond rings!
And one with the family arms! A gold box – with a medal
of his king! And his lady mother's picture! – These were
sacred relics, believe me! See, the waistband of his
breeches have a mine of gold – old Queen Bess's! We have   45

a quarrel to her ever since eighty-eight,* and may
therefore justify the theft, the Inquisition might have
committed it.

LUCETTA See, a bracelet of bowed* gold! These his sisters
tied about his arm at parting. But well – for all this, I fear   50
his being a stranger may make a noise and hinder our
trade with them hereafter.

PHILIPPO That's our security; he is not only a stranger to
us, but to the country too. The common shore* into
which he is descended, thou knowst conducts him into   55
another street, which this light will hinder him from ever
finding again. He knows neither your name, nor that of
the street where your house is, nay, nor the way to his
own lodgings.

LUCETTA And art not thou an unmerciful rogue, not to   60
afford him one night for all this? I should not have been
such a Jew.

PHILIPPO Blame me not, Lucetta, to keep as much of thee
as I can to myself. Come, that thought makes me wanton!
Let's to bed! Sancho, lock up these.   65
This is the fleece which fools do bear,
Designed for witty men to shear.

[*Exeunt*]

Act 3, Scene 4

(*The scene changes, and discovers* BLUNT *creeping out of
a common shore, his face, etc. all dirty*)

BLUNT (*climbing up*) Oh Lord! I am got out at last, and
(which is a miracle) without a clue* – and now to
damning and cursing! But if that would ease me, where
shall I begin? With my fortune, myself, or the quean* that
cozened me? What a dog was I to believe in woman! Oh   5
coxcomb! Ignorant, conceited coxcomb! To fancy she
could be enamoured with my person – at first sight
enamoured! – Oh, I'm a cursed puppy! 'Tis plain, fool

was writ upon my forehead! She perceived it! – Saw the
Essex calf there – for what allurements could there be in   10
this countenance, which I can endure, because I'm
acquainted with it? Oh, dull silly dog! To be thus soothed
into a cozening! Had I been drunk, I might fondly have
credited the young quean! – But as I was in my right wits,
to be thus cheated confirms it, I am a dull believing   15
English country fop. But my comrades! Death and the
devil! There's the worst of all – then a ballad will be sung
tomorrow on the Prado,* to a lousy tune, of the
enchanted 'squire and the annihilated* damsel – but Fred,
that rogue, and the colonel will abuse me beyond all   20
Christian patience. Had she left me my clothes, I have a
bill of exchange at home would have saved my credit, but
now all hope is taken from me. Well, I'll home (if I can
find the way) with this consolation: that I am not the first
kind, believing coxcomb, but there are, gallants, many   25
such good natures amongst ye.
And though you've better arts to hide your follies,
'Adsheartlikins y'are all as arrant cullies.*

                                                [*Exit*]

Act 3, Scene 5

The garden in the night

(*Enter* FLORINDA *in an undress,* * *with a key and a little
box*)

FLORINDA Well, thus far I'm in my way to happiness: I
have got myself free from Callis; my brother too, I find by
yonder light, is got into his cabinet,* and thinks not of
me; I have by good fortune got the key of the garden back
door. I'll open it to prevent Belvile's knocking – a little   5
noise will now alarm my brother. Now am I as fearful as
a young thief. (*unlocks the door*) Hark, what noise is
that? Oh, 'twas the wind that played amongst the boughs

– Belvile stays long, methinks – it's time. Stay – for fear of
a surprise, I'll hide these jewels in yonder jessamin.* (*she*   10
goes to lay down the box)

(*Enter* WILLMORE *drunk*)

WILLMORE What the devil became of these fellows, Belvile
and Frederick? They promised to stay at the next corner
for me, but who the devil knows the corner of a full moon
– now – whereabouts am I? Hah – what have we here, a
garden! A very convenient place to sleep in. Hah – what   15
has God sent us here? – A female! – By this light, a
woman! I'm a dog if it be not a very wench!

FLORINDA He's come! Ha – who's there?

WILLMORE Sweet soul! Let me salute thy shoestring.

FLORINDA 'Tis not my Belvile. Good heavens! I know him   20
not. – Who are you, and from whence come you?

WILLMORE Prithee, prithee, child – not so many hard
questions. Let it suffice I am here, child – come, come kiss
me.

FLORINDA Good gods! What luck is mine!   25

WILLMORE Only good luck, child, parlous* good luck –
come hither – 'tis a delicate shining wench – by this hand,
she's perfumed and smells like any nosegay. Prithee, dear
soul, let's not play the fool, and lose time – precious time
– for as Gad shall save me, I'm as honest a fellow as   30
breathes, though I'm a little disguised* at present. Come,
I say – why, thou mayst be free with me, I'll be very
secret. I'll not boast who obliged me, not I – for hang me
if I know thy name.

FLORINDA Heavens! What a filthy beast is this?   35

WILLMORE I am so, and thou ought'st the sooner to lie
with me for that reason – for look you, child, there will be
no sin in't, because 'twas neither designed nor premedi-
tated. 'Tis pure accident on both sides – that's a certain
thing now. Indeed, should I make love to you, and you   40
vow fidelity – and swear and lie till you believed and
yielded – that were to make it wilful fornication – the

crying sin of the nation. Thou art therefore (as thou art a
good Christian) obliged in conscience to deny me nothing.
Now – come, be kind without any more idle prating.   45

FLORINDA Oh, I am ruined! – Wicked man, unhand me.

WILLMORE Wicked! Egad, child, a judge, were he young
and vigorous and saw those eyes of thine, would know
'twas they gave the first blow – the first provocation.
Come, prithee, let's lose no time, I say – this is a fine   50
convenient place.

FLORINDA Sir, let me go, I conjure you, or I'll call out.

WILLMORE Aye, aye, you were best to call witness to see
how finely you treat me – do –

FLORINDA I'll cry murder! Rape! Or anything, if you do   55
not instantly let me go.

WILLMORE A rape! Come, come, you lie, you baggage, you
lie. What, I'll warrant you would fain have the world
believe now that you are not so forward as I. No, not you.
Why, at this time of night was your cobweb door set   60
open, dear spider, but to catch flies? Hah! Come – or I
shall be damnably angry. Why, what a coil* is here –

FLORINDA Sir, can you think –

WILLMORE That you would do't for nothing? Oh, oh, I
find what you would be at – look here, here's a pistole for 65
you. Here's a work indeed – here – take it I say –

FLORINDA For heaven's sake, sir, as you're a gentleman –

WILLMORE So – now – now – she would be wheedling me
for more. What, you will not take it then – you are
resolved you will not? Come, come take it, or I'll put it up 70
again – for look ye, I never give more. Why how now,
mistress, are you so high i'th'mouth a pistole won't down
with you? Hah – why, what a work's here? – In good
time. Come, no struggling to be gone – but an y'are good
at a dumb wrestle, I'm for ye – look ye – I'm for ye –   75

(*She struggles with him*)

(*Enter* BELVILE *and* FREDERICK)

BELVILE The door is open. A pox of this mad fellow, I'm

angry that we've lost him, I durst have sworn he had
followed us.
FREDERICK But you were so hasty, colonel, to be gone.
FLORINDA Help! Help! Murder! Help – oh, I am ruined.   80
BELVILE Ha! Sure that's Florinda's voice. (*comes up to
them*) A man! Villain, let go that lady!

(*A noise.* WILLMORE *turns and draws.* FREDERICK
interposes)

FLORINDA Belvile! Heavens! My brother too is coming,
and 'twill be impossible to escape. Belvile, I conjure you
to walk under my chamber window, from whence I'll give   85
you some instructions what to do – this rude man has
undone us.

[*Exit*]

WILLMORE Belvile!

(*Enter* PEDRO, STEPHANO, *and other servants with
lights*)

PEDRO I'm betrayed! Run, Stephano, and see if Florinda be
safe.   90

[*Exit* STEPHANO]

(*They fight, and* PEDRO's *party beats 'em out*)

So, whoe'r they be, all is not well. I'll to Florinda's
chamber.

(*Going out, meets* STEPHANO)

STEPHANO You need not, sir, the poor lady's fast asleep
and thinks no harm. I would not wake her, sir, for fear of
frighting her with your danger.   95
PEDRO I'm glad she's there. Rascals, how came the garden
door open?
STEPHANO That question comes too late, sir; some of my
fellow servants masquerading, I'll warrant.
PEDRO Masquerading! A lewd custom to debauch our   100
youth – there's something more in this then* I imagine.
[*Exeunt*]

Act 3, Scene 6

Scene changes to the street

(*Enter* BELVILE *in a rage.* FREDERICK *holding him, and* WILLMORE *melancholy*)

WILLMORE Why, how the devil should I know Florinda?

BELVILE A plague of your ignorance! If it had not been Florinda, must you be a beast – a brute – a senseless swine?

WILLMORE Well, sir, you see I am endured with patience –   5
I can bear – though, egad, y'are very free with me, methinks. I was in good hopes the quarrel would have been on my side, for so uncivilly interrupting me.

BELVILE Peace, brute, whilst thou'rt safe! Oh, I'm distracted.   10

WILLMORE Nay, nay, I'm an unlucky dog, that's certain.

BELVILE Ah, curse upon the star that ruled my birth! Or whatsoever other influence that makes me still so wretched.

WILLMORE Thou break'st my heart with these complaints.   15
There is no star in fault, no influence but sack, the cursed sack I drunk.

FREDERICK Why, how the devil came you so drunk?

WILLMORE Why, how the devil came you so sober?

BELVILE A curse upon his thin skull, he was always   20
beforehand that way.

FREDERICK Prithee, dear colonel, forgive him; he's sorry for his fault.

BELVILE He's always so after he has done a mischief – a plague on all such brutes.   25

WILLMORE By this light, I took her for an arrant harlot.

BELVILE Damn your debauched opinion! Tell me, sot, hadst thou so much sense and light about thee to distinguish her woman, and couldst not see something about her face and person to strike an awful reverence   30
into thy soul?

WILLMORE Faith no, I considered her as mere a woman as I could wish.

BELVILE 'Sdeath, I have no patience – draw, or I'll kill you.

WILLMORE Let that alone till tomorrow, and if I set not all   35
right again, use your pleasure.

BELVILE Tomorrow! Damn it,
The spiteful light will lead me to no happiness.
Tomorrow is Antonio's, and perhaps
Guides him to my undoing. Oh, that I could meet   40
This rival! This powerful fortunate!

WILLMORE What then?

BELVILE Let thy own reason, or my rage, instruct thee.

WILLMORE I shall be finely informed then, no doubt. Hear
me, colonel – hear me – show me the man and I'll do his   45
business.

BELVILE I know him no more than thou, or if I did I should
not need thy aid.

WILLMORE This you say is Angellica's house; I promised
the kind baggage to lie with her tonight. (*offers to go in*)   50

(*Enter* ANTONIO *and his* PAGE. ANTONIO *knocks on the
<door with> the hilt of his sword*)

ANTONIO You paid the thousand crowns I directed?

PAGE To the lady's old woman, sir, I did.

WILLMORE Who the devil have we here?

BELVILE I'll now plant myself under Florinda's window,
and if I find no comfort there, I'll die.   55

[*Exeunt* BELVILE *and* FREDERICK]

(*Enter* MORETTA)

MORETTA Page!

PAGE Here's my lord.

WILLMORE How is this? A picaroon going to board my
frigate? Here's one chase-gun* for you.

(*Drawing his sword, jostles* ANTONIO, *who turns and
draws. They fight,* ANTONIO *falls*)

MORETTA Oh bless us! We're all undone!   60

(*Runs in and shuts the door*)

PAGE Help! Murder!

(BELVILE *returns at the noise of fighting*)

BELVILE Ha! The mad rogue's engaged in some unlucky adventure again.

(*Enter two or three* MASQUERADERS)

MASQUERADERS Ha! A man killed!

WILLMORE How! A man killed! Then I'll go home to sleep. 65
[*Puts up and reels out*]
[*Exeunt* MASQUERADERS *another way*]

BELVILE Who should it be? Pray heaven the rogue is safe, for all my quarrel to him.

(*As* BELVILE *is groping about, enter an* OFFICER *and* SIX SOLDIERS)

SOLDIER Who's there?

OFFICER So, here's one dispatched – secure the murderer.

BELVILE Do not mistake my charity for murder! I came to 70 his assistance.

(*Soldiers seize on* BELVILE)

OFFICER That shall be tried, sir – St Jago,* swords drawn in the carnival!

(*Goes to* ANTONIO)

ANTONIO Thy hand, prithee.

OFFICER Ha! Don Antonio! Look well to the villain there. 75 How is it, sir?

ANTONIO I'm hurt.

BELVILE Has my humanity made me a criminal?

OFFICER Away with him.

BELVILE What a cursed chance is this! 80
[*Exeunt soldiers with* BELVILE]

ANTONIO (*to the* OFFICER) This is the man that has set upon me twice. Carry him to my apartment, till you have farther orders from me.

[*Exit* ANTONIO, *led*]

Act 4, Scene 1

A fine room

Discovers BELVILE *as by dark, alone*

BELVILE When shall I be weary of railing on Fortune, who
is resolved never to turn with smiles upon me? Two such
defeats in one night none but the devil, and that mad
rogue, could have contrived to have plagued me with. I
am here a prisoner, but where, heaven knows – and if   5
there be murder done, I can soon decide the fate of a
stranger in a nation without mercy. Yet this is nothing to
the torture my soul bows with when I think of losing my
fair, my dear Florinda. Hark, my door opens – a light – a
man – and seems of quality – armed, too! Now shall I die   10
like a dog, without defence.

(*Enter* ANTONIO *in a night-gown,* with a light; his arm
in a scarf, and a sword under his arm. He sets the
candle on the table*)

ANTONIO Sir, I come to know what injuries I have done
you, that could provoke you to so mean an action as to
attack me basely, without allowing time for my defence.

BELVILE Sir, for a man in my circumstances to plead   15
innocence would look like fear. But view me well, and
you will find no marks of coward on me, nor anything
that betrays that brutality you accuse me with.

ANTONIO In vain, sir, you impose upon my sense. You are
not only he who drew on me last night, but yesterday   20
before the same house, that of Angellica.
Yet there is something in your face and mien
That makes me wish I were mistaken.

BELVILE I own I fought today in the defence of a friend of
mine, with whom you (if you're the same) and your party   25
were first engaged.
Perhaps you think this crime enough to kill me,
But if you do, I cannot fear you'll do it basely.

ANTONIO No, sir, I'll make you fit for a defence with this.

(Gives him the sword)

BELVILE This gallantry surprises me – nor know I how to   30
use this present, sir, against a man so brave.

ANTONIO You shall not need.
For know, I come to snatch you from a danger
That is decreed against you:
Perhaps your life or long imprisonment;   35
And 'twas with so much courage you offended,
I cannot see you punished.

BELVILE How shall I pay this generosity?

ANTONIO It had been safer to have killed another
Than have attempted me.   40
To show your danger, sir, I'll let you know my
    quality;
And 'tis the viceroy's son whom you have wounded
    here.

BELVILE The viceroy's son!
(aside) Death and confusion! Was this plague reserved
To complete all the rest – obliged by him!   45
The man of all the world I would destroy!

ANTONIO You seem disordered, sir.

BELVILE Yes, trust me, sir, I am, and 'tis with pain
That man receives such bounties,
Who wants the power to pay 'em back again.   50

ANTONIO To gallant spirits 'tis indeed uneasy;
But you may quickly overpay* me, sir.

BELVILE Then I am well. *(aside)* Kind heaven, but set us
    even,
That I may fight with him, and keep my honour safe.
– Oh, I'm impatient, sir, to be discounting   55
The mighty debt I owe you, command me quickly.

ANTONIO I have a quarrel with a rival, sir,
About the maid we love.

BELVILE *(aside)* Death, 'tis Florinda he means –
That thought destroys my reason,   60
And I shall kill him –

ANTONIO My rival, sir,
Is one has all the virtues man can boast of –

BELVILE (*aside*) Death! Who should this be?

ANTONIO He challenged me to meet him on the Molo   65
As soon as day appeared, but last night's quarrel
Has made my arm unfit to guide a sword.

BELVILE I apprehend you, sir, you'd have me kill the
man
That lays a claim to the maid you speak of.
I'll do't – I'll fly to do't!   70

ANTONIO Sir, do you know her?

BELVILE No, sir, but 'tis enough she is admired by you.

ANTONIO Sir, I shall rob you of the glory on't,
For you must fight under my name and dress.

BELVILE That opinion must be strangely obliging that   75
makes you think I can personate the brave Antonio,
whom I can but strive to imitate.

ANTONIO You say too much to my advantage.
Come, sir, the day appears that calls you forth.
Within, sir, is the habit.   80

[*Exit* ANTONIO]

BELVILE Fantastic Fortune, thou deceitful light,*
That cheats the wearied traveller by night,
Though on a precipice each step you tread,
I am resolved to follow where you lead.

[*Exit*]

Act 4, Scene 2

The Molo

(*Enter* FLORINDA *and* CALLIS *in masks with* STEPHANO)

FLORINDA (*aside*) I'm dying with my fears. Belvile's not
coming as I expected under my window,
Makes me believe that all those fears were true.
– Canst thou not tell with whom my brother fights?

STEPHANO No, madam, they were both in masquerade. I   5
was by when they challenged one another, and they had
decided the question then, but were prevented by some

cavaliers, which made 'em put it off till now – but I am
sure 'tis about you they fight.

FLORINDA (*aside*) Nay, then, 'tis with Belvile, for what   10
other lover have I that dares fight for me, except Antonio?
And he is too much in favour with my brother. If it be he,
for whom shall I direct my prayers to heaven?

STEPHANO Madam, I must leave you, for if my master see
me, I shall be hanged for being your conductor – I escaped   15
narrowly for the excuse I made for you last night i' th'
garden.

FLORINDA And I'll reward thee for 't – prithee, no more.
                                    [*Exit* STEPHANO]

(*Enter* DON PEDRO *in his masquing habit*)

PEDRO Antonio's late today, the place will fill, and we may
be prevented.   20

(*Walks about*)

FLORINDA (*aside*) Antonio! Sure I heard amiss.

PEDRO But who will not excuse a happy lover
When soft fair arms confine the yielding neck;
And the kind whisper languishingly breathes,
'Must you be gone so soon?'   25
Sure, I had dwelt forever on her bosom –
But stay, he's here.

(*Enter* BELVILE *dressed in* ANTONIO'S *clothes*)

FLORINDA 'Tis not Belvile, half my fears are vanished.

PEDRO Antonio!

BELVILE (*aside*) This must be he.   30
You're early, sir – I do not use to be outdone this
way.

PEDRO The wretched, sir, are watchful, and 'tis enough
You've the advantage of me in Angellica.

BELVILE (*aside*) Angellica! Or* I've mistook my man, or   35
else Antonio.
Can he forget his interest in Florinda,
And fight for common prize?

PEDRO Come, sir, you know our terms –
BELVILE (*aside*) By heaven, not I.   40
  – No talking, I am ready, sir.

       (*Offers to fight,* FLORINDA *runs in*)

FLORINDA (*to* BELVILE) O, hold! Whoe'er you be, I do
  conjure you, hold!
  If you strike here – I die.
PEDRO Florinda!   45
BELVILE Florinda imploring for my rival!
PEDRO Away, this kindness is unseasonable.

   (*Puts her by, they fight; she runs in just as* BELVILE
           disarms PEDRO)

FLORINDA Who are you, sir, that dares deny my
  prayers?
BELVILE Thy prayers destroy him. If thou wouldst
  preserve him,
  Do that thou'rt unacquainted with and curse him.   50

           (*She holds him*)

FLORINDA By all you hold most dear, by her you love,
  I do conjure you, touch him not.
BELVILE By her I love!
  See – I obey – and at your feet resign,
  The useless trophy of my victory.   55

       (*Lays his sword at her feet*)

PEDRO Antonio, you've done enough to prove you love
  Florinda.
BELVILE Love Florinda!
  Does heaven love adoration, prayer, or penitence! Love
  her! Here, sir – your sword again. (*snatches up the sword* 60
  and gives it him) Upon this truth, I'll fight my life away.
PEDRO No, you've redeemed my sister, and my friendship!

   (*He gives him* FLORINDA *and pulls off his vizard to*
      show his face, and puts it on again)

BELVILE Don Pedro!

PEDRO Can you resign your claims to other women,
And give your heart entirely to Florinda?   65

BELVILE Entire as dying saints' confessions are!
I can delay my happiness no longer.
This minute let me make Florinda mine!

PEDRO This minute let it be – no time so proper,
This night my father will arrive from Rome,   70
And possibly may hinder what we purpose!

FLORINDA Oh heavens! This minute!

(*Enter* MASQUERADERS *and pass over*)

BELVILE Oh, do not ruin me!

PEDRO The place begins to fill, and that we may not be
observed, do you walk off to St Peter's church, where I   75
will meet you and conclude your happiness.

BELVILE I'll meet you there. – (*aside*) If there be no more
saints' churches in Naples.

FLORINDA Oh stay, sir, and recall your hasty doom!
Alas, I have not yet prepared my heart   80
To entertain so strange a guest.

PEDRO Away, this silly modesty is assumed too late.

BELVILE Heaven, madam! What do you do?

FLORINDA Do? Despise the man that lays a tyrant's
claim
To what he ought to conquer by submission.   85

BELVILE You do not know me – move a little this way.
(*draws her aside*)

FLORINDA Yes, you may force me even to the altar,
But not the holy man that offers there
Shall force me to be thine.

(PEDRO *talks to* CALLIS *this while*)

BELVILE Oh, do not lose so blest an opportunity!   90
See – 'tis your Belvile – not Antonio,
Whom your mistaken scorn and anger ruins.

(*Pulls off his vizard*)

FLORINDA Belvile!
    Where was my soul it could not meet thy voice
    And take this knowledge in?   95

(*As they are talking, enter* WILLMORE *finely dressed, and*
FREDERICK)

WILLMORE No intelligence! No news of Belvile yet – well, I
    am the most unlucky rascal in nature – ha – am I
    deceived? Or is it he? Look, Fred – 'tis he – my dear
    Belvile!

(*Runs and embraces him.* BELVILE'*s vizard falls out on's
hand*)

BELVILE Hell and confusion seize thee!   100
PEDRO Ha! Belvile! I beg your pardon, sir.

(*Takes* FLORINDA *from him*)

BELVILE Nay touch her not, she's mine by conquest, sir;
    I won her by my sword.
WILLMORE Didst thou so? And egad, child, we'll keep her
    by the sword.   105

(*Draws on* PEDRO. BELVILE *goes between*)

BELVILE Stand off!
    Thou'rt so profanely lewd, so cursed by heaven,
    All quarrels thou espousest must be fatal.
WILLMORE Nay, an you be so hot, my valour's coy,
    And shall be courted when you want it next. (*puts up* 110
his sword)
BELVILE (*to* PEDRO) You know I ought to claim a
    victor's right.
    But you're the brother to divine Florinda,
    To whom I'm such a slave. To purchase her
    I durst not hurt the man she holds so dear.
PEDRO 'Twas by Antonio's, not by Belvile's sword   115
    This question should have been decided, sir.
    I must confess much to your bravery's due,
    Both now, and when I met you last in arms.

But I am nicely punctual in my word,
As men of honour ought, and beg your pardon.   120
For this mistake another time shall clear.
(*aside to* FLORINDA *as they are going out*)
This was some plot between you and Belvile.
But I'll prevent you.

(BELVILE *looks after her and begins to walk up and
down in rage*)

WILLMORE Do not be modest now and lose the woman,
but if we shall fetch her back so –   125
BELVILE Do not speak to me –
WILLMORE Not speak to you! Egad, I'll speak to you, and
will be answered too.
BELVILE Will you, sir –
WILLMORE I know I've done some mischief, but I'm so dull 130
a puppy, that I'm the son of a whore if I know how, or
where – prithee inform my understanding –
BELVILE Leave me, I say, and leave me instantly.
WILLMORE I will not leave you in this humour, nor till I
know my crime.   135
BELVILE Death, I'll tell you, sir –

(*Draws and runs at* WILLMORE. *He runs out*, BELVILE
after him; FREDERICK *interposes*)

(*Enter* ANGELLICA, MORETTA *and* SEBASTIAN)

ANGELLICA Ha – Sebastian –
Is not that Willmore? Haste, haste and bring him back.
FREDERICK The colonel's mad – I never saw him thus
before. I'll after 'em lest he do some mischief, for I am 140
sure Willmore will not draw on him.

[*Exit*]

ANGELLICA I am all rage! My first desires defeated!
For one for aught he knows that has no
Other merit than her quality –
Her being Don Pedro's sister. He loves her!   145
I know 'tis so – dull, dull, insensible –

He will not see me now though oft invited;
And broke his word last night – false, perjured man!
He that but yesterday fought for my favours,
And would have made his life a sacrifice   150
To've gained one night with me,
Must now be hired and courted to my arms.

MORETTA I told you what would come on't, but Moretta's
an old doting fool. Why did you give him five hundred
crowns, but to set himself out for other lovers? You 155
should have kept him poor, if you had meant to have had
any good from him.

ANGELLICA Oh, name not such mean trifles! Had I given
Him all my youth has earned from sin,
I had not lost a thought, nor sigh upon't.   160
But I have given him my eternal rest,
My whole repose, my future joys, my heart!
My virgin heart, Moretta! Oh 'tis gone!

MORETTA Curse on him, here he comes.
How fine she has made him too.   165

(*Enter* WILLMORE *and* SEBASTIAN. ANGELLICA *turns
and walks away*)

WILLMORE How now, turned shadow!
Fly when I pursue, and follow when I fly!

(*sings*) Stay, gentle shadow of my dove
And tell me ere I go,
Whether the substance may not prove   170
A fleeting thing like you.

(*As she turns she looks on him*)

There's a soft, kind look remaining yet.

ANGELLICA Well, sir, you may be gay; all happiness,
All joys pursue you still. Fortune's your slave,
And gives you every hour choice of new hearts   175
And beauties, till you are cloyed with the repeated
Bliss which others vainly languish for.
But know, false man, that I shall be revenged.

(Turns away in rage)

WILLMORE So, gad, there are of those faint-hearted lovers,
whom such a sharp lesson next their hearts would make   180
as impotent as fourscore. Pox o'this whining! My business is to laugh and love. A pox on't, I hate your sullen
lover: a man shall lose as much time to put you in humour
now, as would serve to gain a new woman.

ANGELLICA I scorn to cool that fire I cannot raise,   185
Or do the drudgery of your virtuous mistress.

WILLMORE A virtuous mistress! Death, what a thing thou
hast found out for me! Why, what the devil should I do
with a virtuous woman? A sort of ill-natured creatures,
that take a pride to torment a lover. Virtue is but an   190
infirmity in woman; a disease that renders even the
handsome ungrateful, while the ill-favoured, for want of
solicitations and address, only fancy themselves so. I have
lain with a woman of quality, who has all the while been
railing at whores.   195

ANGELLICA I will not answer for your mistress's virtue,
Though she be young enough to know no guilt;
And I could wish you would persuade my heart
'Twas the two hundred thousand crowns you courted.

WILLMORE Two hundred thousand crowns! What story's   200
this? What trick? What woman? – Ha!

ANGELLICA How strange you make it; have you forgot the
creature you entertained on the piazza last night?

WILLMORE *(aside)* Ha! My gypsy worth two hundred
thousand crowns! Oh, how I long to be with her – pox, I   205
knew she was of quality.

ANGELLICA False man! I see my ruin in thy face.
How many vows you breathed upon my bosom,
Never to be unjust – have you forgot so soon?

WILLMORE Faith no, I was just coming to repeat 'em – but   210
here's a humour indeed – would make a man a saint.
(aside) Would she would be angry enough to leave me,
and command me not to wait on her.

(Enter HELLENA *dressed in man's clothes)*

HELLENA (*aside*) This must be Angellica! I know it by her
mumping* matron here. Aye, aye, 'tis she! My mad 215
captain's with her too, for all his swearing – how this
unconstant humour makes me love him!
– Pray, good grave gentlewoman, is not this Angellica?

MORETTA My too young sir, it is – (*aside*) I hope 'tis one
from Don Antonio. (*goes to* ANGELLICA) 220

HELLENA (*aside*) Well, something I'll do to vex him for
this.

ANGELLICA I will not speak with him; am I in humour to
receive a lover?

WILLMORE Not speak with him! Why I'll be gone – and 225
wait your idler minutes – can I show less obedience to the
thing I love so fondly?

(*Offers to go*)

ANGELLICA A fine excuse this! Stay –

WILLMORE And hinder your advantage! Should I repay
your bounties so ungratefully? 230

ANGELLICA Come hither, boy.
(*to* WILLMORE) That I may let you see
How much above the advantages you name,
I prize one minute's joy with you.

WILLMORE Oh, you destroy me with this endearment. 235
(*impatient to be gone*) Death! How shall I get away? –
Madam, 'twill not be fit I should be seen with you
– besides, it will not be convenient – and I've a friend –
that's dangerously sick.

ANGELLICA I see you're impatient – yet you shall stay. 240

WILLMORE (*aside*) And miss my assignation with my
gypsy.

(*Walks about impatiently*)

(MORETTA *brings* HELLENA, *who addresses herself to*
ANGELLICA)

HELLENA Madam,
You'll hardly pardon my intrusion,
When you shall know my business! 245

And I'm too young to tell my tale with art;
But there must be a wondrous store of goodness,
Where so much beauty dwells.
ANGELLICA A pretty advocate, whoever sent thee.
Prithee, proceed. – (*to* WILLMORE *who is stealing off*) 250
Nay, sir, you shall not go.
WILLMORE (*aside*) Then I shall lose my dear gypsy forever
– Pox on't, she stays me out of spite.
HELLENA I am related to a lady, madam,
Young, rich, and nobly born, but has the fate   255
To be in love with a young English gentleman.
Strangely she loves him, at first sight she loved him,
But did adore him when she heard him speak;
For he, she said, had charms in every word,
That failed not to surprise, to wound and conquer.   260
WILLMORE (*aside*) Ha! Egad, I hope this concerns me.
ANGELLICA (*aside*) 'Tis my false man he means – would he
were gone. This praise will raise his pride, and ruin me –
(*to* WILLMORE) Well, since you are so impatient to be
gone I will release you, sir.   265
WILLMORE (*aside*) Nay, then, I'm sure 'twas me he spoke
of, this cannot be the effects of kindness in her.
– No, madam, I've considered better on't,
And will not give you cause of jealousy.
ANGELLICA But, sir, I've – business, that –   270
WILLMORE This shall not do, I know 'tis but to try me.
ANGELLICA Well, to your story, boy – (*aside*) though
'twill undo me.
HELLENA With this addition to his other beauties,
He won her unregarding tender heart.
He vowed, and sighed, and swore he loved her dearly; 275
And she believed the cunning flatterer,
And thought herself the happiest maid alive.
Today was the appointed time by both
To consummate their bliss;
The virgin, altar, and the priest were dressed,   280
And while she languished for th'expected bridegroom,
She heard he paid his broken vows to you.

WILLMORE (*aside*) So, this is some dear rogue that's in love
  with me, and this way lets me know it; or if it be not me,
  he means someone whose place I may supply.   285
ANGELLICA Now I perceive
  The cause of thy impatience to be gone,
  And all the business of this glorious dress.
WILLMORE Damn the young prater, I know not what he
  means.   290
HELLENA Madam,
  In your fair eyes I read too much concern,
  To tell my farther business.
ANGELLICA Prithee, sweet youth, talk on, thou mayst
    perhaps
  Raise here a storm that may undo my passion,   295
  And then I'll grant thee anything.
HELLENA Madam, 'tis to entreat you (oh, unreasonable)
  You would not see this stranger;
  For if you do, she vows you are undone,
  Though nature never made a man so excellent,   300
  And sure he' ad been a god, but for inconstancy.
WILLMORE (*aside*) Ah, rogue, how finely he's instructed! –
  'Tis plain; some woman that has seen me *en passant*.*
ANGELLICA Oh, I shall burn with jealousy! Do you know
  the man you speak of?   305
HELLENA Yes, madam, he used to be in buff and scarlet.
ANGELLICA (*to* WILLMORE) Thou, false as hell, what canst
  thou say to this?
WILLMORE By heaven –
ANGELLICA Hold, do not damn thyself –   310
HELLENA Nor hope to be believed.

(*He walks about, they follow*)

ANGELLICA Oh, perjured man!
  Is't thus you pay my generous passion back?
HELLENA Why would you, sir, abuse my lady's faith?
ANGELLICA And use me so inhumanly.   315
HELLENA A maid so young, so innocent –
WILLMORE Ah, young devil.

ANGELLICA Dost thou not know thy life is in my
  power?
HELLENA Or think my lady cannot be revenged?
WILLMORE (*aside*) So, so, the storm comes finely on.   320
ANGELLICA Now thou art silent, guilt has struck thee
  dumb.
  Oh, hadst thou still been so, I'd lived in safety.

> (*She turns away and weeps*)

WILLMORE (*aside to* HELLENA) Sweetheart, the lady's
name and house – quickly, I'm impatient to be with her.

> (*Looks towards* ANGELLICA *to watch her turning, and as
> she comes towards them he meets her*)

HELLENA <*aside*> So, now he is for another woman.   325
WILLMORE The impudentest young thing in nature; I
cannot persuade him out of his error, madam.
ANGELLICA I know he's in the right – yet thou'st a
  tongue
  That would persuade him to deny his faith.

> (*In rage walks away*)

WILLMORE (*said softly to* HELLENA) Her name, her name, 330
  dear boy.
HELLENA Have you forgot it, sir?
WILLMORE (*aside*) Oh, I perceive he's not to know I am a
stranger to his lady.
  – Yes, yes, I do know – but – I have forgot the –   335

> (ANGELLICA *turns*)

  – By heaven, such early confidence I never saw.
ANGELLICA Did I not charge you with this mistress, sir?
  Which you denied, though I beheld your perjury.
  This little generosity of thine, has rendered back my
  heart.   340

> (*Walks away*)

WILLMORE So, you have made sweet work here, my little

mischief. Look your lady be kind and good-natured now,
or I shall have but a cursed bargain on't.

(ANGELLICA *turns towards them*)

– The rogue's bred up to mischief, art thou so great a fool
to credit him?   345
ANGELLICA Yes, I do, and you in vain impose upon me.
– Come hither, boy – is not this he you spake of?
HELLENA I think – it is, I cannot swear, but I vow he has
just such another lying lover's look.

(HELLENA *looks in his face, he gazes on her*)

WILLMORE (*aside*) Ha! Do not I know that face? By 350
heaven, my little gypsy, what a dull dog was I; had I but
looked that way I'd known her. Are all my hopes of a new
woman banished? – Egad, if I do not fit thee* for this,
hang me.
– Madam, I have found out the plot.   355
HELLENA (*aside*) Oh Lord, what does he say? Am I
discovered now?
WILLMORE Do you see this young spark here?
HELLENA He'll tell her who I am.
WILLMORE Who do you think this is?   360
HELLENA (*aside*) Aye, aye, he does know me –
Nay, dear captain! I am undone if you discover me.
WILLMORE Nay, nay, no cogging;* she shall know what a
precious mistress I have.
HELLENA Will you be such a devil?   365
WILLMORE (*aside*) Nay, nay, I'll teach you to spoil sport
you will not make.
– This small ambassador comes not from a person of
quality as you imagine, and he says; but from a very
arrant gypsy: the talking'st, prating'st, canting'st* little 370
animal thou ever saw'st.
ANGELLICA What news you tell me, that's the thing I
mean.
HELLENA (*aside*) Would I were well off the place – if ever I
go a-captain-hunting again –   375

WILLMORE Mean that thing? That gipsy thing? Thou
   mayst as well be jealous of thy monkey, or parrot, as of
   her; a German motion* were worth a dozen of her, and a
   dream were a better enjoyment; a creature of a constitution fitter for heaven than man.   380

HELLENA (*aside*) Though I'm sure he lies, yet this vexes me.

ANGELLICA You are mistaken, she's a Spanish woman
   Made up of no such dull materials.

WILLMORE Materials! Egad, an she be made of any that
   will either dispense or admit of love, I'll be bound to   385
   continence.

HELLENA (*aside to him*) Unreasonable man, do you think
   so?

WILLMORE You may return, my little brazen head,* and
   tell your lady that till she be handsome enough to be   390
   beloved, or I be dull enough to be religious, there will be
   small hopes of me.

ANGELLICA Did you not promise then to marry her?

WILLMORE Not I, by heaven.

ANGELLICA You cannot undeceive my fears and torments,   395
   Till you have vowed you will not marry her.

HELLENA (*aside*) If he swears that, he'll be revenged on me
   indeed for all my rogueries.

ANGELLICA I know what arguments you'll bring against
   me – fortune, and honour –   400

WILLMORE Honour! I tell you I hate it in your sex; and
   those that fancy themselves possessed of that foppery are
   the most impertinently troublesome of all womankind,
   and will transgress nine commandments to keep one; and
   to satisfy your jealousy, I swear –   405

HELLENA (*aside to him*) Oh, no swearing, dear captain.

WILLMORE If it were possible I should ever be inclined to
   marry, it should be some kind young sinner; one that has
   generosity enough to give a favour handsomely to one
   that can ask it discreetly; one that has wit enough to   410
   manage an intrigue of love – Oh, how civil such a wench
   is to a man that does her the honour to marry her.

ANGELLICA By heaven, there's no faith in anything he says.

(*Enter* SEBASTIAN)

SEBASTIAN Madam, Don Antonio –
ANGELLICA Come hither.   415
HELLENA (*aside*) Ha! Antonio! He may be coming hither,
    and he'll certainly discover me. I'll therefore retire
    without a ceremony.

                                            [*Exit* HELLENA]

ANGELLICA I'll see him, get my coach ready.
SEBASTIAN It waits you, madam.   420
WILLMORE (*aside*) This is lucky. – What, madam, now I
    may be gone and leave you to the enjoyment of my rival?
ANGELLICA Dull man, that canst not see how ill, how
        poor,
    That false dissimulation looks: be gone,
    And never let me see thy cozening face again,   425
    Lest I relapse and kill thee.
WILLMORE Yes, you can spare me now – farewell, till
    you're in better humour. (*aside*) I'm glad of this release –
    Now for my gypsy:
    For though to worse we change, yet still we find   430
    New joys, new charms, in a new miss that's kind.

                                          [*Exit* WILLMORE]

ANGELLICA He's gone, and in this ague of my soul
    The shivering fit returns;
    Oh, with what willing haste he took his leave,
    As if the longed-for minute were arrived   435
    Of some blest assignation.
    In vain I have consulted all my charms,
    In vain this beauty prized, in vain believed
    My eyes could kindle any lasting fires.
    I had forgot my name, my infamy,   440
    And the reproach that honour lays on those
    That dare pretend a sober passion here.
    Nice reputation, though it leave behind
    More virtues than inhabit where that dwells,
    Yet that once gone, those virtues shine no more.   445
    – Then since I am not fit to be beloved,

I am resolved to think on a revenge
On him that soothed me thus to my undoing.

[*Exeunt*]

Act 4, Scene 3

A street

(*Enter* FLORINDA *and* VALERIA *in habits different from what they have been seen in*)

FLORINDA We're happily escaped, and yet I tremble still.

VALERIA A lover and fear! Why, I am but half an one, and yet I have courage for any attempt. Would Hellena were here. I would fain have had her as deep in this mischief as we; she'll fare but ill else, I doubt.   5

FLORINDA She pretended a visit to the Augustine nuns, but I believe some other design carried her out; pray heaven we light on her. Prithee, what didst do with Callis?

VALERIA When I saw no reason would do good on her, I followed her into the wardrobe,* and as she was looking   10
for something in a great chest, I toppled her in by the heels, snatched the key of the apartment where you were confined, locked her in, and left her bawling for help.

FLORINDA 'Tis well you resolve to follow my fortunes, for thou darest never appear at home again after such an   15
action.

VALERIA That's according as the young stranger and I shall agree. But to our business – I delivered your note* to Belvile when I got out under pretence of going to mass. I found him at his lodging, and believe me it came   20
seasonably, for never was man in so desperate a condition. I told him of your resolution of making your escape today, if your brother would be absent long enough to permit you; if not, to die rather than be Antonio's.

FLORINDA Thou shouldst have told him I was confined to   25
my chamber upon my brother's suspicion that the business on the Molo was a plot laid between him and I.

VALERIA I said all this, and told him your brother was now
gone to his devotion; and he resolves to visit every church
till he find him, and not only undeceive him in that, but 30
caress him so as shall delay his return home.

FLORINDA Oh heavens! He's here, and Belvile with him
too.

(They put on their vizards)

(Enter DON PEDRO, BELVILE, WILLMORE; BELVILE *and*
DON PEDRO *seeming in serious discourse)*

VALERIA Walk boldly by them, and I'll come at a distance,
lest he suspect us. 35

(She walks by them, and looks back on them)

WILLMORE Ha! A woman, and of an excellent mien.

PEDRO She throws a kind look back on you.

WILLMORE Death, 'tis a likely wench, and that kind look
shall not be cast away – I'll follow her.

BELVILE Prithee, do not. 40

WILLMORE Do not? By heavens, to the Antipodes,* with
such an invitation.

(She goes out, and WILLMORE *follows her)*

BELVILE 'Tis a mad fellow for a wench.

(Enter FREDERICK*)*

FREDERICK Oh colonel, such news!

BELVILE Prithee, what? 45

FREDERICK News that will make you laugh in spite of
fortune.

BELVILE What, Blunt has had some damned trick put upon
him – cheated, banged, or clapped?*

FREDERICK Cheated, sir, rarely cheated of all but his shirt 50
and drawers. The unconscionable whore, too, turned him
out before consummation, so that traversing the streets at
midnight, the watch found him in this *fresco*, and
conducted him home. By heaven, 'tis such a sight, and yet
I durst as well been hanged as laugh at him or pity him; 55

he beats all that do but ask him a question, and is in such
an humour.

PEDRO Who is't has met with this ill usage, sir?

BELVILE A friend of ours whom you must see for mirth's
sake. (*aside*) I'll employ him to give Florinda time for an   60
escape.

PEDRO What is he?

BELVILE A young countryman of ours, one that has been
educated at so plentiful a rate, he yet ne'er knew the want
of money, and 'twill be a great jest to see how simply he'll   65
look without it. For my part I'll lend him none, and* the
rogue know not how to put on a borrowing face and
ask first; I'll let him see how good 'tis to play our parts,
whilst I play his. Prithee, Fred, do you go home and keep
him in that posture till we come.   70

[Exeunt]

(*Enter* FLORINDA *from the farther end of the scene,
looking behind her*)

FLORINDA I am followed still – ha – my brother too,
advancing this way. Good heavens, defend me from being
seen by him.

[She goes off]

(*Enter* WILLMORE, *and after him* VALERIA, *at a little
distance*)

WILLMORE Ah! There she sails; she looks back as she were
willing to be boarded. I'll warrant her prize.*   75

(*He goes out,* VALERIA *following*)

(*Enter* HELLENA, *just as he goes out, with a page*)

HELLENA Ha! Is not that my captain that has a woman in
chase? 'Tis not Angellica. – Boy, follow those people at a
distance, and bring me an account where they go in.

[Exit PAGE]

I'll find his haunts and plague him everywhere. Ha, my
brother!   80

(BELVILE, WILLMORE, PEDRO *cross the stage;* HELLENA
runs off)

Act 4, Scene 4

Scene changes to another street

(*Enter* FLORINDA)

FLORINDA What shall I do? My brother now pursues me.
Will no kind power protect me from his tyranny? Ha!
Here's a door open; I'll venture in, since nothing can be
worse than to fall into his hands. My life and honour are
at stake, and my necessity has no choice.   5

(*She goes in*)

(*Enter* VALERIA *and* HELLENA'S PAGE *peeping after*
FLORINDA)

PAGE Here she went in, I shall remember this house.

[*Exit* BOY]

VALERIA This is Belvile's lodging; she's gone in as readily
as if she knew it. Ha! – here's that mad fellow again, I
dare not venture in; I'll watch my opportunity.

(*Goes aside*)

(*Enter* WILLMORE, *gazing about him*)

WILLMORE I have lost her hereabouts. Pox on't, she must   10
not 'scape me so.

[*Goes out*]

Act 4, Scene 5

Scene changes to BLUNT's *chamber, discovers him sitting
on a couch in his shirt and drawers, reading*

BLUNT So, now my mind's a little at peace since I have

resolved revenge. A pox on this tailor, though, for not
bringing home the clothes I bespoke. And a pox of all
poor cavaliers, a man can never keep a spare suit for 'em;
and I shall have these rogues come in and find me naked,   5
and then I'm undone. But I'm resolved to arm myself – the
rascals shall not insult over me too much.

(*Puts on an old rusty sword, and buff belt*)

Now, how like a morris dancer* I am equipped. A fine
lady-like whore to cheat me thus, without affording me a
kindness for my money. A pox light on her, I shall never   10
be reconciled to the sex more; she has made me as
faithless as a physician,* as uncharitable as a churchman,
and as ill-natured as a poet. Oh, how I'll use all
womankind hereafter! What would I give to have one of
'em within my reach now! Any mortal thing in petticoats,   15
kind Fortune, send me, and I'll forgive thy last night's
malice. Here's a cursed book too – a warning to all young
travellers – that can instruct me how to prevent such
mischiefs now 'tis too late. Well, 'tis a rare convenient
thing to read a little now and then, as well as hawk and   20
hunt.

(*Sits down again and reads. Enter to him* FLORINDA)

FLORINDA This house is haunted, sure; 'tis well furnished
and no living thing inhabits it. Ha – a man; heavens, how
he's attired!* Sure 'tis some rope-dancer, or fencing-
master. I tremble now for fear, and yet I must venture   25
now to speak to him. – Sir, if I may not interrupt your
meditations –

(*He starts up and gazes*)

BLUNT Ha, what's here! Are my wishes granted? And is not
that a she creature? 'Adsheartlikins, 'tis! What wretched
thing art thou, ha?   30
FLORINDA Charitable sir, you've told yourself already
what I am: a very wretched maid, forced by a strange

unlucky accident, to seek a safety here, and must be
ruined, if you do not grant it.

BLUNT Ruined! Is there any ruin so inevitable as that which   35
now threatens thee? Dost thou know, miserable woman,
into what den of mischiefs thou art fallen? What abyss of
confusion – ha? Dost not see something in my looks that
frights thy guilty soul, and makes thee wish to change that
shape of woman for any humble animal, or devil? For   40
those were safer for thee, and less mischievous.

FLORINDA Alas, what mean you, sir? I must confess your
looks have something in 'em makes me fear, but I beseech
you, as you seem a gentleman, pity a harmless virgin that
takes your house for sanctuary.   45

BLUNT Talk on, talk on, and weep too, till my faith return.
Do, flatter me out of my senses again – a harmless virgin
with a pox, as much one as t'other, 'adsheartlikins. Why,
what the devil, can I not be safe in my house for you, not
in my chamber – nay, even being naked too cannot secure   50
me? This is an impudence greater than has invaded me
yet. Come, no resistance.

(*Pulls her rudely*)

FLORINDA Dare you be so cruel?

BLUNT Cruel, 'adsheartlikins, as a galley slave, or a Spanish
whore. Cruel? Yes, I will kiss and beat thee all over, kiss   55
and see thee all over; thou shalt lie with me too, not that I
care for the enjoyment, but to let thee see I have ta'en
deliberated malice to thee, and will be revenged on one
whore for the sins of another. I will smile and deceive
thee, flatter thee and beat thee, kiss and swear, and lie   60
to thee, embrace thee and rob thee, as she did me; fawn
on thee and strip thee stark naked; then hang thee out at
my window by the heels, with a paper of scurvy verses
fastened to thy breast, in praise of damnable women.
Come, come along.   65

FLORINDA Alas, sir, must I be sacrificed for the crimes of
the most infamous of my sex? I never understood the sins
you name.

BLUNT Do, persuade the fool you love him, or that one of you can be just or honest; tell me I was not an easy 70 coxcomb, or any strange impossible tale. It will be believed sooner than thy false showers or protestations. A generation of damned hypocrites to flatter my very clothes from my back! Dissembling witches! Are these the returns you make an honest gentleman that trusts, 75 believes and loves you? But if I be not even with you – come along – or I shall –

(*Pulls her again. Enter* FREDERICK)

FREDERICK Ha! What's here to do?

BLUNT 'Adsheartlikins, Fred, I am glad thou art come, to be a witness of my dire revenge. 80

FREDERICK What's this, a person of quality too, who is upon the ramble to supply the defects of some grave and impotent husband?

BLUNT No, this has another pretence; some very unfortu- nate accident brought her hither, to save a life pursued by 85 I know not who, or why, and forced her to take sanctuary here at Fools' Haven. 'Adsheartlikins, to me of all mankind for protection! Is the ass to be cajoled again, think ye? No, young one, no prayers or tears shall mitigate my rage; therefore prepare for both my pleas- 90 ures, of enjoyment and revenge, for I am resolved to make up my loss here on thy body; I'll take it out in kindness and in beating.

FREDERICK Now, mistress of mine, what do you think of this? 95

FLORINDA I think he will not – dares not – be so barbarous.

FREDERICK Have a care, Blunt, she fetched a deep sigh; she's enamoured with thy shirt and drawers, she'll strip thee even of that. There are of her calling such uncon- 100 scionable baggages, and such dexterous thieves, they'll flay a man, and he shall ne'er miss his skin till he feels the cold. There was a countryman of ours robbed of a row of teeth whilst he was a-sleeping, which the jilt made him

buy again when he waked – you see, lady, how little 105
reason we have to trust you.

BLUNT 'Adsheartlikins, why this is most abominable.

FLORINDA Some such devils there may be; but by all that's
holy, I am none such. I entered here to save a life in
danger.   110

BLUNT For no goodness, I'll warrant her.

FREDERICK Faith, damsel, you had e'en confessed* the
plain truth, for we are not fellows to be caught twice in
the same trap. Look on that wreck, a tight vessel when he
set out of haven, well trimmed and laden; and see how a 115
female picaroon of this island of rogues has shattered
him; and canst thou hope for any mercy?

BLUNT No, no, gentlewoman, come along, 'adsheartlikins,
we must be better acquainted. We'll both lie with her, and
then let me alone to bang her.   120

FREDERICK I'm ready to serve you in matters of revenge
that has a double pleasure in't.

BLUNT Well said. You hear, little one, how you are
condemned by public vote to the bed within; there's no
resisting your destiny, sweetheart.   125

(Pulls her)

FLORINDA Stay, sir, I have seen you with Belvile, an
English cavalier – for his sake use me kindly. You know
him, sir.

BLUNT Belvile? Why, yes, sweeting, we do know Belvile,
and wish he were with us now: he's a cormorant* at 130
whore and bacon; he'd have a limb or two of thee, my
virgin pullet, but 'tis no matter, we'll leave him the bones
to pick.

FLORINDA Sir, if you have any esteem for that Belvile, I
conjure you to treat me with more gentleness; he'll thank 135
you for the justice.

FREDERICK Hark'ee, Blunt, I doubt we are mistaken in this
matter.

FLORINDA Sir, if you find me not worth Belvile's care, use

me as you please, and that you may think I merit better 140
treatment than you threaten – pray take this present –

(*Gives him a ring; he looks on it*)

BLUNT Hum – a diamond! Why 'tis a wonderful virtue now
that lies in this ring, a mollifying virtue. 'Adsheartlikins,
there's more persuasive rhetoric in't than all her sex can
utter. 145

FREDERICK I begin to suspect something; and 'twould
anger us vilely to be trussed up for a rape upon a maid of
quality, when we only believe we ruffle a harlot.

BLUNT Thou art a credulous fellow, but 'adsheartlikins, I
have no faith yet; why, my saint prattled as parlously as 150
this does, she gave me a bracelet too, a devil on her, but I
sent my man to sell it today for necessaries, and it proved
as counterfeit as her vows of love.

FREDERICK However, let it reprieve her till we see Belvile.

BLUNT That's hard, yet I will grant it. 155

(*Enter a* SERVANT)

SERVANT Oh, sir, the colonel is just come in with his new
friend and a Spaniard of quality, and talks of having you
to dinner with 'em.

BLUNT 'Adsheartlikins, I'm undone – I would not see 'em
for the world. Harkee, Fred, lock up the wench in your 160
chamber.

FREDERICK Fear nothing, madam; whate'er he threatens,
you are safe whilst in my hands.

[*Exeunt* FREDERICK *and* FLORINDA]

BLUNT And, sirrah, upon your life, say I am not at home –
or that I am asleep – or – or anything. Away – I'll prevent 165
their coming this way.

[*Locks the door and exeunt*]

Act 5, Scene 1

BLUNT's *chamber*

(After a great knocking at his chamber door, enter
BLUNT, *softly crossing the stage, in his shirt and drawers*
as before)

<VOICES> (*call within*) Ned! Ned Blunt! Ned Blunt!

BLUNT The rogues are up in arms. 'Adsheartlikins, this
villainous Frederick has betrayed me, they have heard of
my blessed fortune.

<VOICES> (*and knocking within*) Ned Blunt! Ned! Ned! –   5

BELVILE Why, he's dead, sir, without dispute dead, he has
not been seen today. Let's break open the door – here,
boy –

BLUNT Ha, break open the door. 'Adsheartlikins, that mad
fellow will be as good as his word.   10

BELVILE Boy, bring something to force the door.

(A great noise within, at the door again)

BLUNT So, now must I speak in my own defence, I'll try
what rhetoric will do. – Hold – hold, what do you mean,
gentlemen, what do you mean?

BELVILE (*within*) Oh, rogue, art alive? Prithee, open the   15
door and convince us.

BLUNT Yes, I am alive, gentlemen – but at present a little
busy.

BELVILE (*within*) How! Blunt grown a man of business!
Come, come, open and let's see this miracle.   20

BLUNT No, no, no, no, gentlemen. 'Tis no great business –
but – I am – at – my devotion – 'Adsheartlikins, will you
not allow a man time to pray?

BELVILE (*within*) Turned religious! A greater wonder than
the first; therefore open quickly, or we shall unhinge, we   25
shall.

BLUNT (*aside*) This won't do. – Why, hark'ee, colonel, to
tell you the plain truth, I am about a necessary affair of
life – I have a wench with me – you apprehend me? – The
devil's in't if they be so uncivil as to disturb me now.   30

WILLMORE How, a wench? Nay then, we must enter and
partake, no resistance – unless it be your lady of quality,
and then we'll keep our distance.

BLUNT So, the business is out.

WILLMORE Come, come, lend's more hands to the door –   35
now, heave all together – so, well done, my boys – (*breaks
open the door*)

(*Enter* BELVILE, WILLMORE, FREDERICK *and* PEDRO.
BLUNT *looks simply;* * *they all laugh at him. He lays his
hand on his sword, and comes up to* WILLMORE)

BLUNT Hark'ee, sir, laugh out your laugh quickly, d'ye
hear, and be gone. I shall spoil your sport else, 'adsheartlikins, sir, I shall. The jest has been carried on too long. –
(*aside*) A plague upon my tailor.   40

WILLMORE 'Sdeath, how the whore has dressed him. Faith,
sir, I'm sorry.

BLUNT Are you so, sir? Keep't to yourself then, sir, I advise
you, d'ye hear; for I can as little endure your pity as his
mirth.   45

(*Lays his hand on's sword*)

BELVILE Indeed, Willmore, thou wert a little too rough
with Ned Blunt's mistress. Call a person of quality
whore? And one so young, so handsome, and so eloquent!
Ha, ha, he!

BLUNT Hark'ee, sir, you know me, and know I can be   50
angry. Have a care – for 'adsheartlikins, I can fight, too –
I can, sir – do you mark me? – no more.

BELVILE Why so peevish, good Ned? Some disappointments, I'll warrant. What, did the jealous count, her
husband, return just in the nick?   55

BLUNT Or the devil, sir – d'ye laugh? –

(*They laugh*)

Look ye, settle me a good sober countenance, and that
quickly too, or you shall know Ned Blunt is not –

BELVILE Not everybody; we know that.

BLUNT Not an ass to be laughed at, sir.   60

WILLMORE Unconscionable sinner, to bring a lover so near
his happiness, a vigorous passionate lover, and then not
only cheat him of his moveables, but his very desires too.

BELVILE Ah, sir, a mistress is a trifle with Blunt. He'll have
a dozen the next time he looks abroad. His eyes have   65
charms not to be resisted; there needs no more than to
expose that taking person to the view of the fair, and he
leads 'em all in triumph.

PEDRO Sir, though I'm a stranger to you, I am ashamed at
the rudeness of my nation; and could you learn who did   70
it, would assist you to make an example of 'em.

BLUNT Why aye, there's one speaks sense now, and
handsomely, and let me tell you, gentlemen, I should not
have showed myself like a jack pudding* thus to have
made you mirth, but that I have a revenge within my   75
power; for know, I have got into my possession a female
who had better have fallen under any curse, than the ruin
I design her. 'Adsheartlikins, she assaulted me here in my
own lodgings, and had doubtless committed a rape upon
me, had not this sword defended me.   80

FREDERICK I know not that, but o' my conscience thou
had ravished her, had she not redeemed herself with a
ring – let's see't, Blunt.

(BLUNT shows the ring)

BELVILE Ha! The ring I gave Florinda, when we exchanged
our vows – Hark'ee, Blunt, –   85

(Goes to whisper to him)

WILLMORE No whispering, good colonel, there's a woman
in the case, no whispering.

BELVILE *(to BLUNT)* Hark'ee, fool, be advised and conceal
both the ring and the story for your reputation's sake. Do
not let people know what despised cullies we English are; 90
to be cheated and abused by one whore, and another
rather bribe thee than be kind to thee, is an infamy to our
nation.

WILLMORE Come, come, where's the wench? We'll see her, let her be what she will, we'll see her. 95
PEDRO Aye, aye, let us see her. I can soon discover whether she be of quality, or for your diversion.
BLUNT She's in Fred's custody.
WILLMORE (to FREDERICK) Come, come, the key.

(<FREDERICK> *gives him the key. They are going*)

BELVILE <aside> Death, what shall I do? – Stay, gentle- 100
men, – <aside> Yet if I hinder 'em, I shall discover all.
– Hold – let's go one at once;* give me the key.
WILLMORE Nay, hold there, colonel, I'll go first.
FREDERICK Nay, no dispute, Ned and I have the propriety of her.* 105
WILLMORE Damn propriety – then we'll draw cuts –

(BELVILE *goes to whisper* WILLMORE)

– Nay, no corruption, good colonel; come, the longest sword carries her.

(*They all draw, forgetting* DON PEDRO, *being as a Spaniard, had the longest*)*

BLUNT I yield up my interest to you, gentlemen, and that will be revenge sufficient. 110
WILLMORE (to PEDRO) The wench is yours. <aside> Pox of his Toledo,* I had forgot that.
FREDERICK Come, sir, I'll conduct you to the lady.
                              [*Exeunt* FREDERICK *and* PEDRO]

BELVILE (aside) To hinder him will certainly discover her.
(to WILLMORE <who is> *walking up and down out of humour*) – Dost know, dull beast, what mischief thou 115
hast done?
WILLMORE Aye, aye, to trust our fortune to lots, a devil on't, 'twas madness, that's the truth on't.
BELVILE Oh, intolerable sot –

(*Enter* FLORINDA *running, masked,* PEDRO *after her;*
        WILLMORE *gazing round her*)

FLORINDA (*aside*) Good heaven, defend me from 120 discovery.

PEDRO 'Tis but in vain to fly me, you're fallen to my lot.

BELVILE Sure she's undiscovered yet, but now I fear there is no way to bring her off.

WILLMORE Why, what a pox! Is not this my woman, the 125 same I followed but now?

PEDRO (*talking to* FLORINDA, *who walks up and down*) As if I did not know ye, and your business here.

FLORINDA (*aside*) Good heaven, I fear he does indeed.

PEDRO Come, pray be kind, I know you meant to be so when you entered here, for these are proper gentlemen. 130

WILLMORE But, sir – perhaps the lady will not be imposed upon, she'll choose her man.

PEDRO I am better bred than not to leave her choice free.

(*Enter* VALERIA, *and is surprised at sight of* DON
PEDRO)

VALERIA (*aside*) Don Pedro here! There's no avoiding him.

FLORINDA (*aside*) Valeria! Then I'm undone.   135

VALERIA (*to* PEDRO, *running to him*) Oh! Have I found you, sir – the strangest accident – if I had breath – to tell it.

PEDRO Speak – is Florinda safe? Hellena well?

VALERIA Aye, aye, sir – Florinda – is safe – <*aside*> from 140 any fears of you.

PEDRO Why, where's Florinda? Speak.

VALERIA Aye, where indeed, sir, I wish I could inform you – but to hold you no longer in doubt –

FLORINDA (*aside*) Oh, what will she say?   145

VALERIA She's fled away in the habit – of one of her pages, sir; but Callis thinks you may retrieve her yet, if you make haste away. She'll tell you, sir, the rest – (*aside*) – if you can find her out.

PEDRO Dishonourable girl, she has undone my aim. Sir, 150 you see my necessity of leaving you, and hope you'll pardon it. My sister, I know, will make her flight to you; and if she do, I shall expect she should be rendered back.

BELVILE I shall consult my love and honour, sir.

[*Exit* PEDRO]

FLORINDA (*to* VALERIA) My dear preserver, let me 155
embrace thee.

WILLMORE What the devil's all this?

BLUNT Mystery, by this light.

VALERIA Come, come, make haste and get yourselves
married quickly, for your brother will return again.   160

BELVILE I'm so surprised with fears and joys, so amazed to
find you here in safety, I can scarce persuade my heart
into a faith of what I see –

WILLMORE Hark'ee, colonel, is this the mistress who has
cost you so many sighs, and me so many quarrels with 165
you?

BELVILE It is. (*to* FLORINDA) – Pray give him the honour
of your hand.

WILLMORE (*kneels and kisses her hand*) Thus it must be
received then. And with it give your pardon too.   170

FLORINDA The friend to Belvile may command me
anything.

WILLMORE (*aside*) Death, would I might, 'tis a surprising
beauty.

BELVILE Boy, run and fetch a father* instantly.   175

[*Exit* BOY]

FREDERICK So, now do I stand like a dog, and have not a
syllable to plead my own cause with. By this hand,
madam, I was never thoroughly confounded before, nor
shall I ever more dare look up with confidence, till you are
pleased to pardon me.   180

FLORINDA Sir, I'll be reconciled to you on one condition:
that you'll follow the example of your friend, in marrying
a maid that does not hate you, and whose fortune, I
believe, will not be unwelcome to you.

FREDERICK Madam, had I no inclinations that way, I 185
should obey your kind commands.

BELVILE Who, Fred marry? He has so few inclinations for
womankind, that had he been possessed of paradise, he

might have continued there to this day, if no crime but
love could have disinherited him.   190

FREDERICK Oh, I do not use to boast of my intrigues.

BELVILE Boast? Why, thou dost nothing but boast; and I
dare swear wert thou as innocent from the sin of the
grape, as thou art from the apple, thou might'st yet claim
that right in Eden which our first parents lost by too much 195
loving.

FREDERICK I wish this lady would think me so modest a
man.

VALERIA She would be sorry then, and not like you half so
well, and I should be loath to break my word with you, 200
which was: that if your friend and mine agreed, it should
be a match between you and I.

(*She gives him her hand*)

FREDERICK (*kisses her hand*) Bear witness, colonel, 'tis a
bargain.

BLUNT (*to* FLORINDA) I have a pardon to beg, too. But, 205
'adsheartlikins, I am so out of countenance that I'm a dog
if I can say anything to purpose.

FLORINDA Sir, I heartily forgive you all.

BLUNT That's nobly said, sweet lady; Belvile, prithee
present her her ring again, for I find I have not courage to 210
approach her myself.

(*Gives* <BELVILE> *the ring,* <who> *gives* <it> *to*
FLORINDA)

(*Enter* BOY)

BOY Sir, I have brought the father that you sent for.

BELVILE 'Tis well, and now my dear Florinda, let's fly to
complete that mighty joy we have so long wished and
sighed for. – Come, Fred, you'll follow?   215

FREDERICK Your example, sir, 'twas ever my ambition in
war, and must be so in love.

WILLMORE And must not I see this juggling* knot tied?

BELVILE No, thou shalt do us better service, and be our

guard, lest Don Pedro's sudden return interrupt the 220
ceremony.

WILLMORE Content; I'll secure this pass.

[*Exeunt* BELVILE, FLORINDA, FREDERICK *and* VALERIA]

(*Enter* BOY)

BOY (*to* WILLMORE) Sir, there's a lady without would
speak to you.

WILLMORE Conduct her in, I dare not quit my post. 225

BOY <*to* BLUNT> And, sir, your tailor waits you in your
chamber.

BLUNT Some comfort yet, I shall not dance naked at the
wedding.

[*Exit* BLUNT *and* BOY]

(*Enter again the* BOY, *conducting in* ANGELLICA *in a*
masquing habit and a vizard. WILLMORE *runs to her*)

WILLMORE This can be none but my pretty gypsy – oh, I 230
see you can follow as well as fly. Come, confess thyself
the most malicious devil in nature, you think you have
done my business with Angellica.

ANGELLICA Stand off, base villain –

(*She draws a pistol, and holds it to his breast*)

WILLMORE Ha, 'tis not she! – Who art thou, and what's 235
thy business?

ANGELLICA One thou hast injured, and who comes to kill
thee for it.

WILLMORE What the devil canst thou mean?

ANGELLICA By all my hopes to kill thee – 240

(*Holds still the pistol to his breast, he going back, she*
following still)

WILLMORE Prithee, on what acquaintance? For I know
thee not.

ANGELLICA (*pulls off her vizard*) Behold this face – so
lost to thy remembrance,
And then call all thy sins about thy soul,

And let 'em die with thee.   245
WILLMORE Angellica!
ANGELLICA Yes, traitor,
  Does not thy guilty blood run shivering through thy
    veins?
  Hast thou no horror at this sight, that tells thee
  Thou hast not long to boast thy shameful conquest?   250
WILLMORE Faith, no, child, my blood keeps its old ebbs
  and flows still, and that usual heat too, that could oblige
  thee with a kindness, had I but opportunity.
ANGELLICA Devil! Dost wanton with my pain? Have at thy
  heart!   255
WILLMORE Hold, dear virago!* Hold thy hand a little,
  I am not now at leisure to be killed –
  Hold and hear me – (aside) – Death, I think she's in
  earnest.
ANGELLICA (aside, turning from him) Oh, if I take not   260
    heed,
  My coward heart will leave me to his mercy.
  What have you, sir, to say? But should I hear thee,
  Thou'dst talk away all that is brave about me:

    (Follows him with the pistol to his breast)

  And I have vowed thy death, by all that's sacred.
WILLMORE Why then, there's an end of a proper handsome   265
  fellow, that might 'a lived to have done good service yet;
  that's all I can say to 't.
ANGELLICA (pausingly) Yet – I would give thee – time for –
  penitence.
WILLMORE Faith, child, I thank God, I have ever took care 270
  to lead a good sober, hopeful life, and am of a religion
  that teaches me to believe I shall depart in peace.
ANGELLICA So will the devil! Tell me,
  How many poor believing fools thou hast undone?
  How many hearts thou hast betrayed to ruin?   275
  Yet these are little mischiefs to the ills
  Thou'st taught mine to commit: thou taught'st it love!
WILLMORE Egad, 'twas shrewdly hurt the while.

ANGELLICA Love, that has robbed it of its unconcern,
  Of all that pride that taught me how to value it.   280
  And in its room
  A mean submissive passion was conveyed,
  That made me humbly bow, which I ne'er did
  To anything but heaven.
  Thou, perjured man, didst this, and with thy oaths,   285
  Which on thy knees thou didst devoutly make,
  Softened my yielding heart – and then, I was a slave –
  – Yet still had been content to've worn my chains;
  Worn 'em with vanity and joy for ever,
  Hadst thou not broke those vows that put them on.   290
  'Twas then I was undone.

(*All this while follows him with the pistol to his breast*)

WILLMORE Broke my vows! Why, where hast thou lived?
Amongst the gods? For I never heard of mortal man that
has not broke a thousand vows.

ANGELLICA Oh impudence!   295

WILLMORE Angellica! That beauty has been too long
tempting, not to have made a thousand lovers languish,
who in the amorous fever,* no doubt have sworn like me:
did they all die in that faith? Still adoring? I do not think
they did.   300

ANGELLICA No, faithless man: had I repaid their vows, as I
did thine, I would have killed the ungrateful that had
abandoned me.

WILLMORE This old general has quite spoiled thee; nothing
makes a woman so vain as being flattered. Your old lover 305
ever supplies the defects of age with intolerable dotage,
vast charge, and that which you call constancy; and
attributing all this to your own merits, you domineer, and
throw your favours in's teeth, upbraiding him still with
the defects of age, and cuckold him as often as he deceives 310
your expectations. But the gay, young, brisk lover, that
brings his equal fires, and can give you dart for dart,
you'll <find> will be* as nice* as you sometimes.

ANGELLICA All this thou'st made me know, for which I

hate thee.
Had I remained in innocent security,   315
I should have thought all men were born my slaves,
And worn my power like lightning in my eyes,
To have destroyed at pleasure when offended.
But when love held the mirror, the undeceiving glass
Reflected all the weakness of my soul, and made me
    know   320
My richest treasure being lost, my honour,
All the remaining spoil could not be worth
The conqueror's care or value.
Oh, how I fell, like a long-worshipped idol,
Discovering all the cheat.   325
Would not the incense and rich sacrifice,
Which blind devotion offered at my altars,
Have fallen to thee?
Why wouldst thou then destroy my fancied power?

WILLMORE By heaven, thou'rt brave, and I admire thee
    strangely.   330
I wish I were that dull, that constant thing
Which thou wouldst have, and nature never meant me.
I must, like cheerful birds, sing in all groves,
And perch on every bough,
Billing the next kind she that flies to meet me;   335
Yet after all could build my nest with thee,
Thither repairing when I'd loved my round,
And still reserve a tributary flame.
To gain your credit, I'll pay back your charity,
And be obliged for nothing but for love.   340

(Offers her a purse of gold)

ANGELLICA Oh, that thou wert in earnest!
So mean a thought of me
Would turn my rage to scorn, and I should pity thee,   345
And give thee leave to live;
Which for the public safety of our sex,
And my own private injuries I dare not do,
Prepare – *(follows still, as before)*

- I will no more be tempted with replies.   350
WILLMORE Sure –
ANGELLICA Another word will damn thee! I've heard thee
talk too long.

(*She follows him with the pistol ready to shoot; he
retires still amazed. Enter* DON ANTONIO, *his arm in a
scarf, and lays hold on the pistol*)

ANTONIO Ha! Angellica!
ANGELLICA Antonio! What devil brought thee hither?   355
ANTONIO Love and curiosity, seeing your coach at the
door. Let me disarm you of this unbecoming instrument
of death. (*takes away the pistol*) Amongst the number of
your slaves, was there not one worthy the honour to have
fought your quarrel? <*to* WILLMORE> Who are you, sir, 360
that are so very wretched to merit death from her?
WILLMORE One, sir, that could have made a better end of
an amorous quarrel without you, than with you.
ANTONIO Sure 'tis some rival. Ha! The very man took
down her picture yesterday – the very same that set on me 365
last night. Blest opportunity!

(*Offers to shoot him*)

ANGELLICA Hold, you're mistaken, sir.
ANTONIO By heaven, the very same!
Sir, what pretensions have you to this lady?
WILLMORE Sir, I do not use to be examined, and am ill at 370
all disputes but this –

(*Draws;* ANTONIO *offers to shoot*)

ANGELLICA (*to* WILLMORE) Oh hold! You see he's armed
with certain death;
– And you, Antonio, I command you hold,
By all the passion you've so lately vowed me.   375

(*Enter* DON PEDRO, *sees* ANTONIO, *and stays*)

PEDRO (*aside*) Ha, Antonio! And Angellica!
ANTONIO When I refuse obedience to your will,

May you destroy me with your mortal hate.
By all that's holy I adore you so,
That even my rival, who has charms enough   380
To make him fall a victim to my jealousy
Shall live, nay, and have leave to love on still.
PEDRO (*aside*) What's this I hear?
ANGELLICA (*pointing to* WILLMORE)
Ah thus, 'twas thus he talked, and I believed.   385
Antonio, yesterday,
I'd not have sold my interest in his heart
For all the sword has lost and won in battle.
(*to* WILLMORE) But now to show my utmost of
   contempt,
I give thee life – which, if thou wouldst preserve,   390
Live where my eyes may never see thee more,
Live to undo someone whose soul may prove
So bravely constant to revenge my love.

(*Goes out,* ANTONIO *follows, but* PEDRO *pulls back*)

PEDRO Antonio – stay.
ANTONIO Don Pedro –   395
PEDRO What coward fear was that prevented thee
   From meeting me this morning on the Molo?
ANTONIO Meet thee?
PEDRO Yes me; I was the man that dared thee to't.
ANTONIO Hast thou so often seen me fight in war,   400
   To find no better case to excuse my absence?
   I sent my sword and one to do thee right,
   Finding myself uncapable to use a sword.
PEDRO But 'twas Florinda's quarrel that we fought,
   And you to show how little you esteemed her,   405
   Sent me your rival, giving him your interest.
   But I have found the cause of this affront,
   And when I meet you fit for the dispute,
   I'll tell you my resentment.
ANTONIO I shall be ready, sir, ere long to do you 410
reason.
                                        [*Exit* ANTONIO]

PEDRO If I could find Florinda now, whilst my anger's high, I think I should be kind, and give her to Belvile in revenge.

WILLMORE Faith, sir, I know not what you would do, but I 415 believe the priest within has been so kind.

PEDRO How! My sister married?

WILLMORE I hope by this time he is, and bedded too, or he has not my longings about him.

PEDRO Dares he do this? Does he not fear my power?   420

WILLMORE Faith, not at all. If you will go in and thank him for the favour he has done your sister, so; if not, sir, my power's greater in this house than yours. I have a damned surly crew here that will keep you till the next tide, and then clap you on board for prize. My ship lies 425 but a league off the Molo, and we shall show your donship a damned tramontana* rover's trick.

(*Enter* BELVILE)

BELVILE This rogue's in some new mischief. Ha! Pedro returned!

PEDRO Colonel Belvile, I hear you have married my sister? 430

BELVILE You have heard truth then, sir.

PEDRO Have I so? Then, sir, I wish you joy.

BELVILE How!

PEDRO By this embrace I do, and I am glad on't.

BELVILE Are you in earnest?   435

PEDRO By our long friendship and my obligations to thee, I am; the sudden change I'll give you reasons for anon. Come, lead me to my sister, that she may know I now approve her choice.

[*Exit* BELVILE *with* PEDRO]

(WILLMORE *goes to follow them. Enter* HELLENA, *as before in boy's clothes, and pulls him back*)

WILLMORE Ha! My gypsy – now a thousand blessings on 440 thee for this kindness. Egad, child, I was e'en in despair of ever seeing thee again; my friends are all provided for within, each man has his kind woman.

HELLENA Ha! I thought they had served me some such 445
trick!

WILLMORE And I was e'en resolved to go aboard, and
condemn myself to my lone cabin, and the thoughts of
thee.

HELLENA And could you have left me behind? Would you
have been so ill-natured? 450

WILLMORE Why, 'twould have broke my heart, child; but
since we are met again, I defy foul weather to part us.

HELLENA And would you be a faithful friend now, if a
maid should trust you?

WILLMORE For a friend I cannot promise; thou art of a 455
form so excellent, a face and humour too good for cold
dull friendship. I am parlously afraid of being in love,
child; and you have not forgot how severely you have
used me?

HELLENA That's all one; such usage you must still look for: 460
to find out all your haunts, to rail at you to all that love
you, till I have made you love only me in your own
defence, because nobody else will love you.*

WILLMORE But hast thou no better quality to recommend
thyself by? 465

HELLENA Faith, none, captain. Why, 'twill be the greater
charity to take me for thy mistress. I am a lone child, a
kind of orphan lover; and why I should die a maid, and in
a captain's hands too, I do not understand.

WILLMORE Egad, I was never clawed away with broad- 470
sides from any female before. Thou hast one virtue I
adore – good nature. I hate a coy demure mistress, she's
as troublesome as a colt; I'll break none. No, give me a
mad mistress when mewed,* and in flying, one* I dare
trust upon the wing, that whilst she's kind will come to 475
the lure.*

HELLENA Nay, as kind as you will, good captain, while it
lasts, but let's lose no time.

WILLMORE My time's as precious to me as thine can be.
Therefore, dear creature, since we are so well agreed, let's 480
retire to my chamber, and if ever thou wert treated with

such savoury love! Come, my bed's prepared for such a
guest, all clean and sweet as thy fair self. I love to steal a
dish and a bottle with a friend, and hate long graces.
Come, let's retire and fall to.   485

HELLENA 'Tis but getting my consent, and the business is
soon done. Let but old gaffer Hymen* and his priest say
amen to't, and I dare lay my mother's daughter by as
proper a fellow as your father's son, without fear or
blushing.   490

WILLMORE Hold, hold, no bug* words child. Priest and
Hymen! Prithee add a hangman to 'em to make up the
consort.* No, no, we'll have no vows but love, child, nor
witness but the lover; the kind deity enjoin naught but
love and enjoy! Hymen and priest wait still upon portion   495
and jointure; love and beauty have their own ceremonies.
Marriage is as certain a bane to love as lending money is
to friendship. I'll neither ask nor give a vow, though I
could be content to turn gypsy and become a left-handed*
bridegroom, to have the pleasure of working that great   500
miracle of making a maid a mother, if you durst venture.
'Tis upse* gypsy that, and if I miss, I'll lose my labour.

HELLENA And if you do not lose, what shall I get? A cradle
full of noise and mischief, with a pack of repentance at
my back? Can you teach me to weave incle* to pass my   505
time with? 'Tis upse gypsy that too.

WILLMORE I can teach thee to weave a true love's knot
better.

HELLENA So can my dog.

WILLMORE Well, I see we are both upon our guards, and I   510
see there's no way to conquer good nature, but by
yielding. Here, give me thy hand – one kiss and I am
thine.

HELLENA One kiss! How like my page he speaks. I am
resolved you shall have none, for asking such a sneaking*   515
sum. He that will be satisfied with one kiss, will never die
of that longing. Good friend single-kiss, is all your talking
come to this? – A kiss, a caudle!* Farewell, captain single-
kiss.

(Going out; he stays her)

WILLMORE Nay, if we part so, let me die like a bird upon a 520
bough, at the sheriff's charge.* By heaven, both the Indies
shall not buy thee from me. I adore thy humour and will
marry thee, and we are so of one humour it must be a
bargain. Give me thy hand. *(kisses her hand)* And now let
the blind ones, Love and Fortune,* do their worst. 525

HELLENA Why, God-a-mercy, captain!

WILLMORE But hark'ee, the bargain is now made: but is it
not fit we should know each other's names, that when we
have reason to curse one another hereafter (and people
ask who 'tis I give to the devil), I may at least be able to 530
tell what family you came of?

HELLENA Good reason, captain; and when I have cause (as
I doubt not but I shall have plentiful), that I may know at
whom to throw my – blessings, I beseech ye your name.

WILLMORE I am called Robert the Constant. 535

HELLENA A very fine name. Pray was it your falconer or
butler that christened you? Do they not use to whistle
when they call you?

WILLMORE I hope you have a better, that a man may name
without crossing himself, you are so merry with mine. 540

HELLENA I am called Hellena the Inconstant.

(*Enter* PEDRO, BELVILE, FLORINDA, FREDERICK,
VALERIA)

PEDRO Ha, Hellena!

FLORINDA Hellena!

HELLENA The very same. Ha, my brother! Now, captain,
show your love and courage; stand to your arms and 545
defend me bravely, or I am lost for ever.

PEDRO What's this I hear? False girl, how came you hither,
and what's your business? Speak.

(Goes roughly to her)

WILLMORE *(puts himself between)* Hold off, sir, you have
leave to parley only. 550

HELLENA I had e'en as good tell it, as you guess it. Faith,

brother, my business is the same with all living creatures
of my age: to love and be beloved, and here's the man.

PEDRO Perfidious maid, hast thou deceived me too,
deceived thyself and heaven?   555

HELLENA 'Tis time enough to make my peace with that,
Be you but kind, let me alone with heaven.

PEDRO Belvile, I did not expect this false play from you.
Was't not enough you'd gain Florinda (which I par-
doned), but your lewd friends too must be enriched with 560
the spoils of a noble family?

BELVILE Faith, sir, I am as much surprised at this as you
can be. Yet, sir, my friends are gentlemen, and ought to be
esteemed for their misfortunes, since they have the glory
to suffer with the best of men and kings.* 'Tis true he's a 565
rover of fortune, yet a prince aboard his little wooden
world.

PEDRO What's this to the maintenance of a woman of her
birth and quality?

WILLMORE Faith, sir, I can boast of nothing but a sword 570
which does me right where'er I come, and has defended a
worse cause than a woman's; and since I loved her before
I knew either her birth or name, I must pursue my
resolution and marry her.

PEDRO And is all your holy intent of becoming a nun 575
debauched into a desire of man?

HELLENA Why, I have considered the matter, brother, and
find the three thousand crowns my uncle left me (and you
cannot keep from me), will be better laid out in love than
in religion, and turn to as good an account. Let most 580
voices carry it: for heaven, or the captain?

ALL CRY A captain! A captain!

HELLENA Look ye, sir, 'tis a clear case.

PEDRO Oh, I am mad! (aside) If I refuse my life's in danger.
– Come, there's one motive induces me. Take her: I shall 585
now be free from fears of her honour; guard you it now, if
you can, I have been a slave to 't long enough.

(Gives her to him)

WILLMORE Faith, sir, I am of a nation that are of opinion a
woman's honour is not worth guarding when she has a
mind to part with it.   590

HELLENA Well said, captain.

PEDRO (*to* VALERIA) This was your plot, mistress, but I
hope you have married one that will revenge my quarrel
to you.

VALERIA There's no altering destiny, sir.   595

PEDRO Sooner than a woman's will; therefore I forgive you
all, and wish you may get my father's pardon as easily,
which I fear.

(*Enter* BLUNT *dressed in a Spanish habit, looking very
ridiculously; his man adjusting his band*)*

MAN 'Tis very well, sir.

BLUNT Well, sir! 'Adsheartlikins, I tell you 'tis damnable 600
ill, sir. A Spanish habit, good Lord! Could the devil and
my tailor devise no other punishment for me but the mode
of a nation I abominate?

BELVILE What's the matter, Ned?

BLUNT Pray view me round, and judge – (*turns round*)   605

BELVILE I must confess thou art a kind of an odd figure.

BLUNT In a Spanish habit with a vengeance! I had rather be
in the Inquisition for Judaism, than in this doublet and
breeches; a pillory were an easy collar to this three
handfuls high; and these shoes, too, are worse than the 610
stocks, with the sole an inch shorter than my foot. In fine,
gentlemen, methinks I look altogether like a bag of bays*
stuffed full of fool's flesh.

BELVILE Methinks 'tis well, and makes thee look *en
cavalier.** Come, sir, settle your face, and salute our 615
friends, lady –

BLUNT Ha, sayst thou so, my little rover! (*to* HELLENA)
Lady, if you be one, give me leave to kiss your hand, and
tell you, 'adsheartlikins, for all I look so, I am your
humble servant. A pox of my Spanish habit!   620

(*Music is heard to play*)

WILLMORE Hark – what's this?

(*Enter* BOY)

BOY Sir, as the custom is, the gay people in masquerade
who make every man's house their own, are coming up.

(*Enter several men and women in masquing habits with
music; they put themselves in order and dance*)

BLUNT 'Adsheartlikins, would 'twere lawful to pull off
their false faces, that I might see if my doxy* were not 625
amongst 'em.

BELVILE (*to the masquers*) Ladies and gentlemen, since you
come so apropos, you must take a small collation with us.

WILLMORE Whilst we'll to the good man within, who stays
to give us a cast of his office. (*to* HELLENA) Have you no 630
trembling at the near approach?

HELLENA No more than you have in an engagement or a
tempest.

WILLMORE Egad, thou 'rt a brave girl, and I admire thy
love and courage.   635
Lead on, no other dangers they can dread,
Who venture in the storms o' th' marriage bed.

[*Exeunt*]

Epilogue

The banished cavaliers! A roving blade!
A popish carnival! A masquerade!
The devil's in't if this will please the nation,
In these our blessed times of reformation,
When conventicling* is so much in fashion.   5
And yet –
That mutinous tribe less factions do beget
Than your continual differing in wit;
Your judgement's (as your passion's) a disease;
Nor muse nor miss* your appetite can please;   10
You're grown as nice as queasy consciences,
Whose each convulsion, when the spirit moves,
Damns everything that maggot* disapproves.

   With canting* rule you would the stage refine,
And to dull method all our sense confine.   15
With th' insolence of commonwealths you rule,
Where each gay fop, and politic grave fool,
On monarch wit impose, without control.
As for the last, who seldom sees a play,
Unless it be the old Blackfriars* way,   20
Shaking his empty noddle o'er bamboo,*
He cries, 'Good faith, these plays will never do.
Ah, sir, in my young days, what lofty wit,
What high-strained scenes of fighting there were writ;
These are slight airy toys. But tell me, pray,   25
What has the House of Commons done today?'
Then shows his politics, to let you see,
Of state affairs he'll judge as notably
As he can do of wit and poetry.
The younger sparks who hither do resort,   30
Cry, –
'Pox o'your genteel things, give us more sport;
Damn me, I'm sure 'twill never please the court.'
   Such fops are never pleased, unless the play
Be stuffed with fools as brisk and dull as they.   35

Such might the half-crown spare,* and in a glass
At home, behold a more accomplished ass,
Where they may set their cravats, wigs, and faces,
And practise all their buffoonery grimaces –
See how this huff* becomes, this damny,* – stare –   40
Which they at home may act, because they dare,
But must with prudent caution do elsewhere.
Oh, that our Nokes, or Tony Leigh* could show
A fop, but half so much to th' life as you.

Postscript

This play had been sooner in print, but for a report about the town (made by some either very malicious or very ignorant) that 'twas *Thomaso* altered;* which made the booksellers fear some trouble from the proprietor* of that admirable play, which indeed has wit enough to stock a poet, and is not to be pieced or mended* by any but the excellent author himself. That I have stolen some hints from it, may be a proof that I valued it more than to pretend to alter it; had I had the dexterity of some poets, who are not more expert in stealing than in the art of concealing, and who even that way outdo the Spartan boys,* I might have appropriated all to myself; but I, vainly proud of my judgement, hang out the sign of Angellica (the only stolen object), to give notice where a great part of the wit dwelt; though if the play of *The Novella** were as well worth remembering as *Thomaso*, they might (bating the name) have as well said I took it from thence. I will only say the plot and business (not to boast on't) is my own. As for the words and characters, I leave the reader to judge and compare with *Thomaso*, to whom I recommend the great entertainment of reading it; though had this succeeded ill, I should have had no need of imploring that justice from the critics, who are naturally so kind to any that pretend to usurp their dominion, especially of our sex,* they would doubtless have given me the whole honour on't. Therefore I will only say in English what the famous Virgil does in Latin: I make verses, and others have the fame.*

FINIS

THE KIND KEEPER

or

MR LIMBERHAM

A Comedy

By

JOHN DRYDEN

Κἤν με φάγῃς ἐπὶ ῥίζαν, ὁμῶς ἔτι καρποφορήσω*
(Ἀνθολογία Δεύτερα)

Hic nuptarum insanit amoribus; his meretricum;
Omnes hi metuunt versus; odere poetas.*
<Horace, Satires>

<DEDICATION>
*To the Right Honourable John, Lord Vaughan, &c.**

My Lord,

I cannot easily excuse the printing of a play at so
unseasonable a time, when the great plot of the nation,* like
one of Pharaoh's lean kine,* has devoured its younger
brethren of the stage.* But however weak my defence might
be for this, I am sure I should not need any to the world for   5
my dedication to your lordship. And if you can pardon my
presumption in it, that a bad poet should address himself to
so great a judge of wit, I may hope at least to scape with the
excuse of Catullus, when he writ to Cicero:

> Gratias tibi maximas Catullus   10
> Agit, pessimus omnium poeta;
> Tanto pessimus omnium poeta,
> Quanto tu optimus omnium patronus.*

I have seen an epistle of Flecknoe's* to a nobleman who
was by some extraordinary chance a scholar (and you may   15
please to take notice, by the way, how natural the
connection of thought is betwixt a bad poet and Flecknoe),
where he begins thus: 'Quatuordecim iam elapsi sunt anni,
etc.'* – his Latin, it seems, not holding out to the end of the
sentence. But he endeavoured to tell his patron, betwixt two   20
languages which he understood alike, that it was fourteen
years since he had the happiness to know him. 'Tis just so
long (and as happy be the omen of dullness to me as it is to
some clergymen and statesmen), since your lordship has
known that there is a worse poet remaining in the world   25
than he of scandalous memory who left it last.* I might
enlarge upon the subject with my author, and assure you
that I have served as long for you as one of the patriarchs
did for his Old Testament mistress.* But I leave those
flourishes, when occasion shall serve, for a greater orator to   30
use, and dare only tell you that I never passed any part of
my life with greater satisfaction or improvement to myself,

than those years which I have lived in the honour of your
lordship's acquaintance; if I may have only the time abated
when the public service called you to another part of the   35
world,* which, in imitation of our florid* speakers, I might
(if I durst presume upon the expression) call the parenthesis
of my life.

That I have always honoured you, I suppose I need not
tell you at this time of day. For you know I stayed not to   40
date my respects to you from that title which now you
have,* and to which you bring a greater addition by your
merit, than you receive from it by the name. But I am proud
to let others know how long it is that I have been made
happy by my knowledge of you, because I am sure it will   45
give me a reputation with the present age and with
posterity. And now, my lord, I know you are afraid lest I
should take this occasion, which lies so fair for me, to
acquaint the world with some of those excellencies which I
have admired in you. But I have reasonably considered that   50
'to acquaint the world' is a phrase of a malicious meaning;
for it would imply that the world were not already
acquainted with them. You are so generally known to be
above the meanness of my praises, that you have spared my
evidence and spoiled my compliment. Should I take for my   55
commonplaces your knowledge both of the old and new
philosophy;* should I add to these your skill in mathematics
and history; and yet farther, your being conversant with all
the ancient authors of the Greek and Latin tongues, as well
as with the modern; I should tell nothing new to mankind.   60
For when I have once but named you, the world will
anticipate all my commendations, and go faster before me
than I can follow. Be therefore secure, my lord, that your
own fame has freed itself from the danger of a panegyric;
and only give me leave to tell you that I value the candour of   65
your nature, and that one character of friendliness and (if I
may have leave to call it) kindness in you, before all those
other which make you considerable in the nation.

Some few of our nobility are learned, and therefore I will
not conclude an absolute contradiction in the terms of   70

nobleman and scholar; but as the world goes now, 'tis very
hard to predicate one upon the other; and 'tis yet more
difficult to prove that a nobleman can be a friend to poetry.
Were it not for two or three instances in Whitehall and in
the town, the poets of this age would find so little   75
encouragement for their labours, and so few understanders,
that they might have leisure to turn pamphleteers, and
augment the number of those abominable scribblers, who in
this time of licence* abuse the press almost every day with
nonsense and railing against the government.   80

It remains, my lord, that I should give you some account
of this comedy, which you have never seen, because it was
written and acted in your absence at your government of
Jamaica. 'Twas intended for an honest satire against our
crying sin of keeping.* How it would have succeeded, I can   85
but guess, for it was permitted to be acted only thrice. The
crime for which it suffered was that which is objected
against the *Satires* of Juvenal, and the *Epigrams* of Catullus:
that it expressed too much of the vice which it decried. Your
lordship knows what answer was returned by the elder* of   90
those poets whom I last mentioned, to his accusers:

> Castum esse decet pium poetam
> Ipsum. Versiculos nihil necesse est:
> Qui tum denique habent salem ac leporem
> Si sint molliculi et parum pudici.*   95

But I dare not make that apology for myself, and
therefore have taken a becoming care that those things
which offended on the stage might be either altered, or
omitted in the press.* For their authority is, and shall be
ever sacred to me, as much absent as present, and in all   100
alterations of their fortune, who for those reasons have
stopped its further appearance on the theatre. And whatsoever hindrance it has been to me in point of profit, many of
my friends can bear me witness, that I have not once
murmured against that decree. The same fortune once   105
happened to Molière on the occasion of his *Tartuffe*;*
which, notwithstanding, afterwards has seen the light in a

country more bigot than ours, and is accounted amongst the best pieces of that poet. I will be bold enough to say that this comedy is of the first rank of those which I have written, 110 and that posterity will be of my opinion. It has nothing of particular* satire in it; for whatsoever may have been pretended by some critics in the town, I may safely and solemnly affirm that no one character has been drawn from any single man;* and that I have known so many of the 115 same humour, in every folly which is here exposed, as may serve to warrant it from a particular reflection. It was printed in my absence from the town this summer, much against my expectation. Otherwise I had overlooked the press,* and been yet more careful that neither my friends 120 should have had the least occasion of unkindness against me, nor my enemies of upbraiding me. But if it live to a second impression, I will faithfully perform what has been wanting in this.* In the meantime, my lord, I recommend it to your protection, and beg I may keep still that place in 125 your favour which I have hitherto enjoyed; and which I shall reckon as one of the greatest blessings which can befall,

My lord,

Your lordship's most obedient, faithful servant,

John Dryden 130

Prologue

True wit has seen its best days long ago.
It ne'er looked up since we were dipped in show;*
When sense in doggerel rhymes and clouds* was lost,
And dullness flourished at the actors' cost.
Nor stopped it here: when tragedy was done,   5
Satire and humour the same fate have run;
And comedy is sunk to trick and pun.
Now our machining lumber will not sell,
And you no longer care for heaven or hell.
What stuff will please you next, the Lord can tell.   10
Let them who the rebellion first began
To wit, restore the monarch if they can.
Our author dares not be the first bold man.
He, like the prudent citizen, takes care
To keep for better marts his staple ware;   15
His toys* are good enough for Stourbridge Fair.*
Tricks were the fashion; if it now be spent,
'Tis time enough at Easter to invent;
No man will make up a new suit for Lent.
If now and then he takes a small pretence   20
To forage for a little wit and sense;
Pray pardon him, he meant you no offence.
Next summer, Nostradamus* tells, they say,
That all the critics shall be shipped away,
And not enough be left to damn a play.   25
To every sail beside, good heaven, be kind;
But drive away that swarm with such a wind
That not one locust* may be left behind.

DRAMATIS PERSONAE

The play was first performed in March 1678 by the Duke's Company at the Dorset Garden Theatre, but was stopped after three days. No cast is recorded.

ALDO an honest, good-natured, free-hearted old gentleman of the town

WOODALL his son, under a false name; bred abroad, and new returned from travel

LIMBERHAM a tame, foolish keeper, perusaded by what is last said to him, and changing next word

BRAINSICK a husband, who being well conceited of himself,* despises his wife; vehement and eloquent, as he thinks, but, indeed, a talker of nonsense

GERVASE Woodall's man: formal,* and apt to give good counsel

GILES Woodall's cast* servant

<GEOFFERY Aldo's servant>

MRS SAINTLY an hypocritical, fanatic* landlady of the boarding-house

MRS TRICKSY a termagant kept mistress

MRS PLEASANCE supposed daughter to Mistress Saintly; spiteful and satirical, but secretly in love with Woodall

MRS BRAINSICK

JUDITH a maid of the house

<assorted whores: MRS OVERDON; PRU, her daughter; MRS PAD; MRS TERMAGANT; MRS HACKNEY>

Scene: A boarding-house in town

Act 1, Scene 1

An open garden-house;* a table in it, and chairs

(*Enter* WOODALL, GERVASE)

WOODALL Bid the footman receive the trunks and portmanteaux, and see 'em placed in the lodgings you have
taken for me, while I walk a turn here in the garden.

GERVASE 'Tis already ordered, sir. But they are like to stay
in the outer room, till the mistress of the house return   5
from morning exercise.

WOODALL What, she's gone to the parish church, it seems,
to her devotions?

GERVASE No, sir. The servants have informed me that she
rises every morning, and goes to a private meeting-house*   10
where they pray for the government, and practise against
the authority of it.

WOODALL And hast thou trepanned* me into a tabernacle
of the godly? Is this pious boarding-house a place for me,
thou wicked varlet?   15

GERVASE According to human appearance, I must confess,
'tis neither fit for you, nor you for it; but have patience,
sir, matters are not so bad as they may seem. There are
pious bawdy-houses in the world, or conventicles would
not be so much frequented.* Neither is it impossible but a   20
devout, fanatic landlady of a boarding-house may be a
bawd.

WOODALL Aye, to those of her own church, I grant you,
Gervase; but I am none of those.

GERVASE If I were worthy to read you a lecture in the   25
mystery of wickedness, I would instruct you first in the art
of seeming holiness. But, heaven be thanked, you have a
toward and pregnant genius* to vice, and need not any
man's instruction; and I am too good, I thank my stars,
for the vile employment of a pimp.   30

WOODALL Then thou art e'en too good for me; a worse
man will serve my turn.

GERVASE I call your conscience to witness how often I have
given you wholesome counsel; how often I have said to
you, with tears in my eyes, 'Master', or 'Master Aldo' –   35

WOODALL 'Mr Woodall', you rogue! That's my *nom de
guerre*.* You know I have laid by Aldo, for fear that
name should bring me to the notice of my father.

GERVASE Cry you mercy, good Mr Woodall. How often
have I said, 'Into what courses do you run?' Your father   40
sent you into France at twelve year old, bred you up at
Paris; first, in a college,* and then at an academy.* At the
first, instead of running through a course of philosophy,
you ran through all the bawdy-houses in town. At the
later, instead of managing the great horse,* you exercised   45
on your master's wife. What you did in Germany, I know
not, but that you beat 'em all at their own weapon,
drinking, and have brought home a goblet of plate* from
Munster, for the prize of swallowing a gallon of Rhenish*
more than the bishop.   50

WOODALL Gervase, thou shalt be my chronicler; thou
losest none of my heroic actions.

GERVASE What a comfort are you like to prove to your
good old father! You have run a-campaigning among the
French these last three years without his leave. And now   55
he sends for you back to settle you in the world, and
marry you to the heiress of a rich gentleman of whom he
had the guardianship, yet you do not make your application to him.

WOODALL Prithee, no more.   60

GERVASE You are come over; have been in town above a
week incognito, haunting playhouses and other places,
which for modesty I name not; and have changed your
name from Aldo to Woodall for fear of being discovered
to him. You have not so much as enquired where he is   65
lodged, though you know he is most commonly in
London. And lastly, you have discharged my honest
fellow-servant Giles, because –

WOODALL Because he was too saucy, and was ever offering
to give me counsel. Mark that, and tremble at his destiny.   70

GERVASE I know the reason why I am kept: because you cannot be discovered by my means. For you took me up in France, and your father knows me not.

WOODALL I must have a ramble* in the town. When I have spent my money, I will grow dutiful; see my father, and   75 ask for more. In the meantime, I have beheld a handsome woman at a play; I am fallen in love with her, and have found her easy. Thou, I thank thee, hast traced her to her lodging in this boarding-house, and hither I am come to accomplish my design.   80

GERVASE Well, heaven mend all.

(*Noise <from outside>*)

I hear our landlady's voice without; and therefore shall defer my counsel to a fitter season.

WOODALL Not a syllable of counsel. The next grave sentence, thou marchest after Giles. Woodall's my name;   85 remember that.

(*Enter* MRS SAINTLY)

Is this the lady of the house?

GERVASE Yes, Mr Woodall, for want of a better, as she will tell you.

WOODALL (*saluting* her) She has a notable smack with   90 her! I believe zeal first taught the art of kissing close.

MRS SAINTLY You're welcome, gentleman. Woodall is your name?

WOODALL I call myself so.

MRS SAINTLY You look like a sober, discreet gentleman.   95 There is grace in your countenance.

WOODALL Some sprinklings of it, madam; we must not boast.

MRS SAINTLY Verily, boasting is of an evil principle.

WOODALL Faith, madam –   100

MRS SAINTLY No swearing, I beseech you. Of what church are you?

WOODALL Why, of Covent Garden church,* I think.

GERVASE (*aside*) How lewdly and ignorantly he answers!
<to him> She means, of what religion are you?   105

WOODALL Oh, does she so? (*to* MRS SAINTLY) Why, I am
of your religion. Be it what it will, I warrant it a right one.
I'll not stand with you for a trifle. Presbyterian, Independent, Anabaptist – they are all of 'em too good for us,
unless we had the grace to follow 'em.   110

MRS SAINTLY I see you are ignorant; but verily, you are a
new vessel, and I may season* you. I hope you do not use
the parish church.*

WOODALL Faith, madam – cry you mercy, I forgot again! –
I have been in England but five days.   115

MRS SAINTLY (*aside*) I find a certain motion within me to
this young man, and must secure him to myself, ere he see
my lodgers. <to him> Oh, seriously, I had forgotten; your
trunk and portmanteaux are standing in the hall. Your
lodgings are ready, and your man may place 'em, if he   120
please, while you and I confer together.

WOODALL Go, Gervase, and do as you are directed.

[*Exit* GERVASE]

MRS SAINTLY In the first place, you must know we are a
company of ourselves, and expect you should live con-
formably and lovingly amongst us.   125

WOODALL There you have hit me. I am the most loving
soul, and shall be conformable to all of you.

MRS SAINTLY And to me especially. Then, I hope you're no
keeper of late hours.

WOODALL No, no, my hours are very early; betwixt three   130
and four in the morning, commonly.

MRS SAINTLY That must be amended; but to remedy the
inconvenience, I will myself sit up for you. I hope you
would not offer violence* to me?

WOODALL I think I should not, if I were sober.   135

MRS SAINTLY Then if you were overtaken* and should
offer violence, and I consent not, you may do your filthy
part, and I am blameless.

WOODALL (*aside*) I think the devil's in her; she has given

me the hint again. (*to her*) Well, it shall go hard, but I will 140
offer violence sometimes. Will that content you?

MRS SAINTLY I have a cup of cordial water* in my closet,
which will help to strengthen nature and to carry off a
debauch. I do not invite you thither, but the house will be
safe abed, and scandal will be avoided.   145

WOODALL Hang scandal; I am above it, at those times.

MRS SAINTLY But scandal is the greatest part of the
offence; you must be secret. And I must warn you of
another thing. There are, besides myself, two more young
women in my house.   150

WOODALL (*aside*) That 'besides herself' is a cooling card.
<*to her*> Pray, how young are they?

MRS SAINTLY About my age; some eighteen, or twenty, or
thereabouts.

WOODALL Oh, very good! Two more young women 155
besides yourself – and both handsome?

MRS SAINTLY No, verily, they are painted outsides.* You
must not cast your eyes upon 'em, nor listen to their
conversation. You are already chosen for a better work.

WOODALL I warrant you, let me alone.* I am chosen, I. 160

MRS SAINTLY They are a couple of alluring, wanton
minxes.

WOODALL Are they very alluring, say you? Very wanton?

MRS SAINTLY You appear exalted when I mention those
pitfalls of iniquity.   165

WOODALL Who I? Exalted? Good faith, I am as sober a
melancholy poor soul! –

MRS SAINTLY I see this abominable sin of swearing is
rooted in you. Tear it out! Oh, tear it out! It will destroy
your precious soul.   170

WOODALL I find we two shall scarce agree. I must not
come to your closet when I have got a bottle; for, at such
a time, I am horribly given to it.

MRS SAINTLY Verily, a little swearing may be then allow-
able. You may swear you love me, 'tis a lawful oath; but 175
then, you must not look on harlots.

WOODALL <*aside*> I must wheedle her, and whet my

courage first on her, as a good musician always preludes
before a tune. (*embracing her*) Come, here's my first oath.

(*Enter* ALDO)

ALDO How now, Mrs Saintly! What work have we here 180
towards?

WOODALL (*aside*) Aldo, my own natural father, as I live! I
remember the lines of that hidebound* face. Does he
lodge here? If he should know me, I am ruined.

MRS SAINTLY (*aside*) Curse on his coming! He has dis- 185
turbed us. <*to* WOODALL> Well, young gentleman, I shall
take a time to instruct you better.

WOODALL You shall find me an apt scholar.

MRS SAINTLY I must go abroad upon some business; but
remember your promise to carry yourself soberly, and 190
without scandal in my family; and so I leave you to this
gentleman, who is a member of it.

[*Exit* MRS SAINTLY]

ALDO (*aside*) Before George,* a proper fellow! And a
swinger* he should be, by his make! The rogue would
bumble* a whore, I warrant him! <*to* WOODALL> You 195
are welcome, sir, amongst us – most heartily welcome, as
I may say.

WOODALL <*aside*> All's well: he knows me not. <*to*
ALDO> Sir, your civility is obliging to a stranger, and may
befriend me in the acquaintance of our fellow-lodgers. 200

ALDO Hold you there, sir. I must first understand you a
little better; and yet, methinks, you should be true to love.

WOODALL Drinking and wenching are but slips of youth. I
had those good qualities from my father.

ALDO (*hugging him*) Thou, boy! Aha, boy! A true Trojan,* 205
I warrant thee! Well, I say no more; but you are lighted
into such a family, such food for concupiscence, such
bona robas!*

WOODALL One I know indeed, a wife. But *bona robas* say
you?
210

ALDO I say, *bona robas* in the plural number.

WOODALL Why, what a Turk Mahomet shall I be!* No, I

will not make myself drunk, with the conceit of so much
joy. The fortune's too great for mortal man, and I, a poor
unworthy sinner.   215

ALDO Would I lie to my friend? Am I a man? Am I a
Christian? There is that wife you mentioned, a delicate
little wheedling devil, with such an appearance of simplicity. And with that she does undermine, so fool her
conceited husband, that he despises her!   220

WOODALL Just ripe for horns. His destiny, like a Turk's, is
written in his forehead.*

ALDO Peace, peace; thou art yet ordained for greater
things. There's another too, a kept mistress, a brave,
strapping jade, a two-handed* whore!   225

WOODALL A kept mistress too! My bowels yearn to her
already. She's certain prize.

ALDO But this lady is so termagant an empress! And he, so
submissive, so tame, so led a keeper, and as proud of his
slavery as a Frenchman. I am confident he dares not find   230
her false, for fear of a quarrel with her, because he is sure
to be at the charges of the war. She knows he cannot live
without her, and therefore seeks occasions of falling out
to make him purchase peace. I believe she's now aiming at
a settlement.*   235

WOODALL Might not I ask you one civil question? How
pass you your time in this noble family? For I find you are
a lover of the game,* and should be loath to hunt in your
purlieus.*

ALDO I must first tell you something of my condition. I am 240
here a friend to all of 'em. I am their factotum, do all their
business. For, not to boast, sir, I am a man of general
acquaintance. There's no news in town, either foreign or
domestic, but I have it first; no mortgage of lands, no sale
of houses, but I have a finger in 'em.   245

WOODALL Then, I suppose, you are a gainer by your pains.

ALDO No, I do all gratis, and am most commonly a loser;
only a buck sometimes from this good lord, or that good
lady, in the country. And I eat it not alone; I must have
company.   250

WOODALL Pray, what company do you invite?

ALDO Peace, peace, I am coming to you. Why, you must
know I am tender-natured; and if any unhappy difference
have arisen betwixt a mistress and her gallant, then I
strike in to do good offices betwixt 'em; and, at my own   255
proper* charges, conclude the quarrel with a reconciling
supper.

WOODALL I find the ladies of pleasure are beholden to you.

ALDO Before George, I love the poor little devils. I am
indeed a father* to 'em, and so they call me. I give 'em my   260
counsel, and assist 'em with my purse. I cannot see a
pretty sinner hurried to prison by the land-pirates,* but
nature works,* and I must bail her; or want a supper, but
I have a couple of crammed* chickens, a cream tart and a
bottle of wine to offer her.   265

WOODALL Sure, you expect some kindness in return.

ALDO Faith, not much. Nature in me is at low water mark;
my body's a jade,* and tires under me. Yet I love to
smuggle* still in a corner; pat 'em down and purr over
'em; but after that, I can do 'em little harm.   270

WOODALL Then I'm acquainted with your business. You
would be a kind of deputy-fumbler under me.

ALDO You have me right. Be you the lion, to devour the
prey. I am your jackal, to provide it for you. There will be
a bone for me to pick.   275

WOODALL Your humility becomes your age. For my part I
am vigorous, and throw at all.

ALDO As right as if I had begot thee! Wilt thou give me
leave to call thee son?

WOODALL With all my heart.   280

ALDO Ha, mad son!

WOODALL Mad daddy!

ALDO Your man told me you were just returned from
travel. What parts have you last visited?

WOODALL I came from France.   285

ALDO Then, perhaps, you may have known an ungracious
boy of mine there.

WOODALL Like enough. Pray, what's his name?

ALDO George Aldo.

WOODALL I must confess I do know the gentleman. Satisfy 290
yourself he's in health, and upon his return.

ALDO That's some comfort; but, I hear, a very rogue, a
lewd young fellow.

WOODALL The worst I know of him is that he loves a
wench, and that good quality he has not stolen.   295

(*Music at the balcony overhead.* MRS TRICKSY *and*
JUDITH *appear*)

Hark! There's music above.

ALDO 'Tis at my daughter Tricksy's lodging, the kept
mistress I told you of – the lass of mettle. But for all she
carries it so high, I know her pedigree. Her mother's a
seamstress in Dog and Bitch Yard, and was, in her youth, 300
as right* as she is.

WOODALL Then she's a two-piled punk,* a punk of two
descents.*

ALDO And her father, the famous cobbler, who taught
'Walsingham' to the blackbirds.* How stand thy affec- 305
tions to her, thou lusty rogue?

WOODALL All o'fire; a most urging creature!

ALDO Peace! They are beginning.

A Song

I

'Gainst keepers we petition,
Who would enclose the common;   310
'Tis enough to raise sedition
In the free-born subject, woman.
Because for his gold
I my body have sold,
He thinks I'm a slave for my life.   315
He rants, domineers;
He swaggers and swears,
And would keep me as bare as his wife.

2

'Gainst keepers we petition, etc.
'Tis honest and fair   320
That a feast I prepare;
But when his dull appetite's o'er,
I'll treat with the rest
Some welcomer guest,
For the reck'ning was paid me before.   325

WOODALL A song against keepers! This makes well for us
lusty lovers.

MRS TRICKSY (<calls from> above) Father, father Aldo!

ALDO Daughter Tricksy, are you there, child? Your friends
at Barnet* are all well; and your dear Master Limberham,   330
that noble Hephaestion,* is returning with 'em.

MRS TRICKSY And you are come upon the spur before to
acquaint me with the news.

ALDO Well, thou art the happiest rogue in a kind keeper!
He drank thy health five times, supernaculum,* to my son 335
Brainsick; and dipped my daughter Pleasance's little
finger, to make it go down more glibly. And, before
George, I grew tory rory,* as they say, and strained a
brimmer through the lilywhite smock,* i'faith.

MRS TRICKSY You will never leave these fumbling* tricks, 340
father, till you are taken upon suspicion of manhood, and
have a bastard laid at your door. I am sure you would
own it for your credit.

ALDO Before George, I should not see it starve for the
mother's sake. For, if she were a punk, she was good-   345
natured, I warrant her.

WOODALL (aside) Well, if ever son was blessed with a
hopeful father, I am.

MRS TRICKSY Who's that gentleman with you?

ALDO A young monsieur returned from travel. A lusty   350
young rogue; a true-milled whoremaster, with the right
stamp.* He's a fellow-lodger, incorporate in our society.
For whose sake he came hither, let him tell you.

WOODALL (*aside*) Are you gloating* already? Then there's
hopes, i'faith.   355

MRS TRICKSY You seem to know him, father.

ALDO Know him! From his cradle – (*to* WOODALL) What's
your name?

WOODALL Woodall.

ALDO Woodall of Woodall! I knew his father. We were   360
contemporaries and fellow-wenchers in our youth.

WOODALL (*aside*) My honest father stumbles into truth, in
spite of lying.

MRS TRICKSY I was just coming down to the garden-house
before you came.   365

ALDO I'm sorry I cannot stay to present my son Woodall to
you; but I have set you together, that's enough for me.
                                                        [*Exit*]

WOODALL (*alone*) 'Twas my study to avoid my father, and
I have run full into his mouth. And yet I have a strong
hank upon* him too, for I am private to as many of his   370
virtues, as he is of mine. After all, if I had an ounce of
discretion left, I should pursue this business no farther.
But two fine women in a house! Well, 'tis resolved, come
what will on't, thou art answerable for all my sins, old
Aldo.   375

   (*Enter* MRS TRICKSY *with a box of essences*)*

Here she comes, this heir apparent of a seamstress and a
cobbler! And yet, as she's adorned, she looks like any
princess of the blood.

                 (*Salutes her*)

MRS TRICKSY (*aside*) What a difference there is between
this gentleman and my feeble keeper, Mr Limberham!   380
He's to my wish, if he would but make the least advances
to me. <*to* WOODALL> Father Aldo tells me, sir, you're a
traveller. What adventures have you had in foreign
countries?

WOODALL I have no adventures of my own can deserve   385
your curiosity; but, now I think on't, I can tell you one

that happened to a French cavalier, a friend of mine, at
Tripoli.

MRS TRICKSY No wars, I beseech you. I am so weary of
father Aldo's Lorraine and Créquy.*   390

WOODALL Then this is as you would desire it, a love-
adventure. This French gentleman was made a slave to the
dey* of Tripoli; by his good qualities gained his master's
favour; and after, by corrupting an eunuch, was brought
into the seraglio privately, to see the dey's mistress.   395

MRS TRICKSY This is somewhat; proceed, sweet sir.

WOODALL He was so much amazed when he first beheld
her, leaning over a balcony, that he scarcely dared to lift
his eyes, or speak to her.

MRS TRICKSY (aside) I find him now. <to him> But what   400
followed of this dumb interview?

WOODALL The nymph was gracious, and came down to
him; but with so goddess-like a presence, that the poor
gentleman was thunderstruck again.

MRS TRICKSY That savoured little of the monsieur's gallan-   405
try, especially when the lady gave him encouragement.

WOODALL The gentleman was not so dull but he understood the favour, and was presuming enough to try if she
were mortal. He advanced with more assurance, and took
her fair hands. Was he not too bold, madam? And would   410
not you have drawn back yours, had you been in the
sultana's place?

MRS TRICKSY If the sultana liked him well enough to come
down into the garden to him, I suppose she came not
thither to gather nosegays.   415

WOODALL Give me leave, madam, to thank you, in my
friend's behalf, for your favourable judgement. (kisses her
hand) He kissed her hand with an exceeding transport;
and finding that she pressed his at the same instant, he
proceeded with a greater eagerness to her lips. But,   420
madam, the story would be without life, unless you give
me leave to act the circumstances.

(Kisses her)

MRS TRICKSY Well, I'll swear you are the most natural historian!

WOODALL But now, madam, my heart beats with joy, 425 when I come to tell you the sweetest part of his adventure. Opportunity was favourable, and love was on his side. He told her the chamber was more private and a fitter scene for pleasure. Then, looking on her eyes, he found 'em languishing; he saw her cheeks blushing, and heard her 430 voice faltering in a half denial. (*takes her hand*) He seized her hand with an amorous ecstasy, and –

MRS TRICKSY Hold, sir, you act your part too far. Your friend was unconscionable,* if he desired more favours at the first interview.   435

WOODALL He both desired, and obtained 'em, madam, and so will –

(Noise <outside>)

MRS TRICKSY Heavens! I hear Mr Limberham's voice. He's returned from Barnet.

WOODALL I'll avoid him.   440

MRS TRICKSY That's impossible; he'll meet you. Let me think a moment. Mrs Saintly is abroad, and cannot discover you. Have any of the servants seen you?

WOODALL None.

MRS TRICKSY Then you shall pass for my Italian merchant 445 of essences. Here's a little box of 'em just ready.

WOODALL But I speak no Italian, only a few broken scraps which I picked up from scaramouch and harlequin at Paris.*

MRS TRICKSY You must venture that. When we are rid of 450 Limberham, 'tis but slipping into your chamber, throwing off your black periwig and riding-suit, and you come out an Englishman. No more; he's here.

(Enter LIMBERHAM)

LIMBERHAM Why, how now, Pug?* Nay, I must lay you over the lips, to take handsel* of 'em, for my welcome. 455

MRS TRICKSY (*putting him back*) Foh! How you smell of sweat, dear!

LIMBERHAM I have put myself into this same unsavoury heat out of my violent affection to see thee, Pug. Before George, as father Aldo says, I could not live without thee. 460 Thou art the purest* bedfellow, though I say it, that I did nothing but dream of thee all night; and then I was so troublesome to father Aldo (for you must know, he and I were lodged together) that, in my conscience, I did so kiss him and so hug him in my sleep! 465

MRS TRICKSY I dare be sworn 'twas in your sleep; for when you are waking you are the most honest, quiet bedfellow that ever lay by woman.*

LIMBERHAM Well, Pug, all shall be amended. I am come home on purpose to pay old debts. But who is that same 470 fellow there? What makes he in our territories?

MRS TRICKSY You oaf, you! Do you not perceive it is the Italian signior, who is come to sell me essences?

LIMBERHAM Is this the signior? I warrant you, 'tis he the lampoon* was made on. 475

(*Sings the tune of 'Signior', and ends with 'Ho, ho'*)

MRS TRICKSY Prithee, leave thy foppery that we may have done with him. He asks an unreasonable price, and we cannot agree. Here, signior, take your trinkets and be gone.

WOODALL (*taking the box*) A dio, seigniora.* 480

LIMBERHAM Hold; pray, stay a little, signior. A thing is come into my head o' the' sudden.

MRS TRICKSY What would you have, you eternal sot? The man's in haste.

LIMBERHAM But why should you be in your frumps,* Pug, 485 when I design only to oblige you? I must present you with this box of essences. Nothing can be too dear for thee.

MRS TRICKSY Pray let him go. He understands no English.

LIMBERHAM Then how could you drive a bargain with him, Pug? 490

MRS TRICKSY Why, by signs, you coxcomb!

LIMBERHAM Very good. Then I'll first pull him by the sleeve. That's a sign to stay. <*to* WOODALL> Look you, Mr Signior, I would make a presence of your essences to this lady. For I find I can't speak too plain to you because 495 you understand no English. Be not you refractory now, but take ready money – that's a rule.

WOODALL *Seignioro, non intendo Inglese.**

LIMBERHAM This is a very dull fellow! He says he does not intend English. How much shall I offer him, Pug?   500

MRS TRICKSY If you will present me,* I have bidden him ten guineas.

LIMBERHAM And, before George, you bid him fair. Look you, Mr Seignior, I will give you all these: <*counts out guineas*> one, two, three, four, five, six, seven, eight, nine 505 and ten. Do you see, seignior?

WOODALL *Seignior, si.*

LIMBERHAM Lo' you* there, Pug, he does see. Here, will you take me at my word?

WOODALL (*shrugging up*) *Troppo poco, troppo co.**   510

LIMBERHAM *A poco, a poco!* Why, a pox o'you, too, and* you go to that. Stay, now I think on't, I can tickle him up with French; he'll understand that, sure. <*to* WOODALL> *Mounsieur, vouley-vous prendre ces dix guinnees pour ces essences? Mon foy c'est assez.**   515

WOODALL *Chi vala, amici. Ho di casa! Taratapa, taratapa, eus, matou, meau!** (<*aside*> *to her*) I am at the end of my Italian, what will become of me?

MRS TRICKSY (<*aside*> *to him*) Speak anything and make it pass for Italian. But be sure you take his money.   520

WOODALL *Seignior, jo non canno takare ten guinneo, possibilmentè; 'tis to my losso.*

LIMBERHAM That is, Pug, he cannot possibly take ten guineas, 'tis to his loss. Now I understand him. This is almost English.   525

MRS TRICKSY English! Away, you fop!* 'Tis a kind of lingua franca as I have heard the merchants call it; a certain compound language made up of all tongues that passes through the Levant.*

LIMBERHAM This *lingua*-what-you-call-it, is the most rar- 530
est language. I understand it as well as if it were English.
You shall see me answer him. <*to* WOODALL> *Seignioro,
stay a littlo, and consider wello, ten guinnio is monyo, a
very considerablo summo.*

MRS TRICKSY Come, you shall make it twelve, and he shall 535
take it for my sake.

LIMBERHAM Then, *seignioro, for Pugsakio, addo two
moro. Je vous donne bon advise. Prenez vistement. Prenez
me a mon mot.*

WOODALL *Jo losero molto. Ma per gagnare it vestro* 540
*costumo, datemi hansello.**

LIMBERHAM There is both *hansello* and *guinnio. Tako,
tako;* and so good morrow.

MRS TRICKSY Good morrow, *seignior*, I like your spirits
very well. Pray let me have all your essence you can spare. 545

LIMBERHAM Come, *Puggio*, let us retire in *secreto*, like
lovers, into our *chambro*; for I grow *impatiento*. <*to*
WOODALL> *Bon matin, mounsieur, bon matin et bon
jour.*

[*Exeunt* LIMBERHAM, MRS TRICKSY]

WOODALL Well, get thee gone, squire *Limberhamo*, for the 550
easiest fool I ever knew, next my naunt of fairies in *The
Alchemist*.* I have escaped, thanks to my mistress's
lingua franca. I'll steal to my chamber, shift my periwig
and clothes, and then, with the help of resty* Gervase,
concert the business of the next campaign. My father 555
sticks in my stomach still; but I am resolved to be
Woodall with him, and Aldo with the women.

[*Exit*]

Act 2, Scene 1

(*Enter* WOODALL, GERVASE)

WOODALL Hitherto, sweet Gervase, we have carried matters swimmingly. I have danced in a net* before my

father, almost checkmated the keeper, retired to my
chamber undiscovered, shifted my habit, and am come
out an absolute monsieur to allure the ladies. How sits my   5
chedreux?*

GERVASE Oh, very finely! With the locks combed down,
like a mermaid's on a signpost.* Well, you think now
your father may live in the same house with you till
doomsday and never find you; or, when he has found you,   10
he will be kind enough not to consider what a property*
you have made of him. My employment is at end. You
have got a better pimp, thanks to your filial reverence.

WOODALL Prithee, what should a man do with such a
father but use him thus? Besides, he does journey-work*   15
under me; 'tis his humour to fumble, and my duty to
provide for his old age.

GERVASE Take my advice yet. Down o' your marrow-
bones, and ask forgiveness; espouse the wife he has
provided for you; lie by the side of a wholesome woman,   20
and procreate your own progeny in the fear of heaven.

WOODALL I have no vocation to it, Gervase. A man of
sense is not made for marriage. 'Tis a game which none
but dull, plodding fellows can play at well; and 'tis as
natural to them as crimp* is to a Dutchman.   25

GERVASE Think on't however, sir. Debauchery is upon its
last legs in England. Witty men began the fashion; and
now the fops are got into't, 'tis time to leave it.

(*Enter* ALDO)

ALDO Son Woodall, thou vigorous young rogue, I congratulate thy good fortune. Thy man has told me of the   30
adventure of the Italian merchant.

WOODALL Well, they are now retired together like Rinaldo
and Armida,* to private dalliance; but we shall find a
time to separate their loves and strike in betwixt 'em,
daddy. But I hear there's another lady in the house, my   35
landlady's fair daughter. How came you to leave her out
of your catalogue?

ALDO She's pretty, I confess, but most damnably honest.*

Have a care of her, I warn you, for she's prying and
malicious.   40

WOODALL A tang of the mother; but I love to graff* on
such a crab-tree. She may bear good fruit another year.

ALDO No, no, avoid her. I warrant thee, young Alexander,
I will provide thee more worlds to conquer.

GERVASE (aside) My old master would fain pass for Philip   45
of Macedon,* when he is little better than Sir Pandarus of
Troy.*

WOODALL If you get this keeper out of doors, father, and
give me but an opportunity –

ALDO Trust my diligence. I will smoke him out as they do   50
bees, but I will make him leave his honeycomb.

GERVASE (aside) If I had a thousand sons, none of the race
of the Gervases should ever be educated by thee, thou vile
old Satan.

ALDO Away boy, fix thy arms and whet,* like the lusty   55
German boys before a charge. He shall bolt immediately.

WOODALL Oh, fear not the vigorous five and twenty.

ALDO Hold, a word first. Thou saidst my son was shortly
to come over.

WOODALL So he told me.   60

ALDO Thou art my bosom friend.

GERVASE (aside) Of an hour's acquaintance.

ALDO Be sure thou dost not discover my frailties to the
young scoundrel. 'Twere enough to make the boy my
master. I must keep up the dignity of old age with him.   65

WOODALL Keep but your own counsel, father; for whatever he knows must come from you.

ALDO The truth on't is, I sent for him over, partly to have
married him, and partly because his villainous bills came
so thick upon me, that I grew weary of the charge.   70

GERVASE He spared for nothing; he laid it on, sir, as I have
heard.

WOODALL Peace, you lying rogue. Believe me, sir, bating
his necessary expenses of women, which I know you
would not have him want: in all things else, he was the   75
best manager of your allowance and, though I say it –

GERVASE (*aside*) That should not say it —

WOODALL The most hopeful young gentleman in Paris.

ALDO Report speaks otherwise. And before George, I shall read him a wormwood lecture,* when I see him. But 80 hark, I hear the door unlock; the lovers are coming out. I'll stay here, to wheedle him abroad; but you must vanish.

WOODALL Like night and the moon in *The Maid's Tragedy*: I into mist; you into day.*   85

[*Exit* WOODALL *and* GERVASE]

(*Enter* LIMBERHAM *and* MRS TRICKSY)

LIMBERHAM Nay, but dear, sweet, honey Pug, forgive me but this once. It may be any man's case when his desires are too vehement.*

MRS TRICKSY Let me alone; I care not.

LIMBERHAM But then thou wilt not love me, Pug.   90

ALDO How now, son Limberham? There's no quarrel towards, I hope!

MRS TRICKSY You had best* tell now, and make yourself ridiculous!

LIMBERHAM She's in passion. Pray, do you moderate this 95 matter, father Aldo.

MRS TRICKSY Father Aldo! I wonder you are not ashamed to call him so! You may be his father, if the truth were known.

ALDO Before George, I smell a rat, son Limberham. I 100 doubt, I doubt here has been some great omission in love affairs.

LIMBERHAM I think all the stars in heaven have conspired my ruin. I'll look in my almanac — as I hope for mercy, 'tis cross-day,* now.   105

MRS TRICKSY Hang your pitiful excuses. 'Tis well known what offers I have had, and what fortunes I might have made with others, like a fool as I was, to throw away my youth and beauty upon you. I could have had a young, handsome lord that offered me my coach and six; besides 110 many a good knight and gentleman that would have

parted with their own ladies, and have settled half they
had upon me.

LIMBERHAM Aye, you said so.

MRS TRICKSY I said so, sir! Who am I? Is not my word as 115
good as yours?

LIMBERHAM As mine, gentlewoman? Though I say it, my
word will go for thousands.

MRS TRICKSY The more shame for you, that you have done
no more for me. But I am resolved I'll not lose my time 120
with you; I'll part.

LIMBERHAM Do. Who cares? Go to Dog and Bitch Yard
and help your mother to make footmen's shirts.

MRS TRICKSY I defy you, slanderer, I defy you.

ALDO Nay, dear daughter!   125

LIMBERHAM I defy her too.

ALDO Nay, good son!

MRS TRICKSY Let me alone. I'll have him cudgelled by my
footman.

(*Enter* MRS SAINTLY)

MRS SAINTLY Bless us! What's here to do? My neighbours 130
will think I keep a nest of unclean birds here.

LIMBERHAM <*to* MRS TRICKSY> You had best preach
now, and make her house be thought a bawdy-house!

MRS TRICKSY No, no; while you are in't, you'll secure it
from that scandal. Hark hither, Mrs Saintly.   135

(*Whispers <to her>*)

LIMBERHAM Do; tell, tell, no matter for that.

MRS SAINTLY Who would have imagined you had been
such a kind of man, Mr Limberham! Oh, heaven! Oh,
heaven!

[*Exit*]

LIMBERHAM So, now you have spit your venom, and the 140
storm is over.

ALDO (*crying*) That I should ever live to see this day!

MRS TRICKSY To show I can live honest, in spite of all
mankind, I'll go into a nunnery, and that's my resolution.

LIMBERHAM Don't hinder her, good father Aldo. I'm sure 145
she'll come back from France before she gets halfway o'er
to Calais.

ALDO Nay, but son Limberham, this must not be. A word
in private. <takes him aside> You'll never get such another
woman for love nor money. Do but look upon her; she's a 150
mistress for an emperor.

LIMBERHAM Let her be a mistress for a pope, like a whore
of Babylon* as she is.

ALDO Would I were worthy to be a young man, for her
sake. She should eat pearl,* if she would have 'em. 155

LIMBERHAM She can digest 'em, and gold too. Let me tell
you, father Aldo, she has the stomach of an ostrich.*

ALDO Daughter Tricksy, a word with you.

MRS TRICKSY I'll hear nothing. I am for a nunnery.

ALDO (takes her aside) I never saw a woman before you, 160
but first or last she would be brought to reason. Hark you
child, you'll scarcely find so kind a keeper. What if he has
some impediment one way? Everybody is not a Hercules.* You shall have my son Woodall to supply his
wants. But as long as he maintains you, be ruled by him 165
that bears the purse.

(LIMBERHAM singing)

I my own jailor was; my only foe,
Who did my liberty forego;
I was a pris'ner, 'cause I would be so.

ALDO Why, look you now, son Limberham, is this a song 170
to be sung at such a time, when I am labouring your
reconcilement? Come daughter Tricksy, you must be
ruled. I'll be the peacemaker.

MRS TRICKSY No, I'm just going.

LIMBERHAM The devil take me, if I call you back. 175

MRS TRICKSY And his dam take me, if I return; except you
do.

ALDO So, now you'll part for a mere punctilio!* Turn to
him, daughter. Speak to her, son. Why should you be so
refractory both, to bring my grey hairs with sorrow to the 180

grave?

LIMBERHAM I'll not be forsworn; I swore first.

MRS TRICKSY Thou art a forsworn man however; for thou swor'st to love me eternally.

LIMBERHAM Yes, I was such a fool, to swear so.　185

ALDO And will you have that dreadful oath lie gnawing on your conscience?

MRS TRICKSY Let him be damned; (*going*) and so farewell for ever.

LIMBERHAM Pug!　190

MRS TRICKSY Did you call, Mr Limberham?

LIMBERHAM It may be, aye; it may be, no.

MRS TRICKSY Well, I am going to the nunnery. But to show I am in charity, I'll pray for you.

ALDO Pray for him! Fie, daughter, fie! Is that an answer for　195 a Christian?

LIMBERHAM What did Pug say? Will she pray for me? Well, to show I am in charity, she shall not pray for me. Come back, Pug. But did I ever think thou couldst have been so unkind to have parted with me?　200

(*Cries*)

ALDO Look you, daughter, see how nature works in him!

LIMBERHAM I'll settle two hundred a year upon thee, because thou saidst thou wouldst pray for me.

ALDO Before George, son Limberham, you'll spoil all, if you underbid so. Come, down with your dust,* man.　205 What, show a base mind, when a fair lady's in question?

LIMBERHAM Well, if I must give three hundred –

MRS TRICKSY No, 'tis no matter; my thoughts are on a better place.

ALDO Come, there's no better place, than little London.　210 You sha'not part for a trifle. What, son Limberham? Four hundred a year's a square sum, and you shall give it.

LIMBERHAM 'Tis a round sum, indeed. I wish a three-cornered sum would have served her turn. Why should you be so pervicatious* now, Pug? Pray take three　215 hundred. (*she frowns*) Nay, rather than part, Pug, it shall be so.

ALDO It shall be so, it shall be so. Come now, buss,* and seal the bargain.

MRS TRICKSY (*kissing <LIMBERHAM>*) You see what a   220
good-natured fool I am, Mr Limberham, to come back into a wicked world for love of you. You'll see the writings drawn, father?

ALDO Aye; and pay the lawyer too. Why, this is as it should be! I'll be at the charge of the reconciling supper.   225
(*to her, aside*) Daughter, my son Woodall is waiting for you. <*to* LIMBERHAM> Come away, son Limberham, to the Temple.*

LIMBERHAM With all my heart, while she's in a good humour: it would cost me another hundred, if I should   230
stay till Pug were in wrath again. Adieu, sweet Pug.

[*Exeunt* ALDO <*and*> LIMBERHAM]

MRS TRICKSY That he should be so silly to imagine I would go into a nunnery! 'Tis likely; I have much nun's flesh* about me! But here comes my gentleman.

(*Enter* WOODALL, *not seeing her*)

WOODALL Now the wife's returned, and the daughter too,   235
and I have seen 'em both, and am more distracted than before. I would enjoy all, and have not yet determined with which I should begin. 'Tis but a kind of clergy-covetousness in me to desire so many. If I stand gaping after pluralities, one of 'em is in danger to be made a   240
sinecure.* (*sees her*) Oh, fortune has determined for me. 'Tis just here, as it is in the world: the mistress will be served before the wife.

MRS TRICKSY How now, sir? Are you rehearsing your lingua franca by yourself, that you walk so pensively?   245

WOODALL No, faith, madam. I was thinking of the lady who at parting bespoke so cunningly of me all my essences.

MRS TRICKSY But there are other beauties in the house, and I should be impatient of a rival. For I am apt to be   250 partial to myself, and think I deserve to be preferred before 'em.

WOODALL Your beauty will allow of no competition; and I am sure my love could make none.

MRS TRICKSY Yes, you have seen Mrs Brainsick; she's a 255 beauty.

WOODALL You mean, I suppose, the peaking* creature, the married woman, with a sidling* look, as if one cheek carried more bias than the other –

MRS TRICKSY Yes, and with a high nose, as visible as a 260 landmark.

WOODALL With one cheek blue, the other red – just like the covering of Lambeth Palace.*

MRS TRICKSY Nay, but her legs, if you could see 'em.

WOODALL She was so foolish to wear short petticoats and 265 show 'em. They are pillars gross enough to support a larger building – of the Tuscan order,* by my troth.

MRS TRICKSY And her little head, upon that long neck, shows like a traitor's skull upon a pole. Then, for her wit – 270

WOODALL She can have none. There's not room enough for a thought to play in.

MRS TRICKSY I think, indeed, I may safely trust you with such charms; and you have pleased me with your description of her. 275

WOODALL I wish you would give me leave to please you better. But you transact as gravely with me as a Spaniard, and are losing love, as he does Flanders.* You consider and demur, when the monarch is up in arms and at your gates. 280

MRS TRICKSY But to yield upon the first summons, ere you have laid a formal siege – tomorrow may prove a luckier day to you.

WOODALL Believe me, madam, lovers are not to trust tomorrow. Love may die upon our hands or opportunity 285 be wanting. 'Tis best securing the present hour.

MRS TRICKSY No, love's like fruit; it must have time to

ripen on the tree. If it be green gathered, 'twill but wither
afterwards.

WOODALL Rather 'tis like gunpowder; that which fires   290
quickest is commonly the strongest. By this burning kiss –

MRS TRICKSY You lovers are such froward* children, ever
crying for the breast; and, when you have once had it, fall
fast asleep in the nurse's arms. And with what face should
I look upon my keeper after it?   295

WOODALL With the same face that all mistresses look upon
theirs. Come, come.

MRS TRICKSY But my reputation!

WOODALL Nay, that's no argument, if I should be so base
to tell. For women get good fortunes nowadays, by losing 300
their credit, as a cunning citizen does by breaking.*

MRS TRICKSY But I'm so shamefaced! Well, I'll go in, and
hide my blushes.

[Exit]

WOODALL I'll not be long after you; for I think I have
hidden my blushes where I shall never find 'em.   305

(Re-enter MRS TRICKSY)

MRS TRICKSY As I live, Mr Limberham and father Aldo are
just returned. I saw 'em entering. My settlement will
miscarry if we are found here. What shall we do?

WOODALL Go you into your bedchamber, and leave me to
fortune.   310

MRS TRICKSY That you should be so dull! Their suspicion
will be strong still, for what should you make here?

WOODALL The curse on't is, too, I bid my man tell the
family I was gone abroad; so that if I am seen, you are
infallibly discovered.   315

(Noise <outside>)

MRS TRICKSY Hark, I hear 'em! Here's a chest which I
borrowed of Mrs Pleasance. Get quickly into it and I will
lock you up. There's nothing in't but clothes of Limberham's and a box of writings.

WOODALL I shall be smothered.   320

MRS TRICKSY Make haste, for heaven's sake. They'll quickly be gone, and then –

WOODALL That 'then', will make a man venture anything.

(He goes in, and she locks the chest)

(Enter LIMBERHAM *and* ALDO)

LIMBERHAM Dost thou not wonder, to see me come again so quickly, Pug?   325

MRS TRICKSY No, I am prepared for any foolish freak of yours. I knew you would have a qualm when you came to settlement.

LIMBERHAM Your settlement depends most absolutely on that chest.   330

MRS TRICKSY Father Aldo, a word with you, for heaven's sake.

ALDO No, no, I'll not whisper. Do not stand in your own light, but produce the keys, daughter.

LIMBERHAM Be not musty,* my pretty Saint Peter,* but produce the keys. I must have the writings out that concern thy settlement.   335

MRS TRICKSY Now I see you are so reasonable, I'll show you I dare trust your honesty. The settlement shall be deferred till another day.   340

ALDO No deferring, in these cases, daughter.

MRS TRICKSY But I have lost the keys.

LIMBERHAM That's a jest! Let me feel in thy pocket, for I must oblige thee.

MRS TRICKSY You shall feel nowhere. I have felt already, and am sure they are lost.   345

ALDO But feel again, the lawyer stays.

MRS TRICKSY Well, to satisfy you, I will feel. *<feels in her pocket>* They are not here. *<feels again>* Nor here neither.   350

(She pulls out her handkerchief and the keys drop after it. LIMBERHAM *takes 'em up)*

LIMBERHAM Look you now, Pug! Who's in the right? Well, thou art born to be a lucky Pug, in spite of thyself.

MRS TRICKSY (*aside*) Oh, I am ruined! – One word, I beseech you, father Aldo.

ALDO Not a syllable. What's the devil in you, daughter? 355 Open, son, open.

MRS TRICKSY (*aloud*) It shall not be opened. I will have my will, though I lose my settlement. Would I were within the chest; I would hold it down, to spite you. I say again, would I were within the chest, I would hold it so fast, you 360 should not open it. <*aside*> The best on't is, there's good incle* on the top of the inside, if he have the wit to lay hold on't.

LIMBERHAM (*going to open it*) Before George, I think you have the devil in a string,* Pug. I cannot open it, for the 365 guts of me. *Hictius Doctius!** What's here to do? I believe, in my conscience, Pug can conjure. Marry, God bless* us all good Christians.

ALDO Push hard, son.

LIMBERHAM I cannot push; I was never good at pushing. 370 When I push, I think the devil pushes too. Well, I must let it alone, for I am a fumbler. Here, take the keys, Pug.

MRS TRICKSY (*aside*) Then all's safe again.

(*Enter* JUDITH *and* GERVASE)

JUDITH Madam, Mrs Pleasance has sent for the chest you borrowed of her. She has present occasion for it; and has 375 desired us to carry it away.

LIMBERHAM Well, that's but reason. If she must have it, she must have it.

MRS TRICKSY Tell her, it shall be returned some time today. At present we must crave her pardon, because we 380 have some writings in it which must first be taken out, when we can open it.

LIMBERHAM Nay, that's but reason too. Then she must not have it.

GERVASE Let me come to't. I'll break it open, and you may 385 take out your writings.

LIMBERHAM That's true. 'Tis but reasonable it should be broke open.

MRS TRICKSY Then I may be bound to make good the loss.

LIMBERHAM 'Tis unreasonable it should be broken open. 390

ALDO Before George, Gervase and I will carry it away; and
a smith shall be sent for to my daughter Pleasance's
chamber, to open it without damage.

LIMBERHAM Why, who says against it? Let it be carried;
I'm all for reason.   395

MRS TRICKSY Hold; I say it shall not stir.

ALDO What? Everyone must have their own: *Fiat Justitia
aut ruat Mundus.**

LIMBERHAM Aye, *fiat Justitia,* Pug. She must have her
own; for *Justitia* is Latin for justice.   400

(ALDO *and* GERVASE *lift at it*)

ALDO I think the devil's in't.

GERVASE There's somewhat bounces* like him in't. 'Tis
plaguy heavy; but we'll take t'other heave.

MRS TRICKSY (*taking hold of the chest*) Then you shall
carry me too. Help, murder! Murder!   405

(*A confused gabbling among 'em*)

(*Enter* MRS SAINTLY)

MRS SAINTLY Verily, I think all hell's broke loose among
you. What, a schism in my family! Does this become the
purity of my house? What will the ungodly say?

LIMBERHAM No matter for the ungodly; this is all among
ourselves. For look you, the business is this: Mrs 410
Pleasance has sent for this same business here, which she
lent to Pug. Now Pug has some private businesses within
this business, which she would take out first, and the
business will not be opened; and this makes all the
business.   415

MRS SAINTLY Verily, I am raised up for a judge amongst
you; and I say –

MRS TRICKSY I'll have no judge: it shall not go.

ALDO Why son, why daughter, why Mrs Saintly – are you
all mad? Hear me, I am sober, I am discreet. Let a smith 420
be sent for hither; let him break open the chest; let the

things contained be taken out, and the thing containing be restored.

LIMBERHAM Now hear me, too, for I am sober and discreet. Father Aldo is an oracle. It shall be so.   425

MRS TRICKSY Well, to show I am reasonable, I am content Mr Gervase and I will fetch an instrument from the next smith. In the meantime, let the chest remain where it now stands, and let everyone depart the chamber.

LIMBERHAM That no violence be offered to the person of 430 the chest, in Pug's absence.

ALDO Then this matter is composed.

MRS TRICKSY (aside) Now I shall have leisure to instruct his man, and set him free without discovery. Come, Mr Gervase.   435

[Exeunt all but MRS SAINTLY]

MRS SAINTLY There is a certain motion put into my mind, and it is of good. I have keys here which a precious brother, a devout blacksmith, made me; and which will open any lock of the same bore. Verily, it can be no sin to unlock this chest therewith, and take from thence the 440 spoils of the ungodly. I will satisfy my conscience by giving part thereof to the hungry and the needy; some to our pastor, that he may prove it lawful; and some I will sanctify to my own use.

(She unlocks the chest, and WOODALL starts up)

WOODALL Let me embrace you, my dear deliverer!   445

(She shrieks)

Bless us! Is it you, Mrs Saintly?

MRS SAINTLY (shrieking) Heaven, of his mercy! Stop thief, stop thief.

WOODALL What will become of me now?

MRS SAINTLY According to thy wickedness, shall it be 450 done unto thee. Have I discovered thy backslidings, thou unfaithful man? Thy treachery to me shall be rewarded, verily; for I will testify against thee.

WOODALL Nay, since you are so revengeful, you shall

suffer part of the disgrace. If you testify against me for 455
adultery, I shall testify against you for theft. There's an
eighth for your seventh.*

(*Noise*)

MRS SAINTLY Verily, they are approaching. Return to my
embraces and it shall be forgiven thee.

WOODALL Thank you, for your own sake. Hark! They are 460
coming. Cry 'Thief' again, and help to save all yet.

MRS SAINTLY Stop thief! Stop thief!

WOODALL Thank you, for your own sake; but I fear 'tis
too late.

(*Enter* MRS TRICKSY, LIMBERHAM)

MRS TRICKSY (*entering*) The chest open, and Woodall 465
discovered, I am ruined!

LIMBERHAM Why all this shrieking, Mrs Saintly?

WOODALL (*rushing him down*) Stop thief! Stop thief! Stop
thief! (*to* LIMBERHAM) Cry you mercy, gentleman, if I
have hurt you. 470

LIMBERHAM (*rising*) 'Tis a fine time to cry a man mercy,
when you have beaten his wind out of his body.

MRS SAINTLY As I watched the chest, behold, a vision
rushed out of it on the sudden; and I lifted up my voice,
and shrieked. 475

LIMBERHAM A vision, landlady? What, have we Gog and
Magog* in our chamber?

MRS TRICKSY A thief, I warrant you, who had gotten into
the chest.

WOODALL Most certainly a thief. For hearing my landlady 480
cry out, I flew from my chamber to her help, and met him
running downstairs; and then he turned back to the
balcony, and leapt into the street.

LIMBERHAM I thought, indeed, that something held down
the chest when I would have opened it. But my writings 485
are there still. That's one comfort! (*to* WOODALL) Oh,
seignioro, are you here?

WOODALL Do you speak to me, sir?

MRS SAINTLY This is Mr Woodall, your new fellow-lodger.

LIMBERHAM Cry you mercy, sir; I durst have sworn you 490
could have spoken lingua franca. I thought in my
conscience, Pug, this had been thy Italian *merchanto*.

WOODALL Sir, I see you mistake me for some other. I
should happy to be better known to you.

LIMBERHAM Sir, I beg your pardon with all my *hearto*. 495
Before George, I was caught again there! But you are so
very like a paltry fellow who came to sell Pug essences
this morning, that one would swear those eyes and that
nose and mouth belonged to that rascal.

WOODALL You must pardon me, sir, if I don't much relish 500
the close of your compliment.

MRS TRICKSY Their eyes are nothing like. *<aside to him>*
You'll have a quarrel.

LIMBERHAM Not very like, I confess.

MRS TRICKSY Their nose and mouth are quite different. 505

LIMBERHAM As Pug says, they are quite different, indeed.
But I durst have sworn it had been he; and therefore, once
again, I demand your *pardono*.

MRS TRICKSY Come, let us go down. By this time Gervase
has brought the smith, and then Mrs Pleasance may have 510
her chest. Please you, sir, to bear us company.

WOODALL At your service, madam.

LIMBERHAM Pray lead the way, sir.

WOODALL 'Tis against my will, sir, but I must leave you in
possession.   515

[*Exeunt*]

Act 3, Scene I

(*Enter* MRS SAINTLY *and* MRS PLEASANCE)

MRS PLEASANCE Never fear it, I'll be a spy upon his
actions. He shall neither whisper nor gloat on either of
'em, but I'll ring him a peal!*

MRS SAINTLY Above all things, have a care of him
yourself; for sure there is witchcraft betwixt his lips. He is 5

a wolf within the sheepfold, and therefore I will be earnest* that you may not fall.

[*Exit*]

MRS PLEASANCE Why should my mother be so inquisitive about this lodger? I half suspect old Eve herself has a mind to be nibbling at the pippin.* He makes love to one 10 of 'em, I am confident. It may be to both; for methinks I should have done so if I had been a man; but the damned petticoats have perverted me to honesty and therefore I have a grudge to him, for the privilege of his sex. He shuns me too, and that vexes me; for though I would deny 15 him, I scorn he should not think me worth a civil question.

(*Re-enter** WOODALL, *with* MRS TRICKSY, MRS BRAINSICK, JUDITH *and music*)

MRS BRAINSICK Come, your works, your works; they shall have the approbation of Mrs Pleasance.
MRS TRICKSY No more apologies. Give Judith the words; 20 she sings at sight.
JUDITH I'll try my skill. <*sings*>

A Song from the Italian

By a dismal cypress lying,
Damon cried, all pale and dying,
'Kind is death that ends my pain,   25
But cruel she I loved in vain.
The mossy fountains
Murmur my trouble,
And hollow mountains
My groans redouble: 30
Every nymph mourns me,
Thus while I languish;
She only scorns me,
Who caused my anguish,
No love returning me, but all hope denying.'   35
By a dismal cypress lying,
Like a swan so sung he dying:

'Kind is death that ends my pain,
But cruel she I loved in vain.'

MRS PLEASANCE By these languishing eyes, and those 40
simagres* of yours, we are given to understand, sir, you
have a mistress in this company. Come, make a free
discovery which of 'em your poetry is to charm; and put
the other out of pain.

MRS TRICKSY No doubt 'twas meant to Mrs Brainsick. 45

MRS BRAINSICK We wives are despicable creatures. We
know it, madam, when a mistress is in presence.

MRS PLEASANCE Why this ceremony betwixt you? 'Tis a
likely, proper fellow, and looks as he could people a new
Isle of Pines.* 50

MRS BRAINSICK 'Twere a work of charity to convert a fair
young schismatic* like you, if 'twere but to gain you to a
better opinion of the government.

MRS PLEASANCE If I am not mistaken in you two, he has
works of charity enough upon his hands already. But 'tis 55
a willing soul, I'll warrant him, eager upon the quarry,
and as sharp as a governor of Covent Garden.*

WOODALL Sure, this is not the phrase of your family. I
thought to have found a sanctified sister, but I suspect
now, madam, that if your mother kept a pension* in your 60
father's time, there might be some gentleman-lodger in
the house; for I humbly conceive, you are of the half-
strain at least.

MRS PLEASANCE For all the rudeness of your language, I
am resolved to know upon what voyage you are bound. 65
You privateer of love, you Argiers man,* that cruise up
and down for prize in the Strait's mouth; which of the
vessels would you snap* now?

MRS TRICKSY We are both under safe convoy, madam: a
lover, and a husband. 70

MRS PLEASANCE Nay, for your part, you are notably
guarded, I confess; but keepers have their rooks,* as well
as gamesters. But they only venture under 'em till they
pick up a sum, and then push for themselves.

WOODALL (*aside*) A plague of her suspicions; they'll ruin   75
me on that side.

MRS PLEASANCE So, let but little minx go proud,* and the
dogs in Covent Garden* have her in the wind immediately. All pursue the scent.

MRS TRICKSY Not to a boarding-house, I hope!   80

MRS PLEASANCE If they were wise, they would rather go to
a brothel-house. For there, most mistresses have left
behind 'em their maidenheads of blessed memory, and
those which would not go off in that market, are carried
about by bawds and sold at doors, like stale flesh in   85
baskets. Then, for your honesty, or justness, as you call it,
to your keepers: your kept mistress is originally a punk;
and let the cat be changed into a lady never so formally,
she still retains her natural property of mousing.

MRS BRAINSICK You are very sharp upon the mistresses;   90
but I hope you'll spare the wives.

MRS PLEASANCE Yes, as much as your husbands do after
the first month of marriage. But you requite their
negligence in household duties, by making them husbands
of the first head* ere the year be over.   95

WOODALL (*aside*) She has me there too!

MRS PLEASANCE And as for you, young gallant –

WOODALL Hold, I beseech you, a truce for me.

MRS PLEASANCE In troth, I pity you, for you have
undertaken a most difficult task, to cozen two women,   100
who are no babies in their art. If you bring it about, you
perform as much as he that cheated the very lottery.*

WOODALL Ladies, I am sorry this should happen to you for
my sake. She's in a raging fit, you see. 'Tis best
withdrawing till the spirit of prophecy* has left her.   105

MRS TRICKSY I'll take shelter in my chamber – (*aside*)
whither, I hope, he'll have the grace to follow me.

MRS BRAINSICK And, now I think on't, I have some letters
to dispatch.

[*Exeunt* MRS TRICKSY *and* MRS BRAINSICK *severally*]

MRS PLEASANCE Now, good John among the maids,* how   110
mean you to bestow your time? Away to your study, I

advise you. Invoke your muses and make madrigals upon
absence.

WOODALL I would go to China or Japan, to be rid of that
impetuous clack of yours. Farewell, thou legion of 115
tongues in one woman.

MRS PLEASANCE Will you not stay, sir? It may be I have a
little business with you.

WOODALL Yes, the second part of the same tune! Strike by
yourself, sweet 'larm,* you're true bell metal, I warrant 120
you.

[*Exit*]

MRS PLEASANCE This spitefulness of mine will be my ruin.
To rail them off was well enough, but to talk him away
too! O tongue, tongue! Thou wert given for a curse to all
our sex!   125

(*Enter* JUDITH)

JUDITH Madam, your mother would speak with you.

MRS PLEASANCE I will not come. I'm mad, I think. I come
immediately. Well, I'll go in, and vent my passion by
railing at them and him too.

[*Exit*]

JUDITH You may enter in safety, sir, the enemy's marched 130
off.

(*Re-enter* WOODALL)

WOODALL Nothing, but the love I bear thy mistress, could
keep me in the house with such a fury. When will the
bright nymph appear?

JUDITH Immediately; I hear her coming.   135

WOODALL That I could find her coming,* Mrs Judith!

(*Enter* MRS BRAINSICK)

You have made me languish in expectation, madam. Was
it nothing, do you think, to be so near a happiness, with
violent desires, and to be delayed?

MRS BRAINSICK Is it nothing, do you think, for a woman 140

of honour to overcome the ties of virtue and reputation; to do that for you which I thought I should never have ventured for the sake of any man?

WOODALL But my comfort is that love has overcome. Your honour is, in other words, but your good repute; and 'tis my 145 part to take care of that. For the fountain of a woman's honour is in the lover, as that of the subject is in the king.

MRS BRAINSICK You had concluded well if you had been my husband. You know where our subjection lies.

WOODALL But cannot I be yours without a priest? They 150 were cunning people, doubtless, who began that trade to have a double hank upon us for two worlds: that no pleasure here, or hereafter, should be had without a bribe to them.

MRS BRAINSICK Well, I'm resolved I'll read against the 155 next time I see you; for, the truth is, I am not very well prepared with arguments for marriage. Meanwhile, farewell.

WOODALL I stand corrected. You have reason, indeed, to go, if I can use my time no better. We'll withdraw, if you 160 please, and dispute the rest within.

MRS BRAINSICK Perhaps, I meant not so.

WOODALL I understand your meaning at your eyes. You'll watch, Judith?

MRS BRAINSICK Nay, if that were all, I expect not my 165 husband till tomorrow. The truth is, he's so oddly humoured that if I were ill-inclined, it would half justify a woman. He's such a kind of man.

WOODALL Or if he be not, we'll make him such a kind of man. 170

MRS BRAINSICK So fantastical, so musical, his talk all rapture and half nonsense. Like a clock out of order, set him a-going and he strikes eternally. Besides, he thinks me such a fool that I could half resolve to revenge myself in justification of my wit. 175

WOODALL Come, come, no half resolutions among lovers. I'll hear no more of him till I have revenged you fully. Go out, and watch, Judith.

[*Exit* JUDITH]

MRS BRAINSICK Yet, I could say, in my defence, that my
    friends* married me to him against my will.   180
WOODALL Then let us put your friends, too, into the
    quarrel. It shall go hard but I'll give you a revenge for
    them.

            (*Enter* JUDITH *again, hastily*)

How now? What's the matter?
MRS BRAINSICK Canst thou not speak? Hast thou seen a   185
    ghost?

        (JUDITH *looks ghastly, and signs horns*)

As I live, she signs horns! That must be for my husband.
    He's returned.
JUDITH I should have told you so, if I could have spoken
    for fear.   190

                (*Knocking*)

MRS BRAINSICK Hark, a knocking! What shall we do?
    There's no dallying in this case. Here you must not be
    found, that's certain; but Judith hath a chamber within
    mine. Haste quickly thither. I'll secure the rest.
JUDITH Follow me, sir.   195
            [*Exeunt* WOODALL, JUDITH]

    (*Knocking again. She opens; enter* BRAINSICK)

BRAINSICK What's the matter, gentlewoman? Am I
    excluded from my own fortress, and by the way of
    barricado? Am I to dance attendance at the door as if I
    were some base plebeian groom? I'll have you know that
    when my foot assaults, the lightning and the thunder are 200
    not so terrible as the strokes. Brazen gates shall tremble,
    and bolts of adamant dismount from off their hinges to
    admit me.
MRS BRAINSICK Who would have thought that 'nown*
    dear would have come so soon? I was e'en lying down on   205
    my bed and dreaming of him. Tum a' me and buss,* poor
    dear, piddee* buss.

BRAINSICK I nauseate these foolish feats of love.

MRS BRAINSICK Nay, but why should he be so fretful 210
now? And knows I dote on him. To leave a poor dear so
long without him, and then come home in an angry
humour! Indeed I'll ky.*

BRAINSICK Prithee, leave thy fulsome fondness; I have
surfeited on conjugal embraces.

MRS BRAINSICK I thought so. Some light huswife* has 215
bewitched him from me. I was a little fool, so I was, to
leave a dear behind at Barnet, when I knew the women
would run mad for him.

BRAINSICK I have a luscious air* forming like a Pallas in
my brain-pan;* and now thou comest across my fancy, to 220
disturb the rich ideas with the yellow jaundice of thy
jealousy.

(*Noise within*)

Hark, what noise is that within, about Judith's bed?

MRS BRAINSICK I believe, dear, she's making it. <aside>
Would the fool would go.   225

BRAINSICK Hark, again!

MRS BRAINSICK (*aside*) I have a dismal apprehension in
my head that he's giving my maid a cast of his office,* in
my stead. Oh, how it stings me!

(WOODALL *sneezes*)

BRAINSICK I'll enter and find the reason of this tumult. 230

MRS BRAINSICK (*holding him*) Not for the world. There
may be a thief there, and should I put 'nown dear in
danger of his life? <aside> What shall I do? Betwixt the
jealousy of my love and fear of this fool, I am distracted. I
must not venture 'em together, what e'er comes on't. 235
<aloud> Why, Judith, I say! Come forth, damsel.

WOODALL (*within*) The danger's over. I may come out
safely.

JUDITH (*within*) Are you mad? You sha'not.

MRS BRAINSICK (*aside*) So, now I'm ruined unavoidably. 240

BRAINSICK Whoe'er thou art, I have pronounced thy

doom. Dreadful Brainsick bares his brawny arm in tearing terror. Kneeling queens in vain should beg thy being.* – Sa, sa, there.*

MRS BRAINSICK (*aside*) Though I believe he dares not 245 venture in, yet I must not put it to the trial. <*calls*> Why Judith, come out, come out, huswife.

(*Enter* JUDITH, *trembling*)

What villain have you hid within?

JUDITH Oh lord, madam, what shall I say?

MRS BRAINSICK How should I know what you should say? 250 Mr Brainsick has heard a man's voice within. If you know what he makes there, confess the truth. I am almost dead with fear, and he stands shaking.

BRAINSICK Terror, I? 'Tis indignation shakes me. With this sabre I'll slice him small as atoms. He shall be doomed by 255 the judge and damned upon the gibbet.

JUDITH (*kneeling*) My master's so outrageous, sweet madam, do you intercede for me, and I'll tell you all in private. (*whispers*) If I say it is a thief, he'll call up help. I know not what o'th' sudden to invent.   260

MRS BRAINSICK <*aside to* JUDITH> Let me alone. (*laughs*) And is this all? Why would you not confess it before, Judith? When you know I am an indulgent mistress.

BRAINSICK What has she confessed?

MRS BRAINSICK A venial love-trespass, dear. 'Tis a sweet- 265 heart of hers, one that is to marry her; and she was unwilling I should know it, so she hid him in her chamber.

(*Enter* ALDO)

ALDO What's the matter, trow?* What, in martial posture, son Brainsick?   270

JUDITH Pray, father Aldo, do you beg my pardon of my master. I have committed a fault. I have hidden a gentleman in my chamber, who is to marry me without his friends' consent, and therefore came in private to me.

ALDO　That thou shouldst think to keep this secret! Why, I 275
know it as well as he that made thee.

MRS BRAINSICK　(*aside*) Heaven be praised, for this knower
of all things. Now will he lie three or four rapping
volunties* rather than be thought ignorant in anything.

BRAINSICK　Do you know his friends, father Aldo?　280

ALDO　Know 'em! I think I do. His mother was an archdea-
con's daughter; as honest a woman as ever broke bread.
She and I have been cater-cousins* in our youth. We have
tumbled together between a pair of sheets, i'faith.

BRAINSICK　An honest woman, and yet you two have 285
tumbled together! Those are inconsistent.

ALDO　No matter for that.

MRS BRAINSICK　<*aside*> He blunders; I must help him. <*to
ALDO*> I warrant 'twas before marriage that you were so
great.　290

ALDO　Before George, and so it was; for she had the
prettiest black mole upon her left ankle, it does me good
to think on't! His father was Squire What-d'you-call-him,
of What-d'you-call-'em-shire. What think you, little
Judith? Do I know him now?　295

JUDITH　I suppose you may be mistaken. My servant's
father is a knight of Hampshire.

ALDO　I meant of Hampshire. But that I should forget he
was a knight, when I got him knighted at the king's
coming in!* Two fat bucks, I am sure, he sent me.　300

BRAINSICK　And what's his name?

ALDO　Nay, for that, you must excuse me. I must not
disclose little Judith's secrets.

MRS BRAINSICK　All this while the poor gentleman is left in
pain. We must let him out in secret; for I believe the 305
young fellow is so bashful, he would not willingly be seen.

JUDITH　The best way will be for father Aldo to lend me the
key of his door, which opens into my chamber; and so I
can convey him out.

ALDO　(*giving her a key*) Do so, daughter. Not a word of 310
my familiarity with his mother, to prevent bloodshed

betwixt us. But I have her name down in my almanac,* I
warrant her.

JUDITH What, kiss and tell, father Aldo; kiss and tell?

MRS BRAINSICK I'll go and pass an hour with Mrs Tricksy. 315
[*Exit*]

(*Enter* LIMBERHAM)

BRAINSICK What, the lusty lover, Limberham?

(*Enter* WOODALL *at another door*)

ALDO Oh, here's a monsieur new come over, and a fellow-
lodger. I must endear you two to one another.

BRAINSICK Sir, 'tis my extreme ambition to be better
known to you. You come out of the country I adore. And 320
how does the dear Battist?* I long for some of his new
compositions in the last opera. Apropos! I have had the
most happy invention this morning, and a tune trolling in
my head. I rise immediately in my nightgown and
slippers, down I put the notes slapdash, made words to 325
'em like lightning, and I warrant you have 'em at the
circle* in the evening.

WOODALL All were complete, sir, if Saint André* would
make steps to 'em.

BRAINSICK Nay, thanks to my genius, that care's over. 330
You shall see, you shall see. But first the air. – (*sings*) Is't
not very fine? Ha, *messieurs*!

LIMBERHAM The close of it is the most ravishing I ever
heard!

BRAINSICK I dwell not on your commendations. (*to* 335
WOODALL) What say you, sir? Is't not admirable? Do you
enter into't?

WOODALL Most delicate cadence!

BRAINSICK Gad, I think so, without vanity. Battist and I
have but one soul. But the close, the close! (*sings it thrice* 340
over) I have words, too, upon the air, but I am naturally
so bashful!

WOODALL Will you oblige me, sir?

BRAINSICK You might command me, sir; for I sing too *en cavalier*,* but –   345

LIMBERHAM But you would be entreated, and say, 'Nolo, nolo, nolo,'* three times, like any bishop when your mouth waters at the diocese.*

BRAINSICK I have no voice; but, since this gentleman commands me, let the words commend themselves. (*sings*)   350 'My Phyllis is charming' –

LIMBERHAM But why, of all names, would you choose a Phyllis? There have been so many Phyllises in songs,* I thought there had not been another left, for love or money.   355

BRAINSICK If a man should listen to a fop! (*sings*) 'My Phyllis' –

ALDO Before George, I am on t'other side. I think, as good no song, as no Phyllis.

BRAINSICK Yet again! – (*sings*) 'My Phyllis' –   360

LIMBERHAM Pray, for my sake, let it be your Chloris.

BRAINSICK (*looking scornfully at him, sings*) 'My Phyllis' –

LIMBERHAM You had as good call her your *succuba*.*

BRAINSICK *Morbleu!** Will you not give me leave? I am full of Phyllis. (*sings*) 'My Phyllis' –   365

LIMBERHAM Nay, I confess, Phyllis is a very pretty name.

BRAINSICK *Diable!** Now I will not sing, to spite you. By the world, you are not worthy of it. Well, I have a gentleman's fortune; I have courage, and make no inconsiderable figure in the world. Yet I would quit my   370 pretensions to all these, rather than not be author of this sonnet* which your rudeness has irrevocably lost.

LIMBERHAM Some foolish French *quelque chose*,* I warrant you.

BRAINSICK *Quelque chose!* O ignorance in supreme perfec-   375 tion! He means a kickshaw.

LIMBERHAM Why, a kickshaw let it be, then! And a kickshaw for your song!

BRAINSICK I give to the devil such a judge. Well, were I to be born again, I would as soon be the elephant* as a wit;   380 he's less a monster in this age of malice. I could burn my sonnet out of rage.

LIMBERHAM You may use your pleasure with your own.

WOODALL His friends would not suffer him; Virgil was not permitted to burn his *Æneids.** 385

BRAINSICK Dear sir, I'll not die ungrateful for your approbation. (*aside to* WOODALL) You see this fellow? He's an ass already; he has a handsome mistress and you shall make an ox of him, ere long.

WOODALL <*aside to* BRAINSICK> Say no more, it shall be 390 done.

LIMBERHAM <*aside to* WOODALL> Hark you, Mr Woodall; this fool Brainsick grows insupportable. He's a public nuisance; but I scorn to set my wit against him. He has a pretty wife; I say no more, but if you do not graff him* – 395

WOODALL <*aside to* LIMBERHAM> A word to the wise. I shall consider him, for your sake.

LIMBERHAM Pray do, sir. Consider him much.

WOODALL Much is the word. (*aside*) This feud makes well for me. 400

BRAINSICK (<*aside*> *to* WOODALL) I'll give you the opportunity and rid you of him. – Come away, little Limberham; you and I and father Aldo will take a turn together in the square.

ALDO We'll follow you immediately. 405

LIMBERHAM Yes, we'll come after you, bully Brainsick; but I hope you will not draw upon us there.

BRAINSICK If you fear that, bilbo* shall be left behind.

LIMBERHAM Nay, nay, leave but your madrigal behind. Draw not that upon us, and 'tis no matter for your sword. 410

[*Exit* BRAINSICK]

(*Enter* MRS TRICKSY *and* MRS BRAINSICK, *with a note for each*)*

WOODALL (*aside*) Both together! Either of 'em apart, had been my business; but I shall ne'er play well at this three-hand game.

LIMBERHAM Oh, Pug, how have you been passing of your
time?   415

MRS TRICKSY I have been looking over the last present of
orange gloves* you made me; and methinks I do not like
the scent. – Oh lord, Mr Woodall, did you bring those
you wear from Paris?

WOODALL Mine are Roman, madam.   420

MRS TRICKSY The scent I love of all the world. Pray let me
see 'em.

MRS BRAINSICK Nay, not both, good Mrs Tricksy; for I
love that scent as well as you.

WOODALL (*pulling 'em off and giving each one*) I shall find   425
two dozen more of women's gloves among my trifles, if
you please to accept 'em, ladies.

MRS TRICKSY Look to't; we shall expect 'em. <*aside*> Now
to put in my billet-doux!

MRS BRAINSICK <*aside*> So, now I have the opportunity to   430
thrust in my note.

MRS TRICKSY Here, sir, take your glove again; the perfume's too strong for me.

MRS BRAINSICK Pray take the other to't; though I should
have kept it for a pawn.   435

(MRS BRAINSICK's *note falls out,* LIMBERHAM *takes it
up*)

LIMBERHAM What have we here? <*reads*> 'For Mr
Woodall' –

BOTH WOMEN Hold, hold, Mr Limberham.

(*They snatch it*)

ALDO Before George, son Limberham, you shall read it.

WOODALL By your favour, sir, but he must not.   440

MRS TRICKSY <*aside*> He'll know my hand and I am ruined!

MRS BRAINSICK <*aside*> Oh, my misfortune! Mr Woodall,
will you suffer your secrets to be discovered?

WOODALL (*aside*) It belongs to one of 'em, that's certain. –
Mr Limberham, I must desire you to restore this letter; 'tis   445
from my mistress.

MRS TRICKSY *<aside>* The devil's in him; will he confess?

WOODALL This paper was sent me from her this morning; and I was so fond of it that I left it in my glove. If one of the ladies had found it there, I should have been laughed 450 at most unmercifully.

MRS BRAINSICK *<aside>* That's well come off!

LIMBERHAM *aside* My heart was at my mouth, for fear it had been Pug's. *<hands the note to* WOODALL*>* There 'tis again. – Hold, hold; pray let me see 't once more. A 455 mistress, said you?

ALDO Yes, a mistress, sir. I'll be his voucher; he has a mistress, and a fair one too.

LIMBERHAM Do you know it, father Aldo?

ALDO Know it! I know the match is as good as made 460 already. Old Woodall and I are all one. You, son, were sent for over on purpose. The articles for her jointure are all concluded, and a friend of mine drew 'em.

LIMBERHAM Nay, if father Aldo knows it, I am satisfied.

ALDO But how came you by this letter, son Woodall? Let 465 me examine you.

WOODALL Came by it! *<aside>* Pox, he has nonplussed me! *<to him>* How do you say I came by it, father Aldo?

ALDO Why, there's it now. This morning I met your mistress's father, Mr You-know-who – 470

WOODALL Mr Who, sir?

ALDO Nay, you shall excuse me for that; but we are intimate. His name begins with some vowel or consonant, no matter which – well, her father gave me this very numerical* letter, superscribed,* 'for Mr Woodall'. 475

LIMBERHAM Before George, and so it is.

ALDO Carry me this letter, quoth he, to your son Woodall. 'Tis from my daughter such a one, and then whispered me her name.

WOODALL Let me see; I'll read it once again. 480

LIMBERHAM What? Are you not acquainted with the contents of it?

WOODALL Oh, your true lover will read you over a letter from his mistress a thousand times.

MRS TRICKSY Aye, two thousand, if he be in the humour. 485

WOODALL Two thousand! Then it must be hers. (*reads to himself*) 'Away to your chamber immediately, and I'll give my fool the slip' – The fool! That may be either the keeper, or the husband; but commonly the keeper is the greater. Humh! Without subscription!* It must be 490 Tricksy. – Father Aldo, prithee rid me of this coxcomb.

ALDO Come, son Limberham, we let our friend Brainsick walk too long alone. Shall we follow him? We must make haste, for I expect a whole bevy of whores, a chamber-full of temptation, this afternoon. 'Tis my day of audience. 495

LIMBERHAM Mr Woodall, we leave you here, you remember?

[*Exeunt* LIMBERHAM, ALDO]

WOODALL Let me alone. Ladies, your servant; I have a little private business with a friend of mine.

MRS BRAINSICK <*aside*> Meaning me. – Well, sir, your 500 servant.

MRS TRICKSY Your servant, till we meet again.

[*Exeunt severally*]

Act 3, Scene 2

MR WOODALL's *chamber*. MRS BRAINSICK *alone*

MRS BRAINSICK My note has taken as I wished. He will be here immediately. If I could but resolve to lose no time, out of modesty; but 'tis his part to be violent, for both our credits. Never so little force and ruffling, and a poor weak woman is excused. 5

(*Noise* <outside>)

Hark, I hear him coming – Ah me! The steps beat double. He comes not alone. If it should be my husband with him! Where shall I hide myself? I see no other place but under his bed. I must lie as silently as my fear will suffer me.

Heaven send me safe again to my own chamber. (*creeps* 10
under the bed)

(*Enter* WOODALL *and* MRS TRICKSY)

WOODALL Well, fortune at the last is favourable, and now
you are my prisoner.

MRS TRICKSY After a quarter of an hour, I suppose I shall
have my liberty upon easy terms. But pray let us parley a
little first.   15

WOODALL Let it be upon the bed then. Please you to sit?

MRS TRICKSY No matter where. I am never the nearer to
your wicked purpose. But you men are commonly great
comedians* in love-matters; therefore you must swear, in
the first place –   20

WOODALL Nay, no conditions. The fortress is reduced to
extremity and you must yield upon discretion, or I storm.

MRS TRICKSY Never to love any other woman.

WOODALL I kiss the book upon 't. (*kisses her.* MRS
BRAINSICK *pinches him from underneath the bed*) Oh, 25
are you at your love-tricks already? If you pinch me thus,
I shall bite your lip.

MRS TRICKSY I did not pinch you. But you are apt, I see, to
take any occasion of gathering up more close to me. Next,
you shall not so much as look on Mrs Brainsick.   30

WOODALL Have you done? These covenants are so
tedious!

MRS TRICKSY Nay, but swear then.

WOODALL I do promise – I do swear – I do anything.
(MRS BRAINSICK *runs a pin into him*) Oh, the devil! 35
What do you mean to run pins into me? This is perfect
caterwauling.*

MRS TRICKSY You fancy all this. I would not hurt you for
the world. Come, you shall see how well I love you.
(*kisses him.* MRS BRAINSICK *pricks her*) Oh! I think you 40
have needles growing in your bed.

(*Both rise up*)

WOODALL I'll see what's the matter in' t.

MRS SAINTLY (*within*) Mr Woodall, where are you, verily?

WOODALL Pox (verily) her! 'Tis my landlady. Here, hide
yourself behind the curtains, while I run to the door to 45
stop her entry.

MRS TRICKSY Necessity has no law. I must be patient.

(*She gets into the bed, and draws the clothes over her*)

(*Enter* MRS SAINTLY)

MRS SAINTLY In sadness, gentleman, I can hold no longer.
I will not keep your wicked counsel how you were locked
up in the chest; for it lies heavy upon my conscience and 50
out it must, and shall.

WOODALL You may tell, but who'll believe you? Where's
your witness?

MRS SAINTLY Verily, heaven is my witness.

WOODALL That's your witness, too, that you would have 55
allured me to lewdness; have seduced a hopeful young
man, as I am. You would have enticed youth. Mark that,
beldam.*

MRS SAINTLY I care not. My single evidence is enough to
Mr Limberham. He will believe me that thou burn'st in 60
unlawful lust to his beloved. So thou shalt be an outcast
from my family.

WOODALL Then will I go to the elders of thy church and
lay thee open before them: that thou didst feloniously
unlock that chest with wicked intentions of purloining. 65
So, thou shalt be excommunicated from the congregation,
thou Jezebel, and delivered over to Satan.

MRS SAINTLY Verily, our teacher* will not excommunicate
me for taking the spoils of the ungodly to clothe him. For
it is a judged case amongst us that a married woman may 70
steal from her husband to relieve a brother. But yet thou
mayst atone this difference betwixt us. Verily, thou
mayst.

WOODALL Now thou art tempting me again. Well, if I had
not the gift of continency, what might become of me? 75

MRS SAINTLY The means have been offered thee, and thou
hast kicked with the heel.* I will go immediately to the

tabernacle* of Mr Limberham, and discover thee, O thou
serpent, in thy crooked paths.

(*Going*)

WOODALL Hold, good landlady, not so fast. Let me have   80
time to consider on't. I may mollify, for flesh is frail. An
hour or two hence, we will confer together upon the
premises.*

MRS SAINTLY Oh, on the sudden, I feel myself exceedingly
sick! Oh! Oh!   85

WOODALL Get you quickly to your closet, and fall to your
mirabilis.* This is no place for sick people. Begone,
begone.

MRS SAINTLY Verily, I can go no farther.

WOODALL But you shall, verily. I will thrust you down, out   90
of pure pity.

MRS SAINTLY Oh, my eyes grow dim! My heart quops,*
and my back acheth! Here I will lay me down, and rest
me.

(*Throws herself suddenly down upon the bed;* MRS
TRICKSY *shrieks, and rises.* MRS BRAINSICK *rises from
under the bed in a fright*)

WOODALL <aside> So! Here's a fine business! My whole   95
seraglio up in arms!

MRS SAINTLY So, so! If providence had not sent me hither,
what folly had been this day committed!

MRS TRICKSY Oh, the old woman in the oven!* We both
overheard your pious documents.* Did we not, Mrs   100
Brainsick?

MRS BRAINSICK Yes, we did overhear her, and we will
both testify against her.

WOODALL I have nothing to say for her. Nay, I told her her
own; you can both bear me witness. If a sober man   105
cannot be quiet in his own chamber for her –

MRS TRICKSY For you know, sir, when Mrs Brainsick and I
overheard her coming – having been before acquainted

with her wicked purpose – we both agreed to trap her
in it.   110

MRS BRAINSICK And now she would scape, herself, by
accusing us! But let us both conclude to cast an infamy
upon her house, and leave it.

MRS SAINTLY Sweet Mr Woodall, intercede for me, or I
shall be ruined.   115

WOODALL Well, for once, I'll be good-natured, and try my
interest. Pray, ladies, for my sake, let this business go no
farther.

MRS TRICKSY ⎱
MRS BRAINSICK ⎰ You may command us.

WOODALL For, look you, the offence was properly to my   120
person; and charity has taught me to forgive my enemies.
I hope, Mistress Saintly, this will be a warning to you, to
amend your life. I speak like a Christian, as one that
tenders the welfare of your soul.

MRS SAINTLY Verily, I will consider.   125

WOODALL Why, that's well said. (aside) Gad, and so must
I too; for my people is dissatisfied, and my government in
danger. But this is no place for meditation. (to them)
Ladies, I wait on you.

                                                      [Exeunt]

Act 4, Scene 1

(Enter ALDO, GEOFFERY)

ALDO Dispatch, Geoffery, dispatch. The outlying* punks
will be upon us ere I am in a readiness to give audience. Is
the office well provided?

GEOFFERY The stores are very low, sir: some doily*
petticoats and mantos* we have; and half a dozen pair of   5
laced shoes, bought from court at second-hand.

ALDO Before George, there's not enough to rig out a
mournival of* whores. They'll think me grown a mere
curmudgeon.* Mercy on me, how will this glorious trade
be carried on, with such a miserable stock?   10

GEOFFERY I hear a coach already stopping at the door.

ALDO Well, somewhat in ornament for the body, somewhat in counsel for the mind. One thing must help out
another in this bad world. Whoring must go on!

(*Enter* MRS OVERDON, *and her daughter* PRU)

MRS OVERDON Ask blessing, Pru. He's the best father you   15
ever had.

ALDO Bless thee, and make thee a substantial, thriving
whore. Have your mother in your eye, Pru; 'tis good to
follow good example. How old are you, Pru? Hold up
your head, child.   20

PRU Going o'my sixteen, father Aldo.

ALDO And you have been initiated but these two years?
Loss of time, loss of precious time. Mrs Overdon, how
much have you made of Pru since she has been man's
meat?   25

MRS OVERDON A very small matter, by my troth, considering the charges I have been at in her education. Poor Pru
was born under an unlucky planet; I despair of a coach
for her. Her first maidenhead brought me in but little; the
weather-beaten old knight that bought her of me beat   30
down the price so low. I held her at an hundred guineas
and he bid ten, and higher than thirty he would not rise.

ALDO A pox of his unlucky handsel. He can but fumble,
and will not pay neither.

PRU Hang him; I could never endure him, father. He's the   35
filthiest old goat; and then he comes every day to our
house and eats out his thirty guineas; and at three
months' end, he threw me off!

MRS OVERDON And since then, the poor child has
dwindled and dwindled away. Her next maidenhead   40
brought me but ten; and from ten she fell to five; and at
last to a single guinea. She has no luck to keeping. They
all leave her, the more my sorrow.

ALDO We must get her a husband then in the city. They
bite rarely at a stale whore o' this end o'th' town, new   45
furbished up in a tawdry* manto.

MRS OVERDON No. Pray let her try her fortune a little longer in the world first. By my troth, I should be loath to be at all this cost in her French and her singing, to have her thrown away upon a husband. 50

ALDO Before George, there can come no good of your swearing, Mrs Overdon. Say your prayers, Pru, and go duly to church o' Sundays; you'll thrive the better all the week. Come, have a good heart, child; I'll keep thee myself. Thou shalt do my little business; and I'll find thee 55 an able young fellow to do thine.

(*Enter* MRS PAD)*

Daughter Pad; you are welcome. What, you have performed the last Christian office to your keeper? I saw you follow him up the heavy hill to Tyburn.* Have you had never a business since his death? 60

MRS PAD No, indeed, father; never since execution day. The night before, we lay together most lovingly in Newgate. And the next morning, he lift up his eyes and prepared his soul with a prayer, while one might tell twenty; and then mounted the cart as merrily, as if he had 65 been a-going for a purse.

ALDO You are a sorrowful widow, daughter Pad; but I'll take care of you. Geoffery, see her rigged out immediately for a new voyage. Look in figure nine in the upper drawer, and give her out the flowered justaucorps,* with 70 the petticoat belonging to't.

MRS PAD Could you not help to prefer me, father?

ALDO Let me see! Let me see! Before George, I have it, and it comes as pat too! Go me* to the very judge who sat upon him. 'Tis an amorous, impotent, old magistrate, and 75 keeps admirably. I saw him leer upon you from the bench. He'll tell you what's sweeter than strawberries and cream, before you part.

(*Enter* MRS TERMAGANT)

MRS TERMAGANT Oh, father, I think I shall go mad.

ALDO You are of the violentest temper, daughter Terma-   80
gant. When had you a business last?

MRS TERMAGANT The last I had was with young Caster,*
that son of a whore gamester. He brought me to taverns
to draw in young cullies,* while he bubbled* 'em at play.
And when he had picked up a considerable sum, and   85
should divide, the cheating dog would sink my share and
swear, damn him, he won nothing.

ALDO Unconscionable villain, to cozen* you in your own
calling!

MRS TERMAGANT When he loses upon the square,* he   90
comes home 'Zoundsing' and 'Blooding'; first beats me
unmercifully, and then squeezes me to the last penny. He
has used me so, that, Gad forgive me, I could almost
forswear my trade. The rogue starves me too. He made
me keep Lent last year till Whitsuntide, and outfaced me   95
with oaths it was but Easter. And what mads me most, I
carry a bastard of the rogue's in my belly, and now he
turns me off and will not own it.

MRS OVERDON (*laying her hand on her belly*) Lord, how it
quops!* You are half a year gone, madam –   100

MRS TERMAGANT I feel the young rascal kicking already,
like his father. Oh, there's an elbow thrusting out! I think
in my conscience he's palming and topping* in my belly,
and practising for a livelihood before he comes into the
world.   105

ALDO Geoffery, set her down in the register, that I may
provide her a midwife, and a dry and wet nurse. When
you are up again, as heaven send you a good hour, we'll
pay him off at law, i'faith. You have him under black and
white, I hope.   110

MRS TERMAGANT Yes, I have a note under his hand for
two hundred pounds.

ALDO A note under's hand! That's a chip in porridge;* 'tis
just nothing. Look, Geoffery, to the figure twelve for old
half-shirts* for childbed linen.   115

(*Enter* MRS HACKNEY)

MRS HACKNEY Oh, Madam Termagant, are you here! Justice, father Aldo, justice!

ALDO Why, what's the matter, daughter Hackney?

MRS HACKNEY She has violated the law of nations; for yesterday she inveigled my own natural* cully from me, a 120 married lord, and made him false to my bed, father.

MRS TERMAGANT Come, you are an illiterate whore. He's my lord now, and though you call him fool, 'tis well known he's a critic, gentlewoman. You never read a play in all your life; and I gained him by my wit, and so I'll 125 keep him.

MRS HACKNEY My comfort is, I have had the best of him. He can take up* no more till his father dies. And so, much good may <it> do you with my cully and my clap* into the bargain. 130

ALDO Then there's a father for your child – my lord's son and heir by Mr Caster. But henceforward, to preserve peace betwixt you, I ordain that you shall ply no more in my daughter Hackney's quarters. You shall have the City from Whitechapel to Temple Bar,* and she shall have to 135 Covent Garden downwards.* At the playhouses, she shall ply the boxes because she has the better face; and you shall have the pit, because you can prattle best out of a vizor-mask.*

MRS PAD Then all friends and confederates. Now, let's 140 have 'Father Aldo's Delight',* and so adjourn the House.*

ALDO Well said, daughter. Lift up your voices, and sing like nightingales, you tory rory jades. Courage, I say! As long as the merry pence hold out, you shall none of you 145 die in Shoreditch.*

(*Enter* WOODALL)

A hey, boys, a hey! Here he comes that will swinge* you all! Down, you little jades, and worship him. 'Tis the genius* of whoring.

WOODALL And down went chairs and table, and out went 150 every candle. Ho, brave old patriarch in the middle of the

church militant! Whores of all sorts; forkers and ruin-
tailed:* Now come I jingling in with my bells,* and fly at
the whole covey.

ALDO A hey, a hey, boys, the town's thy own. Burn, ravish 155
and destroy!

WOODALL We'll have a night on't; like Alexander when he
burnt Persepolis.* *Tue, tue, tue! Point de quartier!**

(*He runs in amongst 'em, and they scuttle about the
room*)

(*Enter* MRS SAINTLY, MRS PLEASANCE, JUDITH *with
broomsticks*)

MRS SAINTLY What, in the midst of Sodom?* O thou lewd
young man! My indignation boils over against these 160
harlots; and thus I sweep 'em from out my family.

MRS PLEASANCE Down with the suburbians,* down with
'em.

ALDO Oh, spare my daughters, Mrs Saintly! Sweet Mrs
Pleasance, spare my flesh and blood!   165

WOODALL Keep the door open and help to secure the
retreat, father. There's no pity to be expected.

(*The* WHORES *run out, followed by* MRS SAINTLY, MRS
PLEASANCE *and* JUDITH)

ALDO Welladay, welladay! One of my daughters is big
with bastard, and she laid at her gaskins* most unmercifully! Every stripe she had, I felt it. The first fruit of 170
whoredom is irrecoverably lost!

WOODALL Make haste, and comfort her.

ALDO I will, I will; and yet I have a vexatious business
which calls me first another way. The rogue, my son, is
certainly come over; he has been seen in town four days 175
ago!

WOODALL 'Tis impossible. I'll not believe it.

ALDO A friend of mine met his old man, Giles, this very
morning, in quest of me; and Giles assured him his master
is lodged in this very street.   180

WOODALL In this very street! How knows he that?

ALDO He dogged him to the corner of it; and then my son
turned back and threatened him. But I'll find out Giles,
and then I'll make such an example of my reprobate!

[*Exit* ALDO]

WOODALL If Giles be discovered, I am undone! <*calls*> 185
Why, Gervase! Where are you, sirrah? Hey, hey!

(*Enter* GERVASE)

Run quickly to that betraying rascal, Giles – a rogue who
would take Judas his* bargain out of his hands, and
undersell him. Command him strictly to mew himself up
in his lodgings till farther orders. And in case he be 190
refractory, let him know I have not forgot to kick and
cudgel. That memento would do well for you too, sirrah.

GERVASE Thank your worship, you have always been
liberal of your hands to me.

WOODALL And you have richly deserved it.   195

GERVASE I will not say who has better deserved it of my
old master.

WOODALL Away, old Epictetus,* about your business, and
leave your musty morals, or I shall –

GERVASE Nay, I won't forfeit my own wisdom so far as to 200
suffer for it. Rest you merry: I'll do my best, and heaven
mend all.

[*Exit*]

(*Enter* MRS SAINTLY)

MRS SAINTLY Verily, I have waited till you were alone, and
am come to rebuke you, out of the zeal of my spirit.

WOODALL 'Tis the spirit of persecution. Diocletian and 205
Julian the Apostate* were but types* of thee! Get thee
hence, thou old Geneva Testament.* Thou art a part of
the ceremonial law, and hast been abolished these twenty
years.*

MRS SAINTLY All this is nothing, sir. I am privy to your 210
plots. I'll discover 'em to Mr Limberham, and make the
house too hot for you.

WOODALL What, you can talk in the language of the world, I see!

MRS SAINTLY I can, I can, sir; and in the language of the 215 flesh and devil too, if you provoke me to despair. You must, and shall, be mine this night.

WOODALL The very ghost of Queen Dido* in the ballad.

MRS SAINTLY Delay no longer, or –

WOODALL 'Or'? You will not swear, I hope? 220

MRS SAINTLY Uds niggers,* but I will; and that so loud, that Mr Limberham shall hear me.

WOODALL 'Uds niggers', I confess, is a very dreadful oath. You could lie naturally before, as you are a fanatic. If you can swear such rappers* too, there's hope of you; you 225 may be a woman of the world in time. Well, you shall be satisfied to the utmost farthing tonight, and in your own chamber.

MRS SAINTLY Or expect tomorrow –

WOODALL All shall be atoned ere then. Go, provide the 230 bottle of clary,* the Westphalia ham, and other fortifications of nature. We shall see what may be done. (*chucks her*)* What! An old woman must not be cast away!

MRS SAINTLY Then, verily, I am appeased.

WOODALL Nay, no relapsing into 'verily'; that's in our 235 bargain. Look how she weeps for joy! 'Tis a good old soul, I warrant her.

MRS SAINTLY You wi' not fail?

WOODALL Dost thou think I have no compassion for thy grey hairs? Away, away; our love may be discovered. We 240 must avoid scandal; 'tis thy own maxim.

[Exit MRS SAINTLY]

They are all now at ombre,* and Brainsick's maid has promised to send her mistress up.

(*Enter* MRS PLEASANCE)

That fury here again!

MRS PLEASANCE (*aside*) I'll conquer my proud spirit, I'm 245 resolved on't, and speak kindly to him. <*to him*> What, alone, sir? If my company be not troublesome; or a tender

young creature, as I am, may safely trust herself with a
man of such prowess in love affairs – *<aside>* It wonnot
be.   250

WOODALL (*aside*) So! There's one broadside already. I
must sheer off.

MRS PLEASANCE What? You have been pricking* up and
down here upon a cold scent; but at last you have hit it
off, it seems! Now for a fair view at the wife or mistress! 255
Up the wind, and away with it. Heigh, Jowler!* *<aside>* I
think I am bewitched, I cannot hold.

WOODALL (*going*) Your servant, your servant, madam. I
am in a little haste at present.

MRS PLEASANCE Pray resolve me first, for which of 'em 260
you lie in ambush. For, methinks, you have the mien of a
spider in her den. Come, I know the web is spread, and,
whoever comes, Sir Cranion* stands ready to dart out,
hale her in and shed his venom.

WOODALL (*aside*) But such a terrible wasp as she, will spoil 265
the snare if I durst tell her so.

MRS PLEASANCE 'Tis unconscionably done of me to debar
you the freedom and civilities of the house. Alas, poor
gentleman! To take a lodging at so dear a rate, and not to
have the benefit of his bargain! (*aside*) Mischief on me, 270
what needed I have said that?

WOODALL The dialogue will go no farther. Farewell,
gentle, quiet lady.

MRS PLEASANCE Pray stay a little; I'll not leave you thus.

WOODALL I know it; and therefore mean to leave you first. 275

MRS PLEASANCE Oh, I find it now; you are going to set up
your bills, like a love-mountebank,* for the speedy cure
of distressed widows, old ladies, and languishing maids in
the green sickness.* A sovereign remedy!

WOODALL That last, for maids, would be thrown away. 280
Few of your age are qualified for the medicine. What the
devil would you be at, madam?

MRS PLEASANCE I am in the humour of giving you good
counsel. The wife can afford you but the leavings of a fop;
and to a witty man, as you think yourself, that's 285

nauseous. The mistress has fed upon fool* so long, she's
carrion too, and common into the bargain. Would you
beat a ground for game in the afternoon, when my Lord
Mayor's pack* had been before you in the morning?

WOODALL I had rather sit five hours at one of his greasy 290
feasts, than hear you talk.

MRS PLEASANCE Your two mistresses keep both shop and
warehouse; and what they cannot put off in gross* to the
keeper and the husband, they sell by retail to the next
chance customer. Come, are you edified? 295

WOODALL I'm considering how to thank you for your
homily. And to make a sober application of it, you may
have some laudable design yourself in this advice.

MRS PLEASANCE Meaning, some secret inclination to that
amiable person of yours? 300

WOODALL I confess, I am vain enough to hope it. For why
should you remove the two dishes, but to make me fall
more hungrily on the third?

MRS PLEASANCE Perhaps, indeed, in the way of honour –

WOODALL Pah, pah! That word 'honour' has almost 305
turned my stomach. It carries a villainous interpretation
of matrimony along with it. But, in a civil way, I could be
content to deal with you, as the church does with the
heads of your fanatics: offer you a lusty benefice to stop
your mouth – if fifty guineas, and a courtesy more worth, 310
will win you.

MRS PLEASANCE Out upon thee! Fifty guineas! Dost thou
think I'll sell myself? And at playhouse price* too?
Whenever I go, I go altogether; no cutting from the whole
piece. He who has me, shall have the fag end* with the 315
rest, I warrant him. Be satisfied, thy shears shall never
enter into my cloth. But look to thyself, thou impudent
belswagger.* I'll be revenged; I will.

[*Exit*]

WOODALL The maid will give warning, that's my comfort;
for she is bribed on my side. I have another kind of love to 320
this girl, than to either of the other two. But a fanatic's

daughter and the noose of matrimony are such intolerable terms! Oh, here she comes who will sell me better cheap!*

(*Enter* MRS BRAINSICK)

MRS BRAINSICK How now, sir? What impudence is this of yours, to approach my lodgings?*   325

WOODALL You lately honoured mine, and 'tis the part of a well-bred man to return your visit.

MRS BRAINSICK If I could have imagined how base a fellow you had been, you should not then have been troubled with my company.   330

WOODALL How could I guess that you intended me the favour, without first acquainting me?

MRS BRAINSICK Could I do it, ungrateful as you are, with more obligation to you, or more hazard to myself, than by putting my note into your glove?   335

WOODALL Was it yours then? I believed it came from Mrs Tricksy.

MRS BRAINSICK You wished it so; which made you so easily believe it. I heard the pleasant dialogue betwixt you.   340

WOODALL I am glad you did. For you could not but observe with how much care I avoided all occasions of railing at you; to which she urged me, like a malicious woman, as she was.

MRS BRAINSICK By the same token, you vowed and swore   345 never to look on Mrs Brainsick!

WOODALL But I had my mental reservations in a readiness. I had vowed fidelity to you before; and there went my second oath, i'faith. It vanished in a twinkling, and never gnawed my conscience in the least.   350

MRS BRAINSICK Well, I shall never heartily forgive you.

JUDITH (*within*) Mr Brainsick, Mr Brainsick, what do you mean to make my lady lose her game thus? Pray come back, and take up her cards again.

MRS BRAINSICK My husband, as I live! Well, for all my   355 quarrel to you, step immediately into that little dark

closet. 'Tis for my private occasions.* There's no lock,
but he wi'not stay.

WOODALL (*goes in*) Thus am I ever tantalised?

(*Enter* BRAINSICK)

BRAINSICK What, am I become your drudge? Your slave? 360
The property of all your pleasures? Shall I, the lord and
master of your life, become subservient; and the noble
name of husband be dishonoured? No, though all the
cards were kings and queens, and Indies to be gained by
every deal –   365

MRS BRAINSICK My dear, I am coming to do my duty. I
did but go up a little (I whispered you for what), and am
returning immediately.

BRAINSICK Your sex is but one universal ordure; a nuisance, and encumbrance of that majestic creature, man. 370
Yet I myself am mortal too; nature's necessities have
called me up. Produce your utensil of urine.

MRS BRAINSICK 'Tis not in the way,* child. You may go
down into the garden.*

BRAINSICK The voyage is too far. Though the way were 375
paved with pearls and diamonds, every step of mine is
precious as the march of monarchs.

MRS BRAINSICK Then my steps, which are not so precious,
shall be employed for you. I'll call up Judith.

BRAINSICK I will not dance attendance. At the present, 380
your closet shall be honoured.

MRS BRAINSICK Oh lord, dear, 'tis not worthy to receive
such a man as you are.

BRAINSICK Nature presses; I am in haste.

MRS BRAINSICK (*aside*) He must be discovered, and I 385
unavoidably undone!

(BRAINSICK *goes to the door, and* WOODALL *meets him;*
she shrieks out)

BRAINSICK Monsieur Woodall!

WOODALL Sir, begone, and make no noise, or you'll spoil
all.

BRAINSICK Spoil all, quoth a! What does he mean, in the 390
name of wonder?

WOODALL (*taking him aside*) Hark you, Mr Brainsick, is
the devil in you, that you and your wife come hither to
disturb my intrigue, which you yourself engaged me in
with Mrs Tricksy, to revenge you on Limberham? Why, I 395
had made an appointment with her here; but, hearing
somebody come up, I retired into the closet till I was
satisfied 'twas not the keeper.

BRAINSICK But why this intrigue in my wife's chamber?

WOODALL Why, you turn my brains with talking to me of 400
your wife's chamber! Do you lie in common? The wife
and husband, the keeper and the mistress?

MRS BRAINSICK <*aside*> I am afraid they are quarrelling.
Pray heaven, I get off.

BRAINSICK Once again, I am the sultan of this place. Mr 405
Limberham is the mogul of the next mansion.

WOODALL Though I am a stranger in the house, 'tis
impossible I should be so much mistaken. I say this is
Limberham's lodging.

BRAINSICK You would not venture a wager of ten pounds 410
that you are not mistaken?

WOODALL 'Tis done. I'll lay you.

BRAINSICK Who shall be judge?

WOODALL Who better than your wife? She cannot be
partial, because she knows not on which side you have 415
laid.

BRAINSICK Content. Come hither, lady mine. Whose lodgings are these? Who is lord, and Grand Seignior* of 'em?

MRS BRAINSICK (*aside*) Oh, goes it there? <*to* BRAINSICK>
Why should you ask me such a question, when everybody 420
in the house can tell they are 'nown dear's?

BRAINSICK Now are you satisfied? Children and fools,*
you know the proverb.

WOODALL Pox on me. Nothing but such a positive coxcomb as I am would have laid his money upon such odds. 425
As if you did not know your own lodgings better than I,

at half a day's warning! And that which vexes me more
than the loss of my money, is the loss of my adventure!

[*Exit*]

BRAINSICK It shall be spent; we'll have a treat with it. This
is a fool of the first magnitude.   430

MRS BRAINSICK Let 'nown dear alone, to find a fool out.

(*Enter* LIMBERHAM)

LIMBERHAM Bully Brainsick, Pug has sent me to you on an
embassy to bring you down to cards again. She's in her
mulligrubs* already; she'll never forgive you the last vol*
you won. 'Tis but losing a little to her, out of complais-   435
ance, as they say, to a fair lady; and whate'er she wins, I'll
make up to you again in private.

BRAINSICK I would not be that slave you are, to enjoy the
treasures of the East! The possession of Peru and of
Potosi* should not buy me to the bargain.   440

LIMBERHAM Will you leave your perboles,* and come
then?

BRAINSICK No; for I have won a wager to be spent
luxuriously at Long's,* with Pleasance of the party, and
termagant Tricksy. And I will pass in person to the   445
preparation. <*to his wife*> Come, Matrimony.

[*Exeunt* BRAINSICK, MRS BRAINSICK]

(*Enter* MRS SAINTLY, *and* MRS PLEASANCE)

MRS PLEASANCE To him; I'll second you. Now for
mischief!

MRS SAINTLY Arise, Mr Limberham, arise; for conspiracies
are hatched against you, and a new Faux* is preparing to   450
blow up your happiness.

LIMBERHAM What's the matter, landlady? Prithee, speak
good honest English, and leave thy canting.

MRS SAINTLY Verily, thy beloved is led astray by the young
man Woodall, that vessel of uncleanness. I beheld them   455
communing together. She feigned herself sick, and retired
to her tent in the garden-house. And I watched her out-
going, and, behold, he followed her.

MRS PLEASANCE Do you stand unmoved and hear all this?

LIMBERHAM Before George, I am thunderstruck!   460

MRS SAINTLY Take to thee thy resolution, and avenge thyself.

LIMBERHAM But give me leave to consider first. A man must do nothing rashly.

MRS PLEASANCE I could tear out the villain's eyes for   465
dishonouring you while you stand considering, as you call it. Are you a man, and suffer this?

LIMBERHAM Yes, I am a man; but a man's but a man, you know. I am recollecting* myself how these things can be.

MRS SAINTLY How they can be! I have heard 'em. I have   470
seen 'em.

LIMBERHAM Heard 'em, and seen 'em! It may be so; but yet I cannot enter into this same business. I am amazed, I must confess; but the best is, I do not believe one word on't.   475

MRS SAINTLY Make haste, and thine own eyes shall testify against her.

LIMBERHAM Nay, if my own eyes testify, it may be so. But 'tis impossible, however, for I am making a settlement upon her this very day.   480

MRS PLEASANCE Look and satisfy yourself, ere you make that settlement on so false a creature.

LIMBERHAM But yet, if I should look and not find her false, then I must cast in another hundred, to make her satisfaction.   485

MRS PLEASANCE Was there ever such a meek, hen-hearted creature!

MRS SAINTLY Verily, thou hast not the spirit of a cock-chicken.

LIMBERHAM Before George, but I have the spirit of a lion,   490
and I will tear her limb from limb – if I could believe it.

MRS PLEASANCE <aside> Love, jealousy and disdain, how they torture me at once! And this insensible creature – were I but in his place – (to him) Think, that this very instant she's yours no more! Now, now she's giving up   495

herself, with so much violence of love that if thunder
roared, she could not hear it.

LIMBERHAM I have been whetting all this while. They shall
be so taken in the manner, that Mars and Venus* shall be
nothing to 'em.   500

MRS PLEASANCE Make haste; go on then.

LIMBERHAM Yes, I will go on – and yet my mind misgives
me plaguily.

MRS SAINTLY Again backsliding!

MRS PLEASANCE Have you no sense of honour in you?   505

LIMBERHAM Well, honour is honour, and I must go. But I
shall never get me such another Pug again! Oh, my heart!
My poor tender heart! 'Tis just breaking with Pug's
unkindness!

[*They drag him out*]

Act 4, Scene 2

WOODALL *and* MRS TRICKSY *discovered* in the garden-
house

(*Enter* GERVASE *to them*)

GERVASE Make haste, and save yourself, sir; the enemy's at
hand. I have discovered him from the corner where you
set me sentry.

WOODALL Who is't?

GERVASE Who should it be, but Limberham? Armed with a   5
two-hand fox.* Oh, lord! Oh, lord!

MRS TRICKSY Enter quickly into the still-house* both of
you, and leave me to him. There's a spring-lock within, to
open it when we are gone.

WOODALL Well, I have won the party and revenge,   10
however. A minute longer, and I had won the tout.*

(*They go in; she locks the door*)

(*Enter* LIMBERHAM, *with a great sword*)

LIMBERHAM Disloyal Pug.

MRS TRICKSY   What humour's this? You're drunk, it seems. Go sleep.

LIMBERHAM Thou hast robbed me of my repose for ever. I am like Macbeth after the death of good King Duncan. Methinks a voice says to me, 'Sleep no more; Tricksy has murdered sleep'.*

MRS TRICKSY Now I find it. You are willing to save your settlement, and are sent by some of your wise counsellors to pick a quarrel with me.

LIMBERHAM I have been your cully above these seven years; but at last my eyes are opened to your witchcraft, and indulgent heaven has taken a care of my preservation. In short, madam, I have found you out; and, to cut off preambles, produce your adulterer.

MRS TRICKSY If I have any, you know him best. You are the only ruin of my reputation. But if I have dishonoured my family for the love of you, methinks you should be the last man to upbraid me with it.

LIMBERHAM I am sure you are of the family of your abominable great-grandam Eve; but produce the man, or, by my father's soul –

MRS TRICKSY Still I am in the dark.

LIMBERHAM Yes, you have been in the dark; I know it. But I shall bring you to light immediately.

MRS TRICKSY You are not jealous?

LIMBERHAM No; I am too certain to be jealous. But you have a man here that shall be nameless. Let me see him.

MRS TRICKSY Oh, if that be your business, you had best search. And when you have wearied yourself, and spent your idle humour, you may find me above, in my chamber, and come to ask my pardon.

(*Going*)

LIMBERHAM You may go, madam; but I shall beseech your ladyship to leave the key of the still-house door behind you. I have a mind to some of the sweetmeats you have

locked up there, you understand me. Now, for the old
dog-trick!* You have lost the key, I know already, but I
am prepared for that. You shall know you have no fool to
deal with.   50

MRS TRICKSY No; here's the key. Take it, and satisfy your
foolish curiosity.

LIMBERHAM (*aside*) This confidence amazes me! If those
two gypsies* have abused me, and I should not find him
there now, this would make an immortal quarrel.   55

MRS TRICKSY (*aside*) I have put him to a stand.

LIMBERHAM <*aside*> Hang't, 'tis no matter; I will be
satisfied. If it comes to a rupture, I know the way to buy
my peace. <*to her*> Pug, produce the key.

MRS TRICKSY (*takes him about the neck*) My dear, I have it   60
for you. Come and kiss me. Why would you be so unkind
to suspect my faith now? When I have forsaken all the
world for you. (*kiss again*) But I am not in the mood of
quarrelling tonight. I take this jealousy the best way, as
the effect of your passion. Come up, and we'll go to bed   65
together and be friends. (*kiss again*)

LIMBERHAM (*aside*) Pug's in a pure* humour tonight and
'twould vex a man to lose it; but yet I must be satisfied.
And therefore, <*to her*> upon mature consideration, give
me the key.   70

MRS TRICKSY You are resolved then?

LIMBERHAM Yes, I am resolved; for I have sworn to myself
by Styx,* and that's an irrevocable oath.

MRS TRICKSY Now, see your folly. There's the key. (*gives
it to him*)

LIMBERHAM Why, that's a loving Pug. I will prove thee   75
innocent immediately, and that will put an end to all
controversies between us.

MRS TRICKSY Yes, it shall put an end to all our quarrels.
Farewell for the last time, sir. Look well upon my face,
that you may remember it. For, from this time forward, I   80
have sworn it irrevocably, too, that you shall never see it
more.

LIMBERHAM Nay, but hold a little, Pug. What's the meaning of this new commotion?

MRS TRICKSY No more; but satisfy your foolish fancy, for 85 you are master. And besides, I am willing to be justified.

LIMBERHAM Then you shall be justified.

(Puts the key in the door)

MRS TRICKSY I know I shall. Farewell.

LIMBERHAM But, are you sure you shall?

MRS TRICKSY No, no, he's there. You'll find him up in the 90 chimney, or behind the door; or, it may be, crowded into some little gallipot.*

LIMBERHAM But you will not leave me, if I should look?

MRS TRICKSY You are not worth my answer. I am gone.

(Going out)

LIMBERHAM Hold, hold, divine Pug, and let me recollect a 95 little. <*aside*> This is no time for meditation, neither. While I deliberate, she may be gone. She must be innocent, or she could never be so confident and careless. <*to her*> Sweet Pug, forgive me. (*kneels*)

MRS TRICKSY I am provoked too far. 100

LIMBERHAM 'Tis the property of a goddess to forgive. Accept of this oblation. (*offers the key*) With this humble kiss, I here present it to thy fair hand. I conclude thee innocent without looking, and depend wholly upon thy mercy. 105

MRS TRICKSY No, keep it, keep it. The lodgings are your own.

LIMBERHAM If I should keep it, I were unworthy of forgiveness. I will no longer hold this fatal instrument of our separation. 110

MRS TRICKSY (*taking it*) Rise, sir. I will endeavour to overcome my nature, and forgive you. For I am so scrupulously nice* in love, that it grates my very soul to be suspected. Yet, take my counsel, and satisfy yourself.

LIMBERHAM I would not be satisfied to be possessor of 115 Potosi, as my brother Brainsick says. Come, to bed, dear

Pug. Now, would not I change my condition to be an eastern monarch.

[Exeunt]

(*Enter* WOODALL *and* GERVASE)

GERVASE Oh, lord, sir, are we alive?

WOODALL Alive! Why, we were never in any danger. Well, 120 she's a rare manager of a fool!

GERVASE Are you disposed yet to receive good counsel? Has affliction wrought upon you?

WOODALL Yes, I must ask thy advice in a most important business. I have promised a charity to Mrs Saintly, and 125 she expects* it with a beating heart, abed. Now, I have at present no running-cash to throw away; my ready money is all paid to Mrs Tricksy, and the bill is drawn upon me for tonight.

GERVASE Take advice of your pillow.*   130

WOODALL No, sirrah. Since you have not the grace to offer yours, I will for once make use of my authority, and command you to perform the foresaid drudgery in my place.

GERVASE Zookers,* I cannot answer it to my conscience. 135

WOODALL Nay, and your conscience can suffer you to swear, it shall suffer you to lie, too. I mean in this sense. Come, no denial, you must do it. She's rich, and there's a provision for your life.

GERVASE I beseech you, sir, have pity on my soul.   140

WOODALL Have you pity of your body. There's all the wages you must expect.

GERVASE Well, sir, you have persuaded me. I will arm my conscience with a resolution of making her an honourable amends by marriage. For tomorrow morning, a parson 145 shall authorise my labours, and turn fornication into duty. And moreover, I will enjoin myself, by way of penance, not to touch her for seven nights after.

WOODALL Thou wert predestinated for a husband I see, by that natural instinct. As we walk, I will instruct thee how 150 to behave thyself with secrecy and silence.

GERVASE I have a key of the garden to let us out the back
way into the street, and so privately to our lodging.

WOODALL 'Tis well. I'll plot the rest of my affairs abed.
For 'tis resolved that Limberham shall not wear horns 155
alone, and I am impatient till I add to my trophy the
spoils of Brainsick.

[*Exeunt*]

Act 5, Scene 1

(*Enter* WOODALL, JUDITH)

JUDITH Well, you are a lucky man! Mrs Brainsick is fool
enough to believe you wholly innocent, and that the
adventure of the garden-house last night was only a vision
of Mrs Saintly's.

WOODALL I knew if I could once speak with her, all would 5
be set right immediately; for, had I been there, look you –

JUDITH As you were, most certainly.

WOODALL Limberham must have found me out. That fee-
fa-fum of a keeper would ha' smelt the blood of a
cuckold-maker.* They say, he was peeping and butting 10
about* in every cranny.

JUDITH But one. You must excuse my unbelief, though
Mrs Brainsick is better satisfied. She and her husband,
you know, went out this morning to the New Exchange.*
There, she has given him the slip; and pretending to call at 15
her tailor's, to try her stays for a new gown –

WOODALL I understand thee. She fetched me a short turn,
like a hare before her muse,* and will immediately run
hither to covert?

JUDITH Yes; but because your chamber will be least 20
suspicious, she appoints to meet you there; that, if her
husband should come back, he may think her still abroad,
and you may have time –

WOODALL To take in the horn-work. It happens as I wish,
for Mistress Tricksy and her keeper are gone out with 25
father Aldo to complete her settlement. My landlady is

safe at her morning exercise with my man Gervase, and
her daughter not stirring. The house is our own, and
iniquity may walk barefaced.

JUDITH And, to make all sure, I am ordered to be from   30
home. When I come back again, I shall knock at your
door, with (*singing*) 'Speak brother, speak; is the deed
done?'

WOODALL 'Long ago, long ago.'* And then we come
panting out together. Oh, I am ravished with the   35
imagination on't!

JUDITH Well, I must retire. Good morrow to you, sir.
                                                  [*Exit*]

WOODALL Now do I humbly conceive that this mistress in
matrimony will give me more pleasure than the former.
For your coupled spaniels, when they are once let loose,   40
are afterwards the highest rangers.*

(*Enter* MRS BRAINSICK *running*)

MRS BRAINSICK O dear Mr Woodall, what shall I do?

WOODALL Recover breath, and I'll instruct you in the next
chamber.

MRS BRAINSICK But my husband follows me at heels.   45

WOODALL Has he seen you?

MRS BRAINSICK I hope not. I thought I had left him sure
enough, at the Exchange; but, looking behind me, as I
entered into the house, I saw him walking a round rate*
this way.   50

WOODALL Since he has not seen you, there's no danger.
You need but step into my chamber, and there we'll lock
ourselves up, and transform him in a twinkling.

MRS BRAINSICK I had rather have got into my own; but
Judith is gone out with the key, I doubt.   55

WOODALL Yes, by your appointment. But so much the
better, for when the cuckold finds no company, he will
certainly go a-sauntering again.

MRS BRAINSICK Make haste then.

WOODALL Immediately. (*goes to open the door hastily*,   60

and breaks his key) What's the matter here? The key turns
round, and will not open! As I live, we are undone! With
too much haste 'tis broken!

MRS BRAINSICK Then I am lost; for I cannot enter into my
own.   65

WOODALL This next room is Limberham's. See! The door's
open, and he and his mistress are both abroad.

MRS BRAINSICK There's no remedy, I must venture in. For
his knowing I am come back so soon must be cause of
jealousy enough, if the fool should find me.   70

WOODALL (*looking in*) See there! Mrs Tricksy has left her
Indian gown* upon the bed. Clap it on, and turn your
back. He will easily mistake you for her if he should look
in upon you.

MRS BRAINSICK I'll put on my vizor-mask, however, for   75
more security.

(*Noise*)

Hark! I hear him. (*Goes in*)

(*Enter* BRAINSICK)

BRAINSICK What, in a musty musing, Monsieur Woodall?
Let me enter into the affair.

WOODALL You may guess it by the post I have taken up.   80

BRAINSICK Oh, at the door of the damsel Tricksy! Your
business is known by your abode; as the posture of a
porter before a gate denotes to what family he belongs.
(*looks in*) 'Tis an assignation I see; for yonder she stands,
with her back toward me, dressed up for the duel with all   85
the ornaments of the east. Now for the judges of the field
to divide the sun and wind betwixt the combatants, and a
tearing* trumpeter to sound the charge.

WOODALL 'Tis a private quarrel to be decided without
seconds; and therefore you would do me a favour to   90
withdraw.

BRAINSICK Your Limberham is nearer than you imagine. I
left him almost entering at the door.

WOODALL Plague of all impertinent cuckolds! They are ever troublesome to us honest lovers, so intruding!   95

BRAINSICK They are indeed, where their company is not desired.

WOODALL Sure, he has some tutelar devil to guard his brows! Just when she had bobbed* him, and made an errand home to come to me!   100

BRAINSICK 'Tis unconscionably done of him. But you shall not adjourn your love for this. The Brainsick has an ascendant over him. I am your guarantee; he's doomed a cuckold, in disdain of destiny.

WOODALL What mean you?   105

BRAINSICK To stand before the door with my brandished blade and defend the entrance. He dies upon the point if he approaches.

WOODALL If I durst trust it, 'tis heroic.

BRAINSICK 'Tis the office of a friend. I'll do't.   110

WOODALL (aside) Should he know hereafter his wife were here, he would think I had enjoyed her though I had not. 'Tis best venturing for something. He takes pains enough o'conscience for his cuckoldom; and, by my troth, has earned it fairly. (to him) But may a man venture upon   115 your promise?

BRAINSICK Bars of brass and doors of adamant could not more secure you.

WOODALL I know it; but still, gentle means are best. You may come to force at last. Perhaps you may wheedle him   120 away. 'Tis but drawing a trope* or two upon him.

BRAINSICK He shall have it with all the artillery of eloquence.

WOODALL Aye, aye, your figure breaks no bones. With your good leave.   125

(Goes in)

BRAINSICK Thou hast it, boy. Turn to him, madam. To her, Woodall! And Saint George for merry England. Tan ta ra ra ra, ra ra! Dub, a dub, dub! Tan ta ra ra ra!

(Enter LIMBERHAM)

LIMBERHAM How now, bully Brainsick! What, upon the
tan ta ra, by yourself?   130

BRAINSICK Clangor, taratantara, murmur.

LIMBERHAM Commend me to honest lingua franca. Why,
this is enough to stun a Christian, with your Hebrew and
your Greek and suchlike Latin.

BRAINSICK Out, Ignorance!   135

LIMBERHAM <trying to get in> Then, Ignorance, by your
leave; for I must enter.

BRAINSICK Why in such haste? The fortune of Greece
depends not on't.

LIMBERHAM But Pug's fortune does. That's dearer to me   140
than Greece, and sweeter than ambergris.

BRAINSICK You'll not find her here. Come, you are
jealous.* You're haunted with a raging fiend that robs
you of your sweet repose.

LIMBERHAM Nay, and you are in your perboles again!   145
Look you, 'tis Pug is jealous of her jewels. She has left the
key of her cabinet behind; and has desired me to bring it
back to her.

BRAINSICK <aside> Poor fool! He little thinks she's here
before him! <to him> Well, this pretence will never pass 150
on me, for I dive deeper into your affairs. You are jealous.
But rather than my soul should be concerned for a sex so
insignificant – Ha! The gods! If I thought my proper* wife
were now within and prostituting all her treasures to the
lawless love of an adulterer, I would stand as intrepid, as 155
firm and as unmoved as the statue of a Roman gladiator.

LIMBERHAM (in the same tone) Of a Roman gladiator!
Now are you as mad as a March hare. But I am in haste
to return to Pug. Yet, by your favour, I will first secure the
cabinet.   160

BRAINSICK No, you must not.

LIMBERHAM Must not? What, may not a man come by
you to look upon his own goods and chattels in his own
chamber?

BRAINSICK No. With this sabre I defy the destinies, and 165
dam up the passage with my person, like a rugged rock

opposed against the roaring of the boisterous billows.
Your jealousy shall have no course through me, though
potentates and princes –

LIMBERHAM Prithee what have we to do with potentates 170
and princes? Will you leave your troping and let me pass?

BRAINSICK You have your utmost answer.

LIMBERHAM If this maggot* bite a little deeper, we shall
have you a citizen of Bet'lem* yet ere dog-days.* Well, I
say little; but I'll tell Pug on't.   175

[Exit]

BRAINSICK She knows it already, by your favour. (knocking) Sound a retreat, you lusty lovers, or the enemy will
charge you in the flank with a fresh reserve. March off,
march off upon the spur, ere he can reach you.

(Enter WOODALL)

WOODALL How now, Baron Tell-clock,* is the passage 180
clear?

BRAINSICK Clear as a level without hills or woods, and
void of ambuscade.*

WOODALL But Limberham will return immediately when
he finds not his mistress where he thought he left her.   185

BRAINSICK Friendship, which has done much, will yet do
more. (shows a key) With this passe par tout, I will
instantly conduct her to my own chamber, that she may
outface the keeper she has been there. And when my wife
returns, who is my slave, I will lay my conjugal com- 190
mands upon her to affirm they have been all this time
together.

WOODALL I shall never make you amends for this kindness, my dear padron. But would it not be better if you
would take the pains to run after Limberham and stop 195
him in his way ere he reach the place where he thinks he
left his mistress; then hold him in discourse as long as
possibly you can, till you guess your wife may be
returned, that so they may appear together?

BRAINSICK I warrant you. Laissez faire à Marc Antoine!* 200

[Exit]

WOODALL Now, madam, you may venture out in safety.

MRS BRAINSICK (*entering*) Pray heaven I may.

(*Noise*)

WOODALL Hark! I hear Judith's voice. It happens well that
she's returned. Slip into your chamber immediately and
send back the gown.   205

MRS BRAINSICK I will. But are not you a wicked man, to
put me into all this danger?

[*Exit*]

WOODALL Let what can happen, my comfort is at least I
have enjoyed. But this is no place for consideration. Be
jogging, good Mr Woodall, out of this family while you   210
are well; and go plant in some other country where your
virtues are not so famous. (*going*)

(*Enter* MRS TRICKSY, *with a box of writings*)

MRS TRICKSY What, wandering up and down as if you
wanted an owner? Do you know that I am Lady of the
Manor, and that all wefts* and strays belong to me?   215

WOODALL I have waited for you above an hour; but Friar
Bacon's head* has been lately speaking to me that time is
past. In a word, your keeper has been here and will return
immediately. We must defer our happiness till some more
favourable time.   220

MRS TRICKSY I fear him not. He has this morning armed
me against himself by this settlement. The next time he
rebels, he gives me a fair occasion of leaving him for ever.

WOODALL But is this conscience in you? Not to let him
have his bargain, when he has paid so dear for't?   225

MRS TRICKSY You do not know him. He must perpetually
be used ill or he insults.* Besides, I have gained an
absolute dominion over him. He must not see when I bid
him wink. If you argue after this, either you love me not,
or dare not.   230

WOODALL Go in, madam. I was never dared before. I'll but
scout a little and follow you immediately.

(MRS TRICKSY *goes in*)

I find a mistress is only kept for other men; and the keeper
is but her man in a green livery, bound to serve a warrant
for the doe* whene'er she pleases, or is in season.   235

(*Enter* JUDITH, *with the night-gown*)

JUDITH Still you're a lucky man! Mr Brainsick has been
exceeding honourable. He ran as if a legion of bailiffs had
been at his heels, and overtook Limberham in the street.
Here, take the gown. Lay it where you found it, and the
danger's over.   240

WOODALL Speak softly; Mrs Tricksy is returned. (*looks in*)
Oh, she's gone into her closet to lay up her writings. I can
throw it on the bed ere she perceive it has been wanting.

(*Throws it in*)

JUDITH Every woman would not have done this for you
which I have done.   245

WOODALL I am sensible of it, little Judith. There's a time to
come shall pay for all. I hear her a-returning. Not a word.
Away.

[*Exit* JUDITH]

(*Re-enter* MRS TRICKSY)

MRS TRICKSY What, is a second summons needful? My
favours have not been so cheap* that they should stick 250
upon my hands. It seems you slight your bill of fare
because you know it, or fear to be invited to your loss.

WOODALL I was willing to secure my happiness from
interruption. A true soldier never falls upon the plunder
while the enemy is in the field.   255

MRS TRICKSY He has been so often baffled* that he grows
contemptible. Were he here, should he see you enter into
my closet; yet –

<Noise>

WOODALL You are like to be put upon the trial, for I hear
his voice.   260

MRS TRICKSY 'Tis so. Go in, and mark the event now. Be
but as unconcerned as you are safe, and trust him to my
management.

WOODALL I must venture it; because to be seen here would
have the same effect as to be taken within. Yet I doubt 265
you are too confident.

(*He goes in*)

(*Enter* LIMBERHAM *and* BRAINSICK)

LIMBERHAM How now, Pug? Returned so soon!

MRS TRICKSY When I saw you came not for me, I was
loath to be long without you.

LIMBERHAM But which way came you, that I saw you not? 270

MRS TRICKSY The back way, by the garden door.

LIMBERHAM How long have you been here?

MRS TRICKSY Just come before you.

LIMBERHAM Oh, then all's well. For to tell you true, Pug, I
had a kind of villainous apprehension that you had been 275
here longer. But whate'er thou sayst is an oracle, sweet
Pug, and I am satisfied.

BRAINSICK (*aside*) How infinitely she gulls him! And he so
stupid not to find it! (*to her*) If he be still within, madam –
you know my meaning? – here's bilbo* ready to forbid 280
your keeper entrance.

MRS TRICKSY (*aside*) Woodall must have told him of our
appointment. <*to* LIMBERHAM> What think you of
walking down, Mr Limberham?

LIMBERHAM I'll but visit the chamber a little first.   285

MRS TRICKSY What new maggot's this? You dare not sure
be jealous!

LIMBERHAM No, I protest, sweet Pug, I am not – only to
satisfy my curiosity. That's but reasonable, you know.

MRS TRICKSY Come, what foolish curiosity?   290

LIMBERHAM You must know, Pug, I was going but just
now, in obedience to your commands, to enquire of the
health and safety of your jewels, and my brother Brainsick most barbarously forbade me entrance. <*to him*>
Nay, I dare accuse you, when Pug's by to back me. But 295

now I am resolved I will go see 'em, or somebody shall
smoke for't.

BRAINSICK But I resolve you shall not. If she pleases to
command my person, I can comply with the obligation of
a cavalier.*   300

MRS TRICKSY But what reason had you to forbid him then,
sir?

LIMBERHAM Aye, what reason had you to forbid me then,
sir?

BRAINSICK 'Twas only my *capriccio*,* madam. <*aside*> 305
Now must I seem ignorant of what she knows full well.

MRS TRICKSY We'll enquire the cause at better leisure.
Come down, Mr Limberham.

LIMBERHAM Nay, if it were only his *capriccio*, I am
satisfied. Though, I must tell you, I was in a kind of huff 310
to hear him 'Tan ta ra, tan ta ra', a quarter of an hour
together. For 'Tan ta ra' is but an odd kind of sound, you
know, before a man's chamber.

(*Enter* MRS PLEASANCE)

MRS PLEASANCE (*aside*) Judith has assured me he must be
there; and I'm resolved I'll satisfy my revenge at any rate 315
upon my rivals.

MRS TRICKSY Mrs Pleasance is come to call us. Pray, let us
go.

MRS PLEASANCE Oh dear, Mr Limberham, I have had the
dreadfullest dream tonight, and am come to tell it you. I 320
dreamed you left your mistress's jewels in your chamber,
and the door open.

LIMBERHAM In good time be it spoken; and so I did, Mrs
Pleasance.

MRS PLEASANCE And that a great swingeing* thief came in 325
and whipped 'em out.

LIMBERHAM Marry, heaven forbid.

MRS TRICKSY This is ridiculous. I'll speak to your mother,
madam, not to suffer you to eat such heavy suppers.

LIMBERHAM Nay, that's very true. For you may remember 330

she fed very much upon larks and pigeons, and they are
very heavy meat, as Pug says.

MRS TRICKSY The jewels are all safe; I looked on 'em.

BRAINSICK Will you never stand corrected, Mrs Pleasance?

MRS PLEASANCE Not by you. Correct your Matrimony. 335
And methought, of a sudden, this thief was turned to Mr
Woodall and that hearing Mr Limberham come, he
slipped for fear into the closet.

MRS TRICKSY I looked all over it. I'm sure he is not there.
Come away, dear.   340

BRAINSICK What, I think you are in a dream too, brother
Limberham.

LIMBERHAM If her dream should come out now! 'Tis good
to be sure, however.

MRS TRICKSY You *are* sure. Have not I said it? You had 345
best make Mr Woodall a thief, madam.

MRS PLEASANCE I make him nothing, madam. But the
thief in my dream was like Mr Woodall, and that thief
may have made Mr Limberham something.

LIMBERHAM Nay, Mr Woodall is no thief, that's certain. 350
But if a thief should be turned to Mr Woodall, that may
be something.

MRS TRICKSY Then I'll fetch out the jewels. Will that
satisfy you?

BRAINSICK That shall satisfy him.   355

LIMBERHAM Yes, that shall satisfy me.

MRS PLEASANCE Then you are a predestinated fool, and
somewhat worse that shall be nameless. Do you not see
how grossly she abuses you? My life on't, there's
somebody within, and she knows it; otherwise she would 360
suffer you to bring out the jewels.

LIMBERHAM Nay, I am no predestinated fool; and therefore, Pug, give way.

MRS TRICKSY I will not satisfy your humour.

LIMBERHAM Then I will satisfy it myself. For my gener- 365
ous* blood is up, and I'll force my entrance.

BRAINSICK Here's bilbo, then, shall bar you. Atoms are
not so small as I will slice the slave. Ha! Fate and furies!

LIMBERHAM Aye, for all your 'fate and furies', I charge you, in his majesty's name, to keep the peace. Now, disobey authority, if you dare. 370

MRS TRICKSY Fear him not, sweet Mr Brainsick.

MRS PLEASANCE (to BRAINSICK) But if you should hinder him, he may trouble you at law, sir, and say you robbed him of his jewels. 375

LIMBERHAM That's well thought on. I will accuse him heinously, there – and therefore fear and tremble!

BRAINSICK My allegiance charms me. I acquiesce. (aside) Th'occasion's plausible to let him pass. Now let the burnished beams upon his brow blaze broad for the brand 380 he cast upon the Brainsick.

MRS TRICKSY Dear Mr Limberham, come back, and hear me.

LIMBERHAM Yes, I will hear thee, Pug.

MRS PLEASANCE Go on; my life for yours, he's there. 385

LIMBERHAM I am deaf as an adder.* I will not hear thee, nor have no commiseration.

(*Struggles from her, and rushes in*)

MRS TRICKSY Then I know the worst, and care not.

(**LIMBERHAM** *comes running out with the jewels,* followed by **WOODALL**, *with his sword drawn <and concealing a box>*)

LIMBERHAM Oh, save me, Pug, save me!

(*Gets behind her*)

WOODALL A slave, to come and interrupt me at my 390 devotions! But I'll –

LIMBERHAM Hold, hold! Since you are so devout, for heaven sake, hold!

BRAINSICK Nay, Monsieur Woodall!

MRS TRICKSY For my sake, spare him. 395

LIMBERHAM Yes, for Pug's sake, spare me.

WOODALL I did his chamber the honour, when my own

was not open, to retire thither; and he to disturb me, like a profane rascal as he was.

LIMBERHAM (*aside*) I believe he had the devil for his 400 chaplain* and a man durst tell him so.

WOODALL What's that you mutter?

LIMBERHAM Nay, nothing, but that I thought you had not been so well given. I was only afraid of Pug's jewels.

WOODALL What, does he take me for a thief? Nay then – 405

LIMBERHAM Oh, mercy, mercy!

MRS PLEASANCE Hold, sir; 'twas a foolish dream of mine that set him on. I dreamed a thief, who had been just reprieved for a former robbery, was venturing his neck a minute after in Mr Limberham's closet. 410

WOODALL Are you thereabouts, i'faith! A pox of Artemidorus!*

MRS TRICKSY I have had a dream, too, concerning Mrs Brainsick, and perhaps –

WOODALL Mrs Tricksy, a word in private with you, by 415 your keeper's leave.

LIMBERHAM Yes, sir, you may speak your pleasure to her; and, if you have a mind to go to prayers together, the closet is open.

WOODALL (*to* MRS TRICKSY) You but suspect it at most, 420 and cannot prove it. If you value me, you will not engage me in a quarrel with her husband.

MRS TRICKSY <*to him*> Well, in hope you'll love me, I'll obey.

BRAINSICK Now, damsel Tricksy, your dream, your 425 dream!

MRS TRICKSY 'Twas something of a flageolet* that a shepherd played upon so sweetly that three women followed him for his music; and still* one of 'em snatched it from the other. 430

MRS PLEASANCE (*aside*) I understand her, but I find she's bribed to secrecy.

LIMBERHAM That flageolet was, by interpretation – but let that pass; and Mr Woodall, there, was the shepherd that played the 'Tan ta ra' upon't. But a generous heart like 435 mine will endure the infamy no longer. Therefore, Pug, I banish thee forever.

MRS TRICKSY Then farewell.

LIMBERHAM Is that all you make of me?

MRS TRICKSY I hate to be tormented with your jealous 440 humours, and am glad to be rid of 'em.

LIMBERHAM Bear witness, good people, of her ingratitude! Nothing vexes me but that she calls me jealous when I found him as close as a butterfly in her closet.

MRS TRICKSY No matter for that. I knew not he was there. 445

LIMBERHAM Would I could believe thee.

WOODALL You have both our words for't.

MRS TRICKSY Why should you persuade him against his will?

LIMBERHAM Since you won't persuade me, I care not 450 much. Here are the jewels in my possession, and I'll fetch out the settlement immediately.

WOODALL (showing the box) Look you, sir, I'll spare your pains. Four hundred a year will serve to comfort a poor cast mistress. 455

LIMBERHAM I thought what would come of your devil's paternosters!*

BRAINSICK Restore it to him for pity, Woodall.

MRS TRICKSY I make him my trustee; he shall not restore it. 460

LIMBERHAM Here are jewels that cost me above two thousand pounds; a queen might wear 'em. Behold this orient* necklace, Pug! 'Tis pity any neck should touch it after thine, that pretty neck! But, oh, 'tis the falsest neck that e'er was hanged in pearl. 465

WOODALL 'Twould become your bounty to give it her at parting.

LIMBERHAM Never the sooner for your asking. But, oh, that word 'parting'! Can I bear it? If she could find in her heart but so much grace as to acknowledge what a 470 traitress she has been, I think in my conscience I could forgive her.

MRS TRICKSY I'll not wrong my innocence so much, nor

this gentleman's. But, since you have accused us falsely, four hundred a year betwixt us two will make us some 475 part of reparation.

WOODALL I answer you not, but with my leg,* madam.

MRS PLEASANCE (aside) This mads me; but I cannot help it.

LIMBERHAM What, wilt thou kill me, Pug, with thy 480 unkindness when thou know'st I cannot live without thee? It goes to my heart that this wicked fellow –

WOODALL How's that, sir?

LIMBERHAM Under the rose,* good Mr Woodall. But I speak it with all submission in the bitterness of my spirit 485 that you, or any man, should have the disposing of my four hundred a year gratis. Therefore, dear Pug, a word in private, with your permission, good Mr Woodall.

MRS TRICKSY Alas, I know by experience I may safely trust my person with you.   490

[*Exeunt* LIMBERHAM, MRS TRICKSY]

(Enter ALDO)

MRS PLEASANCE Oh, father Aldo, we have wanted you! Here has been made the rarest discovery!

BRAINSICK With the most comical catastrophe!

WOODALL Happily arrived, i'faith, my old sub-fornicator. I have been taken upon suspicion here with Mrs Tricksy. 495

ALDO To be taken to be seen! Before George, that's a point next the worst, son Woodall.

WOODALL Truth is, I wanted thy assistance, old Methusalem.* But my comfort is I fell greatly.

ALDO Well, young Phaëton,* that's somewhat yet, if you 500 made a blaze at your departure.

(*Enter* GILES, MRS BRAINSICK *and* JUDITH)

GILES By your leave, gentlemen. I have followed an old master of mine, these two long hours, and had a fair course* at him up the street. Here he entered, I'm sure.

ALDO Whoop, holiday! Our trusty and well-beloved Giles, 505

most welcome! Now for some news of my ungracious
son.

WOODALL (*aside*) Giles here! Oh rogue, rogue! Now,
would I were safe stowed over head and ears in the chest
again.   510

ALDO Look you now, son Woodall, I told you I was not
mistaken. My rascal's in town, with a vengeance to him.

GILES Why, this is he, sir; I thought you had known him.

ALDO Known whom?

GILES Your son here, my young master.   515

ALDO Do I dote?* Or art thou drunk, Giles?

GILES Nay, I am sober enough, I'm sure. I have been kept
fasting almost these two days.

ALDO Before George, 'tis so! I read it in that leering look.
What a Tartar have I caught!*   520

BRAINSICK Woodall, his son?

MRS PLEASANCE What, young father Aldo?

ALDO (*aside*) Now cannot I for shame hold up my head to
think what this young rogue is privy to!

MRS BRAINSICK The most dumb interview I ever saw!   525

BRAINSICK What, have you beheld the gorgon's head* on
either side?

ALDO <*aside*> Oh, my sins! My sins! And he keeps my
book of conscience too! He can display 'em, with a
witness! Oh, treacherous young devil!   530

WOODALL (*aside*) Well, the squib's run to the end of the
line,* and now for the cracker. I must bear up.

ALDO <*aside*> I must set a face of authority on the matter,
for my credit. <*to his son*> Pray, who am I? Do you know
me, sir?   535

WOODALL Yes, I think I should partly know, sir. You may
remember some private passages betwixt us.

ALDO (*aside*) I thought as much; he has me already! <*to
him*> But pray, sir, why this ceremony* amongst friends?
Put on, put on; and let us hear what news from France. 540
Have you heard lately from my son? Does he continue
still the most hopeful and esteemed young gentleman in
Paris? Does he manage his allowance with the same

discretion? And lastly, has he still the same respect and
duty for his good old father?   545

WOODALL Faith, sir, I have been too long from my
catechise* to answer so many questions. But, suppose
there be no news of your quondam* son, you may
comfort up your heart for such a loss. Father Aldo has a
numerous progeny about the town, heaven bless 'em.   550

ALDO 'Tis very well, sir. I find you have been searching for
your relations then, in Whetstone's Park!*

WOODALL No, sir, I made some scruple of going to the
'foresaid place, for fear of meeting my own father there.

ALDO Before George, I could find in my heart to disinherit 555
thee.

MRS PLEASANCE Sure, you cannot be so unnatural.

WOODALL I am sure I am no bastard; witness one good
quality I have. If any of your children have a stronger
tang of the father in 'em, I am content to be disowned.   560

ALDO Well, from this time forward, I pronounce thee – no
son of mine.

WOODALL Then you desire I should proceed to justify I am
lawfully begotten? The evidence is ready, sir; and, if you
please, I shall relate before this honourable assembly,   565
those excellent lessons of morality you gave me at our
first acquaintance. As, in the first place –

ALDO Hold, hold! I charge thee hold, on thy obedience. I
forgive thee heartily. I have proof enough thou art my
son. But tame thee that can, thou art a mad one.   570

MRS PLEASANCE Why, this is as it should be.

ALDO (to him) Not a word of any passages betwixt us. 'Tis
enough we know each other. Hereafter we'll banish all
pomp and ceremony, and live familiarly together. I'll be
Pylades, and thou mad Orestes,* and we'll divide the   575
estate betwixt us, and have fresh wenches and *ballum
rankum** every night.

WOODALL A match, i'faith, and let the world pass.

ALDO But hold a little; I had forgot one point. I hope you
are not married nor engaged?   580

WOODALL To nothing but my pleasures, I.

ALDO A mingle of profit would do well though. Come, here's a girl; look well upon her. 'Tis a mettled toad,* I can tell you that. She'll make notable work betwixt two sheets in a lawful way.   585

WOODALL What, my old enemy, Mrs Pleasance?

MRS BRAINSICK Marry Mrs Saintly's daughter?

ALDO The truth is, she has passed for her daughter by my appointment; but she has good blood running in her veins, as the best of you. Her father, Mr Palms, on his 590 deathbed, left her to my care and disposal, besides a fortune of twelve hundred a year. A pretty convenience,* by my faith.

WOODALL Beyond my hopes, if she consent.

ALDO I have taken some care of her education, and placed 595 her here with Mrs Saintly, as her daughter, to avoid her being blown upon* by fops and younger brothers. So now, son, I hope I have matched your concealment with my discovery! There's hit for hit ere I cross the cudgels.*

MRS PLEASANCE You will not take 'em up, sir?   600

WOODALL I dare not, against you, madam. I'm sure you'll worst me at all weapons. All I can say is, I do not now begin to love you.

ALDO Let me speak for thee. Thou shalt be used, little Pleasance, like a sovereign princess. Thou shalt not touch 605 a bit of butcher's meat* in a twelve month, and thou shalt be treated –

MRS PLEASANCE Not with *ballum rankum* every night, I hope!

ALDO Well, thou art a wag, no more of that. Thou shalt 610 want neither man's meat nor woman's meat, as far as his provision will hold out.

MRS PLEASANCE But I fear he's so horribly given to go a-house-warming abroad, that the least part of the provision will come to my share at home.   615

WOODALL You'll find me so much employment in my own family, that I shall have little need to look out for journey-work.*

ALDO Before George, he shall do thee reason ere thou sleep'st. 620

MRS PLEASANCE No; he shall have an honourable truce for one day at least. For 'tis not fair, to put a fresh enemy upon him.

MRS BRAINSICK (to MRS PLEASANCE) I beseech you, madam, discover nothing betwixt him and me. 625

MRS PLEASANCE (to her) I am contented to cancel the old score. But take heed of bringing me an after-reckoning.

(Enter GERVASE leading MRS SAINTLY)

GERVASE Save you, gentlemen, and you, my quondam master. You are welcome all, as I may say.

ALDO How now, sirrah? What's the matter? 630

GERVASE Give good words, while you live, sir. Your landlord and Mr Saintly, if you please.

WOODALL Oh, I understand the business; he's married to the widow.

MRS SAINTLY Verily, the good work is accomplished. 635

BRAINSICK But, why Mr Saintly?

GERVASE When a man is married to his betters, 'tis but decency to take her name. A pretty house, pretty situation and prettily furnished! I have been unlawfully labouring at hard duty, but a parson has soldered up* the matter. 640 Thank your worship, Mr Woodall. <sees GILES> How? Giles here!

WOODALL The business is out, and I am now Aldo. My father has forgiven me, and we are friends.

GERVASE When will Giles, with his honesty,* come to this? 645

WOODALL Nay, do not insult too much, good Mr Saintly. Thou wert but my deputy. Thou know'st the widow intended it to me.

GERVASE But I am satisfied she performed it with me, sir. Well, there is much goodwill in these precise old women; 650 they are the most zealous bedfellows. Look and* she does not blush now! You see there's grace in her.

WOODALL Mr Limberham, where are you? Come, cheer up

man. How go matters on your side of the country? Cry
him, Gervase.   655

GERVASE (*calls*) Mr Limberham, Mr Limberham, make your
appearance in the court and save your recognizance.*

(*Enter* LIMBERHAM *and* MRS TRICKSY)

WOODALL Sir, I should now make a speech to you in my
own defence; but the short of all is this: if you can forgive
what's passed – your hand, and I'll endeavour to make up 660
the breach betwixt you and your mistress. If not, I am
ready to give you the satisfaction of a gentleman.

LIMBERHAM Sir, I am a peaceable man and a good
Christian, though I say it, and desire no satisfaction from
any man. Pug and I are partly agreed upon the point 665
already. And therefore lay thy hand upon thy heart, Pug,
and if thou canst from the bottom of thy soul defy
mankind, naming nobody, I'll forgive thy past enormities;
and, to give good example to all Christian keepers, will
take thee to my wedded wife. And thy four hundred a 670
year shall be settled upon thee, for separate maintenance.*

MRS TRICKSY Why, now I can consent with honour.

ALDO This is the first business that was ever made up
without me.   675

WOODALL Give you joy, Mr Bridegroom.

LIMBERHAM You may spare your breath, sir, if you please.
I desire none from you. 'Tis true, I'm satisfied of her
virtue, in spite of slander; but, to silence calumny, I shall
civilly desire you henceforth, not to make a chapel of 680
ease* of Pug's closet.

MRS PLEASANCE (*aside*) I'll take care of false worship, I'll
warrant him. He shall have no more to do with Bel and
the dragon.*

BRAINSICK Come hither, Wedlock, and let me seal my 685
lasting love upon thy lips. Saintly has been seduced, and
so has Tricksy, but thou alone art kind and constant.
Hitherto, I have not valued modesty according to its

merit, but hereafter, Memphis* shall not boast a monument more firm, than my affection.   690

WOODALL A most excellent reformation and at a most seasonable time! The moral on't is pleasant, if well considered. Now, let's to dinner. Mr Saintly, lead the way, as becomes you in your own house.

(The rest going off)

MRS PLEASANCE Your hand, sweet moiety.*   695
WOODALL And heart too, my 'comfortable importance'.*
Mistress and wife, by turns, I have possessed:
He who enjoys 'em both in one, is blessed.

<Exeunt>

Epilogue

I beg a boon, that ere you all disband,
Someone would take my bargain off my hand.
To keep a punk is but a common evil,
To find her false, and marry, that's the devil.
Well, I ne'er acted part in all my life,   5
But still I was fobbed off with some such wife.
I find the trick; these poets take no pity
Of one that is a member of the city.
We cheat you lawfully and in our trades,
You treat us basely with your common jades.   10
Now I am married, I must sit down by it,
But let me keep my dear-bought spouse in quiet.
Let none of you damned Woodalls of the pit,
Put in for shares to mend our breed in wit.
We know your bastards from our flesh and blood: 15
Not one in ten of yours e'er comes to good.
In all the boys, their fathers' virtues shine,
But all the female fry* turn pugs* like mine.
When these grow up, Lord! – With what rampant
    gadders*
Our counters* will be thronged, and roads with
    padders!*   20
This town two bargains has not worth one farthing:
A Smithfield horse, and wife of Covent Garden.*

THE ORPHAN
or
THE UNHAPPY MARRIAGE

A Tragedy

By

THOMAS OTWAY

Qui pelago credit magno, se faenore tollit;
Qui pugnas et castra petit, praecingitur auro;
Vilis adulator picto jacet ebrius ostro;
Et qui sollicitat nuptas, ad praemia peccat:
Sola pruinosis horret facundia pannis,
Atque inopi lingua desertas invocat artes.*

[Petronius Arbiter, *Satyricon*]

<DEDICATION>
*To Her Royal Highness the Duchess**

Madam,

    After having a great while wished to write something that might be worthy to lay at your Highness's feet, and finding it impossible: since the world has been so kind to me to judge of this poem to my advantage, as the most pardonable fault which I have made in its kind; I had sinned against myself if I had not chosen this opportunity to implore (what my ambition is most fond of) your favour and protection.   5

    For though fortune would not so far bless my endeavours as to encourage them with your Royal Highness's presence* when this came into the world; yet I cannot but declare it   10 was my design and hopes it might have been your divertisement in that happy season when you returned again to cheer all those eyes that had before wept for your departure, and enliven all hearts that had drooped for your absence.* When wit ought to have paid its choicest tributes in, and joy have   15 known no limits, then I hoped my little mite would not have been rejected; though my ill fortune was too hard for me, and I lost a greater honour by your Royal Highness's absence, than all the applauses of the world besides can make me reparation for.   20

    Nevertheless, I thought myself not quite unhappy, so long as I had hopes this way* yet to recompense my disappointment past; when I considered also that poetry might claim right to a little share in your favour. For Tasso and Ariosto,* some of the best, have made their names eternal   25 by transmitting to after-ages the glory of your ancestors. And under the spreading of that shade where two of the best have planted their laurels, how honoured should I be, who am the worst, if but a branch might grow for me.

    I dare not think of offering at anything in this address that   30 might look like a panegyric, for fear lest when I have done my best, the world should condemn me for saying too little, and you yourself check me for meddling with a task unfit for my talent.

For the description of virtues and perfections as rare as yours are ought to be done by as deliberate as skilful a hand. The features must be drawn very fine to be like; hasty daubing would but spoil the picture, and make it so unnatural as must want false lights to set it off. And your virtue can receive no more lustre from praises, than your beauty can be improved by art; which, as it charms the bravest prince that ever amazed the world with his virtue,* so let but all other hearts enquire into themselves, and then judge how it ought to be praised.

Your love, too, as none but that great hero who has it could deserve it, and therefore, by a particular lot from heaven, was destined to so extraordinary a blessing, so matchless for itself and so wondrous for its constancy, shall be remembered to your immortal honour, when all other transactions of the age you live in shall be forgotten.

But I forget that I am to ask pardon for the fault I have been all this while committing; wherefore I beg your Highness to forgive me this presumption, and that you will be pleased to think well of one who cannot help resolving with all the actions of life, to endeavour to deserve it. Nay, more, I would beg and hope it may be granted that I may, through yours, never want an advocate in his favour, whose heart and mind you have so entire a share in. It is my only portion and my fortune. I cannot but be happy so long as I have but hopes I may enjoy it; and I must be miserable, should it ever be my ill fate to lose it.

This, with eternal wishes for your Royal Highness's content, happiness and prosperity, in all humility is presented by

Your most obedient and devoted servant,

Thomas Otway

Prologue

To you, great judges in this writing age,
The sons of wit and patrons of the stage,
With all those humble thoughts which still have swayed
His pride, much doubting, trembling and afraid
Of what is to his want of merit due,   5
And awed by every excellence in you,
The author sends to beg you would be kind,
And spare those many faults you needs must find.
You to whom wit a common foe is grown,
The thing ye scorn and publicly disown,   10
Though now perhaps y'are here for other ends,
He swears to me you ought to be his friends:
For he ne'er called ye yet insipid tools,
Nor wrote one line to tell you ye were fools;
But says of wit ye have so large a store,   15
So very much, you never will have more.
He ne'er with libel treated yet the town,
The names of honest men bedaubed and shown;
Nay, never once lampooned* the harmless life
Of suburb virgin, or of city wife.   20
Satire's the effect of Poetry's disease,
Which, sick of a lewd age, she vents for ease;*
But now her only strife should be to please,
Since of ill fate the baneful cloud's withdrawn,
And happiness again begins to dawn;*   25
Since back with joy and triumph he is come,
That always drove fears hence, ne'er brought 'em home.
Oft has he ploughed the boist'rous ocean o'er,
Yet ne'er more welcome to the longing shore,
Not when he brought home victories before.*   30
For then fresh laurels* flourished on his brow,
And he comes crowned with olive branches* now.
Receive him! Oh, receive him as his friends;
Embrace the blessings which he recommends,
Such quiet as your foes shall ne'er destroy;   35
Then shake off fears, and clap your hands for joy.

DRAMATIS PERSONAE

The play was first performed February/March 1680 by the Duke's Company at the Dorset Garden Theatre with the cast listed below.

ACASTO a nobleman retired from court, and living privately in the country — Mr Gillow

CASTALIO ⎫ his sons — Mr Betterton
POLYDORE ⎭ — Mr John Williams

CHAMONT a young soldier of fortune — Mr Smith

ERNESTO ⎫ servants in the family — Mr Norris
PAULINO ⎭ — Mr Wiltshire

CORDELIO Polydore's page — The Little Girl*

CHAPLAIN — Mr Percival

MONIMIA the orphan, left under the guardianship of old Acasto — Mrs Barry*

SERINA Acasto's daughter — Mrs Butler

FLORELLA Monimia's woman — Mrs Osborn

<SERVANTS, ATTENDANTS>

Scene: Bohemia

Act 1, Scene 1

(Enter PAULINO *and* ERNESTO*)*

PAULINO 'Tis strange, Ernesto, this severity
  Should still reign powerful in Acasto's mind,
  To hate the court, where he was bred and lived,
  All honours heaped on him that power could give.
ERNESTO 'Tis true, he came thither a private gentleman,   5
  But young and brave, and of a family
  Ancient and noble as the empire* holds.
  The honours he has gained are justly his,
  He purchased them in war. Thrice has he led
  An army against the rebels, and as often   10
  Returned with victory; the world has not
  A truer soldier, or a better subject.
PAULINO It was his virtue that first made me serve him;
  He is the best of masters as of friends.
  I know he has lately been invited thither;   15
  Yet still he keeps his stubborn purpose, cries
  He's old, and willingly would be at rest.
  I doubt there's deep resentment in his mind,
  For the late slight his honour suffered there.
ERNESTO Has he not reason? When for what he had
    borne,   20
  Long, hard and faithful toil, he might have claimed
  Places in honour, and employments high,
  A huffing,* shining, flattering, cringing coward.
  A canker-worm of peace was raised above him.
PAULINO Yet still he holds just value for the king,   25
  Nor ever names him but with highest reverence.
  'Tis noble that –
ERNESTO Oh! I have heard him wanton in his praise,
  Speak things of him might charm the ears of envy.
PAULINO Oh, may he live till Nature's self grow old,   30
  And from her womb no more can bless the earth!
  For when he dies, farewell all honour, bounty,

All generous encouragement of arts,
For Charity herself becomes a widow.

ERNESTO No, he has two sons that were ordained to be   35
As well his virtue's, as his fortune's heirs.

PAULINO They're both of nature mild, and full of
    sweetness.
They came twins from the womb, and still they live,
As if they would go twins too, to the grave:
Neither has anything he calls his own,   40
But of each other's joys, as griefs, partaking;
So very honestly, so well they love,
As they were only for each other born.

ERNESTO Never was parent in an offspring happier;
He has a daughter too, whose blooming age   45
Promises goodness equal to her beauty.

PAULINO And as there is a friendship 'twixt the
    brethren,
So has her infant nature chosen, too,
A faithful partner of her thoughts and wishes,
And kind companion of her harmless pleasures.   50

ERNESTO You mean the beauteous orphan, fair
    Monimia?

PAULINO The same, the daughter of the brave Chamont.
He was our lord's companion in the wars,
Where such a wondrous friendship grew between 'em,
As only death could end. Chamont's estate   55
Was ruined in our late and civil discords.
Therefore, unable to advance her fortune,
He left this daughter to our master's care,
To such a care as she scarce lost a father.

ERNESTO Her brother to the emperor's wars went early,   60
To seek a fortune or a noble fate;
Whence he with honour is expected back,
And mighty marks of that great prince's* favour.

PAULINO Our master never would permit his sons
To launch for fortune in th'uncertain world;   65
But warns to avoid both courts and camps,
Where dilatory Fortune plays the jilt

With the brave, noble, honest, gallant man,
To throw herself away on fools and knaves.
ERNESTO They both have forward, gen'rous, active
        spirits;   70
'Tis daily their petition to their father
To send them forth where glory's to be gotten;
They cry they're weary of their lazy home,
Restless to do something that fame may talk of.
Today they chased the boar, and near this time   75
Should be returned.
PAULINO   Oh, that's a royal sport!
We yet may see the old man in a morning,
Lusty as health, come ruddy to the field,
And there pursue the chase as if he meant
To o'ertake time and bring back youth again.   80
               [*Exeunt* ERNESTO *and* PAULINO]

(*Enter* CASTALIO, POLYDORE *and* PAGE)

CASTALIO Polydore! Our sport
Has been today much better for the danger.
When on the brink the foaming boar I met,
And in his side thought to have lodged my spear,
The desperate savage rushed within my force,   85
And bore me headlong with him down the rock.
POLYDORE But then –
CASTALIO Aye, then, my brother, my friend, Polydore,
Like Perseus mounted on his winged steed,*
Came on, and down the dang'rous precipice leapt,   90
To save Castalio. 'Twas a god-like act.
POLYDORE But when I came, I found you conqueror.
Oh, my heart danced to see your danger past!
The heat and fury of the chase was cooled,
And I had nothing in my mind but joy.   95
CASTALIO So, Polydore, methinks we might in war
Rush on together; thou shouldst be my guard,
And I'd be thine; what is't could hurt us then?
Now half the youth of Europe are in arms,
How fulsome must it be to stay behind,   100

And die of rank diseases here at home?
POLYDORE No, let me purchase in my youth renown,
  To make me loved and valued when I'm old.
  I would be busy in the world and learn,
  Not, like a coarse and useless dunghill weed,   105
  Fixed to one spot and rot just as I grew.
CASTALIO Our father
  Has ta'en himself a surfeit of the world,
  And cries it is not safe that we should taste it.
  I own I have duty very powerful in me,   110
  And though I'd hazard all to raise my name,
  Yet he's so tender and so good a father,
  I could not do a thing to cross his will.
POLYDORE Castalio, I have doubts within my heart,
  Which you, and only you, can satisfy –   115
  Will you be free and candid to your friend?
CASTALIO Have I a thought my Polydore should not
    know?
  What can this mean?
POLYDORE   Nay, I'll conjure you too,
  By all the strictest bonds of faithful friendship,
  To show your heart as naked in this point,   120
  As you would purge you of your sins to Heaven.
CASTALIO I will.
POLYDORE And should I chance to touch it nearly, bear
  it
  With all the suff'rance of a tender friend.
CASTALIO As calmly as the wounded patient bears   125
  The artist's* hand, that ministers his cure.
POLYDORE That's kindly said. You know our father's
  ward,
  The fair Monimia; is your heart at peace?
  Is it so guarded that you could not love her?
CASTALIO Suppose I should.
POLYDORE   Suppose you should not, brother.   130
CASTALIO You'd say I must not.
POLYDORE   That would sound too roughly
  'Twixt friends and brothers as we two are.

CASTALIO Is love a fault?

POLYDORE   In one of us it may be;
  What if I love her?

CASTALIO   Then I must inform you,
  I loved her first, and cannot quit the claim,   135
  But will preserve the birthright of my passion.

POLYDORE You will?

CASTALIO   I will.

POLYDORE   No more, I've done.

CASTALIO   Why not?

POLYDORE I told you, I had done;
  But you, Castalio, would dispute it.

CASTALIO   No –
  Not with my Polydore, though I must own   140
  My nature obstinate and void of suff'rance.
  Love reigns a very tyrant in my heart,
  Attended on his throne by all his guards
  Of furious wishes, fears, and nice* suspicions.
  I could not bear a rival in my friendship,   145
  I am so much in love, and fond of thee.

POLYDORE Yet you would break this friendship?

CASTALIO   Not for crowns.*

POLYDORE But for a toy you would, a woman's toy,*
  Unjust Castalio!

CASTALIO   Prithee, where's my fault?

POLYDORE You love Monimia.

CASTALIO   Yes.

POLYDORE   And you would kill me,   150
  If I'm your rival.

CASTALIO   No, sure we're such friends,
  So much one man, that our affections too
  Must be united and the same as we are.

POLYDORE I dote upon Monimia.

CASTALIO   Love her still;
  Win, and enjoy her.

POLYDORE   Both of us cannot.   155

CASTALIO No matter
  Whose chance it proves, but let's not quarrel for't.

POLYDORE You would not wed Monimia, would you?
CASTALIO   Wed her!
  No! Were she all desire could wish, as fair
  As would the vainest of her sex be thought,   160
  With wealth beyond what woman's pride could waste,
  She should not cheat me of my freedom. Marry?
  When I am old and weary of the world,
  I may grow desperate
  And take a wife to mortify withal.   165
POLYDORE It is an elder brother's duty so
  To propagate his family and name;
  You would not have yours die and buried with you?
CASTALIO Mere vanity, and silly dotage all,
  No, let me live at large, and when I die –   170
POLYDORE Who shall possess th' estate you leave?
CASTALIO   My friend,
  If he survives me, or if not, my king,
  Who may bestow't again on some brave man,
  Whose honesty and services deserve one.
POLYDORE 'Tis kindly offered.
CASTALIO   By yon heaven, I love   175
  My Polydore beyond all worldly joys,
  And would not shock his quiet to be blest
  With greater happiness than man e'er tasted.
POLYDORE And by that heaven eternally I swear,
  To keep the kind Castalio in my heart.   180
  Whose shall Monimia be?
CASTALIO   No matter whose.
POLYDORE Were you not with her privately last night?
CASTALIO I was, and should have met her here again;
  But th'opportunity shall now be thine;
  Myself will bring thee to the scene of love.   185
  But have a care, by friendship I conjure thee,
  That no false play be offered to thy brother.
  Urge all thy powers to make thy passion prosper,
  But wrong not mine.
POLYDORE   Heaven blast me if I do.
CASTALIO If't prove thy fortune, Polydore, to conquer,   190

(For thou hast all the arts of fine persuasion!),
Trust me, and let me know thy love's success,
That I may ever after stifle mine.
POLYDORE Though she be dearer to my soul than rest
    To weary pilgrims, or to misers, gold,   195
    To great men, pow'r, or wealthy cities, pride,
    Rather than wrong Castalio, I'd forget her.
    For if ye powers have happiness in store,
    When ye would shower down joys on Polydore,
    In one great blessing all your bounty send,   200
    That I may never lose so dear a friend.
       [*Exeunt* CASTALIO, POLYDORE. *Manet** PAGE]

       (*Enter* MONIMIA)

MONIMIA So soon returned from hunting? This fair day
    Seems as if sent t' invite the world abroad.
    Passed not Castalio and Polydore this way?
PAGE Madam, just now.
MONIMIA   Sure some ill fate's upon me.   205
    Distrust and heaviness sits round my heart,
    And apprehension shocks my timorous soul.
    Why was I not lain in my peaceful grave
    With my poor parents, and at rest as they are?
    Instead of that, I am wand'ring into cares.   210
    Castalio! Oh, Castalio! thou hast caught
    My foolish heart; and like a tender child,
    That trusts his plaything to another hand,
    I fear its harm, and fain would have it back.
    – Come near, Cordelio, I must chide you, sir.   215
PAGE Why, madam, have I done you any wrong?
MONIMIA I never see you now. You have been kinder;
    Sat by my bed and sung me pretty songs.
    Perhaps I've been ungrateful, here's money for you.
    Will you oblige me? Shall I see you oft'ner?   220
PAGE Madam, indeed I'd serve you with my soul;
    But in a morning when you call me to you,
    As by your bed I stand and tell you stories,
    I am ashamed to see your swelling breasts,

It makes me blush, they are so very white.   225
MONIMIA Oh, men, for flattery and deceit renowned!
  Thus, when y'are young, you learn it all like him,
  Till as your years increase, that strengthens too,
  T'undo poor maids and make our ruin easy.
  Tell me, Cordelio, for thou hast oft heard   230
  Their friendly converse and their bosom secrets,
  Sometimes at least, have they not talked of me?
PAGE Oh, madam, very wickedly they have talked;
  But I'm afraid to name it, for they say
  Boys must be whipped that tell their master's secrets.   235
MONIMIA Fear not, Cordelio! It shall ne'er be known,
  For I'll preserve the secret as 'twere mine;
  Polydore cannot be so kind as I.
  I'll furnish thee for all thy harmless sports
  With pretty toys, and thou shalt be my page.   240
PAGE And truly, madam, I had rather be so.
  Methinks you love me better than my lord,
  For he was never half so kind as you are!
  What must I do?
MONIMIA   Inform me how th'hast heard
  Castalio and his brother use my name.   245
PAGE With all the tenderness of love,
  You were the subject of their last discourse.
  At first I thought it would have fatal proved,
  But as the one grew hot, the other cooled,
  And yielded to the frailty of his friend;   250
  At last, after much struggling 'twas resolved.
MONIMIA What, good Cordelio?
PAGE   Not to quarrel for you.
MONIMIA I would not have 'em, by my dearest hopes,
  I would not be the argument of strife.
  <aside> But surely my Castalio won't forsake me,   255
  And make a mockery of my easy love.
  – Went they together?
PAGE   Yes, to seek you, madam.
  Castalio promised Polydore to bring him
  Where he alone might meet you,

And fairly try the fortune of his wishes.   260
MONIMIA *<aside>* Am I then grown so cheap, just to be
  made
  A common stake, a prize for love in jest?
  – Was not Castalio very loth to yield it?
  Or was it Polydore's unruly passion
  That heightened the debate?   The fault was Polydore's.   265
PAGE
  Castalio played with love, and smiling showed
  The pleasure, not the pangs of his desire.
  He said no woman's smiles should buy his freedom
  And marriage is a mortifying thing.
MONIMIA Then am I ruined; if Castalio's false,   270
  Where is there faith or honour to be found?
  Ye gods that guard the innocent, and guide
  The weak, protect and take me to your care.
  Oh, but I love him! There's the rock will wrack* me!
  Why was I made with all my sex's softness,   275
  Yet want* the cunning to conceal its follies?
  I'll see Castalio, tax him with his falsehoods;
  Be a true woman, rail, protest my wrongs,
  Resolve to hate him, and yet love him still.

                (*Enter* CASTALIO *and* POLYDORE)

He comes, the conqueror comes! Lie still, my heart,   280
And learn to bear thy injuries with scorn.
CASTALIO Madam, my brother begs he may have leave
  To tell you something that concerns you nearly.
  I leave you, as becomes me, and withdraw.
MONIMIA My Lord Castalio!
CASTALIO   Madam!
MONIMIA   Have you purposed   285
  To abuse me palpably? What means this usage?
  Why am I left with Polydore alone?
CASTALIO He best can tell you. Business of importance
  Calls me away, I must attend my father.
MONIMIA Will you then leave me thus?
CASTALIO   But for a moment.   290

MONIMIA It has been otherwise: the time has been
  When business might have stayed, and I been heard.
CASTALIO I could forever hear thee, but this time
  Matters of such odd circumstances press me,
  That I must go –   295
MONIMIA Then go; and if't be possible, forever.
                                      [*Exit* CASTALIO]

  Well, my Lord Polydore, I guess your business,
  And read the ill-natured purpose in your eyes.
POLYDORE If to desire you more than misers wealth,
  Or dying men an hour of added life;   300
  If softest wishes, and a heart more true
  Than ever suffered yet for love disdained,
  Speak an ill nature, you accuse me justly.
MONIMIA Talk not of love, my lord, I must not hear it.
POLYDORE Who can behold such beauty and be silent?   305
  Desire first taught us words. Man, when created
  At first alone, long wandered up and down,
  Forlorn, and silent as his vassal beasts;
  But when a heaven-born maid, like you, appeared,
  Strange pleasures filled his eyes, and fired his heart,   310
  Unloosed his tongue, and his first talk was love.
MONIMIA The first created pair indeed were blest;
  They were the only objects of each other;
  Therefore he courted her, and her alone.
  But in this peopled world of beauty, where   315
  There's roving room, where you may court and ruin
  A thousand more, why need you talk to me?
POLYDORE Oh, I could talk to thee forever! Thus
  Eternally admiring, fix and gaze
  On those dear eyes, for every glance they send   320
  Darts through my soul, and almost gives enjoyment.
MONIMIA How can you labour thus for my undoing?
  I must confess, indeed, I owe you more
  Than ever I can hope to think to pay.
  There always was a friendship 'twixt our families;   325
  And therefore when my tender parents died,
  Whose ruined fortunes, too, expired with them,

Your father's pity and his bounty took me,
A poor and helpless orphan, to his care.
POLYDORE 'Twas Heaven ordained it so to make me
    happy.   330
Hence with this peevish virtue, 'tis a cheat,
And those who taught it first were hypocrites.
Come, those soft, tender limbs were made for yielding.
MONIMIA (*kneels*) Here on my knees, by Heaven's blest
    power I swear,
If you persist, I never henceforth will see you;   335
But rather wander through the world a beggar,
And live on sordid scraps at proud men's doors.
For though to fortune lost, I'll still inherit
My mother's virtues and my father's honour.
POLYDORE Intolerable vanity! Your sex   340
Was never in the right, y'are always false,
Or silly. Even your dresses are not more
Fantastic than your appetites. You think
Of nothing twice! Opinion you have none.
Today y'are nice, tomorrow not so free,   345
Now smile, then frown; now sorrowful, then glad;
Now pleased, now not; and all you know not why!
Virtue you affect, inconstancy's your practice;
And when your loose desires once get dominion,
No hungry churl feeds coarser at a feast,*   350
Every rank fool goes down –
MONIMIA   Indeed, my lord,
I own my sex's follies, I have 'em all,
And to avoid its faults must fly from you.
Therefore, believe me, could you raise me high,
As most fantastic woman's wish could reach,   355
And lay all nature's riches at my feet,
I'd rather run a savage in the woods
Amongst brute beasts, grow wrinkled and deformed
As wildness and most rude neglect could make me,
So I might still enjoy my honour safe   360
From the destroying wiles of faithless man.
                       [*Exit* MONIMIA]

POLYDORE Who'd be that sordid, foolish thing called
   man,
  To cringe thus, fawn, and flatter for a pleasure,
  Which beasts enjoy so very much above him?
  The lusty bull ranges through all the field,   365
  And from the herd singling his female out,
  Enjoys her, and abandons her at will.
  It shall be so; I'll yet possess my love,
  Wait on, and watch her loose, unguarded hours,
  Then, when her roving thoughts have been abroad,   370
  And brought in wanton wishes to her heart,
  I' th' very minute when her virtue nods,
  I'll rush upon her in a storm of love,
  Bear down her guard of honour all before me,
  Surfeit on joys till even desire grows sick: 375
  Then by long absence liberty regain,
  And quite forget the pleasure and the pain.
                     [*Exeunt* POLYDORE *and* PAGE]

Act 2, Scene 1

(*Enter* ACASTO, CASTALIO, POLYDORE, ATTENDANTS)

ACASTO Today has been a day of glorious sport.
  When you, Castalio, and your brother left me,
  Forth from the thickets rushed another boar,
  So large he seemed the tyrant of the woods,
  With all his dreadful bristles raised up high,   5
  They seemed a grove of spears upon his back.
  Foaming he came at me, where I was posted
  Best to observe which way he'd lead the chase,
  Whetting his huge long tusks, and gaping wide,
  As if he already had me for his prey;   10
  Till brandishing my well-poised javelin high,
  With this cold,* executing arm, I struck
  The ugly, brindled monster to the heart.
CASTALIO The actions of your life were always

wondrous.

ACASTO No flattery, boy! An honest man can't live by't;   15
 It is a little sneaking art, which knaves
 Use to cajole and soften fools withal.
 If thou hast flattery in thy nature, out with't,
 Or send it to a court, for there 'twill thrive.

POLYDORE Why there?

ACASTO   'Tis next to money current there,   20
 To be seen daily in as many forms
 As there are sorts of vanities and men:
 The superstitious* statesman has his sneer,
 To smooth a poor man off with that can't bribe him;
 The grave dull fellow of small business soothes   25
 The humorist,* and will needs admire his wit.
 Who without spleen* could see a hot-brained atheist
 Thanking a surly doctor* for his sermon;
 Or a grave councillor meet a smooth young lord,
 Squeeze him by the hand, and praise his good
  complexion?   30

POLYDORE Courts are the places where best manners
  flourish,
 Where the deserving ought to rise, and fools
 Make show. Why should I vex and chafe my spleen
 To see a gaudy coxcomb shine, when I
 Have seen enough to soothe him in his follies   35
 And ride him to advantage as I please?

ACASTO Who merit ought indeed to rise i' the world,
 But no wise man that's honest should expect.
 What man of sense would rack his generous mind
 To practise all the base formalities   40
 And forms of business; force a grave starched face,
 When he's a very libertine in's heart?
 Seem not to know this or that man in public,
 When privately perhaps they meet together,
 And lay the scene of some brave fellow's ruin?   45
 Such things are done –

CASTALIO   Your lordship's wrongs have been
 So great that you with justice may complain;

But suffer us, whose younger minds ne'er felt
Fortune's deceit, to court her as she's fair.
Were she a common mistress, kind to all,   50
Her worth would cease, and half the world grow idle.
ACASTO Go to, y'are fools, and know me not, I've learnt
Long since to bear, revenge, or scorn my wrongs,
According to the value of the doer.
You both would fain be great, and to that end   55
Desire to do things worthy your ambition.
Go to the camp, preferment's noble mart,
Where honour ought to have the fairest play, you'll
    find
Corruption, envy, discontent, and faction
Almost in every band. How many men   60
Have spent their blood in their dear country's service,
Yet now pine under want, while selfish slaves,
That ev'n would cut their throats whom now they
    fawn on,
Like deadly locusts eat the honey up
Which these industrious bees so hardly toiled for?   65
CASTALIO These precepts suit not with my active mind,
Methinks I would be busy.
POLYDORE   So would I,
Not loiter out my life at home, and know
No farther than one prospect gives me leave.
ACASTO Busy your minds then; study arts and men.   70
Learn how to value merits though in rags,
And scorn a proud, ill-mannered knave in office.

(*Enter* SERINA, MONIMIA *and* MAID)

SERINA My lord, my father!
ACASTO   Blessings on my child,
My little cherub, what hast thou to ask me?
SERINA I bring you, sir, most glad and welcome news,   75
The young Chamont, whom you've so often wished
    for,
Is just arrived and ent'ring.
ACASTO   By my soul,

And all my honours, he's most dearly welcome,
Let me receive him like his father's friend.

(*Enter* CHAMONT)

Welcome, thou relic of the best loved man;   80
Welcome from all the turmoils, and the hazards
Of certain danger, and uncertain fortune;
Welcome as happy tidings after fears.

CHAMONT Words would but wrong the gratitude I owe
    you.
Should I begin to speak, my soul's so full   85
That I should talk of nothing else all day.

MONIMIA My brother!

CHAMONT   Oh my sister! Let me hold thee
Long in my arms. I've not beheld thy face
These many days. By night I've often seen thee
In gentle dreams, and satisfied my soul   90
With fancied joy, till morning cares awaked me.
(*to* SERINA) Another sister? Sure it must be so;
Though I remember well I had but one.
But I feel something in my heart that prompts
And tells me she has claim and interest there.   95

ACASTO Young soldier, you've not only studied war;
Courtship I see has been your practice too,
And may not prove unwelcome to my daughter.

CHAMONT Is she your daughter? Then my heart told
    true!
And I'm at least her brother by adoption.   100
For you have made yourself to me a father,
And by that patent I have leave to love her.

SERINA (*aside*) Monimia, thou hast told me men are
    false,
Will flatter, feign and make an art of love.
Is Chamont so? No, sure he's more than man,   105
Something that's near divine, and truth dwells in him.

ACASTO Thus happy, who would envy pompous power,
The luxury of courts, or wealth of cities?
Let there be joy through all the house this day!

In every room let plenty flow at large,   110
It is the birthday of my royal master.
You have not visited the court, Chamont,
Since your return?
CHAMONT   I have no business there;
  I have not slavish temperance enough
  T'attend a favourite's heels, and watch his smiles,   115
  Bear an ill office done me to my face,
  And thank the lord that wronged me for his favour.
ACASTO (*to his sons*) This you could do.
CASTALIO   I'd serve my prince.
ACASTO   Who'd serve him?
CASTALIO I would, my lord.
POLYDORE   And I, both would.
ACASTO   Away,
  He needs not any servants such as you!   120
  Serve him! He merits more than man can do!
  He is so good, praise cannot speak his worth;
  So merciful, sure he ne'er slept in wrath;
  So just, that were he but a private man,
  He could not do a wrong. How would you serve him? 125
CASTALIO I'd serve him with my fortune here at home,
  And serve him with my person in his wars.
  Watch for him, fight for him, bleed for him.
POLYDORE Die for him,
  As every true-born loyal subject ought.   130
ACASTO Let me embrace you both. Now by the souls
  Of my brave ancestors, I'm truly happy!
  For this be ever blest my marriage day,
  Blest be your mother's memory that bore you,
  And doubly blest be that auspicious hour   135
  That gave ye* birth. Yes, my aspiring boys,
  Ye shall have business when your master wants you,
  You cannot serve a nobler. I have served him;
  In this old body yet the marks remain
  Of many wounds. I've with this tongue proclaimed   140
  His right, even in the face of rank rebellion.
  And when a foul-mouthed traitor once prophaned

His sacred name, with my good sabre drawn,
Ev'n at the head of all his giddy rout
I rushed and clove the rebel to the chine.*   145

(*Enter* SERVANT)

SERVANT My lord, the expected guests are just arrived.
ACASTO Go you, and give 'em welcome and reception.
  <*Exeunt all but* ACASTO, CHAMONT, *and* MONIMIA>

CHAMONT My lord, I stand in need of your assistance
In something that concerns my peace and honour.
ACASTO Spoke like the son of that brave man I loved;   150
So freely, friendly we conversed together.
Whate'er it be, with confidence impart it,
Thou shalt command my fortune and my sword.
CHAMONT I dare not doubt your friendship nor your
      justice.
Your bounty shown to what I hold most dear,   155
My orphan sister, must not be forgotten.
ACASTO Prithee, no more of that, it grates my nature.
CHAMONT When our dear parents died, they died
      together;
One fate surprised 'em, and one grave received 'em.
My father, with his dying breath, bequeathed   160
Her to my love. My mother, as she lay
Languishing near him, called me to her side,
Took me in her fainting arms, wept and embraced me,
Then pressed me close, and as she observed my tears,
Kissed 'em away, said she, 'Chamont, my son,   165
By this, and all the love I ever showed thee,
Be careful of Monimia, watch her youth,
Let not her wants betray her to dishonour.
Perhaps kind Heaven may raise some friend.' Then
      sighed,*
Kissed me again, so blessed us, and expired.   170
– Pardon my grief.
ACASTO   It speaks an honest nature.
CHAMONT The friend Heaven raised was you – you took
      her up,

An infant to the desert world exposed,
And proved another parent.

ACASTO   I've not wronged her.

CHAMONT Far be it from my fears.

ACASTO   Then why this argument? 175

CHAMONT My lord, my nature's jealous, and you'll bear
  it.

ACASTO Go on.

CHAMONT   Great spirits bear misfortunes hardly;
  Good offices claim gratitude, and pride,
  Where power is wanting, will usurp a little,
  May make us (rather than be thought behindhand)   180
  Pay over-price.

ACASTO   I cannot guess your drift.
  Distrust you me?

CHAMONT   No, but I fear her weakness
  May make her pay a debt at any rate;
  And to deal freely with your lordship's goodness,
  I've heard a story lately much disturbs me.   185

ACASTO Then first charge her; and if th'offence be found
  Within my reach, though it should touch my nature
  In my own offspring, by the dear remembrance
  Of thy brave father, whom my heart rejoiced in,
  I'd prosecute it with severest vengeance.   190

CHAMONT I thank you from my soul.

                              <Exit ACASTO>

MONIMIA   Alas, my brother!
  What have I done? And why do you abuse me?
  My heart quakes in me; in your settled face
  And clouded brow methinks I see my fate.
  You will not kill me!

CHAMONT   Prithee, why dost talk so?   195

MONIMIA Look kindly on me then, I cannot bear
  Severity; it daunts, and does amaze me.
  My heart's so tender, should you charge me roughly,
  I should but weep, and answer you with sobbing;
  But use me gently like a loving brother,   200
  And search through all the secrets of my soul.

CHAMONT Fear nothing, I will show myself a brother,
  A tender, loving, and an honest brother.
  You've not forgot our father?
MONIMIA   I shall never.
CHAMONT Then you'll remember too, he was a man   205
  That lived up to the standard of his honour,
  And prized that jewel more than the mines of wealth.
  He'd not have done a shameful thing but once,
  Though kept in darkness from the world, and hidden,
  He could not have forgiven it to himself.   210
  This was the only portion that he left us,
  And I more glory in't than if possessed
  Of all that ever fortune threw on fools.
  'Twas a large trust, and must be managed nicely;
  Now if by any chance, Monimia,   215
  You have soiled this gem and taken from its value,
  How will y'account with me?
MONIMIA   I challenge envy,
  Malice, and all the practices of hell,
  To censure all the actions of my past
  Unhappy life, and taint me if they can!   220
CHAMONT I'll tell thee then. Three nights ago, as I
  Lay musing in my bed, all darkness round me,
  A sudden damp struck to my heart, cold sweat
  Dewed all my face, and trembling seized my limbs;
  My bed shook under me, the curtains started,   225
  And to my tortured fancy there appeared
  The form of thee thus beauteous as thou art,
  Thy garments flowing loose, and in each hand
  A wanton lover, which by turns caressed thee
  With all the freedom of unbounded pleasure.   230
  I snatched my sword, and in the very moment
  Darted it at the phantom – straight it left me –
  Then rose and called for lights, when, oh, dire omen!
  I found my weapon had the arras pierced
  Just where that famous tale was interwoven   235
  How th'unhappy Theban* slew his father.
MONIMIA And for this cause my virtue is suspected!

Because in dreams your fancy has been ridden,
I must be tortured waking!
CHAMONT   Have a care,
  Labour not to be justified too fast;   240
  Hear all, and then let justice hold the scale.
  What followed was the riddle that confounds me:
  Through a close lane, as I pursued my journey,
  And meditated on the last night's vision,
  I spied a wrinkled hag, with age grown double,   245
  Picking dry sticks, and mumbling to herself.
  Her eyes with scalding rheum were galled and red,
  Cold palsy shook her head, her hands seemed
    withered,
  And on her crooked shoulders she had wrapped
  The tattered remnant of an old stripped* hanging,   250
  Which served to keep her carcass from the cold;
  So there was nothing of a piece about her.
  Her lower weeds* were all o'er coarsely patched
  With different coloured rags, black, red, white, yellow,
  And seemed to speak variety of wretchedness.   255
  I asked her of my way, which she informed me;
  Then craved my charity, and bade me hasten
  To save a sister: at that word I started.
MONIMIA The common cheat of beggars every day!
  They flock about our doors, pretend to gifts   260
  Of prophecy, and telling fools their fortunes.
CHAMONT Oh! But she told me such a tale, Monimia,
  As in it bore great circumstance of truth –
  Castalio, and Polydore, my sister.
MONIMIA   Ha!
CHAMONT What, altered? Does your courage fail you?   265
  Now, by my father's soul, the witch was honest.
  Answer me, if thou hast not lost to them
  The honour at a sordid game.
MONIMIA   I will,
  I must – so hardly my misfortune loads me:
  That both have offered me their love's most true –   270

CHAMONT And 'tis as true too, they have both undone
    thee.
MONIMIA Though they both with earnest vows
    Have pressed my heart, if e'er in thought I yielded
    To any but Castalio –
CHAMONT   But Castalio!
MONIMIA Still will you cross the line of my discourse?   275
    Yes, I confess that he has won my soul
    By generous love and honourable vows,
    Which he this day appointed to complete,
    And make himself by holy marriage mine.
CHAMONT Are thou then spotless? Hast thou still
    preserved   280
    Thy virtue white without a blot, untainted?
MONIMIA When I'm unchaste may Heaven reject my
    prayers!
    Or more, to make me wretched, may you know it!
CHAMONT Oh, then, Monimia, are thou dearer to me
    Than all the comforts ever yet blessed man;   285
    And let not marriage bait thee to thy ruin.
    Trust not a man: we are by nature false,
    Dissembling, subtle, cruel and unconstant.
    When a man talks of love, with caution trust him;
    But if he swears, he'll certainly deceive thee.   290
    I charge thee, let no more Castalio soothe thee.
    Avoid it, as thou wouldst preserve the peace
    Of a poor brother, to whose soul th'art precious.
MONIMIA I will.
CHAMONT Appear as cold when next you meet, as great
    ones   295
    When merit begs, then shalt thou see how soon
    His heart will cool and all his pains grow easy.
                                    [*Exit* CHAMONT]

MONIMIA Yes, I will try him, torture him severely;
    For, oh, Castalio, thou too much hast wronged me
    In leaving me to Polydore's ill usage!   300
    He comes, and now for once, O Love, stand neuter
    Whilst a hard part's performed! For I must tempt,

Wound his soft nature, though my own heart aches
for't.

[*Exit* MONIMIA]

(*Enter* CASTALIO)

CASTALIO Monimia, Monimia – she's gone,
And seemed to part with anger in her eyes.   305
I am a fool, and she has found my weakness.
She uses me already like a slave
Fast bound in chains, to be chastised at will.
'Twas not well done to trifle with my brother:
I might have trusted him with all the secret,   310
Opened my silly* heart and shown it bare.
But then he loves her too – but not like me;
I am a doting, honest slave, designed
For bondage, marriage bonds, which I've sworn
To wear. It is the only thing I e'er   315
Hid from his knowledge, and he'll sure forgive
The first transgression of a wretched friend
Betrayed to love and all its little follies.

(*Enter* POLYDORE, *and* PAGE *at the door*)

POLYDORE Here place yourself, and watch my brother
throughly.*
If he should chance to meet Monimia, make   320
Just observation of each word and action;
Pass not one circumstance without remark.
Sir, 'tis your office: do't and bring me word.

[*Exit* POLYDORE]

(*Enter* MONIMIA)

CASTALIO Monimia, my angel, 'twas not kind
To leave me like a turtle* here alone,   325
To droop and mourn the absence of my mate.
When thou art from me every place is desert,
And I, methinks, am savage and forlorn.
Thy presence only 'tis can make me blest,
Heal my unquiet mind, and tune my soul.   330
MONIMIA Oh, the bewitching tongue of faithless men!

'Tis thus the false hyena* makes her moan,
To draw the pitying traveller to her den.
Your sex are so — such false dissemblers all:
With sighs and plaints y'entice poor women's hearts,   335
And all that pity you are made your prey.

CASTALIO What means my love? Oh, how have I
    deserved
This language from the sovereign of my joys?
Stop, stop those tears, Monimia, for they fall
Like baneful dew from a distempered sky;   340
I feel 'em chill me to the very heart.

MONIMIA Oh, you are false, Castalio, most forlorn!*
Attempt no farther to delude my faith,
My heart is fixed, and you shall shake't no more.

CASTALIO Who told you so? What hell-bred villain durst 345
Prophane the sacred business of my love?

MONIMIA Your brother, knowing on what terms I'm
    here,
Th'unhappy object of your father's charity,
Licentiously discoursed to me of love,
And durst affront me with his brutal passion.   350

CASTALIO 'Tis I have been to blame, and only I,
False to my brother, and unjust to thee.
For, oh, he loves thee too, and this day owned it;
Taxed me with mine, and claimed a right above me.

MONIMIA And was your love so very tame to shrink,   355
Or rather than lose him, abandon me?

CASTALIO I, knowing him precipitate and rash,
To calm his heat, and to conceal my happiness,
Seemed to comply with his unruly will;
Talked as he talked, and granted all he asked,   360
Lest he in rage might have our loves betrayed,
And I forever had Monimia lost.

MONIMIA Could you then? Did you? Can you own it
    too?
'Twas poorly done, unworthy of yourself,
And I can never think you meant me fair.   365

CASTALIO Is this Monimia? Surely no! Till now

I ever thought her dove-like, soft, and kind.
Who trusts his heart with woman's surely lost!
You were made fair on purpose to undo us,
Whilst greedily we snatch th'alluring bait,   370
And ne'er distrust the poison that it hides.

MONIMIA When love ill-placed would find a means to
    break –

CASTALIO It never wants pretences nor excuse.

MONIMIA Man, therefore, was a lord-like creature made,
Rough as the winds, and as inconstant too;   375
A lofty aspect given him for command,
Easily softened when he would betray.
Like conquering tyrants you our breasts invade,
Where you are pleased to forage for a while,
But soon you find new conquests out, and leave   380
The ravaged province ruinate and waste.
If so, Castalio, you have served my heart,
I find that desolation's settled there,
And I shall ne'er recover peace again.

CASTALIO Who can hear this and bear an equal mind?   385
Since you will drive me from you, I must go;
But, oh, Monimia, when th'hast banished me,
No creeping slave, though tractable and dull
As artful woman for her ends would choose,
Shall ever dote as I have done; for, oh,   390
No tongue my pleasure nor my pain can tell:
'Tis heaven to have thee, and without thee hell.

MONIMIA Castalio, stay! We must not part. I find
My rage ebbs out, and love flows in apace.
These little quarrels love must needs forgive,   395
They rouse up drowsy thoughts, and wake the soul.
Oh, charm me with the music of thy tongue;
I'm ne'er so blest as when I hear thy vows,
And listen to the language of thy heart.

CASTALIO Where am I? Surely paradise is round me!   400
Sweets planted by the hand of Heaven grow here,
And every sense is full of thy perfection.
To hear thee speak might calm a madman's frenzy,

Till by attention he forgot his sorrows;
But to behold thy eyes, th'amazing beauties,   405
Might make him rage again with love, as I do.
To touch thee's heaven, but to enjoy thee, oh,
Thou nature's whole perfection in one piece!
Sure, framing thee, Heaven took unusual care,
As its own beauty it designed thee fair,   410
And formed thee by the best-loved angel there.

                                        [*Exeunt*]

Act 3, Scene 1

(*Enter* POLYDORE, *and* PAGE)

POLYDORE Were they so kind? Express it to me all
    In words may make me think I saw it too.
PAGE At first I thought they had been mortal foes:
    Monimia raged, Castalio grew disturbed;
    Each thought the other wronged, yet both so haughty,   5
    They scorned submission; though love all the while
    The rebel played, and scarce could be contained.
POLYDORE But what succeeded?
PAGE   Oh, 'twas wondrous pretty!
    For of a sudden all the storm was past,
    A gentle calm of love succeeded in;   10
    Monimia sighed and blushed, Castalio swore –
    As you, my lord, I well remember, did
    To my young sister in the orange grove,
    When I was first preferred to be your page.
POLYDORE (*aside*) Happy Castalio! Now, by my great
    soul.   15
    M'ambitious soul, that languishes to glory,
    I'll have her yet, by my best hopes I will;
    She shall be mine, in spite of all her arts.
    But for Castalio why was I refused?
    Has he supplanted me by some foul play?   20
    Traduced my honour? Death! He durst not do't.
    It must be so: we parted, and he met her,

Half to compliance brought by me, surprised
Her sinking virtue till she yielded quite.
So poachers basely pick up tired game,   25
Whilst the fair hunter's cheated of his prey.
– Boy!

PAGE My lord?

POLYDORE Go to your chamber and prepare your lute;
Find out some song to please me, that describes   30
Women's hypocrisies, their subtle wiles,
Betraying smiles, feigned tears, inconstancies,
Their painted outsides and corrupted minds,
The sum of all their follies and their falsehoods.

<Exit PAGE>

(Enter SERVANT)

SERVANT Oh, the unhappiest tidings tongue e'er told!   35
POLYDORE The matter?
SERVANT   Oh, your father, my good master,
As with his guests he sat in mirth raised high,
And chased the goblets*round the joyful board,
A sudden trembling seized on all his limbs;
His eyes distorted grew, his visage pale,   40
His speech forsook him, life itself seemed fled;
And all his friends are waiting now about him.

(Enter ACASTO leaning on two)

ACASTO Support me, give me air, I'll yet recover.
'Twas but a slip decaying nature made,
For she grows weary near her journey's end.   45
Where are my sons? Come near, my Polydore,
– Your brother – where's Castalio?

SERVANT   My lord,
I've searched, as you commanded, all the house;
He or Monimia are not to be found.

ACASTO Not to be found? Then where are all my
    friends?   50
'Tis well;
I hope they'll pardon an unhappy fault

M'unmannerly infirmity has made.
Death could not come in a more welcome hour,
For I'm prepared to meet him, and methinks   55
Would live and die with all my friends about me.

(*Enter* CASTALIO <*and* MONIMIA>)

CASTALIO Angels preserve my dearest father's life,
Bless it with long and uninterrupted days!
Oh, may he live till time itself decay!
Till good men wish him dead, or I offend him!   60
ACASTO Thank you, Castalio, give me both your hands
And bear me up – I'd walk. So, now methinks
I appear as great as Hercules himself,
Supported by the pillars he had raised.*
CASTALIO My lord, your chaplain.
ACASTO   Let the good man enter. 65

<*Enter* CHAPLAIN>

CHAPLAIN Heaven guard your lordship, and restore your
    health!
ACASTO I have provided for thee, if I die.
No fawning! 'Tis a scandal to thy office.
My sons, as thus united ever live;
And for the estate, you'll find when I am dead   70
I have divided it betwixt you both,
Equally parted, as you shared my love;
Only to sweet Monimia I've bequeathed
Ten thousand crowns, a little portion for her,
To wed her honourably as she's born.   75
Be not less friends because you're brothers; shun
The man that's singular: his mind's unsound,
His spleen o'erweighs his brains. But above all,
Avoid the politic, the factious fool,
The busy, buzzing, talking, hardened knave,   80
The quaint, smooth rogue, that sins against his reason,
Calls saucy loud suspicion, public zeal,
And mutiny, the dicates of his spirit.
Be very careful how ye make new friends:

Men read not morals now – 'twas a custom,   85
But all are to their fathers' vices born,
And in their mothers' ignorance are bred.
Let marriage be the last mad thing ye do,
For all the sins and follies of the past.
If you have children, never give them knowledge,   90
'Twill spoil their fortune, fools are all the fashion.
If y'ave religion, keep it to yourselves;
Atheists will else make use of toleration
And laugh ye out on't; never show religion
Except* ye mean to pass for knaves of conscience,   95
And cheat believing fools that think ye honest.

<Enter SERINA and CHAMONT>

SERINA My father!
ACASTO   My heart's darling!
SERINA   Let my knees
   Fix to the earth. Ne'er let my eyes have rest,
   But wake and weep till Heaven restore my father!
ACASTO Rise to my arms, and thy kind prayers are
      answered;   100
   For thou'rt a wondrous extract of all goodness,
   Born for my joy, and no pain's felt when near thee.
   Chamont!
CHAMONT My lord, may't prove not an unlucky omen!
   Many, I see, are waiting round about you,   105
   And I am come to ask a blessing too.
ACASTO Mayst thou be happy!
CHAMONT   Where?
ACASTO   In all thy wishes!
CHAMONT Confirm me so, and make this fair one mine.
   I am unpractised in the trade of courtship,
   And know not how to deal love out with art.   110
   Onsets in love seem best like those in war,
   Fierce, resolute, and done with all the force.
   So I would open my whole heart at once,
   And pour out the abundance of my soul.
ACASTO What says Serina? Canst thou love a soldier?   115

One born to honour and to honour bred?
One that has learned to treat ev'n foes with kindness,
To wrong no good man's fame, nor praise himself?

SERINA Oh, name not love, for that's allied to joy,
And joy must be a stranger to my heart   120
When you're in danger. May Chamont's good fortune
Render him lovely to some happier maid!
Whilst I at friendly distance see him blest,
Praise the kind gods, and wonder at his virtues.

ACASTO Chamont, pursue her, conquer and possess her,   125
And as my son, a third of all my fortune
Shall be thy lot.
But keep thy eyes from wandering, man of frailty!
Beware the dangerous beauty of the wanton;
Shun their enticements; ruin, like a vulture,   130
Waits on their conquests. Falsehood too's their
    business;
They put false beauty off to all the world;
Use false endearments to the fools that love 'em,
And when they marry, to their silly husbands
They bring false virtue, broken fame, and fortune.   135

MONIMIA <aside> Hear ye that, my lord?

POLYDORE <aside> Yes, my fair monitor, old men
    always talk thus.

ACASTO Chamont, you told me of some doubts that
    pressed you.
Are you not satisfied that I am your friend?

CHAMONT My lord, I would not lose that satisfaction   140
For any blessing I could wish for.
As to my fears – already I have lost 'em;
They ne'er shall vex me more, nor trouble you.

ACASTO I thank you. Daughter, you must do so too.
– My friends, 'tis late, or we would yet be company,   145
For my disorder seems all past and over,
And I methinks begin to feel new health.

CASTALIO Would you but rest, it might restore you
    quite.

ACASTO Yes, I'll to bed; old men must humour

weakness.
Let me have music then, to lull and chase   150
This melancholy thought of death away.
Good night, my friends! Heaven guard ye all! Good
    night!
Tomorrow early we'll salute the day,
Find out new pleasures, and redeem lost time.

                [*Exeunt all but* CHAMONT *and* CHAPLAIN]

CHAMONT Hist! hist! Sir Gravity! a word with you.   155
CHAPLAIN With me, sir?
CHAMONT If you're at leisure, sir, we'll waste an hour.
  'Tis yet too soon to sleep, and 'twill be charity
  To lend your conversation to a stranger.
CHAPLAIN Sir, you are a soldier?
CHAMONT   Yes.
CHAPLAIN   I love a soldier,   160
  And had been one myself, but my old parents
  Would make me what you see of me – yet I'm honest,
  For all I wear black.
CHAMONT   And that's a wonder.
  Have you had long dependence on this family?
CHAPLAIN I have not thought it so, because my time's   165
  Spent pleasantly.
  My lord's not haughty nor imperious,
  Nor I gravely whimsical.
  He has good nature, and I have manners.
  His sons too are civil to me, because   170
  I do not pretend to be wiser than they are.
  I meddle with no man's business but my own;
  I rise in a morning early, study moderately,
  Eat and drink cheerfully, live soberly
  Take my innocent pleasures freely.   175
  So I* meet with respect, and am not the jest of the
    family.
CHAMONT I'm glad you are so happy.
  <aside> A pleasant fellow this, and may be useful.
  Knew you my father, the old Chamont?
CHAPLAIN I did, and was most sorry when we lost him.   180

CHAMONT Why? Didst thou love him?

CHAPLAIN Everybody loved him; besides he was my
    master's friend.

CHAMONT I could embrace thee for that very notion.
  If thou didst love my father, I could think
  Thou wouldst not be an enemy to me.   185

CHAPLAIN I can be no man's foe.

CHAMONT   Then prithee tell me,
  Think'st thou the Lord Castalio loves my sister?
  Nay, never start. Come, come, I know thy office
  Opens thee all the secrets of the family.
  Then, if thou art honest, use this freedom kindly.   190

CHAPLAIN Love your sister?

CHAMONT Aye, love her.

CHAPLAIN Sir, I never asked him,
  And wonder you should ask it me.

CHAMONT Nay, but th'art an hypocrite. Is there not one 195
  Of all your tribe that's honest in your schools?*
  The pride of your superiors makes ye slaves.
  Ye all live loathsome, sneaking, servile lives,
  Not free enough to practise generous truth,
  Though ye pretend to teach it to the world.   200

CHAPLAIN I would deserve a better thought from you.

CHAMONT If thou wouldst have me not contemn thy
    office
  And character, think all thy brethren knaves,
  Thy trade a cheat, and thou its worst professor.
  Inform me – for I tell thee, priest, I'll know.   205

CHAPLAIN Either he loves her, or he much has wronged
    her.

CHAMONT How wronged her? Have a care, for this may
    lay
  A scene of mischief to undo us all.
  But tell me, wronged her saidst thou?

CHAPLAIN   Aye, sir, wronged her.

CHAMONT This is a secret worth a monarch's fortune.   210
  What shall I give thee for't? Thou dear physician
  Of sickly souls, unfold this riddle to me,

And comfort mine –

CHAPLAIN I would hide nothing from you willingly.

CHAMONT Nay, then again th'art honest. Wouldst thou
    tell me?   215

CHAPLAIN Yes, if I durst.

CHAMONT   Why, what affrights thee?

CHAPLAIN   You do,
Who are not to be trusted with the secret.

CHAMONT Why, I am no fool.

CHAPLAIN   So indeed you say.

CHAMONT Prithee, be serious then.

CHAPLAIN   You see I am so,
And hardly shall be mad enough tonight   220
To trust you with my ruin.

CHAMONT   Art thou then
So far concerned in't? What has been thy office?
Curse on that formal steady villain's face!
Just so do all bawds look. Nay, bawds, they say,
Can pray upon occasion, talk of Heaven,   225
Turn up their goggling eyeballs, rail at vice,
Dissemble, lie, and preach like any priest.
Art thou a bawd?

CHAPLAIN   Sir, I'm not often used thus.

CHAMONT Be just then.

CHAPLAIN   So I will be to the trust
That's laid upon me.

CHAMONT   By the reverenced soul   230
Of that great honest man that gave me being,
Tell me but what thou know'st concerns my honour,
And if I e'er reveal it to thy wrong,
May this good sword ne'er do me right in battle!
May I ne'er know that blessed peace of mind,   235
That dwells in good and pious men like thee!

CHAPLAIN I see your temper's moved, and I will trust
    you.

CHAMONT Wilt thou?

CHAPLAIN   I will, but if it ever 'scape you –

CHAMONT It never shall.

CHAPLAIN   Swear, then.
CHAMONT   I do, by all
  That's dear to me, by th'honour of my name,   240
  And that power I serve, it never shall.
CHAPLAIN Then this good day, when all the house was
  busy,
  When mirth and kind rejoicing filled each room,
  As I was walking in the grove I met them.
CHAMONT What? Met them in the grove together? Tell
  me   245
  How? Walking, standing, sitting, lying? Ha!
CHAPLAIN I by their own appointment met them there,
  Received their marriage vows and joined their hands.
CHAMONT How! Married?
CHAPLAIN   Yes, sir.
CHAMONT   Then my soul's at peace.
  But why would you delay so long to give it?   250
CHAPLAIN Not knowing what reception it may find
  With old Acasto, maybe I was too cautious
  To trust the secret from me.
CHAMONT   What's the cause
  I cannot guess – though 'tis my sister's honour,
  I do not like this marriage,   255
  Huddled i' th' dark and done at too much venture.
  The business looks with an unlucky face.
  Keep still the secret; for it ne'er shall 'scape me,
  Not ev'n to them, the new-matched pair. Farewell.
  Believe my truth and know me for thy friend.   260
                                       [Exeunt]

(*Enter* CASTALIO *and* MONIMIA)

CASTALIO Young Chamont, and the chaplain – sure, 'tis
  they!
  No matter what's contrived or who consulted,
  Since my Monimia's mine; though this sad look
  Seems no good boding omen to our bliss;
  Else, prithee, tell me why that look cast down?   265
  Why that sad sigh, as if thy heart were breaking?

MONIMIA Castalio, I am thinking what we've done.
  The heavenly powers were sure displeased today!
  For at the ceremony as we stood,
  And as your hand was kindly joined with mine,   270
  As the good priest pronounced the sacred words,
  Passion grew big and I could not forbear,
  Tears drowned my eyes, and trembling seized my soul.
  What should that mean?
CASTALIO   Oh, thou art tender all!
  Gentle and kind, as sympathising nature!   275
  When a sad story has been told, I've seen
  Thy little breasts with soft compassion swelled,
  Shove up and down, and heave like dying birds –
  But now let fear be banished, think no more
  Of danger, for there's safety in my arms;   280
  Let them receive thee. Heav'n grow jealous now!
  Sure, she's too good for any mortal creature!
  I could grow wild, and praise thee ev'n to madness.
  But wherefore do I dally with my bliss?
  The night's far spent and day draws on apace;   285
  To bed, my love, and wake till I come thither.

        (<Enter> POLYDORE at the door)

POLYDORE <aside> So hot, my brother?
MONIMIA   'Twill be impossible.
  You know your father's chamber's next to mine,
  And the least noise will certainly alarm him.
CASTALIO Impossible? Impossible? Alas!   290
  Is't possible to live one hour without thee?
  Let me behold those eyes, they'll tell me truth.
  Hast thou no longing? Art thou still the same
  Cold, icy virgin? No; th'art altered quite.
  Haste, haste to bed, and let loose all thy wishes.   295
MONIMIA 'Tis but one night, my lord, I pray be ruled.
CASTALIO Try if th'ast the power to stop a flowing tide,
  Or in a tempest make the seas be calm;
  And when that's done, I'll conquer my desires.
  No more, my blessing. What shall be the sign?   300

When shall I come? For to my joys I'll steal
As if I ne'er had paid my freedom for them.
MONIMIA Just three soft strokes upon the chamber door,
And at that signal you shall gain admittance;
But speak not the least word, for if you should,   305
'Tis surely heard, and all will be betrayed.
CASTALIO Oh, doubt it not, Monimia, our joys
Shall be as silent as the ecstatic bliss
Of souls that by intelligence* converse:
Immortal pleasures shall our senses drown,   310
Thought shall be lost, and every power dissolved.
Away, my love – first take this kiss – now haste.
I long for that to come, yet grudge each minute past.

                              [*Exit* MONIMIA]

My brother wandering too so late this way?
POLYDORE Castalio!
CASTALIO   My Polydore, how dost thou?   315
How does our father? Is he well recovered?
POLYDORE I left him happily reposed to rest;
He's still as gay as if his life were young.
But how does fair Monimia?
CASTALIO   Doubtless well.
A cruel beauty with her conquests pleased   320
Is always joyful and her mind in health.
POLYDORE Is she the same Monimia still she was?
May we not hope she's made of mortal mode?
CASTALIO She's not woman else;
Though I'm grown weary of this tedious hoping,   325
W'ave in a barren desert strayed too long.
POLYDORE Yet may relief be unexpected found,
And love's sweet manna cover all the field.
Met ye today?
CASTALIO   No, she has still avoided me.
Her brother too is jealous of her grown,   330
And has been hinting something to my father.
I wish I'd never meddled with the matter,
And would enjoin thee, Polydore –
POLYDORE   To what?

CASTALIO To leave this peevish beauty to herself.

POLYDORE What, quit my love? As soon I'd quit my
  post   335
  In fight, and like a coward run away.
  No, by my stars, I'll chase her till she yields
  To me, or meets her rescue in another.

CASTALIO Nay, she has beauty that might shake the
  leagues
  Of mighty kings, and set the world at odds.   340
  But I have wondrous reasons on my side,
  That would persuade thee, were they known.

POLYDORE   Then speak 'em.
  What are they? Came ye to her window here
  To learn 'em now? Castalio, have a care;
  Use honest dealing with your friend and brother.   345
  Believe me, I'm not with my love so blinded,
  But can discern your purpose to abuse me.
  Quit your pretences to her.

CASTALIO   Grant I do;
  You love capitulation, Polydore,
  And but upon conditions would oblige me.   350

POLYDORE You say you've reasons. Why are they
  concealed?

CASTALIO Tomorrow I may tell you.
  It is a matter of such circumstance,
  As I must well consult e'er I reveal.
  But, prithee, cease to think I would abuse thee,   355
  Till more be known.

POLYDORE   When you, Castalio, cease
  To meet Monimia unknown to me,
  And then deny it slavishly, I'll cease
  To think Castalio faithless to his friend.
  Did I not see you part this very moment?   360

CASTALIO It seems you've watched me then?

POLYDORE   I scorn the office.

CASTALIO Prithee, avoid a thing thou mayst repent.

POLYDORE That is henceforward making leagues with
  you.

CASTALIO Nay, if y'are angry, Polydore, good night.
POLYDORE Good night, Castalio, if y'are in such haste.   365
                              \<Exit CASTALIO\>

He little thinks I've overheard the appointment,
But to his chamber's gone to wait a while,
Then come and take possession of my love.
This is the utmost point of all my hope,
Or now she must, or* never can be mine.   370
Oh, for a means now how to counterplot
And disappoint this happy elder brother!
In everything we do, or undertake,
He soars above me, mount what height I can,
And keeps the start he got of me in birth.   375
– Cordelio!

                    (*Enter* PAGE)

PAGE   My lord?
POLYDORE   Come hither, boy.
Thou hast a pretty, forward, lying face,
And mayst in time expect preferment. Canst thou
Pretend to secrecy? Cajole and flatter
Thy master's follies, and assist his pleasures?   380
PAGE My lord, I could do anything for you,
And ever be a very faithful boy.
Command whate'er's your pleasure, I'll observe:
Be it to run, or watch, or to convey
A letter to a beauteous lady's bosom.   385
At least I am not dull, and soon should learn.
POLYDORE 'Tis pity then thou shouldst not be
    employed.
Go to my brother, he's in's chamber now
Undressing and preparing for his rest.
Find out some means to keep him up a while,   390
Tell him a pretty story that may please
His ear; invent a tale, no matter what.
If he should ask of me, tell him I'm gone
To bed, and sent you there to know his pleasure,
Whether he'll hunt tomorrow. *\<aside\>* Well said,

Polydore: 395
Dissemble with thy brother! *<to the* PAGE> That's one
  point –
But do not leave him till he's in his bed;
Or if he chance to walk this way again,
Follow, and do not quit him, but seem fond
To do him little offices of service.   400
Perhaps at last it may offend him, then
Retire and wait till I come in. Away!
Succeed in this, and be employed again.
PAGE Doubt not, my lord. He has been always kind
  To me; would often set me on his knees,   405
Then give me sweetmeats, call me pretty boy,
And ask me what the maids talked of at nights.
POLYDORE Run quickly then, and prosperous be thy
  wishes.

                                         [*Exit* PAGE]

Here I'm alone and fit for mischief. Now
To cheat this brother – will't be honest that   410
I heard the sign she ordered him to give?
Oh, for the art of Proteus* but to change
The happy Polydore to blest Castalio!
She's not so well acquainted with him yet,
But I may fit her arms as well as he.   415
Then, when I'm happily possessed of more
Than sense can think, all loosened into joy,
To hear my disappointed brother come
And give the unregarded signal – oh!
What a malicious pleasure will that be!   420
'Just three soft strokes against the chamber door,
But speak not the least word, for if you should,
It is surely heard, and we are both betrayed.'
How I adore a mistress that contrives
With care to lay the business of her joys!   425
One that has wit to charm the very soul,
And give a double relish to delight!
Blest Heaven, assist me but in this dear hour,
And my kind stars be but propitious now;

Dispose of me hereafter as you please.   430
– Monimia! Monimia! (*gives the sign*)
MAID (*at the window*)   Who's there?
POLYDORE 'Tis I.
MAID   My Lord Castalio?
POLYDORE   The same.
How does my love, my dear Monimia?
MAID   Oh!
She wonders much at your unkind delay!
You've stayed so long that at each little noise   435
The wind but makes, she asks if you are coming.
POLYDORE Tell her I'm here, and let the door be
    opened.

(MAID *descends*)

Now boast Castalio, triumph now and tell
Thyself strange stories of a promised bliss.

(*The door unbolts*)

It opens – ha! What means my trembling flesh!   440
Limbs, do your office and support me well.
Bear me to her, then fail me if you can.

                                                        [*Exit*]

(*Enter* CASTALIO *and* PAGE)

PAGE Indeed, my lord, 'twill be a lovely morning.
Pray let us hunt.
CASTALIO   Go, you're an idle prattler.
I'll stay at home tomorrow; if your lord   445
Thinks fit, he may command my hounds. Go, leave
    me,
I must go to bed.
PAGE   I'll wait upon your lordship,
If you think fit, and sing you to repose.
CASTALIO No, my kind boy, the night is too far wasted;
My senses too are quite disrobed of thought,   450
And ready all with me to go to rest.
Good night: commend me to my brother.

PAGE   Oh!
　 You never heard the last new song I learned.
　 It is the finest, prettiest song indeed,
　 Of my lord and lady, you know who, that were caught 455
　 Together, you know where, my lord, indeed it is.
CASTALIO You must be whipped, youngster, if you get
　 such songs as those are. <aside> What means this boy's
　 impertinence tonight?
PAGE Why, what must I sing, pray, my dear lord?   460
CASTALIO Psalms, child, psalms.
PAGE Oh, dear me! Boys that go to school learn psalms,
　 but pages that are better bred sing lampoons.*
CASTALIO Well, leave me, I'm weary.
PAGE Oh, but you promised me last time I told you 465
　 what colour my Lady Monimia's stockings were of, and
　 that she gartered them above knee, that you would give
　 me a little horse to go a-hunting upon, so you did. I'll
　 tell you no more stories, except you keep your word
　 with me.   470
CASTALIO Well, go, you trifler, and tomorrow ask me.
PAGE Indeed, my lord, I can't abide to leave you.
CASTALIO Why, wert thou instructed to attend me?
PAGE No, no, indeed, indeed, my lord, I was not; but I
　 know what I know.   475
CASTALIO What dost thou know? Death! What can all this
　 mean?
PAGE Oh! I know who loves somebody.
CASTALIO What's that to me, boy?
PAGE Nay, I know who loves you too.   480
CASTALIO That is a wonder, prithee, tell it me.
PAGE 'Tis – 'tis – I know who – but will you give me the
　 horse then?
CASTALIO I will, my child.
PAGE It is my Lady Monimia, look you – but don't you 485
　 tell her I told you. She'll give me no more playthings then.
　 I heard her say so as she lay a-bed, man.
CASTALIO Talked she of me when in her bed, Cordelio?
PAGE Yes, and I sung her the song you made too. And

she did so sigh, and so look with her eyes; and her   490
breasts did so lift up and down, I could have found
in my heart to have beat 'em, for they made me
ashamed.

CASTALIO Hark, what's that noise?
    Take this, be gone, and leave me.   495
    You knave, you little flatterer, get you gone.

[Exit PAGE]

Surely it was a noise. Hist! – Only fancy.
For all is hushed, as Nature were retired,
And the perpetual motion standing still,
So much she from her work appears to cease,   500
And every warring element's at peace.
All the wild herds are in their coverts couched;
The fishes to their banks or ooze repaired,
And to the murmurs of the waters sleep;
The feeling air's at rest and feels no noise,   505
Except of some soft breaths among the trees,
Rocking the harmless birds that rest upon 'em.
'Tis now that guided by my love I go
To take possession of Monimia's arms.
Sure Polydore's by this time gone to bed.   510
At midnight thus the usurer steals untracked
To make a visit to his hoarded gold,
And feast his eyes upon the shining Mammon.*

        (*Knocks*)

She hears me not, sure she already sleeps.
Her wishes could not brook my so long delay,   515
And her poor heart has beat itself to rest.

        (*Knocks again*)

Monimia! My angel – ha – not yet?
How long's the softest moment of delay
To a heart impatient of its pangs like mine,
In sight of ease and panting to the goal.   520
Once more –

        (*Knocks again*)

MAID *<at the window>* Who's there,
That comes thus rudely to disturb our rest?
CASTALIO 'Tis I.
MAID   Who are you? What's your name?
CASTALIO   Suppose
The Lord Castalio.
MAID   I know you not;   525
The Lord Castalio has no business here.
CASTALIO Ha! Have a care! What can this mean?
Whoe'er thou art, I charge thee to Monimia fly;
Tell her I'm here and wait upon my doom.
MAID Whoe'er you are, you may repent this outrage.   530
My lady must not be disturbed. Good night!
CASTALIO She must – tell her she shall – Go, I'm in
haste,
And bring her tidings from the state of love;
Th'are all in consultation met together,
How to reward my truth, and crown her vows.   535
MAID Sure, the man's mad.
CASTALIO   Or this will make me so.
Obey me, or by all the wrongs I suffer,
I'll scale the window and come in by force,
Let the sad consequence be what it will.

<MAID goes from the window>

This creature's trifling folly makes me mad.   540
MAID *<at the window>* My lady's answer is, you may
depart.
She says she knows you: you are Polydore
Sent by Castalio as you were today,
T'affront and do her violence again.
CASTALIO I'll not believe 't.
MAID   You may, sir.
CASTALIO   Curses blast thee! 545
MAID Well, 'tis a fine cool evening, and I hope
May cure the raging fever in your blood.
Good night!
CASTALIO   And farewell all that's just in woman!

This is contrived, a studied trick to abuse   550
My easy nature, and torment my mind.
Sure, now sh'has bound me fast and means to lord it,
To rein me hard, and ride me at her will,
Till by degrees she shape me into fool
For all her future uses. Death and torment!
'Tis impudence to think my soul will bear it.   555
Oh, I could grow ev'n wild and tear my hair.
'Tis well, Monimia, that thy empire's short,
Let but tomorrow, but tomorrow come,
And try if all thy arts appease my wrong;
Till when, be this detested place my bed,   560
(*lies down*) Where I will ruminate on woman's ills,
Laugh at myself and curse th'inconstant sex.
Faithless Monimia! Oh, Monimia!

                    (*Enter* ERNESTO)

ERNESTO   Either
  My sense has been deluded, or this way
  I heard the sound of sorrow; 'tis late night,   565
  And none whose mind's at peace would wander now.
CASTALIO Who's there?
ERNESTO   A friend.
CASTALIO   If thou art so, retire,
  And leave this place, for I would be alone.
ERNESTO Castalio! My lord, why in this posture
  Stretched on the ground? Your honest true old servant, 570
  Your poor Ernesto, cannot see you thus –
  Rise, I beseech you.
CASTALIO   If thou art Ernesto,
  As by thy honesty thou seemest to be,
  Once leave me to my folly.
ERNESTO   I can't leave you,
  And not the reason know of your disorders.   575
  Remember how, when young, I in my arms
  Have often borne you, pleased you in your pleasures,
  And sought an early share in your affection.
  Do not discard me now, but let me serve you.

CASTALIO Thou canst not serve me.
ERNESTO   Why?
CASTALIO   Because my thoughts 580
  Are full of woman. Thou, poor wretch, art past 'em.
ERNESTO I hate the sex.
CASTALIO   Then I'm thy friend, Ernesto. (*rises*)
  I'd leave the world for him that hates a woman.
  Woman, the fountain of all human frailty!
  What mighty ills have not been done by woman?   585
  Who was't betrayed the Capitol?* A woman.
  Who lost Mark Anthony the world?* A woman.
  Who was the cause of a long ten years' war,
  And laid at last Old Troy in ashes?* Woman.
  Destructive, damnable, deceitful woman.   590
  Woman, to man first as a blessing given,
  When innocence and love were in their prime;
  Happy a while in paradise they lay,
  But quickly woman longed to go astray;
  Some foolish new adventure needs must prove,   595
  And the first devil she saw she changed her love.
  To his temptation lewdly she inclined
  Her soul, and for an apple damned mankind.

<Exeunt>

Act 4, Scene 1

(ACASTO *solus*)

ACASTO Blest be the morning that has brought me
    health;
  A happy rest has softened pain away,
  And I'll forget it, though my mind's not well.
  A heavy melancholy clogs my heart,
  I droop and sigh I know not why. Dark dreams,   5
  Sick fancy's children, have been over-busy,
  And all the night played farces in my brains.
  Methought I heard the midnight raven cry,

Waked with th'imagined noise, my curtains seemed
To start, and at my feet my sons appeared   10
Like ghosts, all pale and stiff. I strove to speak,
But could not; suddenly the forms were lost,
And seemed to vanish in a bloody cloud.
'Twas odd, and for the present shook my thoughts,
But was th'effect of my distempered blood;   15
And when the health's disturbed, the mind's unruly.

(Enter POLYDORE)

Good morning, Polydore.
POLYDORE   Heaven keep your lordship.
ACASTO Have you yet seen Castalio today?
POLYDORE My lord, 'tis early day, he's hardly risen.
ACASTO Go, call him up, and meet me in the chapel.   20
                        [Exit POLYDORE]

I cannot think all has gone well tonight:
For as I waking lay (and sure my sense
Was then my own), methought I heard my son
Castalio's voice, but it seemed low and mournful;
Under my window, too, I thought I heard it.   25
M'untoward fancy could not be deceived
In everything, and I will search the truth out.

(Enter MONIMIA, and her MAID)

Already up, Monimia! You rose
Thus early surely to outshine the day!
Or was there anything that crossed your rest?   30
They were naughty thoughts that would not let you
    sleep.
MONIMIA Whatever are my thoughts, my lord, I've
    learned
By your example to correct their ills,
And morn and evening give up th'account.
ACASTO Your pardon, sweet one, I upbraid you not;   35
    Or if I would, you are so good I could not.
    Though* I'm deceived, or you are more fair today,
    For beauty's heightened in your cheeks, and all

Your charms seem up, and ready in your eyes.

MONIMIA The little share I have's so very mean, 40
  That it may easily admit addition;
  Though you, my lord, should most of all beware
  To give it too much praise, and make me proud.

ACASTO Proud of an old man's praises! No, Monimia!
  But if my prayers can work thee any good, 45
  Thou shalt not want the largest share of 'em.
  Heard you no noise tonight?

MONIMIA   Noise, my good lord?

ACASTO Aye, about midnight.

MONIMIA Indeed, my lord, I don't remember any.

ACASTO You must, sure! Went you early to rest? 50

MONIMIA About the wonted hour. (aside) Why this
    enquiry?

ACASTO And went your maid to bed too?

MONIMIA My lord, I guess so;
  I've seldom known her disobey my orders.

ACASTO Sure, goblins then, fairies haunt the dwelling. 55
  I'll have enquiry made through all the house,
  But I'll find out the cause of these disorders.
  Good day to thee, Monimia – I'll to chapel.

MONIMIA I'll but dispatch some orders to my woman,
  And wait upon your lordship there. 60

                                   [Exit ACASTO]

I fear the priest has played us false; if so
My poor Castalio loses all for me.
I wonder though, he made such haste to leave me –
Was't not unkind, Florella? Surely 'twas!
He scarce afforded one kind parting word, 65
But went away so cold. The kiss he gave me
Seemed the forced compliment of sated love.
Would I had never married!

MAID   Why?

MONIMIA   Methinks
  The scene's quite altered. I am not the same;
  I've bound up for myself a weight of cares, 70
  And how the burden will be borne, none knows.

A husband may be jealous, rigid, false;
And should Castalio e'er prove so to me,
So tender is my heart, so nice my love,
'Twould ruin and distract my rest for ever.   75
MAID   Madam, he's coming.
MONIMIA   Where, Florella? Where?
Is he returning? To my chamber lead,
I'll meet him there. The mysteries of our love
Should be kept private, as religious rites,
From the unhallowed view of common eyes.   80

            [*Exeunt* MONIMIA *and* MAID]

(*Enter* CASTALIO)

CASTALIO   Wished morning's come! And now upon the
   plains
And distant mountains, where they feed their flocks,
The happy shepherds leave their homely huts,
And with their pipes proclaim the new-born day.
The lusty swain comes with his well-filled scrip*   85
Of healthful viands, which, when hunger calls,
With much content and appetite he eats,
To follow in the fields his daily toil,
And dress* the grateful glebe* that yields him fruits.
The beasts that under the warm hedges slept,   90
And weathered out the cold bleak night, are up,
And looking towards the neighbouring pastures, raise
The voice, and bid their fellow brutes good morrow.
The cheerful birds too, on the tops of trees,
Assemble all in choirs, and with their notes   95
Salute and welcome up the rising sun.
There's no condition sure so cursed as mine;
I'm married – 'sdeath, I'm sped!* How like a dog
Looked Hercules, thus to a distaff chained!*
Monimia! Oh, Monimia!   100

(*Enter* MONIMIA, *and* MAID)

MONIMIA   I come,
I fly to my adored Castalio's arms,

My wishes' lord. May every morn begin
Like this, and with our days our loves renew.
Now I may hope y'are satisfied – (*looking
  languishingly on him*)

CASTALIO   I am
Well satisfied, that thou art – oh –

MONIMIA   What? Speak –   105
Art thou not well, Castalio? Come, lean
Upon my breasts and tell me where's thy pain.

CASTALIO 'Tis here! 'Tis in my head; 'tis in my heart,
'Tis everywhere; it rages like a madness,
And I most wonder how my reason holds.   110
Nay, wonder not, Monimia; the slave
You thought you had secured within my breast
Is grown a rebel, and has broke his chain;
And now he walks there like a lord at large.

MONIMIA Am I not then your wife, your loved
  Monimia?   115
I once was so, or I've most strangely dreamt.
What ails my love?

CASTALIO   What e'er thy dreams have been,
Thy waking thoughts ne'er meant Castalio well.
No more, Monimia, of your sex's arts,
They're useless all. I'm not that pliant tool,   120
That necessary utensil you'd make me,
I know my charter better – I am man,
Obstinate man, and will not be enslaved.

MONIMIA You shall not fear't. Indeed my nature's easy;
I'll ever live your most obedient wife,   125
Nor ever any privilege pretend
Beyond your will, for that shall be my law.
Indeed I will not.

CASTALIO   Nay, you shall not, madam.
By yon bright heaven, you shall not. All the day
I'll play the tyrant, and at night forsake thee,   130
Till by afflictions and continued cares,
I've worn thee to a homely household drudge.
Nay, if I've any too, thou shalt be made

Subservient to all my looser pleasures,
For thou hast wronged Castalio.

MONIMIA   No more!   135
Oh, kill me here, or tell me my offence;
I'll never quit you else, but on these knees,
Thus follow you all day, till th'are worn bare,
And hang upon you like a drowning creature.
Castalio –

CASTALIO   Away! Last night, last night –   140

MONIMIA   It was our wedding night.

CASTALIO   No more, forget it –

MONIMIA   Why? Do you then repent?

CASTALIO   I do.

MONIMIA   Oh heav'n!
And will you leave me thus? Help, help, Florella –

   (*He drags her to the door and breaks from her*)

                              <*Exit* CASTALIO>

Help me to hold this yet loved, cruel man.
Oh, my heart breaks – I'm dying – Oh – stand off –   145
I'll not indulge this woman's weakness; still
Chafed and fomented, let my heart swell on,
Till with its injuries it burst, and shake
With the dire blow this prison to the earth.

MAID   What sad mistake has been the cause of this?   150

MONIMIA   Castalio! Oh, how often has he swore
Nature should change, the sun and stars grow dark,
E'er he would falsify his vows to me.
Make haste, confusion, then! Sun, lose thy light,
And stars drop dead with sorrow to the earth;   155
For my Castalio's false –

MAID   Unhappy day!

MONIMIA   False as the wind, the water, or the weather!
Cruel as tigers o'er their trembling prey.
I feel him in my breast, he tears my heart,
And at each sigh he drinks the gushing blood –   160
Must I be long in pain?

                              [*Exit* MAID]

(*Enter* CHAMONT)

CHAMONT In tears, Monimia?

MONIMIA   Whoe'er thou art,
Leave me alone to my beloved despair.

CHAMONT Lift up thy eyes and see who comes to cheer
   thee.
Tell me the story of thy wrongs, and then   165
See if my soul has rest till thou hast justice.

MONIMIA My brother!

CHAMONT   Yes, Monimia, if thou think'st
That I deserve the name, I am thy brother.

MONIMIA Oh, Castalio!

CHAMONT Ha!   170
Name me that name again! My soul's on fire
Till I know all. There's meaning in that name:
I know he is thy husband, therefore trust me
With all the following truth –

MONIMIA   Indeed, Chamont,
There's nothing in it but the fault of nature.   175
I'm often thus seized suddenly with grief,
I know not why.

CHAMONT   You use me ill, Monimia;
And I might think with justice most severely
Of this unfaithful dealing with your brother.

MONIMIA Truly, I am not to blame. Suppose I'm fond,   180
And grieve for what as much may please another:
Should I upbraid the dearest friend on earth
For the first fault? You would not do so, would you?

CHAMONT Not if I'd cause to think it was a friend.

MONIMIA Why do you then call this unfaithful dealing?   185
I ne'er concealed my soul from you before.
Bear with me now, and search my wounds no farther,
For every probing pains me to the heart.

CHAMONT 'Tis sign there's danger in't and must be
   prevented.
Where's your new husband? Still that thought disturbs
   you.   190
What, only answer me with tears? Castalio!

Nay, now they stream –
Cruel, unkind Castalio! Is't not so?
MONIMIA I cannot speak, grief flows so fast upon me,
It chokes, and will not let me tell the cause.   195
Oh!
CHAMONT   My Monimia! To my soul thou'rt dear
As honour to my name; dear as the light
To eyes but just restored and healed of blindness.
Why wilt thou not repose within my breast
The anguish that torments thee?
MONIMIA   Oh! I dare not.   200
CHAMONT I have no friend but thee – we must confide
In one another. Two unhappy orphans,
Alas, we are, and when I see thee grieve,
Methinks it is a part of me that suffers.
MONIMIA Oh, shouldst thou know the cause of my
    lamenting,   205
I am satisfied, Chamont, that thou wouldst scorn me.
Thou wouldst despise the abject lost Monimia,
No more wouldst praise this beauty. But
When in some cell distracted, as I shall be,
Thou seest me lie – these unregarded locks   210
Matted like furies' tresses; my poor limbs
Chained to the ground, and 'stead of the delights
Which happy lovers taste, my keeper's stripes,
A bed of straw, and a coarse wooden dish
Of wretched sustenance – when thus thou seest me,   215
Prithee have charity and pity for me.
Let me enjoy this thought.
CHAMONT   Why wilt thou rack
My soul so long, Monimia? Ease me quickly,
Or thou wilt run me into madness first.
MONIMIA Could you be secret?
CHAMONT   Secret as the grave.   220
MONIMIA But when I've told you, will you keep your
    fury
Within its bounds? Will you not do some rash
And horrid* mischief? For indeed, Chamont,

You would not think how hardly I've been used
From a near friend; from one that has my soul   225
A slave, and therefore treats it like a tyrant.

CHAMONT I will be calm, but has Castalio wronged
    thee?
  Has he already wasted all his love?
  What has he done? Quickly! For I'm all trembling
  With expectation of a horrid tale.   230

MONIMIA Oh, could you think it!

CHAMONT   What?

MONIMIA   I fear he'll kill me.

CHAMONT Ha!

MONIMIA Indeed I do, he's strangely cruel to me,
  Which, if it lasts, I'm sure must break my heart.

CHAMONT What has he done?

MONIMIA   Most barbarously used me.   235
  Nothing so kind as he, when in my arms,
  In thousand kisses, tender sighs and joys,
  Not to be thought again, the night was wasted.
  At dawn of day, he rose and left his conquest;
  But when we met, and I with open arms   240
  Ran to embrace the lord of all my wishes,
  Oh then! –

CHAMONT Go on!

MONIMIA   He threw me from his breast,
  Like a detested sin.

CHAMONT   How!

MONIMIA   As I hung too
  Upon his knees, and begged to know the cause,
  He dragged me like a slave upon the earth,   245
  And had no pity on my cries.

CHAMONT   How! Did he
  Dash thee disdainfully away with scorn?

MONIMIA He did; and more, I fear, will ne'er be friends,
  Though I still love him with unbated passion.

CHAMONT What, throw thee from him?

MONIMIA   Yes, indeed he did.   250

CHAMONT So may this arm

Throw him to the earth, like a dead dog despised!
Lameness and leprosy, blindness and lunacy,
Poverty, shame, pride, and the name of villain
Light on me, if, Castalio, I forgive thee!   255
MONIMIA Nay, now, Chamont, art thou unkind as he is.
Didst thou not promise me thou wouldst be calm?
Keep my disgrace concealed? Why shouldst thou kill
    him?
By all my love, this arm should do him vengeance.
Alas, I love him still, and though I ne'er   260
Clasp him again within these longing arms,
Yet bless him, bless him, gods, where'er he goes.

(*Enter* ACASTO)

ACASTO Sure, some ill fate is towards me. In my house
I only meet with oddness and disorder:
Each vassal has a wild distracted face,   265
And looks as full of business as a blockhead
In times of danger. Just this very moment
I met Castalio, too –
CHAMONT   Then you met a villain.
ACASTO Ha!
CHAMONT   Yes, a villain.
ACASTO   Have a care, young soldier.
How thou'rt too busy with Acasto's fame!   270
I have a sword, my arm's good old acquaintance.
Villain, to thee –
CHAMONT   Curse on thy scandalous age
Which hinders me to rush upon thy throat,
And tear the root up of that cursed bramble!
ACASTO Ungrateful ruffian! Sure my good old friend   275
Was ne'er thy father; nothing of him's in thee.
What have I done in my unhappy age,
To be thus used? I scorn to upbraid thee, boy,
But I could put thee in remembrance –
CHAMONT   Do.
ACASTO I scorn it –
CHAMONT   No, I'll calmly hear the story,   280

For I would fain know all, to see which scale
Weighs most – Ha! Is not that good old Acasto?
What have I done? Can you forgive this folly?
ACASTO Why dost thou ask it?
CHAMONT   'Twas the rude overflowing
  Of too much passion; pray, my lord, forgive me.
    (*kneels*)   285
ACASTO Mock me not, youth, I can revenge a wrong.
CHAMONT I know it well, but for this thought of mine,
  Pity a madman's frenzy and forget it.
ACASTO I will, but henceforth, prithee, be more kind.
  (*raises him*) Whence came the cause?
CHAMONT   Indeed, I've been to blame,   290
  But I'll learn better, for you've been my father –
  You've been her father, too – (*takes* MONIMIA *by the
    hand*)
ACASTO   Forbear the prologue –
  And let me know the substance of thy tale.
CHAMONT You took her up a little tender flower,
  Just sprouted on a bank, which the next frost   295
  Had nipped; and with a careful loving hand
  Transplanted her into your own fair garden,
  Where the sun always shines. There long she
    flourished,
  Grew sweet to sense, and lovely to the eye,
  Till at the last a cruel spoiler came,   300
  Cropped this fair rose, and rifled all its sweetness,
  Then cast it like a loathsome weed away.
ACASTO You talk to me in parables, Chamont.
  You may have known that I'm no wordy man:
  Fine speeches are the instruments of knaves   305
  Or fools, that use 'em when they want good sense;
  But honesty
  Needs no disguise nor ornament: be plain.
CHAMONT Your son –
ACASTO   I've two, and both I hope have honour.
CHAMONT I hope so too – but –
ACASTO   Speak.

CHAMONT	I must inform you	310

Once more, Castalio –

ACASTO   Still Castalio!

CHAMONT   Yes,

Your son Castalio has wronged Monimia.

ACASTO Ha! Wronged her?

CHAMONT   Married her.

ACASTO   I'm sorry for't.

CHAMONT Why sorry?

By yon blest heaven there's not a lord   315

But might be proud to take her to his heart.

ACASTO I'll not deny't.

CHAMONT   You dare not, by the gods,

You dare not – all your family combined

In one damned falsehood to outdo Castalio

Dare not deny't.

ACASTO   How has Castalio wronged her?   320

CHAMONT Ask that of him. I say my sister's wronged;

Monimia, my sister, born as high

And noble as Castalio – do her justice,

Or by the gods, I'll lay a scene of blood

Shall make this dwelling horrible to nature.   325

I'll do't. Hark you, my lord, your son Castalio –

Take him to your closet, and there teach him manners.

ACASTO You shall have justice.

CHAMONT   Nay – I will have justice.

Who'll sleep in safety that has done me wrong?

My lord, I'll not disturb you to repeat   330

The cause of this. I beg you (to preserve

Your house's honour) ask it of Castalio.

ACASTO I will.

CHAMONT   Till then, farewell –

                           [*Exit* CHAMONT]

ACASTO   Farewell, proud boy.

Monimia!

MONIMIA   My lord?

ACASTO   You are my daughter.

MONIMIA I am, my lord, if you'll vouchsafe to own me. 335

ACASTO When you'll complain to me, I'll prove a father.

[*Exit* ACASTO]

MONIMIA Now I'm undone for ever. Who on earth
  Is there so wretched as Monimia?
  First by Castalio cruelly forsaken;
  I've lost Acasto: his parting frowns   340
  May well instruct me rage is in his heart.
  I shall be next abandoned to my fortune,
  Thrust out a naked wanderer to the world,
  And branded for the mischievous Monimia.
  What will become of me? My cruel brother   345
  Is framing mischief too, for aught I know,
  That may produce bloodshed, and horrid murder.
  I would not be the cause of one man's death
  To reign the empress of the earth – nay, more,
  I'd rather lose for ever my Castalio,   350
  My dear, unkind Castalio.

(*Enter* POLYDORE)

POLYDORE   Monimia, weeping!
  So morning dews on new-blown roses lodge,
  By the sun's amorous heat to be exhaled.
  I come, my love, to kiss all sorrow from thee.
  What mean these sighs? And why thus beats thy heart? 355
MONIMIA Let me alone to sorrow. 'Tis a cause
  None shall e'er know, but it shall with me die.
POLYDORE Happy, Monimia, he to whom these sighs,
  These tears, and all these languishings are paid!
  I am no stranger to your dearest secret;   360
  I know your heart was never meant for me,
  That jewel's for an elder brother's price.
MONIMIA My lord?
POLYDORE   Nay, wonder not; last night I heard
  His oaths, your vows, and to my torment saw
  Your wild embraces; heard the'appointment made – 365
  – I did, Monimia, and I cursed the sound.
  Wilt thou be sworn, my love? Wilt thou be ne'er
  Unkind again?

MONIMIA   Banish such fruitless hopes!
  Have you sworn constancy to my undoing?
  Will you be ne'er my friend again?   370
POLYDORE What means my love?
MONIMIA   Away! What meant my lord
  Last night?
POLYDORE Is that a question now to be demanded?
  I hope Monimia was not much displeased.
MONIMIA Was it well done to treat me like a prostitute? 375
  T'assault my lodging at the dead of night,
  And threaten me if I denied admittance?
  You said you were Castalio –
POLYDORE   By those eyes,
  It was the same. I spent my time much better:
  I tell thee, ill-natured fair one, I was posted   380
  To more advantage on a pleasant hill
  Of springing joy, and everlasting sweetness.
MONIMIA Ha – have a care –
POLYDORE   Where is the danger near me?
MONIMIA I fear y'are on a rock will wreck your quiet,
  And drown your soul in wretchedness for ever;   385
  A thousand horrid thoughts crowd on my memory.
  Will you be kind and answer me one question?
POLYDORE I'd trust thee with my life on those soft
    breasts;
  Breathe out the choicest secrets of my heart,
  Till I had nothing in it left but love.   390
MONIMIA Nay, I'll conjure you by the gods and angels,
  By the honour of your name, that's most concerned,
  To tell me, Polydore, and tell me truly,
  Where did you rest last night?
POLYDORE   Within thy arms
  I triumphed – rest had been my foe.
MONIMIA   'Tis done – (she faints) 395
POLYDORE She faints! – No help? Who waits? A curse
  Upon my vanity that could not keep
  The secret of my happiness in silence.
  Confusion! We shall be surprised anon,

And consequently all must be betrayed –   400
Monimia! She breathes – Monimia! –

MONIMIA   Well –
Let mischiefs multiply! Let every hour
Of my loathed life yield me increase of horror!
Oh, let the sun to these unhappy eyes
Ne'er shine again, but be eclipsed forever!   405
May everything I look on seem a prodigy
To fill my soul with terrors – till I quite
Forget I ever had humanity,
And grow a curser of the works of nature!

POLYDORE What means all this?

MONIMIA   Oh, Polydore, if all   410
The friendship e'er you vowed to good Castalio
Be not a falsehood; if you ever loved
Your brother, you've undone yourself and me.

POLYDORE Which way? Can ruin reach the man that's
    rich,
As I am in possession of your sweetness?   415

MONIMIA Oh, I'm his wife!

POLYDORE   What says Monimia? Ha! –
Speak that again –

MONIMIA   I am Castalio's wife.

POLYDORE His married, wedded wife?

MONIMIA   Yesterday's sun
Saw it performed.

POLYDORE   And then have I enjoyed
My brother's wife?

MONIMIA   As surely as we both   420
Must taste of misery, that guilt is thine.

POLYDORE Must we be miserable then?

MONIMIA   Oh!

POLYDORE Oh! Thou mayst yet be happy.

MONIMIA   Couldst thou be
Happy with such a weight upon thy soul?

POLYDORE It may be yet a secret. I'll go try   425
To reconcile and bring Castalio to thee,
Whilst from the world I take myself away.

And waste my life in penance for my sin.

MONIMIA Then thou wouldst more undo me: heap a
  load
  Of added sins upon my wretched head.   430
  Wouldst thou again have me betray thy brother
  And bring pollution to his arms? Cursed thought!
  Oh, when shall I be mad indeed!

POLYDORE   Nay, then,
  Let us embrace, and from this very moment
  Vow an eternal misery together.   435

MONIMIA And wilt thou be a very faithful wretch?
  Never grow fond of cheerful peace again?
  Wilt with me study to be unhappy,
  And find out ways how to increase affliction?

POLYDORE We'll institute new arts unknown before,   440
  To vary plagues, and make 'em look like new ones.
  First, if the fruit of our detested joy,
  A child, be born, it shall be murdered –

MONIMIA   No!
  Sure, that may live.

POLYDORE   Why?

MONIMIA   To become a thing
  More wretched than its parents, to be branded   445
  With all our infamy, and curse its birth.

POLYDORE That's well contrived! Then thus let's go
    together
  Full of our guilt, distracted where to roam,
  Like the first wretched pair expelled their Paradise.
  Let's find some place where adders nest in winter,   450
  Loathsome and venomous; where poisons hang
  Like gums upon the walls; where witches meet
  By night and feed upon some pampered imp,
  Fat with the blood of babes. There we'll inhabit,
  And live up to the height of desperation: 455
  Desire shall languish like a withering flower,
  And no distinction of the sex be thought of;
  Horrors shall fright me from those pleasing harms,
  And I'll no more be caught with beauty's charms –

But when I'm dying, take me in thy arms.   460

                                              [*Exeunt*]

Act 5, Scene 1

(CASTALIO, *lying on the ground <music playing>*)

Song*

Come, all ye youths, whose hearts e'er bled
    By cruel beauty's pride,
Bring each a garland on his head
    Let none his sorrows hide,
But hand in hand around me move   5
Singing the saddest tales of love;
And see, when your complaints ye join,
If all your wrongs can equal mine.

2

The happiest mortal once was I,
    My heart no sorrows knew.   10
Pity the pain with which I die,
    But ask not whence it grew.
Yet if a tempting fair you find
That's very lovely, very kind,
Though bright as Heaven whose stamp she bears,   15
Think of my fate, and shun her snares.

CASTALIO See where the deer trot after one another:
    Male, female, father, daughter, mother, son,
    Brother and sister mingled all together;
    No discontent they know, but in delightful   20
    Wildness and freedom, pleasant springs, fresh herbage,
    Calm harbours, lusty health and innocence
    Enjoy their portion. If they see a man,
    How will they turn together all and gaze
    Upon the monster –   25
    Once in a season too, they taste of love:

Only the beast of reason is its slave,
And in that folly drudges all the year.

(*Enter* ACASTO)

ACASTO Castalio! Castalio!
CASTALIO   Who's there
So wretched but to name Castalio?   30
ACASTO I hope my message may succeed.
CASTALIO   My father!
'Tis joy to see you, though where sorrow's nourished.
ACASTO I'm come in beauty's cause, you'll guess the
    rest.
CASTALIO A woman! If you love my peace of mind,
Name not a woman to me; but to think   35
Of woman were enough to taint my brains,
Till they foment to madness! Oh, my father!
ACASTO What ails my boy?
CASTALIO   A woman is the thing
I would forget, and blot from my remembrance.
ACASTO Forget Monimia?
CASTALIO   She to choose – Monimia!   40
The very sound's ungrateful to my sense.
ACASTO This might seem strange, but you I've found
    will hide
Your heart from me – you dare not trust to your
    father.
CASTALIO No more Monimia.
ACASTO   Is she not your wife?
CASTALIO So much the worse: who loves to hear of
    wife?   45
When you would give all worldly plagues a name
Worse than they have already, call 'em wife!
But a new-married wife's a seeming mischief,
Full of herself. Why, what a deal of horror
Has that poor wretch to come that wedded yesterday!   50
ACASTO Castalio, you must go along with me,
And see Monimia.
CASTALIO   Sure my lord but mocks me –

Go see Monimia? Pray, my lord, excuse me,
And leave the conduct of this part of life
To my own choice.

ACASTO   I say, no more dispute.   55
Complaints are made to me that you have wronged
    her.

CASTALIO Who has complained?

ACASTO Her brother to my face proclaimed her
    wronged,
And in such terms they've warmed me.

CASTALIO What terms? Her brother? Heavens!   60
Where learned she that?
What, does she send her hero with defiance?
He durst not sure affront you?

ACASTO   No, not much,
But –

CASTALIO Speak, what said he?

ACASTO   That thou wert a villain:
Methinks I would not have thee thought a villain.   65

CASTALIO Shame on the ill-mannered brute!
Your age secured him, he durst not else have said so.

ACASTO By my sword,
I would not see thee wronged and bear it vilely,*
Though I have passed my word she shall have justice. 70

CASTALIO Justice! To give her justice would undo her.
Think you this solitude I now had chosen,
Left joys just opening to my sense, sought here
A place to curse my fate in, measured out
My grave at length, wished* to have grown one piece 75
With this cold clay – and all without a cause?

(*Enter* CHAMONT)

CHAMONT Where is the hero famous and renowned
For wronging innocence, and breaking vows;
Whose mighty spirit, and whose stubborn heart,
No woman can appease, nor man provoke?   80

ACASTO I guess, Chamont, you come to seek Castalio?

CHAMONT I come to seek the husband of Monimia.

CASTALIO The slave is here.

CHAMONT   I thought e'er now to'ave found you
  Atoning for the ills you've done Chamont;
  For you have wronged the dearest part of him.   85
  Monimia, young lord, weeps in this heart;
  And all the tears thy injuries have drawn
  From her poor eyes, are drops of blood from hence.

CASTALIO Then you are Chamont?

CHAMONT   Yes, and I hope no stranger
  To great Castalio.

CASTALIO   I've heard of such a man   90
  That has been very busy with my honour:
  I own I'm much indebted to you, sir,
  And here return the villain back again
  You sent me by my father.

CHAMONT   Thus I'll thank you. (draws)

ACASTO By this good sword, who first presumes to
    violence   95
  Makes me his foe – (draws and interposes)
  (to CASTALIO) Young man, it once was thought
  I was fit guardian of my house's honour,
  And you might trust your share with me – (to
    CHAMONT) For you,
  Young soldier, I must tell you, you have wronged me.
  I promised you to do Monimia right,   100
  And thought my word a pledge I would not forfeit;
  But you, I find, would fright us to performance.

CASTALIO Sir, in my younger years with care you taught
    me
  That brave revenge was due to injured honour;
  Oppose not then the justice of my sword,   105
  Lest you should make me jealous* of your love.

CHAMONT Into thy father's arms thou fly'st for safety,
  Because thou know'st the place is sanctified
  With the remembrance of an ancient friendship.

CASTALIO I am a villain if I will not seek thee   110
  Till I may be revenged for all the wrongs
  Done me by that ungrateful fair thou plead'st for.

CHAMONT She wrong thee! By the fury in my heart,
Thy father's honour's not above Monimia's;
Nor was thy mother's truth and virtue fairer.   115
ACASTO Boy, don't disturb the ashes of the dead
With thy capricious follies. The remembrance
Of the loved creature that once filled these arms –
CHAMONT Has not been wronged.
CASTALIO   It shall not.
CHAMONT   No, nor shall
Monimia, though a helpless orphan, destitute   120
Of friends and fortune, though the unhappy sister
Of poor Chamont, whose sword is all his portion,
Be oppressed by thee, thou proud imperious traitor.
CASTALIO <to ACASTO who holds him>
Ha! Let me free.
CHAMONT Come both.

(*Enter* SERINA)

SERINA   Alas! Alas!
The cause of these disorders, my Chamont?   125
Who is't has wronged thee?
CASTALIO   Now where art thou fled
For shelter?
CHAMONT Come from thine, and see what safeguard
Shall then betray my fears.
SERINA   Cruel Castalio,
Sheathe up thy angry sword, and don't affright me.
Chamont, let once Serina calm thy breast: 130
If any of thy friends have done thee injuries,
I'll be revenged, and love thee better for't.
CASTALIO Sir, if you'd have me think you did not take
This opportunity to show your vanity,
Let's meet some other time, when by ourselves   135
We fairly may dispute our wrongs together.
CHAMONT Till then I am Castalio's friend.
CASTALIO   Serina,
Farewell, I wish much happiness attend you.
SERINA Chamont's the dearest thing I have on earth;

Give me Chamont, and let the world forsake me. 140
CHAMONT Witness the gods, how happy I am in thee!
No beauteous blossom of the fragrant spring,
Though the fair child of Nature newly born,
Can be so lovely. Angry, unkind Castalio,
Suppose I should a while lay by my passions, 145
And be a beggar in Monimia's cause,
Might I be heard?
CASTALIO   Sir, 'twas my last request
You would; though you, I find, will not be satisfied:
So, in a word, Monimia is my scorn.
She basely sent you here to try my fears; 150
That was your business.
No artful prostitute, in falsehoods practised,
To make advantage of her coxcomb's follies,
Could have done more – disquiet vex her for't.
CHAMONT Farewell!
CASTALIO   Farewell.

                    [*Exeunt* CHAMONT *and* SERINA]

                    – My father, you seem
troubled. 155
ACASTO Would I had been absent when this boisterous
    brave
Came to disturb thee thus. I'm grieved I hindered
Thy just resentment – But Monimia –
CASTALIO   Damn her!
ACASTO Don't curse her.
CASTALIO   Did I?
ACASTO   Yes.
CASTALIO   I'm sorry for it.
ACASTO Methinks, if, as* I guess, the fault's but small, 160
    It might be pardoned.
CASTALIO   No.
ACASTO   What has she done?
CASTALIO That she's my wife, may Heaven and you
    forgive me.
ACASTO Be reconciled then.
CASTALIO   No.

ACASTO   Go see her.
CASTALIO   No.
ACASTO I'll send and bring her hither.
CASTALIO   No.
ACASTO   For my sake,
    Castalio, and the quiet of my age.   165
CASTALIO Why will you urge a thing my nature starts
    at?
ACASTO Prithee forgive her.
CASTALIO   Lightnings first shall blast me.
    I tell you were she prostrate at my feet,
    Full of her sex's best dissembled sorrows,
    And all that wondrous beauty of her own,   170
    My heart might break, but it should never soften.

(Enter FLORELLA)

FLORELLA My lord, where are you? Oh, Castalio!
ACASTO Hark –
CASTALIO What's that?
FLORELLA Oh, show me quickly where's Castalio.   175
ACASTO Why, what's the business?
FLORELLA   Oh, the poor Monimia!
CASTALIO Ha?
ACASTO   What's the matter?
FLORELLA   Hurried by despair,
    She flies with fury over all the house,
    Through every room of each apartment crying,
    'Where's my Castalio? Give me my Castalio!'   180
    Except she sees you, sure she'll grow distracted.
CASTALIO Ha! Will she? Does she name Castalio?
    And with such tenderness? Conduct me quickly
    To the poor lovely mourner. Oh, my father.
ACASTO Then wilt thou go? Blessings attend thy
      purpose!   185
CASTALIO I cannot hear Monimia's soul's in sadness,
    And be a man – my heart will not forget her –
    But do not tell the world you saw this of me.
ACASTO Delay not then, but haste and cheer thy love.

CASTALIO Oh, I will throw m'impatient arms about her,   190
  In her soft bosom sigh my soul to peace,
  Till through the panting breast she finds the way
  To mould my heart, and make it what she will.
  Monimia! Oh!

                    [*Exeunt* ACASTO, CASTALIO]

            (*Enter* MONIMIA)

MONIMIA   Stand off and give me room.
  I will not rest till I have found Castalio,   195
  My wishes' lord, comely as rising day,
  Amidst ten thousand eminently known.
  Flowers spring where'er he treads,* his eyes
  Fountains of brightness cheering all about him!
  When will they shine on me? Oh stay, my soul!   200
  I cannot die in peace till I have seen him.

            (CASTALIO *re-enters*)

CASTALIO Who talks of dying with a voice so sweet
  That life's in love with it?
MONIMIA   Hark! 'Tis he that answers:
  So in a camp, though at the dead of night,
  If but the trumpet's cheerful noise is heard,   205
  All at the signal leap from downy rest,
  And every heart awakes as mine does now.
  Where art thou?
CASTALIO Here, my love.
MONIMIA   No nearer, lest I vanish.
CASTALIO Have I been in a dream then all this while?   210
  And art thou but the shadow of Monimia?
  Why dost thou fly me thus?
MONIMIA Oh, were it possible that we could drown
  In dark oblivion but a few past hours,
  We might be happy.   215
CASTALIO Is it then so hard, Monimia, to forgive
  A fault, where humble love, like mine, implores thee?
  For I must love thee, though it prove my ruin.
  Which way shall I court thee?

What shall I do to be enough thy slave,   220
And satisfy the lovely pride that's in thee?
I'll kneel to thee, and weep a flood before thee.
Yet prithee, tyrant, break not quite my heart;
But when my task of penitence is done,
Heal it again and comfort me with love.   225

MONIMIA If I am dumb, Castalio, and want words
  To pay thee back this mighty tenderness,
  It is because I look on thee with horror,
  And cannot see the man I so have wronged.

CASTALIO Thou hast not wronged me.

MONIMIA   Ah! Alas, thou talk'st 230
  Just as thy poor heart thinks. Have I not wronged
    thee?

CASTALIO No.

MONIMIA   Still thou wand'rest in the dark, Castalio.
  But wilt e'er long stumble on horrid danger.

CASTALIO What means my love?

MONIMIA   Couldst thou but forgive me?

CASTALIO What?   235

MONIMIA For my fault last night. Alas, thou canst not.

CASTALIO I can, and do.

MONIMIA   Thus crawling on the earth
  Would I that pardon meet, the only thing
  Can make me view the face of Heaven with hope.

CASTALIO Then let's draw near.

MONIMIA   Ah me!

CASTALIO   So in the fields, 240
  When the destroyer has been out for prey,
  The scattered lovers of the feathered kind,
  Seeking when danger's passed to meet again,
  Make moan, and call, by such degrees approach;
  Till joying thus they bill and spread their wings, 245
  Murmuring love and joy, their fears are over.

MONIMIA Yet have a care – be not too fond of peace,
  Lest in pursuance of the goodly quarry,
  Thou meet a disappointment that distracts thee.

CASTALIO My better angel, then do thou inform me   250

What danger threatens me, and where it lies.
Why didst thou (prithee smile and tell me why),
When I stood waiting underneath the window,
Quaking with fierce and violent desires –
The dropping dews fell cold upon my head,   255
Darkness enclosed, and the winds whistled round me,
Which, with my mournful sighs, made such sad music
As might have moved the hardest heart – why wert
  thou
Deaf to my cries and senseless of my pains?
MONIMIA Did I not beg thee to forbear inquiry?   260
  Read'st thou not something in my face that speaks
  Wonderful change and horror from within me?
CASTALIO Then there is something yet which I've not
  known.
  What dost thou mean by horror and forbearance
  Of more inquiry? Tell me, I beg thee, tell me;   265
  And do not betray me to a second madness.
MONIMIA Must I?
CASTALIO   If labouring in the pangs of death
  Thou wouldst do anything to give me ease,
  Unfold this riddle e'er my thoughts grow wild
  And let in fears of ugly form upon me.   270
MONIMIA My heart won't let me speak it; but
  remember,
  Monimia, poor Monimia, tells thee this:
  We ne'er must meet again –
CASTALIO   What means my destiny?
  For all my good or evil fate dwells in thee.
  Ne'er meet again?
MONIMIA   No, never.
CASTALIO   Where's the power   275
  On earth that dares not look like thee and say so?
  Thou art my heart's inheritance, I served
  A long and painful, faithful slavery for thee,*
  And who shall rob me of the dear-bought blessing?
MONIMIA Time will clear all, but now let this content
  you: 280

Heaven has decreed, and therefore I've resolved
(With torment I must tell it thee, Castalio)
Ever to be a stranger to thy love;
In some far distant country waste my life,
And from this day to see thy face no more.   285
CASTALIO Where am I? Sure I wander midst
    enchantment,
And never more shall find the way to rest.
But, oh Monimia, art th'indeed resolved
To punish me with everlasting absence?
Why turn'st thou from me? I'm alone already: 290
Methinks I stand upon a naked beach,
Sighing to winds, and to the seas complaining,
Whilst afar off the vessel sails away
Where all the treasure of my soul's embarked.
Wilt thou not turn? Oh, could those eyes but speak   295
I should know all, for love is pregnant in 'em.
They swell, they press their beams upon me still.
Wilt thou not speak? If we must part for ever,
Give me but one kind word to think upon
And please myself withal whilst my heart's breaking.   300
MONIMIA Ah, poor Castalio!

                                        [*Exit* MONIMIA]

CASTALIO   Pity, by the gods!
She pities me! Then thou wilt go eternally?
What means all this? Why all this stir to plague
A single wretch? If but your words can shake
This world to atoms, why so much ado   305
With me? Think me but dead and lay me so.

                    (*Enter* POLYDORE)

POLYDORE To live, and live a torment to myself –
What dog would bear't that knew but his condition?
We have little knowledge, and that makes us cowards,
Because it cannot tell us what's to come.   310
CASTALIO Who's there?
POLYDORE Why, what art thou?
CASTALIO My brother Polydore!

POLYDORE My name is Polydore.

CASTALIO Canst thou inform me? 315

POLYDORE Of what?

CASTALIO Of my Monimia.

POLYDORE No. Good day.

CASTALIO In haste?
Methinks my Polydore appears in sadness.

POLYDORE Indeed, and so to me does my Castalio.

CASTALIO Do I?

POLYDORE Thou dost.

CASTALIO Alas, I've wondrous reason! 320
I'm strangely altered, brother, since I saw thee.

POLYDORE Why?

CASTALIO Oh, to tell thee would but put thy heart
To pain. Let me embrace thee but a little,
And weep upon thy neck. I would repose
Within thy friendly bosom all my follies, 325
For thou wilt pardon 'em, because they're mine.

POLYDORE Be not too credulous. Consider first,
Friends may be false. Is there no friendship false?

CASTALIO Why dost thou ask me that? Does this appear
Like a false friendship, when with open arms 330
And streaming eyes I run upon thy breast?
Oh, 'tis in thee alone I must have comfort.

POLYDORE I fear, Castalio, I have none to give thee.

CASTALIO Dost thou not love me then?

POLYDORE Oh, more than life.
I never had a thought of my Castalio 335
Might wrong the friendship we had vowed together.
Hast thou dealt so by me?

CASTALIO I hope I have.

POLYDORE Then tell me, why this mourning, this
disorder?

CASTALIO Oh, Polydore, I know not how to tell thee.
Shame rises in my face, and interrupts 340
The story of my tongue.

POLYDORE I grieve my friend
Knows anything which he's ashamed to tell me.

Or didst thou e'er conceal thy thoughts from Polydore?

CASTALIO Oh, much too oft.
  But let me here conjure thee,   345
  By all the kind affection of a brother
  (For I am ashamed to call myself thy friend),
  Forgive me.

POLYDORE Well, go on.

CASTALIO Our destiny contrived   350
  To plague us both with one unhappy love!
  Thou like a friend, a constant, generous friend,
  In its first pangs didst trust me with thy passion,
  Whilst I still smoothed my pain with smiles before
    thee,
  And made a contract I ne'er meant to keep.   355

POLYDORE How!

CASTALIO Still new ways I studied to abuse thee,
  And kept thee as a stranger to my passion,
  Till yesterday I wedded with Monimia.

POLYDORE Ah, Castalio! Was that well done?   360

CASTALIO No, to conceal't from thee was much a fault.

POLYDORE A fault! When thou hast heard
  The tale I'll tell, what wilt thou call it then?

CASTALIO How my heart throbs!

POLYDORE   First, for thy friendship, traitor,
  I cancel 't thus: after this day, I'll ne'er   365
  Hold trust or converse with the false Castalio!
  This, witness heav'n.

CASTALIO   What will my fate do with me?
  I've lost all happiness, and know not why.
  What means this, brother?

POLYDORE   Perjured, treacherous wretch,
  Farewell.

CASTALIO   I'll be thy slave, and thou shalt use me 370
  Just as thou wilt – do but forgive me.

POLYDORE   Never!

CASTALIO Oh, think a little what thy heart is doing;
  How from our infancy, we hand in hand
  Have trod the path of life, in love together.

One bed has held us, and the same desires,   375
The same aversions still employed our thoughts.
Whene'er had I a friend, that was not Polydore's,
Or Polydore a foe, that was not mine?
Even in the womb we embraced, and wilt thou now,
For the first fault, abandon and forsake me,   380
Leave me amidst afflictions to myself,
Plunged in the gulf of grief, and none to help me?

POLYDORE Go to Monimia. In her arms thou'lt find
Repose. She has the art of healing sorrows.

CASTALIO What arts?

POLYDORE   Blind wretch, thou husband! There's
    a question!   385
Go to her fulsome bed, and wallow there
Till some hot ruffian, full of lust and wine,
Come storm thee out, and show thee what's thy
    bargain.

CASTALIO Hold there, I charge thee.

POLYDORE   Is she not a –

CASTALIO   Whore?

POLYDORE Aye, whore – I think that word needs no
    explaining.   390

CASTALIO Alas, I can forgive ev'n this to thee;
But let me tell thee, Polydore, I'm grieved
To find thee guilty of such low revenge,
To wrong that virtue which thou couldst not ruin.

POLYDORE It seems I lie then.

CASTALIO   Should the bravest man   395
That e'er wore conquering sword, but dare to whisper
What thou proclaim'st, he were the worst of liars.
My friend may be mistaken.

POLYDORE   Damn the evasion!
Thou mean'st the worst, and he's a base-born villain
That said I lied.   400

<Draws his sword>

CASTALIO Do, draw thy sword, and thrust it through
    my heart!

There's no joy in life, if thou art lost.
A base-born villain –

POLYDORE   Yes, thou never camest
From old Acasto's loins – the midwife put
A cheat upon my mother, and instead   405
Of a true brother, in the cradle by me
Placed some coarse peasant's cub, and thou art he!

CASTALIO Thou art my brother still.

POLYDORE   Thou liest.

CASTALIO   Nay, then – (*he draws*)
Yet I am calm.

POLYDORE   A coward's always so.

CASTALIO Ah – ah – that stings home – coward?   410

POLYDORE Aye, base-born coward, villain!

CASTALIO This to thy heart then, though my mother
   bore thee.

(*Fight.* POLYDORE *drops his sword, and runs on*
   CASTALIO*'s*)

POLYDORE Now my Castalio is again my friend.

CASTALIO What have I done! My sword is in thy breast.

POLYDORE So would I have it be, thou best of men,   415
   Thou kindest brother, and thou truest friend.

CASTALIO Ye gods! We're taught that all your works
   are justice,
   Y'are painted merciful, and friends to innocence.
   If so, then why these plagues upon my head?

POLYDORE Blame not the heavens, here lies thy fate,
   Castalio.   420
   Th'are not the gods, 'tis Polydore has wronged thee.
   I've stained thy bed, thy spotless marriage joys
   Have been polluted by thy brother's lust.

CASTALIO By thee!

POLYDORE   By me last night the horrid deed
   Was done, when all things slept but rage and incest.   425

CASTALIO Now, where's Monimia? Oh!

(*Enter* MONIMIA)

MONIMIA   I'm here, who calls me?
　Methought I heard a voice
　Sweet as the shepherd's pipe upon the mountains,
　When all his little flock's at feed before him.
　But what means this? Here's blood –
CASTALIO   Aye, brother's blood – 430
　Art thou prepared for everlasting pains?
POLYDORE Oh let me charge thee by th'eternal justice,
　Hurt not her tender life!
CASTALIO   Not kill her? Rack me,
　Ye powers above, with all your choicest torments,
　Horrors of mind and pains yet uninvented,   435
　If I not practise cruelty upon her,
　And treat revenge some way yet never known.
MONIMIA That task myself have finished. I shall die
　Before we part. I've drunk a healing draught
　For all my cares, and never more shall wrong thee.   440
POLYDORE Oh, she's innocent.
CASTALIO   Tell me that story,
　And thou wilt make a wretch of me indeed.
POLYDORE Hadst thou, Castalio, used me like a friend,
　This ne'er had happened. Hadst thou let me know
　Thy marriage, we had all now met in joy.   445
　But ignorant of that,
　Hearing th'appointment made, enraged to think
　Thou hadst outdone me in successful love,
　I in the dark went and supplied thy place,
　Whilst all the night, midst our triumphant joys,   450
　The trembling, tender, kind, deceived Monimia
　Embraced, caressed, and called me her Castalio.
CASTALIO And all this is the work of my own fortune.
　None but myself could e'er have been so cursed.
　My fatal love, alas! has ruined thee,   455
　Thou fairest, goodliest frame the gods e'er made,
　Or ever human eyes and hearts adored.
　I've murdered too my brother.
　Why wouldst thou study ways to damn me further
　And force the sin of parricide* upon me?   460

POLYDORE 'Twas my own fault, and thou art innocent.
  Forgive the barbarous trespass of my tongue.
  'Twas a hard violence: I could have died
  With love of thee, ev'n when I used thee worst;
  Nay, at each word that my distraction uttered,   465
  My heart recoiled, and 'twas half death to speak 'em.
MONIMIA Now, my Castalio, the most dear of men,
  Wilt thou receive pollution to thy bosom,
  And close the eyes of one that has betrayed thee?
CASTALIO Oh, I'm the unhappy wretch whose cursed fate   470
  Has weighed thee down into destruction with him.
  Why then thus kind to me?
MONIMIA When I'm laid low in the grave, and quite forgotten,
  Mayst thou be happy in a fairer bride;
  But none can ever love thee like Monimia.   475
  When I am dead, as presently I shall be
  (For the grim tyrant grasps my heart already),
  Speak well of me, and if thou find ill tongues
  Too busy with my fame, don't hear me wronged.
  'Twill be a noble justice to the memory   480
  Of a poor wretch, once honoured with thy love.
  How my head swims! 'Tis very dark – good night.
    (dies)
CASTALIO If I survive thee, what a thought was that!
  Thank heaven I go prepared against that curse.

(Enter CHAMONT disarmed, and seized by ACASTO, and
servants)

CHAMONT Gape, hell, and swallow me to quick damnation,   485
  If I forgive your house, if I not live
  An everlasting plague to thee, Acasto,
  And all thy race. Y'have o'erpowered me now,
  But hear me, Heaven – Ah, here's the scene of death,
  My sister, my Monimia! Breathless! Now,   490
  Ye powers above, if y'have justice, strike,

Strike bolts through me, and through the cursed
   Castalio.

ACASTO My Polydore.

POLYDORE   Who calls?

ACASTO   How cam'st thou
   wounded?

CASTALIO Stand off, thou hot-brained, boisterous, noisy
   ruffian,
And leave me to my sorrows.

CHAMONT   By the love   495
I bore her living, I will ne'er forsake,
But here remain till my heart burst with sobbing.

CASTALIO Vanish, I charge thee, or – (*draws a dagger*)

CHAMONT   Thou canst not kill me;
That would be kindness, and against thy nature.

ACASTO What means Castalio? Sure thou wilt not pull   500
More sorrows on thy aged father's head.
Tell me, I beg you, tell me the sad cause
Of all this ruin.

POLYDORE   That must be my task;
But 'tis too long for one in pains to tell.
You'll in my closet find the story written   505
Of all our woes. Castalio's innocent,
And so's Monimia – only I'm to blame:
Inquire no further.

CASTALIO   Thou, unkind Chamont,
Unjustly hast pursued me with thy hate,
And sought the life of him that never wronged thee.   510
Now, if thou wilt embrace a noble vengeance,
Come join with me and curse.

CHAMONT   What?

CASTALIO   First thyself,
As I do, and the hour that gave thee birth.
Confusion and disorder seize the world,
To spoil all trust and converse amongst men: 515
'Twixt families engender endless feuds;
In countries needless fears; in cities factions;
In states rebellion, and in churches schism,

Till all things move against the course of nature;
Till form's dissolved, the chain of causes broken,   520
And the originals of being lost.
ACASTO Have patience.
CASTALIO   Patience! Preach it to the winds,
To roaring seas, or raging fires; the knaves
That teach it laugh at ye, when ye believe 'em.
Strip me of all the common needs of life,   525
Scald me with leprosy, let friends forsake me,
I'll bear it all – but cursed to the degree
That I am now, 'tis this must give me patience:
Thus I find rest, and shall complain no more.

           (Stabs himself)

POLYDORE Castalio! Oh!   530
CASTALIO I come.
Chamont, to thee my birthright I bequeath.
Comfort my mourning father, heal his griefs –

     (ACASTO *faints into the arms of a servant*)

For I perceive they fall with weight upon him.
And for Monimia's sake, whom thou wilt find   535
I never wronged, be kind to poor Serina.
Now all I beg is – lay me in one grave,
Thus, with my love. Farewell, I now am – nothing.
    (dies)
CHAMONT Take care of good Acasto, whilst I go
To search the means by which the fates have plagued
    us.   540
'Tis thus that Heaven its empire does maintain:
It may afflict, but man must not complain.
                              <*Exeunt omnes*>

Epilogue

<Spoken by SERINA>

You've seen one orphan ruined here, and I
May be the next, if old Acasto die.*
Should it prove so, I'd fain amongst you find
Who 'tis would to the fatherless be kind.
To whose protection might I safely go?   5
Is there amongst you no good nature? No.
What should I do? Should I the godly seek,
And go a-conventicling* twice a week?
Quit the lewd stage and its profane pollution,
Affect each form and saint-like institution,   10
So draw the brethren all to contribution?
Or shall I (as I guess the poet may
Within these three days) fairly run away?*
No, to some city lodgings I'll retire,
Seem very grave, and privacy desire;   15
Till I am thought some heiress rich in lands,
Fled to escape a cruel guardian's hands;
Which may produce a story worth the telling
Of the next sparks* that go a-fortune-stealing.

THE ROVER
Part 2

By
APHRA BEHN

<DEDICATION>
To His Royal Highness the Duke &c. *

Great Sir,
    I dread to appear in this humble dedication to your Royal
Highness, as one of those insolent and saucy offenders who
take occasion by your absence* to commit ill-mannered
indecencies unpardonable to a prince of your illustrious
birth and godlike goodness, but that, in spite of seditious   5
scandal, you can forgive; and all the world knows you can
suffer with a divine patience. The proofs you have early and
later given of this have been such as if heaven designed 'em
only to give the world an undeniable testimony of your
noble virtues, your loyalty and true obedience (if I may   10
presume to say so) both to your sacred brother, and the
never-satisfied people. When either one commanded, or
t'other repined, with how cheerful and entire a submission
you obeyed! And though the royal son of a glorious father
who was rendered unfortunate by the unexemplary ingrati-   15
tude of his worst of subjects, and sacrificed to the insatiate
and cruel villainy of a seeming-sanctified faction* who
could never hope to expiate for the unparalleled sin, but by
an entire submission to the gracious offspring of this royal
martyr;* yet you, great sir, denying yourself the rights and   20
privileges the meanest subject claims, with a fortitude
worthy your adorable virtues, put yourself upon a voluntary
exile to appease the causeless murmurs of this again-gather-
ing faction, who make their needless and self-created fears
an occasion to play the old game o'er again; whilst the   25
politic, self-interested and malicious few betray the unconsidering rest with the delicious sounds of liberty and public
good: that lucky cant,* which so few years since so
miserably reduced all the noble, brave and honest to the
obedience of the ill-gotten power and worse-acted greatness   30
of the rabble; so that whilst they most unjustly cried down
the oppression of one of the best of monarchs, and all kingly
government, all England found itself deplorably enslaved by

the arbitrary tyranny of many pageant* kings. Oh, that we should so far forget with what greatness of mind you then 35 shared the common fate, as now again to force your royal person to new perils and new exiles. But such ingratitude we are punished with, and you still suffer for and still forgive it.

This more than human goodness, with the encouragement your Royal Highness was pleased to give the Rover at his 40 first appearance, and the concern you were pleased to have for his second, makes me presume to lay him at your feet. He is a wanderer, too: distressed, beloved, though unfortunate, and ever constant to loyalty.* Were he legions, he should follow and suffer still with so excellent a prince and 45 master. Your infant worth he knew, and all your growing glories; has seen you like young Caesar in the field, when yet a youth, exchanging death for laurels, and wondered at a bravery so early,* which still* made double conquest, not only by your sword, but by your virtues which taught even 50 your enemies so entire an obedience that, ashamed of their rebel gallantry, they have resigned their guilty commissions and vowed never to draw sword more but in the royal cause:* which vow religiously they kept – a noble example for the busy and hot mutineers of this age misled by youth, 55 false ambition and false counsel.

How careless, since your glorious restoration, you have been of your life for the service of your mistaken country, the whole world knows, and all brave men admire.*

Pardon me then, great sir, if I presume to present my 60 faithful soldier (which no storms of fate can ever draw from his obedience), to so great a general. Allow him, royal sir, a shelter and protection, who was driven from his native country with you, forced, as you were, to fight for his bread in a strange land, and suffered with you all the ills of 65 poverty, war and banishment, and still pursues your fortunes. And though he cannot serve your Highness, he may possibly have the honour of diverting you a few moments; which though your Highness cannot want in a place where all hearts and knees are justly bowed in 70 adoration, where all conspire – as all the earth (who have the blessing of your presence) ought – to entertain, serve and please you; yet this humble tribute of a most zealous and devout heart, may find amongst your busier hours of great moment, some one wherein it may have the glory of your 75 regard, and be capable in some small degree of unbending your great mind from royal cares, the weightiest cares of all; which, if it be so fortunate as to do, I have my end and the glory I design: a sufficient reward for her who does and will eternally pray for the life, health and safety of your Royal 80 Highness, as in duty all the world is bound to do, but more especially,

Illustrious sir,

Your Highness' most humble, most faithful and most
obedient servant,
A. Behn

Prologue

In vain we labour to reform the stage:
Poets have caught too the disease o' th' age,
That pest of not being quiet when they're well;
That restless fever, in the brethren,* zeal,
In public spirits, called good o' th' commonweal.* 5
Some for this faction cry, others for that;
The pious mobile* for they know not what;
So though by different ways the fever seize,
In all 'tis one and the same mad disease.
Our author, too, as all new zealots do, 10
Full of conceit and contradiction too,
'Cause the first project took, is now so vain
To attempt to play the old game o'er again.
The scene is only changed, for who would lay
A plot so hopeful just the same dull way?* 15
Poets like statesmen, with a little change,
Pass off old politics for new and strange.
Though the few men of sense decry't aloud,
The cheat will pass with the unthinking crowd.
The rabble 'tis we court, those powerful things, 20
Whose voices can impose even laws on kings.
A pox of sense and reason, or dull rules;*
Give us an audience that declares for fools!
Our play will then stand fair: we've monsters too,
Which far exceed your city pope* for show. 25
Almighty rabble, 'tis to you this day
Our humble author dedicates the play.
From those who in our lofty tier* sit,
Down to the dull state-cullies of the pit,*
Who have much money and but little wit; 30
Whose useful purses, and whose empty skulls,
To private interest* make ye public tools:
To work on projects which the wiser frame,
And of fine men of business get the name.

You who have left caballing* here of late,   35
Employed in matters of a mightier weight;
To you we make our humble application,
You'd spare some time from your dear, new vocation
Of drinking deep, then settling the nation,*
To countenance us, whom commonwealths of old*   40
Did the most politic diversion hold.
Plays were so useful thought to government,
That laws were made for their establishment.
How e'er in schools* differing opinions jar,
Yet all agree i' th' crowded theatre,   45
Which none forsook in any change or war;
That like their gods unviolated stood,
Equally needful to the public good.
Throw then, great sirs, some vacant hours away,
And your petitioners shall humbly pray, etc.   50

DRAMATIS PERSONAE

The play was first performed *c*. January 1681 by the Duke's Company at the Dorset Garden Theatre with the cast listed below.

WILLMORE the Rover in love with La Nuche — Mr Smith

BEAUMOND the English ambassador's nephew, in love with La Nuche, contracted to Ariadne — Mr Williams

NED BLUNT an English country gentleman — Mr Underhill*

NICHOLAS FETHERFOOL an English esquire, his friend — Mr Nokes

SHIFT an English lieutenant — Mr Wiltshire

HUNT an ensign — Mr Richards

HARLEQUIN* Willmore's man

ABEVILE page to Beaumond

DON CARLO an old grandee, in love with La Nuche — Mr Norris

ARIADNE the English ambassador's daughter-in-law,* in love with Willmore — Mrs Currer

LUCIA her kinswoman, a girl — <Mrs Price>*

LA NUCHE a Spanish courtesan, in love with the Rover — Mrs Barry*

PETRONELLA ELENORA her bawd — Mrs Norris

AURELIA her woman — Mrs Crofts

SANCHO her bravo

AN OLD JEW guardian to the two monsters — Mr Freeman

A WOMAN GIANT

A DWARF her sister

<TWO SOLDIERS; RAG, Willmore's serving-boy>
SCARAMOUCH,* SERVANTS, MUSICIANS, OPERATORS* and SPECTATORS

Scene: Madrid

Act 1, Scene 1

(Enter WILLMORE, BLUNT, FETHERFOOL and HUNT;
two more in campania dresses;* RAG, the captain's boy)

WILLMORE Stay, this is the English ambassador's. I'll
  inquire if Beaumond be returned from Paris.

FETHERFOOL Prithee, dear captain, no more delays unless
  thou thinkest he will invite us to dinner; for this fine, thin,
  sharp air of Madrid has a most notable faculty of   5
  provoking an appetite. Prithee, let's to the ordinary.*

WILLMORE I will not stay.

(Knocks. Enter a PORTER)

Friend, is the ambassador's nephew, Mr Beaumond,
returned to Madrid yet? If he be, I would speak with him.

PORTER I'll let him know so much.   10

(Goes in. Shut* the door)

BLUNT Why,* how now, what's the door shut upon us?

FETHERFOOL And reason, Ned, 'tis dinner time in the
  ambassador's kitchen, and should they let the savoury
  steam out, what a world of Castilians would there be at
  the door feeding upon't. Oh, there's no living in Spain   15
  when the pot's uncovered.

BLUNT Nay, 'tis a nation of the finest clean teeth.

FETHERFOOL Teeth! Gad, and they use their swords no
  oftener, a scabbard will last an age.

(Enter SHIFT from the house)

WILLMORE Honest lieutenant.   20

SHIFT My noble captain, welcome to Madrid. What, Mr
  Blunt, and my honoured friend, Nicholas Fetherfool,
  esquire.

FETHERFOOL Thy hand, honest Shift.

(They embrace him)

WILLMORE And how, lieutenant, how stand affairs in this   25

unsanctified town? How does love's great artillery, the
fair La Nuche, from whose bright eyes the little wanton
god* throws darts to wound mankind?

SHIFT Faith, she carries all before her still; undoes her
fellow-traders in love's art: and amongst the number, old   30
Carlo de Minalta Segosa pays high for two nights in a
week.

WILLMORE Hah, Carlo! Death, what a greeting's here,
Carlo the happy man! A dog, a rascal, gain the bright La
Nuche! O Fortune! Cursed, blind, mistaken Fortune!*   35
Eternal friend to fools! Fortune, that takes the noble rate
from man, to place it on her idol, interest.*

SHIFT Why faith, captain, I should think her heart might
stand as fair for you as any, could you be less satirical –
but by this light, captain, you return her raillery a little   40
too roughly.

WILLMORE Her raillery? By this hand, I had rather be
handsomely abused than dully flattered; but when she
touches on my poverty, my honourable poverty, she
presses me too sensibly* – for nothing is so nice* as   45
poverty. But damn her, I'll think of her no more: for she's
a devil, though her form be angel! Is Beaumond come
from Paris yet?

SHIFT He is, I came with him; he's impatient of your
return. I'll let him know you're here.   50

[*Exit* SHIFT]

FETHERFOOL Why, what a pox ails the captain o'th'
sudden? He looks as sullenly as a routed general, or a
lover after hard service.

BLUNT Oh, something the lieutenant has told him about a
wench, and when Cupid's in his breeches the devil's ever   55
in's head. (*to* WILLMORE) How now, what a pox is the
matter with you, you look so scurvily now? What's the
gentlewoman otherwise provided; has she cashiered ye for
want of pay? Or what other dire mischance, hah?

WILLMORE Do not trouble me –   60

BLUNT 'Adsheartlikins,* but I will, and beat thee too, but
I'll know the cause. I heard Shift tell thee something about

La Nuche, a damsel I have often heard thee fool enough
to sigh for.

WILLMORE Confound the mercenary jilt! 65

BLUNT Nay, 'adsheartlikins, they are all so; though I
thought you had been whore-proof. 'Tis enough for us
fools, country gentlemen, esquires and cullies to miscarry
in their amorous adventures, you men of wit weather all
storms, you. 70

WILLMORE Oh sir, you're become a new man, wise and
wary, and can no more be cozened.

BLUNT Not by womankind; and for man, I think my sword
will secure me. Pox, I thought a two months' absence and
a siege would have put such trifles out of thy head. You 75
do not use to be such a miracle of constancy.

WILLMORE That absence makes me think of her so much;
and all the passions thou find'st about me, are to the sex
alone! Give me a woman, Ned, a fine young amorous
wanton, who would allay this fire that makes me rave 80
thus, and thou shouldst find me no longer particular, but
cold as winter nights to this La Nuche. Yet since I lost my
little, charming gypsy,* nothing has gone so near my
heart as this.

BLUNT Aye, there was a girl, the only she-thing that could 85
reconcile me to the petticoats again after my Naples
adventure,* when the quean robbed and stripped me.

WILLMORE Oh, name not Hellena! She was a saint to be
adored on holy-days.

(*Enter* BEAUMOND)

BEAUMOND Willmore! My careless, wild inconstant – how 90
is't, my lucky rover?

(*Embracing*)

WILLMORE My life! My soul! How glad am I to find thee
in my arms again – and well. When left you Paris? Paris,
that city of pottage and crab wine, swarming with lackeys
and philoes,* whose government is carried on by most 95

hands, not most voices. And prithee, how does Belvile and his lady?*

BEAUMOND I left 'em both in health at St Germain.*

WILLMORE Faith, I have wished myself with ye at the old temple of Bacchus at St Cloud,* to sacrifice a bottle and a damsel to his deity. 100

BEAUMOND My constant place of worship whilst there; though for want of new saints my zeal grew something cold, which I was ever fain to supply with a bottle, the old remedy when Phyllis is sullen or absent. 105

WILLMORE Now thou talk'st of Phyllis, prithee dear Harry, what women hast in store?

BEAUMOND I'll tell thee; but first inform me whom these two sparks* are.

WILLMORE 'Egad, and so they are, child. Salute 'em: they 110 are my friends, true blades, Hal, highly guilty of the royal crime, poor and brave, loyal fugitives.*

BEAUMOND (bowing to BLUNT) I love and honour 'em, sir, as such.

BLUNT Sir, there's neither love nor honour lost. 115

FETHERFOOL Sir, I scorn to be behindhand in civilities.

BEAUMOND (to FETHERFOOL) At first sight I find I am much yours, sir.

FETHERFOOL Sir, I love and honour any man that's a friend to Captain Willmore; and therefore I am yours. 120

(Enter SHIFT)

Well, honest lieutenant, how does thy body? When shall Ned, and thou and I, crack a biscuit o'er a glass of wine, have a slice of treason, and settle the nation, hah?

SHIFT You know, squire, I am devoted yours.

(They talk aside)

BEAUMOND Prithee, who are these? 125

WILLMORE Why, the first you saluted is the same Ned Blunt you have often heard Belvile and I speak of. The other is a rarity of another nature, one Squire Fetherfool of Croydon, a tame Justice o'th' Peace, who lived as

innocently as ale and fool could keep him, till for a 130
mistaken kindness to one of the royal party, he lost his
commission, and got the reputation of a sufferer; he's
rich, but covetous as an alderman.

BEAUMOND What a pox dost keep 'em company for, who
have neither wit enough to divert thee, nor good nature 135
enough to serve thee?

WILLMORE Faith, Harry, 'tis true, and if there were no
more charity than profit in't, a man would sooner keep a
cough o'th' lungs than be troubled with 'em. But the
rascals have a blind side as all conceited coxcombs have, 140
which, when I've nothing else to do, I shall expose to
advance our mirth. The rogues must be cozened,* because
they're so positive they never can be so; but I am now for
softer joys, for woman, for woman in abundance – dear
Hal, inform me where I may safely unlade my heart.   145

BEAUMOND The same man still, wild and wanton!

WILLMORE And would not change to be the Catholic
king.*

BEAUMOND I perceive marriage has not tamed you, nor a
wife who had all the charms of her sex.   150

WILLMORE (*with a sham sadness*) Aye, she was too good
for mortals.

BEAUMOND I think thou hadst her but a month; prithee,
how died she?

WILLMORE Faith, e'en with a fit of kindness, poor soul. She 155
would to sea with me and in a storm, far from land, she
gave up the ghost. 'Twas a loss, but I must bear it with a
Christian fortitude.

BEAUMOND Short happinesses vanish like to dreams.

WILLMORE Aye, faith; and nothing remains with me but 160
the sad remembrance – not so much as the least part of
her hundred thousand crowns. Brussels, that enchanted
court, has eased me of that grief, where our heroes act
Tantalus better than ever Ovid described him:* condemned daily to see an apparition of meat, food in vision 165
only. Faith, I had bowels,* was good-natured, and lent
upon the public faith as far as 'twould go. But come, let's

leave this mortifying discourse, and tell me how the price
of pleasure goes.

BEAUMOND At the old rates still; he that gives most is 170
happiest, some few there are for love!

WILLMORE Ah, one of the last, dear Beaumond, and if a
heart or sword can purchase her, I'll bid as fair as the
best. Damn it, I hate a whore that asks me money.

BEAUMOND Yet I have known thee venture all thy stock 175
for a new woman.

WILLMORE Aye, such a fool I was in my dull days of
constancy, but I am now for change, (and should I pay as
often, 'twould undo me) – for change, my dear, of place,
clothes, wine and women. Variety is the soul of pleasure, 180
a good unknown, and we want faith to find it.

BEAUMOND Thou wouldst renounce that fond opinion,
Willmore,*
Didst thou but see a beauty here in town
Whose charms have power to fix inconstant Nature,
Or Fortune were she tottering on her wheel.*   185

WILLMORE Her name, my dear, her name!

BEAUMOND I would not breathe it, even in my
complaints –
Lest amorous winds should bear it o'er the world,
And make mankind her slaves –
But that it is a name too cheaply known,   190
And she that owns it may be as cheaply purchased.

WILLMORE Hah, cheaply purchased too! I languish for
her.

BEAUMOND Aye, there's the devil on't, she is – a whore.

WILLMORE Ah, what a charming sound that mighty 195
word bears.

BEAUMOND Damn her, she'll be thine or anybody's.

WILLMORE I die for her –

BEAUMOND Then for her qualities –

WILLMORE No more, ye gods, I ask no more;   200
Be she but fair and much a whore.
Come, let's to her.

BEAUMOND Perhaps tomorrow you may see this woman.

WILLMORE Death, 'tis an age.

FETHERFOOL Oh, captain, the strangest news, captain. 205

WILLMORE Prithee, what?

FETHERFOOL Why, lieutenant Shift here, tells us of two monsters arrived from Mexico, Jews of vast fortunes, with an old Jew uncle, their guardian. They are worth a hundred thousand pounds apiece. Mercy upon's, why, 'tis 210 a sum able to purchase all Flanders again from his most Christian Majesty.*

WILLMORE Ha, ha, ha, monsters!

BEAUMOND He tells you truth, Willmore.

BLUNT But hark'ee, lieutenant, are you sure they are not 215 married?

BEAUMOND Married? Who the devil would venture on such formidable ladies?

FETHERFOOL How, venture on 'em! By the Lord, Harry, and that would I, though I'm a Justice o'th' Peace, and 220 they be Jews, which to a Christian is a thousand reasons.

BLUNT (aside) Is the devil in you to declare our design?

FETHERFOOL <to him> Mum, as close as a Jesuit.*

BEAUMOND I admire your courage, sir, but one of them is so little and so deformed, 'tis thought she is not capable of 225 marriage; and the other is so huge an overgrown giant, no man dares venture on her.

WILLMORE Prithee, let's go see 'em; what do they pay for going in?

FETHERFOOL Pay! I'd have you know they are monsters of 230 quality.

SHIFT And not to be seen but by particular favour of their guardian, whom I am got acquainted with from the friendship I have with the merchant where they lay. The giant, sir, is in love with me, the dwarf with Ensign Hunt, 235 and as we may manage matters it may prove lucky.

BEAUMOND And didst thou see the show, the Elephant and the Mouse?

SHIFT Yes, and pleased 'em wondrously with news I brought 'em of a famous mountebank* who is coming to 240 Madrid. Here are his bills,* who, amongst other his* marvellous cures, pretends to restore mistakes in nature, to new-mould a face and body though never so mis-shapen, to exact proportion and beauty. This news has made me gracious to the ladies, and I am to bring 'em 245 word of the arrival of this famous empiric,* and to negotiate the business of their reformation.

WILLMORE And do they think to be restored to moderate sizes?

SHIFT Much pleased with the hope, and are resolved to try 250 at any rate.

(WILLMORE *and* BEAUMOND *read the bill*)

FETHERFOOL Mum, lieutenant – not too much of their transformation; we shall have the captain put in for a share, and the devil would not have him his rival. Ned and I are resolved to venture a cast for 'em as they are – 255 hah, Ned?

BLUNT Yes, if there were any hopes of your keeping a secret.

FETHERFOOL Nay, nay, Ned, the world knows I am a plaguy fellow at your secrets; that, and my share of the 260 charge shall be my part, for Shift says the guardian must be bribed for consent. Now the other moiety of the money and the speeches shall be thy part, for thou hast a pretty knack that way. Now Shift shall bring matters neatly about, and we'll pay him by the day, or in gross, when 265 we are married. Hah, Shift?

SHIFT Sir, I shall be reasonable.

WILLMORE <*aside*> I am sure Fetherfool and Blunt have some wise design upon these two monsters – it must be so; and this bill has put an extravagant thought into my 270 head. Hark'ee, Shift –

(*Whispers to him*)

BLUNT The devil's in't if this will not redeem my reputation with the captain, and give him to understand that all the wit does not lie in the family of the Willmore's, but that this noddle of mine can be fruitful too upon occasion. 275

FETHERFOOL Aye, and Lord, how we'll domineer, Ned,
  hah – over Willmore and the rest of the renegado officers,
  when we have married these lady monsters; hah, Ned!

BLUNT Then to return back to Essex worth a million.

FETHERFOOL And I to Croyden –   280

BLUNT Lolling in coach and six –

FETHERFOOL Be dubbed Right Worshipful –

BLUNT And stand for knight o' th' shire.*

WILLMORE (*aside to* SHIFT) Enough, I must have my share
  of this jest, and for divers and sundry reasons thereunto 285
  belonging, must be this very mountebank expected.

SHIFT Faith, sir, and that were no hard matter. For a day
  or two the town will believe it, the same they look for;
  and the bank,* operators and music are all ready.

WILLMORE Well enough; add but a harlequin and scara- 290
  mouch,* and I shall mount in querpo.*

SHIFT Take no care for that, sir. Your man, and Ensign
  Hunt, are excellent at those two; I saw 'em act 'em the
  other day to a wonder. They'll be glad of the employment; myself will be an operator.   295

WILLMORE No more, get 'em ready, and give it out the
  man of art's arrived. Be diligent and secret, for these two
  politic asses must be cozened.

SHIFT I will about the business instantly.

                                                    [*Exit* SHIFT]

BEAUMOND This fellow will do feats if he keep his word. 300

WILLMORE I'll give you mine he shall; but, dear Beaumond, where shall we meet anon?

BEAUMOND I thank ye for that. 'Gad, ye shall dine with
  me.

FETHERFOOL A good motion.   305

WILLMORE I beg your pardon now, dear Beaumond, I,
  having lately nothing else to do, took a command of horse
  from the general at the last siege, from which I am just
  arrived, and my baggage is behind, which I must take
  order for.   310

FETHERFOOL Pox on't, now there's a dinner lost, 'twas
  ever an unlucky rascal.

BEAUMOND To tempt thee more, thou shalt see my wife
that is to be.

WILLMORE Pox on't, I am the lewdest company in Chris- 315
tendom with your honest women; but what, art thou to
be noosed then?

BEAUMOND 'Tis so designed by my uncle, if an old
grandee, my rival, prevent it not. The wench is very
pretty, young and rich, and lives in the same house with 320
me, for 'tis my aunt's daughter.

WILLMORE Much good may it d' ye, Harry. I pity you, but
'tis the common grievance of you happy men of fortune.

(*Goes towards the house door with* BEAUMOND)

(*Enter* LA NUCHE, AURELIA, PETRONELLA, SANCHO;
<the> women veiled a little)

AURELIA (*looking on* WILLMORE) Heavens, madam, is not
that the English captain?   325

LA NUCHE 'Tis, and with him Don Henrick the ambassador's nephew. How my heart pants and heaves at sight of
him! Some fire of the old flame's remaining, which I must
strive to extinguish. For I'll not bate a ducat of this price
I've set upon myself, for all the pleasures youth or love 330
can bring me. For see, Aurelia, the sad memento of a
decayed, poor old forsaken whore, in Petronella. Consider her, and then commend my prudence.

WILLMORE Hah, women!

FETHERFOOL Egad and fine ones too, I'll tell you that.   335

WILLMORE No matter, kindness is better sauce to woman
than beauty. By this hand, she looks at me. (FETHER-
FOOL *holds him*) Why dost hold me?

FETHERFOOL Why, what a devil, art mad?

WILLMORE Raging! As vigorous youth kept long from   340
beauty: wild for the charming sex, eager for woman! I
long to give a loose to love and pleasure.

BLUNT These are not women, sir, for you to ruffle.

WILLMORE Have a care of your persons of quality, Ned!
(*goes to* LA NUCHE) Those lovely eyes were never made to 345
throw their darts in vain!

LA NUCHE The conquest would be hardly worth the pain.

WILLMORE (*aside*) Hah, La Nuche, with what a proud disdain she flung away. (*holds her*) Stay – I will not part so with you.   350

> (*Enter* ARIADNE *and* LUCIA *with* FOOTMEN)

ARIADNE Who are these before us, Lucia?

LUCIA I know not, madam, but if you make not haste home you'll be troubled with Carlo, your importunate lover, who is just behind us.

ARIADNE Hang me, a lovely man! What lady's that? Stay. 355

PETRONELLA What insolence is this? This villain will spoil all –

FETHERFOOL Why, captain, are you quite distracted? Dost know where thou art? Prithee, be civil –

WILLMORE (*turns* <LA NUCHE> *from him*) Go, proud and 360 cruel!

> (*Enter* CARLO, *and two or three Spanish* SERVANTS
> *following:* PETRONELLA *goes to him*)

CARLO Hah, affronted by a drunken islander, a saucy tramontane!* (*to his servants, whilst he takes* <LA NUCHE>) Draw, whilst I lead her off. <*to* LA NUCHE> Fear not, lady, you have the honour of my sword to guard 365 ye!

WILLMORE Hah, Carlo – ye lie! It cannot guard the boasting fool that wears it. Be gone, and look not back upon this woman. (*snatches her from him*) One single glance destroys thee!   370

> (*They draw and fight;* CARLO *getting hindmost of his
> Spaniards, the* ENGLISH *beat 'em off. The ladies run
> away, all but* ARIADNE *and* LUCIA)

LUCIA Heavens, madam, why d'ye stay?

ARIADNE To pray for that dear stranger! – And see, my prayers are heard, and he's returned in safety. This door shall shelter me to o'er-hear the quarrel. (*steps aside*)

(*Enter* WILLMORE, BLUNT; FETHERFOOL *looking big
and putting up his sword*)

FETHERFOOL The noble captain be affronted by a starched 375
ruff and beard, a coward in querpo, a walking bunch of
garlic, a pickled pilchard! Abuse the noble captain, and
bear it off in state, <like>* a Christmas sweetheart! These
things must not be whilst Nicholas Fetherfool wears a
sword.   380

BLUNT Pox o' these women, I thought no good would come
on't; besides, where's the jest in affronting honest women,
if there be such a thing in the nation.

FETHERFOOL Hang 't, 'twas the devil and all.

WILLMORE Ha, ha, ha! Why, good, honest, homespun, 385
country gentlemen, who do ye think those were?

FETHERFOOL Were? Why, ladies of quality going to their
devotion. Who should they be?

BLUNT Why faith, and so I thought too.

WILLMORE Why, that very one woman I spoke to is ten 390
whores in Surrey.

FETHERFOOL Prithee, speak softly man. 'Slife, we shall be
poniarded for keeping thee company.

WILLMORE Wise Mr Justice, give me your warrant, and if I
do not prove 'em whores, whip me.   395

FETHERFOOL Prithee, hold thy scandalous blasphemous
tongue. As if I did not know whores from persons of
quality.

WILLMORE Will you believe me when you lie with her, for
thou'rt a rich ass and mayst do't?   400

FETHERFOOL Whores! Ha, ha!

WILLMORE 'Tis strange logic now, because your band* is
better than mine, I must not know a whore better than you.

BLUNT If this be a whore, as thou sayst, I understand 405
nothing. By this light, such a wench would pass for a
person of quality in London.

FETHERFOOL Few ladies have I seen at a sheriff's feast
have better faces, or worn so good clothes, and by the
Lord, Harry, if these be of the gentle craft, I'd not give a 410
real* for an honest woman for my use.

WILLMORE Come, follow me into the church, for thither I
am sure they're gone. And I will let you see what a
wretched thing you had been, had you lived seven years
longer in Surrey, stewed in ale and beef broth.   415
FETHERFOOL Oh, dear Willmore, name not those savoury
things. There's no jesting with my stomach. It sleeps now,
but if it wakes, woe be to your shares at the ordinary.
BLUNT (*aside*) I'll say that for Fetherfool, if his heart were
but half so good as his stomach, he were a brave fellow. 420
                                          [*Exeunt*]

ARIADNE I am resolved to follow – and learn, if possible,
who 'tis has made this sudden conquest o'er me.
                                          [*All go off*]

Act 1, Scene 2

*Scene draws, and discovers a church: a great many
people as at devotion; soft music playing*

(*Enter* LA NUCHE, AURELIA, PETRONELLA *and* SANCHO.
To them WILLMORE, FETHERFOOL, BLUNT; *then*
ARIADNE, LUCIA. FETHERFOOL *bows to* LA NUCHE *and*
PETRONELLA)

FETHERFOOL Now as I hope to be saved, Blunt, she's a
most melodious lady. Would I were worthy to purchase a
sin or so with her. Would not such a beauty reconcile thy
quarrel to the sex?
BLUNT No, were she an angel in that shape.   5
FETHERFOOL Why, what a pox, couldst not lie with her if
she'd let thee? By the Lord Harry, as arrant a dog as I
am, I'd fain see any of Cupid's cook-maids put me out of
countenance with such a shoulder of mutton!*
ARIADNE See how he gazes on her. Lucia, go nearer and 10
o'er-hear 'em.

(LUCIA *listens*)

WILLMORE <*aside*> Death, how the charming hypocrite

looks today, with such a soft devotion in her eyes, as if
even now she were a-praising heaven for all th' advantages 't has blest her with.   15

BLUNT Look how Willmore eyes her; the rogue's smitten
heart-deep! Whores!

FETHERFOOL Only a trick to keep her to himself. He
thought the name of a Spanish harlot would fright us
from attempting. I must divert him. – How is 't, captain?   20
Prithee, mind this music; is it not most seraphical?

WILLMORE Pox, let the fiddlers mind and tune their pipes.
I've higher pleasures now.

FETHERFOOL Oh, have ye so; what, with whores, captain?
(aside) 'Tis a most delicious gentlewoman.   25

PETRONELLA Pray, madam, mind that cavalier, who takes
such pains to recommend himself to you?

LA NUCHE Yes, for a fine, conceited fool.

PETRONELLA Catso,* a fool, what else?

LA NUCHE Right, they are our noblest chapmen;* a fool,   30
and a rich fool, and an English rich fool.

FETHERFOOL 'Sbud, she eyes me, Ned. I'll set myself in
order; it may take. Hah –

(Sets himself)

PETRONELLA Let me alone to manage him, I'll to him –

LA NUCHE (aside) Or to the devil, so I had one minute's   35
time to speak to Willmore in.

PETRONELLA And accosting him thus; tell him –

LA NUCHE (in a hasty tone) I am desperately in love with
him, and am daughter, wife, or mistress to some grandee.
Bemoan the condition of women of quality in Spain, who   40
by too much constraint are obliged to speak first, but
were we blest like other nations where men and women
meet –

(<LA NUCHE> speaking so fast, <PETRONELLA> offering
to put in her word, is still prevented by t'other's running
on)

PETRONELLA What herds of cuckolds would Spain breed!

'Slife, I could find in my heart to forswear your service.   45
Have I taught ye your trade, to become my instructor
how to cozen a dull, phlegmatic, greasy-brained Englishman! Go, and expect your wishes.

WILLMORE (*aside*) So, she has sent her matron to our
coxcomb. She saw he was a cully fit for game. Who   50
would not be a rascal to be rich – a dog, an ass, a beaten,
hardened coward! By heaven, I will possess this gay
insensible to make me hate her, most extremely curse her.
See – if she be not fallen to prayer again; from thence to
flattery, jilting and purse-taking, to make the proverb   55
good. <*to* LA NUCHE> My fair, false sibyl,* what
inspirations are you waiting from heaven, new arts to
cheat mankind? Tell me, with what face canst thou be
devout, or ask anything from thence, who hast made so
lewd a use of what it has already lavished on thee?   60

LA NUCHE Oh, my careless rover! I perceive all your hot
shot is not yet spent in battle; you have a volley in reserve
for me still. Faith, officer, the town has wanted mirth in
your absence.

WILLMORE And so might all the wiser part for thee, who   65
hast no mirth, no gaiety about thee, but when thou
wouldst design some coxcomb's ruin. To all the rest, a
soul thou hast so dull, that neither love nor mirth, not wit
or wine, can wake it to good nature. Thou'rt one who
lazily work'st in thy trade, and sell'st for ready money so   70
much kindness; a tame, cold sufferer only, and no more.

LA NUCHE What, you would have a mistress like a squirrel
in a cage, always in action – one who is as free of her
favours as I am sparing of mine? Well, captain, I have
known the time when La Nuche was such a wit, such a   75
humour, such a shape and such a voice (though to say
truth, I sing but scurvily), 'twas comedy to see and hear
me!

WILLMORE Why yes, faith, for once thou wert, and for
once mayst be again, till thou know'st thy man, and   80
know'st him to be poor. At first you liked me, too; you
saw me gay, no marks of poverty dwelt in my face or

dress! And then I was the dearest, loveliest man – all this was to my outside. Death, you made love to my breeches, caressed my garniture and feather, an English fool of 85 quality you thought me. 'Sheart, I have known a woman dote on quality, though he has stunk through all his perfumes; one who never went all to bed to her, but left his teeth, an eye, false back and breast, sometimes his palate too upon her toilet;* whilst her fair arms hugged 90 the dismembered carcass, and swore him all perfection, because of quality.

LA NUCHE But he was rich, good captain, was he not?

WILLMORE Oh, most damnably, and a confounded block-head; two certain remedies against your pride and scorn. 95

LA NUCHE Have you done, sir?

WILLMORE With thee and all thy sex, of which I've tried a hundred and found none true or honest.

LA NUCHE Oh, I doubt not the number! For you are one of those healthy-stomached lovers that can digest a mistress 100 in a night, and hunger again next morning. A pox of your whining, consumptive constitution, who are only con-stant for want of appetite. You have a swingeing stomach to variety; and want having set an edge upon your invention (with which you cut through all difficulties) you 105 grow more impudent by success.

WILLMORE I am not always scorned, then.

LA NUCHE I have known you as confidently put your hand into your pockets for money in a morning, as if the devil had been your banker; when you knew you put 'em off at 110 night as empty as your gloves.

WILLMORE And it may be, found money there, too.

LA NUCHE Then, with this poverty, so proud you are, you will not give the wall to* the Catholic king unless his picture hung upon't. No servants, no money, no meat, 115 always on foot, and yet undaunted still.

WILLMORE Allow me that, child.

LA NUCHE I wonder what the devil makes you so terma-gant on our sex. 'Tis not your high feeding, for your grandees only dine, and that but when fortune pleases. 120

For your parts, who are the poor dependant, brown bread and old Adam's ale* is only current amongst ye; yet if little Eve walk in the garden, the starved, lean rogues neigh after her as if they were in paradise.

WILLMORE Still true to love you see.   125

LA NUCHE I heard an English Capuchin* swear that if the king's followers could be brought to pray as well as fast, there would be more saints amongst 'em than the church has ever canonised.

WILLMORE All this with pride I own, since 'tis a royal 130 cause I suffer for. Go, pursue your business your own way; ensnare the fool. I saw the toils* you set, and how that face was ordered for the conquest: your eyes brimful of dying, lying love, and now and then a wishing glance or sigh thrown as by chance; which, when the happy 135 coxcomb caught, you feigned a blush, as angry and ashamed of the discovery. And all this cunning's for a little mercenary gain: fine clothes, perhaps some jewels too, whilst all the finery cannot hide the whore!

LA NUCHE There's your eternal quarrel to our sex; 'twere a 140 fine trade indeed to keep shop and give our ware for love. Would it turn to account, think ye, captain, to trick and dress, to receive all would enter? Faith, captain, try the trade.

(<PETRONELLA> *returns from discourse with*
FETHERFOOL, *speaks to* SANCHO)

PETRONELLA <*to* LA NUCHE> What, in discourse with this 145 railer! Come away; poverty's catching.

WILLMORE So is the pox, good matron, of which you can afford good pennyworths.

LA NUCHE (*aside*) He charms me even with his angry looks, and will undo me yet.   150

PETRONELLA Let's leave this place, I'll tell you my success as we go.

[*Exeunt all, some one way, some another*]

(*The fore-part of the church shuts over, except*
WILLMORE, BLUNT, ARIADNE *and* LUCIA)

WILLMORE She's gone, and all the plagues of pride go with
her.

BLUNT 'Heartlikins, follow her. Pox on't, an I'd but as 155
good a hand at this game as thou hast, I'd venture upon
any chance.

WILLMORE Damn her, come, let's to dinner. Where's
Fetherfool?

BLUNT Followed a good woodman* who gave him the 160
sign; he'll lodge the deer ere night.

WILLMORE Followed her? He durst not; the fool wants
confidence to look on her.

BLUNT Oh, you know not how a country justice may be
improved by travel. The rogue was hedged in at home 165
with the fear of his neighbours and the penal statutes.
Now he's broke loose, he runs neighing like a stone-
horse* upon the common.

WILLMORE However, I'll not believe this. Let's follow 'em.
[*Exeunt* WILLMORE *and* BLUNT]

ARIADNE He is in love, but with a courtesan – some 170
comfort that.
We'll after him. 'Tis a faint-hearted lover,
Who for the first discouragement gives over.
[*Exeunt* ARIADNE *and* LUCIA]

Act 2, Scene 1

(*Enter* FETHERFOOL *and* SANCHO *passing over the stage;
after them* WILLMORE *and* BLUNT, *followed by*
ARIADNE *and* LUCIA)

WILLMORE 'Tis so, by heaven, he's chaffering* with her
pimp. I'll spare my curses on him, for having her, he has a
plague beyond 'em. Hark ye, I'll never love, nor lie with
woman more: those slaves to lust, to vanity and interest.

BLUNT (*shaking his head and smiling*) Ha, captain!   5

WILLMORE Come, let's go drink damnation to 'em all.

BLUNT Not all, good captain.

WILLMORE All, for I hate 'em all.

ARIADNE (*aside*) Heavens, if he should indeed!

BLUNT But, Robert, I have found you most inclined to a   10
damsel when you had a bottle in your head.

WILLMORE Give me thy hand, Ned. Curse me, despise me,
point me out for cowardice if e'er thou see'st me court a
woman more – nay, when thou know'st I ask any of the
sex a civil question again. A plague upon 'em, how   15
they've handled me! Come, let's go drink, I say. Confusion to the race! A woman? No, I will be burnt with my
own fire to cinders ere any of the brood shall lay my
flame.

ARIADNE (<*aside*> *she passing by*) He cannot be so wicked   20
to keep this resolution sure. Faith, I must be resolved. <*to*
WILLMORE> You've made a pious resolution, sir, had
you the grace to keep it.

(Passing on, he pauses and looks on her)

WILLMORE Hum – what's that?

BLUNT That? Oh, nothing – but a woman; come away.   25

WILLMORE A woman! Damn her, what mischief made
her cross my way just on the point of reformation.

BLUNT I find the devil will not lose so hopeful a sinner.
Hold, hold, captain; have you no regard to your own
soul? 'Dsheartilikins, 'tis a woman, a very arrant woman.   30

<BLUNT *goes to* LUCIA>

ARIADNE Your friend informs you right, sir, I am a
woman.

WILLMORE Aye, child, or I were a lost man; therefore dear
lovely creature –

ARIADNE How can you tell, sir?   35

WILLMORE Oh, I have naturally a large faith, child, and
thou'st a promising form, a tempting motion, clean limbs,
well dressed, and a most damnable, inviting air.

ARIADNE I am not to be sold, and so not fond of praise I
merit not.   40

WILLMORE How, not to be sold, too! By this light, child,

thou speakest like a cherubim; I have not heard so
obliging a sound from the mouth of womankind,
this many a day. I find we must be better acquainted,
my dear.   45

ARIADNE Your reason, good familiar sir? I see no such
necessity.

WILLMORE Child, you are mistaken, I am in great necessity; for first, I love thee desperately. Have I not damned
my soul already for thee, and wouldst thou be so wicked   50
to refuse a little consolation to my body? Then, secondly,
I see thou art frank and good-natured, and wilt do reason,
gratis.

ARIADNE How prove ye that, good Mr Philosopher?

WILLMORE Thou sayst thou'rt not to be sold, and I'm sure   55
thou'rt to be had. That lovely body of so divine a
form, those soft smooth arms and hands, were made
t'embrace as well as be embraced; that delicate white
rising bosom to be pressed, and all thy other charms
to be enjoyed.   60

ARIADNE By one that can esteem 'em to their worth, can
set a value and a rate upon 'em.

WILLMORE Name not those words; they grate my ears
like 'jointure', that dull conjugal cant that frights the
generous lover! 'Rate?' – Death! Let the old dotards talk   65
of rates, and pay it t' atone for the defects of impotence.
Let the sly statesman, who jilts the commonwealth
with his grave politics, pay for the sin that he may dote
in secret. Let the brisk fool inch out his scanted sense
with a large purse more eloquent than he. But tell not me   70
of rates, who bring a heart, youth, vigour, and a tongue to
sing the praise of every single pleasure thou shalt give me.

ARIADNE Then if I should be kind, I perceive you would
not keep the secret.

WILLMORE Secrecy is a damned ungrateful sin, child,   75
known only where religion and small beer* are current;
despised where Apollo* and the vine bless the country.
You find none of Jove's mistresses* hid in roots and
plants, but fixed stars in heaven, for all to gaze and

wonder at; and though I am no god, my dear, I'll do a   80
mortal's part, and generously tell th' admiring world
what hidden charms thou hast. Come, lead me to some
place of happiness.

BLUNT <*to* LUCIA> Prithee, honest damsel, be not so full of
questions. Will a pistole* or two do thee any hurt?   85

LUCIA None at all, sir.

BLUNT Thou speak'st like a hearty wench, and I believe
hast not been one of Venus' handmaids so long but thou
understand'st thy trade.* In short, fair damsel, this honest
fellow here, who is so termagant upon thy lady, is my   90
friend, my particular friend, and therefore I would have
him handsomely and well-favouredly abused – you
conceive me?

LUCIA Truly, sir, a friendly request, but in what nature
abused?   95

BLUNT Nature! Why, any of your tricks would serve –
but if he could be conveniently stripped and beaten, or
tossed in a blanket,* or any such trivial business, thou
wouldst do me a singular kindness. As for robbery, he
defies the devil: an empty pocket is an antidote against   100
that ill.

LUCIA Your money, sir? And if he be not cozened, say a
Spanish woman has neither wit nor invention upon
occasion.

BLUNT 'Sheartlikins, how I shall love and honour thee   105
for't; here's earnest* – and –

(*Talks to her with joy and grimace*)

ARIADNE But who was that you entertained at church but
now?

WILLMORE Faith, one who for her beauty merits that
glorious title that she wears; it was – a whore, child.   110

ARIADNE That's but a scurvy name; yet, if I'm not
mistaken in those false eyes of yours, they looked with
longing love upon that – whore, child.

WILLMORE Thou art i'th' right, and by this hand, my soul
was full as wishing as my eyes. But a pox on't, you   115

women have all a certain jargon, or gibberish, peculiar to yourselves: of value, rate, present, interest, settlement, advantage, price, maintenance, and the devil and all of fopperies, which in plain terms signify ready money, by way of fine before entrance; so that an honest well- 120 meaning merchant of love finds no credit amongst ye, without his bill of lading.

ARIADNE We are not all so cruel; but the devil on't is, your good-natured heart is likely accompanied with an ill face, and worse wit.   125

WILLMORE Faith, child, a ready dish, when a man's stomach is up, is better than a tedious feast. I never saw any man yet cut my piece.* Some are for beauty, some for wit, and some for the secret; but I for all, so it be in a kind girl. And for wit in woman: so she say pretty, fond things 130 we understand, though true or false, no matter.

ARIADNE Give the devil his due, you are a very conscientious lover. I love a man that scorns to impose dull truth and constancy on a mistress.

WILLMORE Constancy, that current coin with fools! No, 135 child, heaven keep that curse from our doors.

ARIADNE Hang it, it loses time and profit. New lovers have new vows and new presents; whilst the old feed upon a dull repetition of what they did when they were lovers. 'Tis like eating the cold meat oneself, after having given a 140 friend a feast.

WILLMORE Yes, that's the thrifty food for the family when the guests are gone. Faith, child, thou hast made a neat and a hearty speech; but prithee, my dear, for the future, leave out that same 'profit' and 'present', for I have a 145 natural aversion to hard words. And for matter of quick dispatch in the business, give me thy hand, child. Let us but start fair, and if thou outstripp'st me, thou'rt a nimble racer.

LUCIA (sees SHIFT: <aside to ARIADNE>) Oh, madam, let's 150 be gone. Yonder's lieutenant Shift, who if he see us, will certainly give an account of it to Mr Beaumond. Let's get in through the garden, I have the key.

ARIADNE Here's company coming, and for several reasons,
I would not be seen.   155

(*Offers to go*)

WILLMORE Gad, child, nor I; reputation is tender. Therefore, prithee, let's retire.

(*Offers to go with her*)

ARIADNE You must not stir a step.

WILLMORE Not stir! No magic circle can detain me if you
go.   160

ARIADNE (*speaking hastily*) Follow me then at a distance,
and observe where I enter; and at night (if your passion
lasts so long) return, and you shall find admittance into a
garden.

<*Exit* ARIADNE *and* LUCIA>

(*He runs out after her*)

(*Enter* SHIFT <*and* BLUNT>)

SHIFT Well, sir, the mountebank's come, and just going to 165
begin in the piazza. I have ordered matters so, that you
shall have a sight of the monsters and leave to court 'em,
and when won, to give the guardian a fourth part of the
portions.

BLUNT Good; but mum – here's the captain, who must by 170
no means know our good fortune, till he see us in state.

(*Enter* WILLMORE, SHIFT *goes to him*)

SHIFT All things are ready, sir, for our design: the house
prepared as you directed me, the guardian wrought, by
the persuasions of the two monsters, to take a lodging
there, and try the baths of reformation. The bank's 175
preparing, and the operators and music all ready, and the
impatient town flocked together to behold the man of
wonders; and nothing wanting but your donship and a
proper speech.

WILLMORE 'Tis well, I'll go fit myself with a dress, and 180 think of a speech the while. In the meantime, go you and amuse the gaping fools that expect my coming.

(*Goes out*)

(*Enter* FETHERFOOL *singing and dancing*)

FETHERFOOL 'Have you heard a Spanish lady, how she wooed an Englishman?'*

BLUNT Why, how now Fetherfool?   185

FETHERFOOL 'Garments gay and rich as may be, decked with jewels, had she on –'

BLUNT Why, how now, justice, what, run mad out of the dog days?*

FETHERFOOL 'Of a comely countenance and grace is she;   190 A sweeter creature in the world there could not be.'

SHIFT Why, what the devil's the matter, sir?

BLUNT Stark mad, 'adsheartlikins.

FETHERFOOL (*singing*) 'Of a comely countenance' – Well, lieutenant, the most heroic and illustrious madonna! 195 Thou saw'st her, Ned. 'And of a comely counte –' – the most magnetic face. Well, I knew the charms of these eyes of mine were not made in vain. I was designed for great things, that's certain – 'And a sweeter creature in the world there could not be.'   200

BLUNT What, then the two lady monsters are forgotten? The design upon the million of money, the coach and six, and patent for Right Worshipful? All drowned in the joy of this new mistress. <*to* SHIFT> But well, lieutenant, since he is so well provided for, you may put in with me 205 for a monster. Such a jest and such a sum is not to be lost.

SHIFT (*aside*) Nor shall not, or I have lost my aim.

FETHERFOOL (*putting off his hat*) Your pardons, good gentlemen, and though I perceive I shall have no great need for so trifling a sum as a hundred thousand pound 210 or so, yet a bargain's a bargain, gentlemen.

BLUNT Nay, 'adsheartlikins, the lieutenant scorns to do a foul thing, d'ye see, but we would not have the monsters slighted.

FETHERFOOL   Slighted! No, sir, I scorn your words, I'd 215

have ye to know, that I have as high a respect for madam
monster, as any gentleman in Christendom, and so I
desire she should understand.

BLUNT Why, this is that that's handsome.

SHIFT Well, the mountebank's come; lodgings are taken at 220
his house, and the guardian prepared to receive you on
the aforesaid terms; and some fifty pistoles to the
mountebank to stand your friend, and the business is
done.

FETHERFOOL Which shall be performed accordingly, I 225
have it ready about me.

BLUNT And here's mine. Put 'em together, and let's be
speedy, lest some should bribe higher and put in before
us.

(FETHERFOOL *takes the money, and looks pitifully on't*)

FETHERFOOL 'Tis a plaguy round sum, Ned, pray God it 230
turn to account.

BLUNT Account! 'Adsheartlikins, 'tis not in the power of
mortal man to cozen me.

SHIFT Oh fie, sir, cozen you, sir! Well, you'll stay here and
see the mountebank; he's coming forth.   235

(*A hollowing. Enter from the front a bank, a pageant**
which they fix on the stage at one side: a little pavilion
on't, music playing, and operators round below or
*antickers.** Music plays, and an antic dance*)

(*Enter* WILLMORE *like a mountebank, with a dagger in*
one hand, and a vial in the other; <HARLEQUIN>;
CARLO *with other* SPANIARDS *below, and rabble;*
ARIADNE *and* LUCIA *above in the balcony, others on the*
other side, FETHERFOOL *and* BLUNT *below*)

WILLMORE (*bowing*) Behold this little vial, which contains
in its narrow bounds* what the whole universe cannot
purchase, if sold to its true value. This admirable, this
miraculous elixir, drawn from the hearts of mandrakes,*
phoenix livers* and tongues of mermaids, and distilled by 240
contracted sun-beams, has, besides the unknown virtue of

curing all distempers both of mind and body, that divine
one of animating the heart of man to that degree, that
however remiss, cold and cowardly by nature, he shall
become vigorous and brave. O stupid and insensible man, 245
when honour and secure renown invites you, to treat it
with neglect; even when you need but passive valour to
become the heroes of the age. Receive a thousand
wounds, each of which would let out fleeting life. Here's
that can snatch the parting soul in its full career, and 250
bring it back to its native mansion; baffles grim death,
and disappoints even fate.

FETHERFOOL Oh pox, an a man were sure of that now.

WILLMORE Behold, here's demonstration.

(HARLEQUIN *stabs himself and falls as dead*)

FETHERFOOL Hold, hold, why, what the devil, is the 255
fellow mad?

BLUNT Why, dost think he 'as hurt himself?

FETHERFOOL Hurt himself! Why he's murdered, man; 'tis
flat felo de se,* in any ground in England, if I understand
law, and I have been a Justice o'th' Peace.   260

WILLMORE See, gentlemen, he's dead.

FETHERFOOL (*going out*) Look ye there now, I'll be gone
lest I be taken as an accessory.

WILLMORE Coffin him, inter him; yet after four and
twenty hours, as many drops of this divine elixir gives 265
him new life again. This will recover whole fields of slain,
and all the dead shall rise and fight again. 'Twas this that
made the Roman legions numerous, and now makes
France so formidable, and this alone may be the occasion
of the loss of Germany.   270

(*Pours in* HARLEQUIN's *wound; he rises*)

FETHERFOOL Why, this fellow's the devil, Ned, that's
certain.

BLUNT Oh plague, a damned conjurer, this.

WILLMORE Come, buy this coward's comfort, quickly buy.
What fop would be amused, mimicked and scorned, for 275

fear of wounds can be so easily cured? Who is't would bear the insolence and pride of domineering great men, proud officers or magistrates? Or who would cringe to statesmen out of fear? What cully would be cuckolded? What foolish heir undone by cheating gamesters? What lord would be lampooned? What poet fear the malice of his satirical brother, or atheist fear to fight for fear of death? Come, buy my cowards' comfort, quickly, buy.

FETHERFOOL Egad, Ned, a very excellent thing this; I'll lay out ten reals upon this commodity.

(They buy, whilst another part of the dance is danced)

WILLMORE Behold, this little paper, which contains a powder, whose value surmounts that of rocks of diamonds and hills of gold. 'Twas this made Venus a goddess, and given her by Apollo, from her derived to Helen, and in the sack of Troy lost, till recovered by me out of some ruins of Asia. Come, buy it, ladies, you that would be fair and wear eternal youth; and you in whom the amorous fire remains, when all the charms are fled. You that dress young and gay, and would be thought so; that patch and paint, to fill up time's old furrows on your brows, and set yourselves for conquest though in vain. Here's that will give you auburn hair, white teeth, red lips, and dimples on your cheeks. Come, buy it all you that are past bewitching, and would have handsome, young and active lovers.

FETHERFOOL Another good thing, Ned.

CARLO I'll lay out a pistole or two on this, if it have the same effect on men.

WILLMORE Come, all you city wives, that would advance your husbands to Lord Mayors, come, buy of me new beauty. This will give it, though now decayed, as are your shop commodities. This will retrieve your customers, and vend your false and out-of-fashioned*wares. Cheat, lie, protest and cozen as you please, a handsome wife makes all a lawful gain. Come, city wives, come, buy.

FETHERFOOL A most prodigious fellow.

(They buy, he sits; the other part is danced)

WILLMORE But here, behold the life and soul of man! This
is the amorous powder which Venus made and gave the
god of love, which made him first a deity. You talk of
arrows, bows and killing darts: fables, poetical fictions 315
and no more! 'Tis this alone that wounds and fires the
heart, makes women kind, and equals men to gods! 'Tis
this that makes your great lady dote on the ill-favoured
fop; your great man be jilted by his little mistress; the
judge cajoled by his seamstress, and your politician by his 320
comedian;* your young lady dote on her decrepit husband; your chaplain on my lady's waiting-woman; and
the young squire on the laundry-maid. In fine, messieurs:
'Tis this that cures the lover's pain,
And Celia of her cold disdain.   325
FETHERFOOL A most devilish fellow this!
BLUNT Hold, 'sheartlikins, Fetherfool, let's have a dose or
two of this powder for quick dispatch with our monsters.
FETHERFOOL Who? Pox, man, Jug,* my giant would
swallow a whole cart-load before 'twould operate.   330
BLUNT No hurt in trying a paper or two, however.
CARLO A most admirable receipt, I shall have need on't.
WILLMORE I need say nothing of my divine baths of
reformation, nor the wonders of the old oracle of the
box,* which resolves all questions; my bills sufficiently 335
declare their virtue.

(Sits down. They buy)

(Enter PETRONELLA ELENORA *carried in a chair, dressed
like a girl of fifteen)*

SHIFT Room there, gentlemen, room for a patient.
BLUNT Pray, seignior, who may this be thus muzzled* by
old gaffer Time?
CARLO One Petronella Elenora, sir, a famous out-worn 340
courtesan.
BLUNT Elenora – she may be that of Troy for her antiquity,
though fitter for god Priapus to ravish than Paris.*

SHIFT Hunt, a word. Dost thou see that same formal*
politician yonder, on the jennet,* the nobler animal of the 345
two?

HUNT What of him?

SHIFT 'Tis the same drew on the captain this morning, and
I must revenge the affront.

HUNT Have a care of revenges in Spain upon persons of his 350
quality.

SHIFT Nay, I'll only steal his horse from under him.

HUNT Steal it! Thou mayst take it by force perhaps, but
how safely is a question.

SHIFT I'll warrant thee. Shoulder you up one side of his 355
great saddle, I'll do the like on t'other; then, heaving him
gently up, Harlequin shall lead the horse from between
his worship's legs. All this in the crowd will not be
perceived, where all eyes are employed on the mountebank.   360

HUNT I apprehend you now.

(*Whilst they are lifting* PETRONELLA *on the stage of the*
MOUNTEBANK, *they go into the crowd, shoulder up*
CARLO's *saddle.* HARLEQUIN *leads the horse forward,*
whilst CARLO *is gazing, and turning up his mustachios;*
they hold him up a little while, then let him drop. He
rises and stares about for his horse)

CARLO This <is> flat conjuration.

SHIFT What's your worship on foot?

HUNT I never saw his worship on foot before.

CARLO Sirrah, none of your jests, this must be by diabolical 365
art, and shall cost the seignior dear. Men of my garb
affronted; my jennet vanished! Most miraculous, by St
Jago,* I'll be revenged – Hah, what here – La Nuche!
(*surveys her at a distance*)

(*Enter* LA NUCHE, AURELIA, SANCHO; BEAUMOND
following)

LA NUCHE We are pursued by Beaumond, who will
certainly hinder our speaking to Willmore, should we 370

have the good fortune to see him in this crowd; and yet
there's no avoiding him.

BEAUMOND (*aside*) 'Tis she, how carefully she shuns me!

AURELIA I'm satisfied he knows us by the jealous concern
which appears in that prying countenance of his.   375

BEAUMOND (*holds* <LA NUCHE>) Stay, cruel: is it love or
curiosity that wings those nimble feet?

(LUCIA *above and* ARIADNE)

ARIADNE (*aside*) Beaumond, with a woman –

BEAUMOND Have* you forgot this is the glorious day
That ushers in the night shall make you mine?   380
The happiest night that ever favoured love!

LA NUCHE Or if I have, I find you'll take care to
remember* me.

BEAUMOND Sooner I could forget the aids of life;
Sooner forget how first that beauty charmed me.

LA NUCHE Well, since your memory's so good, I need
not doubt your coming.   385

BEAUMOND Still cold and unconcerned!
How have I doted, and how sacrificed,
Regardless of my fame, lain idling here,
When all the youth of Spain were gaining honour,
Valuing one smile of thine above their laurels!   390

LA NUCHE And in return, I do submit to yield,
Preferring you above those fighting fools,
Who safe in multitudes reap honour cheaper.

BEAUMOND Yet there is one – one of those fighting
fools,
Which shouldst thou see, I fear I were undone: 395
Brave, handsome, gay, and all that women dote on;
Unfortunate in every good of life,
But that one blessing of obtaining women.
Be wise, for if thou seest him thou art lost –
Why dost thou blush?

LA NUCHE   Because you doubt my heart.   400
(*aside*) 'Tis Willmore that he means.
<*to* BEAUMOND> We've eyes upon us, Don Carlo may

grow jealous, and he's a powerful rival. At night I shall expect ye.

BEAUMOND   Whilst I prepare myself for such a blessing.   405

[*Exit* BEAUMOND]

CARLO (*aside*) Hah! A cavalier in conference with La Nuche; and entertained without my knowledge! I must prevent this lover, for he's young – and this night will surprise her.

WILLMORE (*to* PETRONELLA) And you would be restored?   410

PETRONELLA   Yes, if there be that divinity in your baths of reformation.

WILLMORE   There are.
New flames shall sparkle in those eyes,
And these grey hairs flowing and bright shall rise;   415
These cheeks fresh buds of roses wear,
And all your withered limbs so smooth and clear
As shall a general wonder move,
And wound a thousand hearts with love.*

PETRONELLA   A blessing on you, sir, there's fifty pistoles   420
for you, and as I earn it you shall have more.

(*They lift her down*)

[*Exit* WILLMORE, *bowing*]

<*Exit* PETRONELLA>

SHIFT   Messieurs, 'tis late, and the seignior's patients stay for him at his laboratory. Tomorrow you shall see the conclusion of this experiment, and so I humbly take my leave at this time.   425

<*Exeunt* SHIFT *and* HUNT>

(*Enter* WILLMORE *below, sees* LA NUCHE; *makes up to her, whilst the last part of the dance is dancing*)

LA NUCHE   What makes you follow me, sir?

(*She goes from him, he pursues*)

WILLMORE   Madam, I see something in that lovely face of

yours, which if not timely prevented, will be your ruin.
I'm now in haste, but I have more to say.

[*Goes off*]

LA NUCHE Stay, sir. He's gone – and filled me with a   430
curiosity that will not let me rest till it be satisfied. Follow
me, Aurelia, for I must know my destiny.

[*Goes out*]

(*The dance ended, the bank removes; the people go off*)

FETHERFOOL Come, Ned, now for our amorous visit to
the two lady monsters.

[*Exit* FETHERFOOL *and* BLUNT]

Act 2, Scene 2

Scene changes to a fine chamber

(*Enter* ARIADNE *and* LUCIA)

ARIADNE I'm thoughtful. Prithee, cousin, sing some foolish
song.
<LUCIA (*sings*)>

Song

Phyllis, whose heart was unconfined,
And free as flowers on meads and plains,
None boasted of her being kind,
'Mongst all the languishing and amorous swains;
No sighs nor tears the nymph could move   (*Bis*)*
To pity, or return their love.

Till on a time, the hapless maid
Retired, to shun the heat o'th' day,
Into a grove beneath whose shade,
Strephon, the careless shepherd, sleeping lay.
But, oh, such charms the youth adorn,   (*Bis*)
Love is revenged for all her scorn.

                                                            5

                                                            10

Her cheeks with blushes covered were,   15
And tender sighs her bosom warm;
A softness in her eyes appear,
Unusual pains she feels from every charm.
To woods and echoes now she cries,   (*Bis*)
For modesty to speak denies.   20

ARIADNE   Come, help to undress me, for I'll to this
mountebank to know what success I shall have with my
cavalier.

(*Unpins her things before a great glass that is fastened*)

LUCIA   You are resolved then to give him admittance?
ARIADNE   Where's the danger of a handsome young fellow?   25
LUCIA   But you don't know him, madam.
ARIADNE   But I desire to do, and time may bring it about
without miracle.
LUCIA   Your cousin, Beaumond, will forbid the banns.
ARIADNE   No, nor old Carlo, neither: my mother's precious   30
choice, who is as solicitous for the old gentleman, as my
father-in-law is for his nephew. Therefore, Lucia, like a
good and gracious child, I'll end the dispute between my
father and mother, and please myself in the choice of this
stranger, if he be to be had.   35
LUCIA   I should as soon be enamoured on the north wind, a
tempest, or a clap of thunder. Bless me from such a blast.
ARIADNE   I'd have my lover rough as seas in storms upon
occasion. I hate your dull temperate lover, 'tis such a
husbandly quality! Like Beaumond's addresses to me,   40
whom neither joy nor anger puts in motion; or if it do, 'tis
visibly forced. I'm glad I saw him entertain a woman
today – not that I care, but would be fairly rid of him.
LUCIA   You'll hardly mend yourself in this.
ARIADNE   What, because he held discourse with a   45
courtesan?
LUCIA   Why, is there no danger in her eyes do ye think?
ARIADNE   None that I fear. That stranger's not such a fool
to give his heart to a common woman; and she that's

concerned where her lover bestows his body, were I the 50
man, I should think she had a mind to't herself.

LUCIA And reason, madam, in a lawful way; 'tis your due.

ARIADNE What, all? Unconscionable, Lucia! I am more
merciful. But be he what he will, I'll to this cunning man
to know whether ever any part of him shall be mine. 55

LUCIA Lord, madam, sure he's a conjurer.*

ARIADNE Let him be the devil, I'll try his skill, and to that
end will put on a suit of my cousin Endymion; there are
two or three very pretty ones of his in the wardrobe. Go
carry 'em to my chamber, and we'll fit ourselves and 60
away. Go, haste whilst I undress.

[Exit LUCIA]

(ARIADNE undressing before the glass. Enter BEAUMOND
tricking* himself, and looks on himself)

BEAUMOND Now for my charming beauty, fair La Nuche –
(aside) Hah, Ariadne! Damn the dull property! How shall
I free myself?

(She turns, sees him, and walks from the glass. He takes
no notice of her, but tricks himself in the glass, humming
a song)

ARIADNE (aside) Beaumond! What devil brought him 65
hither to prevent me; I hate the formal matrimonial fop!

(Walks about and sings)

Somme nous pas trop heureux
Belle Irise que nous ensemble?
(aside) A devil on him, he may chance to plague me till
night, and hinder my dear assignation. 70

(Sings again)

La nuit et ses sombres voiles
Couvrit nos désires ardents;
Et l'amour et les étoiles,
Sont nos secrets confidents.*

BEAUMOND Pox on't, how dull am I at an excuse. 75

(*Sets his wig in the glass, and sings*)

A pox of love and womankind,
And all the fops adore 'em.

(*Puts on his hat, cocks it and goes to her*)

How is't, coz?

ARIADNE <*aside*> So, here's the saucy freedom of a husband lover; a blest invention this of marrying, whoe'er   80
first found it out.

BEAUMOND Damn this English dog of a periwig-maker!
What an ungainly air it gives the face, and for a wedding
periwig too! (*uneasy*) How dost thou like it, Ariadne?

ARIADNE As ill as the man. I perceive you have taken more   85
care for your periwig than your bride.

BEAUMOND And with reason, Ariadne. The bride was
never the care of the lover, but the business of the parents:
'tis a serious affair, and ought to be managed by the grave
and wise. Thy mother and my uncle have agreed the   90
matter, and would it not look very sillily in me now to
whine a tedious tale of love in your ear, when the business
is at an end? 'Tis like saying a grace when a man should
give thanks.

ARIADNE Why did not you begin sooner then?   95

BEAUMOND Faith, Ariadne, because I know nothing of the
design in hand. Had I had civil warning, thou shouldst
have had as pretty smart speeches from me as any
coxcomb lover of 'em all could have made thee.

ARIADNE I shall never marry like a Jew in my own tribe.   100
I'd rather be possessed by honest, old, doting age, than by
saucy, conceited youth, whose inconstancy never leaves a
woman safe or quiet.

BEAUMOND You know the proverb of the half-loaf,*
Ariadne: a husband that will deal thee some love is better   105
than one who can give thee none. You would have a
blessed time on't with old father Carlo.

ARIADNE No matter, a woman may with some lawful
excuse cuckold him, and 'twould be scarce a sin –

BEAUMOND Not so much as lying with him, whose 110
reverend age would make it look like incest.

ARIADNE But to marry thee would be a tyranny from
whence there's no appeal. A drinking, whoring husband,
'tis the devil!

BEAUMOND You are deceived if you think Don Carlo more 115
chaste than I – only duller and more a miser; one that
fears his flesh more and loves his money better. Then, to
be condemned to lie with him! Oh, who would not rejoice
to meet a woollen waistcoat and knit nightcap without a
lining; a shirt so nasty, a cleanly ghost would not appear 120
in't at the latter day! Then the compound of nasty smells
about him: stinking breath, mustachios stuffed with
villainous snush* tobacco, and hollow teeth. Thus prepared for delight, you meet in bed where you may lie and
sigh whole nights away. He snores it out till morning and 125
then rises to his sordid business.

ARIADNE All this frights me not; 'tis still much better than
a keeping husband,* whom neither beauty nor honour in
a wife can oblige.

BEAUMOND Oh, you know not the good nature of a man 130
of wit. At least I shall bear a conscience, and do thee
reason,* which heaven denies to old Carlo were he
willing.

ARIADNE Oh, he talks as high, and thinks as well of
himself as any young coxcomb of ye all. 135

BEAUMOND He has reason, for if his faith were no better
than his works, he'd be damned.

ARIADNE Death, who would marry who would be chaf-
fered thus, and sold to slavery! I'd rather buy a friend at
any price that I could love and trust. 140

BEAUMOND Aye! Could we but drive on such a bargain!

ARIADNE You should not be the man. You have a mistress,
sir, that has your heart, and all your softer hours. I
know't, and if I were so wretched as to marry thee, must
see my fortune lavished out on her; her coaches, dress and 145
equipage exceed mine by far; possess she all the day thy
hours of mirth, good humour and expense; thy smiles, thy

kisses, and thy charms of wit. Oh, how you talk and look
when in her presence! But when with me (*sings*):
'A pox of love and womankind,   150
And all the fops adore 'em.'
'How is't cuz?' – Then, slap; on goes the beaver, which
being cocked, you bear up briskly, with the second part to
the same tune. Hark ye, sir, let me advise you to pack up
your trumpery and be gone; your honourable love, your   155
matrimonial foppery, with your other trinkets thereunto
belonging; or I shall talk aloud, and let your uncle hear
you.

BEAUMOND (*aside*) Sure, she cannot know I love La
Nuche? (*to her*) The devil take me, spoiled! What rascal   160
has inveigled thee? What lying, fawning coward has
abused thee? When fell you into this lewdness? Pox, thou
art hardly worth the loving now, that canst be such a fool
to wish me chaste, or love me for that virtue; or that
wouldst have me a ceremonious whelp: one that makes   165
handsome legs* to knights without laughing; or with a
sneaking, modest, squirish countenance, assure you I have
my maidenhead. A curse upon thee! The very thought of
wife has made thee formal.

ARIADNE (*aside*) I must dissemble, or he'll stay all day to   170
make his peace again. <*to him*> Why, have you ne'er a
mistress then?

BEAUMOND A hundred, by this day; as many as I like.
They are my mirth, the business of my loose and wanton
hours; but thou art my devotion; the grave, the solemn   175
pleasure of my soul – <*aside*> Pox, would I were
handsomely rid of thee too! <*to her*> Come, I have
business – send me pleased away.

ARIADNE (*aside*) Would to heaven thou wert gone. <*to
him*> You're going to some woman now.   180

BEAUMOND Oh, damn the sex! I hate 'em all – but thee.
Farewell, my pretty, jealous – sullen – fool –

[*Goes out*]

ARIADNE Farewell, believing coxcomb!

(*Enter* LUCIA)

LUCIA Madam, the clothes are ready in your chamber.
ARIADNE Let's haste and put 'em on then.   185

[*Runs out*]

Act 3, Scene 1

A house

(*Enter* FETHERFOOL *and* BLUNT, *staring about; after
them* SHIFT)

SHIFT Well, gentlemen, this is the doctor's house, and your
fifty pistoles has made him entirely yours; the ladies too
are here in safe custody. Come, draw lots who shall have
the dwarf, and who the giant.

(*They draw*)

FETHERFOOL I have the giant.   5
BLUNT And I the little tiny gentlewoman.
SHIFT Well, you shall first see the ladies, and then prepare
for your uncle Moses, the old Jew guardian, before whom
you must be very grave and sententious. You know the
old law was full of ceremony.*   10
FETHERFOOL Well, I long to see the ladies, and to have the
first onset over.
SHIFT I'll cause 'em to walk forth immediately.

[*Goes out*]

FETHERFOOL My heart begins to fail me plaguily. Would I
could see 'em a little at a distance before they come slap   15
dash upon a man. (*peeping*) Hah! Mercy upon us! What's
yonder! Ah, Ned, my monster<'s> as big as the whore of
Babylon* – Oh, I'm in a cold sweat –

(BLUNT *pulls him to peep, and both do so*)

Oh lord! She's as tall as the St Christopher in Notre Dame

at Paris; and the little one looks like the Christo upon his   20
shoulder.* I shall ne'er be able to stand the first brunt.
BLUNT (*pulls him back*) 'Adsheartlikins, whither art going?
FETHERFOOL Why only – to – say my prayers a little – I'll
be with thee presently.

(*Offers to go, he pulls him*)

BLUNT What a pox, art thou afraid of a woman?   25
FETHERFOOL Not of a woman, Ned, but of a she-Gargan-
tua.* I am <of> a Hercules in petticoats.*
BLUNT The less resemblance the better. 'Sheartlikins, I'd
rather mine were a centaur* than a woman. No, since my
Naples adventure, I am clearly for your monster.   30
FETHERFOOL Prithee, Ned, there's reason in all things –
BLUNT – But villainous woman. 'Adsheartlikins, stand
your ground, or I'll nail ye to't. Why, what a pox, are you
so queasy-stomached a monster won't down with you,
with a hundred thousand pound to boot?   35

(*Pulling him*)

FETHERFOOL Nay, Ned, that mollifies something; and I
scorn it should be said of Nick Fetherfool that he left his
friend in danger, or did an ill thing. Therefore, as thou
sayst, Ned, though she were a centaur, I'll not budge an
inch.   40
BLUNT Why, God a mercy.

(*Enter the* GIANT *and* DWARF; *with them* SHIFT *as an
operator* <*and* HARLEQUIN>)

FETHERFOOL Oh, they come! Prithee, Ned, advance.

(*Puts him forward*)

SHIFT Most beautiful ladies –
FETHERFOOL (*aside*) Why, what a flattering son of a
whore's this!   45
SHIFT These are the illustrious persons your uncle designs
your humble servants, and who have so extraordinary a
passion for your seigniorships.

FETHERFOOL (*aside*) Oh yes, a most damnable one. Would
I were cleanlily off the lay,* and had my money again.   50
BLUNT (*aside*) Think of a million, rogue, and do not hang
an arse* thus.
GIANT (*to* SHIFT) What, does the cavalier think I'll devour
him?
FETHERFOOL Something inclined to such a fear.   55
BLUNT (*aside*) Go and salute* her, or, 'adsheartlikins, I'll
leave you to her mercy.
FETHERFOOL (*aside*) Oh, dear Ned, have pity on me; but
as for saluting her, you speak of more than may be done,
dear heart, without a scaling ladder.   60

[*Exit* SHIFT]

DWARF Sure, Seignior Harlequin, these gentlemen are
dumb.
BLUNT No, my little diminutive mistress, my small epitome
of womankind; we can prattle when our hands are in, but
we are raw and bashful, young beginners; for this is the   65
first time we ever were in love. We are something
awkward, or so; but we shall come on in time, and mend
upon encouragement.
FETHERFOOL (*aside*) Pox on him, what a delicate speech
has he made now. Gad, I'd give a thousand pound a year   70
for Ned's concise wit, but not a groat for his judgement in
womankind.

(*Enter* SHIFT *with a ladder, sets it against the* GIANT,
and bows to FETHERFOOL)

SHIFT Here, seignior, don; approach, mount, and salute the
lady.
FETHERFOOL (*aside*) Mount! Why 'twould turn my brains   75
to look down from her shoulders; but hang't, gad, I will
be brave and venture.

(*Runs up the ladder, salutes her, and runs down again*)

(*aside*) And egad, this was an adventure and a bold one;
but since I am come off with a whole skin, I am fleshed
for the next onset.   80

(*Goes to her, speaks, and runs back;* BLUNT *claps him on the back*)

– Madam, has your greatness any mind to marry?

GIANT What if I have?

FETHERFOOL Why then, madam, without enchanted sword or buckler, I am your man.

GIANT My man? My mouse! I'll marry none whose person 85 and courage shall not bear some proportion to mine.

FETHERFOOL Your Mightiness, I fear, will die a maid then.

GIANT I doubt you'll scarce secure me from that fear, who court my fortune, not my beauty.

FETHERFOOL <*aside*> Huh, how scornful she is, I'll war 90 rant you. <*to her*> Why, I must confess, your person is something heroical and masculine, but I protest to your Highness, I love and honour ye.

DWARF Prithee, sister, be not so coy, I like my lover well enough; and if Seignior Mountebank keep his word in 95 making us of reasonable proportions, I think the gentlemen may serve for husbands.

SHIFT (*aside to the* GIANT) Dissemble, or you betray your love for us.

GIANT And if he do keep his word, I should make a better 100 choice. Not that I would change this noble frame of mine, could I but meet my match and keep up the first race of man* entire; but since this scanty world affords none such, I, to be happy, must be new created, and then I shall expect a wiser lover.   105

FETHERFOOL <*aside*> Why, what a peevish tit's* this! <*to her*> Nay, look ye, madam, as for that matter, your Extraordinariness may do what you please; but 'tis not done like a monster of honour, when a man has set his heart upon you, to cast him off. Therefore, I hope you'll 110 pity a despairing lover, and cast down an eye of consolation upon me; for I vow, most Amazonian* princess, I love ye as if heaven and earth would come together.

DWARF My sister will do much, I'm sure, to save the man 115 that loves her so passionately; she has a heart.

FETHERFOOL (*aside*) And a swinger* 'tis! 'Sbud, she moves like the Royal Sovereign,* and is as long a-tacking about.

GIANT Then your religion, sir.

FETHERFOOL Nay, as for that, madam, we are English: a nation, I thank God, that stands as little upon religion as any nation under the sun, unless it be in contradiction; and at this time, have so many amongst us, a man knows not which to turn his hand to. Neither will I stand with your Hugeness for a small matter of faith or so; religion shall break no squares.

DWARF I hope, sir, you are of your friend's opinion.

BLUNT My little spark of a diamond, I am. I was born a Jew, with aversion to swine's flesh.

DWARF Well, sir, I shall hasten Seignior Doctor to complete my beauty by some small addition, to appear the more grateful to you.

BLUNT Lady, do not trouble yourself with transitory parts. 'Adsheartlikins, thou'rt as handsome as needs be for a wife.

DWARF A little taller, seignior, would not do amiss; my younger sister has got so much the start of me.

BLUNT In troth she has; and now I think on't, a little taller would do well for propagation. I should be loath the posterity of the ancient family of the Blunts of Essex should dwindle into pigmies or fairies.

GIANT Well, seigniors, since you come with our uncle's liking, we give ye leave to hope – hope, and be happy.

(*They* <and HARLEQUIN> *go out*)

FETHERFOOL Egad, and that's great and gracious.

(*Enter* WILLMORE *and an* OPERATOR)

WILLMORE Well, gentlemen, and how like you the ladies?

BLUNT Faith, well enough for the first course, sir.

WILLMORE The uncle, by my endeavour, is entirely yours; but whilst the baths are preparing, 'twould be well if you would think of what age, shape and complexion you would have your ladies formed in.

FETHERFOOL Why, may we choose, Mr Doctor?

WILLMORE What beauties you please.

FETHERFOOL Then will I have my giant, Ned, just such
another gentlewoman as I saw at church today – and
about some fifteen.   155

BLUNT Hum, fifteen – I begin to have a plaguy itch about
me, too, towards a handsome damsel of fifteen; but first
let's marry, lest they should be boiled away in these baths
of reformation.

FETHERFOOL But, doctor, can you do all this without the   160
help of the devil?

WILLMORE Hum, some small hand he has in the business.
We make an exchange with him; give him the clippings of
the giant for so much of his store as will serve to build the
dwarf.   165

BLUNT Why, then, mine will be more than three parts devil,
Mr Doctor.

WILLMORE Not so, the stock is only devil; the graft is your
own little wife inoculated.

BLUNT Well, let the devil and you agree about this matter   170
as soon as you please.

(*Enter* SHIFT *as an operator*)

SHIFT Sir, there is without a person of an extraordinary
size would speak with you.

WILLMORE Admit him.

(*Enter* HARLEQUIN; *ushers in* HUNT *as a giant*)

FETHERFOOL (*aside*) Hah, some o'ergrown rival, on my   175
life!

(FETHERFOOL *gets from it*)

WILLMORE (*aside*) What the devil have we here?

HUNT *Bezolos mano's,** seignior, I understand there is a
lady whose beauty and proportion can only merit me. I'll
say no more, but shall be grateful to you for your   180
assistance.

FETHERFOOL <*aside*> 'Tis so.

HUNT (*aside*) The devil's in't if this does not fright 'em from a farther courtship.

WILLMORE Fear nothing, seignior. Seignor, you may try 185 your chance, and visit the ladies.

(<HUNT> *talks to* WILLMORE)

FETHERFOOL Why, where the devil could this monster conceal himself all this while, that we should neither see nor hear of him?

BLUNT Oh, he lay disguised; I have heard of an army that 190 has done so.

FETHERFOOL Pox, no single house could hold him.

BLUNT No – he disposed himself in several parcels up and down the town, here a leg, and there an arm; and hearing of this proper match for him, put himself together to 195 court his fellow monster.

FETHERFOOL Good Lord! I wonder what religion he's of.

BLUNT Some heathen papist, by his notable plots and contrivances.

WILLMORE (*aside*) 'Tis Hunt, that rogue. – Sir, I confess 200 there is great power in sympathy. Conduct him to the ladies.

(<HUNT> *tries to go in at the door*)

I am sorry you cannot enter at that low door, seignior; I'll have it broken down.

HUNT No, seignior, I can go in at twice.   205

FETHERFOOL How? At twice? What a pox can he mean?

WILLMORE Oh, sir, 'tis a frequent thing by way of enchantment.

(HUNT, *being all doublet, leaps off from another man who is all breeches, and goes out. Breeches follows, stalking*)

FETHERFOOL Oh pox, Mr Doctor, this must be the devil!

WILLMORE Oh fie, sir, the devil? No, 'tis all done by an 210 enchanted girdle. (*aside*) These damned rascals will spoil all by too gross an imposition on the fools.

FETHERFOOL This is the devil, Ned, that's certain – but hark'ee, Mr Doctor, I hope I shall not have my mistress enchanted from me by this enchanted rival, hah? 215

WILLMORE Oh, no, sir, the Inquisition will never let 'em marry, for fear of a race of giants; 'twill be worse than the invasion of the Moors, or the French. But go, think of your mistresses' names and ages; here's company, and you would not be seen. 220

[*Exeunt* BLUNT *and* FETHERFOOL]

(*Enter* LA NUCHE, AURELIA, <SANCHO>; WILLMORE *bows to her*)

LA NUCHE Sir, the fame of your excellent knowledge, and what you said to me this day, has given me a curiosity to learn my fate, at least that fate you threatened.

WILLMORE Madam, from the oracle in the box you may be resolved any question. 225

(*Leads her to the table where stands a box full of balls; stares on her*)

<aside> How lovely every absent minute makes her. – Madam, be pleased to draw from out this box what ball you will.

(*She draws; he takes it and gazes on her and on it*)

Madam, upon this little globe is charactered your fate and fortune; the history of your life to come and past. First, 230 madam, you're – a whore.

LA NUCHE A very plain beginning.

WILLMORE My art speaks simple truth; the moon is your ascendant, that covetous planet that borrows all his light, and is in opposition still to Venus; and – interest more 235 prevails with you than love! Yet here I find a cross, intruding line – that does inform me – you have an itch that way, but interest still opposes. You are a slavish, mercenary prostitute.

LA NUCHE Your art is so, though called divine! And all the 240 universe is swayed by interest; and would you wish this beauty which adorns me, should be disposed about for charity? Proceed, and speak more reason.

WILLMORE But Venus here gets the ascent again, and – spite of interest, spite of all aversion, will make you dote 245 upon a man – (*still looking on and turning the ball*) – wild, fickle, restless, faithless as the winds! A man of arms he is – and by this line – a captain (*looking on her*) – for Mars and Venus were in conjunction at his birth, and love and war's his business – 250

LA NUCHE There thou hast touched my heart, and spoke so true that all thou sayst I shall receive as oracle! Well, grant I love: that shall not make me yield.

WILLMORE I must confess you're ruined if you yield; and yet not all your pride, not all your vows, your wit, your 255 resolution or your cunning, can hinder him from conquering absolutely. Your stars are fixed, and fate irrevocable.

LA NUCHE No! I will control my stars and inclinations, and though I love him more than power or interest, I will be mistress of my fixed resolves. One question more, does 260 this same captain, this wild, happy man – love me?

WILLMORE I do not – find – it here – only a possibility encouraged by your love. Oh that you could resist – but you are destined his, and to be ruined –

(*Sighs and looks on her; she grows in rage*)

LA NUCHE Why do you tell me this? I am betrayed, and 265 every caution blows my kindling flame. Hold, tell me no more – I might have guessed my fate, from my own soul have guessed it; but yet I will be brave. I will resist in spite of inclinations, stars or devils.

WILLMORE Strive not, fair creature, with the net that holds 270 you; you'll but entangle more. Alas, you must submit and be undone!

LA NUCHE Damn your false art! Had he but loved me too, it had excused the malice of my stars.

WILLMORE Indeed, his love is doubtful; for here – I trace 275 him in a new pursuit, which, if you can this night prevent, perhaps you fix him.

LA NUCHE Hah, pursuing a new mistress! There thou hast met the little resolution I had left, and dashed it into nothing; but I have vowed allegiance to my interest. Curse 280 on my stars, they could not give me love where that might be advanced! I'll hear no more – (*gives him money*)

(*Enter* SHIFT)

SHIFT Sir, there are several strangers arrived who talk of the old oracle. How will you receive 'em?

WILLMORE I've business now and must be excused a while. 285 <*aside*> Thus far I'm well, but I may tell my tale so often o'er, till, like the trick of love, I spoil the pleasure by the repetition. Now I'll uncase,* and see what effects my art has wrought on La Nuche, for she's the promised good, the philosophic treasure* that terminates my toil and 290 industry. <*to* SHIFT> Wait you here.

[*Exit* WILLMORE]

(*Enter* ARIADNE *in men's clothes, with* LUCIA *so dressed, and other* STRANGERS)

ARIADNE How now,* Seignior Operator, where's this renowned man of arts and sciences, this Don of Wonders? Hah? May a man have a pistole's worth or two of his tricks? Will he show, seignior?   295

SHIFT Whatever you dare see, sir.

ARIADNE And I dare see the greatest bugbear he can conjure up, my mistress's face in a glass excepted.

SHIFT That he can show, sir, but is now busied in weighty affairs with a grandee.   300

ARIADNE Pox, must we wait the leisure of formal grandees and statesmen! Hah, who's this? The lovely conqueress of my heart, La Nuche.

(*Goes to her; she is talking to* AURELIA)

LA NUCHE What foolish thing art thou?

ARIADNE Nay, do not frown, nor fly; for if you do, I must 305 arrest you, fair one.

LA NUCHE At whose suit, pray?

ARIADNE At love's; you've stolen a heart of mine and used it scurvily.

LA NUCHE By what marks do you know the toy, that I may 310 be no longer troubled with it?

ARIADNE By a fresh wound, which touched by her that gave it bleeds anew; a heart all over kind and amorous.

LA NUCHE When was this pretty robbery committed?

ARIADNE Today, most sacrilegiously, at church, where you 315 debauched my zeal; and when I would have prayed, your eyes had put the change upon my tongue and made it utter railings. Heav'n forgive ye!

LA NUCHE You are the gayest thing without a heart, I ever saw.   320

ARIADNE I scorn to flinch for a bare wound or two. Nor is he routed that has lost the day; he may again rally, renew the fight and vanquish.

LA NUCHE You have a good opinion of that beauty which I find not so forcible, nor that fond prattle uttered with 325 such confidence.

ARIADNE But I have quality and fortune too.

LA NUCHE So you had need. I should have guessed the first by your pertness, for your saucy thing of quality acts the man as impudently at fourteen as another at thirty. Nor is 330 there anything so hateful as to hear it talk of love, women and drinking; nay, to see it marry too at that age, and get itself a playfellow in its son and heir.

ARIADNE This satire on my youth shall never put me out of countenance, or make me think you wish me one day 335 older; and egad, I'll warrant 'em that tries me, shall find me ne'er an hour too young.

LA NUCHE You mistake my humour; I hate the person of a fair, conceited boy.

(*Enter* WILLMORE *dressed,* * *singing*)

WILLMORE *Vole, vole, dans cette cage,*   340
    Petit oiseau dans ce bocage. *
  – How now, fool, where's the doctor?

SHIFT A little busy, sir.

WILLMORE Call him. I am in haste, and come to cheapen
the price of monster.   345

SHIFT As how, sir?

WILLMORE In an honourable way: I will lawfully marry
one of 'em, and have pitched upon the giant. I'll bid as
fair as any man.

SHIFT No doubt but you will speed, sir; please you, sir, to   350
walk in.

WILLMORE I'll follow – <sings> Vole, vole, dans cette
cage, etc.

LUCIA <aside to ARIADNE> Why 'tis the captain, madam.

LA NUCHE <aside> Hah – marry!   355

(As he is going out she pulls him)

Hark ye, sir, a word pray.

WILLMORE Your servant, madam, your servant. <sings>
Vole, vole, etc.

(Puts his hat off carelessly, and walks by, going out)

LUCIA <aside> And to be married, mark that.

ARIADNE <aside> Then there's one doubt over; I'm glad he   360
is not married.

LA NUCHE Come back! <aside> Death, I shall burst with
anger – this coldness blows my flame which, if once
visible, makes him a tyrant.

WILLMORE (shakes his pockets, and walks up and down)
Fool, what's a clock, fool? This noise hinders me from   365
hearing it strike.

LA NUCHE A blessed sound, if no hue and cry pursue it.
What, you are resolved then upon this notable exploit?

WILLMORE What exploit, good madam?

LA NUCHE Why, marrying of a monster, and an ugly   370
monster.

WILLMORE Yes faith, child, here stands the bold knight
that singly and unarmed designs to enter the list with
Thogogandiga, the giant. A good sword will defend a
worse cause than an ugly wife. I know no danger worse   375

than fighting for my living; and I have done't this dozen
years for bread.

LA NUCHE This is the common trick of all rogues, when
they have done an ill thing, to face it out.

WILLMORE An ill thing? Your pardon, sweetheart; com-   380
pare it but to banishment, a frozen sentry with brown
George and Spanish pay,* and if it be not better to be
master of a monster than slave to a damned commonwealth, I submit; and since my fortune has thrown this
good in my way –   385

LA NUCHE You'll not be so ungrateful to refuse it. Besides,
then you may hope to sleep again, without dreaming of
famine or the sword, two plagues a soldier of fortune is
subject to.

WILLMORE Besides cashiering, a third plague.   390

LA NUCHE Still unconcerned! You call me mercenary, but I
would starve ere suffer myself to be possessed by a thing
of horror.

WILLMORE You lie; you would, by any thing of horror. Yet
these things of horror have beauties too, beauties thou   395
canst not boast of, beauties that will not fade: diamonds
to supply the lustre of their eyes, and gold the brightness
of their hair; a well-got million to atone for shape; and
orient pearls, more white, more plump and smooth than
that fair body men so languish for, and thou hast set such   400
price on.

ARIADNE <aside> I like not this so well; 'tis a trick to make
her jealous.

WILLMORE Their hands, too, have their beauties, whose
very mark finds credit and respect; their bills are current   405
o'er the universe. Besides these, you shall see waiting at
my door four footmen, a velvet coach, with six Flanders
beauties* more. And are not these most comely virtues in
a soldier's wife, in this most wicked, peaceable age?

LUCIA (aside) He's poor too, there's another comfort.   410

ARIADNE <aside> The most encouraging one I have met
with yet.

WILLMORE Pox on't, I grow weary of this virtuous poverty. 'There goes a gallant fellow,' says one, but gives him
not an onion. The women, too: 'Faith 'tis a handsome 415
gentleman,' but the devil a kiss he gets gratis.

ARIADNE <aside> Oh, how I long to undeceive him of that
error.

LA NUCHE (aside) He speaks not of me. Sure, he knows me
not. 420

WILLMORE No, child, money speaks sense in a language all
nations understand; 'tis beauty, wit, courage, honour and
undisputable reason. See the virtue of a wager, that new
philosophical way lately found out of deciding all hard
questions. Socrates, without ready money to lay down, 425
must yield.

ARIADNE (aside) Well, I must have this gallant fellow.

LA NUCHE <aside> Sure, he has forgot this trivial thing.

WILLMORE (<in a> soft tone) Even thou, who seest me
dying unregarded, wo't* then be fond and kind, and 430
flatter me. – By heaven, I'll hate thee then; nay, I will
marry to be rich to hate thee. The worst of that is but to
suffer nine days' wonderment. Is not that better than an
age of scorn from a proud, faithless beauty?

LA NUCHE Oh, there's resentment left – Why, yes, faith, 435
such a wedding would give the town diversion. We
should have a lamentable ditty made on it, entitled, 'The
Captain's Wedding', with the doleful relation of his being
overlaid* by an o'ergrown monster.

WILLMORE I'll warrant ye I escape that as sure as cuckold- 440
ing, for I would fain see that hardy wight* that dares
attempt my lady bright, either by force or flattery.

LA NUCHE So, then, you intend to bed her?

WILLMORE Yes, faith, and beget a race of heroes: the
mother's form with all the father's qualities. 445

LA NUCHE Faith, such a brood may prove a pretty
livelihood for a poor decayed officer; you may chance to
get a patent to show 'em in England, that nation of
change and novelty.

WILLMORE A provision old Carlo cannot make for you 450
against the abandoned day.

LA NUCHE He can supply the want of issue a better way;
and though he be not so fine a fellow as yourself, he's a
better friend: he can keep a mistress. Give me a man can
feed and clothe me, as well as hug and all to bekiss me; 455
and though his sword be not so good as yours, his bond's
worth a thousand captains. (*aside*) This will not do; I'll
try what jealousy will do. Your servant, captain. (*takes*
ARIADNE *by the hand*) – Your hand, sir.

WILLMORE <*aside*> Hah! What new coxcomb's that? 460
Hold, sir –

(*Takes her from* <ARIADNE>)

ARIADNE What would you, sir? Aught with this lady?

WILLMORE Yes, that which thy youth will only let thee
guess at. This, child, is man's meat; there are other toys
for children. 465

(*Offers to lead her off*)

LA NUCHE Oh, insolent, and whither wouldst thou lead
me?

WILLMORE Only out of harm's way, child. Here are pretty
neat conveniences within. The doctor will be civil; 'tis
part of 's calling. <*to* ARIADNE> Your servant, sir.

(*Going off with* <LA NUCHE>)

ARIADNE <*aside*> I must huff now though I may chance to 470
be beaten. – Come back – (<*touching*> *his sword*) – or I
have something here that will oblige ye to't!

WILLMORE Yes, faith, thou'rt a pretty youth; but at this
time I've more occasion for a thing in petticoats. Go
home, and do not walk the streets much. That tempting 475
face of thine will debauch the grave men of business, and
make the magistrates lust after wickedness.

ARIADNE (*going to draw*) You are a scurvy fellow, sir.

WILLMORE Keep in your sword for fear it cut your fingers,
child. 480

ARIADNE So 'twill your throat, sir. <aside> Here's company coming that will part us, and I'll venture to draw.

(*Draws;* WILLMORE *draws*)

(*Enter* BEAUMOND)

BEAUMOND Hold, hold – hah, Willmore! Thou man of constant mischief; what's the matter?

LA NUCHE <aside> Beaumond! Undone! 485

ARIADNE <aside> Beaumond!

WILLMORE Why, here's a young spark will take my lady bright from me. The unmannered hotspur would not have patience till I had finished my small affair with her.

(*Puts up his sword*)

ARIADNE <aside> Death, he'll know me. <to WILLMORE> 490 Sir, you see we are prevented – (*draws him aside*) – or –

(*Seems to talk to him.* BEAUMOND *gazes on* LA NUCHE, *who has pulled down her veil*)

BEAUMOND 'Tis she! Madam, this veil's too thin to hide the perjured beauty underneath. Oh, have I been searching thee, with all the diligence of impatient love, and am I thus rewarded; to find thee here encompassed round with 495 strangers, fighting who first should take my right away? Gods, take your reason back! Take all your love; for easy man's unworthy of the blessings.

WILLMORE Hark ye, Harry – the woman, the almighty whore, thou told'st me of today. 500

BEAUMOND Death, dost thou mock my grief? Unhand me straight; for though I cannot blame thee, I must hate thee.

[*Goes out*]

WILLMORE What the devil ails he?

ARIADNE You will be sure to come?

WILLMORE At night in the piazza. I have an assignation 505 with a woman. That once dispatched, I will not fail ye, sir.

LUCIA <aside> And will you leave him with her?

ARIADNE *<aside>* Oh yes, he'll be ne'er the worse for my use when he has done with her.   510

[*Exeunt* LUCIA *and* ARIADNE]

(WILLMORE *looks with scorn on* LA NUCHE)

WILLMORE Now you may go o'ertake him, lie with him – and ruin him; the fool was made for such a destiny – if he escapes my sword.

(*He offers to go*)

LA NUCHE (*aside*) I must prevent his visit to this woman; but dare not tell him so. *<to him>* I would not have ye   515 meet this angry youth.

WILLMORE Oh, you would preserve him for a farther use!

LA NUCHE Stay, you must not fight. By heaven, I cannot see – that bosom – wounded.

(*Turns and weeps*)

WILLMORE Hah! Weep'st thou? Curse me when I refuse a   520 faith to that obliging language of thy eyes. Oh, give me one proof more, and after that thou conquerest all my soul. Thy eyes speak love. Come, let us in, my dear, ere the bright fire allays that warms my heart!

(*Goes to lead her out*)

LA NUCHE Your love grows rude, and saucily demands it.   525

(*Flings away*)

WILLMORE Love knows no ceremony, no respect,*
When once approached so near the happy minute.

LA NUCHE What desperate easiness have you seen in me,
Or what mistaken merit in yourself,
Should make you so ridiculously vain   530
To think I'd give myself to such a wretch;
One fall'n even to the last degree of poverty,
Whilst all the world is prostrate at my feet,
Whence I might choose the brave, the great, the rich?

(*He stands spitefully gazing at her*)

(*aside*) Still, as he fires, I find my pride augment;   535
And when he cools, I burn.

WILLMORE Death, thou'rt a vain, conceited, tawdry jilt,
who'st drawn me in as rooks* their cullies do, to make
me venture all my stock of love, and then you turn me out
despised and poor –   540

(*Offers to go*)

LA NUCHE You think you're gone now?

WILLMORE Not all thy arts nor charms can hold me
longer.

LA NUCHE I must submit – and can you part thus from me?

(*Pulls him*)

WILLMORE I can – nay – by heaven, I will not turn, nor   545
look at thee. No, when I do, or trust that faithless tongue
again, may I be –

LA NUCHE Oh, do not swear –

WILLMORE Ever cursed!

(*Breaks from her, she holds him*)

LA NUCHE You shall not go – (*aside*) Plague of this needless   550
pride! Stay, and I'll follow – all the dictates of my love.

WILLMORE Oh, never hope to flatter me to faith again.

(*His back to her, she holding him*)

LA NUCHE I must, I will; what would you have me do?

WILLMORE (*turning softly to her*) Never – deceive me
more; it may be fatal to wind me up to an impatient   555
height, then dash my eager hopes. (*sighing*) Forgive
my roughness – and be kind, La Nuche, I know thou
wo't.

LA NUCHE And will you then be ever kind and true?

WILLMORE Ask thy own charms; and to confirm thee   560
more, yield, and disarm me quite.

LA NUCHE Will you not marry then? For though you never
can be mine that way, I cannot think that you should be
another's.

WILLMORE No more delays, by heaven, 'twas but a trick! 565

LA NUCHE And will you never see that woman neither, whom you're this night to visit?

WILLMORE Damn all the rest of thy weak sex, when thou look'st thus, and art so soft and charming.

(*Offers to lead her out*)

LA NUCHE (*turns in scorn*) Sancho – my coach. 570

WILLMORE Take heed; what mean ye?

LA NUCHE Not to be pointed at by all the envying women of the town, who'll laugh and cry, 'Is this the high-prized lady, now fall'n so low to dote upon a captain, a poor disbanded captain!' Defend me, from that infamy. 575

WILLMORE Now all the plagues – but yet I will not curse thee; 'tis lost on thee, for thou art destined damned.

(*Going out*)

LA NUCHE Whither so fast?

WILLMORE Why, I am so indifferent grown that I can tell thee now: to a woman, young, fair and honest; for she'll 580 be kind and thankful. Farewell, jilt. Now, shouldst thou die for one sight more of me – thou shouldst not ha't. Nay, shouldst thou sacrifice all thou hast cozened other coxcombs of, to buy one single visit, I am so proud, by heaven, thou shouldst not have it. To grieve thee more, 585 see here, insatiate woman – (*shows her a purse, or hands, full of gold*) – the charm that makes me lovely in thine eyes; 't had all been thine hadst thou not basely bargained with me. Now 'tis the prize of some well-meaning whore, whose modesty will trust my generosity. 590

[*Goes out*]

LA NUCHE Now I could rave, t've lost an opportunity which industry nor chance can give again. When on the yielding point, a cursed fit of pride comes cross my soul, and stops the kind career. I'll follow him – yes, I will follow him, even to the arms of her to whom he's gone. 595

AURELIA Madam, 'tis dark, and we may meet with insolence.

LA NUCHE No matter; Sancho, let the coach go home, and
do you follow me.
Women may boast their honour and their pride,   600
But love soon lays those feebler pow'rs aside.

<Exeunt>

Act 4, Scene I

The street or back-side of the piazza, dark

(Enter WILLMORE *alone)*

WILLMORE A pox upon this woman that has jilted me, and
I for being a fond, believing puppy to be in earnest with
so great a devil. Where be these coxcombs too, this Blunt
and Fetherfool? When a man needs 'em not, they are
plaguing him with their unseasonable jests. Could I but   5
light on them, I would be very drunk tonight, but first I'll
try my fortune with this woman. Let me see – hereabouts
is the door –

(Gropes about for the door)

(Enter BEAUMOND, *followed by* LA NUCHE *and*
SANCHO)

LA NUCHE 'Tis he, I know it by his often and uneasy
pauses.   10
BEAUMOND And shall I home and sleep upon my injury,
whilst this more happy rover takes my right away? No,
damn me then for a cold, senseless coward!

(Pauses, and pulls out a key)

WILLMORE This damsel, by the part o' th' town she lives
in, should be of quality, and therefore can have no   15
dishonest design on me; it must be right-down substantial
love that's certain.
BEAUMOND Yet I'll in and arm myself for the encounter,
for 'twill be rough between us, though we're friends.

(Groping about; finds the door)

WILLMORE Oh, 'tis this I'm sure, because the door is open.   20
BEAUMOND Hah, who's there?

(BEAUMOND *advances to unlock the door, runs against*
WILLMORE, *draws*)

WILLMORE That voice is of authority; some husband,
lover, or a brother, on my life. This is a nation of a word
and a blow; therefore I'll betake me to Toledo.* *(draws)*

(WILLMORE *in drawing, hits his sword against that of*
BEAUMOND, *who turns and fights.* LA NUCHE *runs into
the garden frighted*)

BEAUMOND Hah, are you there?   25
SANCHO I'll draw in defence of the captain.

(SANCHO *fights for* BEAUMOND *and beats out*
WILLMORE)

WILLMORE Hah, two to one –

(Turns and goes in)

BEAUMOND The garden door clapped to; sure, he's got in.
Nay, then, I have him sure.

Act 4, Scene 2

The scene changes to a garden; LA NUCHE *in it*

(*To her* BEAUMOND, *who takes hold of her sleeve*)

LA NUCHE Heavens, where am I?
BEAUMOND Hah, a woman! And by these jewels should be
Ariadne – *(feels)* 'Tis so! Death, are all women false?

(She struggles to get away, he holds her)

Oh, 'tis in vain thou fly'st, thy infamy will stay behind
thee still.   5

LA NUCHE (*aside*) Hah, 'tis Beaumond's voice! Now for an art to turn the trick upon him. I must not lose his friendship.

(*Enter* WILLMORE *softly, peeping behind*)

WILLMORE What a devil have we here, more mischief yet! Hah, my woman with a man! I shall spoil all – I ever had   10 an excellent knack of doing so.

BEAUMOND Oh modesty, where art thou! Is this the effect of all your put-on jealousy, that mask to hide your own new falsehood in? New? By heaven, I believe thou'rt old in cunning, that couldst contrive – so near thy wedding   15 night – this, to deprive me of the rights of love!

LA NUCHE (*aside*) Hah, what says he?

WILLMORE (*aside*) How! A maid, and young, and to be married too; a rare wench this to contrive matters so conveniently! Oh, for some mischief now to send him   20 neatly off.

BEAUMOND Now you are silent, but you could talk today loudly of virtue and upbraid my vice! Oh, how you hated a young, keeping husband, whom neither beauty nor honour in a wife could oblige to reason. Oh, damn your   25 honour, 'tis that's the sly pretence of all your domineer- ing, insolent wives. Death! What didst thou see in me should make thee think that I would be a tame, contented cuckold?

(*Going; she holds him*)

LA NUCHE (*aside*) I must not lose this lavish, loving fool.   30

WILLMORE So, I hope he will be civil and withdraw, and leave me in possession.

BEAUMOND No, though my fortune should depend on thee; nay, every* hope of future happiness – by heaven, I scorn to marry thee, unless thou couldst convince me thou   35 wert honest – a whore! Death, how it cools my blood.

WILLMORE And fires mine extremely!

LA NUCHE (*aside*) Nay, then I am provoked though I spoil all. <*to* BEAUMOND> And is a whore a thing so much

despised? Turn back, thou false forsworn. Turn back, and   40
blush at thy mistaken folly.

(*He stands amazed*)

BEAUMOND La Nuche!

(*Enter* ARIADNE *peeping, advancing cautiously,
undressed;* LUCIA *following*)

ARIADNE Oh, he is here – Lucia, attend me in the orange
grove.

[*Exit* LUCIA]

Hah, a woman with him!   45

WILLMORE Hum – what have we here, another damsel?
She's gay too, and seems young and handsome. Sure, one
of these will fall to my share; no matter which, so I am
sure of one.

LA NUCHE Who's silent now? Are you struck dumb with   50
guilt? Thou shame to noble love! Thou scandal to all
brave debauchery; thou fop of fortune; thou slavish heir
to estate and wife, born rich and damned to matrimony.

WILLMORE Egad, a noble wench; I am divided yet.

LA NUCHE Thou formal ass, disguised in generous
lewdness!*   55
See, when the vizor's off, how sneakingly
That empty form appears. Nay, 'tis thy own:
Make much on't, marry with it, and be damned!

(*Offers to go*)

WILLMORE I hope she'll beat him for suspecting her.

(*He holds her, she turns*)

ARIADNE Hah, who the devil can these be?   60

LA NUCHE What silly honest fool did you mistake me for;
what senseless modest thing? Death, am I grown so
despicable, have I deserved no better from thy love than
to be taken for a virtuous changeling?

WILLMORE (*aside*) Egad, 'twas an affront.   65

LA NUCHE I'm glad I've found thee out to be an arrant

coxcomb, one that esteems a woman for being chaste, forsooth! 'Sheart, I shall have thee call me pious shortly, a most – religious matron!

WILLMORE *<aside>* Egad, she has reason.   70

BEAUMOND (*sighing*) Forgive me, for I took ye – for another.

LA NUCHE Oh, did you so? It seems you keep fine company the while. Death, that I should e'er be seen with such a vile dissembler; with one so vain, so dull and so   75 impertinent as can be entertained by honest women!

WILLMORE A heavenly soul, and to my wish, were I but sure of her.

BEAUMOND Oh, you do wondrous well t'accuse me first! Yes, I am a coxcomb, a confounded one, to dote upon so 80 false a prostitute; nay to love seriously and tell it too. Yet such an amorous coxcomb I was born: to hate the enjoyment of the loveliest woman, without I have the heart. The fond, soft prattle, and the lolling dalliance; the frowns, the little quarrels, and the kind degrees of making 85 peace again, are joys which I prefer to all the sensual; whilst I endeavour to forget the whore, and pay my vows to wit, to youth and beauty.

ARIADNE Now hang me, if it be not Beaumond!

BEAUMOND Would any devil less than common woman 90 have served me as thou didst? Say, was not this my night? My paid-for night? My own by right of bargain, and by love? And hast not thou deceived me for a stranger?

WILLMORE (*hugs himself*) So! Make me thankful, then she will be kind.   95

BEAUMOND Was this done like a whore of honour think ye, and would not such an injury make me forswear all joys of womankind, and marry in mere spite?

LA NUCHE Why, where had been the crime had I been kind?   100

BEAUMOND Thou dost confess it then?

LA NUCHE Why not?

BEAUMOND Those bills of love the oftener paid and drawn, make women better merchants than lovers.

LA NUCHE And 'tis the better trade.   105

WILLMORE Oh pox, there she dashed all again. I find they
   calm upon't and will agree. Therefore, I'll bear up to this
   small frigate and lay her aboard.

(*Goes to* ARIADNE)

LA NUCHE However, I am glad the vizor's off. You might
   have fooled me on and sworn I was the only conqueror of   110
   your heart, had not good nature made me follow you, to
   undeceive your false suspicions of me. How have you
   sworn never to marry? How railed at wives, and satired*
   fools obliged to wedlock? And now at last, to thy eternal
   shame, thou hast betrayed thyself to be a most pernicious,   115
   honourable lover, a perjured – honest – nay, a very
   husband.

(*Turns away, he holds her*)

ARIADNE <*aside*> Hah, sure 'tis the captain.

WILLMORE Prithee, child, let's leave 'em to themselves.
   They'll agree matters, I'll warrant them, when they're   120
   alone; and let us try how love and good nature will
   provide for us.

ARIADNE <*aside*> Sure he cannot know me. – Us? Pray,
   who are you, and who am I?

WILLMORE Why look ye, child, I am a very honest civil   125
   fellow, for my part, and thou'rt a woman for thine; and I
   desire to know no more at present.

ARIADNE <*aside*> 'Tis he, and knows not me to be the same
   he appointed today. – Sir, pursue that path on your right
   hand, that grove of orange trees, and I'll follow you   130
   immediately.

WILLMORE Kind and civil; prithee, make haste, dear child.

[*Exit* WILLMORE]

BEAUMOND (*lovingly*) And did you come to call me back
   again?

LA NUCHE No matter, you're to be married, sir.   135

BEAUMOND No more. 'Tis true, to please my uncle, I have
   talked of some such thing; but I'll pursue it no farther, so

thou wilt yet be mine, and mine entirely. I hate this
Ariadne – for a wife, by heaven, I do.

ARIADNE (*claps him on the back*) A very plain confession. 140

BEAUMOND Ariadne!

LA NUCHE (*aside*) I'm glad of this, now I shall be rid of
him. – How is't, sir? I see you struggle hard 'twixt love
and honour, and I'll resign my place.

(*Offers to go;* ARIADNE *pulls her back*)

ARIADNE (*aside*) Hold, if she take him not away I shall 145
disappoint my man. – Faith, I'll not be outdone in
generosity.

(*Gives him to* LA NUCHE)

Here – love deserves him best; and I resign him. (*to*
BEAUMOND) Pox on't, I'm honest, though that's no fault
of mine; 'twas fortune who has made a worse exchange, 150
and you and I should suit most damnably together.

BEAUMOND (*aside*) I am sure there's something in the
wind, she being in the garden, and the door left open. <*to*
ARIADNE> Yes, I believe you are willing enough to part
with me, when you expect another you like better. 155

ARIADNE I'm glad I was beforehand with you then.

BEAUMOND Very good; and the door was left open to give
admittance to a lover.

ARIADNE 'Tis visible it was to let one in to you, false as you
are. 160

LA NUCHE Faith, madam, you mistake my constitution. My
beauty and my business is only to be beloved not to love; I
leave that slavery for you women of quality, who must
invite, or die without the blessing; for likely the fool you
make choice of wants wit or confidence to ask first. You 165
are fain to whistle before the dogs will fetch and carry,
and then too they approach by stealth. And having done
the drudgery, the submissive curs are turned out for fear
of dirtying your apartment, or that the mongrels should
scandalise ye. Whilst all my lovers of the noble kind 170

throng to adore and fill my presence daily; gay, as if each
were triumphing for victory.

ARIADNE *\<aside\>* Aye, this is something. What a poor,
sneaking thing an honest woman is!

LA NUCHE And if we chance to love, still there's a   175
difference. Your hours of love are like the deeds of
darkness, and mine like cheerful birds in open day.

ARIADNE You may, you have no honour to lose.

LA NUCHE Or if I had, why should I double the sin by
hypocrisy?   180

(LUCIA *squeaks within, crying, 'Help, help!'*)

ARIADNE Heavens, that's Lucia's voice!

BEAUMOND Hah, more caterwauling?

(*Enter* LUCIA *in haste*)

LUCIA Oh, madam, we're undone, and, sir, for heaven's
sake, do you retire.

BEAUMOND What's the matter?   185

LUCIA Oh, you have brought the most villainous mad
friend with you. He found me sitting on a bank and did so
ruffle me!

ARIADNE *\<aside\>* Death, she takes Beaumond for the
stranger, and will ruin me.   190

LUCIA Nay, made love so loud, that my lord, your father-
in-law, who was in his cabinet, heard us from the orange
grove, and has sent to search the garden. And should he
find a stranger with you – (*to* BEAUMOND) Do but you
retire, sir, and all's well yet.   195

ARIADNE (*aside*) The devil's in her tongue.

LUCIA For if Mr Beaumond be in the house, we shall have
the devil to do with his jealousy.

ARIADNE So, there 'tis out.

BEAUMOND (*aside*) She takes me for another. I am jilted 200
everywhere – What friend? I brought none with me. (*to*
LA NUCHE) Madam, do you retire.

LA NUCHE Glad of my freedom, too –

[*Goes out*]

(A *clashing of swords within. Enter* WILLMORE *fighting,*
pressed back by THREE *or* FOUR MEN *and* ABEVILE.
ARIADNE *and* LUCIA *run out*)

BEAUMOND Hah, set on by odds! (*puts himself between*
their swords, and speaks to WILLMORE *aside*) Hold, 205
though thou be'st my rival, I will free thee on condition
thou wilt meet me tomorrow morning in the piazza by
daybreak.

WILLMORE By heaven, I'll do it.

BEAUMOND Retire in safety then, you have your pass.   210

ABEVILE Fall, fall on, the number is increased!

(<*They*> *fall on* BEAUMOND)

BEAUMOND Rascals, do you not know me?
[*Falls in with 'em and beats 'em back and exit with them*]

WILLMORE Nay, and you be so well acquainted, I'll leave
you. Unfortunate still I am. My own well meaning, but ill
management, is my eternal foe. Plague on 'em, they have 215
wounded me; yet not one drop of blood's departed from
me that warmed my heart for woman! And I'm not
willing to quit this fairy ground till some kind devil have
been civil to me.

(*Enter* ARIADNE *and* LUCIA)

ARIADNE I say, 'tis he: thou'st made so many dull mistakes 220
tonight, thou darest not trust thy senses when they're
true. – How do you, sir?

WILLMORE That voice has comfort in't, for 'tis a woman's.
Hah, more interruption?

ARIADNE A little this way, sir.   225
[*Exeunt* ARIADNE *and* WILLMORE *into the garden*]

(*Enter* BEAUMOND; ABEVILE *in a submissive posture*)

BEAUMOND No more excuses. By all these circumstances, I
know this Ariadne is a gypsy.* What difference, then,
between a money-taking mistress and her that gives her
love? Only, perhaps, this sins the closer* by't, and talks of

honour more. What fool would be a slave to empty name, 230
or value woman for dissembling well? I'll to La Nuche –
the honester o'th' two. Abevile, get me my music ready,
and attend me at La Nuche's.

[*Exeunt severally*]

LUCIA He's gone, and to his mistress too.

(*Enter* ARIADNE *pursued by* WILLMORE)

WILLMORE My little Daphne, 'tis in vain to fly; unless like 235
her you could be changed into a tree. Apollo's self
pursued not with more eager fire than I.*

(*Holds her*)

ARIADNE Will you not grant a parley e'er I yield?
WILLMORE I'm better at a storm.
ARIADNE Besides, you're wounded too.   240
WILLMORE Oh, leave those wounds of honour to my
surgeon; thy business is to cure those of love. Your true-
bred soldier ever fights with the more heat for a wound or
two.
ARIADNE Hardly in Venus' wars.   245
WILLMORE Herself ne'er thought so when she snatched her
joys between the rough encounters of the god of war.
Come, let's pursue the business we came for. See, the kind
night invites, and all the ruffling winds are hushed and
still; only the zephyrs* spread their tender wings, courting 250
in gentle murmurs the gay boughs. 'Twas in a night like
this, Diana taught the mysteries of love to the fair boy
Endymion.* I am plaguy full of history and simile tonight.
ARIADNE You see how well he fared for being modest.
WILLMORE He might be modest, but 'twas not over-civil to 255
put her goddess-ship to asking first. Thou seest I'm better
bred. Come, let's haste to silent grots that attend us, dark
groves where none can see, and murmuring fountains.
ARIADNE Stay, let me consider first. You are a stranger;
inconstant, too, as island winds; and every day are 260
fighting for your mistresses, of which you've had at least
four since I saw you first, which is not a whole day.

WILLMORE I grant ye, before I was a lover I ran at random, but I'll take up now, be a patient man, and keep to one woman a month.   265

ARIADNE A month!

WILLMORE And a fair reason, child. Time was, I would have worn one shirt, or one pair of shoes so long, as have let the sun set twice upon the same sin. But see the power of love! Thou hast bewitched me, that's certain.   270

ARIADNE Have a care of giving me the ascendant over ye, for fear I make ye marry me.

WILLMORE Hold, I bar that cast, child. No, I'm none of those spirits that can be conjured into a wedding ring, and dance in the dull matrimonial circle all my days.*   275

ARIADNE But what think you of a hundred thousand crowns, and a beauty of sixteen?

WILLMORE As of most admirable blessings – but hark ye, child, I am plaguily afraid thou art some scurvy, honest thing of quality by these odd questions of thine, and hast 280 some wicked design upon my* body.

ARIADNE What, to have and to hold, I'll warrant. No; faith, sir, maids of my quality expect better jointures than a buff-coat, scarf and feather. Such portions as mine are better ornaments in a family than a captain and his 285 commission.

WILLMORE Why, well said; now thou hast explained thyself like a woman of honour. Come, come, let's away.

ARIADNE Explained myself? How mean ye?

WILLMORE Thou sayst I am not fit to marry thee; and I 290 believe this assignation was not made to tell me so, nor yet to hear me whistle to the birds.

ARIADNE Faith no, I saw you, liked ye, and had a mind to ye.

WILLMORE Aye, child.   295

ARIADNE In short, I took ye for a man of honour.

WILLMORE Nay, if I tell, the devil take me.

ARIADNE I am a virgin in distress.

WILLMORE Poor heart.

ARIADNE To be married within a day or two to one I like 300
not.

WILLMORE Hum – and therefore wouldst dispose of a
small virgin treasure (too good for silly husbands) in a
friend's hands. Faith, child, I was ever a good, religious,
charitable Christian; and shall acquit myself as honestly 305
and piously in this affair as becomes a gentleman.

(*Enter* ABEVILE *with* MUSIC)

ABEVILE <*to the* MUSICIANS> Come away, are ye all
armed for the business?

ARIADNE <*to* WILLMORE> Hah, armed? We are surprised
again. 310

WILLMORE (*draws*) Fear not.

ARIADNE (*speaking quick, and pushing him forwards*) Oh
god, sir, haste away, you are already wounded! But I
conjure you, as a man of honour, be here at the garden
gate tonight again; and bring a friend in case of danger, 315
with you, and if possible I'll put myself into your hands,
for this night's work has ruined me.

(*Runs off*)

ABEVILE (*peeping, advancing*) My master, sure, not gone
yet.

WILLMORE Rascals, though you are odds, you'll find hot 320
work in vanquishing.

(*Falls on 'em*)

ABEVILE Hold, sir, I am your page. Do you not know me?
And these, the music you commanded. Shall I carry 'em
where you ordered, sir?

WILLMORE (*aside*) They take me for some other, this was 325
lucky. <*to* ABEVILE> Oh, aye, 'tis well; I'll follow.
<*aside*> But whither? Plague of my dull mistakes, the
woman's gone. (*calls 'em*) Yet stay! <*aside*> For now I
think on't, this mistake may help me to another – <*calls
them*> Stay! <*aside*> I must dispose of this mad fire about 330
me which all these disappointments cannot lay. Oh, for

some young, kind sinner in the nick!* How I could souse*
upon her like a bird of prey, and worry* her with
kindness! <to them> Go on, I follow.

[Go out]

Act 4, Scene 3

Scene changes to LA NUCHE's *house*

(*Enter* PETRONELLA *and* AURELIA *with light*)

AURELIA Well, the stranger is in bed, and most impatiently
expects our patrona, who is not yet returned.

PETRONELLA Curse of this love! I know she's in pursuit of
this rover, this English piece of impudence. Pox on 'em, I
know nothing good in the whole race of 'em, but giving   5
all to their shirts when they're drunk. What shall we do,
Aurelia? This stranger must not be put off, nor Carlo
neither, who has fined* again, as if for a new maidenhead.

AURELIA You are so covetous; you might have put 'em off,   10
but now 'tis too late.

PETRONELLA Put off? Are these fools to be put off, think
ye? A fine fop Englishman, and an old doting grandee?
No, I could put the old trick on 'em still, had she been
here but to have entertained 'em. But hark, one knocks.   15
'Tis Carlo, on my life.

(*Enter* CARLO, *gives* PETRONELLA *gold*)

CARLO Let this plead for me –

PETRONELLA Sweet don, you are the most eloquent
person.

CARLO I would regale* tonight. I know it is not mine, but   20
I've sent five hundred crowns to purchase it, because I
saw another bargaining for't; and persons of my quality
must not be refused. You apprehend me?

PETRONELLA Most rightly. That was the reason then she

came so out of humour home, and is gone to bed in such a   25
sullen fit.

CARLO To bed, and all alone? I would surprise her there.
Oh, how it pleases me to think of stealing into her arms
like a fine dream, wench, hah!

AURELIA 'Twill be a pleasant one no doubt.   30

PETRONELLA (aside) He lays the way out how he'll be
cozened. <to him> The seigniora perhaps may be angry,
sir, but I'll venture that to accommodate you; and that
you may surprise her the more readily, be pleased to stay
in my chamber till you think she may be asleep.   35

CARLO Thou art a perfect mistress of thy trade.

PETRONELLA <aside> So, now will I to the seigniora's bed
myself, dressed and perfumed, and finish two good works
at once: earn five hundred crowns, and keep up the
honour of the house. <to him> Softly, sweet don.   40

(*Lights him out*)

AURELIA And I will do two more good things: disappoint
your expectations; jilt the young English fool, and have
old Carlo well banged, if t'other have any courage.

(*Enter* LA NUCHE *in rage, and* SANCHO)

LA NUCHE* Aurelia, help! Help me to be revenged
Upon this wretched, unconsidering heart!   45

AURELIA Heavens, have you made the rover happy,
madam?

LA NUCHE Oh, would I had! Or that, or any sin
Would change this rage into some easier passion.
Sickness and poverty, disgrace and pity,   50
All met in one, were kinder than this love,
This raging fire of a proud, amorous heart.

(*Enter* PETRONELLA)

PETRONELLA Heavens, what's the matter?

AURELIA <to LA NUCHE> Here's Petronella, dissemble but
your rage a little.   55

LA NUCHE Damn all dissembling now, it is too late;

The tyrant love reigns absolute within,
And I'm lost, Aurelia.

PETRONELLA How, love? Forbid it, heaven! Will love
maintain ye?   60

LA NUCHE Curse on your maxims, will they ease my
heart?
Can your wise counsel fetch me back my rover?

PETRONELLA Hah, your rover! A pox upon him!

LA NUCHE He's gone – gone to the arms of some gay,
generous maid,
Who nobly follows love's diviner dictates;   65
Whilst I, 'gainst nature studying thy dull precepts,
And to be base and infamously rich,
Have bartered all the joys of human life.
Oh, give me love! I will be poor and love!

PETRONELLA <aside> She's lost. – But hear me –   70

LA NUCHE I won't.
From childhood thou hast trained me up in cunning;
Read lectures to me of the use of man,
But kept me from the knowledge of the right;
Taught me to jilt, to flatter and deceive,   75
And hard it was to learn th' ungrateful lessons.
But oh, how soon plain nature taught me love,
And showed me all the cheat of thy false tenets!
No, give me love with any other curse.

PETRONELLA But who will give you that when you are   80
poor? When you are wretchedly despised and poor?

LA NUCHE Hah!

PETRONELLA Do you not daily see fine clothes, rich
furniture, jewels and plate are more inviting than beauty
unadorned? Be old, diseased, deformed, be anything; so   85
you be rich and splendidly attended, you'll find yourself
loved and adored by all. But I'm an old fool still. Well,
Petronella, hadst thou been half as industrious in thy
youth as in thy age, thou hadst not come to this. (*weeps*)

LA NUCHE She's in the right.   90

PETRONELLA What can this mad, poor captain do for you?
Love you whilst you can buy him breeches, and then leave

you? A woman has a sweet time on't with any soldier
lover of 'em all, with their iron minds and buff hearts.
Feathered inamoratos* have nothing that belongs to Love 95
but his wings. The devil clip 'em, for Petronella!

LA NUCHE (*pausing*) True, he can ne'er be constant.

PETRONELLA Heaven forbid he should! No, if you are so
unhappy as that you must have him, give him a night or
two and pay him for't, and send him to feed again. But 100
for your heart, 'sdeath, I would as soon part with my
beauty or youth; and as necessary a tool 'tis for your
trade – a courtesan and love! But all my counsel's thrown
away upon ye. (*weeps*)

LA NUCHE No more, I will be ruled. I will be wise, be rich, 105
and since I must yield somewhere and some time,
Beaumond shall be the man, and this the night. He's
handsome, young and lavishly profuse. This night he
comes, and I'll submit to interest. Let the gilded apartment be made ready, and strew it o'er with flowers; adorn 110
my bed of state; let all be fine. Perfume my chamber like
the phoenix's nest,* I'll be luxurious in my pride tonight,
and make the amorous, prodigal youth my slave.

PETRONELLA Nobly resolved; and for these other two who
wait your coming, let me alone to manage. 115

[*Goes out*]

Act 4, Scene 4

Scene changes to a chamber, discovers FETHERFOOL *in
bed*

FETHERFOOL This gentlewoman is plaguy long in coming;
some nicety now, some perfumed smock, or point*
nightclothes to make her more lovely in my eyes. Well,
these women are right city cooks, they stay so long to
garnish the dish till the meat be cold – but hark, the door 5
opens –

(*Enter* CARLO *softly, half-undressed*)

CARLO This wench stays long, and love's impatient. This is
the chamber of La Nuche, I take it. If she be awake, I'll let
her know who I am; if not, I'll steal a joy before she
thinks of it.   10

FETHERFOOL Sure 'tis she; pretty modest rogue, she comes
i' th' dark to hide her blushes. Hum, I'm plaguy eloquent
o' th' sudden – (*whispering*) Who's there?

CARLO 'Tis I, 'tis I, my love.

FETHERFOOL Hah, sweet soul, make haste. There 'twas   15
again.

CARLO (*to himself*) So kind, sure she takes me for some
other, or has some inkling of my design. Where are you,
sweetest?

FETHERFOOL Here my love, give me your hand.   20

(*Puts out his hand,* CARLO *kneels and kisses it*)

CARLO Here let me worship the fair shrine, before I dare
approach so fair a saint.

(*Kissing the hand*)

FETHERFOOL (*aside*) Hah! What a pox have we here?
Would I were well out o' th' t'other side. Perhaps 'tis her
husband, and then I'm a dead man if I'm discovered.   25

(*Removes to t'other side,* CARLO *holds his hand*)

CARLO Nay, do not fly – I know you took me for some
happier person.

(FETHERFOOL *struggles;* CARLO *rises, and takes him in
his arms and kisses him*)

FETHERFOOL (*in a shrill voice*) What, will you ravish
me?

CARLO Hah, that voice is not La Nuche's! Lights there,   30
lights.

FETHERFOOL (*holds* CARLO) Nay, I can hold a bearded
Venus, sir, as well as any man.

CARLO What art thou, rogue, villain, slave?

(*They fall to cuffs, and fight till they are bloody; fall*

from the bed, and fight on the floor)

(*Enter* PETRONELLA, SANCHO, *and* AURELIA)

PETRONELLA Heaven, what noise is this! We are undone,   35
part 'em, Sancho.

(*They part 'em*)

FETHERFOOL Give me my sword; nay, give me but a knife,
that I may cut yon fellow's throat!

CARLO Sirrah, I'm a grandee, and a Spaniard, and will be
revenged.   40

FETHERFOOL And I'm an Englishman, and a justice, and
will have law, sir.

PETRONELLA (*aside to* SANCHO, *who whispers him*) Say
'tis her husband, or anything to get him hence. (*to* CARLO
aside) These English, sir, are devils; and, on my life, 'tis 45
unknown to the seigniora that he's i'th' house.

CARLO Come, I'm abused, but I must put it up for fear of
my honour; a statesman's reputation is a tender thing.
Convey me out the back way. I'll be revenged.

[*Goes out*]

(AURELIA *aside whispers* <*to* FETHERFOOL>)

FETHERFOOL How, her husband? Prithee, convey me out.   50
My clothes, my clothes, quickly –

AURELIA Out, sir? He has locked the door, and designs to
have ye murdered.

FETHERFOOL Oh, gentle soul – take pity on me! Where?
Oh, what shall I do? My clothes, my sword and money!   55

AURELIA Quickly, Sancho, tie a sheet to the window, and
let him slide down by that. Be speedy, and we'll throw
your clothes out after ye. Here, follow me to the window.

FETHERFOOL Oh, any whither, any whither – that I could
not be warned from whoring in a strange country by my   60
friend, Ned Blunt's example! If I can but keep it secret
now, I care not.

[*Exeunt*]

Act 4, Scene 5

The street

(A sheet tied to the balcony, and FETHERFOOL *sitting cross to slide down)*

FETHERFOOL So now, your neck or your throat; choose ye either, wise Mr Nicholas Fetherfool – but stay, I hear company. Now dare not I budge an inch.

(Enter BEAUMOND *alone)*

BEAUMOND Where can this rascal, my page, be all this while? I waited in the piazza so long that I believed he had   5
mistook my order, and gone directly to La Nuche's house
– but here's no sign of him.

FETHERFOOL Hah! I hear no noise; I'll venture down.

(Goes halfway down and stops)

(Enter ABEVILE, MUSIC, <HARLEQUIN> *and* WILLMORE)

WILLMORE Whither will this boy conduct me? But since to a woman, no matter whither 'tis.   10

FETHERFOOL Hah, more company. Now dare not I stir up nor down; they may be bravoes to cut my throat.

BEAUMOND Oh, sure, these are they.

WILLMORE Come, my heart, lose no time, but tune your pipes.   15

*(HARLEQUIN *plays on his guitar, and sings)*

BEAUMOND How! Sure, this is some rival.

(Goes near and listens)

WILLMORE Hark ye, child, hast thou ne'er an amorous ditty, short and sweet, hah?

ABEVILE Shall I not sing that you gave me, sir?

WILLMORE *<aside>* I shall spoil all with hard questions. –   20
Aye, child, that.

(The boy <ABEVILE> *sings;* BEAUMOND *listens, and seems angry the while)*

Song

A pox upon this needless scorn,
Sylvia, for shame the cheat give o'er;
The end to which the fair are born,
Is not to keep their charms in store,   25
But lavishly dispose in haste
Of joys which none but youth improve;
Joys which decay when beauty's passed,
And who, when beauty's past, will love?

When age those glories shall deface,   30
Revenging all your cold disdain,
And Sylvia shall neglected pass
By every once-admiring swain;
And we can only pity pay,
When you in vain too late shall burn;   35
If love increase, and youth delay,
Ah, Sylvia, who will make return?

Then haste, my Sylvia, to the grove,
Where all the sweets of May conspire
To teach us every art of love,   40
And raise our charms of pleasure higher;
Where, whilst embracing, we should lie
Loosely in shades, on banks of flowers,
The duller world whilst we defy,
Years will be minutes, ages hours.   45

BEAUMOND *<aside>* 'Sdeath, that's my page's voice. Who
the devil is't that ploughs with my heifer!
AURELIA Don Henrick, Don Henrick!

(*The door opens,* BEAUMOND *goes up to't.* WILLMORE
puts him by and offers to go in; he pulls him back)

WILLMORE How now, what intruding slave art thou?
BEAUMOND What thief art thou that basely, and by dark,   50
robb'st me of all my rights?

(*Strikes him; they fight, and blows light on* FETHERFOOL
who hangs down. SANCHO *throws* FETHERFOOL'*s*

clothes out; HARLEQUIN *takes 'em up in confusion. They fight out* BEAUMOND; *all go off, but* WILLMORE *gets into the house.* HARLEQUIN *and* FETHERFOOL *remain.*

FETHERFOOL *gets down, runs against* HARLEQUIN *in the dark; both seem frightened*)

HARLEQUIN *Que questo?* *

FETHERFOOL Ah, *un pouer dead home,* * murthered, killed!

HARLEQUIN (*in Italian*) You are the first dead man I ever 55 saw walk.

FETHERFOOL Hah, Seignior Harlequin!

HARLEQUIN Seigniore Nicholas!

FETHERFOOL A pox, Nicholas, ye! I have been mauled and beaten within doors, and hanged and bastinadoed* 60 without doors; lost my clothes, my money, and all my moveables; but this is nothing to the secret taking air. Ah, dear seignior, convey me to the mountebank's. There I may have recruit* and cure under one.*

[*Exeunt*]

Act 5, Scene 1

A chamber, LA NUCHE *on a couch in an undress;* WILLMORE *at her feet, on his knees, all unbraced;* * his hat, sword, etc. on the table at which she is dressing her head*

WILLMORE O gods! No more!
  I see a yielding in thy charming eyes:
  The blushes on thy face, thy trembling arms,
  Thy panting breast, and short-breathed sighs confess
  Thou wo't be mine, in spite of all thy art. 5
LA NUCHE What need you urge my tongue then to repeat*
  What from my eyes you can so well interpret?

(*Bowing down her head to him, and sighing*)

Or if – it must – dispose me as you please.

WILLMORE (*rises with joy*) Heaven, I thank thee!
   Who would not plough an age in winter seas;   10
   Or wade seven long years in ruder camps,
   To find out this rest at last!

      (*Leans on, and kisses her bosom*)

Upon thy tender bosom to repose;
To gaze upon thy eyes, and taste thy balmy kisses –

      (*Kisses her*)

Sweeter than everlasting groves of spices,   15
When the soft winds display the opening buds.
Come, haste, my soul, to bed.

LA NUCHE You can be soft, I find, when you would
   conquer absolutely.

WILLMORE Not infant angels, not young sighing cupids
   Can be more. This ravishing joy that thou hast
     promised me,   20
   Has formed my soul to such a calm of love,
   It melts even at my eyes –

LA NUCHE What have I done? That promise will undo
   me!
   This chamber was prepared, and I was dressed,
   To give admittance to another lover.   25

WILLMORE But love and fortune both were on my side.
   Come, come to bed; consider nought but love.

      (*They going out, one knocks*)

LA NUCHE Hark!

BEAUMOND (*without*) By heaven, I will have entrance!

LA NUCHE 'Tis he whom I expect. As thou lov'st life and 30
   me, retire a little into this closet.

WILLMORE Hah, retire!

LA NUCHE He's the most fiercely jealous of his sex,
   And disappointment will enrage him more.

WILLMORE Death, let him rage whoe'er he be; dost

think *   35
I'll hide me from him, and leave thee to his love?
Shall I pent up through the thin wainscot hear
Your sighs, your amorous words and sound of kisses?
No, if thou canst cozen me, do't but discreetly,
And I shall think thee true.   40
I have thee now, and when I tamely part
With thee, may cowards huff and bully me.

(Knocks again)

LA NUCHE And must I be undone because I love ye?
  This is the mine from whence I fetched my gold!
WILLMORE Damn the base trash, I'll have thee poor,
    and mine;   45
  'Tis nobler far, to starve with him thou lov'st,
  Than gay without, and pining all within.

*(Knocking breaking the door, WILLMORE snatches up his
sword)*

LA NUCHE <aside> Heavens, here will be murther done. He
  must not see him.

*(As BEAUMOND breaks open the door, she runs away
with the candle. They are by dark; BEAUMOND enters
with his sword drawn)*

WILLMORE What art thou?   50
BEAUMOND A man.

*(They fight. Enter PETRONELLA with light, LA NUCHE
following; BEAUMOND runs to her)*

Oh thou false woman, falser than thy smiles,
Which serve but to delude good-natured man,
And when thou hast him fast, betray'st his heart.
WILLMORE Beaumond!   55
BEAUMOND Willmore! Is it with thee that I must tug for
  empire?
  For I lay claim to all this world of beauty.

(Takes LA NUCHE, *looking with scorn on* WILLMORE)

LA NUCHE Heavens, how got this ruffian in?

WILLMORE Hold, hold, dear Harry, lay no hands on her
till thou canst make thy claim good.   60

BEAUMOND She's mine, by bargain mine, and that's
sufficient.

WILLMORE In law perhaps, it may, for ought I know; but
'tis not so in love. But thou'rt my friend, and I'll therefore
give thee fair play. If thou canst win her, take her; but a   65
sword and a mistress are not to be lost, if a man can keep
'em.

BEAUMOND I cannot blame thee, thou but acts thyself.
But thou, fair hypocrite, to whom I gave my heart,
And this exception made of all mankind,   70
Why wouldst thou, as in malice to my love,
Give it the only wound that could destroy it?

WILLMORE Nay, if thou didst forbid her loving me, I have
her sure.

BEAUMOND I yield him many charms; he's nobly born,   75
Has wit, youth, courage, all that takes the heart;
And only wants what pleases women's vanity,
Estate, the only good that I can boast,
And that I sacrifice to buy thy smiles.

LA NUCHE *(to* WILLMORE) See, sir, here's a much fairer   80
chapman;* you may be gone.

WILLMORE Faith, and so there is, child, for me. I carry all
about me, and that, by heaven, is thine. I'll settle all upon
thee but my sword, and that will buy us bread. I've two
led horses, too; one thou shalt manage, and follow me   85
through dangers.

LA NUCHE A very hopeful, comfortable life!
No, I was made for better exercises.

WILLMORE Why, everything in its turn, child; but a man's
but a man.   90

BEAUMOND No more, but if thou valuest her,
Leave her to ease and plenty.

WILLMORE Leave her to love, my dear; one hour of

right-down love,
Is worth an age of living dully on.
What is't to be adorned and shine with gold,   95
Dressed like a god, but never know the pleasure?
No, no, I have much finer things in store for thee.

(*Hugs her*)

LA NUCHE <*aside*> What shall I do? Here's powerful
    interest prostrate at my feet,

(*Pointing to* BEAUMOND)

Glory, and all that vanity can boast;
But there, (<*pointing*> *to* WILLMORE) Love unadorned,
    no covering but his wings;   100
No wealth, but a full quiver to do mischiefs,
Laughs at those meaner trifles.
BEAUMOND Mute as thou art, are not these minutes
    mine?
But thou, ah false, hast dealt 'em out already,
With all thy charms of love, to this unknown;   105
Silence and guilty blushes say thou hast.
He all disordered too, loose and undressed,
With love and pleasure dancing in his eyes,
Tell me too plainly how thou hast deceived me.
LA NUCHE (*angrily*) Or if I have not 'tis a trick soon
    done,   110
And this ungrateful jealousy would put it in my head.
BEAUMOND Would! By heaven, thou hast! He is not to
    be fooled,
Be soothed into belief of distant joys,
As easy I have been.
I've lost so kind an opportunity,   115
Where night and silence both conspire with love,
Had made him rage like waves blown up by storms.
No more – I know he has. Oh what, La Nuche,
Robbed me of all that I have languished for?
LA NUCHE If it were so, you should not dare believe it.   120

(Angry, turns away; he kneels and holds her)

BEAUMOND Forgive me; oh, so very well I love,
Did I not know that thou hadst been a whore,
I'd give thee the last proof of love and marry thee.

WILLMORE The last indeed, for there's an end of loving.
Do, marry him, and be cursed by all his family.   125
Marry him and ruin him, that he may curse thee too.
But, hark ye, friend, this is not fair; 'tis drawing sharps on
a man that's only armed with the defensive cudgel. I'm for
no such dead-doing arguments. If thou'rt for me, child, it
must be without the folly 'for better for worse'. There's a   130
kind of nonsense in that vow fools only swallow.

LA NUCHE But when I've worn out all my youth and
beauty, and suffered every ill of poverty, I shall be
compelled to begin the world again without a stock to set
up with. No, faith, I'm for a substantial merchant in love,   135
who can repay the loss of time and beauty; with whom to
make one thriving voyage sets me up forever, and I need
never put to sea again.

(Comes to BEAUMOND)

BEAUMOND Nor be exposed to storms of poverty; the
Indies shall come to thee. See here – this is the merchan-   140
dise my love affords.

(Gives her pearl, and pendants of diamond)

LA NUCHE Look ye, sir, will not these pearls do better
round my neck than those kind arms of yours? These
pendants in my ears than all the tales of love you can
whisper there?   145

WILLMORE So, I am deceived. Deal on for trash and barter
all thy joys of life for baubles! *(aside)* This night presents
me one adventure more: I'll try thee once again inconstant
Fortune, and if thou fail'st me then, I will forswear thee.
<to her> Death, hadst thou loved my friend for his own   150
value, I had esteemed thee. But when this youth and
beauty could not plead, to be the mercenary conquest of

his presents was poor, below thy wit. I could have
conquered so, but I scorn thee at that rate – my purse
shall never be my pimp. – Farewell, Harry.   155
BEAUMOND Thou'st shamed me out of folly – stay!
WILLMORE Faith, I have an assignation – with a woman –
a woman friend! Young as the infant day and sweet as
roses ere the morning sun have kissed their dew away. She
will not ask me money, neither.   160
LA NUCHE Hah! Stay –

(*Holds him and looks on him*)

BEAUMOND <*aside*> She loves him, and her eyes betray her
heart.
WILLMORE I am not for your turn, child. Death, I shall lose
my mistress fooling here – I must be gone.   165

(*She holds him, he shakes his head and sings*)

No, no, I will not hire your bed,
Nor tenant to your favours be;
I will not farm your white and red,
You shall not let your love to me:
I court a mistress, not a landlady.* (*Bis*)   170

BEAUMOND He's in the right; and shall I waste my youth
and powerful fortune on one who all this while has jilted
me, seeing I was a lavish, loving fool? No, this soul and
body shall not be divided.

(*Gives her to* WILLMORE)

WILLMORE I am so much thy friend, another time I might 175
be drawn to take a bad bargain off thy hands – but I have
other business at present. Wo't do a kind thing, Harry?
Lend me thy aid to carry off my woman tonight; 'tis hard
by in the piazza, perhaps we may find resistance.
BEAUMOND Myself and sword are yours. I have a chair 180
waits below, too, may do you service.
WILLMORE I thank ye – madam, your servant.
LA NUCHE Left by both?

BEAUMOND (*bows and smiles carelessly*) You see our
affairs are pressing.   185

> [*Exeunt*, WILLMORE *singing*]

LA NUCHE Gone! Where's all your power, ye poor deluded
eyes! Curse on your feeble fires that cannot warm a heart
which every common beauty kindles! Oh, he is gone
forever!

> (*Enter* PETRONELLA)

PETRONELLA Yes he is gone, to your eternal ruin; not all   190
the race of man could have produced so bountiful and
credulous a fool.

LA NUCHE No, never! Fetch him back, my Petronella.
Bring me my wild inconstant or I die!

> (*Puts her out*)

PETRONELLA The devil fetch him back, for Petronella! Is't   195
he you mean? You've had too much of him. A curse upon
him, he's ruined you!

LA NUCHE He has, he shall, he must complete my ruin.

PETRONELLA <aside> She raves, the rogue has given her a
Spanish philtre.*   200

LA NUCHE My coach, my veil – or let 'em all alone.
Undressed thus loosely to the winds, commit me to
darkness, and no guide but pitying Cupid.

> (*Going out;* PETRONELLA *holds her*)

PETRONELLA What, are you* mad?

LA NUCHE As winds let loose, or storms when they rage   205
high.

> [*Goes out*]

PETRONELLA She's lost, and I'll shift for myself; seize all
her money and jewels, of which I have the keys; and if
Seignior Mountebank keeps his word, be transformed to
youth and beauty again, and undo this La Nuche at her   210
own trade.

> (*Goes in*)

Act 5, Scene 2

The street

(*Enter* WILLMORE, BEAUMOND; CHAIR *following*)

WILLMORE Set down the chair; you're now within call. I'll
to the garden door and see if any lady bright appear. –
Dear Beaumond, stay here a minute, and if I find
occasion, I'll give you the word.

BEAUMOND 'Tis hard by my lodgings. If you want conven-   5
iences, I have the key of the back way through the garden,
whither you may carry your mistress.

WILLMORE I thank thee; let me first secure my woman.
                                                    [*Goes out*]

BEAUMOND I thought I'd loved this false, this jilting fair,
even above my friendship; but I find I can forgive this   10
rogue, though I am sure he's robbed me of my joys.

(*Enter* ARIADNE *with a casket of jewels*)

ARIADNE (*aside*) Not yet, a devil on him, he's dear-hearting
it with some other kind damsel. Faith, 'tis most wickedly
done of me to venture my body with a mad unknown
fellow. Thus, a little more delay will put me into a serious   15
consideration, and I shall e'en go home again, sleep and
be sober.

(*She walks about*)

BEAUMOND Hah, a woman! Perhaps the same he looks
for. I'll counterfeit his voice and try my chance – fortune
may set us even.   20

ARIADNE Hah, is not that a man? Yes, and a chair waiting.

(*She peeps*)

BEAUMOND Who's there?

ARIADNE A maid.

BEAUMOND A miracle. Oh, art thou come, child?

ARIADNE <*aside*> 'Tis he. <*to* BEAUMOND> You are a civil   25 captain, are you not, to make a longing maid expect thus. What woman has detained you?

BEAUMOND Faith, my dear, though flesh and blood be frail, yet the dear hopes of thee has made me hold out with a Herculean courage. *<aside>* Stay, where shall I carry her? Not to my own apartment, Ariadne may surprise me. I'll to the mountebank here i'th' piazza. He has a cure for all things, even for longing love, and for a pistole or two will do reason. Hah, company! *<to her>* Here, step into this chair.   30

                                                                     35

(She goes in; they go off just as WILLMORE *enters)*

WILLMORE Hum, a woman of quality and jilt me. Egad, that's strange now. Well, who shall a man trust in this wicked world!

(Enter LA NUCHE *as before)*

LA NUCHE *<aside>* This should be he, he saunters about like an expecting lover.   40

*(*WILLMORE *peeping and approaching)*

WILLMORE *<aside>* By this light, a woman, if she be the right; but right or wrong, so she be feminine. *<to her>* Hark ye, child, I fancy thee some kind thing that belongs to me.

LA NUCHE *(in a low tone)* Who are you?   45

WILLMORE A wandering lover that has lost his heart, and I have a shrewd guess 'tis in thy dear bosom, child.

LA NUCHE Oh, you're a pretty lover! A woman's like to have a sweet time on't, if you're always so tedious.*

WILLMORE By yon bright starlight, child, I walked here in short turns like a sentinel, all this livelong evening, and was just going (gad forgive me) to kill myself.   50

LA NUCHE I rather think some beauty has detained you. Have you not seen La Nuche?

WILLMORE La Nuche! Why she's a whore! I hope you take me for a civiller person, than to throw myself away on whores. No, child, I lie with none but honest women, I.   55

But no disputing now, come – to my lodging, my dear.
Here's a chair waits hard by.

                                                    [*Exeunt*]

Act 5, Scene 3

WILLMORE's *lodging*

(*Enter* HARLEQUIN *with* FETHERFOOL's *clothes on his
shoulder, leading him halting by one hand,* BLUNT
(drunk) *by the other, by dark:* FETHERFOOL *bloody, his
coat put over his shoulders*)

FETHERFOOL *Peano,** *peano,* seignior. Gently, good
Edward; for I'll not halt before a cripple. I have lost a
great part of my agile faculties.

BLUNT Ah, see the inconstancy of fickle fortune, Nicholas.
A man today, and beaten tomorrow. But take comfort,   5
there's many a proper fellow has been robbed and beaten
on this highway of whoring.

FETHERFOOL Aye, Ned, thou speak'st by woeful experience – but that I should miscarry after thy wholesome
documents! But we are all mortal, as thou say'st, Ned.   10
Would I had never crossed the ferry from Croydon. A few
such nights as these would learn a man experience enough
to be a wizard, if he have but the ill luck to escape
hanging.

BLUNT 'Adsheartlikins, I wonder in what country our   15
kinder stars rule? In England: plundered, sequestered,
imprisoned and banished; in France: starved, walking like
the sign of the Naked Boy,* with Plymouth cloaks* in our
hands; in Italy and Spain: robbed, beaten and thrown out
at windows.   20

FETHERFOOL (*weeps*) Well, how happy am I, in having so
true a friend to condole me in affliction. – I am obliged to
Seignior Harlequin, too, for bringing me hither to the
mountebank's, where I shall not only conceal this catastrophe from those fortunate rogues, our comrades, but   25

procure a little album graecum* for my backside. Come,
seignior, my clothes – but seignior – *un portavera poco
palauea.* *

(*Dresses himself*)

HARLEQUIN Seignior?

FETHERFOOL *Entende vos Signoria Englesa?* *

HARLEQUIN *Em poco,* * em poco*, seignior.   30

FETHERFOOL *Per quelq arts* * did your seigniorship escape
cudgelling?

HARLEQUIN *La art de transformatio.* *

FETHERFOOL *Transformatio?* Why, wert thou not born a   35
man?

HARLEQUIN No, seignior, *un vieule famme.* *

FETHERFOOL How, born an old woman?

BLUNT Good Lord! Born an old woman! And so by
transformation became invulnerable!   40

FETHERFOOL Aye, in – invulnerable. What would I give to
be invulnerable! And, egad, I am almost weary of being a
man, and subject to beating. Would I were a woman; a
man has but an ill time on't. If he has a mind to a wench,
the making love is so plaguy tedious; then paying is, to   45
my soul, insupportable. But to be a woman: to be courted
with presents, and have both the pleasure and the profit;
to be without a beard, and sing a fine treble; and squeak if
the men but kiss me – 'twere fine; and what's better, I am
sure never to be beaten again.   50

BLUNT Pox on't, do not use an old friend so scurvily.
Consider the misery thou't endure to have the heart and
mind of a jilting whore possess thee! What a fit of the
devil must he suffer who acts her part from fourteen to
fourscore. No, 'tis resolved thou remain Nicholas Fether-   55
fool still; shalt marry the monster, and laugh at fortune.

FETHERFOOL 'Tis true. Should I turn whore to the disgrace
of my family, what would the world say? 'Who would
have thought it?' cries one; 'I could never have believed,'
cries another. No, as thou sayst, I'll remain as I am; marry   60
and live honestly.

BLUNT Well resolved; I'll leave you, for I was just going to
serenade my fairy queen when I met thee at the door.
Some deeds of gallantry must be performed. <*to* HARLE-
QUIN> Seignior, *bonus nochus.** 65

[*Exit* BLUNT]

(*Enter* SHIFT *with light*)

FETHERFOOL Hah, a light, undone!

HARLEQUIN *Patientia,** patientia*, seignior.

SHIFT Where the devil can this rogue Hunt be? Just now all
things are ready for marrying these two monsters. They
wait; the house is hushed, and in the lucky minute, to 70
have him out of the way! Sure, the devil owes me a spite.

(*Runs against* HARLEQUIN; *puts out his candle*)

HARLEQUIN *Que et la?**

SHIFT 'Tis Harlequin. <*to him*> Pox on't, is't you?

HARLEQUIN <*aside to* SHIFT> Peace, here's Fetherfool. I'll
secure him, whilst you go about your affair. 75

[*Exit* SHIFT]

FETHERFOOL Oh, I hear a noise. Dear Harlequin, secure
me. If I am discovered, I am undone – hold, hold – here's
a door.

(*They both go in*)

Act 5, Scene 4

The scene changes to a chamber; discovers the
SHE-GIANT *asleep in a great, great chair*

(*Enter* FETHERFOOL *and* HARLEQUIN)

FETHERFOOL Hah, my lady monster! Have I, to avoid
Scylla, run upon Charybdis?* Hah, she sleeps. Now
would some magnanimous lover make good use of this
opportunity, take Fortune by the forelock,* put her to't,

and make sure work. But, egad, he must have a better 5
heart, or a better mistress than I.

HARLEQUIN Try your strength, I'll be civil and leave you.

(In Italian he still speaks)

FETHERFOOL Excuse me, seignior, I should crackle like a
wicker bottle in her arms. No, seignior, there's no
venturing without a grate between us; the devil would not 10
give her due benevolence. No, when I'm married, I'll e'en
show her a fair pair of heels; her portion will pay postage.
But what if the giant should carry her? That's to be
feared. Then I have cocked and dressed, and fed* and
ventured all this while for nothing. 15

HARLEQUIN Faith, seignior, if I were you, I would make
sure of something. See how rich she is in gems!

FETHERFOOL Right; as thou sayst, I ought to make sure of
something, and she is rich in gems. How amiable looks
that neck with that delicious row of pearls about it. 20

HARLEQUIN She sleeps.

FETHERFOOL Aye, she sleeps as 'twere her last. What if I
made bold to unrig* her? So, if I miss the lady, I have at
least my charges paid. What vigorous lover can resist her
charms? *(looks on her)* But should she wake and miss it, 25
and find it about me, I should be hanged – *(turns away)* –
so then, I lose my lady too. But flesh and blood cannot
resist. What if I left the town? Then I lose my lady still,
and who would lose a hog* for the rest of the proverb?
And yet a bird in hand,* friend Nicholas, – yet sweet 30
meat may have sour sauce. And yet refuse when fortune
offers? Yet honesty's a jewel – but a pox upon pride,
when folks go naked.

HARLEQUIN Well said.

(Encouraging him by signs)

FETHERFOOL Aye, I'll do't; but what remedy now against 35
discovery and restitution?

HARLEQUIN Oh, sir, take no care, you shall – swallow 'em.

FETHERFOOL How, swallow 'em? I shall ne'er be able to do't.

HARLEQUIN I'll show you, seignior, 'tis easy.   40

FETHERFOOL 'Gad that may be; 'twere excellent if I could do't; but first, by your leave.

(*Unties the necklace, breaks the string, and* HARLEQUIN *swallows one to show him*)

HARLEQUIN Look ye, that's all.

FETHERFOOL Hold, hold, seignior, an you be so nimble, I shall pay dear for my learning. Let me see, friend   45 Nicholas, thou hast swallowed many a pill for the disease of the body; let's see what thou canst perform for that of the purse. (*swallows 'em*) So, a comfortable business this; three or four thousand pound in cordial pearl. 'Sbud, Mark Anthony was never so treated by his Egyptian   50 crocodile.* Hah, what noise is that?

HARLEQUIN Operator, operator, seignior.

FETHERFOOL How, an operator? Why, what the devil makes he here? Some plot upon my lady's chastity. Were I given to be jealous now, danger would ensue – oh, he's   55 entering, I would not be seen for all the world. Oh, some place of refuge!

(*Looking about*)

HARLEQUIN I know of none.

FETHERFOOL Hah, what's this! A clock-case –

HARLEQUIN Good, good. Look you, sir, do you do thus,   60 and 'tis impossible to discover ye.

(*Goes into the case and shows him how to stand. Then* FETHERFOOL *goes in, pulls off his periwig, his head out, turning for the minutes o'th' top: his hand out, and his finger pointing to a figure*)

(*Enter* SHIFT *and* HUNT)

FETHERFOOL Oh heaven, he's here.

SHIFT See where she sleeps; get you about your business. See your own little marmoset and the priest be ready, that

we may marry and consummate before day; and in the 65
morning, our friends shall see us abed together, give us
the good morrow, and the work's done.

[*Exit* HUNT]

FETHERFOOL Oh, traitor to my bed, what a hellish plot's
here discovered!

(SHIFT *wakes the* GIANT)

GIANT Oh, are you come, my sweetest? 70
FETHERFOOL Hah, the mistress of my bosom false, too!
Ah, who would trust faithless beauty. Oh, that I durst
speak.
SHIFT Come let's away, your uncle and the rest of the
house are fast asleep. Let's away ere the two fools, Blunt 75
and Fetherfool, arrive.
GIANT Hang 'em, pigeon-hearted slaves.
SHIFT A clock – let's see what hour 'tis.

(*Lights up the light to see;* FETHERFOOL *blows it out*)

How! Betrayed – I'll kill the villain.

(*Draws*)

FETHERFOOL Say you so? Then 'tis time for me to uncase. 80
SHIFT Have you your lovers hid?

(*Gets out, all groping in the dark.* FETHERFOOL *gets the*
GIANT *by the hand*)

GIANT Softly, or we're undone. Give me your hand and be
undeceived.
FETHERFOOL 'Tis she, now shall I be revenged.

(*Leads her out*)

SHIFT What, gone? Death, has this monster got the arts of 85
woman?

(HARLEQUIN *meets him in the dark and plays
tricks with him*)

[*Exeunt* ALL]

(Enter WILLMORE *and* LA NUCHE *by dark)*

WILLMORE   Now we are safe and free, let's in my soul,
    And gratefully first sacrifice to love,
    Then to the gods of mirth and wine, my dear.
                    [*Exeunt passing over the stage*]

(Enter BLUNT *with* PETRONELLA, *embracing her, his
    sword in his hand, and a box of jewels)*

PETRONELLA   (*aside*) I was damnably afraid I was pursued.   90

BLUNT   <*aside*> Something in the fray I've got. Pray heaven
    it prove a prize, after my cursed ill luck of losing my lady
    dwarf. <*to her*> Why do you tremble fair one? You're in
    the hands of an honest gentleman, 'adsheartlikins.

PETRONELLA   Alas, sir, just as I approached Seignior   95
    Doctor's door, to have myself surrounded with naked
    weapons; then to drop with the fear my casket of jewels,
    which had not you by chance stumbled on and taken up, I
    had lost a hundred thousand crowns with it.

BLUNT   Ha – um, a hundred thousand crowns: a pretty,   100
    trifling sum. <*aside*> I'll marry her out of hand.

PETRONELLA   (*aside*) This is an Englishman, of a dull
    honest nation, and might be managed to advantage, were
    but I transformed now. <*to him*> I hope you are a man of
    honour, sir. I am a virgin, fled from the rage of an   105
    incensed brother. Could you but secure me with my
    treasure, I would be devoted yours.

BLUNT   Secure thee? By this light, sweet soul, I'll marry
    thee! (*aside*) Belvile's lady ran just so away with him;*
    this must be a prize. But hark, prithee, my dear, step in a   110
    little; I'll keep my good fortune to myself.

PETRONELLA   See what trust I repose in your hands; those
    jewels, sir.

BLUNT   So, there can be no jilting here; I am secured from
    being cozened, however.   115
                    [*Exit* PETRONELLA]

(Enter FETHERFOOL)

FETHERFOOL A pox on all fools, I say, and a double pox
on all fighting fools! Just when I had miraculously got my
monster by a mistake in the dark; conveyed her out and
within a moment of marrying her – to have my friend set
upon me and occasion my losing her, was a catastrophe   120
which none but thy termagant courage (which never did
any man good) could have procured.

BLUNT 'Adsheartlikins, I could kill myself.

FETHERFOOL To fight away a couple of such hopeful
monsters, and two millions – 'Ounds!* Was ever valour   125
so improvident?

BLUNT Your fighting made me mistake; for who the pox
would have looked for Nicholas Fetherfool in the person
of a hero?

FETHERFOOL Fight! 'Sbud, a million of money would have   130
provoked a bully; besides, I took you for the damned
rogue, my rival.

BLUNT Just as I had finished my serenade, and had put up
my pipes to be gone, out stalked me your two-handed*
lady, with a man at her girdle like a bunch of keys, whom   135
I – taking for nothing less than someone who had some
foul design upon the gentlewoman – like a true knight
errant, did my best to rescue her.

FETHERFOOL Yes, yes, I feel you did. A pox of your heavy
hand!   140

BLUNT So whilst we two were lovingly cuffing each other,
comes the rival, I suppose, and carries off the prize.

FETHERFOOL Who must be Seignior Lucifer himself; he
could never have vanished with that celerity else with
such a carriage.* But come, all we have to do is to raise   145
the mountebank and the guardian; pursue the rogues;
have 'em hanged by law for a rape and theft; and then we
stand fair again.

BLUNT (aside) Faith, you may if you please, but fortune has
provided otherwise for me.   150

　　　　　[Exit BLUNT and FETHERFOOL]

　　　(Enter BEAUMOND and ARIADNE)

BEAUMOND Sure, none lives here, or thieves are broken in.
The doors are all left open.

ARIADNE (*aside*) Pray heaven this stranger prove but
honest now.

BEAUMOND Now my dear creature everything conspires to 155
make us happy; let us not defer it.

ARIADNE Hold, dear captain, I yield but on conditions,
which are these: I give you up a maid of youth and
beauty; ten thousand pound in ready jewels here; three
times the value in estate to come, of which here be the 160
writings; you delivering me a handsome, proper fellow,
heart-whole and sound. That's all. Your name I ask not
till the priest declare it who is to seal the bargain. I cannot
deceive, for I let you know I am daughter-in-law to the
English ambassador.   165

BEAUMOND (*aside*) Ariadne!
How vain is all man's industry and care
To make him accomplished; when the gay fluttering
    fool,
Or the half-witted, rough, unmannered brute,
Who in plain terms comes right down to the business, 170
Out-rivals him in all his love and fortunes.

ARIADNE Methinks, you cool upon't, captain.

BEAUMOND Yes, Ariadne!

ARIADNE Beaumond!

BEAUMOND Oh, what a world of time have I mispent 175
For want of being a blockhead! 'Sdeath and hell,
Would I had been some brawny, ruffling fool;
Some forward, impudent, unthinking sloven,
A woman's tool; for all besides, unmanageable.
Come, swear that all this while you thought 'twas I: 180
The devil has taught ye tricks to bring your falsehood
    off.

ARIADNE Know 'twas you? No, faith, I took you for as
arrant a right-down captain as ever woman wished for;
and 'twas uncivil, egad, to undeceive me, I tell you that
now.   185

(*Enter* WILLMORE *and* LA NUCHE *by dark*)

WILLMORE Thou art all charms, a heaven of sweets all
over: plump, smooth, round limbs, small rising breasts, a
bosom soft and panting. I long to wound each sense.
Lights there! Who waits? – There yet remains a pleasure
unpossessed, the sight of that dear face. Lights there! 190
Where are my vermin?

[*Exit* WILLMORE]

ARIADNE My captain with a woman! And is it so?

(*Enter* WILLMORE *with lights, sees* ARIADNE, *and goes
to her*)

WILLMORE By heaven, a glorious beauty! Now, a blessing
on thee for showing me so dear a face. Come, child, let's
retire, and begin where we left off.   195

LA NUCHE <*aside*> A woman!

ARIADNE Where we left off? Pray, where was that good
captain?

WILLMORE Within, upon the bed, child; come, I'll show
thee.   200

BEAUMOND Hold, sir –

WILLMORE Beaumond, come fit to celebrate my happiness!
Ah, such a woman, friend!

BEAUMOND Do ye know her?

WILLMORE All o'er, to be the softest, sweetest creature. 205

BEAUMOND I mean, do ye know who she is?

WILLMORE Nor care; 'tis the last question I ever ask a fine
woman.

BEAUMOND And you are sure you are thus well
acquainted?   210

WILLMORE I cannot boast of much acquaintance; but I
have plucked a rose from her bosom – or so – and given it
her again. We've passed the hour of the bergère* together,
that's all.

BEAUMOND And do you know – this lady is my – wife? 215

(*Draw*)

WILLMORE Hah! Hum, hum, hum, hum.

(*Turns and sings, sees* LA NUCHE, *and returns quick with an uneasy grimace*)

BEAUMOND Did you not hear me? Draw!

WILLMORE Draw, sir? What, on my friend?

BEAUMOND On your cuckold, sir, for so you've doubly made me! Draw, or I'll kill thee!   220

(*Passes at him; he fences with his hat,* LA NUCHE *holds* BEAUMOND)

WILLMORE Hold, prithee, hold –

LA NUCHE Put up your sword; this lady's innocent, at least in what concerns this evening's business. I own, with pride I own, I am the woman that pleased so well tonight.

WILLMORE <*aside*> La Nuche! Kind soul to bring me off 225 with so handsome a lie. How lucky 'twas she happened to be here!

BEAUMOND False as thou art, why should I credit thee?

LA NUCHE By heaven, 'tis true; I will not lose the glory on't.   230

WILLMORE Oh, the dear, perjured creature, how I love thee for this dear, lying virtue. (*to* ARIADNE *aside*) Hark ye, child, hast thou nothing to say for thyself to help us out withal?

ARIADNE I! I renounce ye, false man!   235

BEAUMOND Yes, yes, I know she's innocent of this, for which I owe no thanks to either of you, but to myself who mistook her in the dark.

LA NUCHE And you it seems mistook me for this lady.*
I favoured your design to gain your heart,   240
For I was told that if this night I lost you,
I should never regain you. Now I am yours,
And o'er the habitable world will follow you,
And live and starve by turns as fortune pleases.

WILLMORE Nay, by this light, child, I knew when once 245 thou'dst tried me, thou'dst ne'er part with me. Give me thy hand, no poverty shall part us. (*kisses her*) So, now here's a bargain made without the formal foppery of marriage.

LA NUCHE Nay, faith, captain, she that will not take thy 250
word as soon as the parson's of the parish deserves not
the blessing.

WILLMORE Thou art reformed, and I adore the change.

(*Enter the* GUARDIAN, BLUNT *and* FETHERFOOL)

GUARDIAN My nieces stolen, and by a couple of the
seignior's men! The seignior fled too! Undone, undone! 255

WILLMORE <aside> Hah, now's my cue; I must finish this
jest.

[*Goes out*]

(*Enter* SHIFT *and* GIANT, HUNT *and* DWARF)

GUARDIAN Oh, impudence, my nieces, and the villains
with 'em! I charge ye gentlemen to lay hold on 'em.

DWARF For what, good uncle, for being so courageous to 260
marry us?

GUARDIAN How? Married to rogues, rascals, John
Potages!*

BLUNT Who the devil would have looked for jilting in such
hobgoblins? 265

FETHERFOOL And hast thou deceived me, thou foul, filthy
synagogue?*

(*Enter* WILLMORE *like a mountebank, as before*)

BLUNT The mountebank! Oh, thou cheating quack, thou
sophisticated, adulterated villain!

FETHERFOOL Thou cozening, lying, fortune-telling, fee- 270
taking rascal!

BLUNT Thou juggling, conjuring, canting rogue!

WILLMORE What's the matter, gentlemen?

BLUNT Hast thou the impudence to ask, who took my
money to marry me to this ill-favoured baboon? 275

FETHERFOOL And me to this foul, filthy, o'er-grown
chronicle.*

BLUNT And hast suffered rogues, thy servants, to marry
'em? Sirrah, I will beat thee past cure of all thy hard-
named drugs, thy Guzman medicines.* 280

FETHERFOOL Nay, I'll peach him in the Inquisition for a
wizard, and have him hanged for a witch.

SHIFT (*aside to the* GUARDIAN) Sir, we are gentlemen, and
you shall have the thirds of their portion. What would
you more?   285
Look ye, sir.

(*Pulls off their disguise*)

BLUNT Hunt!

FETHERFOOL Shift! We are betrayed! All will out to the
captain.

WILLMORE He shall know no more of it than he does 290
already for me, gentlemen.

(*Pulls off his disguise*)

BLUNT Willmore!

FETHERFOOL Aye, aye, 'tis he.

BLUNT Draw, sir; you know me –

WILLMORE – For one that 'tis impossible to cozen.   295

(*All laugh*)

BEAUMOND Have a care, sir, we are all for the captain.

FETHERFOOL As for that, sir, we fear ye not, d'ye see, were
you Hercules and all his Myrmidons.*

(*Draws, but gets behind*)

WILLMORE Fools, put up your swords, fools, and do not
publish the jest. Your money you shall have again, on 300
condition you never pretend to be wiser than your other
men, but modestly believe you may be cozened as well as
your neighbours.

(*The* GUARDIAN *talking with* HUNT *and* SHIFT *and*
GIANT *this while*)

FETHERFOOL La you, Ned, why should friends fall out?

BLUNT Cozened! It may be not, sir; for look ye, sir, the 305
Essex fool, the cozened, dull rogue can show moveables
or so – nay, they are right, too. (*shows his jewels*) This is

no Naples adventure, gentlemen, no copper chains;* all substantial diamonds, pearls and rubies.

(WILLMORE *takes the casket and looks in it*)

LA NUCHE Hah, do not I know that casket, and those 310 jewels?

FETHERFOOL How the pox came this rogue by these?

WILLMORE Hum, Edward, I confess you have redeemed your reputation, and shall hereafter pass for a wit. By what good fortune came you by this treasure? What lady? 315

BLUNT Lady, sir! Alas no, I am a fool, a country fop, an ass, I. But that you may perceive yourselves mistaken, gentlemen, this is but an earnest of what's to come; a small token of remembrance, or so. And yet I have no charms, I; the fine captain has all the wit and beauty; but 320 thou'rt my friend, and I'll impart.

(*Brings out* PETRONELLA *veiled*)

(*Enter* AURELIA *and* SANCHO)

AURELIA Hither we traced her, and see, she's yonder.

SANCHO Sir, in the king's name lay hold of this old cheat. She has this night robbed our patrona of a hundred thousand crowns in money and jewels. 325

BLUNT Hah!

(*Gets from her*)

LA NUCHE You are mistaken, friend Sancho, she only seized 'em for my use, and has delivered 'em in trust to my friend the captain.

PETRONELLA Hah, La Nuche! 330

BLUNT How! Cozened again!

WILLMORE Look ye, sir, she's so beautiful, you need no portion; that alone's sufficient for a wit.

FETHERFOOL Much good may <it> do you with your rich lady, Edward. 335

BLUNT Death, this fool laugh at me too! Well, I am an arrant, right-down loggerhead, a dull, conceited, cozened, silly fool, and he that ever takes me for any other,

'adsheartlikins, I'll beat him. I forgive you all, and will
henceforth be good-natured. Wo't borrow any money? 340
Pox on't, I'll lend as far as e'er 'twill go, for I am now
reclaimed.

GUARDIAN (*to* FETHERFOOL) Here is a necklace of pearl
lost, which, sir, I lay to your charge.

FETHERFOOL <*aside*> Hum, I was bewitched I did not rub 345
off* with it when it was mine. <*to the* GUARDIAN> Who
I? If e'er I saw a necklace of pearl, I wish 'twere in my
belly.

BLUNT How, a necklace? Unconscionable rogue, not to let
me share. Well, there is no friendship in this world. I hope 350
they'll hang him.

SHIFT He'll ne'er confess without the rack. Come, we'll
toss him in a blanket.

FETHERFOOL <*aside*> Hah, toss me in a blanket! That will
turn my stomach most villainously, and I shall disem- 355
bogue* and discover all.

SHIFT Come, come, the blanket.

(*They lay hold of him*)

FETHERFOOL Hold, hold, I do confess, I do confess –

SHIFT Restore, and have your pardon.

FETHERFOOL That is not in nature at present; for, gentle- 360
men, I have eaten 'em.

SHIFT (*goes to draw*) 'Sdeath, I'll dissect ye.

WILLMORE Let me redeem him; here, boy, take him to my
chamber, and let the doctor clyster* him soundly, and I'll
warrant you your pearl again.   365

FETHERFOOL If this be the end of travelling, I'll e'en to old
England again; take the Covenant, get a sequestrator's
place,* grow rich, and defy all cavaliering.

BEAUMOND 'Tis morning. Let's home, Ariadne, and try, if
possible, to love so well to be content to marry. If we find 370
that amendment in our hearts to say we dare believe and
trust each other, then let it be a match.

ARIADNE With all my heart.

WILLMORE You have a hankering after marriage still, but I
  am for love and gallantry.   375
  So though by several ways we gain our end,
  Love still, like death, does to one centre tend.

                                          <Exeunt>

Epilogue

Spoken by Mrs Barry

Poets are kings of wit, and you appear
A parliament, by playbill summoned here.
Whene'er in want, to you for aid they fly,
And a new play's the speech that begs supply.*
But now –   5
The scanted tribute is so slowly paid,
Our poets must find out another trade;
They've tried all ways the insatiate clan to please,
Have parted with their old prerogatives:
Their birthright, satiring, and their just pretence   10
Of judging, even their own wit and sense;
And write against their consciences to show
How dull they can be to comply with you.
They've flattered all the mutineers i' th' nation,
Grosser than e'er was done in dedication;   15
Pleased your sick palates with fantastic wit,
Such as was ne'er a treat before to th' pit;
Giants, fat cardinals, Pope Joans and friars,*
To entertain Right Worshipfuls and squires:
Who laugh, and cry 'Ads Nigs,* 'tis woundy* good',   20
When the fuger's* all the jest that's understood.
And yet you'll come but once, unless by stealth,
Except the author be for Commonwealth;*
Then half-crown more you nobly throw away,
And though my Lady seldom see a play,   25
She, with her eldest daughter, shall be boxed that day.
Then prologue comes, 'Ads lightikins',* cries Sir John,
'You shall hear notable conceits anon.
How neatly, sir, he'll bob* the court and French king,
And tickle away* – you know who – for wenching.'   30
   All this won't do, they may e'en spare their
      speeches,
For all their greasing* will not buy 'em breeches.

To get a penny, new-found ways must take,
As forming popes, and squibs and crackers make.*
In coffee-houses some their talent vent,   35
Rail for the Cause* against the government,
And make a pretty thriving living on't.
For who would let a useful member want?
    Things being brought to this distressed estate,
'Twere fit you took the matter in debate.   40
There was a time, when loyally by you,
True wit and sense received allegiance due;
Our king of poets had his tribute paid,*
His peers secured beneath his laurels' shade.
What crimes have they committed they must be   45
Driven to the last and worst extremity?
Oh, let it not be said of Englishmen,
Who have to wit so just and noble been,
They should their loyal principles recant,
And let the glorious monarch of it want.   50

THE WIVES' EXCUSE

or

CUCKOLDS MAKE THEMSELVES

A COMEDY

BY

THOMAS SOUTHERNE

Nihil est his, qui placere volunt,
Tam adversarium, quam expectatio.*

[Cicero]

<DEDICATION>
To the Right Honourable Thomas Wharton, Esq.,*
Comptroller of His Majesty's Household*

Sir,

Every man of fortune* has the power of doing a good turn, but there must be more in the man one would choose to be obliged to. I have a thousand obligations to you, and have confessed 'em upon every occasion, with as much satisfaction as I received 'em. I have enjoyed the benefit of 5 your favours; and have the pride of 'em yet in my heart, that you have not thought so much good nature thrown away upon me. I would make you what amends I could, and a dedication is all that I have in my power to return. 'Tis a poetical payment indeed, which, while it discharges one 10 debt, is running into another, begging your protection for a play which will almost need your interest* to defend. I won't contend a point where most voices* are to carry it, but as I designed this play for you, when some people thought well of it,* I hope it does not lessen the present, that 15 everybody does not. 'Tis only the capacity and commendation of the common mistresses to please everybody, to whom I will leave some of my critics who were affronted at Mrs Friendall. For those sparks* who were most offended with her virtue in public, are the men that lose little by it in 20 private; and if all the wives in town were of her mind, those mettled gentlemen would be found to have the least to do in making 'em otherwise.

But if she was of evil example, Witwoud makes amends for her in the moral of her character, where the women are 25 manifestly safer in the possession of a lover, than in the trust and confidence of a friend. But she was no more understood to the advantage of the men, then* the wife was received in favour of the women. As to the music-meeting,* I always thought it an entertainment reasonably grown up into the 30 liking of the town. I introduced it as a fashionable scene of bringing good company together, without a design of

abusing what everybody likes; being in my temper so far
from disturbing a public pleasure, that I would establish
twenty more of 'em, if I could. And for the billet-doux* that 35
was put into Mrs Sightly's hand upon leading her out,* I
have heard of such a thing in a church before now and never
thought the worse of the place.

These, sir, are capital* objections against me; but they hit
very few faults. Nor have they mortified me into a despair of 40
pleasing the more reasonable part of mankind. If Mr
Dryden's judgement goes for anything, I have it on my side.
For, speaking of this play, he has publicly said the town was
kind* to Sir Anthony Love,* I needed 'em only to be just to
this. And to prove there was more than friendship in his 45
opinion: upon the credit of this play with him,* falling sick
last summer, he bequeathed to my care the writing of half
the last act of his tragedy of Cleomenes;* which, when it
comes into the world, you will find to be so considerable a
trust, that all the town will pardon me for defending this 50
play, that preferred me to it.* If modesty be sometimes a
weakness, what I say can hardly be a crime. In a fair English
trial, parties are allowed to be heard, and, without this
vanity of mentioning Mr Dryden, I had lost the best
evidence of my cause. Sir, I have the privilege of a dedication 55
to say some fine things of my patron. But I will be as little
impertinent as I can, and only beg leave to say some true
ones, and no more than I have always declared in the
absence of Mr Wharton: that (without the advantage of
your family and fortune) you are the very man I would 60
choose to be, if I could. I would have the force of your
understanding and knowledge of mankind to make a
fortune out of the public business of the world. Or, if I were
to mend my condition more to my own humour and a way I
should like better than through the hurry of a crowd: your 65
conversation, your person and address would best recommend me to the women. I don't know, sir, how successful
you have been with the fair sex,* but I would not have it lie
at any fair lady's door (who has a mind to be justified in
disposing of herself)* that she could not distinguish in your 70

favour against all the pretenders* of the town. If you have any enemies among the women, I must think 'tis in a great measure because it was impossible to engage 'em all to be your friends.* Sir, I am a well-wisher to all your interests, and be pleased to accept of this dedication of my respects, as 75 an offering of my inclination, as well as a duty from my gratitude.

I am, sir,

Your very much obliged humble servant,

Thomas Southerne

To Mr Southerne
On His Comedy
Called
The Wives' Excuse

Sure there's a fate in plays; and 'tis in vain
To write while these malignant planets* reign.
Some very foolish influence rules the pit,
Not always kind to sense, or just to wit.
And whilst it lasts, let buffoonry succeed   5
To make us laugh, for never was more need.
Farce, in itself, is of a nasty scent;
But the gain smells not of the excrement.
The Spanish nymph,* a wit and beauty, too,
With all her charms bore but a single show.   10
But let a monster Muscovite* appear,
He draws a crowded audience round the year.
Maybe thou hast not pleased the box and pit,
Yet those who blame thy tale,* commend thy wit:
So Terence plotted; but so Terence writ.*   15
Like his, thy thoughts are true, thy language clean,
Ev'n lewdness is made moral in thy scene.*
The hearers may for want of Nokes* repine,
But rest secure, the readers will be thine.
Nor was thy laboured drama damned or hissed,   20
But with a kind civility dismissed –
With such good manners as the wife* did use,
Who, not accepting, did but just refuse.
There was a glance at parting – such a look
As bids thee not give o'er for one rebuke.*   25
But if thou wouldst be seen, as well as read,
Copy one living author, and one dead.
The standard of thy style, let Etherege be;
For wit, th' immortal spring of Wycherley.*
Learn after both to draw some just design,   30
And the next age will learn to copy thine.

John Dryden

Prologue

Gallants, you're welcome to our homely cheer.
If you have brought your English stomachs* here,
We'll treat you, as the French say, *chere entire*.*
And what we want of humour, or of wit,
Take up with your she-neighbours in the pit.   5
For on the stage whate'er we do, or say,
The vizard-masks* can find you better play.
With all our pains, we can but bring 'em in,
'Tis you must take the damsels out again.
And when we've brought you kindly thus together,   10
'Tis your fault if you're parted by foul weather.*
We hope these natural reasons may produce,
In every whoremaster, a kind excuse
For all our faults, the poet's, and the players'.
(*To the Maskers*) You'll pardon us, if you can find out
   theirs.   15
But to the gentler men, who love at sight,
And never care to come to closer fight:
We have provided work for them tonight.
With safety they may draw their cannon down,
And into a surrender bomb the town;   20
From both side-boxes play their batteries;
And not a bullet shot, but burning eyes.
Those they discharge with such successful arts,
They fire three deep* into the ladies' hearts.
Since each man here finds his diversion,   25
Let not the damning of our play be one.
But to the ladies, who must sit it out
To hear us prate, and see the oglers shoot –
Begging their favour, we have this to say,
In hopes of their protection for the play: 30
'Here is a music-meeting every day.'

DRAMATIS PERSONAE

The play was first performed late in 1691 or early in 1692 by the United Company at the Theatre Royal, Drury Lane, with the cast listed below.

LOVEMORE	Mr Betterton
WELLVILE	Mr Kynaston
WILDING	Mr Williams
COURTALL	Mr Bowman
SPRINGAME	Mr Michael Leigh
FRIENDALL	Mr Mountfort
RUFFLE	Mr Bright
MUSIC-MASTER	Mr Harris
MRS FRIENDALL	Mrs Barry
MRS SIGHTLY	Mrs Bracegirdle
MRS WITWOUD	Mrs Mountfort
MRS TEAZALL	Mrs Corey
FANNY, her niece	
BETTY, Witwoud's maid	Mrs Richardson

TWO PAGES, <SEVEN> FOOTMEN,* <MUSICIANS, THREE LORDS, MASQUERADERS> and LINKBOYS*

Scene: London

Act 1, Scene 1

(The outward room to the music-meeting. SEVERAL
FOOTMEN *at hazard,* some rising from play)*

1ST FOOTMAN A pox on these music-meetings! There's no
fifth act here, a free cost,* as we have at the playhouses,
to make gentlemen of us, and keep us out of harm's way.
Nothing but lice and linkboys in this antechamber; or a
merry main* to divert us; and that merry main, as you   5
call it, makes most of us sad all the week after.

2ND FOOTMAN Why, what hast thou done, Gill?

1ST FOOTMAN Undone myself, and a very good friend of
mine, my belly, for a week forward. I am hungry already
in the apprehension of wanting a supper; for my board-   10
wages* is gone to the devil with his bones.*

3RD FOOTMAN Six is the main, gentlemen.

4TH FOOTMAN That was my last tester.*

5TH FOOTMAN I'll play no more –

(Both rising from play)

3RD FOOTMAN Set out my hand, don't leave me so,   15
gentlemen.

6TH FOOTMAN Come, sir, seven to six, I set you.

3RD FOOTMAN Briskly, my boy.

6TH FOOTMAN I set you this.

3RD FOOTMAN How much?   20

6TH FOOTMAN Three halfperth of farthings.

3RD FOOTMAN Three halfperth of farthings? *(rises from
play)* I see thou retainest the spirit of thy ancestors, and as
thou wert born and bred, wilt live and die a footman.
Three halfpennyworth of farthings!   25

2ND FOOTMAN He sets* like a small-beer butler,* in a
widow-lady's family.

3RD FOOTMAN Mayst thou starve under the tyranny of a
housekeeper, and never know the comfort of board-wages
again.   30

6TH FOOTMAN Well, well, I have my money for all that.

1ST FOOTMAN Why, what a pretty fellow have we here debauched from us and our society, by living in a civil family! But this comes of keeping good hours and living orderly; idleness after supper, in your private houses, is 35 the mother of many mischiefs among the maids.

3RD FOOTMAN Aye, aye, want of employment has thrown him upon some gentle chambermaid, and now he sets up for good husbandry,* to father her failings and to get a wet-nurse for his lady.* 40

6TH FOOTMAN Better so, than to father your master's bastards, as you do sometimes; or now and then cheat him of his wench in the convey,* and steal his clap from him.

4TH FOOTMAN Gad i'mercy, i'faith, lad. 45

3RD FOOTMAN That indeed is a sin I often commit, and sometimes repent of: but, the good with the bad, I have no reason to complain of my service.

6TH FOOTMAN Pray don't trouble your head about mine then. 50

2ND FOOTMAN Come, come, we have all good places if we can keep 'em; and for my part, I am too deep in my master's affairs, to fear the losing of mine. What think you of the family of the Friendalls, my lads? A public private family, newly set up, and of very fair reception.* 55

3RD FOOTMAN Aye, Dick, thou hast the time on't indeed.

2ND FOOTMAN The master of it frank* and free, to make an invitation to the whole town; and the mistress hospitable and handsome, to give 'em welcome and content: for my master knows everybody, and contrives 60 that everybody shall know her.

3RD FOOTMAN Aye, marry, sir, there's a family to breed up a pimp in! You may make a fortune out of such a mistress, before your master can get her with child.

2ND FOOTMAN My master has been married not a quarter 65 of a year, and half the young men in town know his wife already; nay, know that he has known enough of her not to care for her already.

3RD FOOTMAN And that may be a very good argument for

some of 'em to persuade her to know a little of somebody 70
else, and care as little for him.

4TH FOOTMAN A very good argument, if she takes it by
the right handle.

2ND FOOTMAN Some of your masters, I warrant you will
put it into her hand. 75

3RD FOOTMAN I know my master has a design upon her.

2ND FOOTMAN And upon all the women in town.

4TH FOOTMAN Mine is in love with her.

5TH FOOTMAN And mine has hopes of her.

3RD FOOTMAN Every man has hopes of a new-married 80
woman, for she marries to like her man; and if upon trial
she finds she can't like her husband, she'll find somebody
else that she can like, in a very little time, I warrant her;
or change her men till she does.

2ND FOOTMAN Let her like as many as she pleases, and 85
welcome. As they thrive with her, I shall thrive by them. I
grind by her mill,* and some of 'em I hope will set it a-
going. Besides, she has discovered some of my master's
intrigues of late. That may help to fill the sails; but I say
nothing, I will take fees a both sides and betray neither. 90

4TH FOOTMAN If your lady loves play,* as they say she
does, she will be so far in your interest, that he that makes
his court to her, must have money to recommend him.

2ND FOOTMAN To me he must, indeed, if he expects my
assistance. 95

5TH FOOTMAN Come, come, what do you think of my
master, Mr Lovemore, for the lady?

3RD FOOTMAN I don't think of him.

2ND FOOTMAN Not so much as she does, I believe you;
he's a generous gentleman and deserves very well of her, 100
and me.

1ST FOOTMAN My master, Mr Wellvile, is often at your
house.

3RD FOOTMAN He follows Mrs Sightly, I can tell you. But
if your lady, Mrs Friendall, has a mind to be very well 105
used; not to settle to't, but only by the way of a
fashionable revenge or so, to do herself justice upon her

husband; I look upon Mr Wilding, my master, one or other, to be the cleverest cuckold-maker in Covent Garden. 110

2ND FOOTMAN Not to settle to't indeed, for your master is not over-constant.

3RD FOOTMAN He does not stay in a family to be challenged into Westminster Hall* by the husband's action of battery for an assault upon his wife;* he is not 115 so constant.

4TH FOOTMAN Or if your lady be disposed to the more refined part of an amour, without the brutality, or design of enjoyment, only for the pleasure of being talked of, or so forth – 120

3RD FOOTMAN Your master Courtall will fit her to a hair. For he will be as fond of the appearances of an intrigue, as she can be. To see him in the chase, you would think he had pleasure in the sport: for he will be as sure always to follow her, as never to press her. He will take as much 125 pains to put her undeservedly into a lampoon upon his account, as he would to avoid a handsome occasion, in private, to qualify her for the scandal.

2ND FOOTMAN In short, Mr Courtall will do everything, but what he ought to do, with a woman. 130

4TH FOOTMAN He has broke off with three gentlewomen, upon my word, within these two months, for coming on too fast upon that business.

2ND FOOTMAN Well, there are pretenders enow;* so I have the profit, let my lady take the pleasure of the choice: 135 I'm for the fairest bidder.

3RD FOOTMAN What, Harry, hast thou nothing to say of thy mistress, Mrs Witwoud?

7TH FOOTMAN Nothing extraordinary, but that I'm tired of her. 140

3RD FOOTMAN She lives as she used to do,* least at home; has no business of her own, but a great deal of other people's. All the men in town follow her, but 'tis for other women; for she has frightened everyone from a design upon her. Then, she's a general confidante and sometimes 145 reports no more than she knows; but that's a favour indeed, from a wit, as they say she is.

7TH FOOTMAN If she be a wit, I'll be sworn she does not take me for one; for she sends me very often upon very ridiculous errands.   150

3RD FOOTMAN I think you have a correspondent porter in every quarter of the town, to disperse her scandalous letters, which she is always bantering one fool or other withal?

7TH FOOTMAN Four or five always in pay with her.   155

3RD FOOTMAN But when Horn Fair* comes, that's sure to be a holiday, and every married man that has a wife handsomer than she is, at her proper* cost and charges, may expect a fairing,* to put him in mind of his fortune.

7TH FOOTMAN I find you know her too well to desire to 160 live with her.

3RD FOOTMAN I had rather be master of the ceremonies to a visiting lady,* to squire about her how-d'ye's, and usher in the formal salutations of all the fops in town, upon her day – nay, though she kept two days a week – than live in 165 a family with her.

1ST FOOTMAN Will this damned music-meeting never be done? Would the cats' guts were in the fiddlers' bellies.

(TWO PAGES *meeting*)

1ST PAGE My Lady Smirkit's page.

2ND PAGE Who's there? My Lady Woudmore?   170

1ST PAGE At your dear service, madam.

2ND PAGE Oh, lord, madam! I am surprised to see your ladyship here.

2ND FOOTMAN What have we here?

3RD FOOTMAN The monkeys aping their ladies; let 'em go 175 on.

2ND PAGE How can your ladyship descend into these little diversions of the town, the plays and the music-meetings?

1ST PAGE Little diversions indeed, madam, to us, who have seen so much better abroad, and still retain too much of 180 the delicacy of the French, to be pleased with the barbarous performance of these English.

3RD FOOTMAN That's a touch* for some of 'em.

1ST PAGE Yet there's no staying always at home, your ladyship knows.   185

2ND PAGE Nor being always seen in the drawing-room,* I vow and swear.

1ST PAGE So that, madam, we are almost under a necessity of appearing in these public places.

2ND PAGE An absolute necessity of showing ourselves 190 sometimes.

1ST PAGE Aye, but madam, then the men: they do so ogle one –

3RD FOOTMAN Ah, very well, Mr Charles!

1ST PAGE Into all the little confusions that a woman is 195 liable to upon those occasions.

2ND PAGE I swear my Lord Simperwell has an irresistible way with him.

1ST PAGE He ogled me all the music long – I believe everybody took notice of it – so furiously, I could not bear 200 it myself. I vow and swear, he almost made me blush; and I would rather do anything to deserve blushing in another place, than by a country modesty betray such an unpardonable want of breeding, to the censure of so much good company.   205

3RD FOOTMAN I dare swear for her ladyship, she had rather do it than blush for't.

1ST PAGE (to the FOOTMAN) Why, how now, Jack Sauce?* (to the PAGE) But did I blush, madam?

2ND PAGE Only for your friends, madam, to see us so 210 neglected.

1ST PAGE Fie, fie, madam, you made your conquest too. I minded nobody but my lord; and I vow and swear, I must own it, madam, he ogles one more like a man of quality then anybody about town that I know of; and I think I am 215 pretty well acquainted with all the soft looks in town.

2ND PAGE One after another we have 'em all – but, Jesu, madam –

1ST PAGE Aye, madam?

2ND PAGE They say the French fleet will be here next 220
summer, with their Tourvilles,* and their things, and,
Jesu, madam, ravish us all.

1ST PAGE Oh lord, madam, ravishing us is nothing – but
our dear religion, madam, what will they do to that?

2ND PAGE Aye, what, indeed, madam!   225

1ST PAGE I would not lose the gaping galleries* of our
churches for the best religion in Christendom.

3RD FOOTMAN You are precious pages, indeed. Betray
your ladies' secrets, before you come into 'em!

<SERVANT> (*within*) Make way for my lord there; bear 230
back, gentlemen.

1ST FOOTMAN So, so, 'tis done at last. Let's get the
coaches to the door.

[*Exeunt omnes*]

Act I, Scene 2

*The curtain drawn up shows the company at the music-
meeting. After an Italian song,* LOVEMORE, WELLVILE,
WILDING, COURTALL, SPRINGAME, FRIENDALL,
RUFFLE, MRS FRIENDALL, MRS SIGHTLY, MRS
WITWOUD, FANNY *advance to the front of the stage*

FRIENDALL Ladies and gentlemen, how did you like the
music?

MRS SIGHTLY Oh, very fine, sure, sir.

MRS WITWOUD What say you to't, young gentleman?

SPRINGAME (*going aside with her*) I have something to say   5
to you I like a great deal better, provided you won't laugh
at me. (*to the company*) But the music's extremely fine.

WELLVILE Especially the vocal part. For I did not understand a word on't.

FRIENDALL Nor I, faith, Wellvile, but the words were   10
Italian. They sung well, and that's enough for the pleasure
of the ear.

COURTALL By which I find your sense is sound.

FRIENDALL And sound sense is a very good thing, Courtall.   15

(*Goes to* WILDING)

WELLVILE (*aside*) That thou wot* never be the better for.

FRIENDALL Wilding, thou hast been so busy about that young girl there, thou know'st nothing of the matter.

WILDING Oh, sir, you're mistaken, I am a great admirer –

FRIENDALL Of everything in petticoats.   20

WILDING Of these musical entertainments. I am very musical, and love any call* that brings the women together.

COURTALL Though it were a cat-call.*

FRIENDALL Vocal or instrumental, which do you most   25
approve of? If you are for the instrumental, there were the sonatas tonight, and the chaconnes,* which you know –

WILDING The sonatas and the chaconnes which I know! Not I, sir. I don't know 'em. They may be two Italian fiddlers of your acquaintance, for anything I know of 'em.   30

FRIENDALL Fie, fie, fiddlers! Masters, if you please, Wilding, masters – excellent in their art, and famous for many admirable compositions.

(*Mingles with the company*)

COURTALL So, he's fast in his own snare, with his sonatas and chaconnes. But how goes the world, Wilding?   35

WILDING The same women every day, and in every public appearance.

COURTALL Here are some faces, I see, of your acquaintance.

WILDING Aye, pox take 'em. I see 'em too often to forget   40
'em. Would their owners thought as ill of 'em as I do, they would keep 'em at home; but they are for showing their show still, though nobody cares for the sight.

(*They mix with the company*)

MRS WITWOUD Methinks 'tis but good manners in Mr

Lovemore to be particular to your sister, when her 45
husband is so universal* to the company.

SPRINGAME Prithee, leave her to her husband. She has
satisfied her relations enough in marrying this coxcomb;
now let her satisfy herself, if she pleases, with anybody
she likes better. 50

MRS WITWOUD Fie, fie, there's no talking to you. You
carry my meaning further than I designed.

SPRINGAME Faith, I took it up but where you left it, very
near the matter.

MRS WITWOUD No, no, you grow scandalous; and I would 55
not be thought to say a scandalous thing of a friend.

SPRINGAME Since my brother-in-law is to be a cuckold – as
it must be mightily my sister's fault, if he be not – I think
Lovemore as proper a fellow to carry on so charitable a
work, as she could ha' lit upon. And if he has her consent 60
to the business, she has mine, I assure you.

MRS WITWOUD A very reasonable brother!

SPRINGAME Would you would be as reasonable a friend,
and allow me as many liberties as I do her.

MRS WITWOUD Why, so I will: she has the men, and you 65
shall have the women, the whole sex to pick and choose –

SPRINGAME One mistress out of –

MRS WITWOUD As many as you please, and as often as you
have occasion.

SPRINGAME Why, faith, that pleases me very well; you hit 70
my constitution, as if you were familiar with it, or had a
mind to be so.

MRS WITWOUD Not I, indeed, sir.

SPRINGAME And I have, as you were saying –

MRS WITWOUD As I was saying? 75

SPRINGAME Very often an occasion for a mistress.

MRS WITWOUD You say so yourself, I know nothing of
your occasions.

SPRINGAME Shall I bring you acquainted with some of
'em? I have great variety, and have, every day, a new 80
occasion for a new mistress. If you have a mind to be
satisfied in this point, let me go along with you.

MRS WITWOUD Home with me?

SPRINGAME Or home with me will do my business as well.

MRS WITWOUD But it won't do mine, sir.   85

SPRINGAME Then let it be home with you, though my
lodging is very convenient.

MRS WITWOUD Why, this is sudden indeed, upon so small
an acquaintance. But 'tis something too soon for you, and
a little too late for me.*   90

SPRINGAME Not to repent, I hope, madam? Better late
than never, you know. Come, come, I have known a
worse offer better received.

MRS WITWOUD And this offer you will make to every
woman, till it be received, I dare answer for you.   95

SPRINGAME That's more than you can do for yourself for
refusing it. But the folly fall upon your own head. I have
done my part, and 'tis your fault if you're idle.

(Goes away)

MRS SIGHTLY (to her) You have been entertained, cousin –

MRS WITWOUD By a very pretty, prating fellow, cousin; 100
and I could be contented to let him show his parts this
way as often as he pleased.

MRS SIGHTLY What! Like a man of honour, he's for
making good what he says.

MRS WITWOUD And comes so quick upon that business, he 105
won't afford a woman a reasonable liking-time, to make
a decent excuse to herself, if she should allow him a
favour.

MRS SIGHTLY The young officer has heard enough of your
character,* I suppose, not to put it too much into your 110
power of laughing at him.

MRS WITWOUD I'm sorry for't. I would have a man know
just enough of me to make him a lover; and then, in a
time, I should know enough of him to make him an ass.

MRS SIGHTLY This will come home to you one day.   115

MRS WITWOUD In any shape but a husband, cousin.

(Observing LOVEMORE and MRS FRIENDALL)

But, methinks, Lovemore and Mrs Friendall are very
seriously engaged.

MRS SIGHTLY I have had an eye upon 'em.

MRS WITWOUD For such a trifle as cuckolding a husband is 120
in this town.

MRS SIGHTLY The men will always design upon our sex;
but I dare answer for her.

MRS WITWOUD And so will I – that if she should fall from
the frailty of the flesh into that folly, she will appear no 125
monster, whatever her husband may be. What say you to
a ramble* after the music?

MRS SIGHTLY I say nothing to't.

MRS WITWOUD A hackney jaunt,* from one end of the
town to t'other? 130

MRS SIGHTLY 'Tis too late.

MRS WITWOUD I know two several* companies gone into
the city, one to Pontack's and t'other to the Rummer,* to
supper. I want to disturb, strangely;* what say you coz?
Let's put on our masks, draw up the glasses* and send up 135
for the men, to make their women uneasy. There's one of
'em to be married; it may do good upon her, by showing
what she must trust to* if she will have a husband.

MRS SIGHTLY And can you be so mischievous?

MRS WITWOUD Can you resist the temptation? 140

MRS SIGHTLY I came with Mrs Friendall and must go
home with her. <*indicating* FANNY> Look to your charge
there.

MRS WITWOUD I have an eye that way.

MRS SIGHTLY We shall see you tomorrow, cousin? 145

MRS WITWOUD At your toilet,* cousin; you are always my
first visit.

(*Goes to* WILDING *and* FANNY)

MRS FRIENDALL Is this your friendship to Mr Friendall? I
must not hear it.

LOVEMORE You see he gives you leave. 150

MRS FRIENDALL Therefore I can't take it. The confidence*
is so generous, that ev'n that would secure me to him.

LOVEMORE The confidence is as generous on your side; and do you think that will secure him to you?

MRS FRIENDALL I'll ask him, if you please. 155

LOVEMORE You'll but disturb him.

MRS FRIENDALL (*calling him*) Mr Friendall.

FRIENDALL Ha! What's the matter, madam?

MRS FRIENDALL There has happened here a scurvy* dispute between me and one of your friends, sir, as you 160 think fit to call 'em.

FRIENDALL A dispute! About what, prithee? But before I hear a word on't, Lovemore, thou art certainly in the wrong in holding an argument with a woman.

LOVEMORE I begin to think so too, sir, for contending with 165 a lady that will be tried by nobody but her husband.

FRIENDALL But what's the business? Nothing extraordinary between you, I hope?

MRS FRIENDALL Believe me, sir, I think it very extraordinary. 170

LOVEMORE Very extraordinary indeed, madam, to be so publicly exposed for a private opinion.

MRS FRIENDALL And you shall be the judge of the difference.

FRIENDALL No, no; no difference among friends; it must 175 not come to that. I'll make up all differences between you.

LOVEMORE You may do much indeed to set all straight.

FRIENDALL And so I will, i'faith, Lovemore. I'll reconcile all, I warrant you; but come, what is this mighty matter between you? 180

MRS FRIENDALL I think it a mighty matter, Mr Friendall, to be so far suspected in my conduct that anyone, under the title of your friend, should dare, in your absence, to be so very familiar with me –

FRIENDALL How, madam? 185

LOVEMORE (*aside*) All will out, I see.

FRIENDALL In my absence, so very familiar with you?

MRS FRIENDALL As to censure these innocent liberties that the women allow themselves in the company of their husbands. 190

LOVEMORE (*aside*) So, she has saved her credit with me, and mine with her husband.

(MRS FRIENDALL *joins* MRS SIGHTLY *and* MRS WITWOUD)

FRIENDALL Why, Lovemore, thou art in the wrong of all this. I desired you to sport off* a little gallantry with my wife; to entertain and divert her from making her 195 observations upon me,* and thou dost nothing but play the critic upon her.

LOVEMORE I find I was mistaken. But how would you have me behave myself?

FRIENDALL Why, I would have you very frequent in your 200 visits, and very obliging to my wife now and then, to carry on our other pleasures the better. For an amusement or so, you may say a civil* thing to her. For every woman, you know, loves to have a civil thing said to her sometimes; but then you must be very cautious in the 205 expression. If she should in the least apprehend that you had a design upon her, 'twould raise the devil in one of the family, and lay him in another, perhaps, where I had a mind to employ him. Therefore I would have you keep in favour with her. 210

LOVEMORE I'll do my best, I promise you.

FRIENDALL She's inclining, you must know, to speak very well of you; and that she does of very few of the men, I assure you. She approves of the intimacy and friendship between us, and of your coming to the house; and that 215 may stand you in stead with the lady* you wot of* –

LOVEMORE I apprehend you. (*to* MRS FRIENDALL) So, begging the lady's pardon, with a design of doing something to deserve it –

MRS WITWOUD That will never fail with the women, Mr 220 Lovemore.

LOVEMORE I will make an interest with* the masters, to give you a song at parting.

(*Goes to the* MUSIC-MASTERS)

MRS SIGHTLY An English song, good Mr Lovemore.
FRIENDALL Oh, by all means, an English song.   225

(*Goes to the* MUSIC-MASTERS *too*)

WELLVILE Any song, which won't oblige a man to tell you
he has seen an opera at Venice to understand.
FRIENDALL Pray, let him sing the ladies the song I gave
him.
MUSIC-MASTER Which song, sir?   230
FRIENDALL The last.
MUSIC-MASTER 'Tis not set,* sir.
FRIENDALL Not set, sir!

(*Turning from him, to the* LADIES)

LOVEMORE That's a fault he'll never forgive you.
MUSIC-MASTER Why, really, sir, I would serve any gentle- 235
man to my power; but the words are so abominably out
of the way of music, I don't know how to humour 'em.
There's no setting 'em, or singing 'em, to please anybody,
but himself.
MRS SIGHTLY Oh, but we lose by this.   240
FRIENDALL Hang 'em, idle rascals. They care not what
entertainment we lose, so they have but our money.
MRS SIGHTLY Is it your own song, Mr Friendall?
FRIENDALL I must not rob your ladyship of your part in it.
MRS SIGHTLY My part in your song, sir?   245
MR FRIENDALL You were the muse that inspired me. I writ
it upon your ladyship.
MRS SIGHTLY Fie, fie; that pride would ruin me; but I
know you say so to every woman.

(*She turns from him*)

FRIENDALL Egad, she's i'th' right on't. I have told a dozen 250
so already at the music-meeting, and most of 'em believe
me.
MRS SIGHTLY Does Mr Friendall often write songs,
madam?
MRS FRIENDALL He does many things he should not do, 255

madam; but I think he loves me, and that excuses him to
me. Though, you may be sure, 'tis with the tenderest
concern for my own reputation, that I see my husband
daily trifle away his, so notoriously, in one folly or other
of the town.   260

(*Goes to* FRIENDALL)

MRS WITWOUD For her own reputation, it must be; for the
world will believe she turns such a husband to the right
use,* whatever she says to the contrary.

MRS FRIENDALL Mr Friendall, pray be satisfied with a
good estate; and not imagine, because you have that, you 265
have everything else. The business of writing songs should
be over with a married man. And since I can't be
suspected to be the Phyllis, or Chloris,* 'tis an affront to
me to have another woman thought so.

FRIENDALL Indeed, madam, so far are you right. I never 270
heard of any man that writ a song upon his wife.

Song

(By Major General Sackville*)

Ingrateful* Love! Thus every hour,
To punish me by her disdain,
You tyrannise to show your power;
And she, to triumph in my pain.   275

You, who can laugh at human woes,
And victims to her pride decree,
On me, your yielding slave, impose
Your chains; but leave the rebel free.

How fatal are your poisoned darts!   280
Her conquering eyes the trophies boast,
Whilst you ensnare poor wandering hearts
That in her charms and scorn are lost.

Impious and cruel, you deny
A death* to ease me of my care;   285

Which she delays, to make me try*
The force of beauty, and despair.

FRIENDALL Lovemore, we may thank you for this. But
when you keep your promise to me at dinner tomorrow –
(*speaks to all the* MEN) – and you, and you, and all of 290
you, gentlemen – I'll do you reason* to the good
company.

(*Goes to the door*)

Some of my servants there!

COURTALL <*to* MRS FRIENDALL> Madam, I am very
luckily here to offer you my service. 295

MRS FRIENDALL No particular woman must expect it from
so general a follower of the sex as Mr Courtall is.

COURTALL A general follower of the sex indeed, madam,
in my care of 'em.

MRS FRIENDALL Besides, 'tis dangerous to be seen with a 300
man of your character; for if you don't make it an
intrigue, the town makes it for you. And that does most of
your business as well.

COURTALL There's no knowing a man by his character in
this town. The partiality of friends and the prejudice of 305
enemies, who divide it, always make him better or worse
than he deserves.

MRS FRIENDALL If you have no regard to my reputation,
pray be tender of your own. 'Tis nowadays as scandalous
in a man, who would be thought to know the town (as I 310
know you would) to wait upon a bare face to her coach,
as it used to be to lead out a vizard-mask.* But the pit has
got the better of the boxes* with most of you, in that
point of civility; and I don't doubt, but it turns to better
account. 315

SPRINGAME Indeed, sister, it does turn to better account;
and therefore we must provide for ourselves.

(*Takes* COURTALL *with him to* MRS WITWOUD;
LOVEMORE *goes to* MRS FRIENDALL)

Why, here's a woman, Courtall. If she had a vizard-mask
to encourage me, I could go to the world's end* with her.
But, as she is, bare-faced and an honest woman –   320
MRS WITWOUD You'll do a foolish thing, for once; see her
    to her coach, I dare say for you, to make her otherwise.
SPRINGAME (*addressing to her*)* Why, if it must be so –
WILDING <*to* FANNY> You own your aunt is a-bed; and
    you see Mrs Witwoud's too busy to mind your going 325
    away with me.
FANNY I can't tonight, but I'll call upon you tomorrow
    morning, as I go to six o'clock prayers.
LOVEMORE (*to* MRS FRIENDALL) I hope, madam, I may
    without exception* wait upon you.   330
WELLVILE (*to* MRS SIGHTLY) And, madam, I have the title
    of an old servant to your ladyship, to expect that favour
    from you.
MRS SIGHTLY Mr Friendall, having a handsome wife in
    the company, may be jealous;* and you will pardon me, if 335
    I am unwilling to give him a suspicion of a man whom I
    would have everybody think as well of as I do myself.
MRS FRIENDALL <*to* LOVEMORE> Mr Friendall gives you
    more opportunities than I can approve of, and I could
    wish you would not take the advantage of 'em. They'll 340
    turn to no account.
FRIENDALL Come, ladies, I am your man I find.

(*Leads* MRS SIGHTLY, MRS FRIENDALL *following*)

RUFFLE What think you of this occasion?*
LOVEMORE You can't have a better. Follow him – and be
    famous.   345

(SPRINGAME *leads* MRS WITWOUD, WILDING *leads*
FANNY *out.* RUFFLE *after the company*)

WELLVILE What have you now in hand?
LOVEMORE Why, all my hopes of the wife depending upon
    the senseless behaviour of the husband, I have contrived
    by this fellow, before her face, too, to expose him a way

that must ruin him with her for ever. Let's follow and 350
expect* the event.

[*Exeunt*]

Act 1, Scene 3

The scene changes to the street

(*<Enter> several* LINKBOYS *and* FOOTMEN)

1ST LINKBOY Have a light, gentlemen, have a light, sir.

(*Enter* SPRINGAME *with* MRS WITWOUD; WILDING *with*
FANNY, *and several others*)

SPRINGAME Light yourselves to the devil.
2ND LINKBOY Bless you, master, we can find the way in
the dark. Shall I light your worship there?
SPRINGAME Then call a coach and thy wit shall be thy 5
reward.
5TH FOOTMAN* Mr Friendall's coach there!

(FRIENDALL *enters, leading* MRS SIGHTLY *with* HIS
WIFE. RUFFLE *enters after 'em;* LOVEMORE *and*
WELLVILE *in the rear*)

'Tis at the door, sir.
FRIENDALL *<aside to* MRS SIGHTLY> I must improve*
every opportunity with your ladyship, to convince you of 10
the truths I have been telling you tonight; and in this
billet, I give it under my hand* how very much I am your
servant.*
MRS SIGHTLY Fie, fie, before your wife!

(*Throws it behind her;* RUFFLE *takes it up*)

MRS FRIENDALL *<to* RUFFLE> Sir, that paper don't belong 15
to you.

(FRIENDALL *leads* MRS SIGHTLY *off and returns for* HIS
WIFE)

RUFFLE Don't be jealous, lady, I know no design the gentlewoman has as yet upon my person and I'll belong to you, if this gentleman pleases.

FRIENDALL You're pleased to be merry, sir, but no touch-   20
ing her,* I beseech you.

MRS FRIENDALL What would the fellow have?

RUFFLE Why, I would have this fellow gone about his business.

FRIENDALL My business lies here at present, sir.   25

RUFFLE You lie there, sir!

(Hits FRIENDALL *a box on the ear, and draws; the* women shriek, MRS FRIENDALL *pretends to hold her husband; the company come about 'em*)

MRS FRIENDALL Good Mr Friendall, another time; con-
sider where you are. You are more a man of honour, I know, than to draw your sword among the women. I am sorry this has happened in a place where you can't right   30
yourself,* without wronging the company. But you'll find a time to do a justice to yourself,* and the ladies, who have suffered in the apprehension of such a brutality.

SPRINGAME I'll go along with you.

(All go off but MRS WITWOUD)

MRS WITWOUD Would the devil had 'em, for drawing their   35
swords here. I have lost my little captain in the fray. My charge is departed, too, and for this night I suppose left me to make an excuse to the family for her lying abroad* with a country cousin, or so. That rogue Wilding has carried her home with him, and 'tis as well now as a week   40
hence; for when these young wenches once set their hearts upon't, everything gives them an opportunity to ruin themselves. Her Aunt Teazall has made her rise to six o'clock prayers to fine purpose if this be the fruits of her devotion. But since she must fall to somebody, I'm glad   45
Wilding has her, for he'll use her ill enough in a little time, to make her wiser for the future. By the dear

experience and vexation of this intrigue, being disappointed of many things she expects, she may make a virtue of necessity: repent, because she can't keep him to herself, and make an honest man a very good wife yet.   50

[Exit]

(LOVEMORE, WELLVILE, RUFFLE return)

RUFFLE I have done my part, and am satisfied with the honour of the achievement.

LOVEMORE 'Tis a reputation clear-gained,* since there's no danger of accounting for't.   55

RUFFLE So, thanking you for this occasion of showing myself, I am your humble servant.

[Exit]

WELLVILE Who is this hero, pray?

LOVEMORE Why this is a spark that has had the misfortune of being kicked very lately, and I have helped him to this   60 occasion of repairing his honour upon our very good friend, a greater coward than himself. He has served my ends; now let him serve the town's.

WELLVILE But did you observe how the lady behaved herself in the quarrel, to conceal her husband's cowardice?   65

LOVEMORE What a handsome excuse she made in his favour to the company, when she can never make any for him to herself.

WELLVILE This matter well-managed may turn to account. Though you must not be seen to expose him, you may   70 take the advantage of his exposing himself.

LOVEMORE And let her say what she can, upon this subject, I believe no woman can be contented to have her honour, much longer than her fortune, in the possession of a man who has no fund of his own to answer in   75 security for either.

Thus, who a married woman's love would win,
Should with the husband's failings first begin;
Make him but in the fault, and you shall find
A good excuse will make most women kind.*   80

[Exeunt]

Act 2, Scene I

<MRS TEAZALL's *lodgings*>

MRS WITWOUD *at a table, with <her maid>* BETTY, *and a* FOOTMAN *waiting*

MRS WITWOUD No news of my cousin Fanny this morning?

BETTY For God's sake, madam, not a word of her lying out tonight. We shall have the devil to do with the old gentlewoman, if she knows it. 5

MRS WITWOUD That's a secret I can keep from her, for my own sake, Betty. But how comes this about? I'm quite out of gilt paper.* Harry, you fetch me two or three quire from Mr Bentley's* and call at Mrs Da Robe's,* my mantua-woman's,* as you come back, for letters. And – 10 d'you hear? – Give this note to Joe the porter. He needs no instructions; let him leave it for Mr Wilding.

(FOOTMAN *and* MAID *go out*)

I find I must meddle in this business; for her visits at this rate, will not only be troublesome to him (as I would have 'em); but in a little time be public to the whole town. 15 Now, though I am very well pleased with any matter of scandal, I am so nearly related to the interest* of this girl, I would not have her the occasion of it. They say the understanding ought to be suited to the condition, to make anyone happy. Would she were in a condition 20 suitable to her understanding! She has wit enough for a wife, and nothing else that I know of.

(MRS TEAZALL *enters to her*)

MRS TEAZALL Oh, madam, you're welcome home!

MRS WITWOUD Rather good morrow, cousin.

MRS TEAZALL Rather good morrow indeed, that's the 25 properer salutation. For you're never to be seen in your lodging at any other time of the day. And then, too, as soon as you're out o' bed in a morning, you summon a congregation of your fellows together to hear you prate

by the hour, flatter everybody in the company, speak ill of   30
everyone that's absent, and scatter about the scandal of
that day.

MRS WITWOUD   Why, madam, you won't quarrel at that, I
hope. 'Tis one of the most fashionable, innocent diversions of the town. It makes a great deal of mirth, speaking   35
ill of people, and never does anybody any harm.

MRS TEAZALL   Not with any that know you, I believe. How
came you home last night? The night before, you arrived
like a carted bawd,* justly punished for the sins of the
people. You confessed you were forced to bilk* your   40
coach to get rid of the coxcombs that dogged you from
the playhouse; and being pursued by the coachman and
footmen – for I don't doubt but you gave the gentlemen
encouragement enough to come home with you – you
looked as if you belonged to a cellar* in some of the alleys   45
you were hunted through, and had been caterwauling in
all the kennels* in town.

MRS WITWOUD   That was an unfortunate night indeed.

MRS TEAZALL   Well, deliver every good woman's child, I
say, from such daggle-tailed* courses as these are. What   50
will be the end of 'em, I beseech you? You will make
yourself as odious, in a little time, as you endeavour to
make everybody else. This is not the way to get a
husband; the men know too much of you already, to
desire any more of you.   55

MRS WITWOUD   I don't set up for a husband.

MRS TEAZALL   Marry come up,* here! You may have an
occasion for an husband, when you can't get one.
Husbands are not always to be had at a month's
warning,* to finish another's work. What, 'tis beneath the   60
character of a she-wit, I suppose, to be constant? Or is a
husband out of fashion of you, forsooth? Another
woman's husband* can go down with you, to my
knowledge; and as ugly a rogue too, with as hanging a
countenance,* as I could wish any villain I had a mind to   65
be rid of – your diversion, as you call him.

MRS WITWOUD Oh, spare my shame! I own he is my curse, doomed for my plague and pleasure.

MRS TEAZALL Spare your shame! I'll say that for you, you have not been sparing of any endeavour that could bring 70 a shame any way into the family wherever you lived yet; if there was ever a fool soft enough to throw it upon. All your relations know you, and are afraid to have you in a house with 'em. And I suppose you are very well pleased to be from under their roof; to have your fellows come 75 after you to my house, as they do – and as I am fool enough to allow of.

MRS WITWOUD For no harm, cousin, I hope.

MRS TEAZALL Perhaps you think it no harm; and, indeed, it can't do you any harm. But I'm sure I have one of my 80 nieces already undone by your bringing her acquainted with some of 'em. I was forced to marry her, you know, below her rank (for the usual reason* of this end of the town) into the city, where 'twas less scandalous: the wives there having a charter* for what they do. And now 85 Fanny, a very* girl, when I have provided a husband and all for her – for she must have a husband. She takes after her sister – as a little thing will make a precedent for what we are inclined to – she takes after her sister, I say, and is unfortunately engaged in a passion for Mr Wilding. And 90 how to prevent it –

MRS WITWOUD Indeed, I must acknowledge I was, in a great measure, the unfortunate cause of my cousin Biddy's miscarriage.* But for my cousin Fanny, rely upon me; nothing shall come on't. I am now going to Mr 95 Wilding on that account, and have sent a note to secure him at his lodgings till I come.

(BETTY *enters*)

MRS TEAZALL Well, where's this girl? Why does not she come, when I send for her?

BETTY Madam, she went to six-a-clock prayers, and is not 100 come back yet.

MRS TEAZALL God's bodikins!* Has she got the trick on't

of abusing the church into the place of assignation already? Wilding has carried her home with him. That's certain. <*to* MRS WITWOUD> Get you gone after her. 105 Maybe you may prevent his wicked design on her. Go, go, and redeem her, though you leave yourself in her room.*

MRS WITWOUD I'm obliged to you, truly, madam.

MRS TEAZALL I dare venture you; you'll not be in love with him. You'll give him as good as he brings; and, let the 110 worst come to the worst, you have lived too long in the town to be uneasy for any man, or be concerned beyond the pleasure and convenience of the intrigue. Therefore, I may venture you. A little time goes a great way in this business. Deliver her, and I won't find fault with you – 115 these three days, you shall do what you please.

[*Exeunt*]

Act 2, Scene 2

FRIENDALL's *house*

(<*Enter*>MRS FRIENDALL *following* FRIENDALL)

MRS FRIENDALL Nay, Mr Friendall, I know what you will object to me, but you must hear me out. The concern and care of your reputation is as dear to me as it can be tender to you, since I must appear to the world only in that rank of honour which you are pleased to maintain.   5

FRIENDALL Why, madam, you have as handsome an equipage as any man's wife in town that has a father alive.*

MRS FRIENDALL This must not put me off. I see you make little of the matter, to hide it from my fears; and there 10 indeed you're kind. But 'tis in vain to think of concealing from me what you intend. From what you ought to do, I know what you will do after so base a wrong.

FRIENDALL A drunken extravagance. The fellow will be sorry for't when he's sober –   15

MRS FRIENDALL If you would stay till then.

FRIENDALL And beg my pardon.

MRS FRIENDALL That he shall do, if that would satisfy
   you.

FRIENDALL Satisfy me!   20

MRS FRIENDALL And let it satisfy you: it ought to satisfy
   you from such a one. For I believe he would not have
   quarrelled anywhere else, nor there neither, but upon the
   prospect of being prevented, or parted, or secured
   overnight,* in order to beg pardon in the morning.   25

FRIENDALL Aye, madam, but consider –

MRS FRIENDALL Pray consider me, Mr Friendall. I must
   suffer every way if you proceed to a revenge: in your
   danger, which must be mine; in my honour, which ought
   to be more yours, than to expose it upon every little   30
   occasion. Come, come, in other things you have a good
   opinion of my conduct; pray let me govern here. You may
   be assured I'll do nothing to lessen you. The satisfaction
   shall be as public as the affront. Leave it to me for once, I
   wonnot* be denied – he is not worth your danger.   35

FRIENDALL Well, you shall govern me.

MRS FRIENDALL What, you are a married man and have a
   good estate settled upon you; and should not be accountable to every idle rakehell* that has a mind to establish a
   renown from being troublesome to public places.   40

FRIENDALL What, then, would you propose?

MRS FRIENDALL A small request: not to stir abroad, nor be
   at home to anybody, till you hear from me.

FRIENDALL I promise you I won't.

                                                        [*Exit*]

MRS FRIENDALL I dare take your word. His tameness* last   45
   night and backwardness this morning in resenting that
   blow, satisfy me that he is not in a fever for fighting. I
   don't know that he is a coward; but having these reasons
   to suspect him, I thought this was my best way to hinder
   him from discovering himself.* For if he had betrayed   50
   that baseness to me, I should despise him; and can I love
   the man I most despise?

(*<Enter>* SPRINGAME *to her*)

Brother, I sent for you.

SPRINGAME To make up this quarrel, I know; and I come to lend a helping hand to the work. I design to be a second in the business.   55

MRS FRIENDALL You must be my second then, for I have taken the quarrel upon me.

SPRINGAME With all my heart, egad. We, who live all the summer for the public, should live in the winter* for ourselves.   60

MRS FRIENDALL And the women, good captain.

SPRINGAME That's living for ourselves, for 'tis not living without 'em. And a duel now might but interrupt a month of other business, perhaps, that would be more agreeable to my constitution, I assure you. Then we are to have no fighting it seems?   65

MRS FRIENDALL For reasons I'll tell you hereafter.

SPRINGAME Nay, there was no great danger of it. I have found out the gentleman's lodgings, and character. We shall strike up a peace before a bottle's to an end.   70

MRS FRIENDALL This challenge must be delivered as from him. I trust the management to you. Only take this in advice: that Mr Friendall wants your assistance within. You must stand by him, and oblige the gentleman to make him satisfaction, without bringing his person in danger. And he shall satisfy him, or me.   75

SPRINGAME I understand you, and he shall satisfy him, or me.

MRS FRIENDALL See him satisfied, and I'll satisfy you with something shall be better to a younger brother than the false musters* of a winter's quarter.   80

SPRINGAME I warrant you.

[*Exit*]

MRS FRIENDALL Whatever I think of him, I must not let him fall into the contempt of the town. Every little fellow, I know, will be censoriously inquisitive and maliciously witty upon another man's cowardice, out of the pleasure   85

of finding as great a rascal as himself. How despicable a
condition must that matrimony be, when the husband
(whom we look upon as a sanctuary for a woman's   90
honour) must be obliged to the discretion and management of a wife, for the security of his own! Have a care of
thinking that way. For in a married state, as in the public,
we tie ourselves up, indeed, but to be protected in our
persons, fortunes and honours, by those very laces* that   95
restrain us in other things. For few will obey, but for the
benefit they receive from the government.

(SERVANT *enters*)

SERVANT Madam, Mr Lovemore.

[*Goes out*]

MRS FRIENDALL Lovemore here! I know he comes to
tempt me to rebel; but I'm prepared for him.   100

(LOVEMORE *enters*)

Good morrow, Mr Lovemore.

LOVEMORE I could not expect to see your ladyship so
early. I come to Mr Friendall.

MRS FRIENDALL May I thank you for the visit?

LOVEMORE I came as a friend, you may be sure, madam. 105
Where your honour's concerned, I can't be an enemy.

MRS FRIENDALL Not reasonably, indeed, to any man that
would injure it, since you are a professed enemy.

LOVEMORE An enemy!

MRS FRIENDALL Unless you will allow nobody to ruin it, 110
but yourself.

LOVEMORE Indeed, I would allow nobody to defend it, but
myself, if I had the keeping of it. But a happier man has
that title, and I can only hope to be a second in your
service.   115

MRS FRIENDALL I thank you for the service you design me;
but that happier man, as you call him, who has the title,
will maintain it, it seems. For he and my brother
Springame, I'm afraid, are gone about it already.

LOVEMORE Gone, madam!   120

MRS FRIENDALL An hour ago, before I had notice to
prevent 'em. For Mr Friendall, you may be sure, was
impatient for an occasion of righting himself.

LOVEMORE   I might have thought so, indeed, madam.
Would I had come sooner.   125

MRS FRIENDALL You may yet be serviceable to me, sir,
though you are too late for Mr Friendall.

LOVEMORE How, madam, I beseech you?

MRS FRIENDALL By endeavouring to prevent 'em. You are
acquainted with the ways of reconciling matters of this   130
honourable nature. I am going to make an interest* with
a kinsman, a colonel of the guards, myself, to secure 'em.
Let your good nature in this be a proof of your friendship,
and command me to my power.

[*Exit*]

LOVEMORE   Prevent 'em! Yes, yes. That I must do for my   135
own sake. For if he should behave himself better than I
imagined he would, it may secure him in his wife's esteem
and only ruin me with her, who laid the design.

[*Exit*]

Act 2, Scene 3

WILDING's *lodgings*

(<*Enter*> WILDING *and his* MAN)

WILDING Have you disposed of her?

SERVANT Safe into a chair, sir. She's jogging homeward,
lighter by a maidenhead, I presume, than she came, sir.

WILDING The loss is not so light, but she may feel it.

SERVANT Heavy enough, perhaps, nine months hence, sir.   5
But have you sent ever a* lie along with her?

WILDING How, sirrah?

SERVANT Pardon me, sir. Not that I believe your honour
sparing of your conscience in saying anything, and
swearing to't, that she had a mind to believe.   10

WILDING That you may swear, indeed.

SERVANT But she's gone away so very well satisfied with
what you have said and done to her, she's above inventing
a lie for herself. The first angry word they give her at
home, I suppose, you may hear of her. A hackney coach   15
removes her, and her commodes,* upon very little
warning; and I expect when* she will send in half a dozen
bandboxes* to take possession of your lodgings. But,
pray sir, if I may be so bold –

WILDING Yes, yes. At this time you may be so bold. The   20
service of your wit secures you the privilege of your jest.

SERVANT Then pray, sir, why did you take so much pains
to persuade this young creature to come away from her
aunt, when I know you never design to take care of her
yourself?   25

WILDING Why, 'faith, I can't make you a very good
answer. But the best reason I know of is (besides the
reputation of undoing her) it looks kind, at the time, to
talk of providing for the woman that does one the
favour.* 'Twas a very plausible argument to cozen* her   30
into a consent, level to* my design of lying with her, and
carried to the very mark of love.

SERVANT Indeed, it costs nothing to promise, when nothing
can oblige you to pay. And if she depends upon it at her
peril, 'tis she will be disappointed, not you. Though ten to   35
one, poor little rogue, from the fondness of her own
inclinations, she guesses at yours; and fancies, from the
courtesy she has done you, you will be so civil a
gentleman to marry her.

WILDING Not unlikely. There's none of these young girls,   40
let a man's character be never so loose* among 'em, but
from one vanity or other will be encouraged to design and
venture upon him. And though fifty of their acquaintance
have fallen in the experiment, each of them will still
imagine she has something particular in her person,   45
forsooth, to reclaim, and engage him to herself. So most
of 'em miscarry, upon the project of getting husbands.

SERVANT Gad forgive me for swearing, but as I hope to be

saved, and that's a bold word for a footman, I beg your pardon – there's a lady below, in a vizard, to speak with you. 50
WILDING Get you gone, you rascal. Beg her pardon, and leave to wait upon her.

[*Exit* <SERVANT>]

She would have been admitted in less time to a privy counsellor's levee,* though he had laid aside the business of the nation to manage hers. This must be the letter- 55
lady.* She comes a little unseasonable,* if she knew all. If she has experience enough to allow for some natural miscarriages which may happen in the beginning of an amour, I may pacify her that way. 'Tis but swearing heartily, damning the modesty of my constitution, laying 60
its faults upon an over-respect to her, and promising better things for the future. That used be a current* excuse, but 'tis the women's fault if it pass too often upon 'em. If she prove an old acquaintance, the coldness of the entertainment will secure me from the persecution of her 65
visits hereafter. But if it be a face I never saw, I may use her well enough yet, to encourage her to another appointment. So every way does my business, whatever becomes of the lady's.

(MRS WITWOUD *enters masked*)

Oh, madam, I beg your pardon. 70
MRS WITWOUD No excuses, good sir. Men of employment are above good breeding; and I see you have a great deal upon your hands.
WILDING I am a man of business, indeed, madam; and, as you were pleased to signify in your letter, my practice lies 75
among the women. What can I do for you?
MRS WITWOUD Can't you tell what, sir? You are not the man I took you for. But you are like our fortune-tellers, who come into our secrets more by our own folly in betraying ourselves, than by any skill or knowledge of 80
their own.
WILDING Indeed I should ha' proceeded as most of those fellows do: set out impudently at first, taken several

things for granted (as that you were no maid, and so
forth), ventured briskly at everything, and something 85
might have happened to please you.

MRS WITWOUD Did the lady just gone away from you find
it so?

WILDING She had what she came for. You would take it ill
to lose your labour yourself, madam.   90

MRS WITWOUD She ventured at everything as briskly as
you could, I suppose, sir?

WILDING 'Tis a towardly* girl indeed, and comes on finely.
I have no reason to complain of losing my labour upon
her. She's ready for running away from her relations 95
already. Are not you a little that way inclined? Come,
come, if you have any troubles upon your spirits, child –

MRS WITWOUD You can remove 'em into the flesh, I
warrant you.

WILDING If you have ever a husband that lies heavy upon 100
your conscience, I have a cordial will drive the distemper
from your heart.

MRS WITWOUD Why that's kind indeed, to make some
room for the lover. But that is not my distemper. I could
resolve it myself, if I had a husband, whether I would 105
make him a cuckold, or no. But I lie under the difficulty
of disposing of a maidenhead.

WILDING There I must resolve you;* that case I often
handle.

MRS WITWOUD But hear it, I beseech you, before you 110
decide it.

WILDING That would do well in Westminster Hall, I grant
you, but in proceedings of this nature we are always on
the plaintiff's side. Let the sober party* say what they can
to the reason of the thing, you are certainly in the right, in 115
pleasing yourself.

MRS WITWOUD 'Twill come to that, I believe. For you
must know, sir, that being under the discretion and
tyranny of an old aunt –

WILDING You will naturally run away from her.   120

MRS WITWOUD And being considerable enough to be followed for my fortune –

WILDING You will certainly be betrayed, and sold by her –

MRS WITWOUD To some booby of her own breed, who, paying too dear for the purchase, will undo himself, to 125 undo me.

WILDING Come, come, you are now under my care. 'Tis my fault, if you miscarry.

MRS WITWOUD And mine too, if I do.

WILDING Let me be your trustee.*   130

MRS WITWOUD Indeed, the woman should cheat the man as much as she can before marriage, because, after it, he has a title of cheating her as long as he lives.

WILDING If you can't make over your money, make over your –   135

MRS WITWOUD Common conveyances* both in our sex, sir.

WILDING A maidenhead's a jewel of no value in marriage.

MRS WITWOUD 'Tis never set down, indeed, in the particular* of a woman's estate.   140

WILDING And therefore least missed by a husband, of anything she brings along with her.

MRS WITWOUD If, indeed, by the articles of marriage, a man should covenant for a maidenhead, the woman, in a legal honesty, ought to satisfy the bargain; but the men 145 never mention that, for fear of inflaming the jointure.*

WILDING And the women never put 'em upon't.*

MRS WITWOUD Out of a conscience in their dealings, to be sure, for fear they should not always be able to be as good as their words.   150

WILDING I see, madam, we differ only in our sexes; and if you please, we will beget a right understanding between them too.

MRS WITWOUD How, sir!

WILDING I'll show you how. <advances on her; she resists> 155 Have a care what you do, madam, 'tis a very difficult matter, let me tell you, to refuse a man handsomely. Look you, madam, I would have you make a decent resistance.

A little of it enhances the favour and keeps up the value of
your person; but too much on't is undervaluing of mine. 160
Nay, nay, when it once comes to fighting, you often ruin
what you would raise.* Struggling too long is as much to
your disadvantage as not struggling at all; and you know
'tis the same thing to a woman, a man's being indifferent,
as his being incapable to oblige her. Come, come, enough 165
of this –

MRS WITWOUD So I say too, sir; the jest will go no further,
I see.

   (*Unmasks; he declines into a respect* to her*)

WILDING Mrs Witwoud! I did not expect to see you here,
indeed, madam.   170

MRS WITWOUD I came upon business, Mr Wilding, but the
temptation of a vizard-mask, and the pleasure of prating
upon such an occasion, has carried me a little beyond it.

WILDING I am obliged to you for a great deal of wit,
whatever else you design me by this visit.   175

MRS WITWOUD Which now you hardly thank me for; since
'tis impossible for an old acquaintance to answer your
expectations of a new face.

WILDING To show how I value your visit, and the regard I
have for you, I will give some necessary orders in the 180
family* to prevent your being seen in my lodgings, and
wait upon you again.

                                                    [*Exit*]

MRS WITWOUD By this extraordinary care of my reputation I find he has no design upon it himself. Not that I
have any design upon Mr Wilding; but I am sorry to find 185
that every man has not a design upon me. For since want*
is the rate of things, I know no real value of reputation,
but in regard of common women,* who have none; no
extraordinary worth of a maidenhead, but as 'tis a
temptation to the man to take it away; and the best 190
commendation of virtue is that every man has a design to
put it to the trial. It vexes me, though, to think he should
grow so tame upon the sight of me. Not that I believe I

had anything in my face that altered him. Something did, that's certain; by which I find 'tis not enough for a woman 195 to be handsome, there must be a probability of making that handsome woman kind, to make a man in love with her. For no man is in love without some encouragement to hope upon. Now, from one of my character, who have impertinently prated away so much of my time in setting 200 up for a wit to the ruin of other people's pleasure and loss of my own, what encouragement, or probability can there be, but that, as I have lived a fool, I ought to die repenting, unpitied, and a maid? If I had died a maid, 'tis but what I deserved, for laughing so many honest gentle- 205 men off their charitable design of making me otherwise.

(WILDING *enters to her*)

WILDING Now, madam, you command me.
MRS WITWOUD It shall be to do yourself a favour then, Mr Wilding, to rid you of an incumbrance which lies as heavy upon your pleasures as a wife upon her husband. 210
WILDING Oh, defend me from a wife.
MRS WITWOUD And from a silly mistress, sir; the greater burthen of the two. A wife you may lay aside; but a foolish, fond mistress will hang about you like your conscience, to put you in mind of your sins before you are 215 willing to repent of 'em. You know whom I mean, Mr Wilding; you may trust me with the secret, because I know it already.
WILDING That's one very good reason truly, madam.
MRS WITWOUD My cousin Fanny, indeed, is very well* in 220 her person –
WILDING I'm glad on't.
MRS WITWOUD Very well to be liked, I mean.
WILDING I mean so too, madam. (*aside*) Though I have known a clap mistaken for a maidenhead, before now. 225
MRS WITWOUD But she's a girl, and I can guess how very unfit a girl must be to give you any desire beyond undoing her. For I know your temper so well; now you have

satisfied the curiosity or vanity of your love, you would
not bear the punishment of her company another day, to 230
have pleasure of it another night, whatever you have said
to persuade her to the contrary.

WILDING Fie, madam, think better of me.

MRS WITWOUD Better nor worse, than I do of all the
young men in town. For I believe you would now resign 235
her to anybody else, with as much satisfaction as you got
her for yourself. I know most of those matters end in the
benefit of the public; and a little of your ill usage (which
you will take care to supply her withall) may make her
one of the common goods of the town. But that's a ruin I 240
would prevent if I could. Therefore, to save you the
labour of getting rid of her (for that's the only design you
have upon her, I'm sure) I came to spare your good nature
the trouble, by making you a very fair offer.

WILDING Let's see how reasonable you can be, in another 245
body's bargain.

MRS WITWOUD Very reasonable you shall find me, if you
will give over your farther attempts upon her, which now
you may easily be persuaded to, I suppose; and contribute, by your assistance, to my design of marrying her. I 250
will engage myself and interest, which you know is very
considerable in my own sex, to serve you in any other
woman of my acquaintance.

WILDING Faith, madam, you bid like a chapman.*

MRS WITWOUD Any woman, of any family or condition – 255
the best friend I have – I'll befriend you in, and thank you
into the bargain.

WILDING Stay, let me consider, which –

MRS WITWOUD But take this advice along with you. Raise
the scene of your affairs above the conquest of a girl. 260
Some of you sparks think if you can but compass a
maidenhead, though but your tailor's daughter's, you
have settled a reputation for ever. Why, sir, there are
maidenheads among the women of quality, though not so
many perhaps. But there are favours of all kinds to be had 265

among 'em; as easily brought about, and at the same price of pains that you can purchase a chambermaid's.

WILDING I'm glad you tell me so.

MRS WITWOUD Why there's Mrs Newlove and her Cousin Truegame, Mrs Artist, Mrs Dancer, Lady Smirkit, Lady 270 Woudmore, and twenty more of your acquaintance and mine, all very fine women to the eye –

WILDING And of reputation to the world.

MRS WITWOUD Why those very women of reputation to the world have every one of 'em, to my certain knowl- 275 edge, an intrigue upon their hands, at this very time; for I'm intimate with all of 'em.

WILDING I see you are.

MRS WITWOUD But as fine as they seem to the eye, Mr Wilding, what with the false complexions of their skins, 280 their hair and eyebrows; with other defects about 'em, which I must not discover of my friends, you know; with their stinking breath in the morning, and other unsavoury smell all the day after; they are most of them intolerable to any man that has the use of his nose.   285

WILDING That I could not believe, indeed, but that you tell me so.

MRS WITWOUD Then there's Mrs Faceall, a very fair woman indeed, and a great fortune. As much in shape as you see her,* I have been a godmother to two of her 290 children, and she passes for a very good maid still.

WILDING She passed upon me, I assure you, for I was very near marrying her myself once.

MRS WITWOUD Choose where you please, but I would not advise you to any I have named yet.   295

WILDING Is there any hopes of Mrs Friendall?

MRS WITWOUD Little or none, yet a-while, I believe. Mr Lovemore has at present engaged her. But there's my cousin Sightly! Lord, that I should forget her so long! That I should be so backward in serving a friend! She is 300 the fittest woman in the world for you, the most convenient for your purpose in all the town; easy in her

humour and fortune, and able to make her lover so every
way. She shall be the woman.

WILDING Would you would make her so.   305

MRS WITWOUD I can and will make her so. We shall walk
in the Mall* this morning. If you think fit to be there, it
may introduce the acquaintance.

WILDING I'll but dress, and be with you.

MRS WITWOUD I don't doubt but in a little time to give 310
you an opportunity, and the lady an inclination of having
it improved;* but that must be your business. I'm a-going
about mine, to make her a visit. Remember our bargain,
sir.

WILDING I warrant you.   315

> [*Exit* <MRS WITWOUD>]

Let whore-masters rejoice; the times must mend,
If every woman had but such a friend.

> [*Exit*]

Act 3, Scene 1

RUFFLE's *lodgings*

(<*Enter*> RUFFLE *and* SERVANT)

RUFFLE A gentleman to speak with me! I am gone to
Banstead Downs,* to the horse-match.

SERVANT There's no match there, sir, this fortnight.

RUFFLE Not this fortnight? I had forgot myself. But you
may say I went out by five in the morning, and you don't   5
know when I come back. Go, tell him so.

SERVANT I have told him already you were within, sir.

RUFFLE Pox on him, what manner of man is he? Does he
look like a man of business?

SERVANT Not much like a man of business.   10

RUFFLE No, I warrant you; some coxcombly companion or
other, that visits in a morning and makes other people

idle, not to be idle himself. But can't you tell what he would have with me?

SERVANT I'll ask him, if you please.   15

RUFFLE He may be a messenger* for aught I know.

SERVANT I'll bring an account of him.

[Exit]

RUFFLE Would he were a messenger. I could be contented to pay the fees,* to be secured in the hands of the government for a fortnight. Well, this guilt is certainly   20 very terrible. The blow I gave Friendall was a very ill thing done of me. It lies heavier upon my conscience this morning than it did upon his face last night.

(SERVANT *re-enters*)

SERVANT His name is Captain Springame. You know his business, he says.   25

RUFFLE Yes, yes, I guess at it; I thought what it would come to. Show him up to me.

[Exit SERVANT]

I must do as well as I can.

(*Strips into his gown and cap*)*

There comes no good of being too forward upon these occasions – 'twill require some time to dress again. 'Tis   30 gaining time at least.

(SPRINGAME *enters*)

SPRINGAME Good morrow, sir, I have a small bill upon you here.

RUFFLE A challenge, I suppose.

SPRINGAME Payable at sight,* as you will find it.   35

RUFFLE You take me unprovided, you see, sir, to answer you at sight.

SPRINGAME I'll stay till you dress, sir, if that be all, to have you along with me.

RUFFLE Aye, aye, sir. I'll go along with you; never doubt it,   40 sir. You shan't stay long for me. I may dress time enough

for somebody, if that be your business. I'll do the
gentleman reason, I warrant him.

SPRINGAME We ask no more, sir.

RUFFLE You are his friend I suppose? 45

SPRINGAME At your friend's service. I serve upon these
occasions sometimes, by way of second, or so, when I
want employment of my own.

RUFFLE Is fighting your employment?

SPRINGAME 'Tis a soldier's employment. 50

RUFFLE Why really, sir, I beg your pardon. I'm sorry I
must disappoint you. I never make use of a second;
especially in such a quarrel as this is, where I am so much
in the wrong already, that I am almost unwilling to
engage in it any farther myself. Where is our friend, pray? 55

SPRINGAME Below, in a coach, sir.

RUFFLE Oh dear, sir, don't let him wait upon me;* bring
him up, I beseech you. And – d'ye hear, sir? – I'm loath to
justify an ill thing. If he is resolved to be satisfied, why
with all my heart, sir, I'll give him the satisfaction of a 60
gentleman – I'll beg his pardon. Pray tell him so.

[*Exit* SPRINGAME]

If fighting be his employment, would he were at it
anywhere else, and I fairly rid of him. I could discover,*
now, that Lovemore set me on to affront him – that
would throw the quarrel upon Lovemore. But then, 65
Lovemore knows me, and I must expect to be scurvily
used by him if I do. Hang baseness; 'tis but begging
pardon at last.

(SPRINGAME *enters with* FRIENDALL)

SPRINGAME A very civil gentleman, brother. He is not the
man you took him for. 70

RUFFLE No, indeed, sir, the captain's in the right. I never
justify an ill thing.

FRIENDALL 'Tis very well you don't, sir.

RUFFLE I am more a man of honour, I assure you, sir.

FRIENDALL I shall be glad to find you so. 75

RUFFLE Sir, you shall find me so. I scorn to do an ill thing,

as much as any man. I was last night in the wrong, as
every man is sometimes; and I'm sorry for't. What would
you have more, sir?

FRIENDALL That is not enough, sir, I must have more.   80

RUFFLE Why, I beg your pardon, sir.

FRIENDALL What's begging my pardon, sir, for such a
public affront?

SPRINGAME (aside) So, now he grows upon him.*

FRIENDALL That won't do my business, begging my par-   85
don. My reputation's at stake, and that must be satisfied,
before you and I part, sir.

RUFFLE Lord, sir, you are the strangest man in the world.
You won't oblige me to justify an ill thing, would you?

FRIENDALL Damme, sir, what do you mean? Not to give   90
me satisfaction?

RUFFLE I mean, sir, to give you any satisfaction, in reason.
But I can't fight against my conscience, if I were to be
hanged, sir, not I.

SPRINGAME No, brother, that's a little too hard upon the   95
gentleman. You see his conscience won't suffer him to
fight with you.

FRIENDALL Damn him and his conscience; he made no
conscience of affronting me.

SPRINGAME But his conscience has flown in his face since,   100
it seems.

FRIENDALL And now he finds it only in his fears.

SPRINGAME Come, come, you may be satisfied without
fighting.

FRIENDALL If you think so, brother.   105

(LOVEMORE *enters,* <unseen by RUFFLE>)

LOVEMORE <aside> Pox on't, they're here before me.

(*Joins with* FRIENDALL)

RUFFLE Captain, I'll beg your friend's pardon in any public
place – at the music-meeting, if he pleases.

SPRINGAME That's staying too long for't.

RUFFLE Or in full Mall before the beaux or the officers of   110

the guard; or at Will's coffee-house* before the wits; or in
the playhouse, in the pit before the vizard-masks and
orange-wenches; or behind the scenes* before the women
actors; or anywhere else, but upon the stage; and you
know, one would not willingly be a jest to the upper 115
galleries.*

FRIENDALL You hear what he says, Mr Lovemore.

LOVEMORE I'll do you justice, sir.

RUFFLE If none of these offers will serve his turn –

(*Seeing* LOVEMORE, *he takes heart again*)

Sir, if your friend will be satisfied with nothing but 120
extremities, let him look to himself; let what will be the
consequences. I must do as well as I can with him.

LOVEMORE (*aside*) So, he has seen me, I find.

SPRINGAME (*aside*) What the devil, he won't fight at last,
sure! 125

RUFFLE Sir, your most humble servant. You guess these
gentlemen's business, I suppose. I have offered 'em any
satisfaction, in reason. But taking me, as you see, sir, at a
disadvantage, two to one, nothing would content 'em,
without exposing myself as a rascal to all the town, sir. 130
Now, sir, you are more a gentleman I know; and they
shall be damned, before I give 'em any other satisfaction,
now I have a man of honour to stand by me.

LOVEMORE Gentlemen I came to reconcile you, if I can.
What say you? 135

SPRINGAME He offered just now to beg my brother's
pardon in the playhouse.

RUFFLE Make your best on't; I did so.

FRIENDALL Then let it be tonight in the side-box, before
the ladies. 140

RUFFLE With all my heart, sir.

FRIENDALL For they are the part of the town that a man of
pleasure should secure a reputation withal. Your servant,
sir. Lovemore, your humble servant.

[FRIENDALL *and* SPRINGAME *go out*]

LOVEMORE And hast thou begged his pardon? 145

RUFFLE And glad to come off so. I was never so put to't to bring myself off a quarrel before. It had been impossible if the captain had not done a good office between us, but I bore up as soon as I saw you.

LOVEMORE But then 'twas too late. You had sneakingly 150 begged his pardon before. If you had sent to me at first, I would have brought you off cleverly. Suppose he had carried you behind Southampton House,* which he never intended? 'Twas but falling down, or dropping your sword when you came there to have saved all. But now 155 you have ruined your own reputation and my design upon him forever.

RUFFLE What could I do? He not only sent me a challenge, but came himself to carry me along with him.

LOVEMORE How? Send you a challenge and come 160 with it himself! That's something odd. Pray, let's see the challenge.

RUFFLE There 'tis; make your best on't. The paper will make admirable crackers* for a Lord Mayor's Show, every word in't is as hot as gunpowder. I'm glad I'm rid 165 on't.

[*Exit*]

LOVEMORE *<reads the letter>* If this be Friendall's style, 'tis mightly mended of late. I have a note of his about me, upon Child,* for money won at play. I'll compare 'em. *<takes out the note>* 'Tis not his hand, neither. Nay then, 170 there's more in't. This may be a stratagem of his wife's; I've seen her hand and think this very near it. It must be so. But then, Friendall's coming for satisfaction is an argument he might send this challenge. But coming at the same time with it himself is an argument against him that 175 he knew nothing of the matter. For though he delivers his love-letters, he would hardly deliver his challenges himself. And for his coming here, Springame might put him upon't, from a reasonable probability that this fellow was a rascal. I don't know what to fix upon. This challenge 180 will be of use to me with the lady. I'll take it for granted that she writ it, and proceed upon it accordingly.

[*Exit*]

Act 3, Scene 2

Scene changes to St James's Park

(<*Enter*> MR FRIENDALL, SPRINGAME, *with* MRS
FRIENDALL *and* MRS TEAZALL)

SPRINGAME Brother, if you have no further service for me,
I must think of employing myself, my walk lies another
way.

[*Exit*]

MRS FRIENDALL I'm glad you're rid of this business so
handsomely, Mr Friendall, and that Mr Lovemore was by   5
at his begging your pardon.

FRIENDALL When I undertake things of this kind, I always
go through with 'em.

MRS FRIENDALL This is very well over, and I hope you will
take care to keep out of 'em for the future.   10

FRIENDALL Every man has the misfortune of 'em sometimes, madam.

MRS FRIENDALL But 'tis a prudent man's part to keep out
of the occasion* of 'em. And, in order to't, Mr Friendall, I
could wish you would not make your house, as you daily   15
do, one of the public places of the town.

MRS TEAZALL She's in the right on't indeed, Mr Friendall.
You are very happy in the discretion of a good lady, if
you know when you're well. There are very few women
would quarrel with your good nature, in this point, sir;   20
but she has too great a regard to her own and your
reputation, you see, not to apprehend the malice of ill
tongues upon the liberties you allow in your family. The
graver part of your friends take notice of it already, and,
let me tell you, sir, are extremely concerned.   25

FRIENDALL That they are past the pleasures of good
company themselves. Why really, madam, I believe it. But
they may say what they will; I shall do what I please. I live
to myself, and not to the whimsical humour of the graver
part of my friends, and so you may tell 'em, good madam,   30
from your humble servant.

(*Going*)

MRS FRIENDALL You won't leave us, Mr Friendall?

FRIENDALL I'll go home with you like a good husband, madam; but no man of fashion, you know, walks with his wife. Besides, there's a noble lord I must walk with.   35

[*Exit*]

MRS FRIENDALL Anything to be rid of my company.

MRS TEAZALL Why, how have the men, at this rate, the impudence to think the women should not cuckold 'em! If I had such a husband, as old as I am, a' my conscience, I believe I should use him as he deserved. But that's some   40 comfort; use him as you please, nobody will think you wrong him; and let me tell you, 'tis a great thing to have the town on one's side.

MRS FRIENDALL I'll keep 'em so, if I can.

MRS TEAZALL Nay, faith and troth, you have given him   45 fair warning. If he won't take it, he must answer himself for all the miscarriages you can be guilty of in your conduct hereafter.

MRS FRIENDALL There's something more in that, Mrs Teazall.   50

[*Exeunt*]

(<*Enter*> LOVEMORE, WELLVILE *following 'em*)

WELLVILE There's your Mrs Friendall before us. I honour her character as much as I despise her husband's.

LOVEMORE Though he has scaped the public discovery, if she knows him to be a coward, it does my business still as well.   55

WELLVILE If I did not think him one, I would put him to a trial. He should not so easily get clear off for putting a note into Mrs Sightly's hand at the music-meeting.

LOVEMORE How!

WELLVILE But I owe him a good turn for it.   60

LOVEMORE It comes into my head, and you shall pay him the good turn. What if you put Mrs Sightly upon telling his wife of it?

WELLVILE Ha!

LOVEMORE You ought to do it.   65

WELLVILE I think so too, myself; and you may be satisfied
    I'll do't – more out of a regard to the woman I value so
    much, than any design of promoting your cuckolding the
    fool.

LOVEMORE Good, grave sir; the plot is never the worse, I   70
    hope, for carrying your friend's interest along with the
    lady's.

WELLVILE Make your best use on't, Lovemore. I'm con-
    tented we should thrive together.

                                        [*Exeunt*]

(<*Enter*> MRS SIGHTLY *and* MRS WITWOUD *after 'em*)

MRS WITWOUD You are mightily injured indeed, madam,   75
    to be persuaded to come abroad so much to your
    disadvantage, such a delicate* morning as this is, so much
    against your inclinations. But you'll know your interest
    better in a little time, and me for your friend, I suppose,
    when you find the benefit of it.   80

MRS SIGHTLY Nay, cousin, the injury may be forgiven, for
    the pleasure of the walk at this time of the year.

MRS WITWOUD Why, the very walk is to be liked, though
    there were nobody in it to like us. But there's a great deal
    of good company in the Mall, and, I warrant you, we'll   85
    have our share of the commendation of the place, in spite
    of fresher faces. You are sure of your part of it already.

MRS SIGHTLY How so, good Mrs Witwoud?

MRS WITWOUD Why, good Mrs Sightly, there's Mr Well-
    vile before you.   90

MRS SIGHTLY My platonic lover, as you call him.

MRS WITWOUD And as you find him.

MRS SIGHTLY I think him very much my friend.

MRS WITWOUD Very much your friend! I grant you indeed,
    every woman that is not wholly insensible – and one   95
    would not be thought insensible, you know – every
    woman ought to have a platonic passion for one man or
    other. But a platonic lover in a man, is –

MRS SIGHTLY What, pray?

MRS WITWOUD Why, he is a very unmannerly* fellow. He is not what he should be, that's certain. As for the matter of respect, which we keep such a clutter* about and seem to value so much in the men, all that I know of it is, that if any man pretended to follow and like me, I should never believe what he said if he did not do something to convince me. I should think he affronted me extremely if, upon the first handsome occasion, he did not offer me everything in his power.

MRS SIGHTLY How, cousin!

MRS WITWOUD I hate a blockhead that will never give a woman a reputable occasion of refusing him. 'Tis one of the best compliments a lover can make his mistress's pride, and I never knew any man that did his business without it.

MRS SIGHTLY Why, Witwoud, thou art mad, sure.

MRS WITWOUD And for your Mr Wellvile, if I were in your place, I should have something the better opinion of him if he would have a little worse opinion of me. But between you and me, I should not like him for a lover.

MRS SIGHTLY He does not pretend to be one.

MRS WITWOUD Who's here? Wilding and Courtall behind us? That Wilding, cousin, is a very pretty gentleman.

MRS SIGHTLY And Courtall, too, very well.

MRS WITWOUD I must bring you acquainted with Wilding.

MRS SIGHTLY No more acquaintance, good Mrs Witwoud.

MRS WITWOUD For his discretion and conduct, his good behaviour and all that, Wellvile is his acquaintance, and will answer for. But his agreeable, easy wit, and good humour, you may take upon my word. You'll thank me, when you know him.

[*Exeunt*]

(WILDING *and* COURTALL *enter*)

WILDING She's a woman of her word. You see she has brought Mrs Sightly along with her.

COURTALL I never doubted it. She'll carry her to supper in

a night or two. She's never the worse bawd, I hope, for
being a gentlewoman.   135

WILDING A good family indeed gives a countenance to the
profession; and a reputation is necessary to carry on the
credit of a trade.

COURTALL Here's Wellvile just behind us.

WILDING Prithee, stay with him; I'll tell you how I thrive. 140

[Exit]

(WELLVILE enters)

WELLVILE Good morrow, Mr Courtall.

COURTALL Oh, sir, yours.

WELLVILE Was not that Wilding left you?

COURTALL He's in his employment, sir, very busy.

WELLVILE In pursuit of the women, I know. It hardly 145
answers the expense, I doubt.

COURTALL You have no reason to say so. There's a lady
before us of your acquaintance, Mrs Sightly by name, of
another opinion. I suppose she thinks such an assurance*
as his, in coming to the point, is more to the nature of the 150
thing, than all your ceremony and respect.

WELLVILE Mrs Sightly!

COURTALL She, sir, the very same. I could tell you a secret,
Wellvile, but you are one of those fellows that hate
another man should lie with a woman, though you never 155
attempt her yourself. I confess I am something of your
mind; I think the enjoyment the dull part of an intrigue,
and therefore I give it over when I see the lady in earnest.

WELLVILE But the secret, Courtall.

COURTALL Why faith, Welville, if you have temper to 160
manage it,* the secret may be of use to you. Wilding, you
know, never debauches a woman only for himself; where
he visits, in a little time, every man may be received in his
turn. You must know, 'twas Witwoud put him upon Mrs
Sightly. She knew what she did, I suppose, and has 165
promised him a good office,* in her way. Make your
advantage of what I tell you, but not a syllable to anyone.

(SPRINGAME *enters*)

SPRINGAME Oh, Courtall, here are a couple of vizard-masks have set upon me in the next walk, and I wanted thee to take one of 'em off my hands.   170

COURTALL I'll stand by you, my noble captain.

                                              [*Exeunt*]

WELLVILE (*solus*)* I'll think no more on 't, 'tis imposs-ible.* What's impossible? Nothing's impossible to a woman. We judge but on the outside of that sex and know not what they can do, nor what they do, more than 175 they please to show. I have known Mrs Sightly these seven years – known her? I mean I have seen her, observed her, followed her. Maybe there's no knowing a woman. But in all that time, I never found a freedom that allowed me any encouragement beyond a friend. Maybe I 180 have been wanting to myself.* But then, she would not throw herself away upon a common lover; that's not probable. If she had been affectedly reserved, I would suspect the devil in her heart had stamped the sign of virtue in her looks that she might cheat the world, and sin 185 more close. But she is open in her carriage, easy, clear of those arts that have made lust a trade. Perhaps that openness may be design; 'tis easy to raise doubts. And still she may be – I won't think she can, till I know more. But Witwoud is, I know her, everything that's mischievous – 190 abandoned and undone. Undone herself, she would undo the sex. She is to bawd for Wilding. I know her bad enough for any trade. But bawds have some good nature, and procure pleasure for pay. Witwoud has baser ends: a general ruin upon all her friends.   195

(SEVERAL <LORDS> *pass over the stage.*
<Enter>FRIENDALL <who is> *slighted by 'em, one after another*)

1ST LORD I have a little business, at present; but I shall see you at the play.

                                              [*Exit*]

FRIENDALL In the king's box,* my lord. (*to another*) My
dear lord, I'm your humble servant.

2ND LORD Another time, good Mr Friendall; you see 200
I'm engaged.

[*Exit*]

FRIENDALL A pox o'their engagements. A man can't make
one among 'em. <*to a third* LORD> Oh, my most noble
lord –

3RD LORD I know you will upbraid me, Mr Friend- 205
all, but I'll recover your opinion and come and dine with
you. Let's have Jack Dryden and Will Wycherley,* as you
call 'em. Some of these days, we'll be very witty together;
but now I am your servant.

[*Exit*]

FRIENDALL This is a very unfortunate morning with me; I 210
have not walked one turn with a lord since I came in. I see
I must take up with the men of wit today. – Oh, Mr
Wellvile!

WELLVILE Don't let me keep you from better company.

FRIENDALL Faith, sir, I prefer a man of wit to a man of 215
quality.

WELLVILE <*to himself*> If she thinks Witwoud her friend,
after this, 'tis a sign she's pleased with it, and there's an
end on't.

FRIENDALL Why, Wellvile, thou art cogitabund,* as a man 220
may say. Thy head is running upon thy poetry.

WELLVILE I beg your pardon, sir, I did not mind* you,
indeed.

(WILDING *enters to 'em*)

Your servant, Mr Wilding.

FRIENDALL Wilding, yours. But, Welville, prithee, what 225
is't to be? A song? A tribute to the whole sex? Or a
particular sacrifice? Or is't a libel upon the court, ha? –
We'll keep your counsel! Or a lampoon upon the town?
What, I am a great honourer, and humble servant of the
muses myself. 230

WELLVILE A very favourite of 'em, I hear, sir.

FRIENDALL I sometimes scribble, indeed, for my diversion.

WILDING And the diversion of the ladies, Mr Friendall.

WELLVILE And the diversion of all the town, Mr 235
Friendall.

FRIENDALL Why, faith, gentlemen, poetry is a very pretty
amusement; and, in the way of intrigue,* or so, among
the better rank of people, I have known a paper of verses
go further with a lady in the purchase of a favour than a 240
present of fifty pounds would have done.

WILDING Oh, sir, 'tis the only way of purchasing a woman
that is not to be bought.

FRIENDALL But, Wellvile, prithee communicate, man.

WELLVILE Why, if you will have it, I have a design upon a 245
play.

FRIENDALL Gad, so. Let me write a scene in it. I have a
thousand times had it in my head, but never could bring it
about to write a play yet.

WILDING No, no. You had it not in your head, sir. 250

FRIENDALL I vow to gad, but I have then, twenty
times, I'm confident. But one thing or other always kicked
it out again. But I promise you, I'll write a scene for
you.

WILDING Before you know the subject? 255

FRIENDALL Prithee, what is't? But be what it will, here's
my hand upon't; I'll write it for you.

WELLVILE You must know then, sir, I am scandalised
extremely to see the women upon the stage make
cuckolds at that insatiable rate they do in all our modern 260
comedies, without any other reason from the poets, but
because a man is married he must be a cuckold. Now, sir,
I think the women are most unconscionably injured by
this general scandal upon their sex. Therefore to do 'em
what service I can in their vindication, I design to write a 265
play and call it –

FRIENDALL Aye, what, I beseech you? I love to know the
name of a new play.

WELLVILE *The Wives' Excuse; or, Cuckolds Make Themselves.*   270

FRIENDALL A very pretty name, faith and troth; and very like to be popular among the women.

WILDING And true among the men.

FRIENDALL But what characters have you?

WELLVILE What characters? Why I design to show a fine 275 young woman married to an impertinent, nonsensical, silly, intriguing, cowardly, good-for-nothing coxcomb.

WILDING (*aside*) This blockhead does not know his own picture.

FRIENDALL Well, and how? She must make him a 280 cuckold I suppose.

WELLVILE 'Twas that I was thinking on when you came to me.

FRIENDALL Oh, yes, you must make him a cuckold.

WILDING By all means a cuckold.   285

FRIENDALL For such a character, gentlemen, will vindicate a wife in anything she can do to him. He must be a cuckold.

WELLVILE I am satisfied he ought to be a cuckold; and indeed, if the lady would take my advice, she should make 290 him a cuckold.

FRIENDALL She'll hear reason, I warrant her.

WELLVILE I have not yet determined how to dispose of her. But, in regard to* the ladies, I believe I shall make her honest at last.   295

FRIENDALL I think the ladies ought to take it very ill of you, if you do. But if she proves honest to the last, that's certain 'tis more than the fellow deserves. (*to* WILDING) A very pretty character this, faith and troth.

WILDING And very well known in this town.   300

FRIENDALL Gad, I believe I can help you to a great many hints that may be very serviceable to you.

WELLVILE I design to make use of you. We who write plays must sometimes be beholden to our friends. But more of this at leisure.   305

FRIENDALL Will you walk, gentlemen? The ladies are

before us.

WELLVILE I have a little business with Wilding. We'll
follow you.

[*Exit* FRIENDALL]

WILDING Business with me, Wellvile?   310
WELLVILE About a fair lady, I'll tell you as we walk.

[*Exeunt*]

(*Enter* LOVEMORE *with* MRS FRIENDALL, MRS SIGHTLY,
MRS WITWOUD *and* MRS TEAZALL)

MRS TEAZALL Nay, indeed, Mr Lovemore, as matters are
managed between the men and women of the town, 'tis
no less a blessing for a lady to have a husband that will
but so much as offer to fight for her and her honour, than   315
'tis for a husband to have a lady that has any honour to
defend. There's such a depravity in matrimony, o' both
sides, nowadays.

MRS SIGHTLY Why, good madam, is it such a business for
a man to offer to fight for his wife?   320

MRS WITWOUD All that I know is, the man that would not
fight for me, should do nothing else for me.

MRS TEAZALL You'll have your wit, let who's will* blush
for't.

LOVEMORE (*to* MRS TEAZALL) As you say, madam, a man   325
of honour is a great blessing in a husband – such as Mr
Friendall has shown himself to be. And here's a lady will
value the blessing as it deserves.

MRS FRIENDALL (*aside*) I must, indeed, despise him in my
thoughts.   330

MRS WITWOUD Fulsome and foolish! Let's hear no more
on't. They don't think this can blind us.

(*Walking off with* MRS SIGHTLY)

LOVEMORE If you were not inclined to it before, madam,
this last behaviour of his would engage you to value such
a blessing as you ought.   335

MRS FRIENDALL My duty would engage me. (*aside*) What
does he mean by this?

MRS WITWOUD Cousin Teazall, your opinion, pray.

LOVEMORE I have something to tell you, madam, if you
would but allow me; this is no place.   340

MRS FRIENDALL You'll find a time, I warrant you. Ladies,
the Mall begins to thin. (*goes to 'em*)

(*<Enter> WELLVILE and WILDING coming forward*)

WILDING Well, sir, since you declare yourself in love with
the lady, and I am not, I promise you, and you may trust
me, I'll never follow her more.   345

WELLVILE I do trust, and thank you for the promise.
Ladies, your servant.

(*He addresses to* MRS SIGHTLY; WILDING *to* MRS
WITWOUD)

MRS WITWOUD *<aside to* WILDING*>* Oh, he's come at last.
There's nothing to be done here; you've outstayed your
time. But we'll call at the chocolate house in St Albans 350
Street as we go home. You may meet us there by accident,
you know.

WILDING *<aside>* If I were to be hanged now, I must meet
'em there, though I have given my word to the contrary.

MRS TEAZALL *<aside to* MRS WITWOUD*>* Is that the filthy 355
fellow?

MRS WITWOUD That's Wilding, madam.

MRS TEAZALL I see there's no knowing a whore-master by
his face. He looks like a modest, civil gentleman.

WELLVILE (*to* MRS SIGHTLY) Your friend, Mrs Witwoud, 360
madam, may be of that good-natured opinion that
Lovemore is familiar with the husband only to be more
familiar with the wife. But you must be cautious of what
you say, for fear we turn the scandal upon you.

MRS SIGHTLY Upon me, Mr Wellvile?   365

WELLVILE Pardon me, madam, I have the freedom of a
friend. But Mr Friendall declares he is in love with you;
and, after that, the good-natured town (whatever they
believe) will go near to say that your familiarity with his
wife may be in order to the husband.   370

MRS SIGHTLY Contemptible! Sure, nobody would think so.

WELLVILE 'Tis an ill-natured age to handsome women, madam.

MRS SIGHTLY Must I suffer, because he's a fool?

WELLVILE You may suffer, because he's a fool.   375

MRS SIGHTLY This is not only to be accountable for our own conduct, but to answer for all the indiscretion of the men's.

WELLVILE You must, madam, for those men's you allow to be so near you.   380

MRS SIGHTLY It would be but an ungrateful* piece of news to Mrs Friendall if I should be serious enough to tell her of it.

WELLVILE 'Twould be more ungrateful to her, if anybody else did; and would go near to make you serious, if 385 another should tell her for you.

MRS SIGHTLY But who can tell? It may be the cause of a breach between 'em.

WELLVILE Nay, madam, if it be considerable enough to make a breach in marriage, you may be sure 'twill make a 390 breach in friendship. And how much that will be to the advantage of your reputation upon such an occasion –

MRS SIGHTLY I am convinced you are my friend, Mr Wellvile, and thank you for this care of me.

(*They mingle with* LOVEMORE, MRS FRIENDALL, *and the rest*)

MRS WITWOUD <*aside to* WILDING> This is the aunt 395 would ha' been upon your bones,* I assure you, if I had not delivered you.

WILDING How shall I do to appease her?

MRS WITWOUD There's but one way now to please her. You must know she has been in her time, like other 400 women, in at most of the pleasures of this town; but being too passionate a lover of the sport, she has been a bubble* at all games. And having now nothing to lose but her money, she declares for lanterloo* and is contented to be only cheated at cards.   405

(<*Enter*> FRIENDALL *with* SPRINGAME *and* COURTALL)

FRIENDALL Why, what do you think, ladies? These gentlemen here, in spite of the temptation of so much good
company, refuse to dine with me.

SPRINGAME (*to* MRS WITWOUD) Oh, madam! Are you
there?   410

COURTALL (*to* MRS FRIENDALL) Your brother has seduced
me, madam.

SPRINGAME We'll visit you at night, ladies, in masquerade;* when the privilege of a vizard will allow us a
conversation out of your forms* and more to our humour 415
a great deal, ladies.

[*Exeunt* SPRINGAME *and* COURTALL]

FRIENDALL Lovemore, Wellvile, Wilding – you'll follow
us?

LOVEMORE We won't fail you, sir.

[FRIENDALL *goes out with the* LADIES]

MRS WITWOUD St Albans Street –   420
WILDING We'll tell you more of this.
WELLVILE Wilding, you'll take another turn with us?
WILDING Faith, no, I'm tired. We shall meet at Friendall's,
all.

[*Exit*]

WELLVILE At Friendall's be it then,   425
Where the kind husband welcomes every guest.
LOVEMORE He but invites, his wife must make the feast.

[*Exeunt*]

Act 4, Scene 1

FRIENDALL'*s house*

(*All the company enters after dinner*)

LOVEMORE Mr Friendall, you have the best wines and the
greatest choice of any man in town.

FRIENDALL There's an elegance in eating and drinking, gentlemen, as well as in writing.

WELLVILE (*aside*) Or your style would never go down.   5

FRIENDALL How did you like the Lucena I gave you, the Galicia, the Mountain-Alicant?* You taste the sun in them perfectly, gentlemen.

WILDING Oh, plainly, sir!

FRIENDALL Then the Aracena, the Ranchio, and the   10 Peralta, the Carcavelos, the Lacrymae, the Schiveas, the Cephalonia, the Montalcino, with all the Muscatels, and to conclude, my single bottle of Tokay.*

LOVEMORE Admirable all, sir.

FRIENDALL A friend of mine that brought the Tokay from   15 Buda* assures me the stones of all those grapes are gold.

WELLVILE That makes the wine so scarce.

FRIENDALL Nay, not unlikely. But of all the wines of all the climates under the sun –

WILDING Give me the Greek.   20

FRIENDALL Oh, I abominate –

WELLVILE The language, but not the wines. You may relish them without it.

FRIENDALL Aye, that may be. But of all the wines, pagan or Christian, in the world, I think the Borachio* the   25 noblest.

WELLVILE <*aside*> 'Tis of the roughest kind indeed of beasts; would he were in the skin of one of 'em.

WILDING But your Vin de Congress,* Mr Friendall –

FRIENDALL True; but 'tis a Dutch wine and grows in the   30 province of Zeeland.* I have drank it upon the place.

WILDING But, Mr Friendall, pray, in all your variety and interest among your friends in the city, have you not sometimes met with such a wine as the Vin de Short-Neck?*
   35

FRIENDALL Vin de Short-Neck? Yes, I have drank of it at Thompson's,* and was the first that took notice of it. But 'tis a prohibited French wine,* and I have too great an acquaintance with the members of parliament not to drink according to law.   40

WILDING Yours is very good snuff, Mr Friendall.

FRIENDALL Yes, truly, I think 'tis pretty good powder.

WILDING Pray your opinion of mine; you are a critic.

FRIENDALL This is Havana, indeed; but then 'tis washed.*
Give me your dry powders,* they never lose their scent. 45
Besides, yours is made of the leaves of the tobacco.

WELLVILE Why, what the devil's yours?

FRIENDALL Mine, sir, is right Palilio,* made of the fibres,
the spirituous part of the plant. There's not a pinch of it
out of my box in England. 'Twas made, I assure you, to 50
the palate of His Most Catholic Majesty,* and sent me by
a great Don of Spain that's in his prince's particular
pleasures.

(*Goes to the* WOMEN)

WELLVILE And his, it seems, lie in his nose.

FRIENDALL Ladies, what say you to the fresco* of the 55
garden? We'll drink our tea upon the mount,* and be the
envy of the neighbourhood.

MRS WITWOUD Oh, delicately thought upon!*

FRIENDALL Madam, which tea shall we have?

MRS FRIENDALL Which the company pleases, Mr 60
Friendall.

FRIENDALL The plain Canton, the Nankin, the Bohea, the
Latheroon, the Sunloe, or which?* Ha!

WELLVILE Have you any of the Non Amo Te?*

FRIENDALL Faith, no, sir, there came but little of it over 65
this year; but I am promised a whole canister by a friend
of a considerable interest in the committee.*

LOVEMORE Then the Bohea, sir, the Bohea will do our
business.

FRIENDALL My Bohea, at the best hand* too, cost me ten 70
pound a pound. But I have a tea, with a damned
heathenish hard name, that I think I was very much
befriended in, at an Indian house* in the city. If you
please, we'll have some of that.

MRS FRIENDALL 'Tis in my cabinet, Mr Friendall, I must 75
order it* myself for you.

(Goes out)

FRIENDALL That, madam, must make the compliment the
greater to the company. *Allons*, you know the way; I wait
upon you.

(All go out but LOVEMORE)

LOVEMORE This way she must come, she can't avoid me,   80
thanks to the honest husband.

(MRS FRIENDALL *returns*)

MRS FRIENDALL Are you one of the gentlemen that love
the tea with a hard name?
LOVEMORE Faith, madam, I must love anything that gives
me an opportunity –   85
MRS FRIENDALL With any woman that has a mind to
improve it.
LOVEMORE Of adoring you.
MRS FRIENDALL Me, Mr Lovemore! I was going before,
but now you drive me.   90
LOVEMORE <*detaining her and kneeling*> Stay! This
violence,*
    If you can call it violence on my knees,
    Excuses you to all your female forms;
    Nay, to yourself, severer than your forms;
    If you should stay and hear me.   95
MRS FRIENDALL Well, what's the matter?
LOVEMORE Everything is matter of your praise,
    The subject of fresh wonder:
    Your beauty made to tire the painter's art,
    Your wit to strike the poet's envy dumb.   100
MRS FRIENDALL Are you turned poet too?
LOVEMORE Indeed you can inspire me –
MRS FRIENDALL With the spirit of scandal I may. A small
matter conjures up a lampoon against the women. But to
the purpose, sir: you pretend business with me, and have   105
insinuated a great deal of pains all this day to get an
occasion of speaking to me in private; which now, by Mr
Friendall's assistance, you think you have ingeniously

secured. Why, sir, after all, I know no business between
us that is to be carried on by my being alone with you. 110

LOVEMORE I'm sorry for that indeed, madam.

MRS FRIENDALL Suppose, Mr Lovemore, a man should hit
you a box on the ear.

LOVEMORE Only suppose it, good madam.

MRS FRIENDALL Why, sir, any man that's brute enough 115
may do it. Though that brute should beg your pardon
never so publicly for the wrong, you would never heartily
forgive him for pitching upon you.

LOVEMORE Not heartily, I believe, indeed.

MRS FRIENDALL Why, very well. You keep me here
against my will,   120
Against all rules of decency – to me,
My sex and character, the worst of wrongs.
Yet you will think it hard to be condemned
Or hated for your light opinion of me
That first encouraged you to this design.   125

LOVEMORE Hated for loving you!

MRS FRIENDALL   Aye, there's the business.
Who would not stay to see her worshipper
Upon his knees, thus praised, and thus adored?
'Her beauty made to tire the painter's art,
Her wit to strike the poet's envy dumb';   130
And all delivered in such a dying tone,
No lady can outlive it.
Mr Lovemore, you might have known me better than to
imagine your sly flattery could* softly sing me into a
consent to anything my virtue had abhorred. But how 135
have I behaved myself? What have I done to deserve this?
What encouragement have I given you?

LOVEMORE A lover makes his hopes.

MRS FRIENDALL Perhaps 'tis from the general encouragement of being a married woman, supported on your side 140
by that honourable opinion of our sex, that, because some
women abuse their husbands, every woman may. I grant
you, indeed, the custom of England has been very
prevailing in that point. And I must own to you, an ill

husband is a great provocation to a wife when she has a   145
mind to believe as ill of him as she can.

LOVEMORE How if the wife believe too well of him?

MRS FRIENDALL Why then the folly's hers. For my part, I
have known Mr Friendall too long not to know justly
what he deserves. I won't justify his faults, but because he   150
does not take that care of me he should, must not I have
that regard to myself I ought? What I do is for my own
sake.
Nay, what is past,
Which, by your hints, I know you do suspect,   155
I own I did it –
Not for the commendation of your wit,
Nor as a debt to him, but to myself,
Foreseeing a long life of infamy,
Which in his follies I was married to,   160
And therefore saved myself by saving him.

LOVEMORE Your conduct everywhere is excellent;
But there it was a masterpiece, indeed,
And worthy admiration.

MRS FRIENDALL And would you have me lose that
character   165
So 'worthy admiration', which, ev'n you,
An enemy, must praise, when you would ruin?
No, what I've done to raise this character
May be an argument I will do more
To heighten it, to the last act of life.   170

LOVEMORE And all for the reward of being thought
Too good a wife to such a husband.

MRS FRIENDALL   How!
You know him then?

LOVEMORE You and I know him.

MRS FRIENDALL   Fit to bear a wrong?
Is that the reason of your wronging him?   175
I want but that.* Oh, let me but believe
You injure him because you know you may,
And attempt me because you think it safe,
And I will scorn you low, as you do him.

You say you know him. Now, sir, I know you: 180
You, and your practices against us both.
You have encouraged all that has been done,
Exposing him, only to ruin me.
'Tis necessary to believe as ill of you as I can.
And for the future, till you clear yourself –   185
LOVEMORE I can clear myself.
MRS FRIENDALL I'll think you capable of everything,
Of any baseness to advance your ends;
So leave you to your triumph.

(Going)

LOVEMORE Madam, stay – I must be justified.   190
(shows the letter) This challenge here has taught me all
    I know;
Made me suspect who writ it, and presume
All I have said to you.
MRS FRIENDALL Where had you it?
LOVEMORE Ruffle gave it me. I hope you may forgive my 195
knowing it, since, by resigning it into your hands, I give
you up the only evidence that can rise up against him.
Such a piece of news, madam, would have been welcome
enough to the ill nature of the town; and I might have had
my ends* in such a report, had I encouraged the exposing 200
him. But when I saw how near you were concerned, I had
no other pleasure but the thought of serving you. If I have
served you, I am overpaid. If not, I must serve on. For I
but live to serve you.
MRS FRIENDALL My employment calls upon me. Are not 205
you for tea?

(TWO FOOTMEN *with a service of tea enter, and go out*
with MRS FRIENDALL)

LOVEMORE I find I am restored; but I was reduced to the
necessity of a lie to come into favour again. But that's a
necessity that every man of honour must submit to
sometimes, that has anything to manage with the women. 210
For a lover that never speaks more than the truth, is never

believed to be a lover; and he that won't lie to his mistress, will hardly lie with her. So let his honesty reward him; the lady won't, I dare say for her. There must be a cheat upon the sense sometimes, to make a perfect 215 pleasure to the soul. For if the women did but always know what really we are; we should not so often know so much of them as we do. But 'tis their own faults. They know we can't live without 'em, and therefore ask more of us than we have honestly to give for the purchase. So, 220 very often, they put us upon dissimulation, flattery and false love, to come up to their price. Mrs Friendall went away a little abruptly. I'm glad she did; for that methinks confesses an obligation which she has not yet in her power to return.   225

(WELLVILE *enters to him*)

WELLVILE Lovemore, your plot begins to thrive. I left Mrs Sightly telling Mrs Friendall everything between her and Mr Friendall. I thought fit to acquaint you with it, that you might be prepared. You know best what use to turn it to. My business is with Mrs Sightly.   230

LOVEMORE I thank you for the news. They're coming this way. I would not have 'em see us. I must hover here.

[*Exeunt* LOVEMORE *and* WELLVILE]

(*Enter* MRS FRIENDALL *and* MRS SIGHTLY)

MRS FRIENDALL I could not have believed it.

MRS SIGHTLY I am sorry you have reason to believe it upon my account. Indeed, I was unwilling to believe it. I 235 suffered it as long as I could; but finding no end of this persecution –

MRS FRIENDALL You have used me like a friend, and I thank you. His note since dinner desires you would meet him at seven, at Rosamond's Pond.* You can't be so 240 hard-hearted to disappoint him?

MRS SIGHTLY If you have a mind to have a plainer proof of his treachery –

MRS FRIENDALL The proof is plain enough – you say it.

Besides, he has given it under his hand here, and I believe 245
the gentleman, though you won't.

MRS SIGHTLY Or, if you would, let him know you have
discovered him, and upbraid him with his baseness before
me –

MRS FRIENDALL That would but harden him, or make him 250
vain by showing a concern for him.

MRS SIGHTLY If you have any curiosity to be satisfied, I'll
go with you to the place appointed.

MRS FRIENDALL I would not have him know either of us.

MRS SIGHTLY Then we must have a man to secure us.* 255

MRS FRIENDALL We may trust your friend Mr Wellvile.

MRS SIGHTLY Mr Friendall, you must know, thinks him in
love with me; so being a rival, may make him avoid us.
But Mr Lovemore will do as well.

MRS FRIENDALL I would not have him know it. 260

MRS SIGHTLY He knows it already. I made no secret of it,
and Mr Wellvile told it him.

MRS FRIENDALL Then he, or anyone –

(LOVEMORE *enters to 'em*)

MRS SIGHTLY Oh, here he comes! Mr Lovemore, we must
employ you this afternoon. 265

LOVEMORE To serve myself, in waiting upon you.

(*The rest of the company enter to 'em*)

MRS TEAZALL Well, here's such a clutter to get you to
cards. You have drank your tea; what will you do next, I
trow?

MRS WITWOUD Why take a nap, or smoke a pipe, anybody 270
that has a mind to be private.

MRS TEAZALL Would I had one civilly in a corner.

FRIENDALL (*to a* SERVANT) Get the cards in the drawing-
room.

MRS WITWOUD Not till we have the song, Mr Friendall, 275
you promised us.

FRIENDALL Why, faith, I was forced to set it myself. I
don't know how you'll like it with my voice; but, faith

and troth, I believe the masters of the music-meeting may
set their own words, for any trouble I shall give 'em for   280
the future about mine.
WILDING Nay, then you ruin 'em.
MRS WITWOUD The song, the song, sir.

Song

(*Written by a man of quality*)

1

Say, cruel Amoret, how long,
In billet-doux and humble song,   285
 Shall poor Alexis woo?
 If neither writing, sighing, dying,
Reduce you to a soft complying,
Oh, when will you come to?*

2

Full thirteen moons are now past o'er,   290
Since first those stars I did adore
 That set my heart on fire.
The conscious* playhouse, parks and court,
Have seen my sufferings made your sport:
 Yet am I ne'er the nigher.   295

3

A faithful lover should deserve
A better fate, than thus to starve
 In sight of such a feast;
But oh, if you'll not think it fit,
Your hungry slave should taste one bit,   300
 Give some kind looks at least.

WILDING Admirable well —
MRS WITWOUD Set and sung, sir.
LIVEMORE A gentleman does these things always best.
WELLVILE When he has a genius.   305

FRIENDALL Aye, sir, he must have a genius. There's no being a master of anything without a genius.

MRS FRIENDALL Mrs Teazall, Pam* wants you in the next room.

(Scene draws, shows tables and cards)

MRS TEAZALL I'll make the more of him, when I get him into my hands. 310

WELLVILE (*to* MRS SIGHTLY) I have something to tell you, worth more than the cards can win for you.

MRS FRIENDALL Who's for comet?*

LOVEMORE I am your man, madam. 315

MRS FRIENDALL You play too deep for me.

MRS WITWOUD Cousin, you'll make one of us?

MRS SIGHTLY I go your halves,* if you please, I don't care for playing myself.

(They go in to play. The scene shuts upon 'em.
WELLVILE and MRS SIGHTLY stay)

MRS SIGHTLY Now, Mr Wellvile, you have something extraordinary to say to me. 320

WELLVILE I have, indeed, madam, but I should prepare you for the story. There are some friends in it that you will be concerned to have an ill opinion of.

MRS SIGHTLY I have reason to think you my friend. 325

WELLVILE Then pray give me leave to ask how long you have known Mr Wilding?

MRS SIGHTLY I never spoke to him till this morning at the chocolate-house, as we came from the Park.

WELLVILE I think he's Mrs Witwoud's particular acquaintance. 330

MRS SIGHTLY That, I suppose, gave him his title of speaking to us.

WELLVILE And she has a mind to bring him acquainted with you. I'm sorry I must warn you of him; I was in hopes it would have died of itself. But his talking to you at the chocolate-house, after he had promised never to 335 follow you more, makes me apprehend that he is still carrying on his design upon you.

MRS SIGHTLY A design upon me! 340

WELLVILE He has a design upon you. And you have heard enough of his character to suspect the honour of any design he has upon any woman. But such as it is, your cousin Witwoud and very good friend, for ends of her own, which I can inform you in, has undertaken to bring 345 it about. I see you are surprised.

MRS SIGHTLY I pray, sir, go on.

WELLVILE I never pretended to be a friend of Mrs Witwoud's, but now I hate her. And what I tell you is not to ruin her with you, but of nearer consequence* – to save 350 you from being undone by her. This is not a secret. I'll tell her of it myself, and my thoughts of her into the bargain. But, madam, you know best how far she has solicited his cause to you; how far my story is probable; and whether you don't think she persuaded you to walk this morning 355 in the Mall, in order to meet* Mr Wilding. That was the business* of her visit to you, as he tells me, whatever she pretended to the contrary.

MRS SIGHTLY You astonish me!

WELLVILE I am astonished myself, indeed, madam – not to 360 find her, as I always thought her, fit for any mischief; but to think she can pretend to be* a bawd, and provide no better for a friend: to sacrifice you to a man who would tell all the town of it, as well as Courtall, and has confessed to me that he never was in love with you, nor 365 had a thought that way, till she put it into his head and promised to assist him in't.

MRS SIGHTLY Unheard of villainy!

WELLVILE Faith, madam, if I might advise you, it should be to a man of honour at least, that can be so tender of a 370 reputation not to lessen a lady's favour so far to make it the common mirth of the town. If you have any favours to dispose of, dispose of 'em yourself. Let not another run away with the benefit of your good turns. I have been an old admirer, madam, and I hope stand as fair, and have as 375

good a title to put in my claim, as any man of her
providing.

MRS SIGHTLY So, sir, then it seems you think I must be
provided for, and therefore these advances must please
me. I have some reason to believe what you say of my 380
cousin Witwoud, but I have no reason to think you very
much my friend. She has betrayed me, and you are
pleased to think I deserve it. I thank you for your caution;
but it shall secure me for the future, against her and you.
For as much as I thought you my friend – nay, though I 385
languished for you – the encouragement you are pleased
to make from other people's base opinion of me, shall
teach me to despise you.

(*The scene opens: the company rises from play, and
comes forward*)

MRS TEAZALL Nay, nay, I have done with you. If this be
your fair play, there's no danger of your foul.* Why, you 390
make no conscience of cheating anybody out of your own
gang.

MRS WITWOUD Conscience at cards, cousin! You are a
better-bred lady than to expect it.

FRIENDALL Conscience, madam, is for serious affairs; 395
nobody minds it at play.

MRS TEAZALL Nay, I'm even right enough served. I
deserved it, that's the truth on't. I must be playing with
company so much younger than myself, but I shall be
wiser for the future, and play the fool in my own form,* 400
where I may cheat in my turn.

MRS FRIENDALL If you speak of your losings, madam, I
believe my fortune has been harder than yours. In ten
sets* running with Mr Wilding, I never turned one,* nor
had comet in my hand.*   405

MRS WITWOUD <*aside to* WILDING> Nay, if you win her
money, you may win everything of her, if you know how
to manage your game.

(*Goes to* MRS SIGHTLY)

WILDING And, faith, I'll play it as well as I can.

MRS WITWOUD Cousin, I have won an estate for you.   410

MRS SIGHTLY You have undone me.

　　　　　[*Exit* <MRS SIGHTLY>, MRS WITWOUD *following*]

WILDING I'll watch my time, and follow 'em.

FRIENDALL Lovemore, prithee keep the company together.
　　I have an appointment upon my hands, and must leave
　　you. We must serve one another sometimes, you know. 415
　　　　　　　　　　　　　　　　　　　　[*Goes off*]

　　　　　　　　　(SERVANT *enters*)

SERVANT Madam, the Jew, newly turned Protestant,* that
　　my master was godfather to, has brought the essences and
　　sweet-waters* he ordered him to raffle for.*

MRS FRIENDALL Shall we try whether we like any of 'em?

　　　　　　　　　　　(*Going*)

WELLVILE We shall find him a Jew still in his dealings, I 420
　　suppose.

LOVEMORE You would not have him lose by his conver-
　　sion, I hope.

WILDING Like other wise men, he's for saving soul and
　　body together, I warrant him.   425

　　　　　　　　　(*They go in*)

Act 4, Scene 2

Scene changes to the garden

(*Enter* MRS WITWOUD *following* MRS SIGHTLY)

MRS SIGHTLY Never think of denying, or excusing it to me,
　　I am satisfied there's more in't than you ought to defend.
　　There are so many circumstances to convince me of your
　　treachery to me, I must believe it.

MRS WITWOUD I see, cousin, you will believe anything   5
　　against me. But as I hope to be saved, upon the faith of a

Christian, and may I never rise off my knees into your good opinion again, if I don't abhor the villainy you lay to my charge. Something I must confess to you, but I beg you to forgive me. 'Twas unadvised* indeed, but inno- 10 cent, and without a design upon you. Courtall's a coxcomb; and nothing but Wilding's vanity or Wellvile's revenge could be accessory to the ruin of me with you, the only relation I love and value in the world.

MRS SIGHTLY Oh, I had forgot the pains you took to 15 secure me tomorrow night at cards, at your lodgings with Mr Wilding! Cousin, let me tell you, a bawd is the worst part of an intrigue, and the least to be said for't in excuse of the infamy. But you had something more than a lover to provide for me, or you would not have exposed me to a 20 man that would expose me to all the town. Is it because I have been your best and last friend – for you will hardly find such another in your family – that thus you reward me for the folly? Or is it because I am a witness of your shame, that you would be a contriver of mine? I know 25 (and I look upon it as a judgment upon the former follies of your life) that you are notoriously abandoned to the beastly love of a fellow that nobody else can look upon. And, maybe, you are mischievously pleased to make me as despicable as yourself. There must be the devil in the 30 bottom on't, and I'll fly from him in you.

MRS WITWOUD Oh, don't leave me in this passion! I am utterly ruined if you go. Upon my knees, I beg it of you.

MRS SIGHTLY Cousin, I forgive you. What's past shall be a secret for both our sakes. But I'm resolved never more to 35 come into your power; so farewell, and find a better friend than I have been.

[Goes out]

MRS WITWOUD She's lost, and my design upon her, which is yet a greater misfortune to me.

(<WELLVILE and> WILDING <enter> to her)

(to WILDING) Oh sir, I am obliged to you, and you are 40 obliged to yourself for your success with Mrs Sightly. So

like a boy, to discover the secret before 'twas in your
power to expose! Away, I'll have no more to say to you.

[*Goes out*]

WILDING So, sir, you have made fine work on't with the
women.* I thought I had satisfied you in the Mall this   45
morning.

WELLVILE Sir, I must be better satisfied than I was in the
morning. I find there's no relying upon your word, since,
after your promise never to follow her more, you could
excuse yourself to me in the Mall, to meet her at the   50
chocolate-house.

WILDING Nay then, we have both our grievances, <*draws
his sword*> and this must answer 'em.

(*Going to fight.* COURTALL *enters to part them*)

COURTALL Fie, fie, friends, and fighting! That must not be,
gentlemen. Mrs Witwoud has told me the matter; and   55
unless you had a fourth man to entertain me, you had
ev'n as good put up again. We are all in fault, and all
deserve to be swinged* for't, that's certain. Wilding was a
fool for telling me of his design; and I was a fool for
talking on't to Wellvile; and Wellvile no wiser than either   60
for making such a bustle about it. Therefore, pray,
gentlemen, let's agree in this opinion: that by our own
prating and prying into other people's affairs, we often
discover and ruin one another's designs.
For women are by nature well inclined;   65
Our follies frighten 'em from being kind.

[*Exeunt*]

Act 5, Scene 1

MRS WITWOUD's *lodgings*

(*Enter* WILDING *following* MRS WITWOUD)

MRS WITWOUD Nay, I don't wonder you thrive no better
with the women, when you can part with such an

advantage over Mrs Friendall. You say you have won a
sum of her which she would not be known to lose. Why,
another man would take the privilege of a winning   5
gamester upon such on occasion, to press her to a
promise, at least, of coming out of her debt.

WILDING I shall improve, I find, upon the advantage of
your hints. But Mrs Sightly, madam –

MRS WITWOUD Aye, Mrs Sightly, indeed! Was that a   10
woman to throw away upon the vanity of being talked of
for her? In the time you were bragging to other people of
being in her favour, you might have been everywhere you
desired.

WILDING Nay, not unlikely.   15

MRS WITWOUD I have made all the excuse I could for you;
some too, that in my conscience I thought very unreasonable myself, and could pass upon nobody but a woman
that was easily disposed to forgive you.

WILDING If she would but hear what I have to say for   20
myself.

MRS WITWOUD Nay, she's pretty well prepared. But you
must not think of speaking to her bare-faced – that she
can't consent to, for her own sake. You have made the
matter so public, she has eyes upon her, to be sure, now.   25
But it happens very luckily, Friendall has a masquerade
tonight at his house. There, if you please, I can give you
an opportunity of clearing yourself to her.

WILDING I ask no more of you.

MRS WITWOUD Never think of defending yourself; for   30
what's past, you were certainly i' th' wrong; and she
thinks you so. You know well enough what to say to a
woman that has a mind to believe you.

WILDING How shall I know her at the masquerade?

MRS WITWOUD Go, you, and prepare for 't; and depend   35
upon me for your intelligence.*

[WILDING *goes out*]

I find I am declining in my reputation; and will bring
every woman of my acquaintance into my own condition,
of being suspected, at least. I have promised more than I

can do with my cousin Sightly. I have lost my credit with   40
her too lately to betray her in the way of friendship. Let
me see. <calls> Betty!

(BETTY enters)

You know where the man lives that made my cousin
Sightly's scarf. Go to him from me; desire him to borrow
it, that a lady may see it, who likes it and desires to have   45
one made of the same pattern.

[Exit BETTY]

I despair of bringing her to the masquerade. I must
personate* her myself, and meet Wilding in her room.*
But what may be the issue of that? Let what will be the
issue. The farther he presses his design upon me, the   50
farther I carry my design upon her. And for once, in order
to my revenge, rather than not expose her, I'll venture to
grant him the favour* – that he may tell on't, and she
have the benefit of the scandal.

[Goes out]

Act 5, Scene 2

In St James's Park

(<Enter> LOVEMORE, with MRS FRIENDALL, and MRS
SIGHTLY)

LOVEMORE Yonder comes Mr Friendall, madam.
MRS FRIENDALL Would I were at home again. I came upon
  a foolish discovery of his actions, to be surprised in a very
  unaccountable one of my own.
MRS SIGHTLY That is, walking incognito on this side the   5
  Park with a man of your character, Mr Lovemore.
MRS FRIENDALL I hope he won't know us.

(They put on their masks)

MRS SIGHTLY He's too busy in his own affairs.
LOVEMORE He comes upon us. I must speak to him.

(FRIENDALL *enters*)

FRIENDALL You are provided for, I see. The ladies, I   10
suppose, wish I could say as much for them, too. Very
genteel women both, faith and troth. I warrant 'em
women of condition, if not women of quality,* by their
assignation at Rosamond's Pond.

LOVEMORE You fancy that from the quality of your own   15
intrigue.

FRIENDALL Why, there's something in that too. And the
truth on't is, my assignation is with a woman of quality.

LOVEMORE Mrs Sightly, I fancy, Friendall.

FRIENDALL Fie, fie, why should you think so? But let her   20
be who she will, if she disappoint me, I'll own it
tomorrow to everybody –

LOVEMORE That she disappointed you?

FRIENDALL No, that 'twas Mrs Sightly I had an intrigue
with.   25

MRS SIGHTLY <*aside*> A small matter makes an intrigue of
his side, I find.

FRIENDALL (*viewing his wife*) Sure, I have seen somebody
very like this lady?

MRS FRIENDALL <*aside*> I would not be known for the   30
world.

LOVEMORE <*aside to her*> I'll bring you off, I warrant you.

FRIENDALL She has the air and mien very much of a lady
of my acquaintance.

LOVEMORE Not unlikely, faith. It may be she herself, for   35
ought I know to the contrary. But if you have a mind to
be satisfied –

MRS FRIENDALL <*aside*> Lord! What do you do?

LOVEMORE I have no occasion for her at present.
(<*indicates*>MRS SIGHTLY) This is my woman. <*of* MRS   40
FRIENDALL> She's but an ill-natured encumbrance, at
this time; and you'll do me a favour to dispose of her.

FRIENDALL Nay, if you are so free to dispose of her, I'm
satisfied she is not the woman I took her for. For to tell
you the truth, Lovemore, I thought 'twas my wife. And,   45
egad, I began to be very uneasy; not so much for finding

her in your company, as that she should come so
peevishly* to disturb me in an affair so very much above
her.

MRS SIGHTLY Why, sir, they say your wife is a very fine   50
woman.

FRIENDALL A wife a fine woman, madam? I never knew a
husband that thought so in my life.

MRS FRIENDALL But somebody else may, sir, if you allow
her to make these entertainments for the town that I hear   55
you do.

FRIENDALL Gad so, Lovemore, prithee bring the ladies to
my masquerade tonight. There's nobody but people of
quality to be there, for pleasure is my business, you know;
and I am very well pleased to allow my wife the liberties   60
she takes, in favour of my own.* For to tell you the truth,
the chief end of my marrying her (next to having the
estate settled upon me) was to carry on my intrigues more
swimmingly with the ladies.

LOVEMORE That's a convenience in matrimony, I did not   65
think of.

FRIENDALL One of the greatest, upon my word, sir. For
being seen so often abroad, and visiting with my wife, I
pass upon the formal part of the town for a very good
husband; and upon the privilege of that character, I grow   70
intimate with all her acquaintance. And, by the way,
there's hardly a family in town, but I can contrive to come
acquainted with, upon her account. There I pick and
choose in the very face of their reverend relations, and
deliver my billets myself.

MRS FRIENDALL You have 'em ready then?   75

FRIENDALL Two or three, always in my pocket. (*shows
'em*) I write half a dozen in a morning, for the service of
that day.

LOVEMORE Hard service, I assure you.   80

FRIENDALL Not at all. The letters are but copies one of
another; and a love-letter should be a love-letter, you
know – passionate and tender, whoever 'tis designed for.
Ha! Yonder are two women in masks! I must not be seen

with you. Ladies, you know when you're well, I suppose,   85
by the choice of your man. Make much of him, he's my
bosom friend, and confidant of my pleasures.

MRS FRIENDALL And you of his, I suppose? There's no
pleasure without a confidant.

FRIENDALL Faith, madam, I am of your mind. But Love-   90
more's a little too reserved. 'Tis, at present, his fault, from
a want of knowing the town; but he'll mend of it, I hope,
when he comes to have a woman worth talking of.
Lovemore, not a word at home of seeing me here, as you
value the fortune of your friend. Adieu.   95

[*Goes out*]

MRS FRIENDALL Are you the confidant of the gentleman's
pleasures?

LOVEMORE I have not betrayed 'em, madam.

MRS FRIENDALL Methinks a friend should have warned
me of 'em.   100

LOVEMORE I would not be thought to do ill offices,
especially in marriage, madam.

MRS FRIENDALL I don't think you would. (*aside*) Would
Mr Friendall were as tender of wronging me.

MRS SIGHTLY You have had a handsome account of their   105
expedition. And we are both obliged to Mr Friendall.

MRS FRIENDALL I am very well paid for my curiosity of
coming here. I suppose we shall have a rendezvous of his
wenches at the masquerade. Pray, let's be ready to receive
'em.   110

[*Exeunt*]

Act 5, Scene 3

FRIENDALL's *house*

(<*Enter*> MEN *and* WOMEN *in masquerading habit,*
<*including*> WELLVILE, WILDING, COURTALL,
SPRINGAME, MRS WITWOUD *and* BETTY <*with*
MUSICIANS>)

MRS WITWOUD <*to* BETTY> Wilding has his eye upon us, I
see. I have something to say to him in my own person,
and then I must change scarves with you. Be sure you are
i'th'way.*

WELLVILE (*to* BETTY) I thought I had known you.* I beg   5
your pardon, madam, for the mistake.

BETTY You're very welcome to't, sir. I would have you
mistaken, and that you will always be, when you judge
upon the outsides of the women.

WELLVILE You are for a stricter examination, I find. There   10
are conveniences for a full discovery in the next room.
Somebody will show you the way.

(*Leaves her*)

WILDING That's Sightly in the scarf, and Mrs Witwoud
with her, I suppose. I must not be mistaken.

COURTALL I like the freedom of a masquerade, very well;   15
but it confounds* a man's choice.

SPRINGAME Why, faith, I have a mind to be particular* if I
could but hit upon the woman.

MRS WITWOUD <*aside*> And that you shall presently, little
captain, I'll put myself in your way.   20

SPRINGAME (*to* BETTY) Behind a cloud my pretty moon!
Shall I be the man in you?

BETTY With the bush* at your backside! You deserve to be
whipped for your wit, sir.

(*Goes from him*)

SPRINGAME I stand corrected, madam.   25

MRS WITWOUD Does she beat thee, little master? Come
a' me,* and I'll make much of thee.

SPRINGAME As much as you can of me, I dare say for you.

MRS WITWOUD Come, come, I'll use you better.

SPRINGAME To use me worse. Is not that your design? She 30
has given me my answer at once. You, perhaps, would
linger me through a winter's expectation, and not do my
business at last.

MRS WITWOUD What's your business, pray?

SPRINGAME Why your business, any woman's business, 35
that has a mind to employ me in't.

MRS WITWOUD No touching me. I have an unfashionable
husband in the company that won't thank you for making
him a cuckold.

SPRINGAME But you will, I'm sure, if it be but to teach him 40
better manners.

MRS WITWOUD I like your company extremely; but I have
a great deal of business, and would willingly be rid of
you, at this time. But this ring <gives it him> shall answer
for me, till I see you again. 45

(Going)

SPRINGAME Pray redeem it as soon as you can.

MRS WITWOUD Sir, sir, if you have any interest in the
family, pray let's have a song, or a dance to divert us.

SPRINGAME I'll see what I can do for you.

(Goes away)

MRS WITWOUD You should be Wilding. 50

WILDING And you should be as good as your word.

MRS WITWOUD The lady is better than you can expect.
That's she in the embroidered scarf. You must not speak
to her before the company. Take her aside, by and by, in a
corner. She'll thank you for your care of her. Here's more 55
company. I won't be seen with you.

(LOVEMORE *enters with* MRS FRIENDALL *and* MRS
SIGHTLY)

<aside to BETTY> Now, Betty, for the change.

(MRS WITWOUD *and* BETTY *go out*)

WELLVILE Lovemore, I am in disgrace with Mrs Sightly, and can't find her, to come into favour again.

LOVEMORE That's she, that came in just now with Mrs 60 Friendall. I'll direct you to one, by going to the other.

(*They go to 'em. The* MUSICIANS *perform a song*)

Song

(*Written by Thomas Cheek, Esq.*)*

Corinna, I excuse thy face,
The erring lines which Nature drew,
  When I reflect that every grace
  Thy mind adorns is just and true.   65
But oh, thy wit, what god has sent?
  Surprising, airy, unconfined!
Some wonder, sure, Apollo* meant,
  And shot himself into thy mind.

(*After the song,* MRS WITWOUD *and* BETTY, *having
changed scarves, enter, to be ready for the dance, after
which* –)

LOVEMORE <*to* MRS FRIENDALL> Some can't get hus- 70
bands, and others can't get rid of 'em.

MRS FRIENDALL Every woman carries her cross in this world. A husband happens to be mine, and I must bear it, as well as I can.

LOVEMORE I would ease you of it.   75

MRS FRIENDALL No more upon this subject; you have carried the argument so far, 'tis allowing what you say, to listen any longer. But, Mr Lovemore, I will give you what satisfaction I have in my power, and praise is the reward of virtue, you know. I think you have proceeded like a 80 man of experience in this business, and taken the natural road to undermine most women. I must do you this justice, that nothing has been wanting on your side.

LOVEMORE I would have nothing wanting on my side, madam.   85

MRS FRIENDALL And however you came by the knowledge

of Mr Friendall's weaknesses, you have improved 'em* as
much as they could bear upon the conduct of his wife. If
they have not carried me as far as you designed, 'tis the
fault of my heaviness,* perhaps, that can't be transported   90
into the woman you'd have me.

LOVEMORE There's a fault somewhere.

MRS FRIENDALL Mr Lovemore, some women won't speak
so plain, but I will own to you, I can't think the worse of
you for thinking well of me. Nay, I don't blame you for   95
designing upon me. Custom has fashioned it into the way
of living among the men; and you may be i' th' right to all
the town. But let me be i' th' right too, to my sex and to
myself.

Thus far may be excused.   100
You've proved your passion and my virtue tried;
But all beyond that trial* is my crime,
And not to be forgiven.

Therefore, I entreat you, don't make it impossible to me
for the future, to receive you as a friend; for I must own, 105
I would secure you always for my friend.
Nay more, I will confess my heart to you.
If I could make you mine –

LOVEMORE   Forever yours.

MRS FRIENDALL But I am married; only pity me.*

(*Goes from him*)

LOVEMORE Pity her! She does not deserve it, that won't   110
better her condition when she may. But she's married, she
says. Why, that was the best of my reasons of following
her at first; and I like her so well as she's another man's
wife, I should hardly mend the matter by making her my
own. I won't think yet my two months' thrown away on   115
her. One time or other, some way or other, I may be the
better for her, at least with some other women. But I
begin to believe that every man loses his labour this way
sometimes.

MRS SIGHTLY (*observing* WILDING *and* MRS WITWOUD)
Who can that woman be?   120

WELLVILE Wilding's the man, I know.

MRS SIGHTLY Then it may be my good cousin Witwoud.

WELLVILE Presuming upon the scarf, which is very like
   yours, I ventured, and spake to her. I should have known
   Mrs Witwoud, I believe.   125

MRS SIGHTLY Pray try if you can learn who she is.

(They parl* in a low voice)

MRS WITWOUD This place is too public for a vindication of
   this nature. If you retire into the next room, I may accept
   of your excuses upon your promise of good behaviour,
   and better conduct for the future.   130

WILDING I'll follow you.

(MRS WITWOUD *retires,* WELLVILE *<goes> to* WILDING)

WELLVILE You will be the man I see, Wilding. The lady's
   withdrawn, don't let her stay for you.*

WILDING Faith, Wellvile, 'tis a fortune thrown upon me.
   And since it came without my seeking, methinks you   135
   should hardly think it worth your courting. She'll bring it
   about one way or other, you find.

WELLVILE You speak as if I knew the lady.

WILDING I would have you know so much: that she is not
   worth the honourable care you have of her.   140

WELLVILE Of whom?

WILDING As if you did not know her.

WELLVILE Why, 'tis not Mrs Sightly.

WILDING I have declined it as much as I could in regard to
   a friend; but when she follows me –   145

WELLVILE Mrs Sightly follow you!

(FRIENDALL *enters and joins with* LOVEMORE)

WILDING No naming names, good Wellvile.

WELLVILE Nay, then I must convince you. I just left Mrs
   Sightly to come to you. She's now in the company, and I'll
   carry you to hear me speak to her.   150

(Carries WILDING *to* MRS SIGHTLY)

LOVEMORE Why, this was a terrible disappointment.

FRIENDALL There are lampoons, sir, I say no more; but I may do myself reason* in one of 'em, and disappoint her yet to her disappointment.*

(*Among the* WOMEN, <FRIENDALL> *fastens upon* MRS SIGHTLY)

WILDING Why then, Witwoud has put another woman 155 upon me, and abused Mrs Sightly and me. I am satisfied of the cheat, and would be assisting to the revenge of it if I could.

WELLVILE You would not be the instrument, to make it public yourself?   160

WILDING No, that I can't consent to.

WELLVILE Then leave it to me. Friendall's a property* fit for our several interests; but Lovemore must employ him.

(WELLVILE <goes> to LOVEMORE)

FRIENDALL Faith, madam, I am very fit for your purpose, at present. I have met with a little ill usage from a lady by 165 not meeting with her. But you may be the better for it, if you please. You shall have the pleasure, and she shall have the reputation of the intrigue.

MRS SIGHTLY I am for all or none.

(LOVEMORE *comes to him*)

LOVEMORE The rarest accident, Friendall. The reason that 170 you were disappointed in the Park, I can tell you, was the lady had appointed to meet Wilding here. She is now withdrawn into the next room in expectation of him; which Wellvile, her old lover, suspecting, has taxed him of, and ruined the design. Now if you would have me, I'll 175 keep up the jealousy between 'em, and give you an opportunity to go in to her.

FRIENDALL By all means, Lovemore. This was unexpected, and done like a friend. I owe you a good turn for't. Be sure you keep 'em here.   180

(*Sneaks out after* WITWOUD)

MRS SIGHTLY (*to* WELLVILE) What are you designing upon Mr Friendall?

WELLVILE There's mischief in't; and you may all be the better for't.

(*<Enter>* MRS TEAZALL *pressing in with a* FOOTMAN *upon the company*)

MRS FRIENDALL What's the noise there?   185

FOOTMAN Madam, here's a rude, unmannerly gentle-woman presses in upon me, and refuses to pull off her mask,* as your honour ordered.

MRS TEAZALL You saucy rascal you! I show a better face than thy mother had, when she laid thee to the parish,*   190 you rogue! Prate to me, you varlet! And an honester one, though I say it, than any of the company. Here's fine work, indeed, in a civil family! What, are you ashamed of your doings, that you won't discover yourselves?

SPRINGAME Mistress, you have the natural privilege of a   195 mask. And being disguised in your own face, you may say what you please.

MRS TEAZALL Marry come up, here; will nothing but a good face down with you? A woman has a fine time on't, with your finical fancy; but I want leisure to laugh at you.   200

(*Looking everywhere for her* NIECE)

COURTALL Do you know me?

MRS TEAZALL Aye, aye, I guess at you. Learn to speak without a question,* you fool, before you set up for a wit.

COURTALL I know you.

MRS TEAZALL Why then you may be satisfied, I shall think   205 you an ass.

SPRINGAME Nay, good mother, you had e'en as good pull off your mask. You see you are discovered.

MRS TEAZALL Discovered, you snotty-nosed jackanapes! Would I could discover your master; I would send him a   210 note of your name. You are not yet clean from school, and are setting up for the women, forsooth. You have been so used to be turned up for a blockhead,* as you are,

for peeping into everybody's backdoor to find as great a
fool as yourself. Sirrah, sirrah, a good birch rod for your   215
mistress! That would tickle your tail,* as you deserve.

SPRINGAME Nay, good your reverence.

MRS FRIENDALL What's the matter, pray?

MRS TEAZALL Why, the wicked ways of living in this town
are matter enough for the vexation of any woman that   220
has a girl to look after. God's my life! Can't you keep up
your masquerades in the primitive institution of making
cuckolds, as it used to be,* without bringing the young
wenches into the mystery of matrimony before their time?
Where's my niece among you? 'Tis a burning shame to   225
draw away a poor young girl into these deboist,*
galloping doings, as you do.

MRS FRIENDALL Good Mrs Teazall, not so censorious.
Pray, where's the harm of a little innocent diversion?

MRS TEAZALL Innocent diversion, with a pox to't! For that   230
will be the end on't at last. Very innocent diversion
indeed! Why, your music-meetings, dancing-meetings,
masquing-meetings, are all but pretences to bring you
together. And when you meet, we know what you meet
for well enough. 'Tis to the same purpose, in good troth.   235
All ends in the innocent diversion.

WELLVILE Nay, faith, the gentlewoman has reason for
what she says.

MRS TEAZALL Well, make me thankful for it! There's one
civil gentleman among you. And, really, there's a great   240
deal of comfort in opening a poor woman's case* to a
discreet, good-natured gentleman. Pray, sir, hear me; and
if you don't allow that I have some cause for what I do, I
will be contented never to see coat-card,* nor have Pam
in my pocket again.   245

MRS FRIENDALL But who are you looking for all this
while?

MRS TEAZALL An untowardly* girl, to be sure, my cousin
Fanny, madam. She has undone herself, and my hopes of
a husband for her. Gad forgive me, I have no patience,   250
when I think upon't. Last night, Witwoud, forsooth, she

carries her to the music-meeting. Then one Wilding, an impudent, whore-mastering fellow, he carries her home with him, which I could forgive well enough too, if it ended there; but now, when all things were agreed upon, and Mr Buttybun* was to give us a supper and sign the writings,* in order to marry her tomorrow; when the baggage was called upon to perform her part, whip, she has given us the slip, tucked up her tail, and run a-roguing after that fellow again. But I shall light upon her.

LOVEMORE Wilding, what say you to this?

MRS TEAZALL Oh, sir, are you there? If there be any justice in England for the women, I'll have you bound to the good behaviour. I'll swear the peace against you myself. For there's nobody safe, young or old, at this rate, if such whore-masters as you are allowed to do as you do.

WILDING I am bound already to behave myself like a gentleman. I do what good I can, in my generation,* but injure nobody.

MRS TEAZALL Sirrah, sirrah, you shall find you have injured my niece, and me, before I have done with you.

WILDING You won't bring it to Westminster, I hope, to be decided who has most injured her; I, by being civil to her, or you, by telling it to all the town.

MRS TEAZALL Why that's true again.

WILDING And let the company judge who appears to be most her enemy – I, in teaching her a very good trade;* or you, in endeavouring to break* her before she's well set up in't.

COURTALL (to MRS TEAZALL) Nay, now it goes against you.

WILDING I have put her in a very good way. If she manage it well, she'll make more on't, than her mother made of her matrimony.

MRS TEAZALL Nay, 'twas the ruin of her, that I grant you.

WILDING And let the worst come to the worst, if she fails in this calling, she may begin in another, as they do in the city sometimes. 'Tis but setting up for a husband at last.

MRS TEAZALL But that you won't consent to, it seems.

WILDING Faith, madam, I ha'nt seen your niece since 290
morning; and then Mrs Witwoud obliged me to give over
my pretensions to her, upon the promise of procuring Mrs
Sightly for me.

MRS SIGHTLY Without my knowledge, sir?

WILDING Indeed, madam, you were not to know of the 295
bargain.

MRS TEAZALL Then you don't know where Fanny is?

WILDING Not I, faith, madam.

WELLVILE We were just complaining of Mrs Witwoud's
unkindness to you, as you came in. 300

MRS TEAZALL Aye, sir, I am beholding to you.

WELLVILE She has been very busy all this night in carrying
on an intrigue between your niece and somebody. They
are retired into the next room. They went out at that
door, if you have a mind to be satisfied. 305

MRS TEAZALL I'm sorry, sir, I hadn't time to thank you for
this favour. I must make haste, for I'm resolved to be
satisfied.

(Scene draws, shows FRIENDALL and MRS WITWOUD
upon a couch)

Very fine! Here is a sight indeed!

MRS WITWOUD Confusion! 310

FRIENDALL What a pox! Disturb a gentleman's pleasures!
And in his own house too! <sees who she is> Ha!
Witwoud here! Nay then, would you had come sooner.
<to MRS WITWOUD> Madam, I beg your pardon for
some liberties I have taken with your ladyship. But, faith, 315
I took you for Mrs Sightly.

MRS WITWOUD I never was mistaken in you.

WILDING You see I had too great a respect for you, and
therefore provided you a more deserving –

MRS WITWOUD Fool. 320

WELLVILE And one that had as good-natured a design
upon Mrs Sightly, as you had yourself.

MRS TEAZALL Nay, now, gentlewoman, I think 'tis come
home to you, and I am glad on't, with all my heart.

MRS SIGHTLY You have paid dear enough for that scarf; 325
you may keep it for a pattern for your friends, as 'twas
borrowed for. I won't insult over you, and am only
pleased that I have scaped your snares.

MRS WITWOUD That disappointment is my greatest curse;
and disappointments light upon you all! 330

[Goes out]

COURTALL This is your mistress, captain.

SPRINGAME And, egad, she shall be mine now, in spite of
her teeth.* For since I find she can be civil upon occasion,
I shall beat her into good manners, if she refuses me.

(Goes after her)

WELLVILE (to MRS SIGHTLY) Everything has fallen so 335
much to your advantage, that sure the fault I made may
be forgiven. What amends I have in my power, I am ready
to make you.
My liberty, of what I have to give,*
Is what I value most; and that is yours, 340
When you consent to let me make you mine.

MRS SIGHTLY This is too sudden to be serious.
When you're in earnest, you won't need an answer.*

WILDING They are striking up a peace on all hands,
gentlemen; we shall be left out of the treaty. 345

LOVEMORE There's yet a lady to declare herself.

MRS FRIENDALL Mr Friendall, I'm sorry you thought it
necessary to your pleasures to make me a witness of my ill
usage.
You know I can, and have passed* many things 350
Some women would think wrongs,
As such, resent 'em, and return 'em, too.
But you can tell how I've behaved myself.*

FRIENDALL Like a gentlewoman always, madam, and my
wife.
355
MRS FRIENDALL The unjust world,
Let what will be cause* of our complaint
(As there is cause sufficient still at home)
Condemn us to slavery* for life.

And if by separation we get free,   360
Then all our husband's faults are laid on us.
This hard condition of a woman's fate
I've often weighed, therefore resolved to bear.
And I have born. Oh, what have I not born?
But patience tires with such oppressing wrongs,   365
When they come home to triumph over me;
And tell the town how much I am despised.*

FRIENDALL I see we are both disappointed in this affair of
matrimony. It is not the condition you expected; nor has
it the advantages I proposed. Now, madam, since 'tis 370
impossible to make it happy between us, let us ev'n
resolve to make it as easy as we can.

MRS FRIENDALL That must be my business now.

FRIENDALL And mine too, I assure you. Look you,
madam, your own relations shall provide for you at 375
pleasure, out of my estate. I only article* that I may
have a freedom of visiting you, in the round of my
acquaintance.

MRS FRIENDALL I must be still your wife, and still
unhappy.   380

LOVEMORE <aside> What alteration this may make in my
fortune with her, I don't know; but I'm glad I have parted
'em.

FRIENDALL Well, gentlemen, I can't be very much displeased at the recovery of my liberty. I am only sorry 385
Witwoud was the occasion of it. For an old, blown-upon*
she-wit is hardly an intrigue to justify the separation on
my side, or make a man very vain of his fortune.

LOVEMORE <to the audience> This you must all expect,
who marry fools;
Unless you form 'em early in your schools,   390
And make 'em, what they were designed for, tools.*

<Exeunt>

Epilogue

Spoken by Mrs Barry

My character, not being much in vogue,
Has drawn me in to speak the epilogue.
But, pray, conceive me right, not to disparage
That ancient, English perquisite of marriage,
Which, when the priests first made all pleasure sin,   5
Faster than they could cheat us, drew us in
With rites and liberties of cuckolding.
That used to be the custom, and so common,
No girl but wished herself a married woman.
Whether I've done my husband right, or no,   10
Most women may be in the right that do.
Our author does not set up for reforming,*
Or giving hints to fools who won't take warning.
He's pleased that other people are pleased too
To help to reap that harvest which they sow.   15
For among all the cuckolds of this town
Who show themselves, and are as daily shown,
Our poets may make some of 'em their own.
You find in me what may excuse a wife.
Compare at home the picture with the life,   20
And most of you may find a Friendall there,
And most of you more justly used than here.
Our author has his ends, if he can show
The women ne'er want cause for what they do.
For, ladies, all his aim is pleasing you.   25
Some mettled sparks, whom nothing can withstand –
Your velvet* fortune-hunters – may demand
Why, when the means were in the lady's hand,
The husband civil, and the lover near,
No more was made of the wife's character?   30
'Damn me,' cries one, 'had I been Betterton,'*
And struts and cocks,* 'I know what I had done;
She should not ha' got clear of me so soon.'

You only fear such plays may spoil your game.
But flesh and frailty always are the same;   35
And we shall still proceed in our old way,
For all that you can do, or poets say.

Appendix to *The Wives' Excuse*

A Song, in the first scene of the fourth act*

Hang this whining way of wooing,
Loving was designed a sport;
Sighing, talking, without doing,
Makes a silly, idle court.

Don't believe that words can move her,   5
If she be not well inclined;
She herself must be the lover,
To persuade her to be kind.

If at last, she grants the favour
And consents to be undone: 10
Never think your* passion gave her
To your wishes, but her own.

NOTES

The following abbreviations are used in the notes:

Behn. The Works of Aphra Behn, ed. Montague Summers, 6 vols (1915).

Cordner. *Four Restoration Marriage Plays*, ed. Michael Cordner with Ronald Clayton (World's Classics Series, Oxford, 1995).

Dearing & Roper. *The Works of John Dryden*, Vol. XIV, *Plays*, ed. Vinton A. Dearing & Alan Roper (Berkeley, California, 1992).

Ghosh. *The Works of Thomas Otway*, ed. J. C. Ghosh, 2 vols (Oxford, 1932; reprtd 1968).

Hall. Molière, *Le Bourgeois Gentilhomme*, ed. H. Gaston Hall (1966).

Holland. Peter Holland, *The Ornament of Action: Text and Performance in Restoration Comedy* (Cambridge, 1979).

Milhous & Hume. *A Register of English Theatrical Documents 1660–1737*, ed. Judith Milhous & Robert D. Hume (1991).

Jordan & Love. *The Works of Thomas Southerne*, ed. Robert Jordan & Harold Love, 2 vols (Oxford, 1988).

Love. *The Works of John Wilmot, Earl of Rochester*, ed. Harold Love (Oxford, 1999).

Link. Aphra Behn, *The Rover*, ed. Frederick M. Link (Lincoln, Neb., 1967).

OED. *Oxford English Dictionary*.

Q1. The earliest (and, in some cases, the only) quarto edition of the respective play.

Q2. The 2nd quarto edition of the respective play.

Q3. The 3rd quarto edition.

Q4. The 4th quarto edition.

Roxburghe. The Roxburghe Ballads, ed. J. Woodfall Ebsworth (1888; reprtd. AMS Press Inc., New York, 1966), VI.

Shadwell. The Complete Works of Thomas Shadwell, ed. Montague Summers, 5 vols (1927).

Taylor. Thomas Otway, *The Orphan*, ed. Aline Mackenzie Taylor (1977).

Thomaso. Thomas Killigrew, Thomaso, Or The Wanderer (1663).

Thornton. Thomas Southerne, *The Wives' Excuse or Cuckolds Make Themselves*, ed. Ralph R. Thornton (Wynnewood, Pa., 1973).

Tilley. Morris Palmer Tilley, *A Dictionary of Proverbs in England in the Sixteenth and Seventeenth Centuries* (Ann Arbor, Mich., 1950).

Todd. *The Works of Aphra Behn*, ed. Janet Todd, 7 vols (Columbus, Ohio, 1992–6).

Winn. James A. Winn, *John Dryden and His World* (New Haven, 1987).

Works (1713). *The Works of Mr Thomas Southerne*, 2 vols (1713).

References to Shakespeare are to *The Norton Shakespeare*, ed. Stephen Greenblatt, et al. (New York & London, 1997).

Dates given for Restoration plays are those of their earliest recorded performance, unless otherwise stated.

MARRIAGE A-LA-MODE

Epigraph

Quicquid . . . solido: 'Such as I am, however far beneath Lucilius in rank and native gifts, yet Envy, in spite of herself, will ever admit that I have lived with the great, and, while trying to strike her tooth on something soft, will dash upon what is solid.' (Horace, *Satires*, II.1. 74–9, translated by H. R. Fairclough (Loeb Series, Heinemann, London, 1926, reprtd 1970), p.133.)

Dedication

Rochester: John Wilmot, 2nd Earl of Rochester (1647–80): poet, patron and the most brilliant (and notorious) of the Court Wits.

8 Windsor: The king was there from 27 May to 13 July 1671.

12 *ver sacrum*: literally 'holy spring', i.e. sacrifices of the first spring lambs.

17 conversation: circle of acquaintance.

17–18 this way: Dryden always maintained that comedy was not his forte.

30 interest: self-interest.

31 assurance of: trust in.

33 want: lack.

41 their wit: the wit of those.

51 habitude: familiarity.

66 contemned: scorned.

98 policy: craftiness.

107 papers: copies. Rochester's poetry, like that of most Restoration courtiers, circulated mainly in manuscript during his lifetime.

107–8 you ... play: Rochester's only complete play, *Valentinian*, was written probably *c.*1675–6, performed 1684 and published in 1685.

110–13 Your ... them: Warning or foreboding? By 1675 Rochester had fallen out with Dryden and satirised him and other writers in 'An Allusion to Horace'.

116 Swissers: the politically negligible Swiss cantons.

Prologue

The prologue and epilogue were first printed in *Covent Garden Drolery* (1672). There, the prologue is assigned to Charles Hart who created the role of Palamede; and the epilogue to Michael Mohun who acted Rhodophil.

2 braves: fighting men.

gone: to prepare for the 3rd Dutch War (declared March 1672).

3 Fop-corner: front corner of the pit (near the stage) where fashionable young men gathered.

4 White-wig: fop. Blond wigs were then in fashion.

vizard-mask: slang for a prostitute, since vizard-masks (face-masks) were often worn by such. Most editions read 'vizard make' here, but see Paul Hammond, 'The Prologue and Epilogue to Dryden's *Marriage A-la-Mode* and the problem of *Covent Garden Drollery*', *Papers of the Bibliographical Society of America*, 81, 2 (1987), 169–70.

jar: cause a disturbance.

5 France: England's ally against the Dutch.

6 That ... hear: Restoration audiences were noted for rowdiness.

8–9 warriors ... tiring-room: Soldiers wore red coats and had tied-back hair/wigs. The backstage dressing-room ('tiring-room') was much frequented by admirers of the actors.

15 friends: lovers.

16 grinning honour: death. See Falstaff's comment (*I Henry IV*, V. 3.57–8).

20 punk: prostitute.

22 half-crown: the price of a seat in the pit; also, the usual charge for a prostitute.

23 the Mall: fashionable walk (and pick-up spot) near St James's Park.

24 city friends: a condescending reference to middle-class citizens or tradespeople.

26 elsewhere: Dorset Garden Theatre, home to the Duke's Company and sited near the City. Newer and more luxurious than the rival Drury Lane Theatre, its stage could facilitate elaborate scenic effects.

29 cutting Moorcraft ... masquerade: swaggering Moorcraft: a usurer-turned-gallant in Beaumont & Fletcher's play, *The Scornful Lady* (1616), often revived in the Restoration. Hence, a scornful allusion to the popularity of masquerades with the middle classes.

35 a room . . . within: Masked balls notoriously afforded opportunities for sexual adventures. Despite Dryden's hint, however, his characters stop short of this, as the epilogue points out (ll.11–12 & 23–4).

Act 1, Scene 1

40–41 like cormorants: voracious seabirds used for fishing. Their necks were tied with cords to prevent them swallowing their catch.

55 words of course: mere customary compliments.

84 no propriety: no one else's rights.

84–5 servant: lover.

93 premises: the matters just discussed.

104 avaunt mortality: begone mortal fears!

126 shot the gulf: passed the point of no return.

129 good girls: girls of easy virtue.

145 ill-conditioned: bad-tempered.

177 great beds: State beds, or perhaps the newly fashionable double beds.

182 cordials: invigorating medicine, drinks, or food.

198 chapmen: dealers.

203–4 broad-gold: the old, gold 20-shilling coins. Larger than the post-1663 guinea, they had smooth edges and so were easier to clip.

211 prevents: precedes.

212 chemists: physicians. Mercury was often used as an expensive treatment for venereal disease. Rhodophil's jibe turns on the legendary goal of alchemists: to turn base metals into gold.

219 ubiquitary: to be everywhere.

258 standing in the dark to him: unbeknown to him.

376 Venus Urania: Venus in her aspect as patron-goddess of chaste love.

393 s.d. *peruke*: wig.

407 leave: cease.

443 wonnot: will not.

Act 2, Scene 1

4 *billets doux*: love letters.

7 air: manner, style.

10 *étourdie bête*: senseless beast.

12 Aesop's ass: The ass in the fable tried to win his master's caresses by ineptly imitating a pet dog.

14 *maladroitly*: clumsily.

16 **intrigue:** affair.
50 *grand monde*: the great world.
58 **rudeness:** lack of sophistication.
61 *honnête homme*: well-bred gentleman.
63 *menuets*: minuets.
65 *fade*: insipid.
76 *bien tourné*: elegant.
79 *ménage*: household management.
84 *levée*: morning audience in the bedchamber.
90–91 *obligeant ... ravissant*: obliging, charming, ravishing.
94 **s.h.** *solus*: alone.
101 **at cuffs:** fighting.
102 **rising blow:** upper-cut; but also here, with sexual innuendo.
106 *basta*: enough.
112 **woodman:** literally, a forester or huntsman; here, a hunter of women.
132 **'Ods:** God's.
136 *sub sigillo*: under oath.
     numerical: identical.
143 **dogged:** stubborn.
152 **quoth a:** says she.
194 *devoirs*: respects.
221 *à la dérobée*: secretly.
222 *doux yeux*: amorous glances.
     en suite: then.
223 *galanteries*: flattering things.
228 *fierté*: pride.
229 *rebute*: repulse.
231–2 *d'un air enjoué*: with a playful air.
     à d'autre, à d'autre: (tell it) to someone else [who might believe it].
     grimace: pretence.
232–3 **pass upon:** convince.
235 **making a loose:** getting away.
240 *galèche*: light carriage.
307 **cozen:** cheat.
386 **prince his:** prince's.
400 **one hour good:** one hour at least.
456 **strokes in ashes:** The girls made marks in the fallen ashes, from which they deciphered their lovers' initials.
463 **wake:** annual village festival.
     chaplet: garland of victory.
515 **hook ... scrip:** shepherd's crook and bag.

Act 3, Scene 1

14 turtles: turtle-doves; emblems of true love.

27 telling: counting.

67 Styx: a venerated underworld river by which the gods swore inviolable oaths. If such oaths were broken, dire penalties resulted.

68 banes: a then current form of (marriage) 'banns' – with a pun intended.

81 performance of articles: carrying out the terms of an agreement, i.e. here, a husband's sexual duties.

102 sufficient ordinary: adequate meal: Doralice expands on her food/sex, dish/woman metaphors.

107 *chagrin*: put out.

119–20 *raillied . . . mal traitée*: mocked at . . . mistreated.

123 holiday-night: a church festival day when by custom the royal drawing-room at court was open to non-courtiers.

128 the circle: courtiers and ladies in waiting.

143 carrier's day: when the carrier delivered letters.

158 'After the pangs . . . lover, etc.': from Act 2 of Dryden's comedy, *An Evening's Love* (1668).

164 mercer: dealer in silks, velvets etc.

174 vapour: talk exaggeratedly.

179 finical cit: affectedly fastidious (London) citizen.

181 frumity: country gruel made from wheat, milk, sugar and spice.

182–3 *mirabilis . . . gill-glass*: spiced wine cordial . . . a quarter-pint glass.

194 *tender*: affection.

195 *rebutée*: discouraged.

200 do my *baise mains*: pay my respects (literally: 'kiss hands')

201 *spirituelle*: elegant.

202–3 *prendre . . . carrosse*: take the carriage.

211 *usé*: worn out.

224 *Sottises*: foolish things.

236–7 *équivoque*: equivocal.

  éclaircissement: explanation.

  bévue: blunder.

  façon: manner.

  coup d'étourdi: thoughtless mistake.

247 *point gorget*: lace neckerchief.

253 *languissant*: languishing.

254 Indian gown: dressing-gown or négligé of colourful Indian cloth.

256 mere: absolute.

257 gimp: patterned lace-trimmed.

274 *repartee*: witty retort.

291 **gripe**: grasp.

313 **filberts**: hazelnuts.

314 **stare**: starling.

352 **aspic**: the viper with which Cleopatra killed herself.

382 **doom**: judgement.

407 **Eudocia's**: The former spelling, 'Eudoxia' [I.1.401] changes here, possibly for metrical reasons.

491 **want**: feel the lack of.

Act 3, Scene 2

78 **fit**: sexual arousal.

82 *surprenant au dernier*: highly surprising.

94 *bienséance*: propriety.

109–10 **All-cocks hidden**: children's call in the game of 'hide and seek'; but here, with sexual innuendo.

115 **bugbear**: bogy, hobgoblin.

134 **manner**: act.

153 **none**: contraction of 'mine own'.

Act 4, Scene 1

37 **unavailable**: unavailing.

46 **passengers . . . grates**: passers-by . . . barred prison windows.

57 **grateful**: welcome.

107 **false fires**: a reference to the flickering marsh lights, or *ignes fatui*, said to mislead night travellers: a recurrent metaphor in Restoration writing.

120 s.d. *vizor masks*: face masks.

131 **antique habits**: either grotesque, or antique, masquerade costumes.

136 **masquerade . . . debauch**: Since masquerades involved the wearing of disguises as well as masks, the chances (and hazards) of sexual adventures were increased.

141–2 *terra incognita*: undiscovered land.

154 **doubt**: suspect.

181 **course . . . herd**: a metaphor from coursing or hunting.

187 **resty**: sluggish.

193 **well-breathed courser**: well-exercised hunting-horse.

Act 4, Scene 2

5 **moves**: beseeches.

16 **dark lantern**: having a slide or shutter by which its light may be concealed.

57 **die**: achieve orgasm.

Act 4, Scene 3
5 **raw:** immature.
15 **park-time:** time to go to the park.
27 **wicked boy:** Palamede thinks the 'boy' is offering him sex.
58–9 **read me, and take me:** with a sexual innuendo.
65 **steel:** a reference both to his sword and his penis. The comparison is with a magnetic compass.
70 **pragmatical:** meddling.
95 **archest:** most mischievous.
100 **warrant ... discovery:** guarantee you won't be discovered.
107 **barred ... nicked:** voided the throw ... scored against.
111 **picture in the hangings:** Figures portrayed in wall tapestries were not very lifelike.
118 **Old Chios:** matured wine from the Greek island of Chios.
122–3 **seconds ... weak brother:** joiners in the toast ... poor drinker.
135 **well found out:** devised.
140–41 **s.d. *saluting*:** bowing.
votre ... humble: your most humble servant.
142–3 **Votre ... coeur:** Your slave, sir, with all my heart.
148 **new-laced bosom:** beribboned waistcoat in the French style.
clap: venereal disease.
149 **mouth:** open-mouthed.
150 **man *monsieur*:** French servant.
153 **upon salt water:** to go abroad.
155 **entreprenant:** forward.
177 **Mars:** Roman god of war.
212 **Good Old Cause:** the Puritan cause; used ironically here.

Act 4, Scene 4
22 **s.d. *ambo*:** both together.
101 **discover:** reveal.
108 **bands:** bonds.
113 **Or:** either.
123–6 **My reverend city friends ... fear?:** A passage reflecting the distrust and hostility felt by many London citizens concerning Charles II's alliance with France.
138 **w'not:** contraction of 'wonnot': will not.
141 **mean:** wretched.

Act 5, Scene 1
19 **receipts:** remedies.
23 **mere jockey:** a mere lad.

23-4 **make matches**: propose bets (on his dogs, horses, etc. against others).

24 **crack of the field**: sporting gossip.

31 **mark**: a hawk's quarry.

bobbed at retrieve: cheated of any gain.

52 **humour**: temperament.

60 **mien**: bearing.

64 **pieces**: either gold guineas, or twenty-shilling silver pieces.

77 **old Amazons**: fabled race of female warriors.

96-7 **parenthesis of all**: enclosing all.

115 *douceurs*: compliments.

141 *rompre en visière*: take offence.

145-6 **long of**: because of.

150 *Façon, façon*: nonsense.

152 *désespéré au dernier*: desperate to the last degree.

154 *mal à propos*: in such an untimely way.

156-7 *à contretemps*: inconveniently.

158 *mal peste*: wretched nuisance.

159 *j'enrage*: I am furious.

160-62 *Radoucissez-vous . . . gallante*: Please calm yourself, madam. You are in a temper over a trifle. You misunderstand courtly raillery.

163-4 **He mocks . . . of me**: French syntax.

166-7 *qu'il . . . accompli!*: what an accomplished gallant he is!

169-70 *Ah . . . jour*: 'Ah, how beautiful it is in the groves;
                        Ah, what a fine day the heavens give [us].'

171 **with a** *menuet*: The two preceding lines and ll.177-8 come from the 1st minuet-song in the '*Ballet des Nations*' performed at the end of Molière's comedy *Le Bourgeois Gentilhomme* (1670).

177-8 *Ces beaux . . . l'amour*:
'These pleasant surroundings, these sweet leafy bowers,
These pleasant surroundings, invite us to love.'
Molière's text reads 'Ce beau séjour nous invite à l'amour' (Hall, p. 131).

179 *en cavalier*: as a gallant should.

180 **humours**: adapts to.

181-3 *Vois . . . amoureux*: 'See, my Climène,
                            See how under this oak
                            These amorous birds kiss each other.'
(From the 2nd minuet-song in *Le Bourgeois Gentilhomme*, V.6. 5th entry, 1-3.)

187 *chanson à boire*: drinking-song.

187–8 *'toute la terre ... moi'*: 'All the earth is mine.' [Source unknown.]

189 *cabarets*: taverns.

191 *éveillé*: lively, up-to-date person.

202–3 *gaieté d'esprit*: gaiety of spirit.

203–4 *sans ... condition*: with no reservation or condition.

206 *raccommode*: reconcile.

207 *jusqu' à la mort*: until death.

208 *Allons donc*: Come, then.

209 s.d. *solus*: alone.

224 yclept: called: an archaic word used humorously here.

238 strong water: spirits; customarily offered to criminals being carted to execution.

259 'Slife: contraction of 'God's life'.

290 drawn off: i.e. as liquid is drawn off to leave any sediment.

293 piecing: patching up.

299 better cheap: as a better bargain.

325 taking up the glass: lifting the cold frame.

326 Billing: kissing.

333 indenture: sealed agreement.

351 bilbo: sword; Bilbao in Spain was famed for fine steel.

353 Dangerfield: Uncertain. Either a conventional term for a bully, or perhaps the name of a swordsmith.

383–4 delicate screwed gun: gun with a finely grooved bore (*OED*).

399 standing dish: the regular meal.

406 longest cut: (to draw the) longest straw. Also (as with the previous phrases) with sexual innuendo.

419–20 Fall on ... enough: An approximate quote from *Macbeth* (V. 10.33–4).

564 carriage: conduct.

575 vestals: vestal virgins; originally, Roman priestesses sworn to chastity.

579 you: your (Q1).

Epilogue

4 easy phlegm: not easily roused or passionate.

5 poets: early editions read 'poet's'.

stiff: awkward, and/or strictly moral.

limber: easy, and/or limp, flaccid (*OED*, 1.c).

31–2 Since ... city: A final hit at the 'cits'. See notes to Prologue ll.29 & 30.

THE LIBERTINE

Dedication

Newcastle: William Cavendish, 1st Duke of Newcastle (1593–1676).

30 **Welbeck:** Welbeck Abbey, near Nottingham: Newcastle's favourite seat, where he showed generous hospitality to many writers, artists and intellectuals.

Preface

3 **Spanish play:** *El Burlador de Sevilla* (pub. 1630) by Gabriel Téllez (aka Tirso de Molina). For further details and versions of the Don Juan story, see *Shadwell*, I, cxxv–cxli.

5–6 **comedians:** actors.

7 **several:** separate.

French plays: Dorimon's *Le Festin de Pierre* (1658); De Villier's *Le Festin de Pierre* (1659); Molière's *Dom Juan* (1665); Rosimond's *Le Nouveau Festin de Pierre* (1669).

9 **borrowed:** largely from Rosimond. (See *Shadwell*, III, 9.)

36 *Love and Revenge*: Written by Elkanah Settle, Shadwell's rival and *bête noire*. It was performed 1674, printed 1675 and dedicated to Newcastle. Its source is William Hemming's *The Fatal Contract*. Settle's Postscript glances at Shadwell's boasted speed of composition, but does not name him.

43 **fustian:** bombast.

44 *The Conquest of China*: Performed by the Duke's Company, May 1675.

50 **'Vanity of [his] Tribe':** In dedicating his play to his patron, Settle remarks, 'Yet had I the common Vanity of our Tribe, to believe such a Tribute satisfactory, I should want the confidence to think it so here' ('The Epistle Dedicatory', *The Conquest of China by the Tartars*, 1676).

53–4 **'Servant to His Majesty':** This phrase follows Settle's name on the title pages of both the plays noted above. Settle had been sworn as a 'household servant' of the king in February 1671[/2?], along with other King's Company personnel. (See Milhous & Hume, I, no.628.) Such 'servants' received no salary, but were afforded some privileges, e.g. protection from summary arrest.

55 **protections . . . off:** Shadwell's meaning is uncertain: evidently the customary privileges had been recently curtailed.

57 **'Poet in Extraordinary':** a joke. 'In extraordinary' meant 'supernumerary', or of a rank below those listed 'in ordinary'. R. D. Hume remarked in a private communication that 'Settle was presumably

sworn as a "Comedian in Ordinary" ', hence Shadwell's mocking comment.

64–7 to tax ... frailty: 'for, indeed Impudence in Poets, is a Frailty that most of us cannot Resist' ('The Epistle Dedicatory', *The Conquest of China*).

Prologue
3 picaroons: pirates.
6 Ostend privateers: hostile Dutch ships.
7 or ... or: either ... or.
33 Caesar: Charles II.

Dramatis Personae
Several mistakes and omissions in the cast list of Q1 (1676) have been silently corrected here.

Act 1, Scene 1
139 carbonado: hack at, slash.
149–50 I ... labour: venereal disease often destroyed the nose.
215 bowels: pity.
238 s.d. *swounds*: faints.
267 another-guess man: a man of another kind.
292 inapprehensive: uncomprehending, ignorant.
304 bobs: scoffs, jibes.

Act 1, Scene 2
24 punk: whore.
28 *clavis*: slang for 'penis'. (Latin for 'key'.)
59 s.d. *dark lantern*: having a slide or shutter by which its light can be concealed.
83 disperse: 'dispense' (*Shadwell*), but Q1–2 read 'disperse', as do contemporary songbooks which reprint this song.
126 safe: not a threat.
167 bilbo: a sword (Bilbao in Spain was famed for fine steel).
185 pinked: pierced slightly.

Act 2, Scene 1
s.s. *solus*: alone.
22 buffle: fool.
28 admire: marvel, wonder at.
32–3 idle ... awe: a commonplace of heterodox thought.
141 rook: cheat.
195 suddenly: at once.
283 s.h. OMNES: all.
289 Grand Seignior: sultan of Turkey.

369 **Lucrece**: a celebrated Roman matron who killed herself after being raped by Sextus Tarquinius.

415 *re infecta*: unravished. (Literally: 'with the deed undone'.)

499 *then*: than

517 **enow**: enough.

Act 3, Scene 1
2 **Luff**: steer towards the wind.

Act 3, Scene 2
153 **pose**: confuse, perplex.

270 **collop**: slice.

300 **ramble**: wander, rove (with sexual innuendo).

303 **wittol**: complaisant cuckold.

325 **vizor**: mask.

337 **unhooded**: Hawkers hooded their birds when hunting to prevent distraction.

401 **s.d.** *ambo*: both.

465 **rally**: mock.

639 **sower**: sure, trusty.

640 **wasler**: beat.

Act 4, Scene 1
32 **bobbed**: cheated, fooled.

135 **owned**: admitted.

136 **ducatoon**: Italian silver coin.

Act 4, Scene 2
18 **Saturn's ... days**: the Golden Age when the god, Saturn, reigned; before men grew corrupt and sophisticated.

121 **Sabines**: An Italian tribe whose women were carried off as wives by the early Romans.

154 **Tarquin**: See above, note to 2.1.369.

163 **Scorpio**: the astrological sign ruling the genitals.

Act 4, Scene 4
49 **ragout**: meat stew.

50 *cher entire*: literally, 'a complete piece of meat' (often meaning 'a roast meal', rather than a stew); but here, 'a woman' [punning on 'cher' ('meat') and 'chère' ('dear')].

Act 5, Scene 1
7 **tierce**: a fencing position.

28 **chaffering**: bargaining, haggling.

54-5 **brave ... Ephesus**: Eratostratus burnt this famous temple to Diana to eternise his name.

175 s.d. **probationers:** novices.
235 **mobile:** mob, rabble.

Epilogue
9 **solemn ... cov'nants:** The Solemn League and Covenant (1643) required all MPs, ministers, and office-holders to swear they would defend the Parliamentary cause and reform the churches of England and Ireland (i.e. get rid of the bishops).
21–2 **Each ... shoe:** Imprisoned debtors begged for coins to buy food by suspending shoes from their windows.

THE ROVER

Prologue
2 **society:** professional clique, group.
3 **Rabel's drops:** a patent medicine.
9 **cabal:** faction.
12 **elves:** mischief-makers.
18 **Catholic:** all-embracing.
23 **Bating:** except for.
38 **him:** The prologue's author either did not know, or was concealing, the dramatist's gender. Behn's name does not appear on the title page until the third issue of the first edition.
43 **cits:** a derogatory abbreviation for 'citizens', i.e. middle-class tradespeople.
   May-Day coaches: a mocking reference to the custom of hiring coaches to parade around Hyde Park on May Day.

Dramatis Personae
viceroy's son: Naples was under Spanish rule 1503–1707.
bravoes: hired ruffians, minders.
Mrs Barry: Elizabeth Barry joined the Duke's Company in 1675. Hellena was Barry's first recorded leading role in a major, new, box-office success.

Act 1, Scene 1
31 *Anglese:* Englishman.
42 **proper:** fine; well made.
53 **devote:** nun.
56 **Pamplona:** the much-besieged capital of Navarre in Northern Spain.
57 **colonel of French horse:** Belvile, like many exiled English royalists during the interregnum, has sought military service in foreign forces.
62 s.d. *masquing habit:* masquerade costume.
87 **jointure:** estate or sum to be settled on a widow on her husband's death.

100 **bags:** wealth, money bags.

116 **Indian breeding:** Don Vincentio seems to have had a colonial upbringing in the West Indies.

117 **dog days:** hottest part of the year.

120 **King Sancho the First:** a medieval ruler of Navarre.

126 **uncase:** undress.

145 **Hôtel de Dieu:** hospital founded by a religious order.

153 **Gambo:** Gambia in West Africa. The slave trade between Africa and the West Indies was rapidly developing.

154 **bell and bauble:** trifles; also a mocking reference to Vincentio's ineffectual penis.

164 **grate:** grating, barred door or window.

204 **ramble:** wander, rove (with sexual innuendo).

215 **want:** lack.

Act 1, Scene 2

1 **Why:** 'Whe' in Q1. I have regularised such usages to 'why' throughout.

15 **'sheartlikins:** mild, old-fashioned oath (from: 'God's little heart'). It appears in various forms as Blunt's trademark in both parts of *The Rover*.

41 **hogoes:** strong relishes.

54 **protectors:** Oliver Cromwell was proclaimed Lord Protector in 1653.

56 **forfeit . . . cavaliering:** Many royalists had their estates confiscated during the interregnum.

57 **following the court:** the English court in exile was forced to move location frequently from political and/or financial exigencies.

66 **salute:** kiss. (Then the usual form of greeting for either sex.)

70 **prince:** Charles II in exile.

84 **chapmen:** dealers.

101 **still:** distilling-apparatus. Willmore's innuendo refers to the process by which perfume is distilled from rose petals.

108 **pest-house:** hospital for plague victims.

118 **s.d. *horns*:** sign of cuckoldry.

133 **monsieurs:** Frenchmen.

138 **piazza:** public square.

Dutchman . . . Bridge: a reference to the Dutch defeat by French forces (1672) at Niuewerbrug (New Bridge).

144 **cross their hands:** with silver, i.e. pay them.

162 **parlous:** shrewd.

169–70 **Venus . . . element:** Venus, goddess of love, was sea-born.

194 **old law:** Old Testament.
195 **Jephthah's daughter:** Jephthah allowed his daughter two months to lament her virginity before sacrificing her to God in fulfilment of an oath. (Judges 11. 37–40.)
199 **took orders:** took holy orders to become a nun.
216 **swingeing:** huge, mighty.
252 **sibyl:** prophetess.
287 **nicely:** scrupulously.
302 **contrive ... chains:** Jesuits were much feared and persecuted in Protestant England for their supposed equivocations and plots against the state.
305 **bellman:** town crier.
308 **fit him:** punish him.
   sell ... Peru: Mines in the Spanish colony of Peru used slave labour.
311 **banged:** beaten.
329 **piece of eight:** Spanish silver coin.
341 **honest:** chaste.
350 **Paduana:** woman of Padua.
356 **monarch's birthday:** Courtiers customarily sported new clothes on a royal birthday.

Act 2, Scene 1
s.d. *vizard:* carnival mask.
4 **buff:** soldier's leather coat.
39 **little archer:** Cupid.
45 **clap:** venereal disease.
65 **bottom:** ship's hold.
69 **cozened:** cheated.
81 **arrant:** downright, out-and-out.
83 **ycleped:** called.
86 **Essex calf:** idiot, blockhead.
120–21 **portion ... Infanta:** dowry for the Spanish princess.
162 s.d. *anticly:* grotesquely.
218 **Molo:** large pier, breakwater.
276–7 **if ... Flanders:** Parts of the Spanish Netherlands were lost to France in the 1660s and 1670s.
293 **patacoon:** Spanish silver coin.

Act 2, Scene 2
25 **beaten at Worcester:** the final Royalist defeat (1651), after which Charles II fled to the Continent.
31 **high i'th'mouth:** lofty.
44 **pistole:** Spanish gold coin.

black lead: pencil.

65 **contemn**: despise.

152 **pretend**: Q1 has 'pretends'.

171 **shameroon**: trickster.

173 **tatterdemalion**: ragamuffin.

173–4 **picaroon**: pirate.

Act 3, Scene 1

5 **mewed up**: shut up (like a caged hawk).

10 **Loretto**: a renowned pilgrimage centre. It also attracted thieves, beggars and riff-raff.

42 **the pip**: pique, depression.

68 **billets**: love-letters, *billets-doux*.

76 **a**: omitted in Q1.

103 **Are ... windows?**: Seventeenth-century brothels were often the targets of such rowdy abuse.

110 *bona roba*: courtesan.

111 in *fresco*: in the open air.

116 **spigot**: peg or plug to control the flow of liquor in a butt or cask.

122 **balderdash**: cheap, adulterated alcoholic drink.

sack: white wine imported from Spain and the Canaries.

164 **Capuchin**: friar of the austere Franciscan order.

176 **collation**: light meal.

248 **right**: genuine.

bills of exchange: money-orders.

277 **budget**: leather bag or pouch.

Act 3, Scene 2

18 **mind settlements**: care about marriage settlements.

Act 3, Scene 3

10 **an**: if.

18 s.d. *bed descends*: presumably through a large trap-door.

46 **eighty-eight**: 1588 in the reign of Elizabeth I, when the English fleet defeated the Spanish Armada.

49 **bowed**: curved.

54 **common shore**: main drain or sewer.

Act 3, Scene 4

2 **clue**: guiding thread.

4 **quean**: whore.

18 **Prado**: Madrid's main public park, or promenade. Used also of parks elsewhere.

19 **annihilated**: vanished.

28 **cullies:** dupes.

Act 3, Scene 5
s.d. *undress:* casual dress, worn at home.
3 **cabinet:** small private room or study.
10 **jessamin:** jasmine.
26 **parlous:** exceeding, amazing.
31 **disguised:** drunk.
62 **coil:** fuss.
101 **then:** than.

Act 3, Scene 6
59 **chase-gun:** Chase-guns were those mounted ahead or astern on board ship.
72 **St Jago:** St James, patron saint of Spain.

Act 4, Scene 1
11 s.d. *night-gown:* robe, dressing-gown.
52 **overpay:** recompense.
81 **deceitful light:** a reference to the flickering marsh lights, or *ignes fatui*, said to mislead night travellers.

Act 4, Scene 2
35 **Or:** either.
215 **mumping:** sullen.
303 *en passant:* in passing.
353 **fit thee:** pay you back.
363 **cogging:** wheedling.
370 **canting'st:** most insincere.
378 **German motion:** dull, or lifeless, puppet.
389 **brazen head:** impudence.

Act 4, Scene 3
10 **wardrobe:** room where clothes were kept.
18 **your note:** Q2–3 and some copies of Q1 read 'your letter, your note'.
41 **Antipodes:** regions on the opposite side of the earth.
49 **clapped:** infected with a venereal disease.
66 **and:** if.
75 **prize:** fair game (like an enemy ship captured in wartime).

Act 4, Scene 5
8 **morris dancer:** Such dancers' traditional costume included white clothes, bells, ribbons, swords, etc.
12 **faithless ... physician:** Doctors had a reputation for atheism.

24 attired: Blunt's state of undress caused even more concern in the eighteenth century, when this scene was widely held to be indecent.

112 e'en confessed: better have confessed.

130 cormorant: greedy devourer.

Act 5, Scene 1

36 s.d. *simply*: foolishly.

74 jack pudding: buffoon.

102 one at once: one at a time.

104–5 the propriety of her: the ownership of her.

108 s.d. *longest*: The Spanish fashion was for long swords.

112 Toledo: sword. Toledo was famous for fine blades.

175 a father: a priest.

218 juggling: cheating.

256 virago: termagant; warlike woman.

298 fever: Q3. Q1–2 have 'favour'.

313 you'll <find> will be: Link emends from an MS note in the Luttrell copy of Q1. Q1 has 'you'l will be'.

nice: particular; fastidious.

427 tramontana: northern (from beyond the Alps); foreign.

463 you: Q3. Omitted in Q1–2.

474 mewed: see note to 3.1.5.

one: *Behn*, I. Early editions have 'on'.

476 lure: training equipment used by falconers to recall hawks.

487 old gaffer Hymen: old father Hymen. A jocular reference to Hymen, the Greek god of marriage, who was generally represented as a flower-crowned youth.

491 bug: frightening; off-putting.

493 consort: group.

499 left-handed: unofficial.

502 upse: in the manner of.

505 incle: linen tape or braid.

515 sneaking: paltry.

518 caudle: warm, spiced drink for invalids.

520–21 let ... charge: let me be hanged.

525 blind ... fortune: The classical deities Cupid and Fortuna were both depicted blindfolded.

565 best of men and kings: Charles II.

598 s.d. *band*: neckband.

612 bag of bays: bundle of bay leaves and spices used in cooking.

614–15 *en cavalier*: gallant; modish, like a cavalier.

625 doxy: whore.

Epilogue
5 **conventicling**: The religious meetings of Dissenters (nonconformists) were called conventicles. Behn's epilogue is characteristically ironic at the expense of the Dissenters whom royalists often viewed as political subversives and religious fanatics.
10 **miss**: a kept mistress.
13 **maggot**: whimsical idea; here, from a religious, 'inspirational' source.
14 **canting**: hypocritical.
20 **Blackfriars**: a famous pre-Civil War theatre; hence, an old-fashioned style of play and/or performance.
21 **bamboo**: a cane.
36 **the half-crown spare**: Behn suggests the fops might as well spare the price of a seat and practise their mannerisms in their own mirrors.
40 **huff**: bluster.
   damny: variant of 'damn me'.
43 **Nokes . . . Leigh**: James Nokes and Anthony Leigh were the leading 'low' comic actors of the day. Nokes played the role of Fetherfool in *The Rover*, Part 2.

Postscript
The Postscript is only present in Q1.
3 *Thomaso* **altered**: In fact, much in *The Rover*, Parts 1 & 2 derives from Thomas Killigrew's two-part comedy, *Thomaso, Or The Wanderer* (written 1654; published 1663).
4 **proprietor**: As its author, Killigrew owned *Thomaso*. He was also the manager of the rival theatre company, the King's Company.
6 **pieced or mended**: adapted or 'improved'.
11 **Spartan boys**: In ancient Sparta, boys were trained to endure hardship by having to steal through hunger and to conceal such thefts, even at the cost of their lives.
15 *The Novella*: a comedy (1632) by Richard Brome.
24 **especially of our sex**: This phrase is found only in the third issue, and some copies of the 2nd issue, of Q1.
25–7 **Therefore . . . fame**: Behn translates Virgil's riposte to an inferior poet who had claimed as his own some of Virgil's unsigned verses: '*Hos ego versiculos feci tulit alter honores*' (*Behn*, I, 442).

THE KIND KEEPER

Epigraphs
Κῆν με . . . καρποφορήσω: [The Vine speaks:] 'Though thou eatest me to the root, billy-goat, [I will yet bear fruit enough to prepare a libation for thee when thou art sacrificed]'. (Evenus of Ascalon, *The*

Greek Anthology, with an English translation by W. R. Paton, 5 vols (Loeb, Heinemann, London, 1915; 1925), III, Bk. IX, no.75, p.39.)

Hic nuptarum ... poetas: 'One runs mad for the love of married women; another for whores ... All of these men dread verses and hate poets.' (Horace, *Satires*, I.4.27,33, Loeb, adjusted (Heinemann, London, 1926; 1970), p.50.) The original has 'boys' not 'whores'.

Both epigraphs appear to refer to the *furore* aroused by *The Kind Keeper*. The first would seem to be Dryden's riposte to the criticism which forced him to revise the play. The second presumably alludes to the charge of personal satire, which Dryden denies in the Dedication (ll.81–85).

Dedication

John, Lord Vaughan: (1639–1713), one of Dryden's earliest patrons. Son of Richard, Earl of Carbury; MP for Carmarthen (from 1661); president of the Royal Society (1686); and 'one of the lewdest fellows of the age' (*The Diary of Samuel Pepys*, ed. Robert Latham & William Matthews (1974; 1978), 8, 532–3).

2 great plot ... nation: the Popish Plot, which caused great political unrest c.1678–80.

3 Pharaoh's lean kine: In Pharaoh's dream, the lean cattle ate the fat ones (Genesis 41).

3–4 younger ... stage: Both theatre companies, but especially the King's Company, were adversely affected by the political climate.

10–13 Gratias ... patronus: 'Catullus, the worst of all poets, gives to you [Cicero] his warmest thanks; as much the worst poet of all as you are the best advocate of all' (Catullus, XLIX, 4–7).

14 epistle of Flecknoe's: a letter from the prolific poetaster, Richard Flecknoe. Dryden had already ridiculed him in *Mac Flecknoe* (c.1676) for his bad verse.

18 'Quatuordecim ... anni': 'Fourteen years have passed'. Dryden suggests Flecknoe's poor Latin forced him to end the sentence in (equally poor) English.

26 who ... last: Uncertain. Perhaps either Flecknoe or Andrew Marvell, both of whom died c.1678.

28–9 patriarchs ... mistress: Jacob served fourteen years to gain Rachel for his wife. (Genesis 29).

36–7 another part of the world: Vaughan was governor of Jamaica 1674–8.

florid: pompous.

41–2 title ... have: Vaughan acquired his courtesy title on the death of his elder brother (1667).

57 **philosophy:** science (and perhaps also, philosophy).

79 **time of licence:** The 1662 Licensing Act had expired in May 1679, affording the press relative freedom from censorship.

84–5 **our . . . keeping:** our notorious vice of keeping mistresses.

90 **elder:** earlier.

92–5 **Castum . . . pudici:** 'The sacred poet ought to be chaste himself, though his poems need not be so. Why, they only acquire wit and spice if they are rather naughty and immodest' (Catullus, XVI, 4–6, trans. Francis Warre Cornish, in *Catullus, Tibullus, Pervigilium Veneris* (Loeb, Camb., Mass., & London, 2nd edit., 1988), pp.22–3.

98–9 **altered . . . press:** No copy of the original MS survives, though some of Malone's notes on it do. (See Dearing & Roper, pp.365–6.)

106 *Tartuffe:* first performed 1664.

112 **particular:** personal.

114–15 **from . . . man:** The candidate most canvassed was the Earl of Lauderdale. (See Dearing & Roper, pp.374–5).

119–20 **overlooked the press:** corrected or proofed the text.

122–4 **But . . . this:** In fact, Dryden never corrected the 2nd edition (1690).

Prologue

2 **dipped in show:** A dig at the kind of expensive spectacular productions popular at Dorset Garden; (with a pun on 'dipped' meaning also 'in debt').

3 **doggerel . . . clouds:** Brilliant stage effects (including movable clouds) often accompanied poor dialogue.

16 **toys:** cheaper, inferior goods.

Stourbridge Fair: held every September in Cambridge.

23 **Nostradamus:** a joking reference to the famous French astrologer and prognosticator (1503–66).

27–8 **But . . . locust:** Locusts were the eighth plague of Egypt (Exodus 10).

Dramatis Personae

being well conceited of himself: esteeming himself highly.

formal: over-precise.

cast: cast-off, sacked.

fanatic: scornful term for a member of a Dissenting, or nonconformist, congregation.

Act 1, Scene 1

s.s. *garden-house:* summer-house.

10 **private meeting-house:** a conventicle, or meeting-place, where

Dissenters gathered for prayer. Dissenters were associated with political subversion by Tories and government supporters.

13 **trepanned**: inveigled.

19–20 **or . . . frequented**: a standard joke. Royalists routinely accused Dissenters of hypocrisy, especially in sexual matters.

28 **genius**: leaning, talent.

36–7 *nom de guerre*: assumed name.

42 **college**: school.
 academy: riding school.

45 **managing . . . horse**: learning how to control a war horse.

48 **plate**: silver or gold.

49 **Rhenish**: Rhine wine.

74 **ramble**: a walk for pleasure (with sexual connotations).

90 **s.d.** *saluting*: kissing (the usual form of greeting).

103 **Covent Garden church**: St Paul's; also, a noted place to make assignations.

112 **vessel . . . season**: part of Mrs Saintly's Dissenting dialect.

112–13 **I hope . . . parish church**: As a good 'fanatic', she disapproves of the Anglican Church.

134 **violence**: forceful sexual advances.

136 **overtaken**: drunk.

142 **cordial water**: spiced wine.

157 **painted outsides**: painted sepulchres; hypocrites.

160 **let me alone**: trust me.

183 **hidebound**: tight-skinned.

193 **Before George**: a mild oath (from 'by God').

193–4 **a swinger**: a well-hung [fellow].

195 **bumble**: fuck.

205 **true Trojan**: a roistering fellow.

208 *bona robas*: women of easy virtue.

212 **Why . . . be**: referring to Muslims being allowed four wives, and perhaps to the custom of the Turkish harem.

222 **written in his forehead**: predestined.

225 **two-handed**: big, strapping, formidable.

235 **settlement**: legal annuity.

238 **lover of the game**: pursuer of women.

239 **purlieus**: territory.

256 **proper**: individual, private.

260 **father**: pimp.

262 **land-pirates**: bailiffs.

263 **nature works**: sympathy moves [me].

264 **crammed**: fattened in coops.

268 **jade:** worn-out horse.

269 **smuggle:** cuddle.

301 **as right:** as true (a whore).

302 **two-piled punk:** a double whore.

302–3 **punk of two descents:** a second-generation whore.

304–5 **famous cobbler . . . blackbirds:** i.e. someone who was wasting his time attempting the impossible. 'Walsingham' was a popular tune.

330 **Barnet:** about ten miles from central London.

331 **noble Hephaestion:** Hephaestion was Alexander the Great's close friend and lover. Thus, here, perhaps, an old true friend (or, jokingly, rather more than a friend, see 1.1.462–5).

335 *supernaculum:* to the last drop. An emptied glass was up-ended on one's thumbnail to prove all the liquor had been drunk up properly. If a large drop fell, the penance was another drink!

338 **tory rory:** boisterous, rollicking (with approving political overtones).

339 **smock:** petticoat.

340 **fumbling:** sexually inadequate.

351–2 **true-milled . . . right stamp:** genuine (like a full-value coin with proper, milled edges).

354 **gloating:** ogling.

370 **hank upon:** hold over.

375 s.d. *essences:* perfumes.

390 **Lorraine and Créquy:** The famous French general, François, chevalier de Créquy, Marquis de Marines, captured Lorraine (1670), and won many victories thereafter.

393 **dey:** title of the military governor of Algiers.

434 **unconscionable:** unreasonable.

448–9 **scaramouch . . . at Paris:** stock comic characters from the popular *commedia del'arte*. An Italian troupe was based in Paris, and had visited England several times during the 1670s at Charles II's request.

454 **Pug:** playful, affectionate form of address; pet-name.

455 **handsel:** first payment or instalment.

461 **purest:** most excellent.

466–8 **when . . . woman:** the first of many jibes at the keeper's sexual inadequacy (hinted at by his name, since 'limber' can mean 'flaccid').

475 **the lampoon:** probably the bawdy satirical ballad, *Signior Dildo*, often attributed to John Wilmot, Earl of Rochester. (See Love, pp.248–57).

480 *A dio, seigniora:* Farewell, madam.

485 **frumps:** sulks, ill-humour.

498 *Seignioro . . . Inglese*: Sir, I don't understand English.

501 **present me**: give it me.

508 **Lo' you**: look you.

510 *Troppo . . . co*: too little, too little.

511 **and**: if.

514–15 *Mounsieur . . . assez*: Sir, will you take these ten guineas for the perfumes? It's enough, on my faith!

516–17 *Chi . . . meau!*: Possibly this begins, 'Who goes there, friends! Ho, away from the house!' But since Woodall has run out of Italian, it is clearly not meant to make sense.

526 **fop**: fool.

529 **Levant**: eastern Mediterranean.

541 *hansello*: See note to l.455.

551–2 **naunt . . . *Alchemist***: A reference to Jonson's comedy *The Alchemist* (I.2. & III.5), where Dapper is duped into believing the Queen of the Fairies (impersonated there by a whore) is his beneficent aunt.

554 **resty**: recalcitrant.

Act 2, Scene 1

2 **danced in a net**: been undetected.

6 *chedreux*: fashionable French wig.

7–8 **With . . . signpost**: Probably an inn sign. The popular 'Mermaid' tavern in Hackney issued tokens showing a mermaid with long blonde hair and a mirror. Presumably the device on the tokens matched that on the inn's signboard.

11 **property**: tool, cat's paw.

15 **journey-work**: reliable artisan work carried out for a superior craftsman.

25 **crimp**: both 'a card game', and 'cheating'.

32–3 **Rinaldo and Armida**: The enchantress, Armida, seduces and ensnares the knight, Rinaldo, in Tasso's romantic epic *La Gerusalemme Liberata* (Canto XVI, verses 17–26).

38 **honest**: chaste.

41 **graff**: graft.

45–6 **Philip of Macedon**: warrior-king, father of Alexander the Great.

46–7 **Pandarus of Troy**: elderly Trojan courtier; the go-between in Troilus and Cressida's love-affair (hence, the term, 'pander').

55 **whet**: drink (before fighting).

80 **wormwood lecture**: stern [literally, 'bitter'] lecture.

84–5 **Like . . . day**: A reference to Beaumont and Fletcher's *The Maid's Tragedy* (I.2).

88 **too vehement:** Another Limberham failure: presumably premature ejaculation.

93 **best:** better not.

105 **cross-day:** an unpropitious day.

152–3 **whore of Babylon:** Identified by Protestants with the papacy. (See Revelations 17.)

155 **eat pearl:** Pearls were dissolved and drunk as a sign of conspicuous excess.

157 **stomach ... ostrich:** proverbial for a strong stomach.

163–4 **Everybody ... Hercules:** Greek hero and demigod; fabled (among other feats) to have slept with fifty women in one night.

178 **punctilio:** petty scruple.

205 **dust:** money.

215 **pervicatious:** stubborn.

218 **buss:** kiss.

227–8 **to the Temple:** to find a lawyer at the Inns of Court.

233 **nun's flesh:** ascetic temperament.

239–41 **gaping ... made a sinecure:** eager to get several women [like a clergyman trying to get appointed to more than one benefice at once], I'm in danger of missing out on sexual activity with one of them [she may be turned into a 'sinecure' i.e. an appointment which involves no duties].

257 **peaking:** sickly; or moping.

258 **sidling:** inclining to one side.

263 **covering ... Palace:** The gatehouse of Lambeth Palace is decorated with red and blue patterned brickwork.

267 **Tuscan order:** Massive; solidity characterises the Tuscan order of architecture.

278 **as he does Flanders:** During negotiations, the Spanish lost important Flemish towns to the French (1677).

292 **froward:** perverse.

301 **breaking:** going bankrupt.

335 **musty:** peevish.

Saint Peter: In the Scriptures, St Peter holds the keys of heaven.

362 **incle:** linen tape.

365 **have the devil in a string:** have the devil at one's bidding. Proverbial.

366 *Hictius Doctius*: nonsense phrase used by performing conjurers, jugglers, etc.

368 **bless:** defend.

397–8 *Fiat Justitia aut ruat Mundus*: Let Justice be done even though the world falls to ruin. Proverbial.

402 **bounces:** thumps.

457 **eighth for your seventh:** OT commandments.

476–7 **Gog and Magog:** monstrous figures. (Revelations 20.)

Act 3, Scene 1

3 **ring him a peal:** let out a cry.

6–7 **be earnest:** pray, beg.

10 **pippin:** dessert apple.

17 **s.d. *Re-enter*:** perhaps left over from a revision of this scene.

41 **simagres:** grimaces.

50 *Isle of Pines*: a novel by Henry Payne (1668). It tells how George Pine and four women are shipwrecked on a remote island which they repeople unaided.

52 **schismatic:** Mrs Pleasance is assumed to share her supposed mother's Dissenting religion, and, therefore, an anti-government stance.

57 **governor ... Garden:** overseers of the parish charities; noted for sharp practice.

60 **pension:** lodging house.

66 **Argiers man:** pirate from Algiers. The Strait of Gibraltar was notorious for pirates.

68 **snap:** capture.

72 **rooks:** cheats.

77 **go proud:** be on heat.

78 **dogs ... Garden:** young rakes.

94–5 **husbands ... head:** cuckolds.

102 **he ... lottery:** unidentified. The national lottery of the time was popular.

105 **spirit of prophecy:** another glance at Mrs Pleasance's supposed religion.

110 **John ... maids:** colloquial term for a womaniser.

120 **'larm:** alarm.

136 **coming:** keen to make or welcome advances.

180 **friends:** family, relations.

204 **'nown:** my own.

206 **Tum a' me and buss:** baby-talk: 'Come to me and [give me a] kiss'.

207 **piddee:** I beg you (from 'prithee').

212 **ky:** cry.

215 **light huswife:** wanton hussy.

219 **luscious air:** sweet tune.

219–20 **like a Pallas ... brain-pan:** Pallas Athene, the Greek goddess of wisdom, is fabled to have sprung fully formed from the head of Zeus, her father.

228 cast of his office: sample of his abilities.

243–4 Kneeling . . . being: As here, Brainsick often mingles prose and blank verse in his comically inflated speeches.

244 Sa, sa, there: fencer's cry as he thrusts home.

269 trow: do you know?

279 volunties: deliberate lies (*OED*).

283 cater-cousins: close friends.

300 coming in: accession.

312 name . . . almanac: Almanacs often left blank spaces for notes.

321 Battist: Giovanni Battista Lulli (also known as Jean-Baptiste Lully); Louis XIV's (Italian) master of the court music.

326–7 the circle: courtiers in the royal presence.

328 Saint André: famous French dancing-master.

344–5 *en cavalier*: with (apparently) effortless ease.

346–7 *Nolo, nolo*: I do not wish [it].

347–8 bishop . . . diocese: Evidently bishops were noted for first declining proffered (and desired) promotion.

353 so many . . . songs: For a similar view, see *The Libertine*, 1.2.81–2.

363 *succuba*: whore.

364 *Morbleu*: mild expletive.

367 *Diable*: The devil!

372 sonnet: short lyric.

373 *quelque chose*: fancy trifle. (See l.376 for the anglicised term: 'kickshaw'.)

380 the elephant: There was a popular performing elephant in London at this time. (See Dearing & Roper, p.406).

384–5 Virgil . . . *Æneids*: The dying Virgil asked his friends to burn his unrevised *Æneid*; they refused.

395 graff him: graft [horns on] him; cuckold him.

408 bilbo: sword. (Bilbao in Spain was famed for fine blades.)

410 s.d. *with a note for each*: Either a mistake for 'each with a note', or a reminder to the stage manager.

417 orange gloves: orange-scented gloves.

475 numerical: identical.
superscribed: addressed.

490 subscription: signature.

Act 3, Scene 2

19 comedians: actors; pretenders.

37 caterwauling: making love noisily like cats.

58 **beldam**: old woman.

68 **teacher**: minister; elder.

77 **kicked with the heel**: resisted; rejected my offer. Like many of Mrs Saintly's expressions, this sounds vaguely biblical. Cf., e.g., 'It is hard for thee to kick against the pricks' (Acts 9.5).

78 **tabernacle**: literally 'tent' (OT); here, 'private room, chamber'.

82–3 **upon the premises**: Either 'about what we have been discussing'; or 'in this place'.

87 **mirabilis**: spiced wine cordial.

92 **quops**: beats; throbs.

99 **old woman ... oven**: proverb: 'The good wife would not seek her daughter in the oven if she had not been there before' (Tilley, W353).

100 **documents**: instructions.

Act 4, Scene 1

1 **outlying**: not living in central London.

4 **doily**: woollen fabric.

5 **mantos**: cloaks, mantles.

7–8 **a mournival of**: set of four.

9 **curmudgeon**: skinflint, miser.

46 **tawdry**: cheap and showy.

56 s.d. **PAD**: slang for 'a highwayman': presumably her keeper's occupation.

59 **heavy hill to Tyburn**: the usual phrase for 'the way up to the gallows'. Condemned criminals were carted up Holburn Hill to the gallows at Tyburn (now Marble Arch).

70 **justaucorps**: low-necked woman's jacket or waistcoat with sleeves.

74 **me**: for me.

82 **Caster**: an appropriate name for one who throws dice.

84 **cullies**: dupes.

   bubbled: cheated.

88 **cozen**: cheat.

90 **upon the square**: fairly.

100 **quops**: kicks.

103 **palming and topping**: terms for cheating, especially at dice.

113 **a chip in porridge**: proverbial (Tilley, C353).

115 **half-shirts**: lace or cotton 'filler', worn in the open front and neck of a woman's dress.

120 **natural**: foolish.

128 **take up**: borrow.

129 **clap**: venereal disease.

135 **Whitechapel . . . Bar:** from the east to the west side of the City of London.

135–6 **to Covent . . . downwards:** south London along by the Thames.

139 **vizor-mask:** face mask; often worn by prostitutes. The theatre pit was frequented by young gallants and wits, and by masked whores seeking customers.

141 **'Father Aldo's Delight':** a song.

141–2 **adjourn the House:** mock-parliamentary language.

146 **Shoreditch:** a north London suburb, then a slum area.

147 **swinge:** fuck.

149 **genius:** embodiment.

152–3 **forkers . . . ruin-tailed:** young and old (from names used in partridge hunting). 'To fork' could also mean 'to pick pockets' (Dearing & Roper, p.412).

153 **bells:** like those worn by hawks used in falconry.

158 **Persepolis:** Persian city fired by Alexander the Great after a night's drunken excess. (See Dryden's ode, *Alexander's Feast*, 1697.)
    Tue . . . quartier!: Kill, kill, kill! No quarter!

159 **Sodom:** either (unspecifically) a brothel, or the brothel area nicknamed 'Sodom' in Salisbury Court (off Fleet Street).

162 **suburbians:** whores.

169 **gaskins:** upper back thigh area, or garment covering such.

188 **Judas his:** Judas's.

198 **Epictetus:** classical Stoic philosopher.

205–6 **Diocletian and Julian the Apostate:** Roman emperors noted for persecuting Christians.

206 **types:** forerunners.

207 **Geneva Testament:** the Bible translation (1560) most used by Puritans and Dissenters.

208–9 **ceremonial . . . years:** OT or 'ceremonial' teaching was more acceptable to Dissenters than to Anglicans. The latter's view held sway after 1660.

218 **ghost of Queen Dido:** In 'The Wandering Prince of Troy', Dido's ghost warns Aeneas he is about to die. (See *Roxburghe*, VI, 547–51.)

221 **Uds niggers:** homely oath (i.e. 'God's' + made-up, meaningless noun).

225 **rappers:** downright oaths.

231 **clary:** spiced wine or brandy.

232–3 **s.d.** *chucks her*: touches her playfully under the chin.

242 **ombre:** card-game.

253 **pricking:** tracking (game). Here, with sexual innuendo.

256 **Jowler:** popular name for a hound.

263 **Sir Cranion:** Sir Skull, Death's head.

277 **mountebank:** a quack doctor.

279 **green sickness:** a form of anaemia affecting girls at puberty; once thought to be cured by intercourse.

286 **fool:** fruit-fool; a liquid, insubstantial dish.

288–9 **Lord Mayor's pack:** London's Lord Mayor held ancient hunting rights.

293 **in gross:** wholesale.

313 **playhouse price:** i.e. cheaply. A theatre seat in the pit cost two shillings and sixpence, as (usually) did a prostitute.

315 **fag end:** the last part of a piece of cloth (*OED*).

318 **belswagger:** libertine; whoremonger.

323 **better cheap:** a better bargain.

325 **my lodgings:** The scene has changed from Aldo's room to Mrs Brainsick's.

357 **private occasions:** i.e. when she needs her chamber-pot.

373 **in the way:** at hand.

374 **into the garden:** earth-closets were usually at the bottom of the garden.

418 **Grand Seignior:** sultan of Turkey's title.

422 **Children and fools:** cannot lie (Tilley, C328).

434 **mulligrubs:** fit of bad temper.
    vol: (at ombre) winning all the tricks one holds.

439–40 **Peru and of Potosi:** Potosi, then in Peru, now in Bolivia; fabled for its rich silver mines.

441 **perboles:** hyperboles, exaggerations.

444 **Long's:** well-known tavern and eating-house.

450 **Faux:** Guy Fawkes.

469 **recollecting:** reminding.

499 **Mars and Venus:** Hephaestus, Venus' husband, trapped them in a net as they made love, and summoned the other gods to mock them.

Act 4, Scene 2
s.s. ***discovered*:** revealed.

6 **two-hand fox:** sword needing both hands to wield it.

7 **still-house:** outhouse for distilling home-made spirits, boiling down sugar for sweets, etc.

11 **A minute ... the tout:** Woodall was about to make love for the third time ('party', 'revenge' and 'tout' being terms for winning games in cards).

17–18 **Methinks ... sleep':** See *Macbeth*, II.2.33–4.

47–8 **old dog-trick:** low trick.

54 **gypsies:** trollops.

67 **pure:** fine, excellent.

73 **Styx:** A venerated underworld river by which the gods swore inviolable oaths.

92 **gallipot:** small, glazed pot.

113 **nice:** particular.

126 **expects:** awaits.

130 **Take ... pillow:** sleep on it (with sexual innuendo).

135 **Zookers:** homely oath.

Act 5, Scene 1

8–10 **fee-fa-fum ... cuckold-maker:** from the folk tale of Jack the Giant-Killer.

10–11 **butting about:** thrusting with his head (or his 'horns').

14 **New Exchange:** popular row of shops in the Strand.

18 **muse:** gap in a hedge.

32–4 **'Speak ... ago':** alludes to the witches' song in Davenant's version of *Macbeth*, II.2.

41 **highest rangers:** eager beaters of the ground (for game).

49 **round rate:** quickly.

72 **Indian gown:** dressing-gown or négligé of colourful Indian cloth.

88 **tearing:** loud, noisy.

99 **bobbed:** tricked.

121 **trope:** figure of speech.

143 **jealous:** suspicious.

153 **proper:** own.

173 **maggot:** whimsical fancy.

174 **Bet'lem:** Bethlehem or Bedlam Hospital for the mad.
dog-days: hottest time of the year; thought to be when people were most likely to run mad.

180 **Tell-clock:** a watchman or one who counts the hours.

183 **ambuscade:** ambush.

200 *Laissez faire à Marc Antoine*: 'Leave it to Mark Anthony!'. (Source unknown.)

215 **wefts:** waifs.

216–17 **Friar Bacon's head:** the brazen head fabled to have been made by the magus, Friar Bacon, which could foretell events. Its last words were 'Time is past'.

227 **insults:** takes advantage; grows arrogant.

234–5 **her man ... warrant for the doe:** a gamekeeper empowered to present a permit to hunt the doe.

250 **cheap:** lightly esteemed.

256 **baffled:** outwitted, tricked.

280 **bilbo:** See note to 3.1.408.

299–300 **obligation of a cavalier:** i.e. to obey a lady.

305 *capriccio*: caprice, whim.

325 **swingeing:** strapping.

365–6 **generous:** courageous.

386 **deaf as an adder:** proverbial.

400–401 **devil . . . chaplain:** Cf. 'Who preaches war is the devil's chaplain' (Tilley, W52).

412 **Artemidorus:** classical author of a book on the interpretation of dreams.

427 **something of a flageolet:** something to do with a small flute; (with a *double entendre*).

429 **still:** continually.

456–7 **devil's paternosters:** curses; prayers said backwards.

463 **orient:** lustrous.

477 **leg:** i.e. a bow.

484 **Under the rose:** no offence.

498–9 **old Methusalem:** Methusaleh, OT patriarch and type of longevity (Genesis 5.27).

500 **Phaëthon:** son of the god Apollo; he drove his father's sun-chariot recklessly and was consumed in flames.

503–4 **fair course:** fairly pursued him.

516 **Do I dote:** Am I feeble-minded?

520 **Tartar . . . caught:** proverb. See Tilley, 73.

526 **gorgon's head:** In Greek myth, the head of the gorgon, Medusa, turned all who gazed on it to stone.

531–2 **end of the line:** i.e. of gunpowder.

539 **ceremony:** formality. (Woodall has removed his hat as a sign of respect.)

547 **catechise:** The catechism of questions and answers on the Christian faith, learnt by children before confirmation.

548 **quondam:** former.

552 **Whetstone's Park:** a notorious brothel area.

575 **Pylades . . . mad Orestes:** In Greek myth, inseparable friends. Orestes endured a fit of madness after killing his mother to avenge his father's death. Here, however, 'mad' means primarily, 'madcap'.

576–7 *ballum rankum*: obscene dance performed naked at brothels.

583 **mettled toad:** spirited toad (affectionate usage).

592 **convenience:** advantage.

597 **blown upon:** having the bloom taken off, i.e. being seduced.

599 **cross . . . cudgels:** lay down my weapons (one over the other).

606 **butcher's meat:** meaning, perhaps, she will eat expensive fish or game instead.

617–618 **journey-work:** work paid by the hour for which a craftsman is hired out.

640 **soldered up:** patched up, fixed.

645 **honesty:** meaning both 'honest' and 'chaste'.

651 **and:** if.

657 **recognizance:** bail.

671–2 **maintenance:** a jointure.

680–81 **chapel of ease:** a pun, meaning: (1) a room where a chamber pot is kept; (2) a place for prayers for parishioners who live far from the local church (referring to Woodall's claim to have been praying in Tricksy's closet).

683–4 **Bel . . . dragon:** Bel (an idol) and a dragon were worshipped by the Babylonians.

689 **Memphis:** Egyptian city near the pyramids.

695 **moiety:** 'my better half' (Tilley, H49).

696 **'comfortable importance':** a mistress. A current joke from Marvell's (1672) satire against Bishop Parker who had used the phrase in a religious pamphlet. Marvell pretends to think that 'comfortable importance' is Parker's pompous euphemism for 'a mistress' (*The Rehearsal Transpros'd*, ed. D. I. B. Smith (Oxford, 1971), pp.5–6).

Epilogue

18 **fry:** young, offspring.

  pugs: whores.

19 **gadders:** vagrants.

20 **counters:** prisons.

  padders: highwaymen.

22 **Smithfield . . . Garden:** Proverbial: 'Who goes to Westminster for a wife, to Paul's for a man, and to Smithfield for a horse may meet with a whore, a knave, and a jade'. (Tilley, W276). (Covent Garden is in Westminster.)

THE ORPHAN

Epigraph

Qui . . . artes: 'The man who trusts the sea consoles himself with high profits; the man who follows war and the camp is girded with gold; the base flatterer lies drunk on a couch of purple dye; the man who tempts young wives gets money for his sin; eloquence alone shivers in rags and cold, and calls upon a neglected art with unprofitable tongue.' (Petronius, *Satyricon*, translated by Michael Heseltine (Loeb Series, Heinemann, London, 1916), pp.166–7.)

Dedication
the Duchess: Mary, Duchess of York; daughter of Alphonso IV of Este, Duke of Modena.
9 presence: Mary and her husband, James, Duke of York, were intermittently in exile 1679–82. (See notes to the Dedication of *The Rover*, Part 2.)
14 absence: The Duke and Duchess had returned to London 24 February 1680.
22 this way: by a printed dedication, for which the dramatist usually received twenty guineas.
24–5 Tasso and Ariosto: Italian Renaissance epic poets, patronised by the Este family.
42 virtue: manly courage.

Prologue
19 lampooned: lampoons i.e. personally abusive, satiric poems, sometimes intended to be sung, were much in vogue at this time, often for political ends.
21–2 Satire's . . . ease: Satire is imaged as the faeces of diseased poetry.
24–5 Since . . . dawn: with the Duke of York's return from exile. He had to leave again in October when the Exclusion Crisis peaked.
30 Not . . . before: See below, note to ll.57–9 of the Dedication of *The Rover*, Part 2.
31 laurels: emblems of victory.
32 olive branches: emblems of peace. Despite Otway's plea (ll.33–6), the Whig opposition failed to view the Duke as a conciliator.

Dramatis Personae
The Little Girl: sometimes identified as Anne Bracegirdle (then aged about sixteen), who became one of the two most brilliant Restoration actresses; the other being Elizabeth Barry.
Barry: Monimia was Barry's first great tragic role.

Act 1, Scene 1
The expository opening section of this scene (ll.1–80) was often cut in later performance (see A. M. Taylor, *Next to Shakespeare: Otway's 'Venice Preserv'd' and 'The Orphan' and Their History on the London Stage* (Durham, NC, 1950), p.172).
7 empire: Bohemia formed part of a federation of German and central European states ruled by the Hapsburgs.
23 huffing: blustering, bullying.

63 **prince's:** Leopold I.

89 **Perseus . . . steed:** Otway confuses two Greek heroes: Perseus, who had winged sandals; and Bellerophon, who rode the winged horse, Pegasus.

126 **artist's:** physician's, surgeon's.

144 **nice:** hypersensitive.

147 **crowns:** coins worth five shillings.

148 **toy:** trifle; plaything; (also, slang for 'genitals').

201 **s.d. *Manet*:** stays, remains.

274 **wrack:** wreck.

276 **want:** lack.

350 **at a feast:** Q3; Q1-2 read 'at feast'.

Act 2, Scene 1

12 **cold:** deliberate. (Ghosh emends to 'bold'.)

23 **superstitious:** over-punctilious.

26 **humorist:** facetious person.

27 **spleen:** ill-temper.

28 **doctor:** clergyman.

136 **ye:** in later editions; Q1-4 read 'the'.

145 **chine:** backbone.

169 **Then sighed:** set as s.d. in Q1-4. Set as speech in later editions.

236 **Theban:** Oedipus who, unknowingly, killed his father and married his mother.

250 **stripped:** threadbare, ruined.

253 **weeds:** garments.

311 **silly:** deserving of pity.

319 **throughly:** closely.

325 **turtle:** turtle dove, emblem of marital fidelity.

332 **hyena:** emblem of deceit.

342 **forlorn:** morally lost, depraved.

Act 3, Scene 1

38 **chased the goblets:** passed the goblets. Q1 reads 'goblins' but attempts to make sense of this have proved unconvincing.

63-4 **Hercules . . . raised:** The Greek hero is said to have created the Strait of Gibraltar by dividing into two a mountain thereafter known as the Pillars of Hercules.

95 **Except:** unless.

176 **I:** Omitted in Q2-3. Taylor omits 'I' and prints ll.170-87 as prose.

196 **schools:** colleges.

309 **intelligence:** spiritual, intuitive understanding.

370 **Or . . . or:** either . . . or.

412 **Proteus:** a Greek sea-god and fabled shape-shifter.

463 **lampoons:** see note to Prologue, l.19.

513 **Mammon:** wealth personified as a false god.

586 **Who ... Capitol?:** Tarpeia thought to receive gold when she betrayed Rome's citadel, governed by her father, to the Sabine enemy. Instead, she received death.

587 **Who ... world?:** Cleopatra, Mark Anthony's lover, fled with her ships from the battle of Actium, causing his defeat by Octavius Caesar.

588–9 **Who ... ashes?:** Helen fled from her Greek husband to Troy with her lover, Paris, thus precipitating the Trojan War.

Act 4, Scene 1

37 **Though:** either.

85 **scrip:** bag.

89 **dress:** cultivate.

glebe: land.

98 **sped:** in an evil situation.

98–9 **How ... chained:** As Queen Omphale's lover and slave, Hercules wore women's clothes and sat spinning among her maids.

223 **horrid:** terrible.

Act 5, Scene 1

Song: set by Francis Forcer and published in *Choice Ayres and Songs*, The Third Book (1681).

69 **vilely:** abjectly.

75 **wished:** Q1–4 reads 'wish'.

106 **jealous:** doubtful.

160 **if, as:** Q1–2 reads 'as if'.

198 **where'er he treads:** Q1 reads 'wherehe e're treads'.

277–8 **I ... thee:** Jacob served fourteen years to gain Rachel as his wife (Genesis 29.18–28).

460 **parricide:** At this time, the term could mean the killing of any family member by a near relative.

Epilogue

1–2 **I ... die:** The epilogue, delivered by 'Serina', mediates between Mrs Butler's role as Acasto's daughter, and her real life 'role' as a member of the Duke's Company.

8 **a-conventicling:** Dissenters (nonconformists) worshipped at conventicles, and were routinely mocked for alleged sexual impropriety and hypocrisy. (See here, Otway's pun: – 'ticling'.)

12–13 **Or . . . away:** Otway jokes that the play may fail *before* the third day (or 'poet's day') when a play's takings went to the dramatist.

19 **sparks:** fashionable young men (derogatory).

THE ROVER, PART 2

Dedication

the Duke: James, Duke of York: brother and heir to Charles II; much disliked and distrusted as a Roman Catholic convert. Behn, a partisan royalist, routinely endorses the Stuart monarchy in her work, especially, as here, in times of political crisis.

3 **absence:** James had left England in 1679 after widespread unrest and robust parliamentary efforts to have him excluded from the succession. He finally returned in 1682.

17 **seeming-sanctified faction:** hypocritical, puritan party.

19–20 **royal martyr:** The cult of Charles I as a saintly martyr had been promoted in numerous royalist works, notably *Eikon Basilike* ('The King's Image'). Apparently written by the king himself, it was published soon after his execution (1649).

28 **lucky cant:** successful, but insincere, rhetoric.

34 **pageant:** specious, sham.

43–4 **He . . . loyalty:** Tactfully, Behn only hints here at another shared trait: the taste for a libertine lifestyle.

46–9 **Your infant . . . early:** During the interregnum, the exiled James had joined the French army as a volunteer at nineteen (1652). He served courageously with the French, and, later, the Spanish forces. Both Charles and James were often likened by panegyrists to Augustus Caesar, the first Roman emperor.

49 **still:** continually.

50–54 **which taught . . . cause:** 'Some of Oliver's commanders at Dunkirk'. <Behn> An overstatement, though a friendly meeting between James and the commander of the opposing English garrison (1657) had concerned Cromwell.

57–9 **How . . . admire:** As commander of the English navy, James had shown personal courage in fighting the Dutch at sea (1665).

Prologue

Smith: William Smith created the role of Willmore in *The Rover* and reassumed the part in its sequel. He does not speak in character in this highly politicised prologue.

4 **brethren:** dissenters.

5 **good o' th' commonweal:** a frequent plea during the Commonwealth

(1649–60). Revived during the 1680s by the opposition and ironised here.

7 mobile: mob, rabble.

14–15 The scene ... way: *The Rover* is set in Naples; Part 2 takes place in Madrid. Behn's subtext here relates to contemporary political issues: the Exclusion crisis and the Popish Plot. (See e.g. puns on 'plot', 'old game' and 'project', ll. 12–15).

22 dull rules: the 'rules' of dramatic writing; often meaning the notion of the three unities.

25 city pope: Effigies of the pope were paraded through London and burnt during the annual, public celebration of Elizabeth I's accession day (17 November).

28 lofty tier: the upper gallery, containing the cheapest, one-shilling seats.

29 dull ... pit: self-important, political dupes. Bench seats in the pit (in front of the stage) cost two shillings and sixpence.

32 private interest: unscrupulous, self-interested politicians.

35 caballing: plotting.

38–9 You'd ... nation: Cf. Fetherfool, 1.1.121–3.

40 commonwealths of old: the city states of ancient Greece; but glancing also at England's parliamentary government which had closed the theatres (1642).

44 schools: universities.

Dramatis Personae

Underhill: The great comic actor, Cave Underhill, reassumed the role of Blunt which he had famously created in *The Rover*.

Harlequin: trick-playing servant, a *commedia dell'arte* character. Summers suggests this part was acted by Thomas Jevon who played Harlequin in Behn's *The Emperor of the Moon* (1687).

daughter-in-law: stepdaughter.

<Mrs Price>: Q1 gives Mrs Norris here, but since she is also listed as playing Petronella, and the two characters appear together, she cannot have played both roles. Summers suggests Mrs Price played Lucia.

Mrs Barry: Elizabeth Barry had created the role of Hellena in *The Rover*, a character killed off by Behn before the beginning of the action in Part 2.

Scaramouch: a braggart character in the *commedia dell'arte*.

Operators: assistants to the quack-doctor.

Act 1, Scene 1
s.d. *campania dresses:* military uniform.

6 ordinary: eating-house, inn.

10 s.d. *Shut*: Behn often gives stage directions as imperatives to the actor or stage manager.

11 Why: 'Whe' in Q1. As in *The Rover*, I have regularised such usages to 'why', throughout.

27–8 little wanton god: Cupid.

35 blind ... Fortune: the classical goddess Fortuna; often depicted blindfolded, and holding or standing upon a wheel, emblem of her inconstancy.

37 interest: mercenary, monetary concerns; a key term in the play.

45 sensibly: acutely.

nice: sensitive.

61 'Adsheartlikins: mild old-fashioned oath (from: 'God's little heart'). It appears in various forms as Blunt's trademark in both parts of *The Rover*.

83 gypsy: Hellena in *The Rover*. She is disguised as a gypsy when she first meets Willmore (1.2.140–42).

86–7 Naples adventure: In *The Rover*, Act III, Blunt is tricked and fleeced by a 'quean' (whore).

94–5 pottage ... crab wine ... philoes: thick soup; inferior, sour wine; fellows. All three terms are derogatory here.

96–7 Belvile... lady: Belvile, friend to Willmore; married to Florinda at the end of *The Rover*.

98 St Germain: The English court in exile was based at St Germain–en-Laye, outside Paris.

100 temple ... Cloud: a tavern at St Cloud (near St Germain). Bacchus was the Greek god of wine.

109 sparks: fashionable young men. Beaumond is being ironic.

112 loyal fugitives: exiled royalists.

142 cozened: cheated.

147–8 Catholic king: the king of Spain.

163–4 where ... him: In hell, Tantalus was tormented by being placed near tempting, but inaccessible, fruit and water. See Ovid, *Amores*, II.2.43–4; *Metamorphoses*, IV.458–9.

166 bowels: tender feelings.

182–91 Thou ... purchased: Behn often uses blank verse for passages of heightened emotion, though the transition point from prose to verse can be hard to determine. I have set the whole of this passage as loose, blank verse. Only the last two lines (190–91) appear as verse in previous editions.

185 Fortune ... wheel: See note to l.35 above.

212 Christian Majesty: the king of Spain.

223 **Jesuit:** a member of the Society of Jesus, a Catholic order founded (1534) by Ignatius Loyola. By 1681, Jesuits were widely feared and hated in Protestant England for their supposed plots and duplicity.

240 **mountebank:** itinerant quack.

241 **bills:** handbills.

his: of his.

246 **empiric:** quack-doctor.

283 **knight o' th' shire:** MP for the county.

289 **bank:** the stage, or platform, on which the mountebank performed.

290–91 **add . . . scaramouch:** comic characters (especially from the *commedia dell'arte*). Music and dance regularly accompanied mountebank performances.

291 **in querpo:** in disguise (from Spanish *en cuerpo*, without a cloak; in undress).

363 **tramontane:** northerner.

378 **<like>:** *Behn*, and Todd. Q1 reads 'boto'.

402 **band:** bond, security.

411 **real:** a Spanish silver coin.

Act 1, Scene 2

8–9 **Cupid's . . . shoulder of mutton:** assistant cooks to Cupid . . . desirable dish ('mutton' was also slang for prostitute).

29 **Catso:** literally, slang for 'penis'; often used as a (mild) expletive.

30 **noblest chapmen:** best punters.

56 **sibyl:** prophetess.

90 **toilet:** dressing-table.

114 **give the wall to:** let someone take the inner side of the pavement, nearest the wall, where s/he could best avoid mud, etc., from the street, and slops from the windows above.

122 **old Adam's ale:** water.

126 **Capuchin:** austere Franciscan friar.

132 **toils:** net, snare.

160 **woodman:** a pimp (literally, a 'forester', preparing for Blunt's pun on 'deer').

167–8 **stone-horse:** stallion, ungelded horse.

Act 2, Scene 1

1 **chaffering:** haggling.

76 **small beer:** weak beer.

77 **Apollo:** the Greek sun-god.

78 **Jove's mistresses:** Jupiter (also called Jove), the chief of the Roman gods, had many lovers (e.g. Callisto, Cassiopeia and Maia) who were turned into constellations.

85 pistole: Spanish gold coin.

89 thy trade: Blunt takes Lucia for a whore.

98 tossed in a blanket: a form of rough punishment.

106 earnest: an advance payment.

128 cut my piece: share my taste.

183-4 'Have you heard . . . Englishman?': Fetherfool sings snatches from a popular old ballad (c.1603). (See *Roxburghe*, 653-6.)

189 dog days: hottest part of the year.

235 s.d. *pageant*: tableau, device.

s.d. *antickers*: grotesque dancers.

236-52 Behold . . . fate: For this and the other 'mountebank' speeches, Behn draws on *Thomaso* (Pt. 1, IV. 2) and its source, Jonson's *Volpone* (II.1.).

239-40 hearts . . . livers: magical ingredients. Mandrake plants were thought to have roots resembling the human form, and to shriek when pulled from the ground. Myth relates that the phoenix, a unique bird, regenerates from the ashes of its own funeral pyre.

259 felo de se: suicide. A criminal offence in this period.

308 false and out-of-fashioned: defective and unfashionable.

321 comedian: actress.

329 Jug: endearment, especially for a homely woman.

334-35 oracle of the box: A standard mountebank's device, but perhaps also a glance at the notorious 'Black Box', rumoured by the Whigs to hold evidence of the Duke of Monmouth's legitimacy.

338 muzzled: grizzled.

342-3 Elenora . . . Paris: Paris, Prince of Troy, stole the beautiful Helen from her Greek husband, thus occasioning the Trojan War. Priapus, the classical god of gardens and fertility, was often depicted as a grotesque figure with huge genitals.

344 formal: over-precise.

345 jennet: small Spanish horse.

368 Jago: James, patron saint of Spain.

379 Have: From here to the end of the scene, I have set the Beaumond-La Nuche exchanges as loose blank verse. Except for l.394, they appear as prose in Q1 and Todd.

382 remember: remind.

414-19 New . . . love: Cf. *Thomaso*, where the lines are not set as verse: 'You shall have beauty to your Art, such as shall catch each Lovers heart; Such amorous lustre in your Eyes, and your gray Hairs so bright shall rise; Your Cheeks shall such fresh Roses bear, your skin so white a slickness wear, as shall a general wonder move and pierce the hardest hearts with Love.' (Pt.1, IV. 2, p.364).

Act 2, Scene 2

7 s.d. Bis: repeat.

56 conjurer: magician.

61 s.d. *tricking:* dressing up.

67–74 Somme . . . confidents: 'Are we not too happy, / Fair Iris, that we are together? / Night and its dark veils / Cover our burning desires, / And love and the stars / Are our secret confidants.'

104 half-loaf: half a loaf is better than no bread.

123 snush: snuff.

128 a keeping husband: husband who keeps a mistress.

131–2 do thee reason: treat you fairly; (i.e. keep you happy in bed).

166 legs: bows.

Act 3, Scene 1

10 old law . . . ceremony: Old Testament, i.e. Jewish, law was very formal.

17–18 whore of Babylon: anti-Catholic term for the Church of Rome (Revelations 17.1). This may refer also to the kind of huge pageant figures carried in Protestant parades. (See note to Prologue, l.25.)

19–21 She's . . . shoulder: St Christopher bore the Christ-child on his shoulders across a river.

26–7 Gargantua: the eponymous giant-hero of Rabelais' romance (1534).

27 a Hercules in petticoats: Though renowned for his virile strength, Hercules, the classical hero and demigod, submitted to Queen Omphale as her slave and lover; exchanged clothes with her and sat spinning among her maids.

29 centaur: a mythical beast: half-horse, half-human.

50 lay: enterprise.

51–2 hang an arse: hang back.

56 salute: kiss.

102–3 first race of man: i.e. that before the Flood, fabled to have been giants.

106 tit: derogatory term for a girl; minx, hussy.

112 Amazonian: an Amazon, one of a legendary race of female warriors.

117 swinger: a large one.

118 Royal Sovereign: a leading ship of the Royal Navy.

178 Bezolos mano's: I kiss your hands (from Spanish greeting: *beso las manos*).

288 uncase: take off my disguise.

290 philosophic treasure: Willmore likens La Nuche to those elusive goals of alchemists: the philosopher's stone, which turned all to gold; and the elixir of life, which gave immortality.

292 now: Q1 has 'new'.

339 s.d. *dressed*: in his own clothes.

340–1 *'Vole . . . bocage'*: 'Fly, fly, into this cage / Little bird in the grove'.

381–2 brown George and Spanish pay: coarse, brown bread and compliments (but no money).

407–8 Flanders beauties: horses from Flanders were highly valued.

430 wo't: wilt (colloquial form of the 2nd person singular of the verb 'will').

439 overlaid: smothered (by being crushed in bed).

441 wight: person.

526–36 Love . . . burn: Set as prose in earlier editions.

538 rooks: cheats, swindlers; especially at cards or dice.

Act 4, Scene 1
24 Toledo: sword. Toledo was famous for fine sword-blades.

Act 4, Scene 2
34 every: Q1 has 'ever'; *Behn*, and Todd emend to 'all', and 'even', respectively.

55–8 Thou . . . damned: Set partly as verse in other editions.

113 satired: satirised.

227 gypsy: hussy.

229 closer: more secretly.

235–7 My . . . I: Daphne, fleeing from the amorous god, Apollo, escaped by being changed into a bay tree.

250 zephyrs: mild, west winds.

252–3 Diana . . . Endymion: Diana, the moon goddess, fell in love with Endymion as he slept on Mount Latmos, and visited him nightly.

273–5 I'm . . . days: magicians were thought able to conjure spirits into a circle.

281 my: Q1 has 'by'.

332 in the nick: at the critical moment.
   souse: swoop down.

333 worry: devour greedily.

Act 4, Scene 3
8 fined: paid up.

20 regale: entertain lavishly.

44–79 Aurelia . . . curse: La Nuche's speeches are set as prose in other editions.

95 Feathered inamoratos: dashing lovers with feathers in their hats.

112 **phoenix's nest**: the phoenix was said to make its pyre of aromatic twigs. See above, note to 2.1.239–40.

Act 4, Scene 4
2 **point**: lace.

Act 4, Scene 5
52–3 *Que . . . home*: What's that? / Ah, a poor, dead man. The farcical characters often speak a mishmash of cod-Spanish, French, Italian, etc.
60 **bastinadoed**: thrashed with a stick.
64 **recruit**: help.
  under one: together.

Act 5, Scene 1
s.s. *unbraced*: with his clothes unfastened.
6–7: set as prose in Q1 and Todd.
35–42: set partly as prose in Q1 and Todd.
81 **chapman**: bargainer, trader.
166–70 **No . . . landlady**: from: 'That beauty I adored before', *Westminster Drollery* (1671). Probably not by Behn.
200 **Spanish philtre**: aphrodisiac.
204 **you**: Q1 reads 'your'.

Act 5, Scene 2
49 **tedious**: tardy

Act 5, Scene 3
1 *Peano*: gently, softly (Italian, *piano*, softly).
18 **sign of the Naked Boy**: possibly an inn sign.
  Plymouth cloaks: cudgels.
26 **album graecum**: a medicament comprising the dried faeces of dogs (*Behn*, p.447).
27–8 *un . . . palauea*: a few words, please.
29 *Entende . . . Englesa?*: Do you understand English?
30 *Em poco*: a little.
31 *Per quelq arts*: through what arts.
33 *La art de transformatio*: the art of transformation.
37 *un vieule famme*: an old woman.
65 *bonus nochus*: good night.
67 *Patientia*: patience.
72 *Que et la?*: Who's that?

Act 5, Scene 4
2 **Scylla . . . Charybdis**: In Greek myth, a sea-monster (Scylla) inhabited a cave opposite a whirlpool (Charybdis). Thus, to avoid one danger, voyagers had to sail closer to the other.

4 **take ... forelock:** Fortuna (see note to 1.1.35.) was often depicted bald except for a single forelock, emblematising the need to seize an approaching opportunity before it passes.

14 **fed:** Q1 reads 'feed'.

23 **unrig:** divest.

29 **lose a hog:** proverb: a man will not lose a hog for a pennyworth of tar.

30 **bird in hand:** proverb: a bird in the hand is worth two in the bush.

50-1 **Egyptian crocodile:** At a feast, Cleopatra, queen of Egypt, dissolved a pearl in the drinking-cup of her lover, Mark Anthony.

109 **Belvile's ... him:** See *The Rover*, III.5.

125 **'Ounds:** indignant exclamation (abbreviation of 'God's wounds').

134 **two-handed:** strapping.

145 **carriage:** load.

213 **hour of the bergère:** opportune time of love-making (literally, the 'shepherdess's hour').

239-44: set as prose in other editions.

262-3: **John Potages:** peasants, menials. (See note to 1.1.1.94-5.)

267 **synagogue:** Jew.

277 **chronicle:** figuratively, something/someone very long/tall.

280 **Guzman medicines:** fake medicines. (Roger Boyle's farce *Guzman* (1669) includes a quack-astrologer.)

298 **Myrmidons:** a fabled band of indefatigable warriors, changed from ants into men by Zeus (Jupiter) to assist various of the heroes.

308 **no Naples ... chains:** no fake valuables given by whores. See *The Rover*, 2.1.55-7 & 4.5.151-3.

345-6 **rub off:** run off, make off.

355-6 **disembogue:** discharge, throw up.

364 **clyster:** give an enema to.

367-8 **take ... place:** during the interregnum, the Covenant (1643) was an oath requiring all MPs and officials to defend the Parliamentary cause and support church reform. Sequestrators confiscated royalists' forfeited property.

Epilogue

1-4: Behn parallels the theatre companies' financial crisis with that facing the king: Charles II has to summon parliament in the hope it will vote him funds ('supply'); needy dramatists 'summon' audiences by playbills advertising new works.

18 **Pope ... friars:** Among the popular, anti-Catholic works glanced at here are: Settle's *The Female Prelate* (1680); and Dryden's *The Spanish Friar* (1680).

20 **Ads Nigs:** mild, rustic oath.
 woundy: very.
21 **fuger:** Todd suggests 'figure'.
23 **for Commonwealth:** i.e. a Whig.
27 **'Ads lightikins':** mild old-fashioned oath (from: 'God's lights').
29 **bob:** mock.
30 **tickle away:** tease; reprove amusingly.
32 **greasing:** flattery.
34 **forming . . . make:** another reference to the pope-burning pageants which were accompanied by fireworks. (See note to Prologue, l.25.)
36 **the Cause:** that represented by Shaftesbury's anti-Catholic Whig faction, and seen by Tory propagandists as crypto-republican.
43 **Our king . . . paid:** Charles II; but perhaps also with a glance at Dryden, whose salary as Poet Laureate was often in arrears.

THE WIVES' EXCUSE

Epigraph

Nihil . . . expectatio: 'Nothing is so disadvantageous to those [authors] who wish to please as [their public's] expectation.' (Adapted from Cicero, *Academica*, Bk.II, Section 4, Para.10.)
  Southerne's epigraph alludes to the relative failure of *The Wives' Excuse* compared with the popular success achieved by his preceding comedy, *Sir Anthony Love* (1690).

Dedication

The Dedication appears in only three recorded copies of the 1st edition (1692). (See Harold Love, 'The Printing of *The Wives' Excuse* (1692)', *The Library*, 5th ser., XXV (1970), pp.344–9.)

Wharton: Thomas Wharton (1648–1715), later 1st Marquis of Wharton. A keen Whig supporter, racehorse owner and libertine; he had notoriously abused his first wife, the poet, Anne Wharton (d.1685).

Comptroller . . . Household: a middle-ranking Court appointment, held by Wharton 1689–1702.

1 **man of fortune:** wealthy man.
12 **interest:** influence.
13 **most voices:** the opinion of the majority of the audience.
14–15 **some people . . . it:** presumably those who read it in manuscript before the première.
19 **sparks:** fashionable young men (derogatory).
28 **then:** than.
29 **music-meeting:** public concert with instrumentalists and singers; a fairly recent and fashionable form of entertainment.

35 **billet-doux**: love-letter.

36 **upon leading her out**: as she was escorted out.

39 **capital**: the chief.

44 **kind**: generous.

Sir Anthony Love: see note to the epigraph, above.

46 **credit ... him**: on the basis of his esteem for this play.

48 *Cleomenes*: For details, see Winn, pp.451–3.

51 **that preferred me to it**: that earned me the assignment.

67–8 **I ... fair sex**: a disingenuous comment in view of Wharton's reputation.

69–70 **to be justified ... herself**: to justify her choice of lover.

71 **pretenders**: would-be lovers.

74 **friends**: lovers.

To Mr Southerne

2 **malignant planets**: i.e. those hostile to intelligent, well-written plays (such as *The Wives' Excuse*). Lines 1–8 bemoan the contemporary popularity of farce.

9 **The Spanish nymph**: unidentified; presumably referring either to a character in, or title of a recent unsuccessful play.

11 **monster Muscovite**: i.e. a Russian bear. Bear-baiting was still a popular rival attraction.

14 **blame thy tale**: criticise your plot [for immorality].

15 **So Terence plotted ... writ**: The Roman dramatist, Publius Terentius Afer (*c.*190–150 BC) was renowned for risqué but elegantly written comedies.

17 **scene**: play.

18 **want of Nokes**: James Nokes, famous for his 'low' comic roles, had recently retired.

22 **the wife**: 'The wife in the play, Mrs Friendall' (marginal note in Q1).

24–5 **a glance ... rebuke**: This presumably relates to Mrs Barry's handling of the role at 5.3.70–105.

28–9 **Etherege ... Wycherley**: dramatists of the 1670s. Sir George Etherege (*c.*1635–91) wrote three comedies, most notably, *The Man of Mode* (1676), and was renowned for the ease and elegance of his writing. William Wycherley (1641–1715) wrote four comedies. *The Country Wife* (1675) and *The Plain Dealer* (1676) won him fame as a dramatic satirist.

Prologue

2 **English stomachs**: hearty appetites and (in view of the war with France) patriotic tastes, the play having no French source).

3 *chere entire*: both 'a roast meal' (or 'feast'), and 'a woman'. [See note to *The Libertine*, 4.4.50.]

7 **vizard-masks**: prostitutes.

11 **foul weather**: quarrels, disputes.

24 **three deep**: the side-boxes held three rows of seats.

Dramatis Personae

<SEVEN> FOOTMEN: They would seem to be assigned as follows: 1st to Wellvile; 2nd to Friendall; 3rd to Wilding; 4th to Courtall; 5th to Lovemore; 6th to (?)Ruffle; 7th to Mrs Witwoud.

LINKBOYS: employed to carry torches ('links') to light people along streets at night.

Act 1, Scene 1

s.s. **hazard**: dice game. [For the rules, see Charles Cotton, *The Compleat Gamester* (1674; rptd 1972), pp.168–73.]

2 **fifth act ... cost**: Servants were allowed free entry to the upper gallery to watch a play's last act.

5 **main**: a throw at hazard.

10–11 **board-wages**: wages allowed to servants for food.
bones: dice (often called 'the Devil's bones').

13 **tester**: sixpence.

26 **sets**: bets.
small-beer butler: inferior servant.

39 **for good husbandry**: a pun, meaning both 'as a careful manager [of one's income]', and 'as a good "husband"'.

39–40 **to get ... lady**: the maid would breast-feed her mistress's child and her own.

43 **in the convey**: as she was conveyed [to him].

55 **of very fair reception**: generally hospitable.

57 **frank**: open-handed.

87 **grind ... mill**: i.e. take bribes and tips from her would-be lovers (with sexual innuendo, as in much of this dialogue).

91 **play**: card-playing (for money).

114 **Westminster Hall**: site of the chief law courts.

114–15 **husband's ... wife**: a joke. This was not a legal option.

134 **pretenders enow**: enough pursuers.

141 **used to do**: as she has been accustomed to.

156 **Horn Fair**: a joking allusion to cuckoldry. The *real* Horn Fair (for selling horn goods) was held in Kent.

158 **proper**: own.

159 **fairing**: a gift from the 'fair' i.e. a scandal-spreading letter.

163 **visiting lady**: a compulsive maker and receiver of social calls.

183 **touch:** witty glance at.

186 **drawing-room:** the royal family's reception room at Whitehall.

208 **Jack Sauce:** impudent fellow.

221 **Tourvilles:** Anne Hilarion de Cotentin, Comte de Tourville, Admiral of the French fleet which had defeated the English and Dutch forces in 1690. Fears of a French invasion were still current.

226 **gaping galleries:** gallants frequented church galleries to eye women in the pews below.

Act 1, Scene 2

16 **wot:** wilt.

22 **call:** occasion. (Also, 'a whistle to attract birds', the meaning played on by Courtall.)

24 **cat-call:** shrill whistle to show disapproval in theatres. (It could also mean the 'mating call of cats'; and 'cat' was slang for 'prostitute'.)

27 **sonatas ... chaconnes:** The sonata was then considered an Italian form of music; the chaconne, a French.

46 **universal:** generally attentive.

89–90 **something too soon ... too late for me:** a reflection on their disparate ages.

109–10 **your character:** the current gossip about you.

127 **ramble:** a wander about (often with sexual connotations).

129 **hackney jaunt:** a ride in a hired carriage.

132 **several:** separate.

133 **Pontack's ... the Rummer:** two fashionable taverns.

134 **strangely:** exceedingly.

135 **draw up the glasses:** put up the carriage windows.

138 **trust to:** expect, look for.

146 **toilet:** fashionable ladies received morning calls during the later stages of dressing.

151 **confidence:** trust.

159 **scurvy:** sorry, wretched.

194 **sport off:** display, show.

196 **observations upon me:** seeing what I'm doing [and criticising].

203 **civil:** flattering.

216 **lady:** Friendall has been led to believe that Lovemore pursues another (unidentified) lady.

wot of: know of.

222 **make an interest with:** use my influence to persuade [to do something].

232 **set:** set to music.

262–3 **turns ... right use:** i.e. cuckolds him.

268 **Phyllis, or Chloris:** typical fictitious names for addressees.

271 **Major General Sackville:** Edward Sackville. His song, like the others in the play, is set by Purcell.

272 **Ingrateful:** ungrateful.

285 **death:** also meaning 'orgasm'.

286 **try:** test, experience.

291 **do you reason:** show you my appreciation.

312 **vizard-mask:** prostitute (since masks were often worn by such).

312–13 **the pit . . . boxes:** At the theatre, prostitutes frequented the pit on the look-out for custom; respectable, wealthy women occupied the boxes.

319 **world's end:** perhaps a pun, alluding to 'The World's End', a Chelsea haunt of ill-repute.

323 **s.d.** *addressing to her:* falling in beside her.

330 **without exception:** without any moral objection.

335 **jealous:** suspicious.

343 **occasion:** opportunity.

351 **expect:** await.

Act 1, Scene 3
7 **s.h.** 5TH FOOTMAN: perhaps a mistake for the 2nd (i.e. Friendall's) footman. (See Cordner, p.415; Jordan & Love, I, 467.)

9 **improve:** take advantage of.

12 **give it under my hand:** have written.

13 **servant:** suitor, lover.

20–21 **no touching her:** no involving her [in your joking].

30–31 **right yourself:** i.e. by engaging him in a sword-fight.

32 **to do a justice to yourself:** to challenge him to a duel.

38 **lying abroad:** spending the night away from home.

54 **clear-gained:** won with clear profit, at no risk.

80 **kind:** sexually amenable.

Act 2, Scene 1
8 **gilt paper:** writing paper with gilt edges.

9 **Mr Bentley's:** Richard Bentley, Covent Garden publisher of plays and novels.

Mrs Da Robe's: her name may relate to two occupations, since 'bona roba' could mean 'whore' (Thornton, p.131).

10 **mantua-woman's:** maker of mantles, or loose over-gowns.

17 **so nearly . . . interest:** such a close relation.

39 **carted bawd:** To be drawn through the streets in a cart was a common rough punishment for prostitutes.

40 **bilk:** give the slip to (and evade payment).

45 **cellar:** place of low resort.

47 **kennels:** gutters.

50 **daggle-tailed:** having muddied skirts.

57 **Marry come up:** old-fashioned expression of reproof.

60 **warning:** notice.

62–3 **Another woman's husband:** This mysterious character is never seen or identified.

64–5 **as hanging a countenance:** a face that suggests he deserves hanging.

83 **the usual reason:** pregnancy.

85 **charter:** leave or licence. Mrs Teazall reflects the usual upper-class scorn for City wives and their reputed infidelities.

86 **very:** mere.

94 **miscarriage:** mishap.

102 **God's bodikins:** mild, old-fashioned oath ('by God's little body').

107 **room:** place.

Act 2, Scene 2

7–8 **that . . . alive:** i.e. one who hasn't yet come into her inheritance.

24–5 **secured overnight:** arrested, locked up. Duelling was illegal.

35 **wonnot:** will not.

39 **rakehell:** scoundrel.

45 **tameness:** *Works* (1713); Q1 has 'lameness'.

50 **discovering himself:** revealing himself [as a coward].

60 **in the winter:** i.e. when campaigning was impossible.

82 **false musters:** Officers often put the names of dead soldiers on duty rosters and pocketed their pay.

95 **laces:** cords. (*Works* (1713) has 'laws'.)

131 **make an interest:** use my influence.

Act 2, Scene 3

6 **ever a:** any.

16 **commodes:** fashionably high head-dresses.

17 **expect when:** anticipate the time when.

18 **bandboxes:** light protective containers for women's hats, head-dresses, etc.

29–30 **does . . . favour:** allows one to have sex with her.

30 **cozen:** cheat.

31 **level to:** in line with.

41 **loose:** debauched.

54 **levee:** a formal reception.

55–6 **letter-lady:** see 2.1.11–12.

56 **unseasonable:** Wilding needs time to recoup his sexual resources.

62 **current:** acceptable.

93 **towardly:** apt, promising.

108 **resolve you:** put your mind at rest.

114 **sober party:** morally censorious.

130 **trustee:** a means by which a woman could prevent her husband-to-be gaining control of her finances.

136 **conveyances:** transactions.

139–40 **particular:** detailed account.

146 **inflaming the jointure:** having to increase the sum agreed in a woman's marriage contract that she should receive if widowed.

147 **put 'em upon't:** make them do it.

162 **what . . . raise:** i.e. his penis.

168 s.d. *declines . . . respect*: he treats her more respectfully.

181 **family:** the servants, household.

186 **want:** lack.

188 **common women:** whores.

220 **very well:** attractive. Wilding's reply wilfully takes it to mean 'with no sexually transmitted disease'.

254 **chapman:** dealer, trader.

289–90 **As much . . . see her:** though her figure is excellent.

307 **the Mall:** fashionable walk (and pick-up spot) near St James's Park.

311–12 **an inclination . . . improved:** a desire to make the most of it.

Act 3, Scene 1

2 **Banstead Downs:** race-course near Epsom.

16 **messenger:** royal official whose duties included arresting would-be duellists.

19 **fees:** such prisoners were liable to charges and had to pay also for their board.

28 s.d. *gown and cap*: his night-clothes.

35 **Payable at sight:** a challenge, like a 'bill' (money order) required an immediate response.

57 **wait upon me:** be kept waiting for me.

63 **discover:** reveal.

84 **he grows upon him:** he is growing bolder.

111 **Will's coffee-house:** No.1, Bow Street, Covent Garden; a fashionable resort of writers (Southerne included).

113 **behind the scenes:** admirers frequented the actors' dressing rooms.

115–16 **upper galleries:** which held the cheapest seats and rowdiest spectators.

153 **Southampton House:** Great Russell Street. Duels were often fought in the fields behind the house.

164 **crackers:** squibs, fireworks.

169 **Child:** Sir Francis Child, goldsmith and banker, ran an early form of cheque account at his shop. (Jordan & Love, I, 469.)

Act 3, Scene 2

14 **occasion:** way.

77 **delicate:** fine, charming.

100 **unmannerly:** ill-bred.

102 **clutter:** clatter.

149 **assurance:** self-confidence.

160–61 **temper to manage it:** enough self-control to deal with it.

166 **office:** turn, service.

172 **s.h. solus:** alone.

172–95 **I'll think no more on 't, 'tis impossible:** This speech is set as prose in Q1, but (mostly) as blank verse in Jordan & Love, I, pp.309–10.

180–1 **Maybe ... myself:** Perhaps I have done myself down.

198 **the king's box:** the centre box. It was let out when not in use by the royal family.

207 **Dryden ... Wycherley:** Both were friends of Southerne.

220 **cogitabund:** wrapped in thought.

222 **mind:** notice.

238 **intrigue:** courtship, love-making.

294 **in regard to:** out of consideration to.

323 **who's will:** who as will, i.e. 'whoever will', 'no matter who'.

381 **ungrateful:** unwelcome.

396 **ha' been upon your bones:** have harassed you; (literally: 'beaten on/devoured to your bones').

402 **a bubble:** dupe; one who is cheated.

404 **lanterloo:** popular card-game.

413–14 **in masquerade:** wearing masks and in disguised costume. Masquerade balls and entertainments, public and private, were popular and notoriously afforded opportunities for sexual adventures.

415 **out of your forms:** free from your usual proprieties.

Act 4, Scene 1

6–7 **Lucena ... Galicia ... Mountain-Alicant:** Spanish red wines from Lucena (near Córdoba), and Galicia (north-west Spain); and a red dessert wine from Málaga.

10–13 **Aracena:** wine from Aracena (south-west Spain).

Ranchio: aged Spanish dessert wine.

Peralta: a dessert wine from Valencia.

Carcavelos: Portuguese red and white wine.

Lacrymae: an Italian sweet white wine from Mt Vesuvius.

Schiveas: a wine from the Toledo area.

Cephalonia: a Greek wine.

Montalcino: a wine from Montalcino (near Siena).

all the Muscatels: Spanish, Portuguese (and perhaps Greek) sweet white wines.

Tokay: an expensive dessert wine from Hungary.

16 **Buda:** Budapest.

25 **Borachio:** Spanish wine (from an adopted Spanish word meaning 'a large goatskin bag or bottle'; also 'a drunkard').

29 **Vin de Congress:** a spurious wine. The joke may allude to the Congress of the Hague (held January 1691). Hence, perhaps, the deluded Friendall assumes it is a Dutch wine.

31 **Zeeland:** William III was a stadtholder of the province.

34-5 **Vin de Short-Neck:** another joke; perhaps a pun on Charneco, a Portuguese wine (Jordan & Love, I, 471).

37 **Thompson's:** an (unidentified) tavern, or perhaps a vintner's.

38 **prohibited French wine:** because of the on-going war, trade with France was illegal.

44 **Havana . . . 'tis washed:** snuff from Havana tobacco (despite Friendall's assertion) is *not* washed.

45 **dry powders:** snuffs that are ground after fermentation.

48 **right Palilio:** true Palilio (a delicate variety of snuff).

51 **His . . . Majesty:** the King of Spain.

55 **fresco:** fresh air.

56 **mount:** raised garden mound.

58 **delicately . . . upon:** What a charming notion!

62-3 **Canton . . . Sunloe:** Tea-drinking became fashionable in England in the 1660s.

64 **Non Amo Te:** 'I do not love you' [Martial, *Epigrams*, I.32.1]. Another punning leg-pull which Friendall misses.

67 **the committee:** the Board of Governors of the East India Company.

70 **at the best hand:** either (1) from the best supplier, or (2) at the cheapest price.

73 **an Indian house:** perhaps a merchant-trader's premises rather than just a shop.

76 **order it:** see to it.

91 **Stay! This violence:** This speech and those following, set here as verse, appear as prose in Q1.

134 **could:** 'and' in Q1; 'could' in *Works* (1713).

176 **want but that:** (1) That's all I need [to scorn you utterly]. (2) That would be the last straw.

199–200 **had my ends:** achieved my aim.

240 **Rosamond's Pond:** a common place for assignations in St James's Park.

255 **to secure us:** to protect us.

289 **come to:** surrender.

293 **conscious:** observant.

308 **Pam:** the knave of clubs in lanterloo.

314 **comet:** card-game.

318 **go your halves:** undertake to share half of Mrs Witwoud's winnings, or pay half her losses.

350 **of nearer consequence:** affecting you more closely.

356 **to meet:** *Works* (1713); Q1 reads 'to'.

357 **business:** purpose.

362 **pretend to be:** set out to be.

390 **there's no danger of your foul:** either: 'your idea of fair play is the same as cheating', or 'I'm not going to risk it when you *set out* to cheat'.

400 **in my own form:** in my own [school] class, i.e. with people my own age.

404 **sets:** games.

turned one: won one.

405 **comet in my hand:** when playing comet, the most advantageous card to hold (hence its name).

416 **Jew ... Protestant:** to evade the law forbidding Jews to be shopkeepers, and the discriminatory taxes demanded of Jews.

417–18 **essences and sweet-waters:** perfumes.

418 **to raffle for:** he has been required to run a raffle offering goods from his shop as prizes.

Act 4, Scene 2
10 **unadvised:** imprudent.

45 **women:** *Works* (1713); Q1 has 'woman'.

58 **swinged:** beaten.

Act 5, Scene 1
36 **intelligence:** information.

48 **personate:** impersonate.

room: stead, place.

53 **grant him the favour:** let him have sex with me.

Act 5, Scene 2

13 women of condition . . . women of quality: women of some status, even gentlewomen.

48 peevishly: annoyingly.

61 in favour of my own: to promote my own [pleasures].

Act 5, Scene 3

4 i'th'way: close at hand.

5 I thought . . . you: Betty is wearing a copy of Mrs Sightly's scarf.

16 confounds: confuses.

17 to be particular: assail one woman in particular.

23 bush: (1) the bush attributed to the man in the moon (2) a bundle of sticks [for beating boys].

26–7 Come a'me: (1) come to me (2) come at me [sexually].

62 SONG heading *Thomas Cheek*: wit and minor poet in Dryden's circle.

68 Apollo: Greek god of eloquence, music and poetry.

87 improved 'em: exploited.

90 heaviness: dullness.

93–109 Mr Lovemore . . . only pity me: All this passage is set as prose in Q1.

102 trial: attempt.

126 s.d. *parl*: talk.

133 stay for you: have to wait for you.

153 do myself reason: justify myself.

153–4 disappoint . . . disappointment: take away the pleasure she found in my discomfiture.

162 a property: a tool.

187–8 pull off her mask: Guests were asked to unmask briefly on entrance to deter gatecrashers. He is mocking Mrs Teazall who is *not* wearing a mask.

190 laid . . . parish: abandoned illegitimate children were brought up at the parish's expense.

202–3 speak without a question: i.e. without asking a question: one of the legal tests for imbecility (Jordan & Love, I, 474).

213 turned up for a blockhead: bent over the schoolmaster's flogging-block and whipped as a dunce.

216 tickle your tail: a play on meanings of 'tickle-tail': (1) a schoolmaster's stick (2) a whore. (Cordner, p.425.)

223 as it used to be: i.e. with married women (rather than young unmarried girls) having affairs.

226 deboist: debauched.

241 **opening a poor woman's case:** an unconscious innuendo; 'case' was slang for female genitals.

244 **coat-card:** court-card i.e. queen, king, jack.

248 **untowardly:** perverse, difficult.

256 **Mr Buttybun:** 'One lying with a woman who has just lain with another man, is said to have a buttered bun' (Francis Grose, 1758; cited in Jordan & Love, I, 474).

257 **writings:** marriage contract.

268 **in my generation:** a pun.

277 **good trade:** prostitution.

278 **break:** ruin (financially).

333 **teeth:** resistance.

339–41 **My liberty . . . mine:** set as prose in all editions before Jordan & Love.

342–3 **This is . . . answer:** set as prose in all previous editions.

350 **passed:** overlooked.

350–53 **You know I can . . . myself:** set as prose in all previous editions.

356–67 **The unjust world . . . despised:** set as prose in all editions before Jordan & Love.

357 **cause:** *Works* (1713) has 'the cause'.

359 **slavery:** *Works* (1713) has 'a slavery'.

376 **article:** stipulate.

386 **blown-upon:** fly-blown, tainted.

389–91 **This . . . tools:** an ironic variant on the closing couplet of Molière's *L'École Des Maris* (1661). Noted in David Roberts, *The Ladies: Female Patronage of Restoration Drama 1660–1700* (Oxford, 1989), p.153, n.85.

Epilogue

12 **Our author . . . reforming:** a glance at contemporary unease over the supposedly subversive influence of plays on social and (especially) sexual mores. Demands for reform climaxed in Jeremy Collier's *A Short View of the Immorality and Prophaneness of the English Stage* (1698).

27 **velvet:** smooth, seductive.

31 **Betterton:** Famous for his portrayal of rake-heroes over a long and distinguished career, Betterton to an extent epitomised for audiences the figure of the successful rake. For the disrupting here of such audience preconceptions, see Holland, p.142.

32 **cocks:** adjusts his hat – a typically 'rakish' gesture.

Appendix

Heading: A Song ... fourth act: Despite its heading, this song follows 'Corinna, I excuse thy face' (5.3.62–9) in Q1. I find the issue of its positioning unresolved and have therefore placed it in an appendix. (For details of other editors' views, see Thornton, pp.30–31; Jordan & Love, I, 265–6; Cordner, p.427.)

11 your: Q1 reads 'her'.

SELECT BIBLIOGRAPHY

[* Unless otherwise stated, the place of publication is London.]

Theatre Conditions & Performance

Highfill Jr, Philip, Kalman A. Burnim, & Edward A. Langhans (eds). *A Biographical Dictionary of Actors, Actresses, Musicians, Dancers, etc. in London 1660–1800*, 16 vols (Carbondale & Edwardsville, Ill., 1973–93).

Holland, Peter. *The Ornament of Action: Text and Performance in Restoration Comedy* (Cambridge, 1979).

Howe, Elizabeth. *The First English Actresses: Women and Drama 1660–1700* (Cambridge, 1992).

Loftis, John, Richard Southern, Marion Jones & A. H. Scouten (eds). *The Revels History of Drama in English, Vol. V, 1660–1710* (1976).

Love, Harold. 'Who were the Restoration audience?' *The Yearbook of English Studies*, 10 (1980), 21–44.

Milhous, Judith, & R. D. Hume. *Producible Interpretation: Eight English Plays 1675–1707* (Carbondale, Ill., 1985).

Powell, Jocelyn. *Restoration Theatre Production* (1984).

Roberts, David. *The Ladies: Female Patronage of Restoration Drama 1660–1700* (Oxford, 1989).

Scouten, Arthur H., & Robert D. Hume. '"Restoration Comedy" and its Audiences', 1660–1776,' *Yearbook of English Studies*, 10 (1980), 45–69. [Reptd in Robert D. Hume, *The Rakish Stage: Studies in English Drama 1660–1800* (Carbondale, Ill., 1983), pp.46–81.]

Van Lennep, William, Emmett L. Avery & Arthur Scouten (eds). *The London Stage 1660–1800. Part I, 1660–1700* (Carbondale, Ill., 1965).

Wilson, J. H. *All The King's Ladies: Actresses of the Restoration* (Chicago, 1958).

General Criticism

Burns, Edward. *Restoration Comedy: Crises of Desire and Identity* (1987).

Brown, Laura. *English Dramatic Form, 1660–1760: An Essay in Generic History* (New Haven, 1981).

Canfield, J. Douglas, & Deborah C. Payne (eds). *Cultural Readings of Restoration and Eighteenth-Century Theater* (Athens, Georgia, 1995).

Hughes, Derek. *English Drama 1660–1700* (Clarendon, Oxford, 1996).

Hume, Robert D. *The Development of English Drama in the Late Seventeenth Century* (Oxford, 1976).

Jose, Nicholas. *Ideas of the Restoration in English Literature* (Cambridge, Mass., 1984).

Owen, Susan J. *Restoration Theatre and Crisis* (Oxford, 1996).

Rothstein, Eric, & Frances M. Kavenik. *The Designs of Carolean Comedy* (Carbondale & Edwardsville, Ill., 1988).

Smith, J. H. *The Gay Couple in Restoration Comedy* (Cambridge, Mass., 1948).

Staves, Susan. *Players' Sceptres: Fictions of Authority in the Restoration* (Lincoln, Nebraska, 1979).

Wilson, J. H. *The Court Wits of the Restoration* (Princeton, NJ, 1948).

Libertine Drama Criticism

Braverman, Richard. 'Libertines and Parasites', *Restoration* 11 (1987), 73–86.

—— 'The Rake's Progress Revisited: Politics and Comedy in the Restoration', in *Cultural Readings*, pp.141–68.

Hume, Robert D. 'The Myth of the Rake in "Restoration Comedy"', *Studies in the Literary Imagination*, 10 (Spring, 1977), 25–55. [Reptd in *The Rakish Stage: Studies in English Drama, 1600–1800* (Carbondale, Ill., 1983), pp.138–75.]

Jordan, Robert. 'The Extravagant Rake in Restoration Comedy', in *Restoration Critical Approaches*, ed. H. Love (1972).

Markley, Robert. *Two-Edg'd Weapons: Style and Ideology in the Comedies of Etherege, Wycherley, and Congreve* (Oxford, 1988).

Munns, Jessica. 'Change, skepticism, and uncertainty', in *The Cambridge Companion to Restoration Theatre*, ed. Deborah Payne Fisk (Cambridge, 2000), pp.142–57.

Neill, Michael. 'Heroic Heads and Humble Tails: Sex, Politics, and The Restoration Comic Rake', *The Eighteenth Century: Theory & Interpretation* 24 (1983), 115–39.

Novak, Maximilian. 'Margery Pinchwife's "London Disease": Restoration Comedy and the Libertine Offensive of the 1670's', *Studies in the Literary Imagination* 10 (1977), 1–23.

Traugott, John. 'The Rake's Progress from Court to Comedy: a Study in Comic Form', *Studies in English Literature,* 6 (1966), 381–407.

Turner, James Grantham. 'The Libertine Sublime: Love and Death in

Restoration England', *Studies in Eighteenth-Century Culture*, 19 (1989), 99–115.

Underwood, Dale. *Etherege and the Seventeenth-Century Comedy of Manners* (New Haven, 1957).

Weber, Harold. *The Restoration Rake-Hero: Transformations in Sexual Understanding in Seventeenth-Century England* (Univ. of Wisconsin Press, 1986).

Marriage A-la-Mode

Braverman, Richard. *Plots and Counterplots: Sexual Politics and the Body Politic in English Literature, 1660–1730* (Cambridge, 1993).

Brown, Laura S. 'The Divided Plot: Tragicomic Form in the Restoration', *English Literary History*, 47 (1980), 67–89.

Canfield, J. Douglas. 'The Ideology of Restoration Tragicomedy', *English Literary History*, 51 (1984), 447–64.

Hughes. *English Drama 1660–1700*.

Kroll, Richard. 'Instituting Empiricism: Hobbes's *Leviathan* and Dryden's *Marriage à la Mode*', in *Cultural Readings*, pp.39–66.

McKeon, Michael. 'Marxist Criticism and *Marriage à la Mode*', *The Eighteenth Century: Theory and Interpretation* 24 (1983), 141–63.

Maguire, Nancy Klein. *Regicide and Restoration: English Tragicomedy, 1660–1671* (Cambridge, 1992).

Rothstein, Eric, & Frances Kavenik. *The Designs of Carolean Comedy*.

The Libertine

Alssid, Michael W. *Thomas Shadwell* (New York, 1967).

Kunz, Don R. *The Drama of Thomas Shadwell* (Salzburg, 1972).

Hammond, Brean, & Paulina Kewes. '*A Satyre against Reason and Mankind* from Page to Stage', in *That Second Bottle: Essays on John Wilmot, Earl of Rochester*, ed. Nicholas Fisher (Manchester & New York, 2000), pp. 133–52.

Jaffe, Aaron. 'Seditious Appetites and Creeds: Shadwell's Libertine and Hobbes's Foole', *Restoration*, 24, 2 (Fall, 2000).

Mandel, Oscar. *The Theatre of Don Juan* (1963).

Neill, Michael. 'Heroic Heads and Humble Tails'.

Rothstein, Eric. 'Thomas Shadwell', in *Restoration and Eighteenth-Century Dramatists, Dictionary of Literary Biography*, ed. Paula R. Backscheider (Detroit, 1989), 181–95.

Wheatley, Christopher J. *Without God or Reason: The Plays of Thomas Shadwell and Secular Ethics in the Restoration* (London & Toronto, 1993).

The Rover, Parts 1 & 2

Copeland, Nancy. '"Once a whore and ever"? Whore and Virgin in *The Rover* and its Antecedents', *Restoration*, 16, 1 (Spring, 1992), 20–27.

DeRitter, Jones. 'The Gypsy, *The Rover*, and the Wanderer: Aphra Behn's Revision of Thomas Killigrew', *Restoration*, 10, 2 (Fall, 1986), 82–92.

Diamond, Elin. '*Gestus* and Signature in *The Rover*', *English Literary History*, 56, 3 (Fall, 1989), 519–41.

Hughes, Derek. 'The Masked Woman Revealed: or, the Prostitute and the Playwright in Aphra Behn Criticism', *Women's Writing*, 7, 2 (2000), 149–64.

Hutner, Heidi. 'Revisioning the Female Body: Aphra Behn's *The Rover*, Parts I and II', in *Rereading Aphra Behn: History, Theory and Criticism*, ed. Heidi Hutner (Charlottesville & London, 1993), pp.102–20.

Lussier, Mark S. '"Marrying that hated Object": The Carnival of Desire in Behn's *The Rover*', in *Privileging Gender in Early Modern England*, ed. Jean R. Brink (Kirksville, Missouri, 1993), pp.225–39.

Markley, Robert. '"Be impudent, be saucy, forward, bold, touzing, and leud": The Politics of Masculine Sexuality and Feminine Desire in Behn's Tory Comedies', in *Cultural Readings of Restoration and Eighteenth-Century Theater*, pp.114–40.

Munns, Jessica. 'Barton and Behn's *The Rover*: or, The Text Transpros'd', *Restoration and Eighteenth-Century Theatre Research*, 2nd Series, 3, 2 (Winter, 1988), 11–22.

Owen, Susan J. 'Sexual Politics and Party Politics in Behn's Drama, 1678–83', in *Aphra Behn Studies*, ed. Janet Todd (Cambridge, 1996), pp.15–29.

Payne, Deborah, C. '"And Poets Shall by Patron-Princes Live": Aphra Behn and Patronage', in *Curtain Calls: British and American Women and the Theater, 1660–1820*, ed. Mary Ann Schofield & Cecilia Macheski (Athens, Ohio, 1991), 105–19.

Pearson, Jacqueline. *The Prostituted Muse: Images of Women and Women Dramatists, 1642–1737* (New York, 1988).

Spencer, Jane. '*The Rover* and the Eighteenth Century', in *Aphra Behn Studies*, pp.84–106.

Stapleton, M. L. 'Aphra Behn, Libertine', *Restoration*, 24, 2 (Fall, 2000).

Todd, Janet. *The Sign of Angellica: Women, Writing and Fiction 1660–1800* (1989).

Wiseman, S. J. *Aphra Behn*, Writers & Their Work New Series (Plymouth, 1996).

The Kind Keeper

Baker, Van R. 'Heroic Posturing Satirized: Dryden's *Mr Limberham*', *Papers in Language & Literature*, 8 (1972), 370–79.

Canfield, J. Douglas. *Tricksters and Estates: On the Ideology of Restoration Comedy* (Lexington, 1997).

Hughes, Derek. *English Drama 1660–1700*.

Hume, Robert D. *The Development of English Drama in the Late Seventeenth Century*.

Rothstein, Eric, & Frances Kavenik. *The Designs of Carolean Comedy*.

Staves, Susan. 'Why Was Dryden's *Mr Limberham* Banned? A Problem in Restoration Theatre History', *Restoration and Eighteenth-Century Theatre Research*, 13 (1974), 1–11.

Zimbardo, Rose. *A Mirror to Nature: Transformations in Drama and Aesthetics, 1660–1732* (Lexington, 1986).

The Orphan

Canfield, J. Douglas. 'Thomas Otway', in *Restoration and Eighteenth-Century Dramatists, Dictionary of Literary Biography*, vol. 80 (1989), pp.146–71.

Hughes, Derek. 'Otway's *The Orphan*: An Interpretation', *Durham University Journal*, 75 (1983), 45–54.

—— *English Drama 1660–1700*.

Marshall, Geoffrey. 'The Coherence of *The Orphan*', *Texas Studies in Language and Literature*, 2 (1969–70), 931–43.

Morrow, Laurie P. 'Chastity and Castration in Otway's *The Orphan*', *South Central Review*, 2 (Winter, 1985), 17–30.

Munns, Jessica. 'The Interested Heart and the Absent Mind: Samuel Johnson and Thomas Otway's *The Orphan*', *English Literary History*, 60 (1993), 611–23.

—— *Restoration Politics and Drama*, The Plays of Thomas Otuay, 1675–1683 (Newark & London, 1995).

Owen, Susan J. *Restoration Theatre and Crisis* (Oxford, 1996).

Taylor, Aline Mackenzie. *Next to Shakespeare: Otway's 'Venice Preserv'd' and 'The Orphan' and Their History on the London Stage* (Durham, NC, 1950).

The Wives' Excuse

Cordner, Michael. 'Marriage Comedy After the 1688 Revolution: Southerne to Vanbrugh', *Modern Language Review*, 85 (1990), 273–89.

—— Introduction to *Four Restoration Marriage Plays*, ed. Michael Cordner, with Ronald Clayton (Oxford, 1995), pp. xi–xlix.

Drougge, Helga. '"We'll learn that of the men": Female Sexuality in the

Comedies of Thomas Southerne,' *Studies in English Literature*, 33 (1993), 545–63.

Holland, Peter. *The Ornament of Action.*

Hume, Robert D. 'Marital Discord in English Comedy from Dryden to Fielding', *Modern Philology*, 74 (1977), 87–116. [Reprtd in *The Rakish Stage*, pp.176–213].

Kaufman, Anthony. '"This Hard Condition of a Woman's Fate": Southerne's *The Wives' Excuse*, *Modern Language Quarterly*, 34 (1973), 36–47.

—— '"The Smiler with the Knife": Covert Aggression in Some Restoration Epilogues', *Studies in the Literary Imagination*, 17 (1984), 63–74.

Love, Harold. '*The Wives' Excuse* and Restoration Comedy', *Komos*, 2 (1969–70), 148–56.

Milhous, Judith, & Robert D. Hume. *Producible Interpretation.*

Roberts, David. *The Ladies* (1989).

Waith, Eugene M. 'Admiration in the Comedies of Thomas Southerne', in *Evidence in Literary Scholarship*, ed. René Wellek & Alvaro Ribeiro (Oxford, 1979).

Dryden, *Marriage A-la-Mode*
1.1   At the Sicilian court, Doralice, a young wife, sings a libertine song reflecting her discontent with marriage. She meets Palamede, newly returned to court from travel abroad, and they are mutually attracted. She tells him she is married. Palamede is unaware that her husband is his best friend, Rhodophil, captain of the king's guards. Palamede laments both the fact of her marriage, and that his father has engaged him to marry an, as yet unseen, wealthy young heiress within three days. Before Doralice exits, they agree to meet again. Rhodophil now enters, and confesses to Palamede that he is bored after two years of marriage, and is secretly courting a mistress. Though beautiful, she is an affected Francophile, with ambitions to be socially accepted at court. He does not reveal her name. Palamede confides that he, too, is in love, but does not say with whom. As they leave, they greet the king's villainous favourite, Argaleon, his virtuous sister, Amalthea, and Artemis, a court lady.

    Amalthea tells Artemis how King Polydamas usurped the throne on the death of the rightful ruler, and of the consequent disappearance of a loyal courtier, Eubulus, together with the widowed queen, her young son and heir, and Polydamas' pregnant wife, who disapproved of the usurpation. Amalthea reveals that jewels belonging to Polydamas' wife have now come to light, together with a letter saying that she died in childbirth, but not revealing the sex of the child. Polydamas orders the arrest of a noble-looking youth and girl, Leonidas and Palmyra, who were found living nearby with an old country couple. Polydamas recognises their supposed father as Hermogenes, a former courtier who fled with Eubulus, and demands news of the fugitives. Hermogenes says all are now dead except for Polydamas' son whom he identifies as Leonidas, to the displeasure of Argaleon. Left alone, Leonidas and Palmyra speak briefly of their mutual love.

2.1   Palamede meets his fiancée, Melantha, who, it appears, is also

Rhodophil's mistress, comically besotted on fashionable French words. Palamede narrowly avoids disclosing that he loves Doralice to Rhodophil. Doralice appoints to meet Palamede that evening.

Polydamas orders Leonidas to prepare to marry Amalthea. He refuses. Palmyra complains of Argaleon's attentions. Leonidas and Palmyra reminisce and renew their vows of love.

3.1 Rhodophil and Doralice behave lovingly in front of Artemis, but quarrel when she leaves them. Melantha practises French words with her maid. Polydamas threatens Palmyra with a shameful death unless Leonidas abjures her. Hermogenes now provides evidence that Palmyra is Polydamas' true child, and claims Leonidas as his own son. Polydamas hints at a marriage between Palmyra and Argaleon.

3.2 Palamede and Doralice meet for their assignation, only to find that Rhodophil and Melantha arrive at the same place. All are suspicious, but nothing is proven.

4.1 Despite her own love for Leonidas, Amalthea nobly agrees to help him speak with Palmyra at the coming masquerade. Eubulus arrives secretly at court and reveals himself to Leonidas. Rhodophil and Palamede anticipate sexual adventures at the masquerade. Doralice sends word she is unwell and wishes to sleep alone that night. Rhodophil tells Palamede to look after a youth he has just saved from a street brawl. Unknown to both of them, the 'youth' is Doralice in disguise.

4.2 Leonidas and Palmyra meet at the masquerade. The jealous Argaleon informs the king.

4.3 Palamede tries to get rid of the 'boy', until Doralice reveals herself. Rhodophil enters with Melantha, the latter also in boy's clothes. The two 'boys' quarrel. Rhodophil is suddenly summoned to the guard and Palamede goes with him.

4.4 Eubulus and Hermogenes tell Palmyra that Leonidas is in fact the late king's lost son and heir. Leonidas plans an uprising to regain his rightful throne. Palmyra tells Leonidas that she cannot be disloyal to her father, even though he is a usurper. Polydamas and his guard anticipate the plot and capture Leonidas.

5.1 Palamede hears of his father's imminent arrival, and succeeds in winning Melantha's agreement to marry him. Doralice and then Palamede enter, and all four lovers agree reluctantly to remain faithful to their designated partners.

Leonidas is condemned to death. Palmyra pleads unsuccessfully for his life. Amalthea runs to tell Palamede and Rhodophil of

Leonidas' true identity and to beg their aid. They fight and save him. Leonidas pardons Polydamas, but Argaleon chooses to live a prisoner. Amalthea retreats to a religious community. Leonidas and Palmyra prepare for their marriage.

Shadwell, *The Libertine*

1.1 Don Lopez and Don Antonio praise Don John for his leadership in their lives as libertines. They celebrate past crimes, reproved by Jacomo. Leonora arrives unaware of Don John's falsehood; she refuses to believe Jacomo's account of this and spurns his offer to support her, but agrees to return next morning for proof.

1.2 Maria mistakenly throws Don John a letter meant for her lover, Octavio. Don John waits for Octavio's signal to her, kills him and impersonates him. Lopez and Antonio beat off the watch with some cowardly assistance from Jacomo. Don John is discovered, kills Maria's brother and escapes.

2.1 Leonora is spurned by Don John. Six women arrive, all claiming to be his wives; a mock wedding feast for the wives ends riotously. Maria arrives dressed as a man, with her maid Flora; she vows revenge for her lover and brother; the bravoes she sets against Don John are beaten off by him and Flora is killed. Lopez and Antonio have hired a ship for their escape. The Ghost of Don John's father rises to demand repentance, and is rejected.

3.1 The ship sinks in a thunderstorm. The libertines escape by seizing one of the ship's boats.

3.2 The Hermit and Don Francisco assist survivors. Don John, Lopez and Antonio offend the Hermit but are offered shelter by Don Francisco, who tells them his two daughters are to be married the next day. The Hermit rescues Maria and Leonora, then pulls Jacomo up out of the sea. Don Francisco's daughters, Clara and Flavia, lament their approaching marriages. They separate to look for Don John. He meets and flatters Clara, then Flavia. Maria and Leonora are attacked by Antonio and Lopez; Leonora is rescued by peasants and comes upon Don John who silences her by poison.

4.1 Maria reveals the past crimes of Don John and his friends to Don Francisco, who orders them to leave. Clara and Flavia each claim marriage to Don John. Maria and Don Francisco are slain, and the bridegrooms wounded in the subsequent fight. Clara and Flavia vow to join a convent.

4.2 Shepherds, nymphs and shepherdesses celebrate a rural festival. Don John, Don Lopez, Don Antonio and Jacomo seize the shepherdesses. The shepherds capture Jacomo and threaten to geld him, but he is rescued by the libertines. The shepherds vow to track them.

4.3 Don John, Don Lopez, Don Antonio and Jacomo reach a church and discover a statue of Don John's victim Don Pedro. When Don John invites the Statue to supper, the Statue nods its head.

4.4 Don John, Don Lopez, Don Antonio and Jacomo are dining, when Don Pedro's Ghost arrives. The Ghost warns of heaven's vengeance, raising devils as proof, and invites them to a repast at his tomb.

5.1 Jacomo arms himself for defence. Don John suggests to Lopez and Antonio that they set fire to a nunnery to capture and ravish the nuns. Jacomo is left as sentinel, frightening off the shepherds by disguising himself as a devil. Clara and Flavia are among the nuns seized. Two of the shepherds and an officer are killed.

5.2 The ghosts of Don John's victims are assembled in the church, reproaching him. The Statue offers blood to the libertines instead of wine. Devils sing, welcoming them to hell. The Statue invites them to repent. Lopez and Antonio refuse and are swallowed up. Jacomo creeps away. Don John, still defiant, is carried downwards by devils.

Behn, *The Rover*

1.1 Hellena questions her sister Florinda about her lovers, especially the English captain Belvile, and scorns the prospect of becoming a nun herself. Their brother Pedro praises the elderly suitor chosen by his father for Florinda, but admits the viceroy's son Antonio is his own choice. The girls persuade Callis to disobey orders and take them to the masquerade.

1.2 Belvile's friends Frederick and Blunt discover his love for Florinda. Willmore arrives ashore, eager for women. Hellena, disguised as a gypsy, attracts him by her wit. The prostitute Lucetta ensnares Blunt. Florinda asks Belvile to meet her that night in her garden, to elope.

2.1 Willmore, Belvile and Frederick wait outside the house of the fashionable courtesan, Angellica, to see her picture and terms set out. Blunt boasts about the gentlewoman who is in love with him. Willmore finds the picture attractive. Pedro vows to meet Angellica's terms, as does Antonio; they agree to duel next morning, though Antonio fails to recognise Pedro in masquing costume. Willmore causes a fight by seizing a picture of Angellica. Angellica invites him inside.

2.2   Willmore woos Angellica, but rails at her profession. Angellica answers proudly until she admits her love for him. Moretta protests.

3.1   Hellena admits to Florinda and Valeria that she is in love with Willmore. She is jealous to discover he is visiting Angellica. He boasts to Belvile and Frederick, showing the gold Angellica gave him. Hellena mocks him and he courts her, which angers Angellica.

3.2   Lucetta lures Blunt towards her chamber.

3.3   Blunt undresses in the dark and falls down a trapdoor. Lucetta rejoices with her gallant, Philippo.

3.4   Blunt climbs out of the town sewer.

3.5   Florinda opens the garden gate. Willmore enters, drunk, and mistakes her for a whore. Belvile and Frederick interpose, but the house has been roused. Don Pedro's servant, Stephano, shields Florinda by saying a servant has accidentally left the gate unlocked, but Pedro is suspicious.

3.6   Belvile scolds Willmore. Willmore meets Antonio about to enter Angellica's house: they fight and Antonio is wounded, but Belvile gets captured and blamed.

4.1   Belvile expects to be murdered, but instead Antonio offers him the task of duelling with Pedro in his place.

4.2   Assuming that her brother's duel is with Belvile, Florinda tries to stop it. Pedro thinks he's fighting Antonio, and offers an immediate marriage. Willmore enters and recognises Belvile, which spoils this chance. Belvile and Willmore quarrel. Angellica enters, lamenting Willmore's affection for Hellena. She jealously reveals to Willmore that his gypsy is a rich gentlewoman. Hellena enters dressed as a boy and increases the quarrel between Angellica and Willmore.

4.3   Florinda has escaped with Valeria's assistance. She passes Belvile, Pedro and Willmore. Willmore thinks her glance is an invitation and follows her. Frederick describes Blunt's mishap to Belvile and Pedro, who decide to visit him. Hellena sends her page to follow Willmore.

4.4   Florinda thinks Pedro is following her. She enters a house to escape him. The page and Valeria see where she has gone, Willmore does not.

4.5   Blunt, still in his underwear, reviews his wrongs and curses his tailor. Florinda asks for help, but Blunt refuses to be deceived again and threatens to rape her. Frederick enters and encourages him, until Florinda names Belvile and gives Blunt a ring. Belvile is announced: Blunt sends Florinda away in Frederick's care, then locks himself in to avoid mockery.

5.1 Blunt tries to prevent Belvile, Willmore, Frederick and Pedro entering. He boasts of taking revenge and produces the ring, which Belvile recognises as Florinda's. Willmore and Pedro both demand to see Blunt's wench. Pedro wins the draw and fetches the masked Florinda. Pedro leaves when Valeria tells him that Florinda has run away. Belvile and Frederick exit to marry Florinda and Valeria. Angellica enters with a pistol to shoot Willmore, who manages to dissuade her until Antonio enters and seizes the gun. Pedro overhears Antonio's avowals to Angellica, which softens him to Florinda's marriage to Belvile. Hellena enters, and demands marriage when wooed by Willmore. Pedro is angry to discover her, but forgives her because he's out-numbered. Blunt appears, ridiculous in Spanish clothes. Masquers enter and dance.

Dryden, *The Kind Keeper*

1.1 Woodall arrives at his London lodgings, chosen because he has traced a pretty woman there. He orders Gervase, his servant, not to call him by his real name, Aldo, as he plans to enjoy himself before his father learns of his return from France. He meets the hypocritical landlady, Mrs Saintly. He is surprised to encounter his father, Aldo, who does not recognise him but promises assistance in seducing a wife and a mistress who lodge here. Aldo introduces the mistress, Tricksy, who welcomes Woodall's advances until her keeper Limberham returns. She passes Woodall off to Limberham as an Italian perfume seller.

2.1 Aldo praises Woodall's progress with Tricksy but warns him that the third pretty woman, Mrs Saintly's daughter, is both chaste and malicious. Limberham and Tricksy quarrel, but Aldo reconciles them by persuading Limberham to make a handsome settlement and takes him to get this drawn up by a lawyer. Woodall avows his devotion to Tricksy and has to hide in a chest when Limberham and Aldo return. They want documents from the chest. Tricksy surrenders the key, but Woodall holds the lid shut from inside. Mrs Saintly protests at the noise. All exit to find a blacksmith to break the chest open, except for Mrs Saintly. She produces a false key, planning theft, and screams when Woodall emerges. She protects him but demands a promise of sex in return. Limberham is persuaded that all is well.

3.1 Pleasance finds Woodall attractive, but mocks him when he enters with Tricksy and Mrs Brainsick. Woodall makes advances to Mrs Brainsick, but hides in the servant Judith's room when Brainsick arrives. Brainsick overhears him, but is told by Mrs Brainsick and Aldo that the noise was made by Judith's lover, and Woodall is let out unseen. Limberham scorns Brainsick's song. They quarrel and each decides to help Woodall seduce the other's woman. Mrs Brainsick and Tricksy try to pass Woodall notes: one is dropped and each woman thinks it is hers. Woodall decides it is from Tricksy.

3.2   Mrs Brainsick waits for Woodall in his chamber as in her note. She hides under the bed when she hears Woodall and Tricksy approach. Tricksy hides in the bed when Mrs Saintly enters. Mrs Saintly threatens Woodall, then throws herself down on the bed, rousing Mrs Brainsick and Tricksy. After threats and accusations, they all agree to keep quiet.

4.1   Aldo and his servant Geoffrey welcome various whores that Aldo 'protects'. Woodall enters, riotously. Mrs Saintly, Mrs Pleasance and Judith chase the whores out. Aldo tells Woodall that his son's sacked servant, Giles, reports his son is in town. Woodall responds to Mrs Saintly's demands by making an assignation with her. Pleasance and Woodall argue, but are attracted to each other. Woodall approaches Mrs Brainsick, but has to hide in her closet when Brainsick approaches; Woodall pretends he thought the room was Limberham's. Mrs Saintly and Mrs Pleasance tell Limberham that Woodall and Tricksy are together in the summer-house.

4.2   Gervase warns Woodall and Tricksy of Limberham's approach. Woodall and Gervase retreat into the still-house. Limberham demands the key from Tricksy, but is duped into believing her protestations of innocence. Woodall instructs Gervase to keep the assignation with Mrs Saintly in his place.

5.1   Judith tells Woodall that Mrs Brainsick will meet him in his room, but the key breaks in Woodall's door as Brainsick approaches, so he hides Mrs Brainsick in Limberham's room, disguised in Tricksy's robe. Brainsick believes that Woodall is meeting Tricksy, guards the door against Limberham and then goes off with him. Mrs Brainsick escapes discovery. Tricksy enters, hoping for sex with Woodall, but he has to hide in her room as Limberham and Brainsick return. Pleasance persuades Limberham to enter the room and discover Woodall. Woodall chases Limberham out, claiming he's been praying. Limberham threatens to discard Tricksy, but Woodall has seized the settlement documents. Aldo discovers that Woodall is his son and eventually forgives him. He reveals that Mrs Pleasance is *not* Mrs Saintly's daughter, but an heiress. Pleasance and Woodall agree to marry. Gervase reveals that he has married Mrs Saintly. Limberham offers to marry Tricksy, on generous terms.

Otway, *The Orphan*

1.1 Paulino and Ernesto describe Acasto's virtues, those of his twin sons, and his generosity to the orphaned Monimia. The sons, Castalio and Polydore, return from hunting. They both avow love for Monimia, but swear they won't be rivals. Castalio offers Polydore the appointment he had earlier made with her. Monimia soliloquises about her love for Castalio. She learns about his conversation with Polydore from the page. She rejects Polydore's advances. Polydore vows to persist.

2.1 Acasto advises Castalio and Polydore to avoid court life. Monimia's brother, Chamont, arrives. He tells Acasto of his concern for Monimia's honour, and tells Monimia herself about an ominous dream and a beggarwoman's warning. Monimia decides to treat Castalio with caution. Polydore places the page to overhear them. They are reconciled and vow their love.

3.1 Polydore is indignant at the page's report, deciding that the lovers have deceived him. Acasto has a seizure. Later, all celebrate his return to health, and Chamont asks for Serina's hand. Chamont persuades the chaplain to tell him that Castalio and Monimia have just married. Polydore sees the couple embracing and overhears their arrangement to meet that night. Unaware of their marriage, Polydore decides to take his twin's place. He sends the page to delay Castalio and enters Monimia's room. Later, Castalio is furious to be turned away by Monimia's maid, and curses womankind.

4.1 Acasto is troubled and thinks he has heard Castalio in sorrow during the night. Monimia worries that her husband left her hastily. Castalio enters and threatens her. Chamont finds her in tears and threatens vengeance on Castalio. Chamont tells Acasto of the marriage. Monimia is left alone to grieve. Polydore enters and reveals he slept with her last night. Monimia tells him of her marriage. Horrified at their incest, they both lament.

5.1 Acasto seeks to persuade Castalio to meet Monimia. Chamont arrives, bent on vengeance. Serina averts a fight. Castalio still refuses to see Monimia, until the maid reports that she is approaching, distraught. She bids farewell to Castalio. Polydore provokes a duel with Castalio and runs on his sword. Monimia returns, saying she has drunk poison. Polydore confesses. Chamont and Acasto enter. Castalio stabs himself.

Behn, *The Rover*, Part 2

1.1   Willmore arrives with Blunt, Fetherfool and Hunt outside the English ambassador's residence in Madrid. They meet Shift, who tells them about the courtesan, La Nuche's, conquest of Carlo, to Willmore's dismay. Beaumond greets them. Willmore confides that he is planning to make fools of Blunt and Fetherfool. Beaumond and Willmore praise La Nuche's beauty and regret her profession. Fetherfool and Blunt have heard from Shift of two monstrous heiresses, whom they plan to approach. Shift says that a mountebank is coming to Madrid, promising transformations. Willmore plots to impersonate the mountebank, with Shift's aid. Beaumond reveals that he is to be married. La Nuche enters: she loves Willmore, but regrets his poverty. He rebukes her. Ariadne enters, sees Willmore and lingers. Carlo causes a disturbance. Fetherfool refuses to believe that La Nuche is a whore.

1.2   La Nuche's bawd, Petronella, seeks Fetherfool as a suitable client for her mistress. Willmore reproaches La Nuche, who defends herself. Ariadne vows to pursue Willmore.

2.1   Ariadne comments on Willmore's vow against womankind. He courts her, and she promises admittance to the garden at night. Fetherfool celebrates his impending appointment with La Nuche, but agrees with Blunt that they will both try to marry the monsters. Willmore impersonates the mountebank to great acclaim. Petronella seeks the 'mountebank's' aid to regain her youth. Ariadne sees Beaumond wooing La Nuche; so does Carlo who decides to surprise La Nuche later.

2.2   Ariadne tells her maid Lucia that she plans to visit the mountebank. We learn that her stepfather wants her to marry Beaumond, while her mother wants her to marry Carlo, but she prefers Willmore. Beaumond enters. He and Ariadne argue.

3.1   Shift introduces Blunt and Fetherfool to the Giant and her sister, the Dwarf. Hunt pretends to be a male giant. La Nuche visits the disguised Willmore to learn her fortune. He warns her to make sure of her lover that night. Ariadne enters dressed as a boy. She approaches La Nuche and challenges Willmore. Beaumond enters, recognises La Nuche and rebukes Willmore. La Nuche and Willmore quarrel.

4.1   Willmore seeks to keep his rendezvous with Ariadne. He meets Beaumond at the gate. They fight in the darkness, not recognising each other. La Nuche, who has been following, takes refuge in the garden. Willmore retreats into the garden.

4.2   Beaumond seizes La Nuche, thinking she is his fiancée, Ariadne. La Nuche uses his mistake to reproach him. Ariadne and Willmore observe them. Ariadne sends Willmore further off, while she rebukes Beaumond. Willmore frightens Lucia, who mistakenly reveals Ariadne's plans to Beaumond. Beaumond saves Willmore from the servants, but challenges him to a duel. Beaumond decides La Nuche is more honest than Ariadne. Willmore woos Ariadne until she is startled away by Beaumond's page Abevile leading in musicians. She asks him to meet her later, to carry her away.

4.3   La Nuche's servants, Petronella and Aurelia, regret that her love for Willmore may lose her rich clients. Carlo bribes Petronella to gain access to La Nuche. She plans to impersonate her mistress, but Aurelia plans he should encounter Fetherfool. Petronella reproaches La Nuche for risking poverty by favouring Willmore. La Nuche resolves to spend the night with Beaumond.

4.4   In the dark bedchamber, Carlo mistakes Fetherfool for La Nuche. They fight until the servants part them. Carlo leaves, threatening revenge. Fetherfool escapes by the window.

4.5   Fetherfool hangs from the window on a rope. Beaumond overhears Willmore instructing Abevile to serenade below the window. Beaumond and Willmore fight, striking Fetherfool as well, but Willmore gets into the house.

5.1   Willmore and La Nuche avow their love. Beaumond demands entry and at last realises that he's been fighting with Willmore, his friend. La Nuche is unable to decide between them. Willmore decides to keep his appointment with Ariadne. Beaumond agrees to help, not knowing Ariadne is the woman. La Nuche rushes out after them. Petronella decides to steal her jewels.

5.2   Ariadne mistakes Beaumond for Willmore and exits with him. Willmore mistakes La Nuche for Ariadne and exits with her.

5.3   Fetherfool laments to Blunt. Fetherfool is alarmed by the arrival of Shift and runs away.

5.4   He enters a room where the Giant is asleep in a chair. Harlequin persuades Fetherfool to swallow the pearls from her necklace, and to hide in a clock-case as Shift and Hunt enter. Shift plans to marry the Giant, but in the darkness Fetherfool manages to lead her out. Petronella, veiled and carrying La Nuche's jewels, persuades Blunt that she is a young virgin who needs his help. Fetherfool laments that he has lost hold of the Giant. Beaumond realises that he is helping Ariadne to elope. Having slept with La Nuche, Willmore enters to fetch lights. He sees Ariadne, thinks he has slept with her, and tells Beaumond so. A duel is averted by La Nuche: she reveals she was the woman who slept with Willmore, and promises to be his life's partner despite his poverty. Shift has married the Giant, and Hunt, the Dwarf. Blunt and Fetherfool blame the mountebank for their disappointment, until Willmore reveals his earlier disguise. Blunt's deception by Petronella is disclosed, as is Fetherfool's swallowing of the Giant's pearls. Beaumond and Ariadne agree to try marriage, while Willmore opts for love and gallantry.

Southerne, *The Wives' Excuse*

1.1	Footmen and pages gossip as they wait for the concert to end.
1.2	Friendall tries to display his knowledge of the music. Springame courts Mrs Witwoud, Wilding courts the young girl, Fanny. Friendall encourages Lovemore to approach Mrs Friendall to distract her from his own advances to Mrs Sightly. Wellvile courts Mrs Sightly. Ruffle follows Friendall out, incited by Lovemore.
1.3	Ruffle strikes Friendall, making a duel likely. Lovemore tells Wellvile that he has planned this to show Mrs Friendall that Friendall is a coward.
2.1	Mrs Teazall reproves Mrs Witwoud for her reckless behaviour and for not chaperoning Fanny. She agrees that Mrs Witwoud should rescue Fanny from Wilding.
2.2	Mrs Friendall pretends to believe that Friendall really will fight the duel. She sends her brother Springame to Ruffle with a challenge she has written herself. She asks Lovemore to prevent the duel.
2.3	Wilding and his servant discuss Fanny's seduction. Witwoud enters, masked. Wilding courts her at first, until he knows who she is. Witwoud offers to aid him with Mrs Sightly if he leaves Fanny alone.
3.1	Ruffle fears a duel. Springame brings him the challenge. Ruffle apologises to Friendall when he arrives. Lovemore is annoyed his plan has miscarried, but realises the challenge was written by Mrs Friendall.
3.2	In the park, Friendall refuses to listen to his wife's advice. Mrs Witwoud has persuaded Mrs Sightly to come for a walk. Wilding

tells Courtall, who then tells Wellvile that Wilding has an assignation with Mrs Sightly. Wellvile is jealous but suspects Mrs Witwoud is to blame. After being slighted by various lords, Friendall decides to talk with Wellvile and Wilding, as wits. Wellvile reveals he is writing a play with a potential cuckold in it, like Friendall himself. Mrs Teazall is distracted from reproaching Wilding. Wilding promises Wellvile not to court Mrs Sightly. Wellvile advises Mrs Sightly to tell Mrs Friendall that Friendall has been making advances to her. Friendall invites everyone to his house.

4.1 Friendall boasts ignorantly about his selection of wines, snuffs, and teas. Lovemore intercepts Mrs Friendall as she goes to prepare the tea, and avows his love. She rejects him. He gives her the challenge she wrote in Friendall's name as proof that he won't use it against Friendall. Mrs Friendall learns from Mrs Sightly about Friendall's disloyalty: they decide to rendezvous with him later, masked. While the others play cards, Wellvile tells Mrs Sightly about Mrs Witwoud's plan to engage her with Wilding but also angers her against himself. The card game ends, with Mrs Teazall protesting that she's been cheated.

4.2 Mrs Sightly rebukes Mrs Witwoud for treachery. Mrs Witwoud lies to Wilding that the planned seduction is still viable. Wilding and Wellvile quarrel, but Courtall reconciles them.

5.1 Mrs Witwoud tells Wilding that Mrs Sightly will meet him at Friendall's masquerade. She plans to impersonate Mrs Sightly.

5.2 Lovemore escorts Mrs Friendall and Mrs Sightly, masked, in the park. Friendall describes his motives and intrigues to them.

5.3 The masquerade. Mrs Witwoud's maid, Betty, wears Mrs Sightly's scarf at first, then gives it to Mrs Witwoud. Lovemore continues his courtship of Mrs Friendall. Wellvile warns Wilding that the lady with the scarf isn't Mrs Sightly. Lovemore tells Friendall that the disguised lady is Mrs Sightly and he should follow her. Mrs Teazall bursts in looking for Fanny. Friendall and Mrs Witwoud are discovered together *in flagrante*. Springame follows Mrs Witwoud as she storms out. Wellvile proposes to Mrs Sightly. Friendall agrees to a formal separation from Mrs Friendall.